FOR SALE
Slightly used, one owner med school;
great potential but needs work.
Call 333-2984. Ask for Dan.

Medical student T-shirt message, Urbana, Illinois, circa June, 1981.

Dedication

to Franny

Table of Contents

KEYS

—— to the ——

ASYLUM

A Dean, a Medical School,

and Academic Politics

by Daniel K. Bloomfield, M.D.

Published by New Medical Press, Champaign, IL
Produced by Five Star Publications, Incorporated, Chandler, AZ

Keys to the Asylum: A Dean, a Medical School, and Academic Politics
Copyright © 2000 by Daniel K. Bloomfield, M.D.
New Medical Press
Champaign, Illinois

Produced 2000 by Five Star Publications, Incorporated
P.O. Box 6698
Chandler, AZ 85246-6698
(480) 940-8182
Linda F. Radke, President • www.BookProducer.com

Printed in the United States of America

Requests for permissions should be addressed to:
New Medical Press
2403 Lyndhurst Drive
Champaign, Illinois 61820
(217) 351-9009

Library of Congress Cataloging-in-Publication Data

Bloomfield, Daniel K., 1926–
    Keys to the asylum : a dean, a medical school, and academic politics /
    by Daniel K. Bloomfield.
        p. cm.
    1. Bloomfield, Daniel K., 1926– 2. Deans (Education)--Illinois--
Biography. 3. Medical colleges--Administration. I. Title.

R833 .B56 2000
610'.7177366--dc21
    [B]   00-034727

Publishing consultant: Linda F. Radke
Editor: Salvatore Caputo
Book design and typesetting: Kim Scott
Proofreading: Kevin Dietz

Acknowledgements

This book, 10 years in preparation, is the product of two distinct predecessor volumes and two dedicated editors. What began as an effort to document the history of UICOM-UC from its 1970 beginning as SBMS-UC to the end of my deanship when the future of the school was assured (1984), became a personal memoir of that period. The first historical compilation was 1265 pages including 1103 pages of narrative text, 91 pages of footnotes, an 18 page glossary of abbreviations and acronyms, a 14 page chronology, and 39 pages of original documents including copies of the Treaty and the full-page newspaper advertisements which contained the two open letters to the university's president. I am most grateful to Hilda Banks of Champaign, Illinois, who spent many hours in 1996 expertly copy editing this long document and reducing its size to 900 pages including 738 pages of narrative text. Three years later, in the course of my search for a publisher I was referred to Salvatore Caputo of Five Star Publications, Inc., Chandler, Arizona, to whom I am equally grateful for his editing skills. Mr. Caputo first critiqued the 900 page book in 1999 and concluded that its hybrid form (part history and part memoir) should be abandoned in favor of a historical memoir with an engaging narrative free of excessive documentation, footnotes and technical jargon. He then accepted responsibility to edit the book as such and to reduce it to its present size and format. Readers who would like to review the unabridged document which includes the glossary, the chronology and the footnotes, but is not indexed, should contact the author.

I am also indebted to Melody Simeone, my ever-faithful secretary who word-processed draft after draft of each chapter with speed, efficiency, and good humor, and to Paula Treichler who proofread and edited the first seven chapters prior to Mr. Caputo's finishing work. I also wish to thank the staff of the Library of the Health Sciences, and particularly Victoria Pifalo, who always found the obscure reference and who arranged for my access to the UICOM archives in Chicago where documents (mostly sanitized) of Bill Grove, Joe Begando, Morton Creditor and others are available. I also wish to thank the basic science faculty of SBMS-UC who suffered in silence (mostly) as I compromised their scant budget dollars to keep SCM-UC afloat in hard times. Although the basic science program was never threatened, its faculty remained strongly supportive of our efforts to establish a 4 year medical program. Likewise, thanks are due to the faculty of UIUC as represented by their Senate which carefully studied our Medical Scholars Program and concluded that it was a rich asset for the UIUC campus.

Finally, I would like to give credit by name, but I cannot, to each of the nearly 500 physicians of east central Illinois and to the 21 hospital administrators who, with their strong support and commitment to teaching, made all this possible.

Champaign, Illinois, June 2000.

About the Author

Daniel K. Bloomfield hadn't given much thought to medicine as a career. He had graduated from the U.S. Naval Academy in June 1947 and was contemplating making the U.S. Navy his career in 1949, when his father suggested that the 22-year-old should interview at Case Western Reserve University School of Medicine to determine whether he'd be interested in medicine. The student was pleased with what he saw, and the school must have been equally pleased with him. He graduated from the school in 1954 with his M.D. degree.

Dr. Bloomfield took his internship and residency at Beth Israel Hospital, a Harvard teaching hospital in Boston. While at Beth Israel, he met and married his wife, Frances. After two years there, he spent a summer substituting for a general practitioner at a rural practice in Providence, Kentucky, and developed an appreciation of the doctor-patient relationship. Dr. Bloomfield took a third year of internal medicine residency training at Massachusetts General Hospital.

Trained as a clinical cardiologist, he entered a two-year postdoctoral fellowship in biochemistry at the Harvard Department of Chemistry with Professor Konrad Bloch, where he gained an understanding of the pressures academic research scientists face. He then spent a year as an Honorary Assistant Registrar at the National Heart Hospital in London.

Dr. Bloomfield returned from England in 1960 and joined the faculty of his alma mater as an Established Investigator (research scientist) for the American Heart Association and received a National Institutes of Health grant to study the metabolism of cholesterol in the rat. After four years, Dr. Bloomfield decided he was more of a clinician than a research scientist and resigned his fellowship with the Heart Association.

He was one of six founding members of the Community Health Foundation of Cleveland, Ohio, in 1964. It was the first prepaid medical practice in Ohio. With a deepening interest in education and community affairs, Dr. Bloomfield ran for and was elected to a post on the school board of Cleveland Heights-University Heights in 1965. He accepted a teaching post as a full-time cardiologist at Mount Sinai Hospital in Cleveland in 1967, which allowed him to pursue both cardiology and an academic career.

In 1970, as he opened a private cardiology practice, Dr. Bloomfield received the call that led to his greatest challenge, to become the founding dean of the University of Illinois College of Medicine at Urbana-Champaign. He accepted the position and spent the next 14 years as a crusader for the school. After his resignation as dean in 1984, he joined the school's faculty, where he shared teaching and committee work and began his research on this book. Although he retired in 1996, he continues to teach to this day. Dr. Bloomfield has three children and lives with his wife of 45 years in Champaign, Illinois.

Preface

THIS IS THE STORY of the founding, the political maneuvering, and the near-miraculous survival of a medical school ambivalently sponsored by the University of Illinois. The school was one of four regional programs created by the university's College of Medicine in 1970 in response to a short-lived wave of enthusiastic public funding designed to relieve a "doctor shortage" in the state.

The school was the outgrowth of a bitterly negotiated treaty between two rival university campuses, and its leaders had to deal with two difficult and very different academic bureaucracies to establish itself. This story is about a school in which the dean drew educational support from academic departments whose heads reported to other administrators and who never received adequate funding to do the job for which he was charged. It is about a school that was administratively abused by chronic underfunding, seriously threatened with closure on several occasions, and kept fiscally in almost a perpetually vulnerable state. Need I say more to justify the book's title?

This story is about the administrative flexibility required to adapt programs to meet changing societal needs and priorities. It is also a story about contemporary medical education, curriculum innovation, and the heavy hands that would squelch originality.

This story is also about people who interact with the medical-education system: the students; the faculty, both salaried and volunteer; the academic administrators; the patients and their doctors; the hospitals and nursing homes; the regulators and accreditors; and the public, which expects the medical profession to do its best to preserve its health.

This is a story of clashing academic personalities, of leaders strong and weak, of intrigues that take place in the name of "academic quality" and "fiscal responsibility," and of deception both deliberate and accidental.

Finally, this is a mixture of history and autobiography. The book documents my personal view of the academic and political odyssey that makes up *Keys to the Asylum*. Therefore, the narrative reflects my own priorities and is imperfectly balanced in its concentration. Telling the story presents other problems as well.

The actors involved in these "adventures" are real people who are, in many instances, still active at the University of Illinois or otherwise engaged in medical education. Although relevant chapters of this book have been reviewed in manuscript form by some of them, others might view the events described in a very different light, and all may take issue with my conclusions. I have tried to be as fair as possible in telling the story. Many of those referred to remain colleagues and friends with points of view and sensitivities that make it difficult to be entirely candid in reproducing all the tableaux that make up the historical tapestry.

Another problem is that I am not a historian and did not keep a day-to-day running diary of events as they happened. But I did file documents and memoranda as they related to the developmental history and dictated contemporary notes and personal summaries of memorable events as they occurred. These entries summarized salient events on a contemporary basis and proved very valuable in re-creating the atmospheres in which events took place. My appointment calendars from 1970 to the present have also provided a detailed framework for the narrative.

So although the telling of this story depends in part on my own memory (and some dear friends who know me well will say, "Heaven help us!") and that of friends and colleagues who played key roles in the enterprise, most of what follows is constructed from key documents in the form of letters, memoranda, committee minutes, and the like. What follows, then, is an intensely personal account of the beginning of medical education at the University of Illinois at Urbana-Champaign with apologies in advance to those persons whom I omit, misconstrue, or slight, and more apologies to those upon whom I lavish either excessive praise or opprobrium.

PART I

Beginnings

CHAPTER 1

The Invitation

L EVITY FILLED THE AIR. Good food and plenty of spirits elevated the mood. On a warm May evening in 1984, faculty and community gathered to say good-bye to the dean of the University of Illinois College of Medicine at Urbana-Champaign. He was retiring after fourteen years in office. Rather than engage in maudlin sentimentality, well-wishers filled the country club dining room with parting shots as they roasted the poor soul. They relished the task and made the most of it.

The dean, for his part, showed no sign that this was anything but a lark—a time to laugh, ponder the past and consider the future.

When tall, solemn, gray-haired Truman O. Anderson stood at the lectern, he said he wanted to set the record straight about Bloomfield. No one was more qualified than Anderson, former dean of the university's School of Basic Medical Sciences in Chicago, to talk about Bloomfield's administrative style.

He drew his first laugh with this aside: "I should tell you, Dan, that I had an awful time putting my thoughts on paper and to assure that I would remain temperate with my remarks, I wrote this in church last Sunday while the choir was singing."

The laughs increased in intensity. Anderson brought down the house with his closing comment: "In summary, Danny Bloomfield must be ranked among the most easygoing, soft-spoken, compliant, noncontroversial, unimaginative nonentities I have ever met. But for all of these undistinguishing attributes I toast him tonight. I would like to add to all for those here tonight who believe everything I have just said, you may stop at the door on your way out at the conclusion of this dinner and pick up your very own gullibility award and a book entitled 'This and Other Incredible Fairy Tales.'"

Anderson knew me well. The irony with which he described my "personal qualities" and filled the room with laughter were emblematic of my bruising crusade to launch and sustain the four-year medical curriculum at Urbana-Champaign. To have taken on such a crusade was a risk. To have succeeded was a miracle. It was this saga—this epic adventure, in which the speakers and much of the audience had participated—that was being celebrated.

It all began fifteen years earlier when I answered a fateful phone call on a fall morning in 1969. "Hi Dan," it began. My voice recognition intact, I immediately recalled the resonant bass voice of Lowell Hager, a biochemist I had known ten years earlier in Harvard.

"Are you tired of making all that money in private practice?" That was Lowell all right, displaying an aggressive sense of humor in line with the aggressive intellect of a world-class biochemist and a future member of the National Academy of Sciences. Beneath the banter, he was serious. I wasn't prepared for what came next.

"Do you want to be the dean of a new medical school?"

That was a shocker. It was not the kind of question one hears every day—or even in a lifetime. Lowell was serving on a committee that was charged to look for a dean to start a new medical school on the Urbana-Champaign campus of the University of Illinois (UIUC). The medical school they had in mind was limited for the present to a single year of basic medical sciences, but that he was confident that it represented a first step toward a complete four-year M.D. program. The search committee was seeking a person who knew enough about both the basic medical sciences and clinical medicine to do the job of constructing the first-year program and who had the interest and vision to finish the job of developing a full four-year program. He had thrown my name into the hopper because he knew of my biochemical experience a decade earlier and of my clinical training at two Harvard teaching hospitals in Boston. The committee was only in the preliminary phase of its search, he said. "If you're interested, please send me a resume." I told him that I knew several medical scientists and scholars who fit his criteria, but admitted I was flattered to be considered.

The call came at a particularly opportune time for me in November 1969. I had been on the faculty of Case Western Reserve University School of Medicine for 10 years, but was now entangled in a serious disagreement with my current department head. I was on the verge of leaving academe to open a private practice in cardiology.

Lowell was offering the prospect of reentering the academy on very different terms. It was challenging and appealed to the risk-taker in me. I held no illusions: I was already considered something of a maverick, and the chances that I would make the final selection were limited. I continued to prepare for the transition to private practice, which I opened on January 1, 1970, treating the call as merely a preliminary inquiry—and a long shot at that. But on the off chance that it would come through, I had riders built into my lease and purchase agreements that would release me from long-term obligations in Cleveland.

Hager didn't call again until late March 1970. I had all but forgotten our previous conversation. I was very busy with my private practice. I had hired two loyal employees, a secretary and a nurse; purchased equipment; and divided my time between the office and three local hospitals. If that were not enough, I remained an elected member of the local school board, which is the world's busiest and most thankless job.

Lowell was calling again to confirm that I would look seriously at this "new medical school" position. He explained that he was only one member of a sizable search committee charged to find a "Dean" for this new school of basic medical sciences. The new school was "destined" to be a full four-year medical school, but first had to begin as a one-year school of basic medical sciences. I told Lowell that I had no interest whatsoever in being the dean of a one-year medical school, but that if the university truly intended to begin a four-year program at Urbana, then I was definitely interested. In his view, a full four-year program was only a matter of time. We left the matter there. He had done his job. I expressed an interest and a willingness to visit.

I was prepared to look at alternatives. I was forty-three years old and had less than three months in private practice. A number of setbacks had led me to quit academic and organizational medicine for the rewards of solo private practice; nevertheless, I was not yet wedded to that option. In the sixteen years since graduating from medical school, I had had many seminal experiences both within and outside medicine. Some were pleasant and others not; but all were instructive. At the time, I didn't know that many of these experiences would prove indispensable for functioning effectively as the dean of the School of Basic Medical Sciences at Urbana-Champaign.

CHAPTER 2

Seasoning

C HANCE ALTERS LIFE REMARKABLY. Born in December 1926, I was almost thirteen and entering ninth grade when Hitler invaded Poland in 1939. Twenty-one years after the end of "the war to end all wars," war was again visiting Europe. Although the United States remained neutral in the early stages of World War II, there was a pervasive feeling that, sooner or later, America would fight the Axis powers. For me, that feeling translated into an effort to maximize my educational opportunities while I could. I accelerated through my high school years, taking extra courses, and qualified for graduation after only three years. One week short of my fifteenth birthday, the Japanese attacked Pearl Harbor, and war revisited the entire world.

With President Roosevelt's declaration of war, it became clear that I would enter the armed forces when I came of age. As chance would have it, a friend of mine encouraged me to take the competitive examinations offered by my congressional representative for entry into the U.S. Naval Academy as a congressional appointee. I did not think much about the test until I was awakened one morning about six months later by my mother's joyful voice. "Danny, you've been appointed to the U.S. Naval Academy in Annapolis!" She had just picked up the *Cleveland Plain Dealer*. The announcement was on the front page.

At sixteen, I was too young to enter the academy in 1943, so my appointment was delayed until 1944. I was commissioned as Ensign in June 1947, after an accelerated three-year program. I finished eleventh in a class that originally numbered eleven hundred. I was twenty years old.

The academy and my military service would shape a good deal of my educational thinking. Military education was strictly objective-based learning. Instructors were often raw, untrained officers, with limited expertise in the subjects they taught. They were assigned a tour of duty at the academy, where they were provided with texts and learning objectives that had been prepared by a hidden hand at a higher level. Because many of our instructors were often only one step ahead of the class, it was clear that we would have to learn much for ourselves. Comprehensive, spoon-feeding lectures were rare. Study objectives were assigned before every class and would be tested in virtually every class. Self-instruction was the critical element in performing, and continued self-study was critical to proficiency and advancement when later assigned to the fleet.

I was assigned to the destroyer USS Harold J. Ellison for the rest of my service, 1947 to 1950. I was communications officer of the ship and supervised the radio room, cryptography, and the Combat Information Center (radar and sonar). With these responsibilities, I had about twenty-five men under my command.

Although the military runs by its own rules, much of what I learned about military administration and leadership can be applied to civilian work. In general, military personnel follow appropriate orders with enthusiasm when there is mutual confidence between officer and subordinate. When rapport between superiors and subordinates breaks down, the military can still function, but loses some of its luster and efficiency. Above all, I learned that respect for leadership is greatest when it is earned.

If it was sheer chance that brought me to the navy, it was just as much fortuity that brought me into medicine. Home on navy leave in 1949, I was seriously contemplating a naval career. Although I had never given much thought to medicine as a career, my father suggested that I might interview at Western Reserve University's School of Medicine. So I did. I liked what I saw and filled out an application at Western Reserve (the merger with Case Institute of Technology to become Case Western Reserve took place at a later date). I was accepted and resigned from the U.S. Navy a mere eight days before North Korea invaded South Korea and the United States (through the United Nations) was again at war.

I entered medical school in September 1950. Excited by the work, I studied hard and began to gather ideas about medical education and research. After receiving my M.D. degree in 1954, I took my internship and residency at the Beth Israel Hospital in Boston, a Harvard teaching hospital. As an intern and resident, I was exposed to colleagues and faculty who represented the best in academic medicine. It was there that I learned, among other things, the meaning of the word "smart." All through my prior schooling I had little difficulty being at or near the top of my class. At Beth Israel,

I worked with a select group of fellow interns who represented valedictorian positions from some of the best medical schools in the country and felt pressed, struggling to be an "average" intern.

At Beth Israel, I also met and married my dear wife, Frances, who faithfully supported me through the many difficult periods that were to come. After two years at Beth Israel, I arranged for a third year of internal medicine residency training at the Massachusetts General Hospital (MGH), where the intellectual climate was similarly rigorous.

Before beginning work at MGH, though, I had a profound medical educational experience in rural Kentucky that was just as important as the most erudite rounds at the Harvard teaching hospitals. When my residency at Beth Israel ended, I had three months before my residency at MGH was to start. I used that period to serve locum tenens (in short, as a substitute) for a general practitioner in western Kentucky. In 1950, the town of Providence had 4,000 residents, one main street and two physicians, both general practitioners who never spoke to one another. One of the physicians maintained an infirmary, a small in-patient service that was never used by the doctor I replaced, but there was a small, accredited regional hospital in Madisonville, sixteen miles away.

Shortly after the Fourth of July in 1956, I joined Dr. Wainer (I never called him by his first name and cannot recall it as I write about him forty-two years later) for an introduction into the workings of a general practice. What seasoning I acquired on that rotation! Dr. Wainer and I worked together for three weeks. He introduced me to the practice, and helped me get my feet on the ground in an unfamiliar environment. He then left for an eight-week vacation, his first in many years, and returned in September to work with me for two additional weeks. He had a very active practice. When we were working together, we saw as many as 110 patients on a Saturday, but usually the practice saw about 50 patients each day—this in addition to frequent house calls and home deliveries of babies. Dr. Wainer took care of everything, from sore throats to minor surgery. He rarely referred patients to specialists, not that there were many of those available there. His office was a combination ambulatory-care center, surgicenter, and pharmacy. When it was over, I was relieved to return to the "simple" life of a resident in medicine, who worked only twelve-hour days, weekends, and one out of every three nights.

I set broken bones and delivered babies at home and in the regional hospital, even though I had never had a firsthand opportunity to do either. My first hospital delivery was memorable: a breech birth in a thirty-eight-year-old woman, who was already a mother of five. It was the first breech that I had ever seen—or felt! I was astonished and relieved when the obstetrical nurse, moments after the delivery, told me, "Doctor, that's the smoothest breech delivery I have ever seen in twenty years' experience."

Dr. Wainer's rural practice offered additional lessons. For example, the residents of Providence had universal access to medical care. He never turned away anybody for lack of money or for nonpayment of fees. Regardless of color or social status, patients were always seen on a first-come, first-served basis, "Jim Crow" laws notwithstanding. *Brown v. Board of Education* had been decided only two years earlier, and now its effects directly crossed my path in rural Kentucky.

One of my patients was an African-American mother from Clay, eight miles north of Providence. She had protested the busing of her children from Clay to a distant black school when there was a neighborhood school close by. She met with such stiff resistance from the white Clay citizenry (and considerable opposition from her own black community for stirring up so much trouble) that Governor Happy Chandler had to call out the National Guard to protect her right to enroll her child in the neighborhood school. The atmosphere in the community was very tense. Visiting the patient and the school during the unrest, I felt as though I had suddenly entered a police state. There was an army bivouac on the school grounds, and uniformed soldiers controlled entry and exit. Surrounding the school and its playing fields were dozens of army tents together with a variety of military supplies and equipment.

The social turmoil hardly affected the Wainer clinic. Patient integration was a fact of life. Furthermore, he never mailed bills. People paid cash when they came to the clinic at the time of the visit or paid cash later whenever they could. When they did not pay, he just put it on the tab. I remember going through his charge cards, amazed at the amount of accounts receivable that were due him. But Dr. Wainer was no saint. He had a healthy respect for money. More than one patient described him as a man who practiced medicine with one hand, while the other hand was "on your wallet." Nevertheless, as far as I could tell, everyone in Providence and its surroundings had access to affordable care.

The strain of working twelve- to fourteen-hour days and having neither the time nor the energy to read and study was obvious every night as I collapsed exhausted into bed. Although tried-and-true remedies handled many day-to-day medical problems, how could a GP keep up with the quick advances in medical therapeutics? In rural Kentucky and many other areas of the United States at that time, the pharmaceutical industry, although frequently maligned and overtly self-serving, was almost alone in providing new and useful information to the practitioner on a regular basis.

Dr. Wainer knew that the industry was manipulative, but he was well prepared to capitalize on its largess. He would refuse to see a salesman unless provided with enough product samples as tribute to satisfy his demand. The medications had to be the right quantity and the right variety before the doctor would take the time to listen. Although this strange negotiation made me feel at times as if I had walked into a Middle Eastern bazaar, Wainer had his reasons for it. He ran his own pharmacy in the office and was intent on stocking it as much as possible with free samples. This made it difficult for the local druggist (who loathed Wainer) to survive. Wainer, on the other hand, made a significant profit because he charged brand-name prices even though his private pharmacy was stocked entirely with generic drugs and pharmaceutical samples. (Most states now have laws preventing the sale of pharmaceutical samples, and most professional samples are labeled, "Not to be sold.") The fascinating operation helped me understand the complicated mix of generosity and venality of a practitioner who was generous with his time and service, but not with his money. The Wainer style, not uncommon among practitioners of that time, provides insight into the unique characteristics of American medicine as a mix of service and business, caring and money, professional ideals and market realities.

Coming from Boston, I had expected a far less sophisticated environment in Providence. Dr. Wainer was hardly out of date, and in some areas he was ahead of his time. For example, in obstetrics, medical teaching in 1956 was to avoid the use of oxytocin or pitocin, an extract of the pituitary gland that can induce labor in a pregnant woman. The use of pitocin during active labor was considered dangerous because it might cause uterine rupture. Such a restriction hardly served the needs of the busy general practitioner who divided his time each day among fifty to seventy-five outpatients and three to four home deliveries. Wainer found out very early in his career that he could not afford the time for nature to take its course. Instead, he would fill a small syringe with one milliliter of pitocin extract and then emptied it immediately so that the only pitocin remaining in the syringe was that which clung to the walls. He then filled the same syringe with normal saline and injected it. This appeared to provide just the right stimulus to cause the uterus to expel its contents within thirty to sixty minutes, ensuring a prompt, safe and effective delivery. Several years later, pitocin became widely used to induce labor for selected patients.

It became clear that the bright young resident from the Harvard teaching hospitals had plenty to learn from the wily GP. And what Wainer did not know, could often be found in a book he relied upon, *Surgery of the Ambulatory Patient* by Lewis Ferguson. The book allowed me to modify the medical teaching aphorisms, "See one, do one, teach one" and "First do no harm," to "Read one, do one, and above all, do no harm." These were just a smattering of the seasoning experiences I had that summer.

I had never imagined the impact that a general practitioner makes on family lives. The broad responsibilities of the rural family practitioner—not just the mechanical treatment of injury and disease, but the teaching, the counseling and the support that had to be provided—were overwhelming. These responsibilities were impressed upon me with every patient I saw and cared for.

I was reminded of this twenty years later when a senior faculty member of the University of Illinois College of Agriculture phoned to invite me to lunch. Providence, Kentucky, was a distant memory to me, and I was very much occupied and preoccupied as the medical school dean. Everyone approaching me had an agenda of some sort, so I asked him what his was. But he respectfully declined to tell me the reason for the invitation until we met in person. After a pleasant lunch and casual conversation, he revealed that he wanted to thank me for the care I had given his father in Providence twenty years earlier. He and his entire family remained grateful for the kindness and skill I demonstrated during that difficult period in their lives. I was deeply touched, but more than that, I was genuinely moved by the incredible effect that a caring doctor can have on the lives of patients and their families.

Frances and I left Providence with our hearts overflowing. With us in the car were a baked Kentucky ham and a collie pup we named "Clay," both presents from grateful patients, and behind us we towed a fourteen-foot aluminum boat and trailer that was all but given to us by another patient. The transition from "super-doc" to lowly medical resident in training took seventy-two hours, the time it took to drive to Boston and report to MGH.

After completing my residency at MGH, I took a two-year postdoctoral fellowship at the Harvard Department of Chemistry with Professor Konrad Bloch. (It was there that I first met Lowell Hager.)

I learned a great deal about the heart and soul of the biochemist, not to mention the rigors of bench work and the labors of biochemistry. In the atmosphere of an active research laboratory, one that was competing successfully on the world stage, the work was exciting but endless. The definitive experiment, the denouement of the problem, always seemed to rest with the next experiment. But the next experiment always seemed to open up new problems. It was a wholly different type of life characterized by hardworking camaraderie and competition. An enormous pressure to achieve, to obtain grants which are the lifeblood of research, and above all, to publish in the best journals were facts of life. Ten- to fourteen-hour days were the rule. I probably worked just as hard in Dr. Bloch's laboratory as I did in my busiest periods in medicine.

A few years after I left his laboratory, Dr. Bloch won the Nobel prize for his work on the biosynthesis of cholesterol, work that was going on in his laboratory while I was there. The prize work was unrelated to my own project with Dr. Bloch, but I mention it for two reasons: first, because I had the confidence of knowing that I had experienced the best there was in biochemistry as well as in medicine; and second, because thirty years later, following a process that reflects the steady, but often slow progress of medical science, the "statin" drugs that evolved from Bloch's work appear destined to extend life expectancy for millions of persons with coronary heart disease. To have been present at their genesis was a rare privilege.

The lesson learned from this creative synergy between the basic and the applied is that in science (and scientific research is a major medical-school mission) one must seek out the most qualified individuals and support them to the hilt. Results that may have practical value or may lead to the alleviation of human suffering may have a lag time of thirty years or more, but the wait is usually worth the effort.

After two years in biochemistry, I was accepted as an Honorary Assistant Registrar by Dr. Paul Wood at the National Heart Hospital in London. Wood was a superb clinician and observer. Almost single-handedly, he honed the use of the stethoscope as a diagnostic tool for heart disease after it had been rendered virtually obsolete by the relentless advance of cardiac catheterization and X-ray. To this day, his brilliance in correlating the physical findings of heart sounds and murmurs with exact anatomical diagnosis remains a rich legacy for medicine. His text on the heart can still profitably be read as a classic of applied logic. Even today, in a world where diagnosis by ultrasound and magnetic resonance imaging has partially replaced cardiac catheterization, the stethoscope, thanks to Wood, continues to hold its own.

Returning from England in 1960, I joined the medical-school faculty at Case Western as an Established Investigator of the American Heart Association. I received a National Institutes of Health grant to study the metabolism of cholesterol in the rat. Cholesterol is a unique molecule with a multiple ring structure that can be modified by body enzymes to form hormones and bile acid products, but it does not ordinarily break down within the human body. I focused on the biochemical problems surrounding the cholesterol molecule. I worked twelve- to fourteen-hour days for weeks on end alone in the laboratory. I also felt the heavy burden of ever-increasing pressures to publish and prepare grant proposals and renewals. I was dissatisfied with my progress and realized that I was really not the skilled biochemist that my research demanded. The straw that tipped the decision scales for me was the publication of a solution to the chemical-biochemical problem that I had been working on feverishly for four years. I realized that I was more of a clinician than a biochemist, so I resolved to explore clinical options and resigned from my fellowship. The deciding factor was not that another team preempted me, it was they had used a method I would never have imagined.

In May 1964, I joined a group of five other physicians as one of six founding members of the Community Health Foundation of Cleveland, Ohio, later to become Kaiser Permanente of Ohio. The group was the first prepaid medical practice in the state. I served as an internist and a cardiologist, and I also served on the group's executive committee. From that vantage point, I participated in many negotiations over salary, working conditions, and benefits. I learned many practical administrative concepts that would prove helpful in the task ahead at Illinois. Another bonus to my switch to clinical medicine was my perception of having more time on my hands. Fourteen-hour days in the laboratory were behind me. Flushed with renewed enthusiasm, I began to take part in community activities. In six months, I was circulating petitions to run for the local school board.

In 1965, I ran and was elected to the school board of Cleveland Heights-University Heights. In preparation for academic administration, there is no substitute for genuine political experience. School boards face the same problems locally as governing bodies face nationally. Only the stakes are different. As a microcosm of the greater world, the school board had among its members "tax and spend liberals" and true fiscal conservatives. Bridging these differences required patience, pragmatism, the arts of negotiation and compromise—and a tough skin. Furthermore, the school board experience taught me that there are no absolutes in leadership and administration. There were three superintendents of schools with whom I worked during those five years, individuals who approached problems in very different ways. The key to successfully dealing with them, a lesson I never forgot, was to understand that there are no perfect candidates for key positions. There are only good candidates who can be encouraged to function within a constructive atmosphere that will bring out their best.

Despite the rich satisfaction received from both medical practice and school-board service, I was anxious to explore ways to resume my specialty as a cardiologist within an academic career. In 1967, I accepted a teaching post as a full-time cardiologist at Mount Sinai Hospital, a private teaching hospital in Cleveland affiliated with Case Western. I had the opportunity to observe the relationships and interactions between full-time physicians, part-time physicians, and attending physicians in the private community hospital environment. This three-year experience, which was not without pain, included a better understanding of the fee-for-service system, of professional territorial rights, of the physician's struggle to admit sick patients when beds were literally not to be had, of the relationship of doctors to hospital administrators, and of the suspicion of administrators of any type that all doctors sooner or later acquire.

The experience gave me useful and necessary insight into the angst of the community hospital, its medical staff, its administration, and its directors. I learned a great deal about the "community" in the community-based medical school. However, after nearly three years, I found myself trapped in a policy dispute with the chief of medicine, who also was the leader of our four-person medical partnership. That was when I determined to leave the community hospital setting and indeed the academic institutional setting, and open my own cardiology practice.

After Lowell's surprise call from Urbana, I pondered my maverick career. It seemed to me as if everything I had done in the past was a building block to prepare me to be a dean.

CHAPTER 3

Origins of the "Treaty"

MY FIRST MEETING with University of Illinois College of Medicine officials in Chicago was a cordial "getting to know you" session. However, Executive Dean William J. Grove and Deputy Executive Dean Richard Magraw felt compelled to stress that power and reporting responsibility rested with Chicago. Regardless of what was said by the search committee in Urbana, Bill Grove, as the Executive Dean over each regional school's dean, would be the person who would hire me and to whom I would report.

I told them bluntly that I would not take the job in Urbana unless it was clear that a four-year school would evolve there.

Magraw spoke up. Because he was charged with nursing the new clinical programs in Rockford and Peoria until they could stand on their own, he soothingly assured me that a four-year program was entirely possible, once Rockford and Peoria were established.

Magraw welcomed me warmly. He struck me as friendly, but cautious— a competent administrator who brought with him a load of bureaucratic baggage from his previous job with the Public Health Service in Washington.

On the other hand, Grove was an accomplished surgeon who had been enticed into administration by Granville Bennett, dean of the school from 1954 to 1968. Since succeeding Bennett, Grove had led the effort to regionalize medical education in Illinois.

William J. Grove, MD, was a tough-minded and very able surgeon whose entire career—medical school, internship, residency, and faculty and administration—was spent at the University of Illinois. The College of Medicine was his life. Born in 1920, in Ottawa, Illinois, he was 50 years old when I first met him. Tall and fair complected, with a thinning crop of light brown hair, he generally spoke in a soft but commanding voice.

He played his cards close to his chest, so that those of us who worked for him did not always know his goals and objectives. For the most part, he was even tempered but used a controlled anger to intimidate subordinates when they vexed him. On occasion, his anger overflowed and appeared to get the best of him causing him to take an abrupt step, such as his dismissing a subordinate.

Grove was focused on the Medical Center campus in Chicago. His loyalty to that institution was absolute and uncompromising. Although not always open, he was absolutely honest, and although I was able to extract less from him than I preferred, he never reneged on a commitment. I was often angry with him, but always respected him. He was a good person to work for.

Grove's point man for the college reorganization was Alexander M. Schmidt, whom I also met on my Chicago visit. Schmidt, a cardiologist from Utah, headed the Committee to Coordinate Planning, the major panel charged with implementing the reorganization. He was a consummate bureaucrat. He reveled in administration and was destined to become the Commissioner of the Food and Drug Administration in 1973.

In our meeting, Schmidt focused on the reorganization and regionalization. Most of this information was new to me. Schmidt recently had been appointed Dean of the Abraham Lincoln School of Medicine, a three-year clinical school that was the direct descendant of the College of Medicine. In our discourse, "Mack" Schmidt was warm, friendly, urbane, pleasant, and encouraging.

My previous discussions with Hager had made it clear that the reorganization and regionalization process was quite an undertaking, but until I visited Chicago in April 1970, I did not realize what a massive upheaval had been going on in medical education throughout Illinois and the nation. The projected medical school at Urbana-Champaign was only a small part of this larger and inevitable change, growing out of national concerns in the 1960s over the structure of health care.

Although it now seems difficult to imagine, Medicare and Medicaid, instituted in the 1960s to increase the federal government's commitment to senior health care, were originally conceived as the first step towards universal health care. Accordingly, there were widespread predictions of physician manpower shortages in the years ahead. Reacting to the changing times, both state and federal incentives encouraged the founding of new medical schools and expanded enrollments in those already established.

As a result, Illinois had undertaken a comprehensive study to determine the state's need for additional higher educational programs in medicine, dentistry and related fields. Backed by the Illinois Legislature and the Illinois Board of Higher Education, the survey was carried out by Drs. James Campbell and W. Randolph Tucker. The Board of Higher Education urged Campbell and Tucker to "depart when desired from traditional thinking about methods when meeting needs in the health related fields" and "to explore new methods and ideas," and "to be innovative in your concepts."

Campbell and Tucker held a number of hearings around the state over a twenty-month period and received medical-school proposals from Peoria, Rockford, the Quad Cities (Moline, Illinois; and Davenport, Rock Island, and Bettendorf, Iowa), Springfield, Edwardsville, and Urbana-Champaign. All of this was detailed in the surveyors' June 1968 two-volume summary *Education in the Health Fields for the State of Illinois*, subsequently known as "The Campbell Report." The Campbell Report was to have a major historical impact upon health education in Illinois.

The Urbana-Champaign proposal presented at two public hearings cited the proximity of the main campus of the University of Illinois; the area's favorable location as a crossroads for trains, buses, and superhighways; and the rapid expansion of medical facilities in the area, as well as a relatively rapid increase in the number of practicing physicians, particularly specialists. Dr. Thomas Wilson, an obstetrician/gynecologist of the Carle Clinic, noted that the campus served a regional population of 550,000 "within a radius of fifty miles...adequate to provide clinical material" for medical education.

Tucker held a second public hearing at Urbana-Champaign on November 8, 1967. This meeting was very well attended by a wide spectrum of the local community, including significant representation from the university: Lyle Lanier, Provost; Jack Peltason, Chancellor; and Herbert Farber, Comptroller. Dr. Wilson could be excused for concluding, "Without question, the University of Illinois is in all-out support for a medical school in Urbana-Champaign."

Yet, the intense efforts of Dr. Wilson and others notwithstanding, Urbana-Champaign was given only a one-year school of basic medical sciences. A similar, new one-year school was recommended for Carbondale. Chicago, Springfield, Rockford, and Peoria were each given the responsibility to develop three-year schools, while Edwardsville and the Quad Cities were not invited to join the party. Chicago divided its ongoing four-year program along the guidelines of one year of basic medical sciences and three years of clinical teaching. The backers of these proposals were unaware of the academic politics that influenced these decisions.

Under the leadership of Granville Bennett, then dean of the College of Medicine, and Grove, who was his associate dean at that time, the college had positioned itself to take advantage of the imminent changes being demanded of medical education. As early as March 1966, Grove led first the Executive Committee and then the college faculty to recommend to the university that the College of Medicine "(1) increase substantially its production of physicians (2) assume leadership in investigating, with other colleges of the university, various approaches to greater efficiency and productivity in the basic education of personnel for the health professions and explore the need for further basic science facilities; (3) assume leadership in investigating the possibility of establishing additional affiliations in order to provide the clinical facilities necessary for expansion."

Grove had sensed that the perceived doctor shortage in the 1960s would lead to heavy state and national resource allocation to expand medical education. If that were the case, he reasoned, the College of Medicine should lead the way in Illinois. Grove concluded that regionalization was the least-expensive way to expand doctor output. He visualized relatively inexpensive teaching programs "piggybacking" onto existing community hospital facilities, thus avoiding the expensive development of university teaching hospitals. For Urbana-Champaign, it was apparent that an inexpensive basic medical science teaching program could be grafted on to the already strong life-science departments on the campus. There would be no need to develop independent, and expensive, new basic medical science departments, such as biochemistry or microbiology. Regionalization under the auspices of the College of Medicine would also finesse many of the accreditation problems that new medical schools were encountering circa 1970.

Grove also saw regionalization as a way of solidifying political support for the College in the two largest downstate cities, Peoria and Rockford. However, Urbana probably didn't mean as much to him because any College of Medicine student presence there would be minuscule compared with the other thirty-five thousand UIUC students. It would not have a high enough profile to help the College of Medicine politically.

On October 21, 1968, Grove appointed the College Committee to

Coordinate Planning, with Schmidt as chairman. The committee was to coordinate the work of several other committees appointed at the same time to provide the administrative framework for reorganizing the pattern of education at the college.

The previous model in a four-year medical school had been a pattern of two years of basic medical sciences and two years of clinical medicine. The new mode for medical education in Illinois would be a split of one year of basic medical sciences and three years of clinical medicine. Thus, the thinking behind a single-year school at Urbana-Champaign was that it would provide strictly basic medical sciences, while a three-year institution such as the Abraham Lincoln School of Medicine would provide instruction in clinical medicine.

The coordinating committee's final report, issued May 15, 1969, recommended restructuring the College of Medicine as a group of five semi-autonomous medical schools, each headed by a dean, and linked together as a College of Medicine headed by an executive dean. Each school faculty would have the option of having its own faculty organization and committee structure. The school deans would report to the executive dean in Chicago. These recommendations point out that Grove's main interests were structural and economic, not curricular. They also centralized the administration in his hands.

From the outset of regionalization, Grove was careful to protect his central authority. Early on, a bitter power struggle took place between Grove and Campbell, the co-author of the Campbell Report. Campbell interpreted the Illinois Board of Higher Education's mandate for regionalization as a call for separate but equal medical schools within the University of Illinois system. Campbell's unit, which encompassed the strong teaching program at Presbyterian-St. Luke's Hospital, was unparalleled within the Illinois system. Citing the board's mandate, Campbell insisted that his institution have independent reporting responsibility. Grove balked at this challenge to his power, insisting that Campbell report through the executive dean's office. As president of the hospital, Campbell threatened to withdraw Presbyterian-St. Luke's from the College of Medicine's teaching program, unless Grove gave in, but Grove remained firm and elected to forsake this premier institution rather than sacrifice control.

Subsequently, Campbell carried out his threat, withdrew the hospital from the College of Medicine and reactivated its long-shelved charter as the reborn, independent Rush Medical School. This left a huge void in the College of Medicine's teaching program. The end result was that two very headstrong leaders caused a rupture which was not in the best interest of the college.

Faced with the loss of a major teaching resource, second only in importance to the University of Illinois Hospital, Grove hastily negotiated affiliations and teaching contracts with six private Chicago hospitals— Ravenswood, Weiss Memorial, McNeil, Mercy, Lutheran General, and Illinois Masonic—to fill the clinical teaching gap left by Campbell's defection. In doing so, Grove had to commit state resources to these hospitals, further diluting the limited resources available for the regional schools in Urbana-Champaign, Rockford, and Peoria.

Campbell had been envious of Grove's power throughout the process. He had structured his report to permit Springfield to have its own medical school as a branch of Southern Illinois University in Carbondale. Grove, seeking to solidify political support for the College of Medicine downstate, would have gladly welcomed a Springfield campus into his college. The decision to give Springfield to SIU proved very expensive to the state and to the College of Medicine because a large portion of incremental dollars for medical education was drained off to the south. The new medical school for SIU, starting from scratch, then cost and continues to cost about three times as much as the downstate University of Illinois medical programs on a per-student basis.

Grove was committed to making the College of Medicine a model of medical educational excellence. His ambitious expansion plans included increasing enrollment from two hundred to five hundred per year, resources permitting. Within the context of five hundred graduates per year, there was a role for clinical education and a four-year medical school at Urbana-Champaign, but its priority in Grove's mind in 1970 was low.

His experience and tenure within the College of Medicine since his days as a medical student gave him a strong institutional memory. This was very helpful at times but it also encumbered him with some heavy baggage against our efforts to develop the program at Urbana-Champaign. He was sensitive to intercampus rivalries within the university's then three-campus system, and was particularly thin-skinned when he encountered the competitive posturing of the UIUC campus, which claimed being the university's main locus for quality and excellence as its birthright.

A second medical school within the University of Illinois would compete with his college for state resources, and the thought of the College of Medicine losing its exclusive franchise in medical education to a rival campus was very threatening to Grove.

Above all, he fretted that the UIUC campus had always attracted more than its share of resources to the detriment of the College of Medicine. Now that medical education was at the head of the line for state funding, he would oppose allocating one nickel more than was absolutely necessary to the medical program at Urbana-Champaign, even though it was his own program. Furthermore, the thought of an independent medical school on the UIUC campus was a nightmare to him—and he was determined to avoid it.

In dealing with the expansion of medical education to the Urbana-Champaign campus, Grove had to walk a very fine line. Although he was committed to regionalization and, in theory, to institutional cooperation, he was deeply suspicious of the Urbana campus. His goal, I believe, was to permit the Urbana program to develop under tight safeguards that would enable it to contribute to Collge of Medicine, but would never become independently accredited as a medical school and never be administratively responsible to the UIUC administration.

Remember that UIUC was not just another campus. It was the University's original campus with the potential to eclipse its rivals in all fields, including medicine. Moreover, the perception of UIUC as arrogant and uncollegial, widely held at the Chicago campuses of the university, was not without foundation. It was not uncommon to hear Urbana-Champaign campus faculty routinely demean the Medical Center and refer to it as if it were an academic family skeleton, a low-quality operation that did not measure up to the high research standards at UIUC.

Some of these perceptions were a result of the natural rivalry for resources and prestige between the two campuses, but there were also strong gut-level feelings that went beyond that.

Neither Grove nor the people at UIUC were unmindful of the Flexner Report of 1910, which assessed U.S. medical schools and concluded that the mantle of high scientific quality in Illinois rested on the Urbana-Champaign campus so that it would be the optimal site for a state medical school. Mindful that five other medical schools, six counting the born-again Rush Medical School, were all in Chicago, it did not take too much imagination to picture an independent medical school at UIUC challenging the supremacy of the Chicago operation. The power-oriented governance in Chicago gave little thought to the obvious academic value of a strong medical program at UIUC.

The attitude at Urbana-Champaign was quite different. Although the faculty and administration were willing to go along with the College of Medicine to get the operation started, they wanted assurance that they were not to be exploited. They abhorred being thrust into the role of being strictly a service unit for College of Medicine, teaching routine basic science courses to a specified number of medical students who would be at Urbana-Champaign for only one year and would develop no feelings for and make no contributions to the campus and its institutions. The Urbana-Champaign faculty wanted to be absolutely certain that within a reasonable period the program would expand into a four-year medical school in Urbana-Champaign that would become an integral part of UIUC. Moreover, it would be independent of College of Medicine. This put them on a collision course with Bill Grove.

By the summer of 1968, serious medical education planning began at Urbana-Champaign. In August, George J. Schroepfer, a professor of biochemistry, was appointed director of the medical program on the Urbana-Champaign campus and made an assistant dean in the College of Medicine. Schroepfer chaired the UIUC Committee on Medical Education, which was charged with defining the program's goals or objectives, curriculum, organization, and the facilities needed.

On September 25, 1969, Schroepfer's committee released its report in a document entitled "Status of Program in Medical Education on the Urbana-Champaign Campus." The report reproduced a summary of the College of Medicine's Committee to Coordinate Planning. Outlining its recommendations for the organization of a school of basic medical sciences at Urbana-Champaign, the report added that "although not stated in this summary, Urbana-Champaign has been designated as a potential site for a 'clinical school.'"

This set the stage for the committee's clash with Grove. Although defining the objectives of the program, the curriculum, and the physical facilities necessary to house the program required a great deal of work, they produced no controversy. Defining the organizational elements, that is, the power structure, was another matter. The Urbana-Champaign organizational views

clearly diverged from those in Chicago. The Urbana-Champaign members
and Bill Grove's personal representative on the committee, N.J. Cotsonas Jr.,
reached an impasse. Schroepfer's committee outlined the UIUC position on
governance in a March 10, 1969, letter to Executive Vice President and
Provost Lyle Lanier, who had executive authority over both the Urbana-
Champaign campus and the College of Medicine.

In an attempt to avert years of recurrent haggling over administrative
lines, the letter outlined the problems facing the developing medical school
on the Urbana-Champaign campus. The letter proposed a solution totally
inimical to Grove's interests—instead of a program organized under the
College of Medicine, a separate, distinct school of basic medical sciences
would be established at Urbana-Champaign. This would have been an
autonomous school within the College of Medicine, and its dean would have
reported to the college's executive dean and to Urbana-Champaign's chancellor. Funding would be allocated by the Urbana-Champaign chancellor in
consultation with the College of Medicine's executive dean.

Part of the justification for this approach was that the two faculties
teaching basic sciences, Chicago and Urbana, differed significantly in then-
existing and projected educational responsibilities.

The letter also said: "Perhaps of the most importance... is that the establishment of a separate 'school' of basic medical sciences on the Urbana-
Champaign campus will allow the program to develop and evolve as a
distinct, identifiable educational unit looking to the gradual development of
a full curriculum of medicine in Urbana-Champaign. This point will have
very significant implications with respect to the quality of personnel which
will be recruited for the program. This will be especially true with respect to
the recruitment of a quality person as Dean [or Director]."

Lanier, who had a long history of university service at Urbana-
Champaign, who sympathetically understood Schroepfer's position, and
who was now being asked to wrest a portion of power from Grove and
transfer it to Urbana, still hesitated to interfere with Grove's prerogatives.
The Schroepfer committee's letter to Lanier correctly identified governance
as the primary sticking point. The Urbana-Champaign solution, bluntly
proposed, was: "Trust us. We'll get the job done!"

Grove refused to tolerate a branch campus reporting elsewhere but to his
office. Citing reasons of accreditation (which would come through the
College of Medicine), Grove insisted that he would never accept state funding

channeled to the new school through Urbana-Champaign, whether or not it was "in consultation with the Executive Dean of the College of Medicine." Grove had the chips that counted because all new state dollars for medical education were allocated by the University president to the College of Medicine—and thus to Bill Grove.

Grove also concluded that Schroepfer was a firebrand and had to be replaced. Schroepfer understood the stakes better than anyone else at Urbana-Champaign. He fought vigorously for a more well-defined UIUC role in the medical-education expansion. However, Schropfer proved to be a voice crying in the wilderness, unheard and unsung. Bill Grove dismissed Schroepfer from his deanship because of his determined opposition to the College of Medicine's hegemony over what was, in his view, an Urbana-Champaign program. That dismissal opened the door for me, in all innocence, to enter the scene.

Knowing that the Urbana-Champaign faculty was unlikely to accept an in-house administrator that he sent down from Chicago, Grove convinced Lanier and the UIUC planning group to initiate a nationwide search to select the dean. Grove needed someone from the outside who would nevertheless be his inside person in Urbana-Champaign.

Negotiations between the College of Medicine and the UIUC planning group continued in a tense atmosphere. Grove would have pulled back all of the basic science instruction to Chicago if he thought that the Chicago physical plant could handle the increase of five hundred students per year that expansion promised, but he knew it could not. He had to co-opt the basic science teaching resources of Urbana-Champaign in a manner that gave him control. The Urbana-Champaign faculty frequently threatened to abandon the project if it were not to be academically controlled by UIUC. Furthermore, they sought assurance that there would eventually be a four-year complete program on the campus. They refused to be simply the passive repository of a "low quality" operation from Chicago.

After extensive negotiations resulted in a complete deadlock, Lanier was the only person who could settle the dispute. He not only had the authority in his title of Executive Vice-President and Provost, he had the respect of both parties.

To resolve the impasse, Lanier offered a compromise. In doing so, he pointed out that the main sticking points between the College of Medicine and Urbana-Champaign had to do "with the assumptions and expectations as to the development and administration of a full curriculum for the M.D. degree at the Urbana-Champaign campus." In addition, he wisely noted that the compromise likely would not be fully satisfactory to either group.

Lanier wrote that "no commitment to such a program can be made now," but he also added, "At the same time, no commitment can or should be made that a full program of clinical training will not be developed in time at the Urbana-Champaign campus. Indeed, both the University's report of December 1967 and the Board of Higher Education's document of June 1968 specifically mention such a possibility. But the 'Campbell Report' gives priority to Peoria and Rockford as locations for the initial expansion of clinical training by the University outside Chicago. Hence, it seems best to leave the matter of clinical training at Urbana-Champaign indefinite and open—with the understanding that if and when a four-year medical curriculum emerges there, it would be administered as an independent college under the chancellor at that campus."

The compromise, which I'll call the "Lanier Treaty," ultimately was approved by the planning committees of both campuses and by the Board of Trustees. The treaty rested on five principles acceptable to both parties:

1. There would be a one-year curriculum in basic medical sciences.
2. The program would be conducted under the aegis of the College of Medicine.
3. Mutual agreement regarding major policies and procedures would be necessary to the effectiveness of the program because this program would necessarily require close cooperation between the two campuses.
4. Consideration would be given to the expansion of this program into a full curriculum for the M.D. degree as soon as the necessary resources for clinical training became available in the Urbana-Champaign region.
5. In the event of the establishment of an expanded medical curriculum at Urbana-Champaign that would fulfill all requirements for the M.D. degree, formal responsibility for administering the program would be assigned to Urbana-Champaign. More specifically, a College of Medicine would be established whose dean would report to the Urbana-Champaign chancellor and whose educational policies would be subject to the jurisdiction of the Urbana-Champaign Senate.

By giving authority to Chicago and hope to Urbana-Champaign, Lanier settled the issue for the immediate future. Once these five principles were accepted by both parties, the remainder of the treaty document followed in short order. The organization of the new school was specified in more detail, but specifically directed that the Urbana school would be an administrative unit of the College of Medicine and that the dean of the school would report to the executive dean of the College of Medicine in Chicago, even though "the Chancellor at the Urbana-Champaign campus must concur in the appointment of the dean of the Urbana-Champaign School."

The treaty assumed that "the instructional staff of the School at Urbana-Champaign will all be members of appropriate departments in other Colleges at the UIUC campus and that the School will not have separate departments duplicating existing ones." Thus, it established one of the most complicated administrative problems ever faced by an academic administrator. The dean of the Urbana school would report administratively to the executive dean in Chicago, but the faculty of the school in Urbana would be members of departments in Urbana which reported neither to the dean of the School in Urbana nor to the executive dean of the College of Medicine but only to the UIUC administrative chain of command.

Grove won his battles for control, but at what cost?

Grove was a skillful and meticulous administrator who thrived on the manipulation of both his administrative subordinates and his faculty. His record of success speaks for itself. He led a sizable faculty to engage in the largest medical-school expansion in U.S. history.

Grove proved less adept, however, at dealing with forces outside his jurisdiction that worked against the College of Medicine's interest. Losing his major private teaching hospital in Chicago in the reorganization process was a heavy price to pay for the central control that Grove demanded. His failure to ensure that the College of Medicine regional units in Rockford, Peoria, and Urbana-Champaign had budget allocations that kept pace with other state-supported regional programs in Illinois, led by Southern Illinois University Medical School, was nearly catastrophic. Fixated on economy in the regional schools, and restricting their budget requests to bare minimums, Grove permitted Southern Illinois University to capture the lion's share of new state money for its development. SIU quickly and unashamedly became the most costly medical school, on a per-student basis, in the state. At the same time, it assumed medical hegemony for all of the state of Illinois south of Springfield. Richard Moy, dean at SIU, demonstrably bested Grove in the competition for state funds. Grove's failure in this respect had lasting consequences.

In retrospect, convinced that a strong medical school at Urbana-Champaign had much to add to the campus and to the university, I believe that Lanier made a fundamental error in 1969. In yielding the Urbana medical program governance to Bill Grove for an unspecified period of time, he condemned the College of Medicine at Urbana-Champaign to a form of permanent limbo as a tolerated appendage of the Chicago program and a "foreign body" at UIUC. He denied medical education at Urbana-Champaign the opportunity to expand to a size appropriate for its mission and to achieve all of the excellence that was possible were it unshackled.

CHAPTER 4

Taking the Keys to the Asylum

MY FORMAL INTRODUCTION to the cast of characters at the Medical Center in Chicago complete, it was time to explore Urbana. Conveniently, University of Illinois President David Dodds Henry was in Chicago for a meeting and invited me to join him on the plane he had chartered for his return trip to Urbana.

For the better part of an hour, we flew over mile after mile of the richest farmland in the world, with corn and soybean fields spread before me on all sides. This was true culture shock for a city dweller. I had seen farms in Ohio, but I had never confronted the dominance of agriculture lying there in the vast farms below me. "The world's breadbasket" and "supermarket to the world" suddenly had new meaning.

Sitting on my left, the president was warm, jovial, and optimistic. He looked the role of an academic leader. His kindly, bespectacled face masked a forceful personality. Preoccupied with the agricultural panorama, I was startled when he asked me about my views of the College of Medicine.

I responded that I had very little to say about the college at this early stage so we talked about other issues—the need for more doctors in the state, the prominence of the university in the nation, and the like. A dean does not often have the opportunity for leisurely one-on-one discussions with the university president, and as a candidate dean I welcomed the brief intimacy. I did not have another opportunity to speak to President Henry after that flight (except for perfunctory greetings on formal occasions) for twelve years. I was impressed by his humanity, which tempered but did not cloak strength. By the time we landed in Urbana, I felt ready to join his team if the option were offered.

I had never even heard of Urbana before I worked with Lowell Hager in Konrad Bloch's Harvard laboratory a dozen years earlier. I had been east to Istanbul but had never been west of Detroit, so to me Urbana was a remote rural village that seemed to be about the last place in the world I would consider home. Culture shock struck again the first time I turned on a TV set. Advertisements for herbicides, fertilizers, and hybrid corn stocks replaced the urban-centered copy I was accustomed to in Cleveland. Radio somberly reported the prices of corn and soybean futures on the hour with monotonous regularity and all the streets in the city, it seemed, ran only north-south or east-west. Welcome to the Midwest.

On the other hand, Urbana-Champaign was very much a part of the world I lived in. My preliminary visits took place in April and May 1970, when the Vietnam War was still going full tilt and the government's policy was being met with increasing resistance on college campuses. On May 4, four students were killed by panicked National Guard troops at Kent State University, only forty miles from my home in Cleveland. The protests against the war and the killings at Kent State did not leave the University of Illinois unscathed. Nevertheless, I was not prepared for what I saw.

The main quadrangle of the university looked like a war zone. Windows were boarded up on most of the buildings, casualties of stones thrown in student protests. Outside the Student Union, particularly at lunch-time, soapbox oratory against the war displaced the usual cadre of religious evangelists. My hosts warned me that wearing a suit and tie on the campus carried the risk of being too closely linked to the "establishment" being blamed for the war.

I registered at the Lincoln Lodge (in Illinois it is hard to get away from the fact that this is the "Land of Lincoln") and prepared to make the rounds scheduled by the search committee. Most of the persons I met with in two visits to the Urbana-Champaign campus were parties to the Lanier treaty and wanted to know my views on it. I reiterated my position that I would not come to be the dean of a one-year medical school and that I interpreted the treaty literally. I was convinced that there would be a four-year program at Urbana-Champaign within five years. I must have made a hit because that was what they wanted to hear.

Nevertheless, I insisted on my own meeting with Provost Lyle Lanier. My agenda with Lanier had but one item. I told him what I had told everyone else: If there was a reasonable opportunity to develop a full four-year medical school, I was interested in the position; otherwise, I was not a candidate. Lanier smiled and gave me a brilliantly conceived, noncommittally committed answer, much as Magraw had in Chicago. Pointing to the aerial photo of the Urbana-Champaign campus, which hung on his office wall, he said, "Just look at the size, strength and breadth of the institution before you. It is one of the great campuses in the world. Do you think the faculty of this campus will permit only half a medical school to exist here for long?" He advised me to have patience and that in due time it was inevitable that a complete medical-education program would be established at Urbana-Champaign.

My interviews must have gone well because I was invited to become the first and only dean of the School of Basic Medical Sciences at Urbana-Champaign. Although I did not have the ironclad assurances that I sought, I was satisfied by those I had.

Even Bill Grove, ever scrupulously correct regarding his promises, intimated that a four-year program was well within the realm of possibility. The optimist and risk-taker in me took over at this point. When the formal offer came, and after some negotiation regarding my personal status and academic rank, I accepted the position effective August 1, 1970.

On July 22, The Board of Trustees recommended my appointment as "Professor of Medicine on indefinite tenure in the Abraham Lincoln School of Medicine, and Dean of the School of Basic Medical Sciences at Urbana-Champaign." So I was to be dean of the school in Urbana, but my academic rank and tenure status resided in Chicago. Although I was selected for the post by a search committee largely made up of senior Urbana-Champaign faculty and that faculty would accept my credentials as dean, I did not qualify for a professorial appointment in any of the basic science departments in Urbana-Champaign and so my professorial appointment came from Chicago.

Welcome to the asylum!

In the ensuing months, I closed my embryonic private practice, and made preparations to move to Urbana, Illinois.

Arriving on the campus on August 1, I was a true free-floating apex: a dean at the top of an organization with nothing and no one below me. I occupied a temporary office and had the authority to hire a secretary. Vice Chancellor Herb Carter suggested Mrs. Ellen Rhode, a retired administrative secretary who was very knowledgeable about how the campus academic and administrative bureaucracies worked. Also assigned to me as a liaison from the School of Life Sciences was Professor John D. Anderson, a member of the Department of Physiology and Biophysics. Two better, more devoted or knowledgeable individuals could not be found, and they guided me well.

Nothing had prepared me for the intrigue to be met, protocol to be followed and administrative delicacy that would be required to navigate effectively in the tempestuous two-campus sea in which I found myself. Mrs. Rhode knew the administrative side at UIUC as well as any living person, while John Anderson knew the academic side. No one knew the Medical Center campus well.

It was readily apparent that I needed friends and allies on the Urbana-Champaign campus, so on advice from Ellen and John, I set about to meet every senior faculty member and every department head who had anything to do with biology or medicine. Easing my task, many campus leaders sought me out as well.

Even though I was technically assigned to the College of Medicine administration, I was invited to attend regular monthly meetings of the Urbana-Champaign deans and directors. This, together with my regular intercourse with the College of Medicine's counterpart of this group, gave me unique access to the senior administration's thinking on the two campuses, rare among administrators at my level. I quickly developed a working insight into the operations of this giant university, and with it, a growing comprehension of the orphan status that would be the early fate of the medical enterprise at Urbana-Champaign.

I also met with local physicians, both formally at medical society meetings and informally at their offices. I told them all that the medical school would not threaten their stature or income, that there would be no university hospital at Urbana-Champaign, and that the practicing community represented a largely untapped reservoir of teaching talent and that there would be a place in this medical school for practitioners who wanted to teach.

In addition, I advised them that although the School of Basic Medical Sciences was for the moment a one-year basic science school, I had made it clear to university officials that I accepted the deanship only with the tacit assumption that a four-year program would be developed soon. Although some expressed doubts that we could assemble the manpower for a full four-year program, the majority of those with whom I spoke were excited by the prospect.

I also cultivated hospital affiliations. In 1970, the bulk of clinical teaching was hospital based, and my task was to determine how best to co-opt the private, local hospitals into developing as teaching institutions. I targeted four local or nearby hospitals as essential to our effort and met with the administrators. I was invited to the quarterly luncheon meetings of the twenty-one-member East Central Illinois Hospital Association, where I was introduced to every hospital administrator in the region and did what I could to gain their support.

Bill Grove arranged a reception at the University Club in order to formally introduce Franny and me, as representatives of the College of Medicine, to the Urbana-Champaign campus. Although we had been on campus three months already, the turnout was astonishing. I had thought I was learning who was who on campus, but I was completely unprepared to meet and greet the two hundred to three hundred people who came to that reception. I was very grateful to Grove for organizing it. The reception made a huge impact on the campus. It notified almost every important figure at Urbana-Champaign that medical education had really arrived.

CHAPTER 5

Dealing with Scarce Resources

T HERE IS NO TEXT on how to start a medical school on a shoe-
string. Dr. George T. Harrell probably set a record as the founding
dean of three medical schools and wrote a book about his experience. Each new school was funded generously by its sponsor, the latest being
Pennsylvania State University at Hershey, which began with a $36 million
endowment from the Hershey company. That was a "sweet" deal compared
with my endowment-free first year budget of $150,000, half of which went
for the salaries of Mrs. Rhode, John Anderson and me!

I was terribly naive for not hammering out budget issues before
accepting the deanship, but after my discussions in Urbana and Chicago, I
assumed that the state and the University were serious about regionalizing
medical education and would provide the funds to accomplish that goal.
The state did provide substantial medical school start-up funds but SIU
took the lion's share, and of the funds that were under Bill Grove's management, precious little went to Urbana.

Grove, apparently unaware of the lavish amounts dealt to SIU by the
state, asked for and accepted relatively limited funding for the expansion. He
was determined to make the expansion effective and inexpensive. In doing
this, he played his fiscal cards close to his chest. On paper, the five deans of
the reorganized College of Medicine and Grove made up a council that was
to advise the executive dean on budget allocation. As a practical matter, however, Grove alone prepared the college budget request. When funds were
actually received, he presented each dean with his allocation as a *fait
accompli*. At times, we were informed only of the amount of our own school's
allocation, not the allocations to our sister schools. After one or two years
and considerable agitation, Bill opened up the balance sheets so that we
could compare budgets, if not question them. Never, to my recollection, did
our discussions, complaints, arguments, or pleas change the budget distribution already decided by Grove. Although no regional site was over-funded in

the process, Urbana was definitely on the short end of the stick.

Despite the public and political clamor for more medical schools and more doctors, state and federal funding to fulfill the new political mandates were relatively limited. This was particularly true with respect to the amounts that would trickle down to Urbana. The early realization of these unpleasant facts played a decisive role in planning. It was worrisome to me. If funds were tight at this early stage, where on earth would the funds for an Urbana clinical program come from? How does one even plan a school of basic medical sciences with a budget so anemic? There were many times when I would have liked to throw up my hands in disgust and walk away, but I had learned long before, in school-board squabbles back in Cleveland and in the battles between physicians and hospital administrators, that resigning in high dudgeon rarely gets the job done. It makes the one who resigns feel morally superior and good for a few days, but it really plays into the hands of the antagonists. Political survival requires uncommon perseverance, acceptance and absorption of setbacks, careful planning, and above all, keeping the goal in mind. The eye must be fixed on the prize.

So quitting was out of the question. Given my thin faculty, I pushed Grove to the limit for additional funds, as did the other deans, keeping the heat on him to press the funding sources for more generous allocations. Grove was an exceptionally strong administrator in dealing with subordinates, but as I noted earlier when it came to rattling the cages above him, he was less effective. It became clear to me that I would not solve my funding problem solely by pressing Grove for more state dollars. In the end, my school, as the squeakiest wheel in the house, probably received more than it would have otherwise, but the total amounts remained embarrassingly small—so small that had I been able to convince Grove to increase the budget by 10, 20, or even 30 percent, it would not have solved our problem. If it was to survive, our school was destined to be a low-budget medical school (the students dubbed it "K mart Medical School"). The solution to the problem lay in genuine innovation—doing more with less. We needed cost-saving innovation in curriculum definition and delivery; in instructional methods; in the utilization of full-time faculty; in mobilizing community resources; and particularly in using the community-based practicing physicians to assist us.

The format for medical education, and particularly education in the basic medical sciences, had not really changed very much since 1910. It consisted of two years of didactic basic medical sciences in the lecture and laboratory mode, followed by two years of practical, hospital-based clerkship work. Furthermore, because traditional medical education required the employment of a critical mass of full-time faculty in each of ten to twenty research-oriented departments, the typical medical-education program was quite expensive. Unlike undergraduate programs where a single instructor might teach a course almost as easily to one thousand students as to fifteen students, the average medical school of 1970 employed about fifty full-time faculty members to teach basic medical science to one hundred medical students. It was not the need for more teaching or the need for more detailed instruction that led to such a high faculty-student ratio. The medical school demand for ever-larger faculties to teach a fixed number of students was a reflection of the growing medical-school research mission, which complemented and, in some instances, overshadowed its teaching mission. It is close to the truth to describe the modern medical school in the last quarter of the twentieth century as a biomedical research factory that incidentally trains physicians.

The rigid atmosphere of doctrinaire science that pervades U.S. medical schools is reinforced by the accreditation process of the Liaison Committee for Medical Education. The LCME felt obliged to distinguish medical education in the United States from that in virtually any other country. Therefore, far from accrediting the medical-education process per se, LCME site visitors were frequently more interested in the pedigrees and research prowess of the teachers than of their excellence as teachers. The LCME made the tacit, but not unreasonable assumption that if the faculty were of high caliber (i.e., productive in research), the teaching would be satisfactory.

It is to the distinct credit of Bill Grove that he was able to shelter his fledgling units from the rigid demands of the LCME. The three regional schools matriculated their first students under Grove's claim that the existing College of Medicine accreditation provided an adequate umbrella to shelter all the new schools. It's unlikely that any of three regional schools would have been accredited on their own. But functioning as branches of the accredited College of Medicine, and bound together by a complex collegewide committee structure, the schools began matriculating students in 1970 and 1971, without so much as a by-your-leave to the LCME.

Grove had chutzpah. He bypassed the LCME start-up process to the extent that all three new regional schools had a minimum of three years' operating experience before representatives of the LCME ever saw them. It was not easy, and Grove deserves much credit for launching the reorganization and deflecting LCME criticism of his methodology for at least the first four years that followed the college reorganization. We were thus spared the fate of several contemporary new medical schools such as Michigan State University, the University of Missouri at Kansas City, and Eastern Virginia Medical School, which all saw their innovative teaching programs crushed or substantially modified because of LCME pressure.

It was originally intended that the School of Basic Medical Sciences would begin instruction on September 5, 1972. The first thirty-two students would graduate in June 1973 and be promoted to one of the three-year schools that were developing in Chicago, Rockford, and Peoria. However, observing the state budgeting process, the vulnerability of our school, and the perceptible ambivalence toward medical education both within the state and the university, I saw the imperative of a faster start before someone in a dominant position decided that all this new medical education was too much, too soon, and too expensive.

The politics of medical education funding was skewed against us from the outset. Although the College of Medicine was expanding by three hundred physicians per year, SIU-Springfield, which aimed for only seventy-five graduates per year, received the lion's share of new medical education dollars. Although the broad-based state enthusiasm for more doctors was genuine, the ability to translate those feelings into sustained funding for a medical education program in Urbana remained dubious. My first major decision then was to begin instruction in Urbana with as many students as Bill Grove would assign to us in the autumn of 1971 and not to wait the additional year to "get on the books." Grove, on this occasion, was sympathetic. He, too, saw the dollars going south to SIU and wanted his regional schools to be on line as soon as possible as he prepared to fight budget battles with the university, the Board of Higher Education, and the legislature.

My resources in the fall of 1970, besides what was required for Ellen Rhode, John Anderson, and me, included about seventy-five thousand dollars; a small, windowless office in Roger Adams Laboratory; and pockets of goodwill about the campus. I refer to "pockets" of support because not everyone at Urbana-Champaign was certain that they wanted our operation to succeed. But the heads of physiology and biophysics, biochemistry and microbiology, three departments that were critical to the school's success, were all supportive as long as the medical school could pay its own way. From their standpoint, the medical school would be adding positions to their departments at no real cost to themselves and, indeed, all three were busy in joint recruitment efforts to bring new medical-school faculty to the campus.

However, departments were not willing to assign established faculty to help create the medical curriculum unless proper release-time reimbursement was arranged. When it comes to teaching responsibilities on a research university campus, only money talks; faculty members are completely tied up with their obligatory teaching, their committee service duties, and their research. If they are needed for duties not included in their contract, it usually costs.

The most economical way to tap into departmental resources for the curriculum development we needed to do was to hire competent graduate students in selected disciplines. They were usually available for hire as half-time teaching assistants. However, the graduate student pool was very uneven. Some were excellent and capable of producing useful curricular material that would rival a faculty product. Others were a waste of money.

Needing additional space to house our impromptu faculty and to provide classrooms for a program that would have its first students in six months, the medical school was assigned an old Victorian house at 1205 W. California Street, close to both the Life and Chemical Sciences buildings. It would house our program until the scheduled completion of the Medical Sciences building in 1975.

Other potential assets included the Urbana-Champaign medical community of about 150 physicians, plus another 200 practitioners who lived and worked within a fifty-mile radius. Many were relatively isolated in a downstate rural setting but were genuinely interested in participating in medical education as a means of self-fulfillment and to benefit from much needed continuing professional education. What better continuing education experience could a physician have than reviewing the basic medical sciences one on one with an eager medical student? Who would be more capable of applying a relevance test to learning objectives in the basic medical sciences than a physician on the front line? I had played the role of the rural physician fourteen years earlier, and I believed that there was a role for that type of physician in our school, even in the basic medical sciences. Furthermore, I believed that if I could involve a significant fraction of the 350 area physicians in the basic science program, I would have a major constituency to support our fledgling enterprise in case of political need as well as a nucleus for the development of a clinical curriculum when the time came.

Potential medical education assets also included five local hospitals that would close or consolidate to two effective teaching hospitals over the next two decades, but they could hardly have been termed teaching institutions in 1970. There was also a sleepy Veterans Administration Hospital located thirty miles to the east in Danville. It was a sizable chunk of "pork" brought home to Danville by the city's most famous politician, Joseph Cannon, long-time Speaker of the U.S. House of Representatives. The hospital was mainly a nursing home and psychiatric repository. It would need considerable strengthening to make it a credible teaching hospital.

Reviewing all available assets, real and imagined, if we were to begin teaching only twelve months after the free-floating apex arrived, we needed at least one full-time faculty member in biochemistry, microbiology, physiology, anatomy, and histology. I authorized the appropriate Urbana-Champaign departments to begin their searches immediately for faculty who would be paid and be primarily responsible to the medical-school dean, even though their departmental home would be external to the School of Basic Medical Sciences. Research space for the new faculty was reserved in the newly built twenty-thousand-square-foot Burrill Hall addition.

I also had some luck. On the campus and anxious to help was Ray Watterson, a distinguished teacher of embryology, who was willing to be employed on a part-time basis. Ray quickly proved himself to be the most popular lecturer in our school. Although our school de-emphasized the lecture format, he was living proof that if a lecturer is really good, students will listen. Watterson was an exception that we could not count on in other areas. We still had to assemble an operational curriculum by August 1971 that five or six new, unseasoned faculty members could manage, while allowing them ample time to set up their laboratories and begin research. It was a tall order.

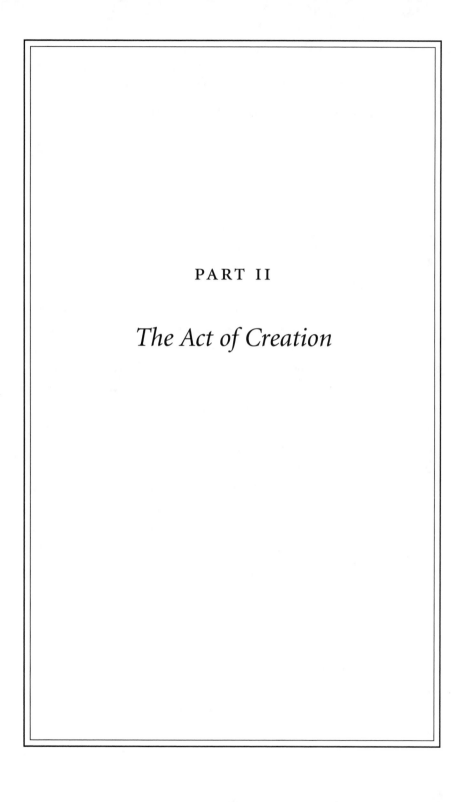

PART II

The Act of Creation

CHAPTER 6

A Curriculum Innovative;
A Curriculum Relevant

PLANNING A NEW MEDICAL SCHOOL CURRICULUM proved to be an exciting challenge. In 1970, there were only two innovative models of medical education that tried to escape the effective but rigid and monolithic confines that Abraham Flexner established in his 1910 report. Case Western Reserve University broke the mold in 1952 under the direction of T. Hale Ham. The earthshaking nature of the new system was not so much its form, but its attention to educational principles. Greater emphasis was placed on instructional relevance. Early clinical experience was introduced by arranging for each medical student to meet a pregnant woman early during the first year of study and to follow mother and child through prenatal care, labor, and delivery, and the continued care of both for the next four years. The student would be notified whenever mother or child sought medical attention and, regardless of current activity, the student would detach in favor of his long-range obligation to participate in the care of his family. In this way, relevance was successfully incorporated into the curriculum.

The main educational structure remained a lecture-laboratory style, but it was more system- than discipline-oriented. Instruction was integrated rather than taught discipline by discipline. For example, the heart was studied as a unit. Its anatomy, physiology, biochemistry and pathology were all presented through team teaching. Organ systems were studied as a unit and tested the same way. The concept of a student multidisciplinary laboratory was introduced in which each student had a single bench assigned for all laboratory exercises.

It was not right for our school, however, because the Case Western system emphasized teaching and required a heavy commitment of faculty teaching time both in planning the integrated instruction and in program delivery. It may not have cost more than traditional schools in direct cash flow, but its teaching burden was heavy. At the School of Basic Medical Sciences, we had resources for a limited number of faculty members, most or all of whom would be junior and untenured and who would be linked to departments which, above all else, demanded research productivity for promotion and tenure. To recruit such faculty and impose a heavy teaching load upon them that would hinder the establishment of their research credentials would have been exploitation, not education.

The search for relevance in medical education had its full expression at McMaster University in Hamilton, Ontario. In 1965, under the guidance of Dean John Evans, McMaster University scrapped the didactic lecture-laboratory system completely for a revolutionary problem-based approach, which emphasized self-learning in a tutorial mode. From the very beginning, students were assigned to tutorial groups that dealt with real or simulated clinical problems. By definition, all knowledge that was essential to the physician in dealing with each clinical problem was relevant. Within each problem, students were expected to identify learning issues ranging from the cellular biology to sophisticated clinical concepts. Tutors functioned as facilitators whose main purpose was to stimulate discussion of relevant basic science and clinical issues. Tutors were not subject experts, although such experts were on hand to consult with tutorial groups. Subject experts also had prepared several hundred audio-visual aids on a wide variety of topics. Many of these were in the form of self-instructional slide-tape packages. It was truly a novel form of medical education that generated much enthusiasm from students and faculty alike. But it too was faculty intensive. When I first visited McMaster in early 1971, the full-time faculty numbered 196, something beyond conception at Urbana, which was planning to begin instruction with eight.

I received curriculum advice from other quarters and quickly discerned that there is never a shortage of ideas and suggestions for curriculum content. Local physicians with whom I talked were especially anxious to help. Practically all physicians who have completed medical school, postgraduate training, and clinical practice can easily think of dozens of ways to improve the curricula. For all the help I received, I was not prepared to begin the organization of a written curriculum without a careful plan. I knew very well that the basic science curriculum of 1970 would be far different from the one I encountered in 1950. Twenty years of scientific progress had created a stunning variety of pathways for potential curricular content.

Moreover, it is difficult to describe in a few sentences the scope and breadth of medical knowledge that we are entrusted to impart in four years to our graduates. At a minimum, the lifetime vocabulary of the medical student doubles during this brief period. In fact, medical education is now acknowledged as a seven-year process. No doctor is adequately prepared to practice modern medicine after graduation from four years of medical school without an additional three to five years of residency training. One could spend a lifetime learning only one or two of the biological sciences basic to medicine. Scientific knowledge is like the "Big Bang" universe, forever expanding. Conventional wisdom declares that medical knowledge doubles every five years, and that's probably a conservative estimate. The more sophisticated we become, the more detailed knowledge we accumulate. Because knowledge begets knowledge, the more we have, the more demands for new knowledge appear.

Individual medical disciplines are losing their autonomy as we probe deeper and deeper into the biology of life and find common denominators. Research efforts in such areas as biochemistry, microbiology, genetics, pharmacology, and pathology gradually lose their disciplinal distinctions as biological research focuses more on molecular biology common to all traditional disciplines. New departmental structures, with names that reflect molecular biology and genetic diagnosis and therapy, are replacing the old.

New technology has even changed the teaching of anatomy, the one discipline that does not change from year to year. However, computerized tomography (CT scans) and magnetic resonance imaging (MRI) have had an enormous impact on how the discipline is presented. Accustomed to visualizing human anatomy in three dimensions as it appears in the human cadaver, medical students must now learn to interpret anatomic clues from planar cross-sectional anatomical views, which are the trademark of the new technology.

Because school time is limited and burgeoning information is unlimited, selectivity is essential and what to teach becomes a serious problem. How to teach, aside from the traditional lecture and laboratory format, is still the subject of considerable discussion and was at the heart of our educational efforts at Urbana. A third variable unique to our fledgling program and its curriculum was that we would be chronically underfunded and would not enjoy a large faculty to equitably share the curriculum-writing burden.

Like all medical schools, we had to jam an infinite amount of material into a finite period of time. Like other medical schools, we had to plan a curriculum that could absorb the new knowledge that was bound to occur. Unlike other medical schools, however, we faced this awesome task with a very small faculty that could ill afford to spend excessive time on instruction. This forced us to ask, "Is there a better way of doing this?"

While searching for suitable models from which to build, I consulted with George Miller who headed the Center for Educational Development. The educational support arm of College of Medicine before regionalization, Miller's center now had the additional responsibility to assist curriculum development in the regional programs. Talking education with George Miller was fun. Relatively unfamiliar with educational literature, I was dazzled by the possibilities our discussions evoked. Coming as I did from a traditional background, Miller's approaches to teaching and learning were entirely new to me.

Miller had co-written a seminal book on medical education, *Teaching and Learning in Medical School.* The book challenged traditional methods of medical education as inconsistent with "good" education and called for better methods of student education and appraisal. He pointed out that many faculty members both within and without the College of Medicine were not only bad teachers, but they also had no idea how to improve or even evaluate their teaching efforts. He argued that advances in research were not limited to the biomedical sciences. There were advances in educational techniques as well, and it was high time to introduce them into medical education.

The book earned Miller international acclaim, but won him few friends at the College of Medicine. Miller was thoroughly disliked by many well-meaning faculty members who saw him as an administrator interfering with faculty prerogatives. His critics claimed that rather than improving educational quality, the implementation of his evaluation ideas was actually lowering the "quality" of medical education. Miller took the criticism in stride and persisted with his message. Grove was convinced that Miller was right and backed him strongly. Eventually Miller's ideas took root and both directly and indirectly influenced the delivery of medical education throughout the college.

At Miller's urging and with Grove's leadership, educational policy, curriculum, and student appraisal were literally wrested from departmental control and made a college function. Departmental curricula now had to be defined by their learning objectives and be approved by a committee of faculty from the entire college. Departments no longer gave their own examinations or were the final pass-fail arbiters for students. The pass-fail option was made exclusively a college function. Departmental examination questions were included in a comprehensive, collegewide examination with a predetermined passing level. Furthermore, examination questions, no matter how clever, that did not "perform" well on any examination were frequently eliminated from the scoring by a collegewide review committee. (Examination questions for certifying examinations were routinely reviewed for their "performance" in effectively discriminating between strong and weak students. Examination items that were improperly answered by more than 50 percent of the class and questions that were answered correctly by the lowest class quintile and incorrectly by the highest class quintile were considered suspect. Each was carefully reviewed by an examination committee that reached a consensus on whether to retain or eliminate the suspect question.) College-level control of these key areas removed the departmental option for tyrannical control of student destinies. The department no longer had the right to fail a student. Only the college could do that. These changes did not endear either Miller or Grove to faculty traditionalists.

Miller advised me to read just one book, if I read nothing else: *Freedom to Learn* by Carl Rogers and H. J. Freiberg. It was a revelation. I read it from cover to cover. Rogers and Freiberg argued that significant learning takes place when the subject matter is genuinely needed by the student and has relevance for the student's own purposes. They cited Marshall McLuhan's example of a young child who moves to a foreign country. The child is allowed to play freely for hours with his new companions, with no language instruction at all. Not only will the child learn another language in a few months, but the child will acquire the proper accent, too. The child is learning in a way that has the most significance and meaning for him and such learning proceeds at an exceedingly rapid rate. "Let someone try to instruct him in a new language, basing the instruction on the elements which have meaning for the teacher, and learning the new language is tremendously slowed or even stopped."

Medical students are not five-year-old children, but they are indeed learning the equivalent of a new language and several new scientific disciplines as well. If we can conclude anything at all from the acquisition of learning in the young child, it is that total immersion with an acute need to learn would seem to be by far the most efficient way to learn basic medical sciences. We already knew that the rigid lecture-laboratory approach leaves many students heavily scarred and without much fondness for the subject matter.

McLuhan's example, the work of Carl Rogers, and George Miller's probing questions clarified for me the concept that teaching and learning are two entirely different modalities. I became convinced that learning, not teaching, was the key to educational success; that once it was determined what the student should learn it was less important who did the teaching. For the first time I could visualize an approach to curricular development that was comprehensive, that could be accomplished within a limited budget, and that might even be ready by September 1971. We did not need, nor could we have afforded, a high-powered faculty to teach. We needed a committed basic-sciences faculty that would identify learning objectives for each discipline and help students learn and master concepts on their own.

By January 1, the framework for the curriculum had come together. It would be a problem-oriented curriculum based upon real patients whose infirmities could be demonstrated to the students and whose clinical problems would serve as a springboard to illustrate basic science principles.

In every basic medical science discipline, students were required to (a) learn the discipline's language; (b) be able to interpret data related to the discipline and be familiar with current literature; (c) be able to interpret signs and symptoms of diseases in terms of basic science principles; (d) achieve minimum passing levels on internal comprehensive examinations and external examinations such as those given by the National Board of Medical Examiners; and (e) achieve self-instructional skills that would allow them to continue to acquire new knowledge over time.

The curriculum departed from the usual medical educational track in another significant manner. Despite concerns about overloading, we enlarged the scope of the first year of instruction. Ordinarily, a first-year medical-school program encompasses the disciplines of anatomy, neuroscience, physiology, biochemistry, immunology, histology, genetics, embryology, and behavioral science. When taught as discrete courses, discipline by discipline, that is a full serving. In addition to preparing the medical student for hospital-based clinical training, the traditional second year in medical school completes basic science education with the disciplines of microbiology, pharmacology, pathology, epidemiology, and biostatistics.

It may have been presumptuous of me to have believed that the right approach could effectively teach virtually all the relevant basic medical sciences in a single academic year (albeit an 11-month academic year), but that was our goal. The key to achieving it was to take advantage of the intellectual merger and reconfiguration of disciplines. With molecular biology burgeoning and constituting a unifying force, there was considerable redundancy in any strictly disciplinary course approach. The biochemist working in search of mammalian DNA secrets overlapped the work of the microbiologist who asked similar questions regarding bacterial DNA. Both disciplines overlapped with that of the genetic scientists who sought answers from DNA as it related to genes present in both higher-organism mammals and less complicated, but fascinating, bacteria.

Because pharmacology can be thought of as chemical physiology; and because pathology combines abnormal histology, abnormal anatomy and abnormal physiology, the first-year medical-school content seemed ripe for integration with that content usually taught in the second year. More important, such an integration better captures students' enthusiasm by linking the notoriously tedious, memory-dependent basic science subjects to exciting clinical applications.

The curriculum design was also an academic political statement. Incorporating pathology and pharmacology in the first year would justify hiring faculty in those disciplines and proved helpful in raising our level of funding. Furthermore, it gave us standing in the second year, and therefore was a major step forward in planning for a clinical program at Urbana.

I was able to enlist the participation of the students and Urbana-Champaign faculty in this experiment, but when I asked a senior scientist at the Medical Center in Chicago to help us carry out our program, it was another story. Widely respected for his research and teaching, Professor Klaus Unna was the head of the Department of Pharmacology at the School of Basic Medical Sciences in Chicago. He was unimpressed with my new approach. He listened politely and carefully to my curriculum proposal, but would have none of it. He insisted there was no substitute for a competent research-oriented department to teach pharmacology in the second year of medical school. A gentleman and a scholar, he wished me well, but that interview showed me that classically trained medical faculty would be a source of resistance to the curriculum. To test an alternative educational approach without established, unimpeachable evidence was unthinkable. I sought no further help from the old guard and was relieved that none of them placed obstacles in our path.

Now that we had decided to incorporate the whole spectrum of basic medical sciences into our one-year program, to enable students to work at their own pace, and to organize material around real clinical problems, our curricular-development tasks were clear. Committees were formed to identify the learning objectives for each basic science discipline, to combine related learning objectives into learning units, and to associate a clinical disease or condition with each unit. Learning objectives provide a flexible, yet stable, approach to curriculum definition. They reflect stability because they are less likely to change with new information. For example, if one objective is "to describe the blood-clotting process," the objective remains constant no matter what revolutionary discoveries are made about blood-clotting mechanisms.

The use of learning objectives within learning units enabled us to generate relatively detailed outlines of each discipline's essentials. As the units were completed, we inverted the process by collecting, under a single disease category, relevant learning units from all disciplines. The end result was a matrix made up of clinical problems on one coordinate, and perpendicular to the diseases was the extensive listing of all learning units, subject-by-subject. Within the matrix, each learning unit was assigned to a clinical problem.

For example, peptic ulcer disease raises topics in the anatomy of the upper gastrointestinal tract, its histology and pathology, the physiology of digestion, the biochemistry of digestive enzyme action, the pharmacology of H2-receptor antagonists and anticholinergic drugs, and microbiology.

Of course, this plan did not always work out neatly. For example, the immunological reactions of blood groups could be studied equally well in the context of erythroblastosis fetalis (severe jaundice of the newborn) or the ABO incompatibilities that complicate transfusions after excessive blood loss from open-heart surgery or trauma. The challenge was to catalogue each unit with an appropriate clinical problem, but at the same time, distribute the learning units equally among all of the clinical problems. Some units intersected with a dozen or more problems, while others related to a single illness. We wished to avoid the asymmetry that would assign five hundred units to one disease, but only fifty units to another. Papering the ample wall of our conference room was sheet after sheet of giant grids charting each intersection between learning units and disease. The concept of relating clinical problems to basic science objectives was enthusiastically accepted by campus and community faculties. It was the lever that effectively mobilized and united our diverse and eclectic faculty. It motivated them to work in concert.

Discipline committees were formed from "faculty": campus scientists who agreed to participate, graduate assistants in the basic medical sciences, pathologists from the community hospitals, and practicing physicians from every medical specialty. Within this unconventional mix were even a few unlicensed physicians, usually émigrés marking time while they prepared for licensure examinations. Most committees consisted of one basic scientist and two or three physicians. The basic scientist generally defined the learning unit and its objectives. The physicians, upholding the principle that basic medical science pertinent to medical education is that which is pertinent to the physician in practice, kept the science relevant and linked the units to the real world of medicine. Physicians and graduate students worked closely together—at 7 a.m. breakfast meetings, after office hours, and in the evenings—to hammer out relevant objectives from which units were created.

Although the task of assigning a relevant disease to each unit usually presented little difficulty, some basic science units were not readily linked to a specific disease. Two generic biomedical problems, "inflammation" and "wound healing," were created to cover these esoteric, yet fundamental, units. Even so, a number of objectives that were considered by both scientists and clinicians to be essential still did not fit in. These were reviewed by Dr. Benjamin T. Williams and me, packaged into units, and arbitrarily assigned to an existing clinical problem.

The concept of curriculum by objectives, together with the unit structure, facilitated the start of the curriculum-writing task long before any full-time faculty members were recruited. Our provisional "basic science faculty" at this juncture consisted of a mixture of graduate assistants, senior faculty in the School of Life Sciences (Stan Stolpe in anatomy and Ray Watterson in embryology, both professors who were no longer engaged in active research and who strongly supported our goal to establish a four-year medical school at Urbana-Champaign) and an eclectic mix of physicians with specialized expertise or interest in a particular field (Ksenja Kokotovic, who had a background in pharmacology; and Stan Bobowski and Ben Williams in pathology).

Among these, Ben Williams deserves special mention. A 1955 Alpha Omega Alpha (the medical school honor society) graduate of the University of Oklahoma and Director of the Mercy Hospital Laboratories (1962–1988), he was a genuinely talented, research-oriented maverick academician who shunned the academy for the "real world." More than any other individual, on or off the campus, Ben contributed to the growth, development, and survival of medical education in Urbana-Champaign. His advice, coupled with prodigious personal effort, provided much of the strength that shielded us amid the rough times that were ahead.

A committed scholar, Williams maintained a sizable personal medical library at home and was widely read in many fields of medicine. He was particularly interested in medical automation, which seemed to be coming of age in 1970. A visionary, he somehow bridged the competing interests of the local doctors and hospitals to found the Regional Health Resource Center, a not-for-profit corporation committed to finding cooperative ways (in the face of destructive local interhospital competition) to use and test the new technologies streaming into medicine. Williams' center (which had a board that included representation from all the hospitals, all forms of medical practice, and the medical school) channeled a significant portion of the unhealthy and costly medical competition into a cooperative effort. Its most notable achievement was the establishment of a communitywide blood bank that would prove to be a leader in providing a reliable, safe blood supply for local hospitals. Under his leadership, the AIDS epidemic was skillfully managed in Champaign-Urbana with minimal blood contamination. More recently, he led the center's program development of computer-based health-risk appraisal that attracted national and international interest. In 1990, he was elected President of the International Health Evaluation Association.

He foresaw the potential of MRI (magnetic resonance imaging), long before it became a household word. His was the intellectual force that arranged for Mercy Hospital to install one of the first clinical MRI units in Illinois, and virtually single-handedly, he recruited Dr. Paul Lauterbur, the inventor of MRI, to the Urbana-Champaign campus. Generous with his time, his knowledge, and his personal resources, Williams served as professor and Head of the Department of Pathology at Urbana-Champaign from 1989 to 1994. He stands as a giant in the history of this school.

It is readily apparent that this was a very mixed bag of provisional faculty—one that might not have been the envy of other medical school deans. But ordinary people, when inspired, are capable of extraordinary achievements, and that is exactly what these pioneers did. They overcame self-doubt and persevered in the curriculum-writing process.

Usually, groups of three or four persons worked in concert to identify curricular objectives for a given discipline. Many local physicians who cast off all kinds of preconceptions to dig into basic science material that they hadn't thought much about for twenty years also were engaged in these pioneering curriculum groups. They worked diligently to make the curriculum scientific and relevant, and they had a great deal of fun as well.

The curriculum assembled and published in July 1971 by this atypical, maverick group of medical teachers was more than adequate for starters. Although it could not boast the authorship of nationally known stellar scientists, I believe that any objective observer would have been duly impressed by the published results.

Meanwhile, the departments of biochemistry, microbiology, and physiology were authorized to search for and recruit those who would become our permanent basic science faculty. These searches illustrated some of the difficulties I faced in initiating the basic science program. The searching departments were not officially in the medical school. Microbiology and physiology were administratively placed in the School of Life Sciences, a school within the College of Liberal Arts and Sciences. The department of biochemistry was administratively a part of the School of Chemical Sciences, which was also a school within the liberal-arts college. These department heads had a moral obligation to assist me. After all, they were parties to the "Treaty" initiating the program. But technically, the department heads were completely independent of the medical school administration. My chain of command to the department heads of physiology and microbiology, for example, was through Bill Grove to the Chicago chancellor, through the president and central administration, to the Urbana-Champaign chancellor, the vice chancellor for academic affairs, the liberal-arts school's dean, and finally to the director of the School of Life Sciences to whom the two department heads directly reported. In other words, I had no real recourse in dealing with department heads other than through powers of persuasion.

In addition, I had all the budgetary clout that seventy-five thousand dollars would bring: a few graduate assistantships, a couple of research assistantships, a little travel support here or lecture sponsorship there; and I had John Anderson who was my bridge to the departments during this critical period. Anderson proved invaluable in easing discomforts caused by conceptual gaps, which opened between a raw, new M.D. dean and the proud, sensitive department heads and a Ph.D. faculty suspicious of medical schools. With John ever-present to remind the department heads of their obligations, they were usually cooperative and helpful. Conversely, without their leadership and support nothing would have moved. However, none were altruistic in their zeal to recruit for School of Basic Medical Sciences, it was an opportunity to strengthen their departments as well.

Assuming that good scientists make good teachers, our mutual goal was to hire the best junior scientists available. The recruitment process worked very well. I had been uneasy at first because I was virtually limited to a veto role in the selection of what were to be my own faculty. But I had drawn up the job description, which was a critical element. The faculty who were recruited, albeit primarily for their scientific skills, were briefed by me so that they clearly understood their medical-education responsibilities. They too would be at the forefront of this endeavor.

Although some departmental faculty who participated in the search did not necessarily agree with our projected process or even like the concept of a medical school on the campus, they too, were committed to attracting high-quality individuals. The end result was nothing short of spectacular. We recruited a superb group of young scientists, recent Ph.D.s and those who had some postdoctoral experience. Without exception, they became committed to our medical-education process, carried more than their share of teaching and committee work, and made it possible for the school to thrive. These initial faculty—Richard Gumport in biochemistry, Michael Gabridge in microbiology, Benita Katzenellenbogen in physiology, Bill Daniel in genetics, Janet Harris in anatomy, and Aulikki Kokko-Cunningham in histology—did an efficient job of managing their areas of the curriculum, while at the same time initiating generally productive research programs. All were true pioneers.

So the first faculty members hired were all junior faculty, who started out on a probationary tenure track that permitted them five or six years at the most to demonstrate research skills and productivity that would qualify them for promotion to associate professor with tenure. I was aware of the burden placed on them, and on their behalf worked with their department heads to limit their classroom and committee responsibilities. Committed to providing them optimal support, I also invested heavily in new IBM word-processing equipment, which in 1970–71 was just beginning to be appreciated. Faculty were given computer priority in writing and editing curricula, grant applications, and publications, a service that made most of them, who had never experienced the power of word processing, very happy and, indeed, sometimes the envy of their departments.

They were ultimately responsible for the delivery of an entire discipline to the medical students, a task usually assigned to anywhere from four to ten faculty members in other medical schools. It is true that the curriculum-development efforts of our provisional faculty gave them a jump-start in their curriculum-management duties, but the curricular gaps and the residual management responsibilities remained formidable. Notwithstanding the program emphasis on self-study, the faculty had to maintain currency in the basic science learning objectives, prepare appropriate testing material, and be available to students for consultation. Their departmental peers who were unattached to the School of Basic Medical Sciences were often appalled at the teaching and administrative burden carried by the young, understaffed medical-school faculty. Yet, the program worked and the faculty thrived.

But that is far ahead of the story, for in January 1971, eight months before our first students were to arrive, and before any searches had been completed, we had no tenure-track academic faculty. We were managing a host of heterogeneous curriculum development teams and were deeply involved in assembling the educational matrix. Some of the teams seemed to find their way; others appeared to flounder and sought direction. On the other hand, pages and pages material were beginning to bury John Anderson and myself in a mountain of paper. But help was on its way. We were about to employ two young administrators who were to make order out of chaos.

CHAPTER 7

Growing Confident

"ADMINISTRIVIA" NEVER WAS one of my strong points. So I was grateful when a college advisor called in the fall of 1970 to ask if I could take on a graduate assistant—a student looking for administrative experience to complement his thesis work! I said I would be glad to interview the student, Tom Gamble, who was working on a Ph.D. in educational administration. Upon interviewing him, I liked Tom immediately and hired him on the spot. He took charge of administrative and student affairs with gusto, and by taking on tasks I never handled very well, he relieved me of an enormous burden. Quickly assuming responsibility for the day-to-day administrivia and management of our small budget, he organized the school administratively and began preparations for the arrival of students.

Aware of the need for public relations, he also began to publish *Hilights*, a monthly report and morale builder from the school, which was circulated to our basic science and clinical constituencies. Tom was a born administrator who loyally gave me credit I did not deserve for the systems he put in place. (When he received his doctoral degree the next year, I immediately offered him a job as Assistant Dean for Business and Student Affairs. He accepted. (Today, Tom is president of a leading junior college in Florida.)

Gamble was not the only graduate student to capitalize on our status as a new organization in a university that was dedicated to research. Graduate students in history, educational psychology, and sociology studied the school's birth and maturation, and in doing so, provided me with timely feedback.

For example, I was approached in October 1970 by Lee Hertzman, a graduate student in the Urbana-Champaign College of Education who was doing his thesis research under the direction of faculty at the Center for Educational Development. By virtue of his interaction with that politically complicated academic structure, he was more worldly than other graduate students. The thrust of his thesis was to compare the development of the two newly formed basic medical science schools within the College of Medicine, but he seemed to be more interested in the politics of establishing a new and innovative curriculum such as ours and the methodology used in recruiting faculty to support it.

Hertzman and I met for an hour every week or two from October 1970 through the next July. While Hertzman was receiving information from me, I was also profiting from information he gave me, particularly as it related to recruiting personnel necessary for educational support. Hertzman took license to ask questions whose answers revealed gaps in my planning process and to discuss alternatives the school had for dealing with such gaps. His role "was that of an active participant and interventionist."

For example, I expressed great frustration with curriculum development since I knew what I wanted, but I didn't know how to get there. I complained to Hertzman that although I found Miller an interesting and stimulating colleague, getting the help that I needed from Miller was entirely another problem. Hertzman knew which "buttons to push" and told me that I needed to ask Miller specifically to send an educational consultant from his "shop."

The curriculum developmental work was going very slowly. It is one thing to have a brilliant educational concept, but it is entirely another to implement the idea. We talked about learning objectives and testing, but putting the concepts down on paper was proving to be difficult. Our hard-working "faculty" members, both salaried and volunteer, were willing but confused. That's when I followed Hertzman's advice to the letter and pinned George Miller down to commit some of his personnel to analyzing and assisting our curriculum development. "What exactly do you need?" he asked. I told him that I knew something was wrong in our curricular development process, but I was at a loss to be more specific. We were engaged in a complex educational innovation, and I felt out of my depth, without any real expertise in education. The process was creating considerable anxiety for all of the participants. George assigned Bill Sorlie to consult, to evaluate our progress in curriculum development and to make recommendations. Bill came down to Urbana in January 1971 and spent three days with us. He gave us a detailed analysis of our problems with suggestions for future action. With that done, he returned to Chicago.

As I recall, his report was couched in educational jargon. This angered me at first because I couldn't get a handle on it. I didn't know how to proceed. On reflection, however, I was convinced that I needed Bill, or some-one like him, at Urbana. In fact, I decided that I needed Bill more at Urbana than George Miller needed him in Chicago. Aware of an unwritten agree-ment about "pirating" personnel from one campus to another, I contacted George and told him of my predicament. He generously advised me that I could retain Bill if I would assume his salary obligation and if Bill were will-ing to move to Urbana. Fortunately for us, he was willing to join us.

Bill, who had a Master's degree in education, had worked only a year at the Center for Educational Development. He had previously served six years as a fourth-grade teacher in Winnetka. Although relatively new to medical education, he quickly mastered many of the principal issues specific to this field. Bill had the perfect background and personality to deal with the broad spectrum of faculty that we would encounter. Above all, he was sensitive and patient with them, as only a fourth-grade teacher could be. He gently coaxed, chided, and persuaded M.D.s and Ph.D.s alike to get their curricu-lum work done and in a form that would be useful. He served a vital func-tion. He gave form and structure to my educational ideas and provided exactly the tonic our curriculum development needed.

Writing objectives proved difficult for many of our faculty members. It was a new experience and a new approach. Often if they were blocked on writing objectives, Bill asked them to write testing questions rather than objectives. He would then modify the question structure to make it into a learning objective. He also introduced into the curriculum a formal method for student evaluation.

The College of Medicine required successful performance on two certi-fying examinations given during the first two years of basic medical sciences: (a) a freshman comprehensive examination assembled by the entire basic science faculty, and (b) the National Board of Medical Examiners Part I (NBME I) exam, an externally prepared and graded test. Satisfactory per-formance on both was necessary for student promotion to the clinical years. Ordinarily, students would take the freshman comprehensive examination at the end of the first year and the NBME I at the end of the second. There were no other required, or certifying, exams, although departments were encouraged to provide students with "diagnostic" exams along the way, as a means to monitor their progress.

When Bill arrived, our curriculum called for only two such examina-tions for each unit of study: a pretest in which the student could evaluate the need for detailed study of that unit (or skip the unit if the pretest showed the student knew the material), and a post-test to inform the student and advisors whether the student had learned the material satisfactorily. These tests were being written simultaneously with the curriculum objectives. They were to be self-administered and self-evaluated. Bill argued that independent self-evaluation was inadequate and that the school needed an examination system that gave objective feedback on student progress from sources other than the freshman comprehensive and the NBME I examinations. Under Bill's leadership, the "Level III" examination system ("Level I" and "Level II" being the self-administered pre- and post-tests) was initiated. These exams, organized by clinical problem, and encompassing as many as two hundred learning objectives, played a major role in evaluating student progress through the problems posed in the curriculum.

With Bill's guidance, graduate student Les Jones created a sophisticated diagnostic examination system whereby students were able to take a Level III examination covering all of the basic science material within a single clinical problem. This gave the school important information in following each student's progress, and was particularly useful in identifying students who were having trouble with the program. So successful was the Level III system that as time went on, the school could accurately predict student success or failure on the year-end certifying examinations.

By the spring of 1971, we had begun to look like a medical school. About fifty people were working on curriculum. We were planning the budget for the 1972 fiscal year. We supervised the finishing touches on the Burrill Hall addition, which provided twenty thousand square feet of attractive office and laboratory space for newly recruited faculty, and we reviewed drawings for the soon-to-be-built Medical Sciences Building, which we would occupy in 1975. The faculty members, both Ph.D. and M.D., were enthusiastic. There was an air of excitement as everyone sensed we were embarked on a revolutionary new course in medical education, a direction that began to make more and more sense to the people involved. When word came down from Chicago on May 18 that we would register sixteen students on September 9 and that classes would begin on the September 13, it acted like a shot in the arm that helped us redouble our efforts.

Much remained to be done. The curriculum was still in flux. We constantly adjusted the projected number of clinical problems. As new objectives were defined, refined, and prepared for final approval, Ben Williams and I charted progress on huge, gridded, easel-size sheets, assigning each basic science learning objective to a relevant clinical problem. On the first pass, our curriculum committees identified 485 clinical problems that covered all of the basic science objectives. Consolidation was clearly in order.

We reasoned at that time, in complete naiveté, that perhaps the ideal number of clinical problems would be forty, or about one per week. In addition, the student would spend four hours per week in a clinical setting with a Medical Doctor Advisor (MDA), a practicing physician who would serve as an advisor and mentor for a student during the basic science year. This would allow the student to see patients and would provide relevance to the heavy dose of science. After completing each Level III examination, the student would also undergo a two-hour interview with a Medical Doctor Evaluator (MDE), a physician who reviewed test results to ensure the student was on the right track. The MDE was the designated gatekeeper for the student's progression from one problem to the next. We selected mainly internists and pathologists as MDEs; volunteers from all medical specialties served as MDAs.

Many Beginning Doctors, as we called the students then, considered this contact with practicing physicians the most productive learning experience they had. It gave the students a necessary break in their studies that was productive and stimulating at the same time. It generated great enthusiasm for proceeding with the basic science curriculum.

Meanwhile, learning objectives continued to pour in from our curriculum committees, impressing us as no other mechanism could, of the enormous breadth of basic science material that we expected our students to master. Individually, each objective could be justified. In the aggregate, there were too many. The number of learning objectives would haunt us as the program grew and as new basic science information cascaded from the world's research laboratories. Watching the expansion of these objectives on our matrix, Ben and I intuitively realized that forty problems were too many; the matrix would have to be condensed.

Two computer scientists, Daniel Slotnik, Director of the Center for Advanced Computation and Peter Alsberg, graciously advised us to apply a program called PERT, for Project Evaluation and Review Techniques, to our problem. Under their guidance, we estimated learning times for each objective in our curriculum. This added a new dimension to our curriculum database, which was already enormous and still growing. But time was short and we needed to know whether or not the computer model of our grand design would prove feasible. So Ben Williams and I spent the next five days and nights arbitrarily assigning learning-time estimates for each of the several thousand basic science learning objectives; an hour for this objective, ninety minutes for that, etc. We also made assumptions regarding the time students would devote to their studies, to testing, to leisure, sleep, vacation, and travel to the MDA and MDE offices. The data was key-carded at Slotnik's center and entered into a computer.

The computer model predicted that the average student, in a self-study mode, could complete the program in nineteen weeks! We knew we had a good program, but it wasn't that good. We had seriously underestimated the time necessary for mastery of many objectives. How long should it take the average medical student to master the concept of oxidative phosphorylation? Of blood-type immunology? Of dorsal-column neuroanatomy? We didn't exactly know, but we knew one thing—it would take significantly longer than we had estimated.

Computer modeling proved invaluable as it gave us a feeling for what could and could not be done in the first forty weeks of medical school. It became obvious that we had to reduce the number of clinical problems and spread the learning objectives from the deleted problems to those that remained. Agonizing over the loss of relevance that would result from this process, we finally settled on a sixteen-problem base, but even that number, over the years, proved to be excessive.

One guide we used in selecting clinical problems was the frequency distribution of Champaign-Urbana hospital admission diagnoses. We retained the ten most prominent diagnoses as curriculum clinical problems so that when students undertook a study problem, they would likely encounter a real patient who suffered from that illness.

There were many other tasks to complete before we were ready to begin instruction. Once collated, the curriculum had to be printed for distribution to students and faculty. It also had to be approved at the College level by the College Committee on Educational Policy. Student registration and record systems had to be established. Furthermore, since the students were to see living patients within a few weeks of entry, we had to prepare them to deal with patients. That meant developing an abbreviated curriculum for the execution of a rudimentary history and physical diagnosis, preparing students emotionally to deal with patient problems, and finally to somehow provide them with a sense of collegiality for meetings with their MDAs and MDEs.

The term "Beginning Doctor," or BD, was coined to encourage professional collegiality. It also provided students with a certain comfort level when meeting patients for the first time. To prepare the BDs to perform a history and physical examination, we developed a three-day curriculum in the first week of study, by the end of which all students had completed the physical examination of a peer. Finally, to prepare students to meet patients in a private-practice setting and to assist them in learning discretion and professional decorum, I wrote ten short scripts for "trigger" videos. These were designed to introduce students to a variety of patient reactions to their disease, to their doctor, and to the student. Patients were portrayed as aggressive, passive-aggressive, manipulative, seductive, depressed, garrulous, etc.—in fact, demonstrating about every type of difficult behavior that I had experienced in my own practice. Bill Sorlie took the scripts to Center for Educational Development, where some educator-actors, including him, portrayed the problem patients on videotape. These productions were shown to our students on the very first day of class. The videos broke the ice and were an instant hit.

Bill Sorlie wrote MDA and MDE job descriptions and organized much-needed workshops to prepare our physician volunteers for teaching. We had no money to pay them, but we did provide personal copies of current texts of their choice that would be helpful in their teaching function.

Meanwhile, recruiting of full-time faculty went forward with the basic science departments leading the way. The departments were very careful to select faculty with strong research backgrounds, and it was my job to explain to the young Ph.D. prospects their role in this new enterprise, a role at variance with their background and training. All the new or projected faculty came from traditional graduate programs with strong research interests. The projected independent-study mode in our new curriculum, the physician input into basic medical science education, and the absence of traditional courses altered the customary duties of the full-time campus faculty. I explained to the recruits that they were not here to teach through a series of lectures and laboratories, that they were essentially relieved of formal course delivery, but were to identify areas where the curriculum needed strengthening and where student learning was less than satisfactory. They were to concentrate on updating curriculum and seminar teaching of those curricular problems that were not readily solved by students and their advisors. The Ph.D. faculty members were also to serve as personal basic science advisors to three or four students. This encouraged basic scientists to review the objectives of other disciplines, eliminating duplication and waste, and to broaden their outlook both in the basic sciences and in the clinic.

By limiting their functions to curriculum management, the basic science faculty would have adequate time to initiate their own laboratory research and to make significant progress so as to qualify for promotion to associate professor after five or six years.

Not all recruiting went smoothly. When major, well-organized departments took responsibility, the results were impressive. But when there was no existing departmental commitment to a discipline, it proved very difficult to attract top-notch faculty, much less find them a departmental home. We had recruitment difficulties in fields such as anatomy, neurosciences, and pharmacology. These disciplines had no departmental or divisional representation in the UIUC schools of life and chemical sciences. Neuroscience, for example, fell into that convenient category known as "interdisciplinary studies," a concept that is supported verbally by all university administrators, but in deed and resources by few.

Shortly after I arrived in August 1970, I was approached by Bill Sleator, head of the Department of Physiology and Biophysics, who was looking to share a salary line in the recruitment of a senior physiologist from another university. The physiologist was working in an area deemed important by the department, but Sleator lacked a full salary line to hire him; he had only one-half of the amount required. It looked like a good opportunity for me to gain at half-price, a senior, experienced professor to lead the medical-school effort in physiology, and to serve as a bridge between the department and the school. A senior professor on the faculty would add a component of maturity to our otherwise young and inexperienced group. Therefore, sight unseen, I agreed to share the appointment with Sleator's department, with the understanding that the new faculty member's sole teaching responsibility in the present year would be to define the physiology learning objectives within three months of arrival. This was agreed upon by all concerned, including the recruit, who immediately relegated the curriculum development task to an unprepared graduate student and apparently, thereafter, hardly gave it another thought.

Three, four, and five months elapsed without any physiology product.

Despite my repeated requests to both the professor and the department head, nothing was submitted. Not only was the physiology curriculum, an absolutely vital discipline, not being developed, but I had committed half of a salary line out of scarce resources to a tenured professor who behaved in a manner openly hostile to the medical school. I was furious. Finally, after six months without tangible progress and with our September starting date only five months away, I insisted that the physiology professor deliver to me whatever work had been completed for my review. What arrived on my desk was a series of penciled scratch sheets that were difficult to discern as relating to physiology, much less having any use at all as a self-study curriculum. It was junk.

The junk curriculum, however, had its uses. As I reviewed the university statutes, it was clear that even a tenured faculty member could be terminated for "due cause" if "a faculty member has been grossly neglectful of or grossly inefficient in the performance of his University duties and functions." I told Bill Sleator that either the professor resign from the medical school or I would move to have his tenure revoked on the basis of incompetence and use the material that he submitted as a physiology curriculum as evidence.

Apparently, nobody in recent memory had ever challenged the tenure of a tenured faculty member, much less openly accused a full professor of incompetence. But, in this instance, I had the documents to prove malfeasance and informed the department that I was very willing to let unbiased outside observers review the documents. The department was not too happy to be pushed around that way by the new medical school dean, and an M.D. at that. But Sleator reluctantly agreed that physiology had not kept its part of the bargain. Furthermore, he agreed that the department would make amends by producing a physiology curriculum in time for the fall semester. Miraculously, in the next two months an acceptable, although just barely acceptable, physiology curriculum was put together by several conscientious members of the embarrassed department.

Meanwhile, the department head and I agreed that the professor who was initially requested to do the job would withdraw completely from the medical school and his salary line be used to hire another physiologist who would be committed to the medical school and its program.

Pharmacology and pathology recruitment and curriculum development raised a separate set of issues. By including these two disciplines in the first-year curriculum, we were departing from conventional wisdom and putting the college regionalization plan off balance. The three-year "clinical" schools at Chicago, Peoria, and Rockford each planned to teach these two disciplines and were nonplused about what to do if the Urbana students arrived already competent in those subjects. Furthermore, the School of Basic Medical Sciences at the Medical Center in Chicago also did not include either subject in its first-year curriculum. So there was considerable uneasiness within the college caused by this upstart program in Urbana.

I was challenged on the issue in administrative meetings. I argued that it made good sense to integrate the abnormal with the normal in the learning process. Pathology was largely abnormal histology and anatomy, and pharmacology was the science of chemically modified normal physiology. Integrated studies in either of these disciplines, a process that had never before been tried, seemed to be well worth the attempt. I also argued that, given the limited amount of time available in medical education, this approach would place a tangible relevance into the curriculum that would magnify the benefits of early clinical exposure.

I also had a hidden agenda. The inclusion of pathology and pharmacology in the first-year curriculum was also a statement that Urbana was determined to develop a full M.D. program. Had I not included a pharmacology and pathology curriculum for the first-year program and dedicated a portion of the limited resources available to me to acquire faculty for those subjects at the outset, the opportunity for clinical development at Urbana would never have occurred.

Although I won the battle of innovation and the right to proceed with the curriculum, I eventually lost the war because, in my overconfidence and naiveté, I made a critical strategic error by agreeing to a single, collegewide, year-end freshman certifying examination. Such an examination, in deference to the first-year program in Chicago, did not include testing of pharmacology and pathology. In accepting that agreement, we lost control of our product. Medical students, like any other students, will only learn what they must learn in order to pass examinations or to meet standards. That which is not critical to their medical-school success is not studied with the same intensity as the required core material. This was evident in the analysis of Level III and other progress examinations.

The curricula for pathology, neuroscience and behavioral science were all assembled by volunteer physicians. A reasonable pharmacology curriculum was assembled through the efforts of a graduate student from the College of Veterinary Medicine Department of Pharmacology who worked with two community physicians. Each author was guided by a list of topics published by the National Board of Medical Examiners. It was a prodigious amount of unpaid, volunteer effort, but it got us to the starting gate with a curriculum corpus that, although not perfect, was certainly perfectible.

At the end of all this curriculum effort, we had covered all bases and had assembled a document that was unique in the annals of medical education in that it contained a version of all the learning objectives in the basic medical sciences. Textbooks had been written and curricular outlines had been written, but never before had such a detailed listing of basic medical science learning objectives been compiled. Dated July 1971, the document contained two thousand pages and was eleven inches thick. It was assembled on time and within our $150,000 budget. In all the annals of U.S. medical education, no state in the union had ever enjoyed such a bargain.

CHAPTER 8

Self-study Technology

W HEN I THINK ABOUT that developmental year from August 1970 to September 1971, it seems I was busy all the time. I had come to Urbana thinking that I would relax more than I did in Cleveland and play some golf. I enjoyed golf, but rarely had the time to pursue it. I joined an Urbana country club, but my golf game never worked out.

One day as I was playing a round with Bill Sorlie, I had so many school issues on my mind that I just couldn't concentrate on hitting the ball. I begged Bill's forgiveness as I left him in the middle of the seventh fairway and returned to my office to work on some pressing matter. I can still see him standing there in the fairway, nonplused, staring at me as I walked off the course with my clubs in tow.

The work also included considerable travel. At least twice a month, there were round trips to Chicago for College of Medicine meetings. There were in addition, trips to medical society meetings in Danville, Decatur, Bloomington/Normal and Charleston/Mattoon, and trips to other medical schools. Urbana-Champaign, which had so many academic resources, maintained a fleet of university-owned airplanes and ran flight-school courses. I enrolled in Aviation 101, basic pilot instruction. By June of 1971, I had earned a pilot's license. Instead of driving, I began flying to and from Chicago and to the communities around Champaign. What a pleasure it was to fly to Chicago rather than to drive a very boring 140 miles there and 140 miles back.

Although flying saved some time, its chief benefit was the relaxation it provided. For example, the drive to Chicago took two and a half hours, door to door, while the flight to Chicago took about sixty minutes of flying time, with half an hour on either end coming and going, perhaps saving thirty minutes each way. However, after a long day's work in Chicago—many times devoted to unpleasant discussions, disagreements and arguments, or to the strenuous defense of our program and its budget—flying the 140 miles back to Urbana was infinitely preferable to the long drive or to an undependable Illinois Central train ride. There are few real luxuries in life, but one of them certainly is taking a single-engine airplane up to six thousand feet at the end of a tiring day and totally relaxing as the plane carries you, almost effortlessly, towards home.

Flying also gave me flexibility to visit other medical schools, something that John Anderson encouraged me to do because he had found such trips helpful in the past. I took his advice. Weather permitting, I could always set my own timetable for arrival and departure, an enormous convenience. I visited Michigan State University College of Human Medicine in East Lansing, Michigan; McMaster University School of Medicine in Hamilton, Ontario; and Ohio State University in Columbus, Ohio.

Although all these institutions were developing unique educational systems, none of the systems were adaptable to our local initiative. A trip to the National Medical Audio-Visual Center in Atlanta, Georgia, was helpful in planning the audiovisual components of our curriculum. Both McMaster and the Audio-Visual Center were very generous in allowing us to copy at will from their extensive audiovisual archives, but the role played by A-V materials in medical education turned out to be smaller than I anticipated.

Among the magnets that had attracted me to Champaign-Urbana was the elegant PLATO (Programmed Logic for Automatic Teaching Operations) system, which had been developed on the campus and had the potential to be an important self-instructional aid. Educational programs on PLATO could proceed at the student's own pace. There were options for reinforcement, encouragement, and references, all available with the press of a key.

Boosting PLATO as the ultimate computer-instruction tool was Professor Donald Bitzer, its inventor and an inveterate enthusiast and optimist. As far as Don was concerned, there was no educational problem that could not be portrayed usefully on PLATO. However, with computers, as with many so-called teaching aids, all that glitters is not gold. They were not a panacea. Although our engagement with computers was destined to be extensive, their main use prior to the development of the PC, would be for automated testing and record-keeping rather than for teaching basic medical sciences.

Computers were also being tested and used at the Center for Educational Development. George Miller, who led the effort there, was interested in establishing a collegewide system of Computer Assisted Instruction. The concept of a network centered in Chicago and ranging to Rockford, Peoria and Urbana-Champaign seemed an appropriate goal. It would unite the College of Medicine electronically.

I met with Miller on July 28, 1971, and told him that I was looking for soft money sources to support the development of Computer Assisted Instruction (CAI) at Urbana. Miller's center had developed two IBM-based CAI programs, *Case* and *Crib.* Neither was very popular with students. The *Case* program, a prototype of many problem-oriented CAI programs used today, was designed to teach problem-solving. Clinical parameters were entered into the computer, and the student would be required to make clinical decisions such as ordering laboratory tests, starting medications, or ordering procedures. Time was entered as a factor so that ultimately the student would diagnose and treat a case to its final outcome, which could be wellness or death. The *Crib* program was much simpler in design. It was limited to multiple-choice questions with immediate feedback provided to the user. Because Miller had been funded for his systems, I thought he might help me in looking for soft money.

Miller complained that my plans were too vague, as indeed they were. He wanted me to define more specifically how I intended to use CAI. He was particularly interested in adapting the *Case* program to basic medical sciences and hoped that we could work together in that area. He hinted that if my school could find a way to employ the *Case* system, he might be able to find some resources for me. But *Case* on an IBM mainframe computer was incompatible with PLATO on the Control Data Corporation computer. It was impossible for me to make a commitment to use *Case* when PLATO was developing rapidly and seemed to be on the verge of becoming a universitywide system. Nothing ever came of these discussions.

The College of Education at Urbana-Champaign was also interested in CAI development and had recommended graduate student Les Jones, who was developing CAI programs in biochemistry. Bill Sorlie persuaded me to give Jones a try, so I hired him as a half-time graduate assistant to develop biochemistry education programs on PLATO. He immediately began working on the biochemistry software, but curriculum-development work progressed very slowly. Jones played a more important role in the development of our teaching program by adapting the Level III examination system to PLATO.

However, the development of problem-oriented software required more investment, resources, time and energy than any of us could appreciate at that time. Unknown to us at the time, the personal-computer and floppy-disk explosion was barely visible on the intellectual horizon.

CHAPTER 9

Sources of Tension

RUMAN ANDERSON and I became staunch friends from the day we first met. Given the budgetary problems and differences in outlook looming between the Chicago administration and myself, I would need all the friends I could get. Anderson, the dean of the School of Basic Medical Sciences in Chicago, and I were assigned as roommates at a management-training conference held in Hershey, Pennsylvania, in September of 1970. It was there my friendship with him began. The mutual respect we developed for each other at that meeting has remained intact over the years.

Whenever there was a college problem that needed interpretation, I could always count on Truman to be frank and helpful. When he learned of our plan to integrate all basic medical sciences into the first-year program, he encouraged us to proceed with our novel approach. He also kept me informed of the backlash originating from some traditional Chicago-based faculty members who, as might be expected, believed that the first-year curriculum was already overloaded and who argued that it would be difficult to do a high-quality job in all disciplines.

With low-key but firm support from Truman, my educational flank was protected so that my primary administrative problem rested with the budget and budgetary allocations for the Urbana teaching program. As time went on during the first year, even during those halcyon days for funding new medical-education programs, it became all too apparent to me that the budget was going to be very tight under any circumstance. Because of that, it remained difficult to foresee how and when an Urbana clinical program would be initiated. I was recruiting junior faculty at the time who were faced with a completely different teaching role and who needed substantial funding support so that they could fulfill their teaching obligations and get a good start on their research. That meant I had to support their laboratories, their graduate assistants, and their travel to scientific meetings until their grant applications were successfully funded. Grove never said "no" to me, that I could not spend my allocation as I chose, but he insisted that I would have to live within my budget.

In January 1971, eight months before the entry of our first basic science students, I presented Grove with a long-range enrollment plan and a budget for the projected growth at Urbana-Champaign to a four-year program. Envisioned was a total Urbana enrollment of 248 students by 1976; 128 first-year, basic science students, and 120 clinical students (40 each of second-, third-, and fourth-year students). This very early push reflected my concern that resources would run out before a clinical program could be started at Urbana. Grove looked over my figures and cautiously agreed with the development "in principle," although he doubted we could follow such a tight time schedule. He was fixed on establishing the Peoria, Rockford, and the Metropolitan-Six (Metro-6) clinical programs before initiating a new clinical program in Urbana-Champaign. He insisted, first of all, that we plan the Urbana-Champaign expansion to 128 students so that we could send an appropriate share of second-year students to those clinical sites. As for me, I saw my school in a Catch-22 situation: 128 was the maximum number of students that Urbana could handle; if they were allocated to the other clinical sites, from where would the second-year students for Urbana come?

When Grove unveiled his budget plan for the 1972 fiscal year to us at the Administrative Advisory Council meeting on July 31, 1971, it was again clear that our school was being grossly underfunded. I received a paltry $246,000 allocation. I was angry and did not care who knew it. Although I have no proof, it seemed to me that Grove very likely talked budget first with his Chicago deans and that Urbana received the leftovers.

The deans and their allocations at that meeting were (in addition to myself with $246,000): Bill Grove with $272,000 for the Office of the Executive Dean; Alexander M. (Mack) Schmidt of the Abraham Lincoln School of Medicine, $5,900,000; Bob Evans of Rockford, $489,000; Nicholas J. Cotsonas of Peoria, $589,000; Truman Anderson from the School of Basic Medical Sciences in Chicago, $2,272,000; and George Miller of the Center for Educational Development, $330,000. Also present was Jerry Hahn, who was responsible for the integration of the Metro-6 hospitals into the system and was allocated $431,000.

We were also notified that the overall university budget was very tight, that there was no money for new equipment, there were to be no salary raises regardless of the source of funds, and that there would be no overtime paid to nonacademic help. Dollars for doctors lasted barely a year. I argued that that we were spread too thin for the amount of new state dollars given to the college, and that if we were truly going to regionalize, it made little sense to pour $431,000 into a new Chicago clinical school, the Metro-6. This argument went nowhere. I suspected that reliance on the Metro-6 hospital teaching programs was temporary in nature and that the $431,000 allocated to Metro-6 was really a convenient place to bank money for future use of the Lincoln school. Over the course of time that is exactly what happened; the $431,000 wound up in the Lincoln budget, and the unit we called Metro-6 vanished.

After further discussion of the Grove allocation, Cotsonas moved that "we all congratulate the Executive Dean for a job well done in distributing the limited funds." Much to the consternation of all, I abstained from supporting the motion because I had no input on the relative need of each campus and could make no judgment as to whether Grove's distribution was wise. I also had private reservations about excessive funds being channeled to the existing clinical schools.

I left that meeting with a fewer friends on the council. The word was out on me—I was not a "team player." The label is a convenient scapegoating ploy used by administrators who neither wish to defend their arbitrary decisions nor receive alternate views. I made it clear to Bill Grove and to my other critics on the council that if I were to be a team player, I wanted to be on the team as a participant decision maker, not as a water boy. Bill Grove was clearly angry at my position, and we were to spar over budgets many times in the next several years.

Any critique of the college budgetary process had to include the management of the resource-devouring university hospital under the Lincoln school's dean. One might legitimately inquire, "Is this hospital, one block removed from Cook County Hospital necessary?" The university hospital—deemed essential to the teaching programs of the Abraham Lincoln school, as well as the colleges of nursing, dentistry, and allied health—was always losing money. Demands for more state resources to keep it in business were clearly on the horizon. Bill Grove also had a capital plan for a $60 million replacement hospital, because the existing plant, although only fifteen years old, had been built on 1930s specifications that were badly outdated in 1971.

Meetings of the advisory council were dominated by Mack Schmidt, the Lincoln school dean, seeking solutions to the difficult problems caused by the hospital. For virtually his entire tenure as dean, he appeared to be frustrated and enmeshed by the eternal and insoluble problems presented by an underfunded, underused, under-reimbursed, and financially insolvent university hospital. His faculty members' morale was low because they perceived, in mirror image perception of the difficulties, it was their own financial resources that were being drained off to begin three new medical schools downstate. Mack, however, was always the consummate "company man" and "team player" (in 1973 he was appointed Commissioner of the Food and Drug Administration by Richard Nixon) and after unburdening himself to his agonized peers, usually went along with Bill Grove's leads.

Tensions also developed between the Peoria dean, Nick Cotsonas, and me. Nicholas J. Cotsonas was no less of a "company man" than Mack Schmidt. Cotsonas was very loyal to Grove and made no apologies about it. My school was clearly a sibling rival to Cotsonas, who could not suppress his negative attitude toward us even though it was commonly and maladroitly masked by a veneer of joviality. In October 1970, barely two months after I had arrived in Urbana, I paid a courtesy visit to Cotsonas in order to get better acquainted. Nick had called me shortly after my arrival in Urbana to congratulate me on my appointment and invited me to visit Peoria. My impressions of him from that telephone conversation and from the Hershey management conference were a mixed bag. Nick was an inveterate punster who seemed oblivious to the fact that his puns were often ill-timed, inappropriate and, worst of all to my mind, not very funny. But my first meeting with him in his temporary office in a Peoria bank building gave no clues about our future relationship. He was warm, forthcoming about the college, and very gracious in greeting me. We discussed everything from the problems associated with the development of a community-based medical school to the unexpected presence of an autumn smog hanging over Peoria. The visit went so well that I was really not prepared for the hostility he exhibited later toward Urbana. In meeting after meeting of the advisory council, Cotsonas gave knee-jerk opposition to any proposal that came from my faculty or me. Particularly threatening to Cotsonas was any discussion of a clinical program at Urbana. Although it took me some time to appreciate it, it soon became apparent that Cotsonas viewed a complete M.D. program in Urbana as an existential threat to Peoria. For this reason, he was not and never would be an enthusiastic supporter of medical education in Urbana-Champaign.

Other factors played a role in Cotsonas' loyalty to Bill Grove. Nick and Bill were long-time friends and colleagues at the University of Illinois. Bill persuaded Nick to take the deanship in Peoria and maneuvered the Peoria medical community to accept Nick as their dean. It appeared to me that with Nick at the helm in Peoria, Grove was assured that his own control of Peoria was not in jeopardy. Grove wanted an "insider" in charge of Peoria because that city was the most well-developed in medical education. Peoria's Saint Francis Hospital was quite proud that it already had a panoply of residency postgraduate programs, including internal medicine, surgery, pediatrics and obstetrics and gynecology. Bill Grove wanted to capitalize on these programs as a basis for medical school growth. Unfortunately for Grove, Saint Francis Hospital was led by a strong and determined CEO, Edward McGrath, who was not about to hand over to the university the fruits of many years' labor without certain protected rights.

There appeared to be one other factor that placed me at a disadvantage in the contest for autonomy, respect, and budget. This stemmed from the long-standing interpersonal relationships that existed between Grove and the principals of the council, men who were my colleagues and peers. An outsider, I often felt disadvantaged. Grove, Miller, Schmidt, Cotsonas, and Anderson were all appointments from within the University of Illinois. All easily qualified as team players. Rockford's Bob Evans and myself were not team players. Instead, we were outsiders—a handicap we couldn't change, and therefore, found difficult to overcome.

These, then, were some of the contrasting moments, highs and lows, that characterized my first year at Urbana-Champaign. It was a year of preparation, of excitement, of energy, and of accomplishment. It was also a year of tension and maneuver, both in relation to budget and to mission. By September 13, 1971, we had progressed from a free-floating apex to the outward substance of a legitimate medical school. A two-thousand-page first-year curriculum based on guided self-learning had been produced and was about to be tested. A budget proposal had been submitted for a four-year program as well. Although the new medical curriculum was not yet complete and certainly crude in many of its sections, it represented a strong entry into innovative learning.

Shortly before classes began, I proudly distributed that first curriculum, in its entirety, to our faculty with the following memo: "This curriculum is by no means complete or in its final form. It was assembled in a nine-month period and represents our best efforts with limited funds. Eventually, the entire curriculum will be structured on the unit system, as exemplified by the physiology, genetics, and immunology sections. In addition to the enclosed curriculum, a separate section is being made up of evaluation materials for each unit. Furthermore, other tutorial units are continuously being developed and purchased to relate to various units of the curriculum."

With that, our preparation was finished. The students arrived on September 9, 1971 for registration. Classes began on September 13. Looking back after twenty-nine years on our thirteen-month effort, it is difficult to believe we could have accomplished so much in so little time. If the "proof of the pudding is in the eating," then we were about ready to feast on the new Urbana-Champaign program that had matriculated its first cohort of students.

CHAPTER 10

Real Students, Real Feedback

O**UR FIRST SIXTEEN STUDENTS** matriculated through a bicampus registration process without too much difficulty. All showed up for class in our schoolhouse at 1205 West California Street. "Twelve-oh-five," as we affectionately called it, was one of several *fin de siècle* houses that the campus had surrounded during the course of its growth and expansion. A wooden frame structure with creaking, hardwood floors, it had served as temporary quarters for several other new and growing campus units that had preceded us. The sitting room, dining room, and bedrooms were large enough to provide small classroom and administrative space. My first office had been in the chemistry building, Roger Adams Laboratory, which was just next door. I was happy to move from there into 1205.

Anticipating our gala beginning, we scheduled a September 7 reception for our prospective students and their parents. This informal affair at 1205 reduced the inevitable tension that accompanied a new school with new students, new faculty, and new curriculum. I greeted our new BDs (beginning doctors) officially on Thursday, September 8, and gave them the background and philosophy of the program. I told them that it was new and untried; that each student would go at his or her own pace; and that the order of progress through the curriculum was up to the student and his or her Medical Doctor Advisor (MDA). We had shaved the program down to fifteen problems by then and suggested that their course through the curriculum would depend somewhat on the clinical material available. I told them that more than one hundred people had worked on the development of the program and that every single one of them wished them success.

The students were advised not to expect the MDAs to teach them the basic medical sciences. No, these advisors would give their studies relevance that could be attained in no other way. We prepared the students for their first clinical experience by showing them the previously mentioned ten video vignettes designed to trigger a discussion and to alert students to some of the troubles they might encounter as raw trainees in clinical situations.

For example, one trigger film displayed a communications problem that cautioned the student to listen carefully to what the patient, or in this case the patient's mother, was saying. It went like this:

> Doctor: Hello Mrs. Jones. How long has Johnny been sick?
> Mrs. Jones: He's not six, doctor; he's five.
> Doctor: Well, if he is fine, why did you bring him in to the clinic?

For the first eight years of the school's existence, we showed these trigger films to every class that entered. Some provoked laughter, but all were usually followed by serious discussion of professional conduct. I believe they did the job they were intended to do, because in all those years of significant early clinical exposure of freshman medical students, we never had a physician complain that a student had acted improperly before a patient.

We also reassured the students that the program was extremely flexible and that to adapt it to their needs and to improve it for those students who were to follow, we would try to get as much feedback from them as possible. I told them that I—together with Tom Gamble, and Bill Sorlie, and available faculty—would meet with them regularly to hear their perceptions and concerns. They were advised that they would also be approached separately by sociology researchers John Kimberly and Michael Counte, who would be seeking their objective input into curriculum development. In addition, there would be beer and pretzels at the dean's home on the fourth Friday of each month. Then to emphasize to the students that the program was committed to clinical relevance and to reassure our physician base that they were to play a key role in the school, I scheduled a senior Carle Clinic physician, Tom Wilson, to give the first lecture in the School of Basic Medical Sciences-UC on the clinical topic of professional behavior.

Then came the introductions. Subject coordinators introduced themselves and told the BDs where and when consultation would be available. Some coordinators recommended texts and study guides; others did not go beyond the basic science objectives that were published in the curriculum. Students were shown their cadavers, and plans were made for cooperative joint dissections. Ray Watterson, a very popular UIUC campus teacher, gave the students an outline of embryology and told them he would give lectures to any who wished to attend. Independent study or not, so strong was Watterson's reputation, that most BDs attended his lectures.

John Kimberly introduced himself and his graduate students to the group and administered a baseline attitudinal summary. Feedback from the Kimberly studies proved to be very helpful over the next few months and years. Although he intended to perform a strictly observational study on the development of a new institution, he understood that the feedback he would provide would influence the outcome.

We scheduled three afternoons that first week of study to teach rudimentary skills in history taking and physical diagnosis. By the end of the third session, each BD had done at least one complete physical examination on a fellow student. To add zest to the exercise, one student had the physical signs of mitral valve prolapse and served as guinea pig for his classmates. Although this experience left much to be desired, we believed that most of the students were now ready to meet their MDAs, who joined the class at an evening reception. At this time, all the MDAs and MDEs were from the Champaign-Urbana area, so the logistics of such a meeting were simple. This gave the student and MDA an opportunity to plan for their first combined clinical experience, based upon one of the fifteen clinical problems.

From here, the students took off in every direction. Together with their MDAs, they chose the clinical problems they would work on, the units they would study, and their own rate of progress. When the BD selected a clinical problem that did not commonly appear in the MDA's practice, the MDA was asked to request colleagues for assistance. Those with a strong bioscience background were free to omit those elements of the program that would have been redundant for them. After completing a problem, the student would take a Level III examination at a PLATO terminal, obtain a printout of the results, and schedule two hours with a Medical Doctor Evaluator (MDE), who would review the Level III report, explore areas in which the student appeared weak, and in general evaluate his or her mastery of the problem. If the MDE was satisfied with the student's progress, the MDE would authorize the student to select another problem. If the MDE found the student's performance on the Level III examination too weak to continue, the student was referred to a campus faculty advisor who was to prescribe remediation.

The students were enthusiastic and excited about the program from day one. They loved the independence, the self-study, the self-pacing and above all, they were enthralled by the early clinical experience. Those who participated in live births called the experience "truly unbelievable." Hospital emergency room activity was very satisfying. In fact, during that first year, every MDA experience was considered positive. The BDs worked hard, twelve to fourteen hours per day, but the work was energized by a psychological high from the clinical experience. There is little doubt in my mind that one full day of clinical experience each week measurably enhanced the students' ability to grasp the basic sciences. It provided a day free from study, yet productive in its own right and incredibly motivating. To this day, those students who still keep in touch with the school remain very positive about the MDA experience, and MDAs remember with great fondness the students they worked with in those early years.

It was not long before the glitches began to appear. Successful as the program seemed to be, the students were not without anxieties. Were they learning enough, and if so, how could they tell? After all, the program at Urbana might be great, but they still had to pass the Chicago freshman comprehensive exam at the end of the year and NBME I later. And the learning objectives were perplexing. The curriculum did not differentiate priorities between one learning objective and another. Determining what was important (or what would be covered on the freshman comprehensive exam) became a critical issue for the students when they realized that they were not going to be able to cover all the material in a single nine-month period.

This brought to light troubles with the exams. Levels I and II, the pretest and posttest for each learning unit, were often too simplistic, lacked depth, and were not always representative of the unit material. In many instances, these diagnostic tests did not provide proper guidance for the student to decide whether or not to study a particular unit.

The Level III exams were the most severely criticized. The students could accept a faulty pretest and posttest, but the Level III exam was a major element in the gating process between clinical problems. The Level III was supposed to cover as many as one hundred learning units, each having as many as twenty different learning objectives divided among thirteen disciplines. Given the plan to cover fifteen clinical problems in the first year of study, each Level III examination theoretically tested almost seven percent of the entire package. As such, the Level III should have been a high-quality examination that covered representative material. It was to be a major milestone marking the student's progress, but here, within the shallow structures of the first year's Level III exams, the weaknesses brought about by our quick startup time and our lack of high-quality, full-time faculty lay exposed. (When full-time faculty did come aboard, the curricular details were quickly improved and Level III exams gained in stature and effectiveness. Administration can have the best ideas on earth, but there is no substitute for a committed and competent faculty.)

In addition, some students felt that the Level III exam, per se, interfered with the basic concept of independent study. They argued that we had sold the BDs on independent study and that the Level III violated that concept.

Early qualms and basic doubts were expressed about the independent-study mode. Students were more used to learning from lectures, with lecture notes that not only provided definition of what specifics the students were to know, but limited the amount they would have to learn. They had won their way into medical school in that fashion. It was upsetting to some that independent study, even when accompanied by a detailed curriculum, extended the bounds of required knowledge, often leaving those bounds undefined.

Other student concerns were recorded by Tom Gamble, the graduate student I was training in administration, but who was by that time functioning as my administrator for student affairs, as well as my administrative right arm.

For example, Tom sent me a memorandum regarding a counseling session on December 9, 1971 with student A.B. (Student identity is disguised. The letters are not the true initials of the students described in this chapter.) Although this student was destined to do well through the remainder of his medical training, A.B. was one giant anxiety package three months into the SBMS-UC program. He complained to Gamble that he believed his background and experience were not adequate to meet the rigors of this demanding curriculum. He said that he studied hard but felt he was forgetting as much as he was learning because of the amount of new information he had to cram in place. He had discussed his feelings with his MDA who tried, unsuccessfully, to reassure him. Married with one child, he was concerned about shortchanging his family. He described his home life as nothing but eating, studying, and sleeping. His moments of relaxation were flooded with guilty feelings. "As the session continued, it was noticeable that A.B. relaxed, and apparently just talking about his feelings was of considerable cathartic value," Gamble said of the counseling session. "He left an hour later feeling a lot better about the program and a lot better about his involvement in it."

Tom also met with C.D., who reported problems with the Levels I, II, and III examinations and who said there appeared to be more in the curriculum than students could possibly learn in the given time. C.D. was particularly concerned about the lack of positive reinforcement to replace the grading system. Although the Level III exam yielded a score, the examinations were so long and detailed and covered so much material that the score was of limited value in assessing his own learning. He was depressed by a feeling that study was never-ending because there was always so much he did not know.

C.D. also expressed the common anxiety felt by all students toward the forthcoming freshman comprehensive examination and the NBME I. Both were scheduled for June 1972. Failure to achieve the minimal passing level on the former would lead to dire results, among which were repeating the first year or being dropped from medical school. According to Gamble, C.D. told him that "there was a general feeling among the students that they really were not assured of the breadth and inclusiveness of the program" and the students were anxious that the program was not "going to teach them the things they needed to know to pass these major progress examinations." Some of the more confident students presented the flip side of that argument, expressing concern that there would not be recognition of their achievements in pharmacology and pathology by the clinical schools.

If the students were apprehensive, so were the participating physicians, the MDAs, and MDEs. All of them had been trained at more traditional medical schools and were concerned about our program. Some expressed the need for more structure in the form of seminars, for better definition of what the students should learn, and for more time to master the curriculum. Many physicians thought that nine months was not enough time for this program, suggesting that if it could be extended to twelve months, it might be more successful. The doctors also expressed their concern with the time demands that the program placed on them. They were unpaid faculty and had obligations to their work and families. Nevertheless, most of the participating doctors wanted to continue with the program, although some skeptics doubted that we could manage a program of 128 students with this form of teaching.

A typical meeting with MDAs and MDEs took place at 6:00 p.m. on a snowy January evening in 1972. (One of the remarkable features of the physician support we enjoyed was that after a full day in hospital and office,

physicians were still willing to meet in the evenings to make this program a
success.) We covered a number of different issues. First on the list, I
explained to them that the budgetary situation was tight, but that we
planned to go from sixteen to thirty-two students next year. We were now
evaluating the problem of whether to use thirty-two new physicians for
thirty-two students or to continue with the same sixteen if they were willing.

Mike Russo, a Christie Clinic surgeon, suggested that the students might
do better to start the program in lock step on a smaller, easier problem, one
with a limited number of learning objectives. He believed that every one of
the first five problems his student undertook was too extensive and time-
consuming. The overwhelming amount of material depressed rather than
stimulated his student. He thought that if all the BDs could start together on
a smaller problem with maximum faculty help at the beginning, it would
ease the group into the curriculum with less trauma. There was general
agreement with this position.

No one present believed that any student could complete fifteen clinical
problems, but they all thought the students could complete ten. There was
such unanimity among the MDAs and MDEs at that time that we decided
then and there that in the coming year the students would be required to
complete a minimum of ten clinical problems instead of fifteen. There was
also a general agreement that classes next year begin in July rather than
September, allowing eleven months, rather than nine to complete the ten
problems. To cover some of the gaps left by reducing the problems to ten, I
agreed to consult with the campus-based faculty about adding a didactic
element to the curriculum with lectures and laboratories according to perceived need. These exercises would be tailored to learning objectives that our
Level III data showed were not being mastered by the students and to those
objectives that could not be covered within the ten problems.

The political problems generated by the inclusion of pathology and
pharmacology in the course of study were commonly raised at these feedback conferences both by BDs and their advisors and evaluators. Some students expressed fear that they would not be given credit for these studies at
SBMS-UC and would be forced to repeat those disciplines in the clinical
schools. Several physicians thought that the inability of the clinical schools
to be flexible on this issue was an excellent reason for us to consider an
independent clinical program at Urbana-Champaign. All the MDAs were
concerned that the laboratory experience in gross anatomy was inadequate.

Many of the MDAs enjoyed teaching and particularly enjoyed their relationship with the BDs. Some BDs were invited to dinner and to social events with physician advisors, which provided very positive contributions to the students' progress. We never rationalized the MDA function as a basic science learning experience. The MDA was not there to teach a specific discipline. The MDA was a personal role model for the BD and provided a threefold learning stimulus: a) to give the student a strong sense of the relevance of the basic sciences to clinical medicine; b) to help the student learn the vocabulary of medicine; and c) to provide a productive break from the long hours of study, thus relaxing the student and improving the opportunities for learning.

Furthermore, although most MDAs came from traditional medical schools, many often described their own basic science and preclinical education as "lousy" or "garbage," thus reassuring the students of the value of our program. One doctor, for example, expressed his belief that after one year of medical school at SBMS-UC, these sixteen BDs were better doctors than he was after three or four years in a traditional medical school.

Some of the physicians appreciated their new exposure to and review of the basic medical sciences, and at least one doctor felt that his experience with a freshman medical student had made him a better physician. But most physicians who participated did so because they wanted to be involved in what appeared to be a new departure for medical education and to do their share.

Meanwhile, as the newly recruited SBMS-UC faculty members assumed more and more ownership of the program they were teaching and administering, they became increasingly conflicted by strong gravitational pulls from their respective departments at UIUC. The basic science departments, quite naturally, were fixed mainly on their own internal sense of quality and were less interested in the success of the medical school. Indeed, the departments had very little stake invested in the medical program. It appeared to me that were the program to fail, the UIUC life sciences would have been happy to pick up whatever pieces were left and proceed indifferently on their chosen paths.

At SBMS-UC Executive Committee meetings, department heads frequently reiterated their beliefs that curriculum development and delivery should be the responsibility of the departments as a whole rather than the responsibility of individual faculty members, even though the responsible individuals were being paid by SBMS-UC. Salary is a symbol of control, and without salary control other powers of administration are often rendered moot. The departments were not administratively responsible to my office. We were operating for the time being on goodwill, but a more formal linkage would be necessary before I would relinquish my budget to the departments. What the departments wanted were the salary lines with no strings attached. "Trust us," they said. So, for the time being, the school relied principally on those members of the department who had been hired specifically for the purpose of delivering medical education.

As the first class of BDs progressed through one clinical problem after another, the faculty gained confidence that our students would do well on both the June comprehensive examination and NBME I. The students in the College of Medicine did not have to take the National Board exam after only one year, but because that exam was a useful external measure of our progress, we asked all sixteen BDs to take the exam in early June as "non-candidates." A failure would not count against a student, but if he or she passed with a score that was satisfactory to the student, the performance could be recorded as if the BD were a "candidate." Such students would not be required to take the exam again after their second year, when the vast majority of U.S. medical students took the exam.

Before the examinations, most of the science faculty scheduled review seminars to be voluntarily attended by the students. There was also a feeling of faculty satisfaction. They were not only promoting the learning of basic science in these future physicians, they were also teaching them skills they needed for continuing self-education for the rest of their professional careers. Indeed, for these reasons, all of us believed that the students who mastered this curriculum had the potential to be more competent, self-motivated physicians.

During that first year, the faculty also concluded that not everything could be assimilated effectively through self-study. Some curricular areas definitely needed a lecture or seminar-type presentation for better understanding. Several members noted that students, who were each on very different tracks through the curriculum, came to them serially at different times during the year asking the same questions about the same units. The faculty response to this was to organize seminars on those topics that required active teaching. The faculty also gradually concluded that students should be paced together through the curriculum so that they would gain the necessary breadth of basic science coverage. Despite the very tangible benefits of BD independence and freedom, the faculty were gradually drawn to the view that if all students were studying the same problem area at the same time, an efficiency could be achieved that offset the loss of student independence. Furthermore, this would permit a rational order to the seminars that the faculty had been preparing based on student need. They reasoned that the seminars, which were now being held for two or three students at a time, would be appropriate for large-scale presentations to all the students because of the inherent difficulties in grasping the full meaning of some subject material.

This represented another major departure from the individual and random course of study. The faculty argued that such a change toward a planned course of study was not only called for early in the program, but looking ahead to our projected complement of 128 students per class, they saw it as mandatory. I argued that ordering the approach to clinical problems would inherently remove some of the relevance from the curriculum, because it would be much more difficult for the MDA to provide the relevant case material on a scheduled basis. When the student and the MDA selected the clinical problem to be studied at any given time, that problem could be tailored more easily to the MDA's practice. After some reflection, I agreed to the proposed change, and the curriculum has been ordered ever since.

Also critiqued by students, MDAs, and MDEs was the dean's own mini-course on the patient history and physical examination that had been presented in the first week of study. It was not a self-study course. Although the organization and presentation of a physical examination and history-taking curriculum for a first-year basic medical science student involved many challenges, the motivation gained through this limited commitment of time and effort made it all seem worthwhile.

It was a form of sink-or-swim education. Although we were never entirely satisfied with the process, it did give the students a running head start toward dealing with clinical patients. In fact, many of our students told us they felt light-years ahead of their peers when they met them during their second year in Chicago, Peoria, or Rockford.

CHAPTER 11

Outside Influences

NEW PROGRAM with a new curriculum must have its own evaluation system. That is fundamental. However, we were quickly denied the right to an evaluation system as innovative as our curriculum. Unfortunately, I had agreed with Bill Grove that our students would take the certifying collegewide freshman comprehensive exam in June 1972.

The College of Medicine insisted that student appraisal and promotion was a college function and forced us to adopt the evaluation system developed by the new "semiautonomous" School of Basic Medical Sciences in Chicago, our counterpart there. The system involved diagnostic, non-certifying progress evaluations in December and March, as well as the freshman comprehensive exam in June.

Although the five or six Urbana faculty members were invited to contribute items for all three of these exams, they were fully occupied with curriculum maturation and Level III development. The exams would be wholly prepared by the Chicago school's 68 faculty members. Although the testing was done with thoroughness and integrity, students from SBMS-UC were at a natural disadvantage.

We argued to the College Committee on Instruction and Appraisal that because our overall curriculum design was approved by the college through its Committee on Educational Policy, and the curriculum had its own interim evaluation procedures, we were not bound to take the Chicago school's interim exams. However, because ours was a minority voice on a committee that was not prepared to tolerate too much diversity and was strongly influenced by Bill Grove, we lost that battle.

I argued that it was unfair to burden our students, already at a disadvantage with respect to the June exam, to be subjected to the interim exams prepared by the Chicago faculty. I lost that one, too, but I did extract the commitment that for our students the December and March exams would be diagnostic, not certifying.

Our faculty was allowed to review all questions proposed by the other faculty and was given veto power over questions that dealt with topics not within SBMS-UC objectives. Likewise, our faculty was invited to add questions to the examination pool. It was a fair system on paper, perhaps, but inadvertently biased against our students.

Furthermore the SBMS-UC students were responsible for pharmacology, pathology, and clinical microbiology which went well beyond the traditional first-year Chicago objectives and which could not be tested in an examination that was common to the two schools.

Our students broke their stride and, as directed, sat for the December exam. As expected, because much of it covered areas they had not yet studied, they did very poorly on it as a group. However, they appreciated the experience to view a Chicago exam, and when they took the second interim exam in March they found that they were better prepared than they thought, doing about as well as the average student in Chicago. The real test to come, however, was the all-important freshman comprehensive exam.

Our semiautonomous status meant precious little when it came to preserving our innovative curriculum. It was this issue, more than any other single cause, upon which our educational experiment foundered.

Our school was an exciting experiment—the integrated learning of all basic medical sciences—but the one ingredient necessary for success, control over the evaluation process, was denied us until it was too late to rescue the essence of our educational thrust. There was no need for this to happen. Given the go-ahead sign by one college committee for a freewheeling curricular model, the same freewheeling approach to evaluation should have prevailed.

After all, if there is one given in any educational system, it is that most students will learn what they have to learn to get by. Motivation, excellence in instruction, useful texts, and learning objectives may all contribute to success, but for the medical student who has struggled through four years of the undergraduate jungle to get superior test scores in courses and competitive scores on the Medical College Aptitude Test, testing is the key to learning. If you test for it, the students will learn it. If you do not, they may or may not learn. The majority of our students kept pathology and pharmacology, which were not covered on the Chicago-written exams, low on their priority lists. There was no escape from that hurdle, and no way to modify that exam to evaluate the BDs' achievement in the excluded disciplines.

Everyone gives lip service to innovation, but in fact, most administrators and faculties are extremely conservative when confronting new ideas. Many are simply frightened by the thought of radical movement; others are lazy, concerned about the increased work load in dealing with change. In this instance, conformity was forced upon our "innovative" program by the rigid adherence to an examination system that undermined our program goals from the start.

To borrow a phrase from George Orwell, the six semiautonomous schools of the College of Medicine were equal, but some were more equal than others. This fact remained a continuing source of frustration for the "less equal" schools, but at least we were "semiautonomous"—whatever that meant.

Meanwhile, I was busy lining up area doctors as MDAs and MDEs for our projected expansion to 32, 64, and ultimately 128 first-year students. My message to community physicians was always the same: The medical school would not develop a university hospital with an exclusive full-time staff. We wanted community physicians to be involved as teachers and as advisors. Furthermore, we believed that participation at the level required of an MDA/MDE would not reduce their income. In other words, there was no bogeyman hiding behind me; we would not be an agent to reduce their status or their dignity in the community; and we were no threat to their incomes. I emphasized this message over and over again. I was determined to avoid a town-gown conflict. It was arduous to battle administrative incomprehension in Chicago, to debug our own program, and to attempt to make sense and be a good citizen of the reorganized College of Medicine, which required its own tribute of endless meetings in Chicago.

A typical meeting to recruit MDA/MDEs took place at Decatur Memorial Hospital. I had been to Decatur several times previously, meeting with key physicians who might provide medical leadership for us. The Decatur medical community was disappointed that Decatur was not selected for a medical school of its own in the regionalization process. Furthermore, although many of the doctors there had close ties to the University of Illinois, the new Southern Illinois University medical school in Springfield was closer to Decatur, better funded than we were in Urbana-Champaign, and a four-year program, not just a school of basic medical science.

Accompanying me on the fifty-mile trip to Decatur were two great supporters and advocates of SBMS-UC, Alan Peterson, an able internist and an

MDE, and Dick Ensrud, a respected gastroenterologist and MDA, who during the ensuing years would successfully head up our internal medicine residency program. The leading force for medical education in Decatur was G. Richard "Dick" Locke. Dick, like myself, was a graduate of Case Western Reserve University and a radiologist at Decatur Memorial Hospital. He was very helpful in all of our Decatur negotiations.

When Al Peterson, Dick Ensrud, and I arrived to sell the program to the Decatur medical community, the three of us faced Dr. Locke, about fifteen physicians, and the administrators of Decatur's two hospitals, St. Mary's and Decatur Memorial. Tension was in the air, and the anxiety was almost palpable. It was the same kind of anxiety we had run into when we first discussed the program in Champaign-Urbana, but it was more exaggerated and not as easily resolved. No matter how many times Ensrud and Peterson stated that they enjoyed working with BDs; that they were very comfortable with the concept; that advising and evaluating students was not as difficult as it sounded; that they did not have to teach biochemistry, physiology, etc., the same questions kept recurring: "How will I ever teach basic science to a first-year medical student?" and "Am I good enough?"

One of the physicians, Hines Hoffman, a surgeon and an old-timer, was openly skeptical. He stated categorically that the time, money, and commitment needed for the program were not available in Decatur. I had been forewarned by Dick Locke that Hoffman was in the process of establishing a connection with Southern Illinois University which was then developing its medical school in Springfield, and did not want to do anything that would jeopardize the relations between his hospital, St. Mary's, and the Springfield operation. Hoffman also attributed to Bill Grove a statement to the effect that residency programs, which would be paid for by patient-care dollars, would add twenty-five to twenty-seven dollars per day to the costs of patient care, an expense he opposed. I could neither confirm nor deny that figure, but I answered that if an internal-medicine residency program improved patient care, whatever the cost, it might be worth it to the patients in terms of their own health care. Most of the other physicians were less antagonistic than Hoffman and more willing to listen, but conceptual progress was absent.

I finally spoke to the Decatur physicians rather bluntly, saying in effect, "You gentlemen are confirming all the opinions and stereotypes that academic medicine has laid on the practicing physician. Academicians tend to stereotype the practicing physician as relatively useless for teaching medical students and as mainly interested in maximizing personal income." I told them that I was convinced this was an incorrect perception and that practicing physicians suffered from a poor self-image. I offered reassurance that every one of them had something to offer; that each of them had a vast amount of medical knowledge and personal experience with which to guide medical students; and that I, as the dean of this new enterprise, had faith in them.

Sometimes when I promoted the program in that manner I felt more like a huckster than a dean. Nevertheless, the three of us left Decatur somewhat optimistic that we had cracked a portion of their anxiety and that some Decatur physicians would join the program. I figured that we would need at least nine physicians in Decatur, three evaluators and six advisors. Dick Locke called me a few days later and confirmed that things were going far better than was the case before our visit and that he would probably have six MDAs and three MDEs ready for the 1972–73 academic year. The first phase of our expansion beyond C-U was going well.

As a community-based medical school, we strove to include practicing physicians in as many phases of the medical-education process as possible. One manner of accomplishing this goal was to initiate clinical conferences that centered on one of the clinical problems. Although we could not organize a clinical conference about all fifteen problems that first year, we attempted to present clinical insights to the students about the five most common ones.

The clinical conferences were not always works of art, but the students generally enjoyed them. Turning practicing clinicians into academicians is not an easy task, but we had to start somewhere. I was under no illusions regarding the quality of the product. It was imperfect, but perfectible. I did not share my conclusions with the students, who as noted above were generally enthused by the conferences. However, in staff discussion I stressed that our clinical faculty required significant support for educational development.

Another important constituency to be cultivated was in the political arena. Politicians must be approached carefully in a public university such as the University of Illinois. In my experience, politicians are usually smarter, much more capable, and harder working than most people expect. Whenever I paid a call, as dean of the medical school, to the office of our local state senator or local state representative, I was warmly received and offered support where possible. In reality, the university bureaucracy effectively isolated deans and directors from direct political action. The university president represented all units of the university to the State Legislature, and the entire university budget was assigned to the university president, not to any one unit. There were no line items for specific schools such as SBMS-UC. My chain of command to the legislature was through Bill Grove, to the chancellor at the Medical Center who reported to the president. State funding for a unit such as SBMS-UC was strictly a "trickle-down" phenomenon.

This was in stark contrast to the new Southern Illinois University medical school, which had its own separate line-item budget within the state budget for SIU. With the school located in the state capital, SIU Dean Richard Moy could effectively plead his case directly to the legislature. I had visited Moy early in 1971 to compare notes. It was a very enlightening visit. Moy was open and generous with information. He was charged with developing a one-year medical basic science program at SIU-Carbondale, 160 miles south of Springfield, and a three-year clinical program in Springfield. His budget for the 1972 fiscal year approached $12 million, which was an astronomical sum, nine times the combined budgets of Rockford, Peoria, and Urbana-Champaign. When it came to getting state support for medical education, Moy was clearly the most successful dean in the state and remained so until his retirement. When I informed Bill Grove about Moy's budget, his reaction was one of disbelief. He could not believe that Moy had been so successful in attracting state funds, something that Grove was unable or unwilling to do. Grove's inability to obtain or even to ask for adequate operative funding for his fledgling programs in Rockford, Peoria, and Urbana-Champaign represents his greatest failure, one that has permanently blighted grander prospects for all three of the College of Medicine's downstate regional programs.

One can only speculate on Grove's reluctance to ask for adequate funding for these regional programs. In my opinion, perhaps Grove feared anything that might diminish the luster of the Chicago program, even though that luster faded perceptibly during his administration. He did not want any of the regional programs, and particularly the one in Urbana, to upstage Chicago.

It is also possible that Grove made requests on our behalf that were turned down, but it seems highly unusual that Grove could not sit down with one of his deans and plan a formal request for additional funds.

CHAPTER 12

The Treadmill Agenda

THE MEETINGS, TRAVEL, and curriculum work—a steady diet of twelve- to fourteen-hour days—were taking their toll. Driving home from a late meeting of the Champaign County Medical Society at 11:00 p.m. one evening, I was feeling very tired. I lost concentration for a moment and found myself in the middle of an intersection, running a red light, with a car bearing down on me from my left. I jammed on the brakes quickly enough that when the collision occurred, it was reasonably gentle, and no one was hurt. The car I struck, which was deflected into the corner traffic light, was driven by an elderly African-American man who approached me very concerned. He was certain he had a green light going into the intersection but in the absence of witnesses and at night, who was going to believe him?

Although insurance companies advise clients never to admit fault in a car accident, I could not follow that rule under the circumstances. I told the gentleman not to worry, that the accident was clearly my fault and that my insurance would cover his loss. In a moment his expression transformed from one of pitched anxiety to one of total relief. I think he was about the happiest man ever to walk away from a fender bender. As for me, I was happy to be unharmed.

After the accident, Franny begged me to slow down, but I could not. There was still too much to be done. While the students were proceeding along their individual pathways and the MDAs and the MDEs were adjusting to their teaching harnesses, countless other activities churned in the dean's office—administrative meetings in Chicago, recruiting new MDAs and MDEs and faculty members, fund-raising attempts for our fledgling school, being available as a resource and participant in community issues, among many other activities. It was a treadmill agenda.

At John Anderson's urging, I recruited an executive committee for SBMS-UC to regularly review the school's progress and determine policy.

Executive committees usually comprise elected faculty members, but in the absence of a genuine faculty, the first SBMS-UC executive committee was more akin to an advisory board made up of key individuals from the campus and the community. Such a group was sorely needed and would prove invaluable for steering the school through the difficult times to come. Two minds are usually better than one, and four or five minds working together on a difficult political problem are even better. So even though the school eventually went to a faculty-elected executive committee, I always maintained an informal group of close advisors to guide me. The purpose of such a close advisory group was not to bypass the executive committee, but to tease out the problems we faced in a brainstorming, problem-solving fashion.

I quickly learned that using an executive committee provided an important advantage. The decisions and declarations of the committee gave me considerable leverage in dealing with Bill Grove and the Chicago operation. As major policy issues arose regarding budget, curriculum, and the development of a clinical program, I could present them in Chicago as a representative of the committee, not as personal issues. This gave me the ability over the years to disagree with Bill Grove and with other members of the university administration almost as if I were a third-party messenger, not as a rebellious administrator. The executive committee could make demands on the system that I, as dean, could not. Of course, Grove was not fooled for a minute when I laid blame for an unpopular demand on my executive committee, and in his moments of irritation, he suggested that were I a good leader, I could deflect my executive committee from making such demands.

As the first sixteen students progressed on their multiple pathways through the curriculum, recruitment of full-time faculty proceeded unevenly. The recruitment of faculty who would assimilate well into existing campus departments proved to be no problem. It was easy to recruit biochemists in the presence of a biochemistry department, microbiologists in the presence of a microbiology department, and when I finally resolved the personnel problems in physiology, recruitment of qualified faculty became relatively simple with that department as well. Recruitment went smoothly in those instances because I allowed the departments to lead the recruitment effort with the understanding that they would choose the best person available who, during the interview process, understood and would agree to be fully committed to the medical-education program that was being initiated. In other words, the department recruited, and I had veto power. (It was a good system. Some recruits who did not agree with the SBMS-UC method of education were rejected for that reason.)

However, when there was no departmental structure to provide for a faculty home, recruitment was another story. The Urbana-Champaign departments were reluctant to take maverick professors under their wing and hesitant to accept faculty members whose research seemed far afield from their own special departmental areas of interest. Thus I needed a pharmacologist, but because there was no department of pharmacology within the School of Life Sciences, I had to search elsewhere for a suitable home. The College of Veterinary Medicine was one alternative, but pharmacologists educated and trained in schools of human medicine were reluctant to consider a collegial home in a department that was distanced physically and conceptually from the medical school in which they were to teach.

We faced the same problems in the anatomy and neuroscience fields. Although it was possible for me to put together interdisciplinary search committees from a variety of departments, who diligently reviewed candidate lists and recommended names to me, when it came time to sit down and negotiate with a specific individual, to discuss salary, equipment, space, and a departmental home, the nontraditional medical structure of the Urbana-Champaign campus proved to be a formidable obstacle. In several instances, some excellent potential faculty recruits were lost because of the absence of a suitable collegial and peer atmosphere.

The obvious solution was to create new departments, but I had no money with which to do so. Besides, with what limited funding I did have, I was determined to exploit the economical use of the existing expertise that suffused the Urbana-Champaign departmental structure.

There were other recruiting problems. One that simply could not have been anticipated centered on a social impasse of the times. The students had been quick to recognize the curricular deficiencies in physiology. Most of the students tried to remedy the deficiency by using the text, *Review of Medical Physiology* by W.F. Ganong, which was a concise, down-to-earth summary of the elements of human physiology. In the spring of 1972, the perfect candidate appeared. She was a gifted, widely respected medical-school physiologist with many years of experience who was looking for a new challenge. In addition to directing a well-funded research program, she was considered to be one of the best teachers of physiology at her medical school. I was very pleased that she was seriously interested in coming to

Champaign-Urbana. After her visit to our school, she was universally acclaimed by all who met her as the right person for the job. She, too, was enthusiastic about the new curriculum and appeared ready to join us.

There was just one hitch. She advised me that she was a lesbian and lived with her partner, who was an academic in the humanities. She insisted that a position be found for her companion as well. This was not too difficult because her friend was fully qualified for a job in another department at the Urbana-Champaign campus. I looked into placing her partner, and it appeared that she was acceptable to the appropriate humanities department, which was prepared to offer her an academic position. However, this was 1972, and both the physiologist and her partner expressed concern to me about living together as a couple in a smaller, downstate community such as Champaign-Urbana. I did everything I could to convince them that homophobia was not a major problem in a university community such as Champaign-Urbana, but ultimately they elected to remain together, sheltered within the confines of a larger, urban setting.

While we were actively recruiting faculty, elements of the Urbana-Champaign campus were actively recruiting SBMS-UC. There were numerous faculty consortia on the campus that sought the advantage of a health-related program that might increase their competitive edge in attracting grants for program project research. I was approached from many quarters: animal science, neuroscience, nutritional science, and computer science. Although open to all requests for cooperation, I had to explain repeatedly that we were a school with only six full-time faculty at the time and with very limited financial resources. I could lend the name of the school to meritorious projects, but applicants could not expect too much medical-school faculty involvement.

In addition to performing my duties as dean, I tried to stay somewhat current in the rapidly expanding field of cardiology. I read journals when time and energy permitted, and in November 1971, I decided to fly myself out to Anaheim, California for the annual meeting of the American Heart Association. By this time I was a qualified pilot, but my license to fly was limited to periods when "Visual Flight Rules" applied, in other words, at times when there were no hindrances to vision such as clouds, smog, fog, etc.

I announced my plans to Franny and invited her to join me. She was less than enthusiastic, but still wanted to accompany me. At that time, we still had three children—ages 9, 13, and 15—at home. She felt it was dangerous for us to fly that distance in a single-engine airplane. I argued that the flight was not only safe, but would allow me to accumulate the additional forty hours of flying time I needed for instrument certification, which was vital to ultimate flying safety. We said goodbye to our children, who were left with a graduate student couple, and on Friday, November 5, took off for Los Angeles by way of Liberal, Kansas; Tucumcari, New Mexico; Tucson, Arizona; and the San Bernardino pass.

The flight west was completely uneventful except for the takeoff from Champaign. It was one of those unsettled fall days with brisk, turbulent winds that frequently sweep across the Great Plains. Franny, who had never flown before in a single-engine plane, was terrified to tears as we rumbled down the runway and took off into what was very bumpy weather. Nevertheless, once we rose to an altitude of five thousand feet, the flight went smoothly and continued to do so as we made our way across the country.

The only other difficult period that we encountered was in our approach to Los Angeles, where we were greeted by a giant smog bank that hovered over the city and made visibility very poor. At that time, I wished that I had more instrument qualifications because it seemed as though I were flying in soup. Nevertheless, with some help from the ground controllers, I found Fullerton Airport, where we landed and parked the plane until our return flight after the meeting. The return trip was completely uneventful. The little Piper Cherokee had an airspeed of about 120 miles per hour, and proved very reliable throughout the forty hours of flight. Upon my return, with the necessary hours of experience under my belt, I enrolled in an instrument-training course and shortly thereafter was certified for instrument flying. That permitted me to travel to Chicago by plane for those administrative meetings regardless of the weather.

CHAPTER 13

The Payoff

D ESPITE THE ADMINISTRATIVE DISTRACTIONS, medical education for the first SBMS-UC cohort of sixteen continued. In the
latter part of the year, things seemed to settle down. There was less
nervousness and agitation. The students and faculty knew what they were
doing or what they had to accomplish. Level III examinations, improved and
updated, were very useful in monitoring student progress. We plotted every
BD's Level III result on easel-borne gridded charts, as if each student was a
thoroughbred racing to the finish. Anxious for the success of the entire
group, I scheduled personal talks with two students who seemed, according
to our plots, to be lagging behind. Interestingly enough, both were enjoying
the program and both were confident that they were doing all right even
advising *me* to keep calm and not to worry. This quiet confidence on the
part of the students was reflected in my monthly meetings with them, which
were well attended through January and February, and then, as the students
exhibited more trust in the program and the program itself became more
routine, attendance tapered.

As the end of the first year drew near, my staff and I reviewed the
schedule for the freshman comprehensive and the NBME I examinations,
which were to be given within a few days of one another in June. We agreed
that these examinations would provide sequential acid tests for the program.

I felt confident enough in the program that I spent six weeks—from
May 5 through June 13—in Israel as a consultant on a new medical school
that was planned for Ben Gurion University in Beer Sheva. I was invited by
Dr. Moshe Prywes, head of the Department of Medical Education at Hebrew
University, Hadassah Medical Center in Jerusalem, after George Miller suggested I could help developing curriculum. I was honored that Miller
thought enough of the SBMS-UC effort to anoint me as a bona fide educational consultant.

After six weeks in Israel, which diverted me from worrying about

SBMS-UC, I returned to receive what amounted to an SBMS-UC report card. The students took the freshman comprehensive examination on June 7 and 8 and the National Boards on June 13 and 14. I came home in time to attend our "traditional" year-end party on June 14, at which the faculty could celebrate our successes and examine our failures. As the Ozark plane flew over the broad green plains of Illinois on the last leg of my long return journey from the Middle East, I had the same good feeling I had when flying with President Henry two years before—a feeling of confidence, a belief that the results would be encouraging.

At 4:00 p.m., June 14, 1972, all sixteen students and most of the faculty were present at my house for a final happy hour, a celebration of the first year's end, and above all, to learn the testing results. The results were very encouraging and, in fact, almost overwhelming. The first news that came down from Chicago, where the examinations were machine graded, informed us that all sixteen students had passed the freshman comprehensive examination of a week earlier, and passed with ease. It was great news for all of us. Needless to say, it was a great shot in the arm to provide motivation for the next year. Everyone felt a sense of achievement; the year-end party was the happiest of our many happy hours.

More good news was to come. Scoring and reporting of the NBME examinations took about five weeks. We would find out later in the summer that fifteen of sixteen students also passed Part I of the National Boards with credible scores. The students did well above the national average on all sections of the examination except for pharmacology and pathology. They achieved the 74th percentile in anatomy, 65th percentile in biochemistry, 62nd percentile in microbiology, and 69th percentile in physiology. Only in the disciplines of pharmacology (22nd percentile) and pathology (11th percentile) were our weaknesses apparent. Overall, the results of pathology and pharmacology notwithstanding, our students scored in the 48th percentile nationally.

Given the results in pharmacology and pathology, we could not declare the SBMS-UC curriculum an unqualified success. We had shown that when learning objectives are defined and students are given access to source information that covers the learning objectives, effective learning takes place. We had demonstrated that faculty can function as information managers as well as teachers, so that having neither a classical basic medical-science faculty nor a formal course structure was not the disadvantage an external observer might expect.

Nevertheless, pathology and pharmacology remained a problem. It is easy to postulate that we tried to put too much into the first year curriculum because virtually all medical schools used a major portion of the second year to teach pharmacology and pathology. But that begs the question of the most effective way to deliver these disciplines.

Unfortunately, in our semiautonomy, we were never free enough to be able to do the experiment correctly. We needed control over our admissions, our calendar, and our own freshman comprehensive examination. Except for some leeway on our starting dates, none of these important elements of education were yielded to us by the College of Medicine. As long as the freshman exam was prepared by the College, it would not cover pharmacology and pathology, and as long as SBMS-UC students knew this was the case, they lacked the essential motivation to study these subjects in the depth necessary to master them. As long as we were not able to select our own student body, where we might have sought out the self-starter, independent type of student, we were destined to take a cross section of medical students, which always included a significant fraction who needed to be spoon-fed and who resisted our managed self-study format. In later years, one of the latter group in later years filed a grievance complaint upon failing an examination, claiming she was well prepared for the exam but that the instructor did not ask the right questions.

Such issues notwithstanding, we were now prepared to move on with our development. Our class size would double in the fall of 1972, to thirty-two. The success of our first sixteen students proved to be a great motivator for all parties. I wasted no time in announcing the student examination results to our clinical colleagues throughout east-central Illinois. The news made recruiting MDAs and MDEs a far easier task. In fact, we now had some physicians actively seeking student advisees. SBMS-UC was now well launched and under way, but much work remained to be done.

PART III

Innovation Meets Bureaucracy

CHAPTER 14

Pushing for a Clinical School

I T IS ONE THING TO CONCEIVE of a four-year school; it is another to
deal, or rather duel, with the controlling bureaucracy to make it a
reality. Fortunately, I did not know much about the University of
Illinois bureaucracy before I took the job, because if I had, I probably would
never have accepted. A bureaucrat who occupies a powerful position quickly
learns that life is made simpler and smoother by saying "no" rather than
"yes" to innovation. The former keeps the ship of state on a steady course;
the latter calls for a change of course and threatens misadventures on
unforeseen rocks and shoals. The innovator who seeks to alter a given
course must convince the bureaucratic leadership that mines lie dead ahead
and cannot be avoided without changing course.

On January 11, 1971, less than six months after I arrived on campus, I
began to push plans for a clinical school. Meeting with Bill Grove in Urbana,
I showed him an Urbana enrollment table projected to 1976, an "astronomical" five years hence. The 1976 projection showed 128 basic-science students
together with three clinical classes of 40 students each, a total of 248 students. Our basic-science program was projected to begin with 16 students in
the fall of 1971, doubling in size each year until we reached our projected
maximum of 128. Meanwhile, the clinical school at Urbana, given the green
light, could begin with 10 students as early as the fall of 1972. It could also
double in size each year for three years until a full complement of 40 students per clinical year was reached.

Grove agreed in principle, but expressed doubt that we could follow
such a tight timetable. He asked for only one firm commitment from me,
and that was for SBMS-UC to develop the capability to provide 128 graduates per year from the basic-science school to send to Rockford, Peoria, and
Chicago's Metro 6. I told him that I was certain SBMS-UC would develop
the capability to graduate 128 per year, but that I did not want to be committed to sending all of them away. After all, if we sent 128 away, what

would be the basic-science source for our own clinical program? Grove deftly dodged the question as premature, and the clinical program at the Urbana campus was left up in the air. It would remain suspended, swinging in the wind, for several years to come.

After our second cohort of thirty-two students was well into the first-year program, we began the clinical planning in earnest. I told the physician community that, although we had no authorization to begin planning a clinical program, it remained very important for us to proceed in anticipation that authorization would come. I regularly quoted the "Lanier Treaty" and its near-guarantee of a clinical program. With this in mind, I scheduled an all-day retreat on Saturday, January 27, 1973, with the volunteer faculty to do some serious clinical planning. The physician turnout was magnificent. I emphasized that both time and money were in short supply, and we had to be ready to begin on short notice. The physicians understood and were ready to work.

I told them that the SBMS-UC message was beginning to get across to local leaders. Champaign-Urbana was a university community, and as such, businesses were closely linked to the success of the University of Illinois. A four-year medical school would mean adding millions of dollars of direct and indirect revenue to the community. However, I also told them that Southern Illinois University was the real medical school success story in this state, attracting millions of state dollars to Springfield, the state capital, only ninety miles away. By this time, SIU had a budget of four million dollars and had yet to accept a single student, while SBMS-UC was in its second year of operation with a budget of $450,000 and an enrolled class of thirty-two students. In other words, SIU had a budget that had the potential to focus referral medicine on Springfield to the detriment of the Champaign-Urbana economy, not to mention the two large group practices, the Carle and Christie clinics. So, I explained, the entire community had a stake in seeing a four-year medical school flourish in Champaign-Urbana.

I was also encouraged to move forward by support voiced in other quarters. For instance, Morton Weir, UIUC's Vice Chancellor for Academic Affairs, was genuinely interested in medical education on the Urbana-Champaign campus. He called me on January 11, 1973, after some preliminary discussions with the university president and vice president, to tell me he believed it was important for us to plan promptly for a clinical program of modest size that maintained high quality and remained innovative. Weir expressed the opinion that it was important to set the foundation for a clinical program at UIUC. He wanted a program narrative, a budget projection, and a tentative enrollment schedule (all of which I was happy to provide) to carry into a January 22 meeting in Chicago with Bill Grove and Barry Munitz, the vice president.

A *Champaign-Urbana News Gazette* front-page editorial on Sunday, February 4, 1973 urged a complete medical school for the community. Written as a memo to Gov. Dan Walker, the Illinois Board of Higher Education, and the Champaign-Urbana community, the editorial first praised the progress we had made at SBMS-UC, our economical approach, and our use of volunteer practicing physicians. It went on to identify the extravagances at Southern Illinois University, proposed expenditures of $154,000 per student compared with $22,300 at SBMS-UC, and complained that SIU seemed "to have a lot of friends in the IBHE and elsewhere in the government at Springfield." The editorial continued that "the University of Illinois is being shortchanged" and that SBMS-UC "deserves an opportunity to become a complete medical school."

The editorial at least caught the attention of the university's higher administration. Already concerned about the possibility of four independent medical schools, President John Corbally, who had replaced President David Henry in 1972, was clearly, from the very beginning of his tenure, troubled by the "Lanier Treaty," which postulated even a second university medical school at Champaign-Urbana. Medical schools were notorious usurpers of resources, and Corbally could not conceive that we differed from the giants he was accustomed to working with. He did not want two, much less four, independent medical schools within the University of Illinois, even though he already had two colleges or programs in engineering, liberal arts and sciences, business administration, and social work. Corbally, who came to Illinois from Ohio State University, saw the university through very different eyes from David Henry's. Henry was a respected academician and educator with a lifelong commitment to the University of Illinois and a person who possessed an unparalleled institutional memory. The loss of that memory through Henry's retirement, and shortly thereafter the retirement of treaty-drafter Lyle Lanier, placed our clinical plans, if not our basic-science school, in real jeopardy.

Spurred by the editorial, Corbally met with representatives of the Medical Center and the UIUC campuses. Typical of Corbally, these meetings did not include me, the dean of the affected unit. In all the meetings over the years during which he sought advice regarding the future of our program, never once was I invited to attend. Representing the Medical Center campus was Chancellor Joseph Begando. A very gentle and sensitive individual, Begando was the ideal person to calm troubled waters. Although in the course of the UIUC clinical development I am sure that I provoked him many times, "Gentleman Joe" never displayed anger. Behind his disarming and gentle demeanor was an effective administrator who guided the Medical Center skillfully through some very turbulent waters before his retirement in 1985.

The UIUC chancellor, in the spring of 1973, was Jack Peltason, whose attitude towards a clinical school at Urbana was not entirely clear to me then. Although Peltason was a key party to the Treaty, he seemed willing to wait for as long as necessary for the clinical school to develop at Urbana-Champaign. "When it's time to develop a clinical school, the governance will fall to Urbana like a ripe plum," he once told me. Probably, Peltason's passivity was related to the very cautious attitude of President Corbally, his immediate superior. Although Weir showed some preliminary interest in a four-year school, he was working for Peltason and was unable to show his hand at this time. So with Henry and Lanier out of the picture, Peltason relatively indifferent, and Weir neutralized, the future was anything but clear.

Corbally issued a chilling memorandum on March 1, 1973 to govern the "Planning for Programs in Medical Education." It said that the "initial and basic responsibility for such planning" resided with the Medical Center, Begando and Grove, working with the Administrative Advisory Council. It also said that policy decisions were to be ultimately reviewed by the university president with the advice of the University Council on Health Affairs. Corbally emphasized the point of the Treaty that said that, on major policy matters, mutual agreement between the Medical Center and UIUC would be necessary because the program would require close cooperation between them.

"Questions and concerns about the planning of medical education expansion should be addressed to Chancellor Begando or Executive Dean Grove via Vice President Munitz. If contacts with administrators of College of Medicine units [for example, Bloomfield] must occur, they should be accomplished in such a manner that the Medical Center Chancellor or the College of Medicine Executive Dean are aware of any substantive discussions," Corbally wrote.

The memo pointedly omitted reference to Treaty provisions regarding the expansion of the Urbana-Champaign medical program and the shift of program governance to UIUC.

Corbally did not send me a copy of this bucket of cold water thrown on our plans. Instead, Bill Grove sent me a copy with a letter he wrote March 6. Grove had read in our local newsletter that we had already been hard at work on a clinical curriculum. Bill's letter, which undoubtedly reflected Corbally's position, was as curt as it was strong.

"I note [in the newsletter] that you list the doctors who are working on the clinical curriculum. The public announcement that you are to have a clinical curriculum in the Urbana-Champaign area is presumptive and without mandate...I ask that you desist from further public display of your personal desires until a clear policy has been approved by the appropriate faculty organizations and administrative officers."

The letter was copied to Corbally, Munitz, Begando and the members of the Administrative Advisory Council. Were they readying me to walk the plank?

If not yet on the plank, I was certainly skating on thin ice. Grove (and indirectly Corbally) had told me to "cool it," while I was in the process of heating up local enthusiasm for a clinical program. I took a calculated risk that Grove would not bounce me out of my job for some perceived act of insubordination. However, given Grove's March 6 letter proscribing any further public discussion of a clinical program, I simply took the position that our curriculum development was, at a minimum, an exercise in continuing medical education, and the doctors should proceed with that in mind. Besides, I was an inveterate optimist. Nobody had said, "No." Corbally's cold shower simply revealed the hurdles I would face to establish a clinical program and that the first lay with my colleagues on the Academic Advisory Council. I resolved to place the clinical program on the council's agenda and keep it there until I was successful or I was fired.

It's interesting to note that archival material from the papers of Joe Begando appears to confirm that both he and Grove supported the establishment of the Urbana-Champaign clinical program. In response to an October 9, 1973 letter from Munitz, Begando recommended the development of a School of Clinical Medicine at Urbana and that it should "begin with the assignment of ten second-year medical students in August 1975."

Grove sent Begando a memorandum dated February 11, 1974 summing up the council's view that a clinical program should be started in September 1975 at Urbana-Champaign.

By the end of May 1973, I had the tentative agreement within the Administrative Advisory Council that a clinical program at Urbana would be appropriate "in due course." No timetable was set, but this was better than nothing. I also had verbal approval from Bill Grove that hinged on the elusive concept of "adequate funding." This was all the authorization I had when I went before the SBMS-UC executive committee seeking support to spend some of our limited resources to hire a "clinical" dean. The basic scientists on the committee did not want to see basic-science resources diluted to support a clinical program that was not yet authorized, much less funded. Resources for our basic-science program were very thin to begin with. Nevertheless, they were aware of the need for a clinical school to complement SBMS-UC and were adamant that if a clinical school were not forthcoming, they would resist relegation of the basic-science program on the UIUC campus to permanent status as a one-year program.

The SBMS-UC executive committee, after prolonged debate, agreed with my proposal to begin the search for a clinical dean. The meeting minutes, routinely sent to Bill Grove, provoked the following response, dated June 26, 1973:

> As I reviewed the agenda and minutes of your Executive Committee of June 6, 1973, I noted that you are recruiting for a position entitled "Dean for Clinical Curriculum." Since SBMS-UC has not been authorized to proceed with a clinical curriculum and *since there is resistance to the concept of a clinical school in the U-C area on the part of high level administrative officials* [emphasis added], I suspect that it is very unwise for you to be recruiting for such a person. I recognize that…there are many on the U-C campus who want a full MD degree-granting program. Furthermore, the AAC is in substantial accord that such a program should be developed in due course. I simply want to warn you that you may be compromising your own desires by getting out too far in front of the general understanding of when a clinical curriculum might come into existence in U-C. I will be glad to have a leisurely and unemotional discussion with you about this issue when we can find time.

The letter hardly put me in the mood for a "leisurely and unemotional discussion." In fact it made me fighting mad, but the question was "What to
do?" Showing the letter to my close advisors, I summarized, in the following
memorandum, where we stood at the moment:

> The Campbell Report of 1968, now five years old, has probably outlived
> much of its usefulness as a planning document. The University of
> Illinois, which has so many regional and diverse health initiatives pend-
> ing, seriously needs to look at its own long-range planning in the health
> sciences at this time. The questions to be addressed are:
>
> 1. Is there an intention within the College of Medicine and the
>   University to advance a clinical program at UIUC, and if so, when?
> 2. Is there intention to develop basic-sciences programs at Rockford
>   and Peoria and thus permit them to develop as independent four-
>   year programs?
> 3. Should the University support the expenditure of $60 million for a
>   new public University Hospital located only a city block away from
>   a second public hospital, Cook County Hospital, or could that kind
>   of money be used to develop a downstate medical center at Urbana-
>   Champaign to complement the UIUC campus, keeping in mind
>   that SIU is burgeoning in Springfield?
> 4. Should a four-year medical school on the UIUC campus directly
>   report to the UIUC Chancellor or should it remain within the
>   umbrella of the college of Medicine in Chicago?
> 5. Finally, given prior proscriptions, how do we alert the UIUC
>   campus administration, specifically Peltason and Weir, to all the
>   nuances in this complex struggle for money and status and to have
>   them behind the concept that it is in the best interests of the UIUC
>   campus to incorporate a medical school into its mission?

Consulting with my advisors, a consensus emerged that we had better look
into what Grove meant by "resistance…on the part of high level administrative officials," and that the next step for me was to meet with UIUC Chancellor Jack Peltason and Vice Chancellor Mort Weir to discuss the issues.

   On July 6, 1973, both Peltason and Weir assured me that no resistance
was coming from their offices. By implication, they made it clear that it
was coming either from Chicago's higher administration or from Corbally
himself. I updated the two senior administrators on the Illinois political

landscape, reminding them of the tremendous amount of fiscal resources that were going to SIU in Springfield and that the Medical Center campus in Chicago was about to request $60 million to build a new university hospital. I stressed that medical research was burgeoning everywhere and that UIUC should take whatever steps were necessary to maintain its place as the state's premier research institution. Both Peltason and Weir promised to address the matter of a clinical program at UIUC.

Peltason wrote to Corbally on July 11:

> "As you know, in the agreement signed by Chancellor Begando and me, with the concurrence of Provost Lanier on July 23, 1969 [the Treaty]...it was stipulated that 'consideration would be given to the expansion of this program into a full curriculum for the MD degree.'
>
> "One of the highest priorities of the U-C campus is the development of a clinical program in medicine. It was with the understanding that such a program would be developed in the near future that the faculty members most involved were persuaded of the desirability of launching the first-year program.
>
> "I am fearful that unless the University of Illinois begins to move on this commitment we will find that all of medicine in Illinois south of Peoria and Rockford will be administered by Southern Illinois University. I fear this development...not just for reasons of institutional jealousy but because...by building on the resources already available at UIUC we can provide the State with a more effective program downstate than can other institutions. I am also fearful that unless we participate in the development of a clinical program, our basic sciences, especially in the biological area, will also suffer...I am hopeful that a decision can be made to permit the assignment of planning funds for a clinical program at UIUC no later than fiscal year 1975."

Peltason added an interesting postscript to the letter:

> "There is no personal ego involved in this. I have plenty of 'empire' to administer already. I am fully aware of the kinds of problems the creation of a medical school on this campus will bring. I just honestly believe that it would be foolish for the state to build up a big medical program in Springfield while there is no such program on the largest and most research-oriented campus in the state."

The Peltason letter drew an instant reaction from Bill Grove, who was at that time juggling many different balls besides the clinical program at Urbana-Champaign. He promptly scheduled a meeting with Jack Peltason, Mort Weir, and me that took place on July 20, 1973. How Bill Grove organized and managed this crucial meeting is a tribute to his skill. Grove sold the concept of a new university hospital to Peltason and Weir and neutralized the increasing pressures from the UIUC campus to develop a clinical school at Urbana, which would have fulfilled the Treaty mandate to shift SBMS-UC governance from Chicago to UIUC. Grove reviewed in great detail the history behind the expansion and regionalization of the College of Medicine, including the history that supported the eventual development of a full MD degree-granting school in Urbana. He also pointed out that the Administrative Advisory Council, which he essentially controlled, was "in favor of the development of the clinical school in Urbana-Champaign but had suggested that such a facility should not be developed prior to FY 1976." Grove then made the case for funding a new university hospital at the Medical Center. He called the proposed hospital essential to good relationships between the Abraham Lincoln School of Medicine and the Metro-6 group of hospitals in Chicago, adding that the new university hospital funding had to go forward before any announcement of the development of the clinical school in Urbana-Champaign could take place.

Grove's letter to Chancellor Begando of July 23, 1973, describing the meeting, summarized the polar positions of the two campuses and records the discussion regarding the ultimate governance of the medical school in Urbana-Champaign. He reported, "Vice Chancellor Weir made it very clear that he believes a medical school in Urbana-Champaign should be under the full control of the Chancellor at Urbana-Champaign and have no relationship to the College of Medicine at the Medical Center. Chancellor Peltason also believed that this should be the organizational pattern but is less certain about the timing of establishment of such pattern."

Ignoring the Treaty, Grove advised Chancellor Begando that he believed that governance "is an issue that should be addressed by the Central Administration at an early date." With Grove pounding the table about the need for a $60 million university hospital and the need to continue the $12 million to $15 million annual subsidy of the old university hospital, it took no genius to realize that Central Administration could conclude that one independent medical school within the university was all that we could afford. The treaty was less than four years old, but since the retirement of David Henry and Lyle Lanier, it was being administratively ground to irrelevance.

Finally, Grove co-opted Peltason and Weir by gaining their support for a new university hospital as a first priority. This was evident from Chancellor Peltason's memorandum of the same meeting which confessed, "Dean Grove has understandable and persuasive reasons to be concerned about the necessity for securing proper funding for a new University Hospital…He believes that it would unnecessarily complicate these deliberations to discuss publicly at this time the date for the beginning of the clinical program on the Urbana-Champaign campus."

Grove also had elicited agreement on the sequence of the Urbana clinical-school process:

1. A recommendation from the Administrative Advisory Council of the College of Medicine to the University Council on Health Affairs (the University Council on Health Affairs was a new hurdle interjected by Bill Grove. There may have been such a council, but it was certainly not operating at this time and to the best of my knowledge during my tenure never functioned within the University Of Illinois).
2. A recommendation of the University Council on Health Affairs to the University.
3. A recommendation of the President of the University to the Board of Trustees.
4. The development of a planning task force that would include not only representatives from the Urbana campus but members from the Medical Center campus, Rockford and Peoria as well.

Agreeing to all the above, Peltason still wanted to keep governance on the table and wrote: "It was decided that the issue of how the Urbana-Champaign medical program is to be administered should not be raised at this time." I was most gratified by Weir's unambiguous position of support for the Treaty. I quoted Weir, in a memorandum to file, "When there's a full MD program on this [UIUC] campus, it will be administratively responsible to this campus." That was Weir's irreversible and non-negotiable position.

Responding to Grove and Peltason's separate communications, Vice President Barry Munitz wanted some clarification. He wrote to Joe Begando and Jack Peltason on August 17, to ask a number of questions. First, he wondered whether they both considered agreements they made based on the

Treaty to represent an operative commitment to eventually developing an Urbana clinical school. He also asked whether they agreed on a governance structure for such a school or, at least, a timetable for resolving the issue. Finally, he wanted to know whether the need and resources for such a school had been or could be established?

With the clinical school being considered at the university's highest levels, the fat was now clearly in the fire. The governance issue was front and center, and the results were anything but certain. But time has a way of weakening resolve. On October 9, 1973, backing off from Weir's strong position, Peltason wrote to Munitz, "This campus administration is prepared to see the program in clinical education at Urbana-Champaign and on the Urbana-Champaign campus to continue to be administered in the immediate future by the School of Medicine of the Medical Center campus." While senior administration dithered with our future, I was preoccupied with the present and prepared for the decisive Peoria retreat scheduled for September 11, 1973. At that time, could or would the Administrative Advisory Council formally advocate a clinical program at UIUC?

Meanwhile, I had been recruiting for the position of Associate Dean for Clinical Affairs, the person who would be responsible for developing the clinical curriculum. Good people were not about to jump ship to a school whose future was in doubt. Mort Creditor, the person who eventually took the position, had impressed me as the director of the Illinois Regional Medical Program (IRMP). The handwriting was on the wall for IRMP. Congress was reducing funds, and the program's ultimate demise was within sight. Creditor was looking for an academic position and the challenge of our situation intrigued him. On September 5, he had called me to say that although he was definitely interested in the position of Associate Dean for Clinical Affairs, he would not come to Urbana unless there was a public announcement of a clinical school. I asked him to put that in writing and I would take it with me to the September 11 retreat that would deal with the future of the clinical program.

Bob Evans, dean of the Rockford School of Medicine, called me six days before the retreat to say that he had received a call from Jerry Hahn, who was then acting Dean of the Metro-6 hospitals and Grove's point man. Hahn had told him that, at the retreat, "The deans will be asked to instruct Grove to notify the President that the council is prepared to develop a clinical school at Urbana-Champaign, *provided it is administratively part of the*

Medical Center campus" (emphasis added). So it was to be a package deal. The clinical-school proposal would go forward, but we would have to agree to continue as a stepchild of the Medical Center in order to get it moving. Bob Evans wanted to know my position, whether I would support such a resolution. Although he recognized an element of blackmail in the resolution, he agreed with its thrust. I thanked Evans and told him I would give him my views after some thought. After consulting with close advisors, I came to the same conclusion voiced by Lowell Hager, who said, "Agree to anything, because ultimately the needs of the program will determine the administrative arrangements." I called Weir the next day and discussed the situation with him. Weir stated that he also agreed with that position. I called Bob Evans to tell him that I would support the whole package.

When the council finally met on retreat, presumably to discuss the College of Medicine's strategic planning over the next five to ten years, it was clear to everybody there that the question of the clinical school in Urbana was going to occupy most of the time. Grove opened the retreat by reviewing the Treaty which was ratified by the Board of Trustees on April 23, 1970, and called attention to assumption five, which called for the establishment of the clinical school to also trigger establishment of a full-fledged College of Medicine administered by UIUC.

This was a bombshell! It should not have been, but it was. No one in the council had any idea such a document existed, much less that it had been incorporated into the public record in the Board of Trustees minutes. The group directed considerable anger at Grove for not discussing the Treaty earlier, but Grove explained that, although the document had the approval of the Urbana-Champaign Senate, it had never gone through the Medical Center Senate and was, in essence, "merely a verbal agreement engineered by Provost Lyle Lanier." I reminded Grove that the agreement had been approved by the Board of Trustees, which made it more official than if it had been approved just by the Medical Center Senate. This revelation made nobody happy.

No one else in the room wanted a competing medical school established within the university. There was instant and considerable pressure on me from all sides to agree to the concept of a single College of Medicine, an idea that I had no difficulty in supporting for reasons noted above. I said I would agree to the concept provided that a clinical program to start in September 1975 would be authorized without delay. On the other hand, the group wanted me to agree that we should have one College of Medicine that would have a clinical program at Urbana-Champaign but with no definite starting date.

Dean Nick Cotsonas of Peoria announced how happy he was that I had agreed to the single college concept and asked me to list the reasons for that agreement. I was tempted to tell him that to get the clinical program started I would have agreed to anything, but instead I listed whatever advantages came readily to mind. Facility of accreditation was a key factor, and there may have been others that I do not recall. Once I had listed the reasons for a single College of Medicine, Cotsonas and Grove, as if they had planned it, followed up with a suggestion that I should write an open letter to Weir, explaining my support for a permanent single college and that I should make a definitive public statement about it in Urbana-Champaign. "What is this?" I asked, "A show trial with confessions?"

Bob Evans intervened and took me off the hook by exposing this bullying tactic for what it was. Once Evans spoke, they backed off. In fact, I think that the council, sensing malicious manipulation on the part of Grove and Cotsonas, reached a consensus to support me and to start a clinical program at UIUC, perhaps as early as September 1975.

The council, with my concurrence, resolved that the Treaty's call for a new medical college at Urbana "should no longer be operative" and unanimously reaffirmed that any clinical program launched would be governed by the College of Medicine. With that decided, we broke for lunch.

During lunch, I met privately with Grove, who reiterated the extreme delicacy of negotiations between the Metro 6 and Abraham Lincoln School of Medicine and the extreme sensitivity, if not paranoia, in Peoria about a clinical program in Urbana. I complained to Bill that these problems were not new and that I could not solve them. Grove felt that both of them would be settled shortly but that we should be very careful about timing the announcement of the clinical program. I discussed Creditor's demand with him, which he dismissed as "typical of Mort Creditor's manipulation."

When the retreat reconvened in the afternoon, other issues took over the agenda. We still had not decided when the clinical program in Urbana would begin. We finally returned to the SBMS-UC problem at 8:00 p.m. George Miller began the discussion by saying, "Is there anyone who can find reason for SBMS-UC not starting a clinical program in September 1975?" If he never contributed another educational quantum, may heaven bless

George Miller! I could not have put the question more pointedly and succinctly myself. Having worked on the problem for eight hours already, no rational person, not even Cotsonas, could offer an objection. At that point the ballgame was over. We had defined September 1975 as the "optimal" time to begin a clinical program in Urbana.

The decision came none too soon. The widely read *Blue Sheet*, a weekly newsletter that summarized health policy, headlined its August 1, 1973, issue with this story:

> "STOP SCHOOLS EXPANSION, HEW SAYS. Enrollments at Medical, Dental and Osteopathic Schools should stop expanding, HEW planners told HEW Secretary Weinberger in a health-programs memorandum for fiscal 1975. The document, leaked to Chairman Kennedy (Democrat-Massachusetts) of the Senate House Subcommittee said enrollment capacity already achieved, continued net inflow of foreign-trained MDs, and increasing use of MD assistants is [sic] expected to result in an adequate aggregate supply of health providers by the next decade."

Clearly, the heat was on at the federal level to reduce medical-school enrollments and to reduce expectations of expansion. It was only a matter of time before this information would reach the state level and perhaps bury our clinical-school plans. For the time being, though, we were on track to begin clinical instruction in September 1975. Acknowledging that fact, the College of Medicine put out an enrollment table on October 25, 1973, that for the first time included a clinical school at Urbana-Champaign, with ten students to be enrolled in September 1975, increasing by ten each year until there would be fifty per class in 1979. There was to be considerable slippage in those projections, but reassured by their publication, Mort Creditor agreed to join us early in 1974. Clinical curriculum planning now began in earnest.

Little did I know that I was in for quite an unpleasant surprise.

CHAPTER 15

Feedback

I HAD THE GO-AHEAD I WANTED for the School of Clinical Medicine, but there were still problems at the School of Basic Medical Sciences that needed tending. Because the SBMS program was innovative and untested, we sought feedback of every kind imaginable (all of those involved turned into "feedback junkies"), and the feedback revealed the program's deficiencies. So the development of the clinical school had to proceed on a separate track as we tuned up SBMS.

John Kimberly, Assistant Professor of Sociology, asked me to contribute support for proposed research on our school's organizational development. Kimberly, an expert on the life cycle of organizations, was very interested in the development of the new medical school, particularly because it was beginning *de novo*. Kimberly and his research assistants conducted a comprehensive set of interviews of students, faculty, and MD Advisors (MDAs) and MD Evaluators (MDEs). These interviews were critical to the development and understanding of our process.

Physician response to the question "What are the strengths of the program?" confirmed a common belief that clinical correlation of basic sciences was a major strength. This included both in relating a specific disease to the basic sciences and providing exposure to patients during the student's first year of medical school. Weaknesses were also cited, but without consensus on any particular aspect of the program. Some physicians were concerned that the students had too much freedom and might waste their time. Some believed that the teaching appeared disjointed and lacked sufficient structure. But the most encouraging piece of information we received was that thirty-six of the forty physicians interviewed indicated they would remain in the program. Buoyed by this information, I pressed on to expand our physician base.

As the number of students increased, so did the number of clinical associates, our reservoir of MDAs/MDEs. By September 1973, we had 250 unsalaried, volunteer clinical associates, more than Rockford (219) or Peoria (156). Our 250 clinical associates represented physicians from Champaign-Urbana and the wide range of cities in east central Illinois. To better serve the associates, and to keep them current, I devised a system of regional assistants to the dean, known as RADs. RADs were volunteer physicians who acted as extensions of the school administration into these communities. They not only acted in their usual capacity as MDAs and MDEs, but also played key roles in recruiting and stimulating other volunteer physicians to participate as associates.

The enthusiasm the program engendered among our clinical associates is best exemplified by developments in Decatur, where G. Richard Locke, MD, was among our most supportive and creative RADs. He stimulated a general desire for a more structured approach to student education in Decatur. The physicians there decided to work as a group and have the students come to Decatur two days a month instead of once a week. The key to the Decatur MDA/MDE participation was the scheduled and obligated attendance by the students. The Decatur physicians planned to present eight clinical seminars in accordance with the students' progress and, therefore, to cover the entire curriculum from a clinical standpoint. This was a unique and independent approach that I strongly supported. This gave the Decatur physicians a considerable amount of autonomy, but in the end it worked out very well for the students who were assigned to that city.

The volunteer clinical faculty was becoming too large for me to manage alone. In addition to appointing RADs, I added Dr. Susan Rohrer to my staff in August 1973.

Her full-time task was to keep in contact with all our teaching physicians, to review their job descriptions, and to meet their academic needs as far as they could be defined. In other words, she was to keep our volunteer faculty involved, committed, and content. That was a big job.

Anticipating continued successful use of regional community hospitals, I pushed actively for as many affiliations as I could gather. By the time the University Board of Trustees met on September 20, 1972, affiliations with nine hospitals were ready for approval in addition to the four originally approached. More affiliations were to come, until the number of regional affiliates totaled twenty-one. As noted in the Board of Trustees' agenda, "These hospitals…could form the nucleus of a new clinical school of medicine based at the Urbana-Champaign campus." Together with the hospitals,

I was able to recruit a majority of the physicians within a sixty-five-mile radius of Champaign-Urbana as clinical associates.

Dr. Rohrer helped maintain contact with the twenty-one "teaching" hospitals with which we were affiliated. Not all of them would meet the standards generally expected of a teaching hospital, but because the school controlled the curricular objectives, the hospital served as a passive vehicle to provide clinical material to fulfill those objectives. We were occasionally under fire because of our use of these smaller hospitals. Once, for example, President John Corbally received a call from the resident of a small Illinois community who complained that the local hospital was administered by an individual who was totally incompetent to be the administrator of a teaching hospital associated with the University of Illinois. She described the physicians as being dissatisfied with the administration and stated that many patients occupying the beds should not have been there. She described the institution as being more of a nursing home than a hospital, and noted that the problem was complicated because the administrator of the hospital was also the mayor of the community. Bill Grove relayed these comments, which he received through administrative channels, to me. He agreed with me that as long as the hospital was accredited, we would work with it.

Yet for all our regional efforts, our core strength in the clinical arena was in Urbana-Champaign, which housed the bulk of our physician support and promised the best potential as a major referral center that would provide the broad range of patient problems necessary for teaching. Although Urbana-Champaign was "overbedded" with four hospitals, one could visualize their potential merging and conversion to effective teaching hospitals.

In addition to independent local physicians, Urbana-Champaign had two major multispecialty group clinics: Carle Clinic, which in 1970 had about seventy physicians, and Christie Clinic, with approximately thirty physicians. Negotiating with Carle Clinic was easier because of its corporate nature. Jack Pollard, its medical director during the fourteen years that I was dean, could commit the clinic to negotiated elements of educational support. Christie Clinic members were basically independent fee-for-service practitioners who shared common overhead for space and administrative services. No one could speak definitively for that clinic, so establishing teaching agreements and contracts there was arduous work.

The differences between the two clinics and the complexity of dealing with independent fee-for-service physicians made it tempting for the medical school to consider dealing exclusively with a single clinic, the Carle. Discussions with Pollard dating back to 1972 made it clear that the Carle organization saw medical education as a plus for the community as well as a plus for Carle. There was strong support at Carle Clinic and Carle Foundation Hospital for a full four-year medical-education program as well.

But as attractive as this option seemed to SBMS-UC, there were several drawbacks. Carle was far more conservative than Christie Clinic was, and although one could rely on Carle commitments once made, those commitments were difficult to obtain. Negotiations with Carle still pitted our painfully small budget against a financial gorilla. In addition, not all of the Carle physicians were as enthusiastic about the medical school and as willing to contribute the necessary time and effort as Pollard was. Although Pollard was influential within the corporation, he was by no means "boss." The number of Carle physicians available as potential medical-school faculty looked good on paper, but the figures masked a significant number of nonplayers.

Another factor that had to be considered was that, in starting the school, much of the initiative came from physicians outside the Carle Clinic. They could not be casually disregarded in favor of a premature embrace of Carle. In fact, it is fair to say that without the support of those individuals we could never have succeeded in putting the whole program together. There was good reason to resist placing all our eggs in the Carle basket.

Experience showed us repeatedly that we should maintain good relations with all parties to medical education in our region. Nothing persuaded us more effectively than our efforts to jointly recruit academic faculty with the clinics. We discussed the importance of joint recruiting in depth with both Champaign-Urbana clinics and reached a consensus with the clinic leaders that attracting a moderate number of academic physicians would be helpful to both parties. We had agreed, in principle, on salary payment plans for such physicians. We sought academically oriented physicians who could engage in clinic activity and private practice while carrying on clinical research. We knew that if a clinical program were to develop, we would need a cadre of geographic full-time faculty—teaching physicians who see most of their patients within the geographic bounds of a teaching hospital—to carry out the many functions that volunteer faculty could not or would not perform. This included committee meetings, formal preparation of curricula, and clinical administrative chores that were beyond what we could ask of volunteer faculty.

On the surface, the clinics were very cooperative and seemed to want to work with us in recruiting. However, when we approached them with specific candidates, they proved very hesitant to add "part-time academics" to their rosters. The clinics were uncomfortable with the lengthy university recruitment procedures such as search committees, advertising, equal opportunity, and affirmative action. They commonly recruited for their immediate needs.

We seemed always to be on a one-way street. We told the clinics every-thing we were doing in the area of recruitment; they told us little or nothing in return and continued to recruit and expand independent of the medical-school interests.

As we continued our efforts to obtain feedback, Kimberly's staff also interviewed Beginning Doctors during the course of the 1974-75 academic year, our fourth year of operation. Interviewers found that the most impor-tant source of satisfaction with the program was the independent-study aspect and the second-most-mentioned satisfying item was the clinical experience. The survey also pointed out that the independent nature of the program—followed closely by geographic considerations—was the most fre-quently mentioned reason for deciding to come to SBMS-UC. The students also felt they were performing better because the independent program allowed them to work on their own and to control their own time. This was particularly true for those with strong science backgrounds. Most students reported that seeing patients in the MDA setting was an important motiva-tor. "It keeps you going" was a common statement.

Students complained about the quality and comprehensiveness of the Level III examinations and that these exams were more evaluative in context and not simply a diagnostic tool. Some of the students found that the pro-gram was "not as independent as I had expected it to be." But, on the whole, this survey revealed a good degree of student satisfaction from a largely self-selected student body.

Obtaining feedback was not entirely risk-free. Sometimes, it caused dif-ficulties. One day I received a call from Ben Robbins, MD, a pediatrician at Carle Clinic. He had been approached by one of Kimberly's enthusiastic research assistants and wanted to know whether I expected him to partici-pate in the exercise. Dr. Robbins complained that he had been asked for a thirty-minute interview to which he responded with surprise: "Wow! A whole half-hour?" The research assistant, instead of backing off from the busy physician, cynically challenged him, "Why do you doctors always reply 'Wow' when I ask that question?" I told Ben that I was upset at such behavior on the part of a graduate assistant, reassured him that I would be talking to Kimberly, and promised that it would not happen again. He reassured me that he would go ahead and have the interview with the graduate assistant if only "to meet the son of a gun."

John Kimberly's surveys were not our only source of information. We were avid miners of feedback ourselves. I blush to recall a memo I received from one of my staff about Dr. W, who was one of our oldest and best supporters over the years. He returned a blank MDA/MDE performance form for the "wound healing" problem, writing on the back, "We do not do this!" The educational staff, lacking insight, two days later sent out second performance survey to Dr. W, who by this time was indignant and responded, "I told you, we do not do this!" The staffer's memo went on to describe how the "uncooperative" Dr. W was telephoned and indicated his distress that the role of the MDA was being changed from year to year (no doubt owing to our fine-tuning) and not for the better. He believed that the new medical-history and physical-examination program, which we had inserted into the MDAs' responsibilities, was a device to extract a heavier unsalaried teaching load from the MDAs than he had bargained for. He felt he did not have time to do all that administrative work and teach too. He was particularly upset with all the new paperwork required. Ten comprehensive evaluation forms per year were more than he had ever anticipated. Besides, he pointed out, the detail was unnecessary. He said he knew what he was doing as an MDA and what his student was doing, and he did not need to fill out an evaluation on it. When the staff member pressed him more than she should have, he closed the conversation by saying, "Well, I don't feel very good about the program. That's my personal opinion. Good-bye."

This was a cogent warning from a friend, and we did not ignore the clear signal that we were asking our volunteer physicians to do too much paperwork. In the usual one-on-one situation, teaching can be very gratifying for the physician. However, the administrative nitty-gritty is another category. Physicians are already besieged by paperwork in their practices and in their day-to-day hospital work. They resent the intrusion of additional paperwork that they consider unnecessary. In balancing the pros and cons of these matters, I tended to sympathize with the physicians and told my staff

not to persist when physicians balked at filling out the appropriate evaluation forms. There were always other good sources to tap.

Sometimes the feedback came directly. Always anxious for campus faculty to know the clinicians better, we held several receptions at our home to
which these groups were invited. We also invited clinical associates to our
faculty meetings.

L.W. (Bill) Tanner wrote a letter in December 1975 that pointed out that
the faculty meetings to which the associates had been invited were dominated by on-campus academic concerns. Tanner had been a family practitioner
in Danville for more than thirty years. He was and remains one of the most
widely respected doctors in that community. (It is of interest that in 1995,
Bill's son Joseph brought their "15 minutes of fame" to the family, as an
astronaut on a space shuttle mission.) Bill had discussed the most-recent
meeting with several other clinical associates and wrote, "If future faculty
meetings are to be devoted to such nitpicking procedures, it will be a long
time before many clinical associates come again."

He went on, "One got the impression that each individual department
was worried more about their own little dynasty in the academic world than
they were in the teaching of clinical medicine and basic science medicine to
willing students...

"The majority of physicians, away from the campus, are interested primarily, of course, in practicing medicine and now are becoming secondarily
interested in the teaching of medicine and feel that meetings that involve
their traveling considerable distances and spending that much time away
from both their practice and their homes should be directed more towards
their areas of interest."

Even though there were more than three hundred clinical associates and
only fifteen to twenty-five faculty members on campus, the "faculty meetings" were dominated by the campus faculty agenda. The Ph.D., who was
deferential to the doctor in the clinical setting of office or hospital, became a
nitpicking monster in the academic atmosphere on campus. I tried every
way I could to attract more clinical associates to our faculty meetings,
scheduling them after office hours, in the evenings, and even on Saturdays,
but they were basically uninterested in the detailed governance issues that
inevitably arose at such meetings. Bill was right. Eventually, most clinical
associates did not bother to show up at faculty meetings, but we continued
to visit them in their cities, at their medical society meetings, and at every

chance we got to solidify relationships with that important constituency.

One of our most important sources of feedback was the National Board of Medical Examiners Part I examination (NBME-I). During the first five years of SBMS-UC's operation, students continued to test satisfactorily, although not exceptionally, on the NBME-I. The initial year got off to a rousing start when the first sixteen students' average score was 500, which placed them in the 48th percentile nationally. Keep in mind this was a result for students who had completed one year of studies compared with the two years other students nationwide had undergone. We were very encouraged by these results, but such success was not repeated in subsequent years. The second group of thirty-two students in 1973 averaged 435, which placed them in the 26th percentile nationally and included our first failure. After that, from 1974-76, the mean percentile standings of the SBMS-UC first-year students were 35, 36, and 42 respectively. The topics dragging the scores down were invariably the subjects not required by the College of Medicine Freshman Comprehensive Examination: pathology and pharmacology. I still regret that we never had the chance to really put the program to the test.

Regardless of whether the program could be tested, our feedback confirmed that we were in sore need of full-time instructors in pathology, in which our students averaged in about the 10th percentile over the years, and in pharmacology, in which they averaged near the 20th percentile. So I made two controversial additions to our faculty,

The first was Detlef Bieger, a pharmacologist whose work complemented that of Charles Hockman in neuropharmacology and neuroscience. Bieger assumed responsibility for the pharmacology curriculum on October 1, 1972. The second was Melvin Schoenberg, a Ph.D. pathologist who arrived from Case Western Reserve University in February 1984. The addition of these two instructors bolstered our pathology and pharmacology programs, but the problems involved in hiring Schoenberg and Bieger exposed our tenuous relationship to the School of Life Sciences.

Mel Schoenberg was one of a kind. He was a very thin, pale, and apparently undernourished person, who suffered from a painful and slowly progressive chronic pancreatitis of many years duration. He stood five feet, four inches tall and weighed no more than one hundred five pounds, including the ever-present cigarette dangling from his lips. He had an unmistakable New York accent grafted onto a thin, plaintive voice that I would hear many times in the ensuing years because Mel was in considerable pain for prolonged periods and required codeine analgesics.

Until he moved to Urbana, Melvin Schoenberg had been a member of the Department of Pathology at Case Western Reserve University, but was never happy there. He was not an MD, but had earned a Ph.D. in pathology working on the immune protein, properdin. When the CWRU properdin research team dissolved in the early seventies, Mel was left on his own as a non-MD, second-class citizen in his own department. He was anxious to relocate.

SBMS-UC was a perfect fit for Mel, because he could teach. Whether he lectured to a full auditorium or tutored students one by one from his sickbed at home, he got results. He also filled our need for a full-time academic pathologist. Pathologists with an MD were beyond our budgetary capability to hire full-time, and we were not yet in a position where we could share a pathology position with one of the four local hospitals. Mel posed no threat to the practicing community, with whom he related well, but the campus departments did not exactly embrace him. Where does one place a somewhat dated, teaching (not researching) pathologist on a campus that prides itself as being on the cutting edge of research? I was faced with the problem of getting Mel a departmental home and pushing his appointment past my executive committee. Anatomy was the ideal place for him, but we still did not have an anatomy department on campus. After the departments of physiology and biophysics and microbiology rejected Mel for membership, I explained to my executive committee that I would appoint Mel to the forthcoming School of Clinical Medicine, but he would have teaching duties in SBMS-UC.

Mel was a great success because he could teach. In his own inimitable manner, he put together a sound pathology curriculum that he delivered in a variety of ways. This included self-study outlines, lectures, and home instruction. Mel would invite students to his house at any time of the day or night for pathology instruction. His wife and children knew this was "just Mel" and tolerated the intrusions or even adapted to them as ways of enjoying an extended family. Debilitated by his chronic pancreatitis, and partially under the influence of analgesic medications, he never gave up even though he sometimes had to be carried into the auditorium for his lectures. When his pain was too great to bear, Mel would remain at home and invite the students over for their lessons. Under Mel's guidance, pathology instruction stabilized and the NBME-I scores improved, but we never got by the ultimate impediment that, as far as the College of Medicine was concerned, pathology in the first year did not count. (Melvin Schoenberg died June 28, 1984.)

The appointment of Detlef Bieger as our first full-time pharmacologist was not easy either. Bieger posed the all-too-common problem of being needed while being unacceptable to the very selective departmental gatekeepers. Trained in Germany, he came to us highly recommended from a postdoctoral fellowship in Canada. He was the unanimous choice of the search committee for the position, but there was one hitch: No existing department in the School of Life Sciences or the School of Chemical Sciences would accept him, even though the search committee was made up entirely of SOLS members.

As usual, I found myself between a rock and a hard place: the personnel were absolutely necessary; the usual candidates shied away from the job, and only mavericks were interested, but they were not qualified. That made it awkward. Fortunately, at this time, Bob Metcalf, head of the Department of Zoology, came to the rescue and offered Bieger a departmental home in zoology, which was gratefully accepted. Metcalf's help on this one was not a popular gesture, but I was very grateful to him for getting the zoology appointment.

Feedback could help us patch here and correct there, but it could not guarantee the success of all of our students. We were thrilled with the first-year results, but the second year brought us our first failure and dropout. It was a particular disappointment to me, who by that time thought that everybody who entered our program should do well and score well on final examinations. I was determined to carefully analyze this experience in order to prevent it from happening again.

George G. (not his real name) was living proof that "you can't win them all." George failed both the freshman comprehensive and the NBME-I examinations. He had come to us from a small farming town in Illinois, carrying a terrible burden on his shoulders. He had been valedictorian of his high school graduating class and a straight-A student at a small, remote four-year college. He was the first and only member of his family who had ever been admitted to medical school. He was the family's and the community's pride and joy. But he had never been academically challenged before. Despite the gold-plated academic record in high school and college, his relatively weak performance on the Medical College Aptitude Examination was a clear indication that his knowledge was limited. Nevertheless, there was no clear indication that George could not eventually be successful in medical school.

Our Level III examination system spotted him early as a student in trouble, and my staff assured me that he had been advised and helped by the appropriate faculty. Nevertheless when the two major exams were given in June of 1973, George was the only one of our thirty-two students who failed both, and he failed them badly. He did not come close to the minimum pass level, a sign that we have since learned is a signal to drop the student from medical school for academic reasons. But at that time, we organized summer remediation activities for George, expected him to participate, and to retake the freshman comprehensive examination in the fall. But George did not appear when summer remedial classes began. Tom Gamble attempted to call him at that point, but was told that he was not well and was remaining at home. Unwilling to accept defeat, and anxious to probe every avenue for clues to the cause of this failure, I was also determined to give George every opportunity to become a physician. Although most of our feedback came from Kimberly or from my staff, this time I wanted to collect it myself. If that meant my driving out to George's home to see him (as it did), so be it.

I left my office on a warm summer afternoon and drove to George G.'s hometown, about ninety miles west of Champaign-Urbana. It was typical of any small, Illinois rural farming town. With a population of three hundred, it was identified on the road map by the smallest of open circles. Once there, it wasn't hard to find George's home, because everybody knew George and where he lived. His mother greeted me warmly at the entrance to the white clapboard home. She was somewhat awed by the fact that the medical school dean was visiting, but was very helpful and forthcoming in an effort rekindle George's interest in medical school. She told me that George was feeling very sad and embarrassed and had remained in his bedroom for the past several days.

When I entered George's room, I did not see him at first. The room was dark, the shades were pulled, and no lights were on. George sat in the corner on a chair, stooped forward and holding his head in his hands. He was, of course, shocked that I had come ninety miles to talk to him. He had little to say at first. He was obviously depressed and subdued, but gradually his story came out. He was the oldest of three boys and was always the role model for family accomplishment. Despite his early academic achievements, he was unprepared for the learning environment at SBMS-UC. He was used to an educational process that gave him the information he needed to know, which he memorized, and about which he correctly answered examination questions. He had tried his best, but there was simply too much to commit to memory in the basic medical sciences. Although the educational system was foreign to him, it was not the system that upset him. It was that he had let down his family, his college classmates, and the good people of this closely knit, small farming community. It was a failure he could hardly bear.

I should have realized that the best course of action was to pat him on the back and tell him that he should choose another profession, but I did not. I talked with him for some time, trying to inspire his self-confidence and, indeed, to convince him to come back for the summer and try to pass the freshman comprehensive in the fall. He finally agreed to think it over. A few days later, he showed up in Urbana for summer classes, and we made every effort to see that he had the best remediation program we could arrange for him. At the end of the summer, George actually passed the Freshman Comprehensive. Again, it was a close call, but he rallied this time to exceed the minimum pass level by a single point. This entitled him to move on to one of the clinical schools where in another year his education was again interrupted by failure on the NBME-I examination. On July 31, 1974, I received a note from Tom Gamble, my dean for student affairs, that read, "George G. has withdrawn from the Peoria School of Medicine. Indications are that he just didn't want to continue the battle. He received a 355 (passing level 380) on NBME-I in June. Peoria has been running a special summer remediation course, which he declined to participate in. Your intervention is discouraged…you win some and lose some." There was nothing more I could do. Our new program had its first failure.

However, our successes were far more numerous. By 1973, the word was out to medical students that we had an exciting new program that encouraged independent study. The class of 1973–74 took the promise of independent study seriously, and more than half of them petitioned the executive dean to be registered for an advanced-standing qualifying examination that would allow them, if they passed, to enter clinical training six months earlier than previously planned. The college used such an examination to accept students from other medical schools or students with atypical backgrounds who might qualify for advanced placement in the second-, third-, and fourth-year classes. The examination had never been used internally as a progress instrument.

The SBMS-UC faculty expressed concern regarding the wisdom of allowing first-year medical students who took and passed the fall proficiency examination to petition for advanced placement in the second year. They had set promotion guidelines for the SBMS-UC program that included factors that went beyond pure cognitive testing. To be promoted, SBMS-UC students had to pass our own skills examination and undergo a subjective evaluation of attitude and performance by the campus faculty advisor, the MDA, and the MDE. In effect, the Beginning Doctors were told there was more to performing as an effective scientific physician than merely knowing the facts and mechanically demonstrating skills. The faculty emphasized that attitude and disposition played an important role in professional development. So, the faculty asked me to inform Bill Grove that if passing the proficiency examination meant promotion to the second year, they would not encourage first-year SBMS-UC students to take the test. The faculty believed, however, that the proficiency examination had served as a useful guide for students and as a reference point to evaluate our educational process.

The College of Medicine administration denied the SBMS-UC student petition for the reasons given above and because the qualifying examination was specifically designed for nonmedical graduate students. The SBMS-UC students then argued that if the qualifying examinations were used as an indicator for passing graduate students on to the second or third year of medical studies, then the test must be a proper measure of competency for first-year medical students as well. Bill Grove again denied the petition, but that was not the end of the matter. Soon, he had to face a second petition from the pesky students at SBMS-UC.

The second petition to reach Bill Grove was from those graduates of SBMS-UC who passed both the freshman comprehensive examination and NBME-I. In theory, these students also qualified for admission to the third year of medical school and to begin clinical clerkships. The College of Medicine had an informal independent-study program in operation called the James Scholar Program, which was primarily designed for a small group of gifted students who would include medical research in their already full medical-school schedule. This program, which never anticipated the events at SBMS-UC, was designed to allow students to proceed through medical school independently, subject only to supervision by a designated faculty member. James Scholar students were to schedule clerkships and fulfill other prerequisites for graduation on their own. College policy was very flexible toward James Scholars. As long as the students were admitted to the James Scholar program and were working under the direction of a supervising faculty member, they were permitted to proceed with clinical training somewhat earlier than was the case for medical students who had attended SBMS-Chicago.

For those who qualified as James Scholars, and most of our students did, this effectively reduced the length of medical school from four to three years. However, the college administration became increasingly uneasy with the rapid progress of SBMS-UC students and took steps to eliminate the three-year pathway. The College Committee on Instruction and Appraisal observed "that a significant number of SBMS-UC students were taking NBME-I as noncandidates at the end of their first year." Believing this was unwise because it had a "destabilizing" effect on the other schools of the college, the committee passed a policy resolution that the NBME-I examination would not be available to any students in the College of Medicine until after the second year of medical school had been completed. This new policy, aimed specifically at SBMS-UC was passed over the vigorous objections of our representatives on the committee.

Nevertheless, in those early years, we savored our success stories. An article in the *Peoria Journal Star* of July 15, 1974, highlights the medical-school experience of Dr. Thomas Hoskins, one of our first sixteen SBMS-UC graduates. He had subsequently graduated from the Peoria School of Medicine and had begun his first year of residency at Methodist Hospital in Peoria. He was the only graduate of the new clinical school at Peoria because he graduated in three years instead of four.

Dr. Hoskins was quoted as saying, "We were given a problem, say a peptic ulcer, and we consulted the syllabus to learn what chapters in what basic science text to read to learn about it...All sixteen of us passed the Freshman Comprehensive Examination, and all but one passed the National Boards Part I. That first year at SBMS-UC was a lot of work. There were days when we sat home and studied twelve to fourteen hours a day. Yet we had fun. We were a close group.

"When I chose Peoria, I found myself back in the classroom situation. I had been spoiled at SBMS-UC. Independent study was my bag. I asked the Peoria School of Medicine officials about the possibility of becoming an independent-study student in Peoria and with the help of the Peoria faculty I did my in-hospital training on a solitary basis."

Following his independent work at several hospitals, he passed the National Boards Part II and the Senior Comprehensive Examination. "Having completed those satisfactorily, I was approved for graduation by the Promotions Committees at both the Peoria School of Medicine and the College of Medicine," he told the newspaper.

It is hard to think of more encouraging feedback.

CHAPTER 16

Creative Tension

A S SBMS-UC GREW, tension also grew between the school and the UIUC departments in which our faculty members were appointed. In the early going, we were dependent on good will to solve many problems, but I quickly learned that power solves more. Fortunately, I had some.

By 1975, I had salary lines for about seventeen full-time basic-science faculty members, who were jointly appointed in UIUC campus departments. I held a unique position with respect to my counterparts on the UIUC campus: I was a "department head," when dealing with campus department heads; I was a "director," when dealing with the schools of life and chemical sciences; and I was a "dean," when dealing with higher campus authority. I controlled the salary lines allocated to SBMS and this included the option to raise or diminish salary. Although faculty promotions were largely the prerogative of the departments, I held veto power over departmental actions. I also had absolute control of all space—teaching, research, and administrative—within two buildings: 20,000 square feet of new space in the Burrill Hall addition, which was completed in the year I came, 1970; and 100,000 square feet in the Medical Sciences Building, which was completed in 1975.

As my power grew, I was fortunate to have John Anderson, who time and again helped me to wield it with discretion. John dissuaded me from sending many a hot-tempered memo. One such instance came out of our growing faculty's need and desire for input into governance, that is, for a mechanism to limit the dean's power. Although I saw us all, faculty and administration, as working toward a common educational goal, the faculty wanted to pursue its work as free from administrative interference as possible.

When the bylaws took effect, they gave me the prerogative as dean to sit as a voting member of any standing faculty committee. I reasoned that because I was a voting member who could sit with any faculty committee, such privileges should extend to my staff, particularly Tom Gamble and Bill Sorlie, upon whom I relied most heavily. On being challenged, the faculty caucused privately and passed a resolution to exclude members of the SBMS administration from voting on two major school committees. The faculty resolution upset me, and I carefully crafted the following memo directed to the campus faculty advisors (CFAs), who were the core basic-science faculty on the campus:

> I have reviewed the minutes of the CFA meeting of August 21, 1974, and note that a resolution was passed to exclude members of the school administration from voting on two major school committees. I am committed to a policy of interaction between faculty and administration in all areas of the educational process. I believe they should work more closely together rather than setting up artificial barriers between them. The suggestion that you made is contrary to that policy and for that reason is unacceptable to me. I do not believe that the votes of administration on any committee would significantly change its thrust or direction and would be very happy to review any instances where this is not the case. Meanwhile, since all the committees are appointed by the Dean, I will exercise my prerogative to establish committees and to designate voting membership. Thus far, all committees so appointed have full vote.

Before sending the memo, I sent a copy to John Anderson for his comments. His one-word reply was handwritten on a four-by-five-inch piece of yellow foolscap: "No!"

He was right. The memo was never sent.

Another source of power is information. There is no substitute for having the facts when debating money issues, and in this respect I had the superb talent of Mike Harms, my assistant for business affairs. Mike had worked in the university's overseas extension program in Tehran and was a minor functionary in the College of Liberal Arts and Sciences when I hired him. He was the ideal administrative assistant for business affairs: quiet, confident, capable, and discrete. He collected facts and figures well and provided them to me in usable form

Mike carefully gathered fiscal statistical information for SBMS-UC on the academic effort expended by faculty. His data originated from annual faculty-effort reports in which they were asked to estimate the time spent in all their activities including direct teaching, other activities related to teaching, university administration activities, administration of organized research, departmental research, thesis guidance, counseling activities, and library activities. The departments continually claimed that SBMS was victimizing and exploiting them. They charged that we were expending departmental resources on medical education and that we were using their facilities for our faculty. In return, the departments demanded that I turn over to them complete indirect-cost recovery on research grants.

Indirect costs are essentially the overhead needed to run a research program. As a result, indirect-cost reimbursements (ICRs) are flexible. They can support additional personnel, purchase new equipment, build new research space, and support travel. Although the expenditures must be accounted for, the rules governing their use are far more flexible than the expenditure rules for the direct costs of grants and contracts. Therefore, in universities, everybody wants their piece of the ICR pie. The costs really are earned by the efforts of the faculty investigator who does the basic work to procure the grant. But presidents, vice presidents, deans, directors, and department heads all stand in the stream of indirect-cost money with their hands out taking whatever they can. Usually, very little is left for the primary investigator whose work generated the costs and who may be considered fortunate if he receives 20 to 25 percent of the pie.

Armed with Mike's figures, I knew that many of our SBMS faculty members were carrying significant teaching loads within the several departments apart from the SBMS curriculum, and that, when faculty effort was totaled, SBMS was subsidizing the departments, not the reverse. For example, Harms' academic statistical report revealed in October 1974 that when we looked at our total faculty effort, 53 percent of their direct-teaching clock hours was spent on the medical-sciences courses and 47 percent was spent on departmental courses. Theoretically, faculty members salaried by SBMS owed 100 percent of their teaching time to SBMS. In short, the respective department heads were grossly exploiting our small cadre of non-tenured faculty members. Furthermore, SBMS-UC was providing the space and administrative support for its own faculty. The knowledge gave me good reason to resist spurious claims by the departments, but not the power to convince them that we were right.

The working relationships between SBMS-UC and elements of the UIUC campus were strained in part, because of our different missions.

Academic departments on integrated campuses have commonly assumed responsibility for undergraduate, graduate, and professional education. But many UIUC campus departments were unaccustomed to working with professional schools such as SBMS-UC.

Our goals in working with departments were as follows:

1. Each department was to accept the responsibility for professional education, including curriculum development, maintenance, and updating. The final evaluation of the professional curriculum would be the responsibility of the SBMS-UC and the college committees on educational policy.
2. Each department would assist in developing backup systems for the SBMS-UC curriculum, including tutorials, seminars, advising, remediation, computer-based education exercises, and laboratories.
3. Each department would maintain a medical-school division for those assigned and labeled as SBMS-UC faculty, so they could tend to SBMS-UC roles, such as attending College of Medicine committee meetings and SBMS-UC meetings, and duties as campus faculty advisors to medical students.
4. SBMS and each department would maintain separate budget and space allocations.
5. The distribution of teaching load on any faculty members salaried by SBMS-UC would be a dual responsibility between the school and the department.

Although this formulation of departmental commitment made good sense to me, I knew it was an unpleasant pill for the departments to swallow. It infringed on their absolute sovereignty. But given our exasperating governance, which required my working with departments that did not report to me, these were the gaps we had to bridge. It was these principles that I would try to incorporate into a Memorandum of Understanding when the time came for the original Treaty to be revisited. The 1969–70 Lanier Treaty had been a useful working document that identified the unique structural relationships that SBMS-UC endure, but it was clear that it would need revision.

By mid-1974 and extending on through 1976, working relationships with departments were so uneven and so uneasy, so near to a point of breakdown that I felt obliged to wave my "big stick," a proposed Department of Medical Sciences within SBMS-UC. I did not really want that to happen because it would not only represent a failure, but also estrange the program from the UIUC campus. However, such a department would provide a recognized administrative unit for present and future members whose interests were not served by departments already existing at UIUC.

For instance, the development of an "Anatomy Department" remained an open question. Traditionally at UIUC, the Department of Physiology in the School of Life Sciences taught anatomy. Stan Stolpe, a senior member of the department who no longer engaged in research, served in the role of anatomy instructor for various graduate and undergraduate courses over the years. His anatomy instruction met the needs of nonmedical students who, for one reason or another, required instruction in human anatomy. With the advent of a medical school, it was imperative to strengthen the teaching of anatomy and to find it an appropriate academic home. I was in control of the situation only insofar as I had reserved a salary line for an anatomy department head, but I had no place to put the line. Because it was agreed that all basic-science departments would be existing departments on the campus, usually in the School of Life Sciences (SOLS) or the School of Chemical Sciences (SOCS), I was effectively barred from initiating my own department of anatomy, unless I could get SOLS and its department heads to concur. This was not a simple task because the subject of anatomy was viewed with great skepticism. Human anatomy was not a "cutting edge" research field, and few modern scientists were willing to attach themselves to obsolescent departments.

A Department of Medical Sciences would have incorporated anatomy, and those other departmental orphans: pharmacology and pathology. It also would have relieved the dean of many minor administrative duties that a departmental chair ordinarily would undertake. I was sometimes acting as a dean, sometimes as director, and other times as a department head, switching hats with remarkable frequency. To have my own department of basic medical sciences would have simplified things a great deal, but I knew in my heart that that was not the way to organize.

The faculty also was uncomfortable with the administrative tension that characterized the relationships between SBMS-UC and the campus departments and schools. On December 21, 1976, during a period when we were beset by tensions both in SBMS-UC and the clinical school, thirteen members of our combined SBMS/SCM-UC salaried faculty, more than 50 percent, petitioned Executive Dean Truman Anderson to create a Department of Basic Medical Sciences in SBMS-UC. Joe Larsen, director of the School of Life Sciences, responded strongly, describing the establishment of such a department as "a disaster to medical-school programs on this campus. Such a department would have virtually no standing on the national scene nor in the professional lives of its members. It would be impossible to recruit good faculty to such a department." The proposal was never acted upon.

The tension between SBMS and the other UIUC schools was paralleled by tension between my administration and a faculty that continually wanted more control and more voice over the future of the school. The SBMS faculty resented the disproportionate effort I was pouring into the clinical program and suspected that SBMS-UC funds were being channeled to support clinical initiatives. The faculty was also upset by the PLATO curriculum computer-assisted-instruction contract that I had solicited without adequate faculty input.

As the faculty continued to limit my freewheeling mandate, faculty meetings and executive committee meetings became long and contentious. The faculty often attacked administration on every detail. I, in turn, kept trying to point out that I was in the difficult, if not impossible, position of carrying out Medical Center policy on the Urbana-Champaign campus, an obligation that sometimes led to differences in views and perceptions. I found myself literally fighting a two-front war.

I discussed with Bill Grove my increasingly complicated relationships with the UIUC units, and he agreed with me that a "summit" meeting was called for. He arranged for a meeting on October 24, 1974, between representatives of the medical school and the UIUC campus.

Grove began the meeting by presenting a brief history of health-science centers, pointing out that problems such as we were discussing had usually been solved by the separation of the health-science units from other basic-science units on the campus. There was general agreement that we wanted to avoid this at UIUC, and I strongly indicated that I would consider it a failure of my administration if we could not avoid such a rupture. The principal issue was one of faculty control. The dual-administration responsibility of faculty to a department head and to the director of a UIUC campus school as opposed to the dean of SBMS-UC led to some of these problems. However, some areas of agreement seemed subject to resolution. These included:

1. Because SBMS-UC paid 100 percent of the faculty salary in most instances of dual appointments, department heads could not and should not have unilaterally assigned SBMS-UC faculty to formal graduate and undergraduate course teaching. It was pointed out that this principle, if accepted by department heads, would be a significant step forward. Mike Harms's data illustrated that this principle had been violated extensively in the past.

2. Department heads needed to identify faculty members within their departments, who were unsalaried by SBMS-UC but who nevertheless were interested enough in medical education to participate in the SBMS-UC program in some way on a rotational basis. This would allow salaried SBMS-UC faculty and faculty not salaried in SBMS to exchange roles both within and without the SBMS-UC program. This would establish a medical division within each department to share responsibility not only for teaching but also for the routine service functions of the school, especially service on SBMS school and college committees. To permit realistic shared roles, there had to be a complete functional exchange. Herb Gutowsky noted that if this were in place, good bookkeeping of the rotation responsibilities would be required.

Other issues were not so easily resolved. These included indirect costs and the mechanisms of faculty promotion. On the latter issue, the UIUC campus officials dug in and held their ground. I argued that the SBMS-UC complement had to be identified as a legitimate faculty on the Urbana-Champaign campus and be allowed major input into the promotion of its own personnel. I suggested that a promotion-committee structure be established with equal representation from the SBMS-UC faculty and faculty assigned from a specific department, followed by a parallel review process on the Medical Center and UIUC campuses. This was unacceptable to the UIUC representatives. Although the Medical Center representatives believed that they could accept the promotion criteria of the UIUC campus, Bill Grove, speaking for the Medical Center, still insisted on an equal input in the process. However, the UIUC people believed that it would be exceedingly disruptive for a higher administrative committee to promote someone already rejected at a lower level, particularly at the departmental level, although under questioning from Grove, Vice Chancellor Mort Weir admitted that precedents did exist.

After this meeting ended in a stalemate, I agreed to work on a draft for a

new Memorandum of Understanding to replace the one in the 1969–70
Treaty. A first draft was completed in February 1975. Mike Harms continued
the regular evaluation of faculty effort, and in doing so, he established an
elaborate accounting system for faculty time and faculty credit for instructional units. Mike's figures were consistent and showed repeatedly that,
despite arguments to the contrary, SBMS-UC continued to contribute the
equivalent of two to four full-time employees to the annual instructional
efforts of the basic-science departments.

The administrative relationship of SBMS-UC, SOLS, SOCS, and the
basic-science faculty continued to sputter on. Items such as faculty instructional time and indirect costs were constant bones of contention. Somehow
we managed to make our way through crisis after crisis and process after
process. In the course of these activities, there were plenty of egos bashed,
hurt feelings, and misunderstandings. It is difficult to lay blame except to
posit that the awkward administrative structure was the primary cause of
these problems.

In April 1975, I scheduled a retreat for SBMS faculty to explicitly discuss
the Memorandum of Understanding. I wanted to incorporate faculty ideas
into the document because it was faculty members who were truly caught
between two administrations and subject to the most pressure as a result.
They knew better than anyone else did what was necessary. They recommended that every department in SOLS and SOCS that was linked to the
medical school should have a medical division led by a departmental coordinator to be responsible for the medical program. The faculty observed that
many departmental members throughout SOLS/SOCS were not only
uncommitted to SBMS-UC, but plainly antagonistic to it. They held that a
medical division within each department was essential to preserve the identity of the medical-education program.

Another issue about which the faculty held strong opinions was the
transfer of information from SBMS-UC to the several departments. Igno-
rance of SBMS achievements was hurting the school. Departmental leadership was largely woefully ignorant of what SBMS-UC was doing or had
accomplished. Despite our presence on the campus for five years, despite the
fact that minutes of all meetings were distributed to the relevant department
heads, and despite the fact that department heads regularly sat on our
SBMS-UC Executive Committee, there was little knowledge disseminated
among the nonmedical faculty of SOLS/SOCS.

The faculty also insisted that they be represented on any search committee, departmental or nondepartmental, created to fill a medical-school position. There had been past instances when a medical position had opened, in which department heads had appointed a search committee without regard to the medical school's needs. My input as dean had been limited to approval of the job description and position notice used for advertising purposes and to a veto power once the candidate was selected by the department. For the good of the school, the SBMS-UC faculty wanted much more say in the selection process. However, some department heads, their autonomy threatened, resisted the placement of medical-school faculty on search committees for a medical-school position. This was unacceptable to the SBMS-UC faculty, and they wanted to make sure that their meaningful input into the search process was written into any future agreement with the UIUC campus departments.

Members of the SBMS faculty voiced their strongest feelings in discussions of their own promotion pathways. As they saw it, they were always in double jeopardy, having to satisfy the rigid, research-oriented requirements of a UIUC department while carrying the teaching load of SBMS. They made it clear that if we expected to hold the school together, we had to control promotion at the school itself. If we lost control of promotion, we lost school identity. They pointed out that this was what the departments wanted all along: control of the medical-school salary lines and the right to deliver a service course when and where they desired. An SBMS-UC faculty Appointments and Promotions Committee was essential, they argued, so that our departmental faculty could be judged by peers who were also involved in professional education. I pointed out to them that double jeopardy also meant double opportunity, namely that the promotion process could work in favor of the faculty member who for some reason was denied promotion in one track but was rescued by the second track. Nevertheless, in trying to resolve the promotion issues with the faculty and the UIUC administration, I understood well why medical schools that evolved upon liberal arts and sciences campuses ultimately developed their own basic-science departments. I was determined that would not be the case here and proceeded to negotiate a compromise in these areas that both the departments and the school could live with.

The negotiations on the Memorandum of Understanding with SOLS/SOCS were long and contentious, stretching out over two years. It was difficult for the departments to give up their curriculum sovereignty. At UIUC, departments had complete control over curriculum content in every course. Now, SBMS-UC was demanding that departments submit their curriculum content to an SBMS-UC faculty committee that would have jurisdiction over their content. The issue was more semantic than real because it was unlikely that the SBMS-UC Educational Policy Committee would reject a departmental proposal. But the mere thought that a medical-school committee, an offshoot of Chicago no less, could reject a UIUC departmental curriculum proposal was unacceptable to the departmental elite and unthinkable to the true believers.

However, on May 13, 1975, amid those negotiations and at a time when I was holding out for SBMS-UC rights, Ralph DeMoss (head of microbiology), Lowell Hager (head of biochemistry), and William Sleator (head of physiology and biophysics) jointly wrote a letter addressed to me and to Bob Rogers, Dean of the UIUC College of Liberal Arts and Sciences (LAS). In effect, they said that one way to solve the integration problems between the School of Basic Medical Sciences and the School of Life Sciences would be to appoint a common director of both schools. The letter said that SOLS's then-current search for a director indicated that some of the candidates were concerned by the complications caused by the relationship between the school and SBMS, and that it deterred some of them from considering the position.

They wrote, "Integration of the activities of the faculties of the two schools requires much more coordination than now exists." Therefore, they added, "We believe that these and other problems can be solved by combining the responsibilities of leadership of the two schools…Combining the responsibilities of leadership of the two schools would also make the position more attractive to the kind of outstanding person we would like to attract to this campus."

The letter was a brilliant coup attempt to transfer the entire authority for the SBMS-UC program to the UIUC campus. Bob Rogers forwarded the letter to Chancellor Jack Peltason and Vice Chancellor for Academic Affairs Mort Weir. They promptly arranged a meeting with me where they probed my thoughts about this suggestion. I told them that I was generally sympathetic to the idea and strongly supported a governance shift of SBMS-UC to UIUC. However, in considering the merger of SOLS and SBMS-UC, I registered concern that within my experience, I had not observed a UIUC campus commitment, at all levels, to health-professional education. I told them that I perceived an attitude within SOLS and SOCS that professional education denigrates quality. Furthermore, I reminded them that I had no authority to appoint a director of SBMS-UC either alone or in negotiation with UIUC campus officials and would need the assistance of Bill Grove to study the request and to assign it to a level suitable for intercampus negotiation. Much to my regret, I obviously upset Mort Weir, who vigorously objected to my doubts of the campus commitment to professional education and used the illustration of the high-quality, nationally recognized professional-education programs at UIUC in accountancy, agricultural engineering, journalism, law, library, and music. He seemed favorably disposed to a single directorship if we could make the necessary arrangements. When I asked the question, "To whom would the combined director report, the dean of LAS (Bob Rogers) or myself?" Weir forcefully responded, "As long as I'm Vice Chancellor for Academic Affairs, I will never permit an MD to have control over [nonmedical] academic units of this campus."

I did not take that as a personal rejection, though it may have been, but rather as an indication of the hostility toward MDs that Weir exhibited and that I believed to be endemic within the life-science elements of the campus. But the size of the gulf that separated Weir's view from mine depressed me. Troubles with the clinical school were brewing, and five years of negotiations about administrative difficulties, both verbally and in writing, had taken their toll. Although work on the new Memorandum was progressing, I was less confident than ever that the health-education program could be blended into the UIUC campus. In my view, the record of SBMS-UC cooperation with the UIUC campus was very clear. Even though we were a very small unit on the campus, we contributed far more than just a medical-education program. On the other hand, the record of campus commitment and support of SBMS-UC was much less clear. We seemed to be drifting towards a permanent separation of administrations, a situation that was personally distasteful to me. But I was not willing to compromise the "best medical education program in the country" to the parochial demands of a campus which, unfortunately, after five years of intimate interaction still did not understand what we were about.

Nevertheless, we finally reached agreement on the Memorandum of Understanding (MOU) that would carry us for at least another five years. The new MOU, ratified July 2, 1975, revealed the give and take that went on during the negotiations. It was far from ideal, but I could live with it. One thorny issue that remained to be resolved was that of indirect-cost reimbursement. It would take another year before the seemingly irreconcilable differences between SBMS-UC and SOLS/SOCS on this issue were finally resolved.

In July of 1976, I succeeded in having the respective business managers of SBMS-UC, SOLS, and SOCS meet to develop a specific proposal for distribution of indirect-cost reimbursements. Looking at other examples of how ICR funds were distributed to joint interdisciplinary projects that already functioned on the UIUC campus, they proposed a formula for indirect-cost sharing that recommended that the unit assigning the space that housed the research project receive 60 percent and that 40 percent be retained by the unit providing grant administration. If a unit provided the space in which the research project was performed and administered the project as well, it would retain 100 percent of the indirect costs. They also recommended that specific projects related to the medical-sciences teaching program, such as a major PLATO that was under way, be administered by SBMS-UC and that all ICR funds generated on such projects be distributed to SBMS-UC. This was finally a proposal I could support. It was eminently fair and reasonable and based on prior interdisciplinary experience. It also had the approval of everybody on the campus except for one person, Bob Rogers, Dean of LAS. Rogers thought he was losing some of his leverage and indirect-cost money and advised Mort Weir to block the agreement. Weir supported Rogers and told the business managers to go back to the drawing board.

Here I was again, astride a lonely outpost of the Medical Center on the Urbana-Champaign campus, completely helpless to effect a major agreement such as this because a single dean on the UIUC campus opposed it. The university simply had no process for resolving intercampus conflict at this level. I was determined to make the university think about the isolation of SBMS-UC and the administrative problems caused by the atypical presence of SBMS on the UIUC campus. So, on July 22, 1976, I wrote directly to President John Corbally saying, "I request that you immediately place the subject ICR (indirect-cost reimbursement) funds into an escrow account until the problem is resolved. My reason for this request is that since 1970 all ICR funds covered by the July 9, 1976 memo have been used exclusively and in my view unfairly by the UIUC campus despite the fact that the

Medical Center campus through SBMS-UC has provided a large share of the indirect support for those grants generating the funds."

Bill Grove, who by this time was the Medical Center's vice chancellor for academic affairs, did not support this letter. In fact, he resented my going around him to the president.

The president, of course, was not happy to hear from me either. He courteously acknowledged my letter and kicked it down to the lower channels again. However, he did say in response, "I have expressed my interest in an early and equitable resolution to this matter and will be kept informed." As upset as they were by my direct approach to the president, Rogers, Weir, and Grove finally accepted the business managers' formula for indirect-cost distribution. The issue was at last settled for the remainder of my tenure as dean. If the term "creative tension" applied anywhere, it applied here.

CHAPTER 17

Diversions

I N BUILDING THE MEDICAL SCHOOL, particularly because it was community based, I was involved as dean in many issues and events that had limited impact on the faculty and students, per se. Among such diversions was medical computing, not because it had no impact, it did, but because it seemed always to be a will-o-the-wisp, holding promise for a vision that could not be grasped.

One of the very attractive features of coming to the University of Illinois at Urbana-Champaign was the potential use of the campus computing facilities. In 1970, UIUC was an uncontested world leader in the development of modern computer hardware. The Illiac IV computer, designed by Dan Slotnik and others at the Center for Advanced Computation, was the state-of-the-art operation of its day. The PLATO system, developed by Don Bitzer, claimed to have the potential to put computer-based education into every classroom in the world and certainly into the medical classroom. Although this field was in its infancy, the potential of medical computing seemed to be limitless for education, diagnosis, and patient care. I was no expert in computing. The computer was always a black box to me. Though I've often exploited computers in their word-processing mode, I feel sure that every computer I have ever worked silently laughed when I was at the controls, mocking me with its unused potential.

In any serial process that contains uneven steps, one can usually identify a rate-limiting step. In man's quest for physical endurance, the ability to transport oxygen to the muscles is the rate-limiting step. In the manufacture and sale of automobiles, the speed of the production line can be a rate-limiting step, although it is frequently supplanted by the strength or weakness of marketing. In focusing the computer industry on education, software is the rate-limiting step. As a dean, attempting to adapt his school to the computer age, money was rate limiting, but no more so than the ability to develop educational software. Working with me on the problem was the ever-loyal Ben Williams, who dedicated much of his second career (he was already an accomplished pathologist) to medical computing.

There is an old saying, "Be careful what you wish for, because your wish might come true." This was the case when we received government funds to develop PLATO lessons in basic medical sciences. I was optimistic in 1973 that computer-assisted instruction (CAI) was the perfect complement to our objective-oriented curriculum. PLATO was the wonder education system of its day. It provided graphics for diagrams and was interactive. Touch screens were developed so that the entire system was reasonably user friendly. PLATO's drawback was that it employed a unique computer language, TUTOR, which was used nowhere else in medical computing and thus restricted users to a single type of computer with a single language. Nevertheless, after a foray to the Washington bureaucracy and subsequent grant preparation, I hit pay dirt: SBMS-UC received a $500,000, three-year contract from the federal Bureau of Health Manpower Education to put our basic medical science curriculum units onto PLATO. Little did I know that my faculty would not receive this personal "triumph" kindly. Instead, it proved to be the beginning of other troubles.

I was so preoccupied with getting the contract that I never gave much thought as to who would do the work. Nor had I involved the faculty in the contract preparation or planning. Our basic-science faculty, which numbered about fifteen by the time the contract began, was not enthused by the prospect of spending long hours on preparing curriculum that could be delivered on PLATO. They had worked hard to develop curriculum units, as well as Level I, II, and III examinations, and they felt they had contributed mightily to the development of the school and its educational goals. They also knew that their promotion and tenure status depended heavily not only on their contributions to the School of Basic Medical Sciences, but on their research records in the first five to six years of their probationary period. They were not about to set aside time, nor in reality did they have the time, to develop instructional programs on PLATO. So I had $500,000 in hand and an angry faculty that was not only reluctant to use the money, but refused to use it. I had the choice of returning the money or hiring adjunct faculty who would work for as long as the external funds held up.

Fortunately, there were scientists on the UIUC campus and others available through advertising who were interested and willing to spend one or two years in an attempt to automate the SBMS-UC curriculum. To head the project I found George Hody, a freelance academic internist from San Diego. Hody hired the necessary adjunct faculty and got the project under way. We housed our new adjunct faculty, five or six in all under Hody's direction, in another aging building much like 1205 California. Here we set up a CAI laboratory, gave each adjunct faculty member a PLATO terminal, and asked these individuals to take our curriculum, unit by unit, and come up with a complete PLATO-based curriculum in three years.

It sounded rational, but I was incredibly overoptimistic. Don Bitzer had claimed that it took about twenty hours of programmer time for one hour of PLATO lesson on a computer. In preparing the contract bid, I doubled that figure to forty hours, but experience showed the figure closer to two hundred hours of professional time for one solid hour of PLATO CAI! The work went very slowly for many reasons. First, it proved difficult to translate units verbatim into the TUTOR language and onto the PLATO screen. Second, the new faculty members were not really faculty in the accepted sense of the term. They were adjunct faculty at best. They were not accepted by any of the campus departments, even for temporary membership. As a result, they had little collegial support and interaction and retreated to an isolated society of their own.

I met frequently with George Hody for progress reports in biochemistry, pharmacology, and microbiology, hoping that my direct interest would hasten the creative process, but progress stayed slow during the entire project. We rapidly fell behind our projected schedule, and if that were not bad enough, even when projects were completed, reviews of the completed units by the regular faculty were often less than favorable. It was difficult to ascertain whether faculty condemnation of the new computer-based basic-science units was deserved or brought on by resentment. Particularly discouraging were faculty reports that some reviewed lessons were deemed as doing more harm than good. Overall, it was a discouraging experience. Only a few hours of useful computer instruction were developed at great cost of time, money, and effort.

When it became obvious that we were falling behind schedule on the PLATO contract, I had a discussion with Tom Chen, who was managing the technical aspects (i.e., the hardware and networking problems), and with John Anderson to search for ways to increase our productivity under the grant. We reasoned that the only way to accomplish this was to enlist other medical schools that might have interests in CAI and attempt network development at the earliest possible date. This would ensure that the project would not be solely a University of Illinois effort but one in which we could perhaps involve five or ten other medical schools. We tried to enlist the head of the Lister Hill Center at the National Library of Medicine (NLM) to fund a health-education network, and received considerable interest, but no money. We tried to subcontract our grant to other medical schools but in the end, only one school, the University of Connecticut, made an attempt to work with us. They set up four PLATO terminals to test the new material as it was produced by our adjunct faculty, but closed down the linkage when their funds ran out.

The experience exposed the limitations of CAI. As powerful as it appears to be, it is a modality of limited use in teaching those sciences that are undergoing constant change and discovery such as biochemistry, pharmacology, and microbiology. Enormous resources are required to place what is known at a given time onto the computer. Information in the sciences changes so rapidly that by the time the computer is programmed, the information is already out of date. Furthermore, in the present environment of academic currency, CAI programs are not considered legitimate publications and, thus, writing them does not count toward promotion and tenure. Therefore, the installation and maintenance of any form of CAI requires a permanent set of atypical faculty technicians to create programs.

In the end, we learned that CAI is most useful for teaching the changeless verities such as arithmetic and spelling, not for advancing sciences. We also found PLATO useful in creating the Level III examination system. The faculty would continue to support and maintain the Level III exams because it was in their interests to do so. It was much simpler to update by dropping or creating an examination question than trying to create new software. As time passed on, I could hardly wait until the three years of the contract were over. We gave it our best shot, even though it was wide of the mark. I did not bother to attempt renewal.

Another major diversion of effort followed our response to a federal health manpower initiative in the early 1970s. This was the brainchild of the Bureau of Health Manpower Employment (BHME). In the drive to correct all health manpower shortages that existed or were perceived to exist, BHME offered funds for the establishment of Area Health Education Centers (AHEC). The general purpose of AHECs was to encourage regional educational institutions to form consortia to provide the appropriate paramedical health personnel, such as nurses, nursing assistants, practical nurses, pharmacists, physiotherapists, occupational therapists, and medical illustrators. In retrospect, this was the beginning of another huge federal-funding roller coaster with five years of increased funding and five years of tapering funds. Like all such roller coasters, you end up back where you started after a wild ride and prodigious amount of effort.

On the basis of this major federal initiative, Illinois was divided into six health regions, east central Illinois being known as Region 3B. Because medical-school deans were expected to exert leadership in their respective regions and it was clear that the AHEC legislation in Congress would be generous, I promptly scheduled a meeting with the biology faculty of Eastern Illinois University (EIU) to explore the possibility of their developing some paramedical educational programs. Barry Ruskin, John Anderson, Bill Sorlie and myself, representing SBMS-UC, met in EIU's Student Union with twelve EIU faculty members from the departments of zoology, life sciences, physical therapy, and botany. After we described our program and curriculum, the representatives from EIU expressed some interest in becoming involved in health-professional education but they were noncommittal at best. Aside from the tepid interest they exhibited, no initiatives were made. As I talked with and discussed the possibilities, I observed how they listened politely to the proposals being made but did not volunteer so much as a single suggestion as to how they might participate. They were completely passive. I left the meeting with the definite impression that EIU was a nonstarter for this project.

AHEC had become Area Health Education System (AHES) when UICOM became involved. The new federal initiative promised significant funding for the expansion of all types of health-professional education. Funds were available to increase medical-school enrollment, for the establishment of primary-care residencies, and to increase the numbers of nurses and allied health personnel. It was too much for UICOM to turn down, and indeed, Bill Grove vigorously led us into establishing a UICOM Area Health Education System. He hired Bud Zimmerman as a full-time AHES coordinator and used our regional development as a framework for expanding all aspects of health-professional education.

Unlike the CAI initiative, AHES money came through Chicago. We received our share at first, and we established programs in nursing, medical art, medical dietetics, and occupational and physical therapy. We also established the Danville Family Practice Residency. Danville was one of only two cities in our region that expressed interest in such a residency. After responding to our initial overtures, the other city, Decatur, established a similar residency program with Southern Illinois University.

L. W. (Bill) Tanner, a senior and respected family practitioner in Danville, agreed to lead the Danville Family Practice Residency (DFPR) on condition that he would be adequately supported, with teachers and funding by the school. The residency took its first resident in July 1974 and closed its doors seven years later in 1982. To support the program academically, Mort Creditor and I assisted Bill Tanner and the DFPR with personal time and effort. Each of us drove the thirty miles to Danville once or twice weekly to make rounds at the DFPR and later at the Danville VA Hospital. When Creditor left Urbana-Champaign for Chicago, I continued to make regular rounds at the residency even though I was fully occupied in keeping the medical school afloat.

I tried, but failed to convince the two private Danville hospitals that they that they could qualify as teaching hospitals and use pass-through dollars to support the residency. They shunned the pass-through dollars that support graduate medical education in the United States. So when AHES funds dried up in 1981, Bill Tanner was forced to close the program down. It is consoling to know, however, that some of the graduates of that residency are still located in and about Danville and doing what they came to do, delivering primary care to an appreciative rural population.

On December 8, 1981 I received official notice from Chicago of the discontinuance of forty-three separate AHES-generated courses "which will not appear in the UIUC 1982-84 Courses Catalogue." The forty-three represented an AHES mini-health university on the UIUC campus that we had created from 1974 to 1981 and that were just as quickly undone. In addition to DFPR, many other fine programs, such as the medical arts, medical dietetics, OT and PT programs all went down the drain, more examples of prodigious amounts of federal money and human effort wasted. We were lucky to keep our medical-education and nursing programs. Another message was also clear: Despite a commitment to health-education regionalization, when funds were short, the programs in Chicago would be protected, regardless of the quality of the regional offerings. This was certainly true in the AHES experience.

These diversions were often arduous and time-consuming, but they never diluted our main effort to establish a four-year curriculum at Urbana-Champaign. Sensitive to the resistance at higher levels of the university administration, we quietly continued planning a second-year medical curriculum *de novo*, based upon the principle that when learning objectives are clearly defined, it is less important who teaches them. The second-year curriculum was to lead into the clerkship experiences of the third and fourth years. Once again, we used a largely volunteer faculty, guided expertly in educational techniques by Bill Sorlie and his one or two graduate assistants. The clinical faculty and curriculum authors were practitioners of east central Illinois. Their only rewards were the satisfaction of participation in this bootstraps project and the opportunity for continuing medical education (CME) credit. The doctors who helped in this effort were a dedicated group, as altruistic about the future of medicine as can be imagined. They saw the need for a four-year medical school at UIUC, and they were working to make it happen. The earning of CME credit and the fact that teaching is always a learning experience were side issues as our loyal faculty plugged away at creating an educational document.

Using our experience in the basic sciences, we planned to break down clinical knowledge into a matrix that would define a systematic and interdisciplinary structure to be linked to clinical experiences. Our immediate task was to mobilize the practicing faculty, the internists, family practitioners, and the specialists and to organize them into teams dealing with general categories such as urology, orthopedics, gastroenterology, cardiology, and so on. Bill Sorlie organized the educational support, usually assigning a graduate student in education to each team. The support person was responsible for setting up regular meeting dates and times, calling the doctors on the meeting day to remind them, taking careful notes of the curriculum planning that was accomplished, and fitting the results into our final curriculum product, "Form 1" and "Form 2."

Form 1 focused on the general clinical unit for study. A Form 1 used in urology, for example, would specify: "To understand nephrolithiasis." The general topic was then parceled into four or more cognitive-learning objectives: for example "Predisposing factors and the pathogenesis of urinary tract stones; the differences between calcium oxalate, calcium phosphate, uric acid, and cystine stones; the clinical manifestations and diagnosis of nephrolithiasis; approaches to nephrolithiasis therapy." Skill and experiential objectives were then listed that described objectives for patient contact and work-up. Finally, clinical correlations such as ureteral colic, hyperparathy-roidism, hematuria, gout, cystinuria, and so on, were listed to provide the clinical-problem-based entry into the unit.

In Form 2, key words and definitions were listed (e.g. litholapaxy, false calculi, urea splitting organisms, etc.) that related to the objectives. Essential prerequisites were identified, if appropriate, and specific learning resources relating to the objectives were identified, i.e. texts, journal articles, audio-visual programs, etc. Finally, Form 2 contained items for self-testing and for written and oral examinations that covered the specific objectives. It was no easy task to corral our volunteer physicians into such an organized format. But surprising as it may seem, they began to enjoy the exercise. It made them look at their discipline in a new manner that many found very refreshing.

All this was taking place towards the end of 1974 and throughout 1975. Enrollment in SBMS-UC had expanded to sixty-four students for the academic year 1974–75, and we were operating both programs at this time on a wing and a prayer. We had minimal funds. We had no assured clinical-program starting date. The on-again, off-again nature of our clinical program was a destabilizing factor. Yet I remained hopeful and optimistic at all times. Hope was the most powerful factor in rallying the physicians to our side. But hope was not always enough. On September 26, 1975, Mort Creditor received a memo that said that a particular doctor wished "to discontinue the curriculum development process until he and his committee have a definite 'yes' or a definite 'no' concerning the status of the School of Clinical Sciences." But definite answers were not forthcoming.

CHAPTER 18

Curriculum Scouting

ORT CREDITOR, who had joined us late in 1974 after retiring from the defunded Illinois Regional Medical Program, was placed in charge of the clinical-curriculum development. He received copies of all the early effort that had been focused on Forms 1 and 2. Anxious to view other medical schools' approaches to clinical-curriculum development before proceeding any further, he and I planned a visit to three medical schools that had special relevance to the ongoing emergence of the School of Clinical Medicine at Urbana-Champaign. Michigan State University was a recognized leader in community-based medical education, and McMaster University School of Medicine was continuing to develop the tutorial approach to medical education. The third school, Dartmouth, was appropriate for two reasons. First, it had a strong working relationship with the private Mary Hitchcock Clinic and Hospital and therefore had a special relevance to our own situation with the Carle Clinic and Carle Foundation Hospital. Second, it had cultivated an effective working relationship with the Veterans Administration Hospital at White River Junction, a model that we might try to duplicate as we worked with our local VA hospital in Danville. The trip was to have a seminal effect on our curriculum design and progress.

The College of Human Medicine at Michigan State University had made significant progress in the three-and-a-half years since I last visited. Dean Andrew Hunt had established clinical education in the cities of Kalamazoo, Flint, Grand Rapids, Saginaw, and Lansing. The basic fiscal device they used was the formation of a local educational corporation, headed by a salaried assistant dean from MSU. This permitted active participation by a broad cross section of the health community under academic leadership.

We discussed budget and administration of the regional programs with Dean Hunt and his staff. The school's experience had been that some assistant deans were successful and developed solid programs, while others had to be removed for lack of progress. Michigan State University had also set up effective payment guidelines for community physicians that permitted the school to deliver clinical education at a relatively low cost. The 1975–76 budget at Grand Rapids, for example, was only $540,000 for about fifty-two M-3 and M-4 students, or just over $10,000 a year per student, a very modest expenditure. The main expenses of the program, however, were in East Lansing, where the full-time clinical faculty was based. Factoring in their salaries would have raised the cost per student by 50 percent or more.

The university also instituted a useful policy that teaching physicians from the community would not be paid for less than a quarter-time effort and that all teaching activity up to one hundred hours per year was considered voluntary. This made the last two years of medical education less expensive, but it also concentrated the full-time faculty and the bulk of financial resources in East Lansing. It was not certain that this inequity could be maintained indefinitely. Community-based faculty members were complemented by the presence of full-time MSU faculty members who traveled each week to the several cities for a half-day of consultation and teaching. At the time we visited MSU, this was an unpopular and burdensome responsibility for the full-time faculty.

We carefully reviewed the MSU M-2 curriculum because this was of immediate concern to us. The M-2 year was organized largely as an introduction to clinical medicine run by the East Lansing full-time faculty. Learning was textbook-oriented. Salaried models were used for physical-examination training. The models were also used as simulated patients. The students uniformly agreed that the use of simulated patients was one of the better learning activities available to them.

After the East Lansing learning phases, the students took classical clinical clerkship rotations for approximately the next eighteen months in one or more regional sites. The program was structured so that students could complete their senior year as early as December, in their fourth year of study, making the MSU program essentially three-and-a-half years. There were mixed opinions on the wisdom of that choice because it limited clerkship time and because many students found that they could not find satisfactory residencies to enter in midyear.

During our visits to Kalamazoo and Grand Rapids, it became apparent that the educational experience in practice varied depending on the physicians' teaching commitment and the learning content. At the conclusion of our discussions with MSU students, it was my perception that they were being trained in a conventional pragmatic fashion with too little stress on mechanisms of disease and basic medical sciences. They made very little use of current literature and basically studied only textbooks. It was a model we wanted to avoid.

From Michigan State University, we flew to Toronto and drove to McMaster in Hamilton, Ontario. The travel gave us ample time for animated discussion of medical education, along with "dos and don'ts" derived from the MSU visit. We were determined that clinical students had to be challenged every step of the way to ensure they understood the how, what, why, where, and when of any patient problem. This was noticeably absent in the education of those MSU students we interviewed at Kalamazoo and Grand Rapids. We were determined to incorporate such challenges into our clinical curriculum at SCM-UC.

I had been greatly impressed by the McMaster program in 1971, particularly by its use of audiovisual materials. The school's generous assistance in helping SBMS-UC get started in 1971 will long be remembered. But in 1971, the McMaster program was just starting its own first class and was relatively amorphous. In the three-and-a-half years since, the teaching at McMaster had become highly sophisticated while maintaining the same principles of independent learning that were present earlier. The school had also developed a behavior-oriented curriculum that emphasized doctor behavior along with doctor knowledge, convincing me that McMaster had the potential to become one of the truly great and innovative medical schools of our time.

My reintroduction to McMaster was mind-boggling. It is difficult to imagine a medical school delivering the massive amount of information that most medical educators consider necessary in a period of three years without a single cognitive test. In fact, the first test a student would encounter after entering the McMaster program was the Canadian licensure examination. I thought we were gambling at SBMS-UC with the program we developed, but that risk was nowhere near the risk and excitement of completely casting aside any quantitative cognitive-learning structure to emphasize the importance of motivation and self-directed learning for the medical student. I was one who always found testing to be a strong motivator for study, but here was a school that was trying to develop a successful product, a physician, without a single written test during the course of the curriculum. Furthermore, McMaster appeared to be successful in most instances. Although the program had its information gaps and drawbacks, all appeared to be remediable.

However, the faculty had to cope with dramatic levels of student anxiety as the time for licensing examinations approached. Students who had been immersed in this program for three years without the customary examination benchmarks were understandably nervous at that time. The testing revealed that 10 percent to 15 percent failed on the first sitting for the examination. Those who failed spent an extra year at McMaster. Thus far, all had passed licensure after four years.

It should be noted at the outset that McMaster enjoyed two essentials that were not easy to come by at Urbana-Champaign: space and money. This made it much more difficult to consider a verbatim transfer of McMaster's impressive medical-education system to our campus. The McMaster building was a startling and successful blending of human effort in an attempt to merge medical education with the medical-care and research systems. In designing the building, a deliberate effort was made to reduce territoriality. Mixing professionally thanks to the atmosphere of the building were doctors, paraprofessionals, medical students, patients, scientists, and administrators. The building was constructed in excellent taste, with decorative use of paints and murals on the walls and fine carpeting creating an appealing place in which to live and work. However, it cost $100 million to build and equip, well beyond the $9 million allocated for the medical-sciences buildings at Urbana-Champaign.

McMaster also had a faculty of 83 basic scientists and 191 full-time clinicians, all for three classes of 80 medical students. Although this faculty taught other allied health and graduate students, it nevertheless represented a vast array of scientific and clinical resources, whose main purpose was the delivery of medical education to 240 medical students.

An additional advantage held by McMaster was that the dean controlled its entire budget and was responsible for the hiring and deployment of all faculty members. The faculty, therefore, was totally owned by the school and dedicated to the McMaster philosophy. None were hired unless they had an explicit commitment to dedicate at least 20 percent of their time to the educational program and to the manner in which the program was being delivered. McMaster University Medical School fulfilled a dictum that educational innovation requires total dedication and total monetary control of the situation. We would try to import some of the McMaster ideas to Illinois, but we had nothing like the operating budget necessary to effect a complete tutorial program.

A few of the basic principles of the McMaster program will serve to illustrate their novelty. First of all, the McMaster system denies that sequential learning of medicine is necessary. The school did not have a "basic science" year. The belief is that all essential medical learning stems from clinical problems and particularly from patient-oriented problems. Further, it recognizes that medical problems as not solely biomedical events, but that illness takes place in a family and social environment that must be studied just as carefully as the science. The McMaster introduction to the study of medicine, Phase 1, was a ten-week period in which student teams and tutors had the opportunity to study up to ten different problems.

For instance, a group of four medical students and their tutor were presented with the problem of a mother pregnant with her third child. Of her previous children, one had Down syndrome and the other did not. The situation presented a problem not only in genetics and molecular biology, but also in the social connections and interplay among the mother, siblings, and father. The only requirement for the students and tutor, who was not an expert in genetics, was to examine all aspects of the problem for ten days. They would plan as a group how to attack the problem, its biochemistry, genetics, clinical aspects, and social implications, and assign learning tasks among themselves. Thereafter, they would meet regularly, report to each other, and refine the learning tasks. By the end of ten days, they had assembled and exchanged a huge amount of information about Down syndrome.

After Phase 1, McMaster students entered a second phase that was generally focused on problems rich in basic medical science concepts such as neoplasia, inflammation, and wound healing. The final preclinical phase, Phase 3, was similar to an organ-system approach, but once again was studied by dealing with real or simulated clinical problems. The three preclinical phases took approximately eighteen months, after which the students took traditional core clinical clerkships.

The total commitment to "physicianship" and to problem-based learning was exciting to observe. It is impossible for physicians to know everything, particularly in the basic sciences, but they do have to be able to analyze and solve a vast array of problems, both biological and human, that come before them. We found the McMaster students remarkably comfortable with their knowledge gaps, which they reasoned they would fill when the appropriate clinical problem was encountered. On the other hand, they were not unconcerned about how they would perform on written

examinations for licensure. The McMaster gambit sacrificed a modest
amount of systematic cognitive information to gain a tremendous amount
in physician maturity.

Mort Creditor and I left McMaster stimulated by the educational possibilities the program raised, but unsure as to whether we could pull off a system like that at SCM-UC without the incredible resources McMaster had.

Leaving McMaster we flew to Lebanon, New Hampshire, to visit
Dartmouth Medical School, the Mary Hitchcock Hospital and Clinic, and
the Veterans Administration Hospital in White River Junction, Vermont.
There were two main areas of interest in the Dartmouth model. One was
the successful use of a large private group practice, clinic, and hospital for
teaching, and the second was the successful incorporation of a Veterans
Administration Hospital into the teaching program at Dartmouth.
Dartmouth, for many years, had been a two-year medical school delivering
the basic medical sciences and the introduction to clinical medicine. Medical
students then transferred for clinical clerkship training to medical schools
throughout the country.

Dean James Strickler described this history to us and how the school
had decided to develop a full three-year MD degree program with the aid
and cooperation of the Mary Hitchcock Clinic. The stimulus came from the
clinic's physicians, who wanted to become involved in graduate medical
education. Relatively isolated in Hanover, New Hampshire, they wanted to
incorporate continuing medical education into their daily practice. They
believed this goal would best be achieved through the establishment of a
full, degree-granting medical school. Therefore, the clinic pushed hard for
development of a full medical school in Hanover. By the time we visited
Dartmouth in December 1974, it operated an effective three-year program,
sixty-four students per class, a total enrollment of 192. Serving this cohort
of students were approximately 240 full-time or geographic full-time faculty,
of whom 132 were full-time employees of the Dartmouth Medical School.
Except for sixteen FTEs at the White River Junction VA Hospital, the
remaining faculty was from the Hitchcock Clinic.

We learned two important concepts at Dartmouth. First, the linkage
between a medical school and a privately operated not-for-profit institution
such as the Hitchcock Hospital and Hitchcock Clinic could be negotiated
to the advantage of all parties. They organized the Dartmouth-Hitchcock
Medical Center, an entity comprising four corporations: the Hitchcock

Hospital, a private not-for-profit voluntary hospital; Dartmouth College and the Dartmouth Medical School; the VA hospital; and the for-profit Hitchcock Clinic. Hence, the medical center was essentially a medical-education holding company with the power to set policy centered in a joint executive council. The structure appeared to work very well.

Second, we learned the basis for the very cooperative and productive association between the VA hospital and Dartmouth Medical School. The VA hospital's chief of staff was Dr. Howard Green, a young internist who moved there from the Hitchcock Clinic when it was decided that such a move would be useful to both the Dartmouth-Hitchcock Medical Center and the veterans' hospital. The move carried the explicit assumption that the latter would be converted to a VA teaching hospital. Green emphasized that a successful program requires a tough VA director, who is dedicated to patient care, to improving the hospital, and to improving hospital service. Within a reasonable period, the VA hospital director must see not just good teaching, but better patient care stemming from the medical-school association. All budgetary requests made to the VA central office in Washington, DC, were based entirely on patient-care needs. In approaching the VA in this fashion, the veterans' hospital had increased its budget significantly in the years since the affiliation was developed. In other words, when working with the VA system, good patient care leads to good medical education, not the reverse.

Mort and I returned to Urbana-Champaign, but not before we had taught Midwesterner Mort how to ski on the icy slopes of New England. We were full of ideas about the M-2 curriculum and were charged up as we developed a vision of what was possible.

CHAPTER 19

A Fateful Triad of Events

T HE SBMS-UC BUDGET GREW by minimal increments in both absolute and relative terms, becoming a constant source of friction between Bill Grove and me. I believe he would have fired me because of my outspoken demands for better funding, except that he knew Urbana was doing its job at very low cost. He never complained that the state wasn't getting its money's worth out of Urbana.

The real game that was being played related to the development of a clinical program in Urbana-Champaign. Grove concentrated on reestablishing his clinical teaching base in Chicago and bolstering the clinical teaching programs in Peoria and Rockford. From 1970 through 1976, when Chicago took on an additional 164 students per year, it received $5,587,000 in new operating funds or $34,000 per additional medical student. The regional programs combined received $5,409,000 for programs that taught 307 additional medical students per year, or $17,619 per additional medical student. Most dramatic of all was the anemic $11,100 per new medical student received by SBMS-UC. The disparity is great, especially because there was supposed to be regional expansion.

The picture was the same for capital-expansion funds in that same period. The regional campuses received capital budgets of $7 million to $9 million to provide facilities for the three new programs, a total of about $26 million. The Chicago campus received at a minimum, $65 million for a new University hospital.

Presenting this data at Administrative Advisory Council meetings didn't help my popularity with Bill Grove, or for that matter with anyone else except for Bob Evans of Rockford, who shared my concern regarding the skewed distribution of available resources. The essence of budget distribution was that Chicago-based administrators controlled the money and the power. They took care of their Chicago needs first and threw bones to the downstate programs. To be fair, however, we had a pretty nice bone at

UIUC, the new, 100,000-square-foot, $7 million Medical Sciences Building that we opened with as much fanfare as possible on October 15, 1975. The building housed most of our basic-science faculty and all the instructional facilities for the M-1 year, and had enough flexible space to allow us to plan for the clinical program yet to come. On the other hand, basic medical science faculty in Chicago lectured and taught in relatively outmoded facilities.

It was interesting to note that in a May 3, 1974 memo to President Corbally, Chancellor Begando bemoaned the financial status of every unit in the College of Medicine, except SBMS-UC, of which he said, "The operating funds for this school in FY 73 were adequate." This memo, which was prepared without my knowledge or input, made it readily apparent to me that no one was really listening to my concerns regarding a thin over-stretched and over-stressed faculty.

Our low-cost operating efficiency did catch the eye of President Corbally who, in a public-relations document titled, "Your Money; Your University," endorsed the affirmation of UIUC Chancellor Jack Peltason that "we have worked to develop plans for the addition of a clinical medicine component to the School of Basic Medical Sciences, and the School of Clinical Medicine is expected to be established in the fall of 1974 (sic)."

Corbally then gave us honorable mention in his annual report to the faculty in 1975. He praised the program for its innovative curriculum and learning format, calling it a program that "provides a high quality educational experience for students and is cost-effective. Because the students proceed through a curriculum with built-in evaluation instruments to help measure their progress, the faculty can devote a large proportion of teaching time to direct instruction and to personal interaction with students. This procedure increases both the quality of the program and the productivity of faculty members and students.

"To realize additional dollar savings, we rely upon the interest and cooperation of local area physicians…These voluntary contributions save the school many thousands of dollars in faculty salaries annually and also play an important role in the continuing professional growth of the practicing physicians who participate with us in medical education."

I don't know whether Corbally's praise affected our ultimate progress on the clinical school. Bill Grove laid much of the blame for delay at the feet of "higher administration," particularly Ron Brady, the Vice President for Fiscal Affairs. Brady, a financial and budgeting expert whom Corbally had brought with him from Ohio State University, was a powerful figure who controlled the university's state operating budget, which in those days amounted to $400 million. Bill Grove told me about Brady's role in the approval process during a telephone call on March 28, 1975. Grove spoke of a meeting three days earlier between himself and Weir, Begando, Munitz, and Brady, in which "Brady had finally crossed the bridge." Grove described all present at the meeting as supportive of clinical education at Urbana-Champaign, except for Brady who was responsible for presenting the university's budget before the Illinois Board of Higher Education and the legislature. According to Grove, Brady wanted to be certain there were no mix-ups concerning the priorities of the Peoria and University Hospital's capital projects. Of course, these were exactly Grove's priorities as well.

But despite all that evidence of good will, I am reasonably certain that the medical-education operation at UIUC always was and remained a low priority item for the Medical Center Campus. The repeated budget clashes over the years led to a great deal of anger and dissatisfaction. How does one disagree without being disloyal? Does loyalty to a program such as the Medical Scholars Program at UICOM-UC take precedence over loyalty to an administrative chain of command that guarantees budgetary inadequacy?

I complained to Bill Grove in 1975 that the senior leadership at Chicago knew nothing about the Urbana-Champaign program that was under their jurisdiction, and worse, they knew nothing about the budget of Southern Illinois University-Springfield, which was feeding from the same state trough as the University of Illinois. Grove, in a personal letter to me dated March 7, 1975, estimated that the SIU state budget for fiscal year 1976 was $3.5 million, when the actual figure was $10.9 million, an enormous discrepancy that he was unwilling or unable to take advantage of.

That reflected Bill Grove's biggest problem in guiding the College of Medicine in its expansion program. He was always ready and strong when administering downward, to curb our desires and to set limits. But when it was apparent, as was obvious in the case of SIU, that he was receiving less than he required, he was unable to rattle the cages above him to draw attention to obvious financial deficiencies. As a result, SIU developed its medical-education programs with about three times the amount of funds per medical student as did University of Illinois College of Medicine, an incredibly bad administrative performance.

In this type of atmosphere I continued to press Bill Grove to request the

additional funds to begin a clinical program. I'm not certain that I ever figured out Bill's true attitude towards such a program at Urbana. He claimed
to be a consistent and avid supporter, and suggested that our differences
were only over timing. However, there were other differences. I had argued
for a single-school structure at Urbana to avoid the awkwardness of administering two separate schools, but Grove, afraid that a single four-year program might qualify us as an independent medical school, refused to allow
me to depart from a dysfunctional administrative organization. So I was
destined to be a "double dean," dean of the School of Basic Medical Sciences
and the School of Clinical Medicine at Urbana-Champaign. This called for
separate committee structures, separate budgets, and unnecessary duplica-
tions of time and effort. It was an extra administrative burden on the smallest unit of the college that, even as two separate medical schools had,
combined, the smallest operating budget to begin with.

Although there was general agreement that the SCM-UC would start in
the fall of 1975, Bob Evans had warned me earlier that Bill Grove's hidden
agenda was to delay our start until September 1976. Bob was correct. Grove
remained very concerned about the costs involved, both operating and capital, although I repeatedly told him that they would be less than any comparable operation. Since John Anderson and I had purposefully designed the
Basic Medical Sciences building with maximal flexibility, there was probably
enough teaching space within that building to accommodate both the basic-
science programs and the didactic elements of our evolving clinical program. Furthermore, it was becoming clear that the community hospitals
would be willing to lease space to the medical school at very reasonable cost.

In due course, Grove contacted me to suggest we delay the start of
SCM-UC an additional year. He told me how anxious he was that there be
no hitch in the funding of the new University Hospital. Peoria also had a
$9 million building program in the works, and he said he was hesitant to ask
the higher-ups for three major new programs in a single year: the hospital,
the Peoria School of Medicine building, and SCM-UC. "After all," he argued,
"SCM-UC is a done deal. Why not wait one more year and give yourself
more time to develop your unique clinical curriculum?"

I talked this over with Mort Creditor, who was in charge of the clinical
curriculum's development. By this time, he was hard at work on the logic-
pathways curriculum, a massive undertaking. There were no ready texts or
journals to follow. We knew we had something very good and decided that

an extra year of preparation would be helpful. We agreed to go along with Bill Grove on the one-year delay, even though Mort had received written assurance from Joe Begando that we would have ten second-year medical students on our campus in August 1975. This delay proved almost fatal to medical education in Urbana-Champaign.

Innocently reassured that August 1976 was finally to be the date of our clinical inauguration, Mort Creditor and I energetically continued to develop the clinical curriculum and to recruit a core clinical faculty. The clinical program itself had yet to be approved by the Illinois Board of Higher Education, and we still remained the School of Clinical Medicine, Urbana-Champaign in name only. Bill Grove, to this point, never authorized a budget line for the new school. We were still operating out of the SBMS-UC account.

The university appropriations bill for fiscal year 1976 was scheduled for a routine hearing in the Illinois General Assembly at 10 a.m., June 11, 1975. However, before the hearings even began, Governor Dan Walker presented his new and unexpected views concerning the fiscal resources of the state. There was a fiscal "crisis" which called for a six percent budget reduction across the board. One week later, President Corbally informed the board of trustees that, although he didn't know precisely the amount of dollars such a reduction would cost the University, he was sure it would be "a large sum." His plans to meet the budget crisis would sacrifice the unborn SCM-UC. "We shall scale down our 1976 budgets. We shall do this by eliminating new program thrusts…and…by slowing down our expansion in the health professions."

Six agonizing years of preparation seemed to be shot down in a week of political activity. Once again I turned to my close advisors, and we brainstormed ways to save the clinical program. Things looked very bad. The period of medical-school expansion was rapidly coming to an end. The public's perception of a "doctor shortage" was no longer being translated into a call for more medical schools. State legislatures and governors were entering into a long-term trend to decrease funding for higher education as a given percentage of the overall state budget. We needed a strong reason for the university and the state to continue the development of clinical education in Urbana.

We found two major reasons to argue for the eventual development of our clinical program. The first was the nature of UIUC itself. It was a major university campus with a heavy research mission. There were few other such major campuses that did not have close physical or research connections to a medical school. Biological research in the late twentieth century demanded a close relationship to medical care and research. The second reason lay in a revised vision of our mission. Our original mission emphasized, like every other medical school, the training of capable doctors. It became clear to us that if that were our sole mission, it could be fulfilled by any number of other medical schools. However, given our physical presence on the UIUC campus, we were ideally suited to train research-oriented physicians who would earn both the MD and the Ph.D. degrees. On this issue we had the unqualified support of the School of Life Sciences, the School of Chemical Sciences, and other campus scientists. Despite past tensions between us, when it came to saving the medical school, faculty from across the campus were there in our support. Thus, in cooperation with the UIUC Graduate College, we inaugurated the Medical Scholars Program, an MD-Ph.D. training program that has developed into one of the major combined-degree training programs in the world.

With all state agencies facing a six percent funding rescission, a climate of accelerating inflation, and a University trying to maintain competitive salary levels for its faculty and staff, there was little hope that new funds would be available to start our clinical program. Grove became virtually unapproachable on the matter. He refused to reschedule our starting date and refused to authorize a separate clinical-school account. It is safe to say that from that point on, Bill Grove was firmly opposed to starting our clinical program. As far as he was concerned, SCM-UC was dead.

However, three crucial events took place that year that gave us a tiny opening to squeeze through. In February 1975, four months before Governor Walker called for the budget cut, Bill Grove fired Rockford Dean Bob Evans. This act seriously weakened Grove as an administrator and loosened his grip on his subordinates. Second, the Medical Center Campus was reorganized. This removed Bill Grove from the Executive Deanship of the College and thrust him upward as the medical center's Vice Chancellor for Academic Affairs. Third, Truman Anderson became the College of Medicine's executive dean. Anderson had always seen the potential of a four-year program at Urbana. That these three occurrences happened when they did is one of the minor miracles upon which SCM-UC was built.

The Bob Evans incident took place at a management retreat in

Clearwater, Florida, sponsored by the Association of American Medical Colleges. Besides the contingent from UICOM, senior administrators from six or seven major medical schools, including New York University, University of Connecticut, University of Wisconsin, and the University of Minnesota, were gathered to work on management problems within their institutions under the tutelage of a guest from the MIT Sloan School of Management. The format included some management theory by lecture, followed by unit workshops guided by one member of the MIT-Sloan consulting faculty, and plenary sessions at which problems common to more than one of the schools represented could be discussed. Besides dealing with specific management problems that we planned to tackle, such as the development of areawide health-education systems (AHES), the introduction of "primary care" into our curriculum, and the approach to arcane issues peculiar to the Chicago site, we were instructed by our management consultant to "flag" interpersonal problems should they arise. Flagging interpersonal problems could lead to useful discussions that might resolve both interpersonal and more generic types of issues.

Only two topics were flagged in our first day's discussion, both relating to my insistence on a better cut of the budget pie. Since I was linked to the UIUC campus, my Administrative Advisory Council colleagues believed that I wanted to be independent of them. They perceived that I was using the independence issue as a club to get more than my share of the pie. Aside from Bloomfield vs. the council, we had nothing else to flag. But, at about 10:00 p.m. on our first evening, after we had labored all afternoon and evening to deal with AHES problems in order to be prepared to present our solutions to the plenary session the next day, Bob, who was the only dean who had come to this working retreat with a spouse, asked Bill, "Do you want me there at the presentation?" Bill snapped back at him, "You just want to show off again."

It was a non sequitur brimming with hostility, and it caught us by surprise. In retrospect, there had been clues of trouble brewing between Bill and Bob for well over a year, but none of us was knowledgeable about the depth of Bill's feeling. Our management consultant was loath to let the episode pass without flagging it for later resolution. We dallied a bit over that, unsure whether we were giving the exchange more weight than it deserved. In the end, we flagged it simply as "Bob and Bill," and proceeded with the training activities of the retreat. The flag stared at us innocuously

from its position on the recording easel below my own flag, which seemed
to take precedence because mine represented "treason." I was accused of disloyalty to the cause, of not being a team player.

Two days and no additional flags later, our internal management-
training process focused on "Management Relationships." Bill moderated
the workshop. It began at about 2:00 p.m. after a hard morning's work on
the definition and introduction of primary care into a system that claimed it
was already teaching and delivering primary care. We were pretty tired by
that time. Three days of non-stop discussions centered on difficult problems
had left many of us believing that we had been over-programmed. Nevertheless, Bill proceeded to outline his agenda for the remainder of the afternoon, writing it on a large easel. Topping the list was the fate of the office of
the Executive Dean with the impending administrative reshuffling at the
Medical Center. He then proceeded to outline several other problems as he
saw them, all dealing with management relationships: school-college issues,
the definition of semiautonomous, the advisory council's decision-making
process, etc. Then, almost as an afterthought, he supplanted the top position
on the list with the word "flags," adding cryptically "You guys want to talk
about flags, so I put that at the top of the list. I don't, but you do."

The response to Bill's challenge was divided. Our consultant urged us to
deal with these personal issues that were distracting us from the work that
we were supposed to accomplish. Both Bud Zimmerman and Jerry Hahn
supported the consultant, while Nick Cotsonas and I opted to avoid the flags
at that time. It was plain to me that Grove was loaded for bear, particularly
so because he kept interjecting into the discussion statements such as, "You
may be sorry if you get me on the flags."

Bud Zimmerman pushed hard on the flags, though, saying, "I don't
think there is anything that would blow this college of medicine apart."

Jerry Hahn added an ill-fated diagnosis, "As far as I'm concerned, the
flags are a big bunch of flatus and we've got to get it out before we go on to
anything else."

I could see the tension rising in Bill Grove's face and tried to defuse the
issue by interjecting, "I'm not so sure that this is the correct time to deal
with the Bob-Bill flag, but I have no hesitation in talking about my own
flag issue."

That flag was listed on the easel as "Dan's trump card," which referred to
my supposed threat to seek separate governance if I didn't get everything I

wanted. So, we began to discuss the issue. I explained that every time I made a demand on him, Bill would respond that the only reason I would make such a request was that I had a fall-back position of separate governance with UIUC, which he, in turn would use as a lever to deny me. I explained that I was in a no-win position. "If I make a demand, it is always taken as an implied threat. If I don't make the demand, I can't get the job done properly." I concluded by telling Grove, "In fact, my trump card has been really your trump card, which you've used to manipulate me for fear of being disloyal."

This was not an easy point to get across and it took about an hour of discussion. Of course, that led to the expected retort from Cotsonas, who asked, "Does this mean you are committed to the College of Medicine for all time?"

He always wanted a lifetime guarantee. I responded that I could not predict the future. I also told them that the independence of the Urbana medical program would always be a threat, no matter who was dean. The UIUC campus agreed to this medical enterprise on those terms, and the Medical Center campus knew it. The main issue was that people who are content have no incentive to secede.

After exhausting ourselves on "Dan's trump card," we returned to the Bill-Bob flag. Bill reiterated his warning, "I don't think you really know what you are getting into." However, it was received more as an invitation. So, we began. Grove identified several issues that he deemed as *causus belli*. Grove was infuriated by Evans's hiring policies, claiming that he paid more for services in Rockford than anywhere else in the system.

Bob responded, "Look Bill, anybody I hire, if it is academic, you have to sign the papers and if it is nonacademic, I have got to get permission from the Personnel Office."

Bill replied, "Oh! You are always going around Personnel."

Evans claimed that he couldn't circumvent Personnel, which lead to more argument. Finally, Bob said, "Bill, will you answer a question yes or no? Can I hire any nonacademic without Personnel Office approval?"

After some thought, Bill replied, "No, but I can't explain to you what I mean. I just can't get my point across…The other thing is that you externalize the College of Medicine. When I was up at the groundbreaking (for a new laboratory and teaching building) two weeks ago with President Corbally, you talked and gave credit to many local politicians and faculty, but you never once mentioned the University of Illinois College of Medicine."

At this point Bob became defensive, and enumerated a number of instances when he had mentioned the University of Illinois. Bill countered that he hadn't mentioned the College of Medicine specifically, pointing out that Corbally had leaned over and said to him at the time, "Bill, didn't you have anything to do with this? Wasn't the College of Medicine involved?"

So the argument became more heated and centered on whether Bob considered the Rockford School of Medicine a genuine part of the College of Medicine. At one point, Bob said, "Bill, you have just got to believe me, at some time, just believe me."

Then, in a very controlled voice that expressed consummate anger, Bill Grove replied, "I don't believe anything you say. Your credibility with me is zero."

A shock wave went around the room. Everyone else was silent. Bill and Bob glared at each other, not knowing what to say next. Our management consultant broke the ice by jesting, "You want to know something? I think we need a consultant."

He recognized that we were in deep water and identified the problem as a major break in relationships. He suggested that we continue to work to see whether we could restore rapport between Bill Grove and Bob Evans.

Meanwhile, Nick Cotsonas played to perfection the role of a guilt-ridden sibling whose rival has just been killed. He was flushed, interrupting the dialogue frequently, picking up and amplifying each nuance of hope and denying that real damage had been done. Not that the rest of us felt any better or less guilty to have permitted the exchange to end so violently, but Cotsonas couldn't contain himself. He said, "Nothing has been said here that can't be fixed up. It's all right, don't worry about it."

When Grove repeated himself about Evans' low credibility with him, Nick seized on the word "low" and exclaimed, "Bob, do you hear that? Your credibility with Bill is 'low,' not 'zero.' This is an improvement already."

The room was heavy with anxiety and we decided to take a break.

Bob was quite shaken. He left the room and indicated to us that he wouldn't be back to complete the session, but the consultant spoke with him privately for thirty minutes and persuaded him to return. When we had reassembled, the consultant began, "Look, there has been a rupture. The question is, 'Are the parties willing to work together?'"

Bill Grove emphatically held his ground. There was no room for reconciliation. Bob however, was a changed person. Gone was the self-confidence that characterized his normal behavior. Instead, he regressed to the role of a humble supplicant with an impassioned plea. "Bill, please take me back, please. You know that I work for you Bill. You're my boss. I've given four years of my life to this College of Medicine development. I thought I was doing a good job. I never thought that my actions upset you so much."

To which, Bill Grove simply responded, "Bullshit."

It was a cold-blooded execution that denied a plea for mercy. Discussion was over for the evening. We broke up. Bob went to his room. The rest of the team, the survivors, joined Bill at the hotel bar. After some reflection and a drink, Bill confided to me, "I have only one regret about that. I may have given some indication that I would take Bob back, and that was wrong. I should have said 'No. I will not take him back.'"

He then delivered the same message to the other advisory council members, excused himself and retired to his room.

The next morning, we began working on the advisory council decision-making process. Bob joined us shortly after we had started, acting as though nothing had happened the night before. He didn't say much, but he seemed to be a part of the group. We weren't making much headway on the decision-making process, largely because the council never made any real decisions that Bill Grove had not recommended. Listening to this jabber with increasing frustration, I finally said, "What do you mean by an AAC decision-making process? You are fooling yourselves. This body makes no decisions."

There were immediate denials. Hahn protested, "What do you mean?" George Miller said, "You know, it is a very important decision-making body."

I replied, "Let me tell you something. Yesterday, we saw a unilateral decision of the discharge of a dean from one of our schools and from our own ranks, and we didn't do a thing about it. We were not a part of that decision, and if Bill Grove can do that in broad daylight, the rest of us have no decision-making power at all."

Bob Evans paled and appeared thunderstruck. Apparently, he had deluded himself the night before into thinking that the exchange had been just another dispute with Grove. I was certain it was not. As the meaning of my words sunk in, our management consultant performed a reality check, asking Bill if what I had said was true. Bill confirmed that Bob was through, and that was it. Bob rose from his chair, mumbled something like, "I guess you don't need me in here anymore," and left the room.

After Evans left, the talk promptly reverted to "damage control." "What's going to happen in Rockford?" The day's agenda was scrapped in order to plot the strategy to meet this new crisis. Bill Grove, of all people, explained that he wanted to avoid a "fuss up in Rockford." Once again, we used the consultant as the neutral middleman to approach Bob and explain to him the importance of handling this affair with discretion. Bill informed us that he was prepared to make Bob's departure from Rockford as painless as possible and to offer him generous termination benefits, in other words, hush money. Although Bob was effectively silenced, the city of Rockford was not. Bob had earned a great deal of respect from the community. He exuded confidence. He exhibited great skills in recruiting both salaried and volunteer faculty, selling the school to, and raising money from, the community. He had warm relationships with the local state legislators. Bob Evans was a presence in Rockford that one could not casually dismiss.

The medical community, which had worked for five years to develop the Rockford School of Medicine, was outraged at Grove's arbitrary action and demanded both an explanation and a promise that such a dismissal would never take place again. The Rockford newspapers bitterly criticized the university and particularly Bill Grove. It was a public-relations mess for the university that required repeated visits by the president and the Medical Center chancellor to calm down. By the end of it all, Bud Grulee, retired dean of the University of Cincinnati Medical School was recruited to replace Bob, but more important from my perspective was that Bill Grove was neutralized as an arbitrary hatchet man.

The real loser in this drama was Grove. He had shot his thunderbolt and nothing was left in reserve. The office of the Executive Dean was weakened as well. There was a stiff price to be paid in Rockford, one that the University did not wish to repeat. In the ensuing months and years, and in pursuit of a clinical program at Urbana-Champaign, I took liberties with my office in fighting negative actions by Bill Grove and his successors that went far beyond anything Bob Evans might have designed, without fear of being dismissed. The firing of Bob Evans, although a trauma to the college, to Rockford, Illinois, and to the university, really opened a survival portal for SCM-UC.

One month later, when the fuss at Rockford was dying down, and Bill Grove and Joe Begando had made all the explanations they could to the public and to the University Board of Trustees, Bill wrote an unusual letter to the Administrative Advisory Council. It was the first and only handwritten letter I ever received from Bill. Written on personal stationary and dated March 26, 1975, 6:15 p.m., it read: "It has been a long and difficult day. It has been a day that caps a series of difficult days and weeks. As I watch the sunset, I want you all to know that I believe I understand why each of you react as you do and must. Please try to understand my reactions. From where I view the sunset, the morning should be bright. The college is secure because of you."

Within six months of the Clearwater conference, the office of Vice Chancellor for Academic Affairs (VCAA) was instituted. The chancellor instituted the office for a number of reasons. One of them was that he wanted to reduce the power of the College of Medicine in its relationships with the other Medical Center units: the schools of Pharmacy, Nursing, Public Health, and Dentistry. However, Bill Grove was the first VCAA. So there was considerable speculation that rather than diminish the power of the College of Medicine, Grove's elevation would actually add to it.

The changed governance theoretically gave more autonomy to the college's executive dean but left a question as to whether Grove could manage the entire Medical Center campus without micromanaging the College of Medicine. Also unknown was whether the college could find a new executive dean who could stand up to Bill Grove.

Truman Anderson's ascension to executive dean was the step that finally paved the way for SCM-UC to become a reality.

CHAPTER 20

Leaping Bureaucratic Hurdles

RUMAN ANDERSON BECAME executive dean of the University of
Illinois College of Medicine on June 1, 1976, six months after Bill
Grove left the job. In the interim, Jerry Hahn had been acting executive dean until a nationwide search for a new dean was completed. Truman
Anderson was the unanimous selection of that search. He was a popular
choice on his own merit, but some other able candidates apparently withdrew from consideration once they saw that they would be reporting to Bill
Grove, whose reputation for authoritarianism was becoming well known in
the medical academic community.

No one was more concerned about Grove than Truman Anderson, who
had known him very well for a long time. Truman had scrubbed in surgery
as a student of Grove's and had considerable experience with him in a
student-mentor relationship. Truman had been Grove's choice to lead the
School of Basic Medical Sciences in Chicago when the college was reorganized in 1969. Now, Truman was taking control of one of the largest medical
schools in the country. His main concern was whether Grove would deal
with him as an administrative peer or revert to paternalistic indulgence.
Truman planned to work hard in his new position to assert his and the
college's independence.

One of Truman's first command decisions was to unlock the shackles
of SCM-UC and let it fly. It was an "in your face" act to Bill Grove, who
remained hesitant to let us begin in the absence of start-up funds. Once
Truman held the reins of power he said to me, "Danny, We'll just have to
find the funds to get you started." And that is exactly what he did. He
"found" $650,000 to permit us to do the recruiting and curriculum develop-
ment for SCM-UC.

One person can make a difference, and Truman, who shared my vision
of a unique medical school at UIUC, certainly did. If not for him, there
would have been no SCM-UC, no Medical Scholars Program, and no

UICOM-UC. It was Truman, and only Truman, who turned the asylum key that unlocked the UICOM treasury and sent us on our way.

His decision to support our initial class with $650,000 of new state money put him in direct conflict with Bill Grove, who could not refrain from micromanaging the College of Medicine, as many feared, and trying to keep SCM-UC in check. Grove, whose new office had a campuswide responsibility, never really gave up the executive dean's chair

The conflict with Bill Grove was especially painful to Truman, who had looked up to Grove throughout his professional career.

This was still 1976, and the budget was tight and would remain so for the foreseeable future. The AHES project was a source of somewhat flexible money that could be shifted to Urbana to hire clinical faculty in connection with a primary-care residency program such as the Danville Family Practice Program. Recalling that SCM-UC was originally slated to start in the fall of 1975, delayed by Bill Grove to 1976, delayed by Governor Walker until heaven knows when, Truman assured me that SCM-UC would begin teaching by the fall of 1978, and he was as good as his word.

Before Truman became executive dean, Grove was taking steps to make certain that the section of the 1969–70 Treaty that referred to a shift of governance for the Urbana program remained inoperative. Given the agreements that were solemnized in the Treaty, this could not be done in one step. However, Grove remained firm in his resolve to prevent the independence of SCM-UC. On the other hand, I was resolved to make the university live up to its Treaty obligations, which provided for the transfer of governance to the UIUC campus at an appropriate time. It was becoming increasingly evident that the UICOM-UC program would never thrive under Chicago leadership.

Grove was worried enough about this matter to arrange a meeting with Begando and Peltason to discuss the administrative arrangements of the medical program in Urbana with respect to the two campuses. At this meeting, Grove persuaded the two chancellors to delay any talk of an SCM-UC governance change for a given period. The meeting culminated with a January 27, 1976, letter (the Chancellors' Agreement of 1976) to President Corbally, which Begando and Peltason signed, but which Grove obviously had approved. The agreement said, "We have concluded that the best interests of the several schools of medicine within the University of Illinois College of Medicine will be served by an agreement to preserve for a fixed

number of years the current organizational structure in which several schools
comprise a single College of Medicine. It is our judgment that the present
organizational structure should remain stable for a period of approximately
seven years…with a review…after a period of approximately five."

It was a five-year stall that would dilute the institutional memory that
resided in the Treaty. Corbally responded on February 9, 1976, "I am in
complete agreement with the conclusions outlined in your letter and with
the review timetable proposed."

Regretfully, the Chancellors' Agreement locked us into this difficult,
almost intolerable governance situation for another five years, until 1981 or
beyond. But Grove was not finished with us yet. The Chancellors' Agreement
in hand, his aim then was to bind SBMS/SCM-UC more closely to the
embrace of the Medical Center. On March 15, 1977, without consultation or
warning, he wrote to Vice President for Administration Ron Brady to
request a comprehensive change in our manner of handling funds. Instead
of managing our budget through the very capable business office at Urbana,
he asked that we transfer all of our business affairs to the business office at
the Medical Center. He claimed that "would vastly improve the understanding of the working relationship between the School of Basic Medical
Sciences at Urbana-Champaign and the School of Clinical Medicine at
Urbana-Champaign and its parent body—the College of Medicine at the
Medical Center."

When I received a copy of that letter I was very angry. It was the last
straw. The thought of shifting all budget functions to the tender mercies of
the Medical Center Business Office was really more than I could bear. I had
endured countless Administrative Advisory Council and Advisory Council
of Deans meetings where the leadership from Rockford and Peoria had
complained about the snaillike turnaround time from that office. The office
was considered not only slow, but also inept. Moreover, these business functions were well and conveniently handled at Urbana-Champaign. I wrote
Mort Weir, then Vice Chancellor of Academic Affairs at UIUC, and he wrote
to Grove on March 21, 1977:

> Besides my belief that some of the changes you recommend are unwise,
> I am quite surprised that they were never discussed with me or with
> Chancellor Peltason. It perhaps could be argued that since the school is
> administratively a part of the Medical Center Campus, the moves that

you recommend should be of no concern to the Urbana Campus. But
since nearly all of the faculty of the school hold appointments in
Urbana departments, we are naturally concerned when suggestions are
made that we believe will not be in the best interest of those faculty.

Grove finally backed off from his position, but he had sent a clear message
that he would do everything within his power to make permanent the
SBMS/SCM-UC governance from Chicago.

Given the tight budget in 1976, Grove decided that he would not allow
SCM-UC to begin without approval of both the Illinois Board of Higher
Education and the Liaison Committee on Medical Education, the combined
body of the Association of American Medical Colleges and the American
Medical Association. Once again, the Urbana-Champaign program was
given special treatment. Neither Peoria nor Rockford had to endure those
approvals, because they were blanket approved within the original concept
of expanding and regionalizing health education in Illinois. I argued
strongly with Grove that we did not need separate approval from the IBHE,
but he thought and acted otherwise.

The University of Illinois was invited to testify at a meeting of the
Health Education Subcommittee of the IBHE on April 7, 1976, in Chicago.
I was on administrative leave in Israel at the time and had left Mort Creditor
in charge of the clinical-school development. So Mort organized our presentation to the IBHE. Before the meeting, it was rumored that SIU, with
its well-funded medical school in Springfield, would oppose approval of
SCM-UC. It seems that almost no one wanted a full four-year program at
UIUC. It was too threatening to other medical schools in the state to have
the University of Illinois flagship campus also have such a school.

Fortunately, not everyone was so negative toward us. The Illinois
Hospital Association (IHA) took some interest in the development of
SCM-UC because twenty-one association members were affiliated with our
program. The IHA circulated a memo on April 2, 1976, informing their
members about an IBHE meeting to review the clinical school proposal on
April 7. IHA members generally supported our cause and appeared in
strength at the meeting.

After the meeting, I received a complete telephone and written report
from both John Anderson and Mort Creditor. Mort said, "The entire tone of
the meeting was extremely favorable, and I think we have passed the main

hurdle and are planning as if we had."

Mort added that Jack Pollard, the Medical Director of Carle Clinic, and Charles Dawley, the President of Carle Foundation Hospital, visited Dartmouth Medical School and came back very pleased with what they had seen. Mort went on to say that the negotiations with Carle were progressing well and that he believed that we had made a tremendous step forward in that direction. He also noted that the negotiations with Mercy Hospital "have been a little bit slower but I understand they are on track and if Mercy delayed a year it would be no great problem in view of the small size of the charter class."

Finally, Mort summarized the development of our relationship with the VA hospital. Dr. John Sharp, our first major recruit to the VA hospital, was interested in serving as chief of medicine at the Danville Veterans Administration Medical Center and as head of the Department of Medicine at SCM-UC.

Mort was a very bright, even brilliant, and hard-working individual who, in my judgment, had one major fault. He lacked insight into the impact he made upon others. For example, he reported successful negotiations when, in fact, the other parties were terrified of the outcome that Creditor was pursuing. There were times during his tenure as my associate dean when he would report to me how successful he had been in one negotiation or another, when the other party, usually someone at Carle or Mercy, would take me aside and advise me to get rid of him, that he was damaging the entire program.

Mort was a traditionalist who saw the world largely in black and white. He was honest and direct to a fault. When he came across an inferior product, he made no bones about telling the person or persons involved of his unhappiness.

On the other hand, I could not have turned over the clinical-curriculum development job to a more eager enthusiast than Mort. He did an outstanding job in framing our clinical program. Yet, once he had begun a task like that, he was loath to seek guidance from anyone. During my leave, Bill Sorlie wrote to me on May 11, 1976, to inform me about the status of the PLATO contract, the adjunct faculty, and other educational issues. He ended his letter with the cryptic comment, "I look forward to your return. If and when the clinical school is approved, I look forward with interest to who the 'functional' dean will be. I begin to wonder sometimes." In essence, what Bill was saying was that Mort Creditor seemed to be taking over and running the school as if it were his own responsibility.

On June 8, 1976, the Board of Higher Education took final action consistent with its master plan by approval of "Unit 179—establishment of a School of Clinical Medicine at Urbana-Champaign as a unit the University of Illinois College of Medicine." Mort Creditor deserves much praise for that achievement.

Even though we surmounted the IBHE hurdle, even though SCM-UC had been approved by the University Board of Trustees in 1974, and even though there was much documentation within the college minutes that SCM-UC should begin no later than the fall of 1978, SCM-UC was not yet on the university books. We had no formal identification within the university's budgeting system, and of course, no distinct budget. I had been bootlegging funds for the development of SCM-UC from SBMS-UC and from funds Truman Anderson made available to recruit faculty, but officially, SCM-UC did not exist. The basic scientists were upset with me for two reasons. First, they resented the constant bleeding off of SBMS-UC funds to the clinical program, and second, they resented me placing MD faculty in SBMS-UC where they clearly did not belong. Truman informed me that Bill Grove still insisted on delaying internal budgeting of SCM-UC until there were enough new funds. This could have taken forever. Something had to be done.

On October 15, 1976, I wrote Truman Anderson to discuss the problems we faced in dealing with our basic-science faculty, the AHES obligations in Region 3-B, and the threat of SIU moving into our region in the absence of a clinical program at Urbana-Champaign. I concluded by stating: "The College of Medicine and the Medical Center Campus can no longer delay on the SCM-UC decision...I recommend that SCM-UC be officially recognized and implemented immediately by title and by separate accounts...Because it is my belief that the University of Illinois would be ill-served and irretrievably embarrassed in its medical-expansion program by any other course, I want you to know, in advance, that in accordance with my responsibilities as dean and in accordance with the University Statutes III.3.d.10, I will appeal any negative recommendations as far and as high as I am legally able to carry them."

This was strong stuff to send to a friend, but I was aware that Truman was in constant conflict with Bill Grove who could not let go of the College of Medicine's reins and at times would wrest them from Executive Dean Anderson. I called Truman before sending the letter to assure him that its sharp-toned message was really for Grove and Begando.

Finally, on January 25, 1977, Bill Grove authorized an account at the Medical Center Campus for the School of Clinical Medicine at Urbana-Champaign, but not without a malignant twist. In authorizing the establishment of an SCM-UC account, he ignored his agreement with Weir and Peltason in March 1976. He specifically directed that all SCM-UC funds and accounting be handled through the Medical Center. It was an order that was directly contrary to prior arrangements outlined in the 1969 Treaty and confirmed at the time of the Chancellors' Agreement of 1976. True to form, Bill Grove was not interested in recent history, convenience, or common sense. He was intent on control.

To insert such a qualifier into the approval of SCM-UC was a low blow and was unacceptable. It was difficult enough to administer two Medical Center programs on the UIUC campus without complicating it even further by requiring the accounting for one program on the Urbana-Champaign campus and the accounting for the other program on the Medical Center campus. Mike Harms pointed out in a memo to me that "the conduct of the office function related to SCM-UC operations through the Medical Center Campus Office of Business Affairs would have many serious disadvantages. We would experience serious problems related to payroll, accounting procedures, and grants administration. Intercampus distance and difference in administrative procedures are the main factors (that) will lead to these difficulties."

It was just another indication that Bill Grove did not want the medical program at Urbana-Champaign to be independent from the Medical Center campus—ever. I immediately conferred with Weir and Peltason, who asked Grove to change his position, but Grove held firm. I argued that budget management within the college was not even in Grove's province as VCAA and that it was a matter for the executive dean of the college, but Bill Grove's displeasure with Truman Anderson and his power as VCAA permitted him to ignore the argument. My strategy was to bump the issue up to the presidential level where it was finally resolved. On June 24, 1977, University Vice President Ron Brady established the following administrative arrangements for the School of Basic Medical Sciences at Urbana-Champaign:

1. The budget sheets and printing of the budget will show the School of Basic Medical Sciences at Urbana-Champaign in the Medical Center section.
2. On July 1, the budget as described should be transferred to the Urbana accounts so that the logistical support processes now in effect will continue.
3. Budget memos shall be approved by the Medical Center in consultation with the Urbana campus.

That settled the issue and was very satisfying to me. Although Brady did not mention SCM-UC, all of us, including the Medical Center administration, assumed that the directive applied to SCM-UC as well as to SBMS-UC.

I talked frequently with Truman, who repeatedly complained about how difficult it was for him to work with Bill Grove. I told him that I needed answers. We were recruiting faculty, establishing operational procedures, and making agreements with hospitals, all without formal authorization from the Medical Center administration. Truman was sympathetic, but acknowledged he was somewhat intimidated by Grove's hostility. Nevertheless, he told me, on April 13, 1977, that he was setting aside $650,000 for SCM-UC to draw upon. To clear the air, he also arranged a meeting for the two of us with Bill Grove. We met in Chicago on April 15. It was a peculiar meeting in that I received the authorization I needed, but no one would put it in writing. Grove took the position that if it was acceptable to Truman, it was acceptable to him. In addition, he cautioned that Truman and I should both realize that all funds for SCM-UC would come from the College of Medicine budget and that there would be no assistance from the office of the VCAA. He added, as an afterthought, that the college would need the blessing of accreditation from the Liaison Committee for Medical Education before starting instruction. This was no minor issue, but I was confident we could make our case to the LCME without too much difficulty. It was just another stumbling block to be overcome.

To be fair to Bill Grove, he reassured me that he did not lack confidence in our ability to run a good program and that he believed that a clinical school in Urbana was integral to his concept of regionalized medical education in Illinois. He declared that his only concern was a fiscal one. He stated that he disagreed with Anderson's decision because he thought that the limited college resources were being stretched too far. I left the meeting with what I understood to be a verbal authorization to begin instruction in 1978. So armed, and to prevent any misunderstanding, I wrote to Truman Anderson and Bill Grove on April 21, 1977, to confirm:

1. That SCM-UC will begin its undergraduate medical education program with ten to twelve students in the fall of 1978.
2. That recruiting for additional faculty and staff to effect that program will begin immediately.
3. That I will plan to spend $650,000 (in addition to that which is already allocated) in the SCM-UC budget during the next two fiscal years, FY78 and FY79.
4. That you will be continually apprised of our financial obligations.
5. That the program will be directed specifically towards the utilization of the UIUC campus resources to develop a variety of combined degree programs unique to American medical education.
6. That the LCME will be contacted promptly to arrange a staff visit to SCM-UC.

As was typical in this bureaucratic nightmare, I received no reply to the memo, so I forged ahead on the assumption that since it was not disapproved, it was therefore approved. It was another little victory without a trophy. The trophy would come in August.

Because of the turmoil in which we were all placed, I invited the entire Medical Center campus faculty, nursing, physical therapy, medical art, etc. in Region 3B to a retreat at the Illini Union on Thursday, July 7, 1977. I wanted to determine whether we could work together to offer solutions to some of the problems we faced. The retreat attendees were a very mixed group with a wide variety of agendas. One thing we could all agree upon was the awkward governance structure relating to one campus being dominant over a unit that is operating on another campus. As a result of this retreat, the faculty urged me, as if I had not already tried, to bring the matter to the attention of higher administration. On July 20, 1977, I wrote jointly to Mort Weir and Bill Grove, the two vice chancellors for academic affairs:

> I call your attention to the concerns of forty members of the Region 3B faculty who urged me to bring these matters to your attention...All faculty...are disheartened by the chronically uncertain and ill-defined relationships and commitments between the Urbana-Champaign

campus and the Medical Center Campus towards the delivery of health-education programs in Region 3B. SBMS-UC has had five faculty resignations in the past three months, four of which were directly related to the awkward governance imposed upon this school. This problem requires the immediate attention of the senior administrators of both campuses. It is clearly a two-campus problem and must be recognized, acknowledged, and dealt with in concert by both campuses.

In addition, because I was still getting anxiety-laden messages from Truman that the higher echelons of the university were still not comfortable with the idea of a clinical school in Urbana, I asked for some acknowledgment that the rug wouldn't be pulled out from under SCM-UC, writing, "Furthermore, the University of Illinois seems again poised to decide 'once and for all' whether a full medical-education program will be mounted in the Urbana-Champaign campus...The SCM-UC approval process has assumed the dimensions of a gauntlet rather than a pathway...However, if it is the decision of the University to reverse its commitment to the beginning of Clinical education in Urbana-Champaign in the fall of 1978, common sense dictates that the negative decision must be made immediately at the university level so that timely public and private notifications can be made. For the moment, pending any change of direction, I intend to proceed with the clinical-school development on the same assumptions as per the enclosed memorandum of April 21, 1977."

The letter was sent to the two vice chancellors and copied to Executive Dean Truman Anderson and President John Corbally. On August 8, I received an answer from Weir and Grove acknowledging receipt of my letter to them and that my proposals for problem resolution were "one approach."

They wrote, "It is our understanding that the College of Medicine has committed itself to assign ten students to the School of Clinical Medicine in Urbana-Champaign in the fall of 1978. Funds for this effort must be generated within the existing budget of the College of Medicine.

"We pledge the support of our offices in helping to make the development of the Clinical School and the further operation of the School of Basic Medical Sciences at Urbana-Champaign a success."

It wasn't a love letter, but it would do. We finally had our trophy in writing: a positive confirmation of what we were about from higher administration on the two campuses. The only obstacle that now remained was the LCME.

CHAPTER 21

Complications from Without: LCME

A CCREDITATION IS AN ELABORATE PROCESS, at the heart of which is an on-site survey by an LCME visiting subcommittee made up of four to eight representative persons who have been deputized to apply LCME policy to the school being accredited. Every visit by such a survey team is preceded by a laborious, in-house "self-study" by the school being surveyed for accreditation. The outcome of the accreditation-review process ranges from full accreditation for seven years to a worst-case withdrawal of accreditation. Intermediate outcomes include provisional accreditation, usually reserved for new and developing schools, and probation, both of which require repeat surveys at intervals of one to two years. The LCME, confident that the United States produces the best doctors in the world, has little incentive to change its formula.

Made up of representatives from the American Medical Association and the Association of American Medical Colleges (AAMC), the Liaison Committee for Medical Education has ultimate accreditation authority over U.S. and Canadian medical schools that grant the MD degree. It publishes a document titled *Functions and Structure of a Medical School* that defines standards and the accreditation process for medical-education programs. Approval, provisional or otherwise, is essential for new medical schools before they take their first students.

Medical-school accreditation was no simple obstacle to overcome. Without the imprimatur of the LCME accreditation, a United States medical school might just as well close its doors. The LCME sends out accreditation inspection teams to all U.S. and Canadian medical schools on a rotating basis at selected intervals. Older, more established schools are inspected less frequently, whereas newer schools may be examined more frequently, depending upon the LCME's interpretation of the survey teams' report. The survey teams look into every aspect of a medical school's operations: admissions, student quality, student finances and loans, curriculum, research, test results, faculty qualifications, departmental structure and function, and so on. The teams, which are made up of representatives (not necessarily members) of the two parent organizations, tend to function in an extremely conservative manner. Ordinarily, members of the inspection teams reflect a broad spectrum of academic interests and approaches. But once assembled for an on-site inspection of another medical school, the members, regardless of prior conviction, tend to become more bureaucratic and more conservative. It is as if the heavy responsibility for accreditation—for giving the official stamp of approval to a medical school, for making decisions that will directly affect the health and lives of thousands of persons—weighs even heavier on each team member at the time of the inspection. Team members then, each imbued with a sense of purpose, tend to coalesce and reinforce each other in their internal caucuses and are prone to arrive at conclusions far more conservative, far more negative, and at times far more punitive than individual members might impose if left to their own devices.

Therefore by their very nature, inspection teams generally stick with the familiar and review innovative programs with great care. The burden of proof for effectiveness in medical education falls heavily on the innovator, and even when proof is offered, it is not always accepted as valid. In short, the LCME is a conservative organization that adheres closely to the status quo.

A little historical background provides some perspective on why this is so. The medical school of 1960 was commonly viewed as a medical-research factory that incidentally produced doctors. That is not to say that no thought was given to medical education, but the majority of faculty were primarily driven by their research priorities. The basic sciences were taught departmentally by the traditional lecture-laboratory method. As far as clinical training was concerned, a fundamental belief prevailed that students who were exposed to the academic pattern of patient care in a clinical-research environment would automatically become good doctors. Learning was largely experiential, that is, patient-based. The textbook, no matter how unselective, provided the curriculum.

The results were pretty good. Between the teaching program outlined above, the selectivity of medical schools in choosing the best and the brightest students, and postdoctoral residency and fellowship programs that were extensions of the medical-school clinical-training years, U.S. medical schools indeed turned out, by any objective measure, the best-trained physicians in the world. This is well-documented by the Educational Commission for

Foreign Medical Graduates scores, specialty-board certification scores, and
the practical experience of hundreds of residency-training programs. The
selectivity of U.S. medical schools is confirmed by the relatively poor performance on comparable examinations of U.S. medical school "rejects" who
persist in attaining a medical degree outside of the United States and
Canada. As a group, U.S. citizens with non-U.S. training have consistently
performed far below U.S. medical-school averages.

   The LCME had plenty of cause for concern during the twenty years
from 1965 to 1985, when, in reaction to a perceived doctor shortage, three
dozen or more brand-new medical schools came into being, increasing the
number of U.S. schools to 125. All of them had to be surveyed for accreditation. Furthermore, many schools branched, regionalized, or simply expanded, and in these cases it was not always clear whether LCME approval was
required or not. The number of medical-school graduates per annum
increased from roughly eight thousand to sixteen thousand. Moreover, many
of the new schools evolved in nontraditional forms, UICOM being a prime
example. The LCME therefore assumed a very vigorous, interventional, and
educationally conservative posture that put it in opposition or even conflict
with many of the newer forms of medical education and organization that
were emerging. Above all, LCME site-visit teams tended to look for solid
departmental structures of full-time faculty in both the basic-medical and
clinical sciences; an active research program at all levels funded preferably
by peer-reviewed grants from National Institutes of Health, National Science
Foundation, or from an organization such as the American Cancer Society
or the American Heart Association; and finally, a research-oriented teaching
hospital that provided for the core clinical experiences. The survey teams
focused on financing and personnel. As surprising as it may seem, the
LCME site visitors paid less attention to curricular details on the assumption that if the traditional building blocks were in place, a good educational
program would follow naturally.

   At the center of LCME stalwarts who tended to define educational quality by budget and numbers of full-time faculty stood James Schofield. Jim
was a wry, seasoned conservative who frequently represented the Association
of American Medical Colleges on site visits. Although an anatomist by profession, by 1970 he worked full-time with the AAMC and frequently participated in accreditation surveys as secretary to the LCME site-visit team. He
was well-known and feared as a person who carried the torch for all that

was conservative about the LCME. When Jim Schofield served as secretary to the site-visit team, nontraditional schools took notice.

Bill Grove's nontraditional design of a single college with several semi-autonomous schools gave the LCME accreditation teams severe problems. The teams had difficulty coping with the administrative structure of the College of Medicine and evaluating semiautonomous schools as parts of the whole. The surveyors uniformly would have preferred to accredit each school individually, but could not do that because each of schools was too far from the mode on which accreditation criteria were based. First, the LCME had no procedures to evaluate one-year or three-year medical schools because none had existed in that form previously. Second, none of the new schools created by Bill Grove had either admission authority or degree-granting authority. Third, although each school had its own curriculum, curriculum approval was a college function; similarly, while each school had its own student promotions committee, student promotion was ultimately a college function, and so on.

The regionalization of medical education in Illinois raised many other basic questions for the accrediting body. First of all, how many medical schools did the University of Illinois claim to have? One? Two? Four? Six? At one time or another within the complex Illinois system run by Bill Grove, there were six full deans and one executive dean to head the Abraham Lincoln School of Medicine, the School of Basic Medical Sciences-Medical Center, Peoria School of Medicine, Rockville School of Medicine, and SBMS/SCM-UC, and, of course, I was actually the official dean of two schools. The title "dean" implies a degree of autonomy characteristic of an independent program. Certainly, that was what was meant in California where the University of California at San Francisco was a separately accredited and distinct medical school from the University of California at Los Angeles. However, Bill Grove knew that none of the new-format schools of UICOM was capable of independent accreditation (save the combined ALSM and SBMS-MC). Therefore, he argued that all of the new schools in the Illinois system were part of a whole UICOM and that separate accreditation was not required for each unit. He realized that the separate accreditation of units was not only very expensive, but also would dilute the power and authority that the University of Illinois at the Medical Center held as the only publicly funded medical school in the state. Southern Illinois University became the second publicly funded medical school in Illinois in

1969. Although SIU slipped out of Grove's grasp, and in doing so comman-
deered an extraordinary amount of the new state funding for medical education, he managed to control developments in Rockford, Peoria, and
Urbana-Champaign by creating partial schools that were more than branches, but less than whole units. In the Urbana case, the artifice of SBMS-UC
and SCM-UC, which were forbidden from officially combining, was a prime
example. But for purposes of accreditation, Bill Grove argued that all
UICOM units shared the college's umbrella.

But the LCME had other questions for UICOM. If we claimed to be a
single medical school, how could we guarantee the uniformity of our product? What controls were in place to assure the LCME that a graduate of the
Peoria School of Medicine was equivalent to a graduate of the Abraham
Lincoln School of Medicine? In fact, the organization of UICOM was
sensibly designed on paper with such questions in mind, and answers were
readily available if the LCME representatives and Dr. Schofield were willing
to listen. The real difficulty the college had was in the implementation of the
design. On paper, the college committee structure was organized to assure
curricular uniformity, and the college had installed a senior comprehensive
examination structure that assured that anyone graduating from any regional unit of UICOM possessed a minimal degree of competence. A College
Committee on Instruction and Appraisal (CCIA) had overall jurisdiction of
the curriculum at all four sites, and membership on the CCIA was drawn
from each. In theory, all the curricula of the several semiautonomous
schools were subject to review and approval by the CCIA. This was a somewhat revolutionary concept in medical education because it removed from
the province of the departments the overall responsibility for curriculum
content and appraisal. Although the departments generally designed their
own curricula and created the test items, these elements were subject to
higher authority, a difference that took some getting used to.

The story becomes more complicated, however, because each of the six
semiautonomous schools had its own equivalent of a CCIA to review and
approve the local curricular offerings so that, in effect, the departmental
curricula were subject to both local and collegewide review. Thus, what
seemed so nicely organized on paper became a bureaucratic nightmare for
the faculty. It posed the prospect of endless committee meetings and excessive travel to and from Chicago where the meetings of the CCIA were held.
The travel could have and should have been reduced to a minimum through

the option of teleconferencing, but that was not offered. Faculty members were frequently forced to spend six hours in travel to Chicago and back for a one- or two-hour meeting. So the demand for meetings was an unconscionable drain on faculty time meant to justify to the LCME that the multi-campus organization was a single college.

In September 1976, I did a survey of the time committed to Chicago meetings. Twenty-three faculty and staff members were asked to review their calendars over the preceding twelve months and to provide a reasonable estimate of days spent at Chicago meetings. The total was 234 days or approximately ten days per year per member of the faculty or staff. When pharmacologist Byron Kemper, then in his tenure probationary period, was asked to serve on a college subcommittee of the CCIA to review the curriculum of the Peoria School of Medicine, he responded to the Office of the Executive Dean as follows:

> Thank you for the invitation to serve on a subcommittee of the Educational Policy Committee to review the curriculum of the Peoria School of Medicine. I must respectfully decline. I serve on the College Committee on Student Appraisal, two active subcommittees of CCSA, the Basic Science Skills Subcommittee and the Basic Science Subcommittee, the SBMS-UC Self-Study Task Force for Accreditation, the SBMS-UC Student Affairs Committee, a subcommittee of that committee, the Student Appraisal Subcommittee (which I chair) and the SOLS/SBMS-UC Environmental Health and Safety Committee. In August, September, and the first week of October, I have spent 61 hours in committee and faculty meetings plus an undetermined amount of time preparing and reading reports.
>
> As a junior faculty member, I am required to demonstrate excellence in teaching and research in order to advance professionally. Given these demands on my time and the priorities I must and desire to give to teaching and research, I am sure you understand my rejection of additional administrative burdens.

Kemper's letter told the story far better than shear numbers would indicate. Were we a medical school or an asylum without walls?

Although college committee meetings sometimes were held in Peoria, Rockford, or Urbana, most were held in Chicago, 135 miles away from our campus. The committee responsibilities were particularly onerous for our

SBMS/SCM faculty, which was the smallest group in the college. They not only had to serve on our own site committees, but also had to represent the school on the college committees. We begged for telephone conference calls, but our pleadings were generally ignored for at least the first decade of our existence. There was a conservative element in the college that liked to sit down in a committee meeting to "see the whites of their eyes." Although in-person meetings can be useful and serve an important purpose, most of the business that we did in the college committee meetings, such as Instruction and Appraisal, Student Promotion, Student Admission, and even the College Executive Committee, could have been done just as effectively by telephone conference calls.

Curricular review was another area in which form was followed by dysfunction. In theory, the several curricula of the College of Medicine schools were to be reviewed and approved by the College Committee on Instruction and Appraisal so that we might claim to be a single college with a varied but centrally approved curriculum. Prior to any LCME accreditation visit, considerable attention was paid to this principle, but there was in fact little intellectual cross-fertilization of educational principles or content. Witness the following memo from biochemist Dick Gumport to me on January 26, 1977, before a pending LCME visit: "Yesterday, I met with a subcommittee of Educational Policy from the Chicago campus. I was told that the purpose of the meeting was to review our curriculum. The group of people who visited us appeared almost totally ignorant of our entire operation, including the curriculum. It was evident that some of them never opened the document since, after explaining the overall curriculum, I was asked if each unit merely consisted of a list of objectives. The group appeared to have done little preparation for the visit. I am appalled that a group from the Center for Educational Development did not have a list of objectives to guide them in their review."

It is not difficult to understand, therefore, the mixed signals the LCME received from the college. Bill Grove and the Chicago administration presented the site visitors with a rational and smooth operating plan that had all i's dotted and t's crossed. The committee structure provided the college with central authority while allowing the opportunity for controlled innovation at the regional sites. Furthermore, UICOM, unlike most other U.S. medical schools, had instituted a sophisticated two-day senior comprehensive-examination system that demanded student attainment of a minimum pass level before the MD would be awarded. No student graduated until that examination was passed. This meant that students who had satisfactorily completed all necessary courses and clerkships and had passed National Board Parts I and II examinations still remained at risk for failure until they had passed the College Senior Comprehensive Examination, which was administered in the fourth year of medical school, sometimes as late as three months before scheduled graduation. The "Senior Comp," as it was known, served as a powerful incentive for students to study hard throughout their four years. It also served as a leveler for a large student body with vastly different skills. One and all had to pass that exam.

But the downside of the Senior Comp exceeded its utility. A criterion-based exam, it was theoretically possible to fail the entire class of three hundred if the minimum pass level was set too high. Indeed, on one occasion we were startled to learn barely three months before the graduation date and at a time when the students had already made their commitments to residency training sites, that 25 percent of the senior class had failed the January Senior Comp. The college was faced with a potential catastrophe and massive embarrassment. There was no way the college could or would notify about seventy-five residency programs throughout the nation that the UICOM graduate selected for their program had failed a last-minute examination and would not be showing up on July 1 to begin residency training. A "make up" examination was quickly prepared and administered in April to those who had failed the test given in January. Thankfully, only a few failed the second exam, but I argued strongly against retention of the Senior Comp because it literally determined in January that seventy-five students were unfit to graduate, and three months later reversed that judgment. There had to be a better and fairer way to evaluate students without such a serious gating examination that took place so late in the course of instruction.

The Senior Comp had other disadvantages as well. No other act taken by UICOM generated more lasting hostility toward the college than that examination. Students who had passed all courses and clerkships and who had satisfactory scores on NBME exams, yet who failed the Senior Comp, were required to repeat their fourth year. Needless to say, those students who had performed at satisfactory levels in every other sphere, yet were caught in the Senior Comp mesh, were forever embittered. So too were many of the UICOM graduates who surmounted the Senior Comp hurdle but who were nevertheless very angry with their alma mater for placing before them this formidable obstacle that literally threatened their careers. One result of this anger is that UICOM has a large but relatively detached alumni. Many of them have yet to forgive UICOM for forcing this pregraduation indignity upon them.

Finally, although there were many operational problems with the system, it had been set up in a responsible manner. Its form promised adherence to appropriate standards of quality, even if the function under that form left much to be desired. If the LCME had possessed the will to understand this new organism within its own frame of reference, things might have gone a little smoother between the LCME and the college. As it was, the LCME viewed the college through its own value system and saw a highly disorganized, frequently demoralized, and unnecessarily complex system that somehow turned out qualified physicians, but a system that it believed would ultimately falter, leading to an inferior product. Forced to look at a new theory of medical-school organization, the LCME balked. Not exactly certain of what it would accept, the LCME nevertheless placed heavy pressure on the college to change its form to a more classical, more easily understood model. Although UICOM was not completely without fault in presenting itself to the LCME, the results of this confrontation led to ten tension-ridden years between 1970 and 1980, and to some serious problems for SCM-UC.

Yet, while the LCME was thundering at the management of UICOM and threatening it with probation, UICOM was still graduating three hundred doctors annually who were well-qualified by any standard, and who by NBME test scores were significantly above U.S. averages. Nevertheless, without the accreditation umbrella of the college as a whole, our innovative program at SBMS-UC probably would never have been accredited despite the impressive achievements of our students. The pity of it all was that the same college umbrella that shielded us from the LCME was also attached to a millstone that weighed heavily about our necks and that ultimately prevented us from reaching many of our objectives.

CHAPTER 22

LCME Meets UICOM

THE LCME TOOK NOTICE of the 1969 UICOM reorganization. Last visited in 1962, the college was due for a reaccreditation survey in 1970. The 1970 survey team gave UICOM a favorable report, and the LCME granted UICOM full approval for seven years, which could have lasted until 1977.

The 1970 LCME report noted, "New experimental programs were being launched in Champaign, Peoria, and Rockford, all under the direction of the Executive Dean of the College of Medicine." The LCME also noted its interest in watching these developments and "invited" the college to inform the LCME formally at intervals on the status of these developments. Subsequently, Bill Grove submitted a lengthy status report, dated August 26, 1971, which summarized the clinical developments in Rockford and Peoria and which noted the beginning of a program in the basic medical sciences at Urbana, including the proposed construction of a Medical Sciences facility there. Grove was answered by an LCME letter of "reasonable assurance" that was a signal from the LCME to the college that on the basis of what Grove affirmed, the development of SBMS-UC was proceeding satisfactorily.

Bill Grove sent informal progress reports to the LCME on "the developing units" in 1972 and 1973. However, early in 1973, seeking recognition for his visionary expansion, Grove formally requested that a full LCME survey of the college be made during the 1973–74 academic year, two-and-a-half years earlier than necessary. The change from informal and voluntarily generated progress reports to an official site survey by the LCME was a major turning point in UICOM history. Bill Grove was confident of a favorable outcome from the review team, but he was proved dead wrong. He never anticipated the criticism that would ensue and the crisis that would build over time. Given the mind-set of the LCME, the confrontation was inevitable whether it came in 1974 or 1977.

The fateful survey that opened hostilities between the LCME and

UICOM took place March 4 through 7, 1974. Because of the anticipated complexity, the LCME sent a site-visit team of seven persons to review four sites in three days. The survey team quickly detected widespread faculty discontent and perceived the form-function problems. It was immediately struck by the elaborate committee structure of the college and noted that although the committees were "designed to deal with collegewide problems, the committee structure in itself may produce stresses and misunderstandings," which was a major understatement. The survey team went on to recommend that great care be taken in making appointments to the college committees so as to provide "adequate representation for important and academically productive elements of the faculty." The team urged that the "peripheral" schools downstate remain small until they could be fully evaluated. The team stated its belief that none of the peripheral schools could have expected individual accreditation without the central support and administrative structure of the College of Medicine in Chicago. The committee was commendatory, however, in its review of the curricular development based on educational objectives that was evident throughout the college, but most well-developed at SBMS-UC. They also praised our efforts to develop better methods of student appraisal, particularly the computerized Level III examination system.

However, the team was critical of college plans (predicated on an enrollment scheme that would eventually reach five hundred per year) to increase class size. The team demanded a limit of no more than sixty-four students to enter SBMS-UC in the fall of 1974, a recommendation that was more of a relief than a hardship because our small faculty was already straining with the limited number of students we had. However, the LCME gratuitously added an additional limitation to the number planned for a fall 1975 admission. Additional enrollment increases in the college, we were told, should await the report of the next survey team. The issues were deemed so critical by the LCME that they called for a repeat visit in October 1974, just six months later. Formal LCME action was to be deferred until the second 1974 visit had been completed.

Bill Grove was very secretive about the LCME conclusions. He was obviously disappointed by the results. What he expected to be a minor triumph had turned into a chilling confrontation. He did not share the whole LCME critique with anyone on his administrative team. Instead, he copied for each of us only those elements of the report that referred to our own schools.

Grove was angry and embarrassed by the LCME conclusions. He viewed the enrollment restriction as unacceptable because he saw the mission of the College of Medicine to boost its enrollment level to about four hundred to five hundred students within a few years, and he was shaken by the need to have two surveys within a single year. We discussed among ourselves the possibility that we would ignore the dictates of the LCME and go our own way. We worked from such a different model of medical education that the survey teams did not have the background to appreciate us. Jim Schofield, particularly, was singled out as a reviewer with a rigidly conservative mentality.

Grove believed that it was an error for the survey team to have split when they visited the three campuses remote from Chicago. Groups of two members each visited Rockford, Peoria, and Urbana-Champaign. The divided approach, he argued, prevented the whole team from getting a better understanding of what he was trying to accomplish. As a result, Bill Grove insisted that in October the entire team visit each of the four sites. The LCME agreed to the request.

Not very much changed in the college function between March and October 1974, when the second set of visitors came. We had prepared for the visit with a plea to all parties that they not air "dirty linen" to the visitors. Instead, they should catalogue and underscore our successes whenever the opportunity arose. The second LCME survey team of 1974 tried to be more helpful. The visit was relatively uneventful and nonconfrontational. The visitors saw many of the same faults as did the earlier group, but appeared to be more sympathetic to Grove's explanations of the necessary organizational complexity. Their final report, which was lengthy and detailed, included three reasonable recommendations for SBMS-UC.

First, the visitors noted that some provision should be made to readily identify the student that does not do well in an independent-study program. They correctly picked up on this problem at Urbana-Champaign, a problem inherent in the structure of the college. Students who were self-motivated and independent thrived at SBMS-UC, but having no control over our own admissions, with each passing year we had to accept a larger proportion of students who preferred spoon-fed information. There was no way we could select students who wanted to pursue the independent multifaceted approach that we had initiated. Our lack of control over the makeup of our own student body devalued our program, but there was nothing we could do about it.

Second, the LCME team correctly recognized the conflicts between the UIUC independent departments and the SBMS-UC faculty members who were assigned teaching responsibilities both within and outside of the medical school. The LCME noted an urgent need to clarify faculty responsibility for teaching the basic medical sciences.

Finally, the survey team noted that clinical education at Urbana-Champaign, scheduled to begin in the fall of 1976, appeared feasible if faculty recruiting could proceed apace. On the other hand, the team found multiple problems at Rockford, Peoria, and even the Abraham Lincoln School of Medicine in Chicago, so that the final specific recommendations of the October 1974 LCME survey team, while granting the College of Medicine approval until 1977, also stipulated that the LCME receive annual reports describing progress in those areas of faculty, facilities, and curriculum that were criticized. In the annual reports, the college was directed to include the projected number of students to be admitted into each regional unit of the college each year. The team did not limit our enrollment at this time, but tied enrollment numbers to the acceptability of future progress reports. With respect to starting SCM-UC, the LCME requested one year's notice before any students were matriculated.

Although anger and concern were evident in the rest of the college, we in Urbana saw the 1974 survey as giving us two-and-a-half years of breathing room. By the time the 1977 survey team visited on March 14–18, 1977, Mort Creditor had done substantial work in curriculum development and recruitment, particularly at the veterans' hospital, where we had five acceptable full-time academic faculty members. We were prepared to present the site-visit team with a feasible plan for initiating clinical education at Urbana-Champaign.

Alas, the March 1977 site-visit team was not prepared to evaluate a new clinical program. It was going for bigger game. The visitors seemed aggressively intent on diminishing Bill Grove for daring to persist with the complex organizational system he had created. Yet the brunt of LCME criticism fell on gentle Truman Anderson, not on Bill Grove, who had moved upstairs to the Vice Chancellor position.

As it turned out, the March 1977 visit proved critical to the future of the college and prepared the way for a separate survey of SCM-UC in time for us to begin instruction in the fall of 1978. The LCME by 1977 was fixed on disassembling the complex college administration as unworkable and was determined to pressure UICOM to alter its governance in favor of an organizational model that had some semblance of the single dean and departmental structure that characterized the more traditional schools. At the team's exit interview with the president and the executive dean, contrary to the team's usual policy of providing observations and recommendations, the visitors provided only the former. The LCME had decided that specific recommendations would be withheld from UICOM until the governance issues were clarified and a separate site visit to review the clinical program of SCM-UC in early 1978 had been completed. This left the College of Medicine and the university itself dangling for fifteen months, not knowing whether the medical schools would be accredited. Clearly, it was unlikely that the largest single medical-education program in the United States, which undoubtedly graduated capable physicians, would be placed on probation or even disaccredited. But a struggle of wills had developed between the University of Illinois and the LCME, and its resolution, ironically, devolved not on Bill Grove, but on Truman Anderson.

The team's report called the College of Medicine "an extraordinarily complex organization" that "presents an example of unresolved counterproductive tension between the need for differentiation of operating units versus central managerial requirements for integration, coordination, and control of resources." The team also noted that "numerous secondary problems have emerged to varying degrees in some highly critical areas" because the "structure, function, and authority/responsibility relationships" between the college and the schools were not uniformly agreed upon.

The report then went on to cite examples, such as the limited effectiveness of faculty in bringing about change, which in turn was reflected in widespread frustration and lowered faculty morale. The team sensed futility, apathy, and withdrawal by some faculty members and cited as one of the causes the enormous consumption of faculty time and energy in travel to and from committee meetings. College faculty had differing perceptions regarding their responsibility for student appraisal, evaluation, and promotion. The team observed that some students felt lost as individuals within the large and impersonal educational system. The visitors also noted that several schools and departments had difficulty filling vital leadership posts.

The team acknowledged that despite the problems cited an impressive number of MD degrees were awarded annually without evidence that the graduates were not properly prepared for the next phase of their education.

However, the visitors believed strongly that the managerial difficulties would ultimately lead to downgrading in education.

With respect to our program, the team picked up some of the faculty's discontent and the administration's frustration associated with the on-again, off-again establishment of a clinical program. The visitors also noticed, as had others previously, the delicate and complex relationships that basic-science faculty experienced with the School of Basic Medical Sciences and the university departments.

As we prepared for the 1977 visit, we did not need the LCME to inform us of the tensions within the faculty. These were reflected in the curriculum itself. Gradually, one by one, we were giving up precious elements of the curriculum to accommodate either faculty or administrative needs. A cartoon sent to me by Bill Sorlie in November 1977 emphasized our plight. It showed a series of four dominos and was titled, "Where are we going?" The first domino was labeled *Program as We Know It*, the second *Deletion of Pharmacology and Pathology in the M-1 Year*, the third was *Deletion of the MDA/MDE as a Requirement in the M-1 Year*, and the fourth was *Change to a Lecture Format*. Sometimes, I had so many conflicts swirling around me that it was difficult to pick up and hold onto principles in any one. But it was very clear that the curriculum we had lovingly assembled in 1971 could hardly be recognized six years later.

Otherwise, no major problems were attributed to SBMS-UC as a one-year school. Our disappointment on learning that SCM-UC was not to be reviewed in March 1977 was mollified by the news from the LCME that SCM-UC's survey would take place February 22 and 23, 1978, in time to get started, if approved, by the fall of 1978.

CHAPTER 23

LCME's Green Light and a Machiavellian Deal

AFTER SEVEN YEARS of treading water, we were finally scheduled for an accreditation visit of our own. When the grand event finally did take place in February 1978, it turned out to be a piece of cake. Truman Anderson's indispensable support was evident in an eloquent cover note that he attached to the presurvey material sent January 5, 1978 to the LCME: "I believe [this material] gives the site visit team representing the LCME a sound basis for understanding and judging the very special, innovative approach planned by our Urbana unit. This submission is the product of more than six years of thought, lengthy debate and enormous amounts of hard work by a group of truly gifted, dedicated scientists, educators and physicians…I trust that the site team and subsequently the LCME will find as much excitement in this proposal as do those of us in the university and the College of Medicine. We are most anxious to get on with it."

We were also relieved to learn that Jim Schofield was not on the team. Ed Peterson, who worked for the AMA and who served as team secretary, was much better known to us. Ed was a gentle pragmatist and, in contrast to Schofield, was not an ideologue.

Mort Creditor had updated and improved the documentation that was originally prepared for the 1977 visit. Like his presentation to the Illinois Board of Higher Education two years earlier, his brief to this LCME committee was thorough and convincing. The survey team was much intrigued by the Medical Scholars Program, which undoubtedly contributed to its favorable evaluation of our clinical development. However, some members were skeptical about our chances for clinical success in the absence of a university hospital, although they did acknowledge the excellent facilities at Mercy Hospital and Carle Clinic. We showed our LCME visitors a variety of teaching strengths, including Bill Tanner, Director of the Danville Family

Practice Residency Program, and Paul Yardy, Director of the Carle Foundation Family Practice Residency Program.

The group of physicians that Mort Creditor had assembled at both
Carle and Mercy Hospitals also impressed the survey team. For the most
part, these physicians were very capable professionally and anxious to teach.
They covered practically all specialty and subspecialty teaching. All were
prepared to work on curriculum development, to teach as volunteers, or
both. I had been talking about the development of the clinical program for
eight years and knew practically every physician in the community. The
opening of the clinical school was the event all of us were waiting for.
Indeed, many of the younger doctors had selected Urbana-Champaign as a
place to practice because of the projected medical school. It came as no surprise, therefore, that we could demonstrate a significant physician interest in
a local clinical medical school. Both Carle and Christie Clinics recognized
that the presence of SCM-UC in the community made their own recruitment efforts easier and more effective. The community at large benefited
from the influx of doctors who supported medical education, and those
same physicians at Carle and Christie Clinics responded magnificently to
our request for teaching support.

In summing up the program, the report stated, "The LCME team feels
that the curriculum as a whole, and Phase III [the logic pathways approach
to pathophysiology] especially, represents a truly creative and carefully
worked out approach and that Phases II and III [the preclinical phases] are
ready to proceed."

The team also praised the leadership of the program for fostering the
cooperation of "a variety of existing scholarly faculty to plan educational
programs, particularly in behavioral, traditional non-medical sciences
including computer sciences, nutrition, anthropology, sociology, political
science, economics, business administration, biological sciences, and law."
The visitors added, "Special commendation should be noted for the attempt
to include the social, psychological, environmental, economic, anthropolog-
ic, epidemiological aspects of medicine into Phase III of the curriculum."

After throwing the bouquets, the team registered two main concerns:
Our residency training programs were only minimally developed, and there
were no clear lines of responsibility for educational programs, such as internal medicine and pediatrics, among others.

That latter criticism simply meant that SCM-UC had not departmentalized. I had purposely avoided departmentalization because we knew we were going to be a different kind of medical school without the usual academic clinical department chairs. Therefore, there were no clear lines of responsibility in the departmental sense. We had, instead, an organized volunteer faculty in the necessary clinical core disciplines.

Probing further, the site visit team stated, "There has been no attempt to align such clinical educational programs with already existing accredited programs such as those in Chicago." The visitors discerned correctly that our relationship with Chicago was purely administrative. Aside from a few faculty members participating in the creation of the senior comprehensive examination, there was virtually no intellectual interchange among any of the four sites of the college. The attempt to have us effectively run as a single medical school was a chimera.

Nevertheless, despite the obvious weaknesses for which there were no immediate answers, the team recommended SCM-UC's approval as a "branch clinical campus which must be considered as a part of the accreditation of the University of Illinois medical school." They continued that the clinical school for twelve students be initiated, contingent on the development of an acceptable teaching program in pharmacology. (Although our program was approved for twelve students, by the time the 342 M-2 students were distributed on the four clinical campuses, thirteen had matriculated at SCM-UC.)

On June 30, 1978 the LCME finally delivered to President Corbally its findings and recommendations from three separate surveys:

- the March 14–18, 1977 visit to the College as a whole;
- he February 22–23, 1978 visit to accredit SCM-UC;
- and a May 9–10, 1978 special visit to the Peoria School of Medicine, which had some problems of its own.

On the basis of information gathered from these visits, the LCME voted to confirm full accreditation of the college for five years with a resurvey expected during the 1982–83 academic year. The LCME directed that the entry class should be held at its current level of 342 students and requested that the dean (the LCME didn't recognize the title of executive dean) to submit an annual report dealing with the identified problems. More importantly for

those of us in Urbana, the LCME authorized "the inauguration of the
Medical Scholars Program, comprising twelve students in 1978," mentioning
as well our need to increase the number of full-time faculty members in
major clinical fields, to establish a better departmental structure, to conclude
stronger affiliation agreements with our teaching hospitals, and the need for
residency-training programs, especially in internal medicine.

The favorable review of our nascent clinical program proved to be but a
brief respite in the clash between the LCME and UICOM bureaucracies. The
LCME still recognized our program (as well as the Peoria and Rockford programs) as a mere branch of the "real" medical school in Chicago. Bill Grove
still wanted his regionalization concept to survive, and he defended it vigorously against LCME criticism he thought harsh, uninformed, and unfair.

Caught in the middle of this contest of wills was Truman Anderson.
Although he was the executive dean of UICOM, he perceived his freedom to
manage was severely limited by Grove, who simply couldn't lay aside the
dean's reins of his beloved college. A gentleman to the core, Anderson was
not the kind of street fighter who could parry repeated assaults on his judgment. He recognized the basis for the LCME's complaints and patiently and
carefully cultivated LCME personnel to defuse the tension between that
body and the college. Yet he believed in the validity of the UICOM innovation and defended the college before the LCME. In our private chats, he
looked tired and depressed. Describing his problems to me one day, he summarized his state of mind by saying, "Who needs this bullcrap?" It was clear
that he was thinking of resigning. Indeed, in October 1978, less than three
years after he assumed the position of executive dean and barely two
months after SCM-UC took its first students, Truman Anderson submitted
his resignation, effective January 31, 1979. The Urbana clinical program was
losing an important friend, and SCM-UC was once again vulnerable.

Because of Truman's strong advocacy of SCM-UC, his replacement was
an immediate, critical, and high-priority issue for us. I had to move and to
move quickly. For a number of reasons, I thought of Mort Creditor as a possible successor to Truman. During his four years at SCM-UC, Creditor built
up a strong clinical curriculum and faculty establishment. By the time the
LCME survey team arrived at SCM-UC in February 1978, Mort Creditor
presented the visitors with a scorecard that showed a respectable number of
full-time faculty as well as a sizable and deeply committed volunteer clinical
faculty. When SCM-UC opened July 8, 1978, Mort Creditor personally led

the teaching program, emphasizing the logic pathways and student behavioral skills of thoroughness, reliability, and accuracy. He was a popular and well-respected teacher.

When Truman resigned, Mort was busy shoring up some of our weaknesses and preparing for the first SCM-UC progress report to the LCME. When the report was submitted in February 1979, organization and planning for the core and elective clinical clerkships were virtually complete for all four years. Committees had been formed and charged to review and strengthen each of the core clerkships and to establish evaluation procedures. Clinical Education Centers (CECs) had been designated at Carle, Mercy, and Danville Veterans Administration Medical Center (DVAMC). The CEC in theory was the university presence in each designated teaching hospital, and the CEC director was the salaried individual responsible for coordinating all teaching programs at that site. The concept of the CEC directorship was administratively flawed in that it provided maximum responsibility with limited authority. The CEC director had no budget, and was entirely beholden to volunteer or minimally salaried physicians to deliver the clinical-teaching program. It was not an easy charge, but with proper administrative support and diplomacy, it was a necessary position to establish a smooth flow of activity within the hospital sites. The CEC director also served as an important bridge between the dean's office and the hospital administration.

The February 1979 progress report also boasted twenty-one full-time and six part-time faculty members leading an educational program for thirteen students. Of course, we counted our physician teachers at the DVAMC as full salaried, although their salaries did not come from SCM-UC. Thus, DVAMC accounted for ten of the twenty-one full-salaried faculty members we reported. The plan for our teaching program was to establish a curriculum for every core and elective clerkship that could be delivered at each of the three CECs.

We still lacked a full range of graduate medical education (i.e., residency) programs that some medical educators believe are indispensable to undergraduate medical education. But beginning new residencies in the late 1970s and early 1980s was no simple task. Residencies are expensive operations funded by "pass-through" dollars, which are hidden in the hospital charges or embedded in hospital reimbursements from insurance companies or Medicare. Many early warning signs signaled that hospitals were going to have to tighten their belts to survive the new climate of cost containment sweeping the country. We elected to limit our residency programs to family practice, internal medicine and surgery. Arthur Leonard, CEC Director at Mercy Hospital was also charged with the responsibility of establishing a new Internal Medicine Residency, and the recently appointed Chief of Surgery at DVAMC was charged with the establishment of a new surgical residency. It had been agreed that all residencies would use the facilities of our three teaching hospitals and all of the hospitals were to share in the costs proportionately.

Meanwhile, we reported serious trouble with our family-practice residencies. Funds from AHES had been drastically reduced, and the Danville family-practice residency was on the ropes because neither of the Danville hospitals, Lakeview or St. Elizabeth's, wished to assume fiscal responsibility. Likewise, the Carle Foundation Hospital family-practice residency was failing because of its inability to attract satisfactory residents. Although we were coming up short on residencies, we argued that our curriculum was better for the absence of residents because it meant that our students would be exposed directly to the expertise provided by confident, board-certified specialists.

Mort Creditor was at the heart of all the developments that I have summarized above. During the four years Mort had been with me at SBMS/SCM-UC, he clearly had made monumental contributions. In staff meetings where we developed policy, Mort was vocal and effective. As we worked together, Mort more and more became a "co-dean." My style of administration was to get the best effort possible from staff members by giving them major responsibility and then keeping out of their way as they solved their problems. I tried never to micromanage or second-guess their decisions. This approach worked extraordinarily well with a person like Mort Creditor, who gave 150 percent effort at all times, and, indeed, the style worked well with all my staff.

Over time, however, the relations between Mort and me became strained. It seemed that we argued more and more about smaller and smaller policy differences. In his never-ending search for "quality," Mort often lost sight of the difference between "quality" and "reality," and rejected many of my pragmatic solutions to problems that confronted us. Although Mort and I were in general agreement that it would be many years before we could assemble an effective academic team, he continued to push for excellence in some of the clinical areas where excellence, as he narrowly defined it, was lacking, a thrust that embarrassed some of our clinician teachers. We often argued bitterly in the privacy of our offices—arguments with raised voices that were overheard by our staffs.

From my point of view, Mort never quite understood my close relationship with our main constituency for SCM-UC, the clinicians of Urbana-Champaign, who would ultimately be the backbone of our clinical-teaching program. I had made it my business to know practically every physician within a fifty-mile radius on a first-name basis. They were all my friends for almost ten years, and it hurt me to hear Mort, even in camera, discuss their weaknesses from his "ivory tower" point of view. Mort insisted that he was very sensitive to the feelings of our clinical faculty and believed that he handled them well. This may have been true in many cases, but in too many others it was not an accurate observation. Many physicians felt intimidated and threatened by Mort Creditor.

I began to receive strong signals from hospital clinicians and others that Mort was severely criticizing our own program and its faculty to students and others. Some complained to me that he was undermining my own position as dean and acting as if he were the dean himself. Mort vigorously denied these charges when I discussed them with him. He argued that we might "fight like hell in the privacy of the conference room," but on the street he was very, very (he loved using the repetitive adverb) discreet. I am sure that he believed this was the case, but Mort also exuded body language in unmistakable ways. When he wanted to get a point across, he might deliver friendly and conciliatory words from his mouth but give an entirely different message with his face and body. After one particularly tense discussion regarding his communications with some of our affiliated hospitals, Mort sent a memorandum dated April 22, 1977, which said, "This morning you made it clear to me that I cannot be trusted to deal with the hospitals because I had 'screwed up' in Decatur and Danville. In addition, a few weeks ago, you wondered aloud whether your allowing me to participate in the State of Illinois Department of Public Aid Reimbursement Review Board hadn't biased my negotiating position. Since these are your perceptions, I will no longer engage in any hospital negotiations nor will I participate in any clinical-faculty recruitment activities since these must be carried out in partnership with the hospitals." (To add impact to this memorandum, Creditor blind-copied it to Bill Grove and Truman Anderson, as well as to several local faculty members.)

Having great respect for Mort's ability, drive, and productivity, I neither wanted to follow the advice of some of my closest advisors to "get rid of him," nor did I want to see him withdraw as the memorandum suggested. I did not feel threatened by him. At his best, Mort was of incomparable value to our program; at his worst, he was an overachiever and extremely productive. The thought of finding a comparable replacement daunted me. However, the resignation of Truman Anderson offered an opportunity to resolve the "Mort Creditor problem" in a way that could benefit both SCM-UC and the College of Medicine. If I could sell Mort Creditor to Bill Grove as a replacement for Truman Anderson, not only would I resolve my local problem, but I would also place Mort in a strong position to help *his* school. Machiavelli never made a better deal.

When Truman Anderson threw in the towel, I moved quickly. I met with Grove in Chicago to discuss my problems with Mort Creditor and to suggest to him that Mort be considered a candidate for acting executive dean to replace Truman. Bill Grove knew Mort as an able administrator. I told Grove that I was certain that Mort was never really happy in the small-city atmosphere of Urbana-Champaign and longed to return to Chicago. He and his wife, Una, repeatedly made trips to Chicago to see friends and attend cultural events. For example, they had kept their season tickets for the Chicago Lyric Opera, and reveled in each performance, the long drive from Champaign notwithstanding.

I praised Mort's skills as an administrator, suggesting that Mort would be happier when he was the chief executive officer rather than an associate dean. I told Grove, and believed it to be true, that Mort was relatively unhappy playing second fiddle to me. I added that Mort was a strong organizer who had the ability to lead the college into an acceptable configuration for the LCME. Grove, noncommittal as ever, took the idea under consideration. He asked me whether I would miss Mort's contribution to the clinical program. I replied that although Mort's presence would be missed, I believed the program was established solidly enough that we could do without him in the foreseeable future.

When Bill Grove explored with Mort the possibility of appointing him as acting executive dean pending appointment of a permanent successor, Mort virtually leaped at the idea. He told Grove that he already had plans for attempting to resolve the college governance problems. I do not really know what other options Bill Grove was considering, but he did settle on Morton Creditor on an interim basis and as a major candidate for the permanent position. So on January 31, 1979, barely six months after he had matriculated thirteen students to start the clinical program at Urbana-Champaign as my associate dean, Morton Creditor accepted the position of acting executive dean of the college and moved from his position on my staff to become my boss. I was enthusiastic and delighted at the time and wrote to my faculty on January 23, 1979: "This is to formally announce that Dr. Morton C. Creditor...will be leaving SBMS/SCM-UC on February 1, 1979 to assume responsibility...as the acting executive dean of the College of Medicine. Ms. Una Creditor, assistant to the dean and Mort's wife, will accompany him...This announcement is made with truly mixed feelings. On the one hand, we have lost a valuable and creative teacher, whose contributions to SBMS-UC and SCM-UC were very significant...On the other hand, Mort will assume a key role in the administration of the College of Medicine at a critical period when stabilization is necessary. The SBMS/SCM-UC loss will be the College of Medicine's gain."

Mort Creditor's farewell letter to me was upbeat about the future. In closing, he wrote, "We are going to miss the school, our friends, and the lifestyle of Urbana-Champaign. Fortunately, we will have good reason to stay in touch. I take comfort from the fact that, at least for as long as I am acting as executive dean, my responsibilities include the nurturing of SBMS and SCM."

I thought that I had engineered a genuine coup. I had solved my local, internal problem with Mort Creditor, and at the same time placed him in a position where he would be happy, productive, and content, and where he was in a key position to sustain the newly born and still vulnerable clinical program at Urbana-Champaign.

CHAPTER 24

Domino Effects

ORT CREDITOR'S DEPARTURE left a gaping hole in our clinical program. Once again I had great difficulty in filling the position because of the precarious status of SCM-UC. Nobody wants to join a sinking ship. The survival of our program was not assured and remained a matter of speculation. Although advertisements had turned up candidates for the position, very few of the respondents were qualified. Those who were qualified were too smart to come under the tenuous survival circumstances that existed. Of course, I played the role of perennial optimist, the Candide of our time, and tried to convince potential recruits that there was little doubt that we would develop into a major research-oriented medical school with the Medical Scholars Program as our *raison d'etre*, but there weren't many takers.

Finally, after almost a year, Harold M. Swartz, an MD and Ph.D. joined SBMS/SCM-UC in January 1980 as professor of medicine and associate dean for clinical affairs. An internationally acknowledged expert in the field of electron spin resonance, he also promptly accepted a joint appointment as a member of the Department of Physiology and Biophysics. Hal Swartz turned out to be an excellent choice. (I always kidded him that anyone with the same initials as Harvard Medical School couldn't be all that bad.) He brought with him a keen intellect, an enormous capacity for work, outstanding research skills, and when the going got rough, the ability to slug it out in the streets with the toughest of our opposition.

When Hal negotiated the terms under which he would join us, he insisted on two firm conditions. The first was that in his role as dean for academic affairs, I would provide him with full authority to run the clinical program and to recruit and assign faculty. That was no problem for me, because that was the same deal I had given Mort Creditor. I insisted only on being kept fully informed at all times and agreed that, for the most part, I would intervene only when requested.

His second condition was that he be allowed 20 percent of his time for research. He directed an electron spin resonance laboratory at the Medical College of Wisconsin, Milwaukee, and eventually wanted to move a part of that laboratory to UIUC. I told him that I did not think it would be possible to carry out significant research with the academic responsibilities he was about to assume, but nevertheless, I agreed to his second condition as well. What I did not know then, but would soon learn, was that he was probably one of the brightest, most hard-working, and productive people I could have chosen. He not only assumed a full administrative burden, but he also developed a sound research presence on the campus and was the school's leading generator of funds from indirect cost reimbursements.

Swartz was a gem, albeit a diamond in the rough. In some ways, he was quite similar to Mort Creditor in that he did not suffer fools easily. Also, he was so bright and analyzed situations so quickly that those mortal creatures that were not blessed with such skills were often left behind in a cloud of misunderstanding.

I received criticism at times from every direction and from all sorts of people about Hal, but the criticism was usually about his abrupt, potentially offensive style. The contrast with Mort was striking in two dimensions. First, no one ever claimed that he wanted to undermine or displace me, he was loyal to the core. Second, he was accepted well by the large majority of clinical faculty.

Hal was not "smooth." His frequently abrupt manner drove my staff— Art Leonard (clinical affairs), Rick Schimmel (fiscal affairs), Paula Treichler, and later Bill Sorlie (student affairs)—to distraction. However, Hal did what he promised he would do. He organized the clinical program, to which he added a major component related to Medicine and Society, took control of the Medical Scholars Program, and at the same time developed the most productive research program in the school. (The only drawback to Hal's presence was that the logic pathways approach to pathophysiology languished and was lost without Mort Creditor's leadership.)

Hal Swartz helped out in the political arena as well. He quickly joined my group of close advisors, as we plotted strategy day after day to ward off the political assaults from those who would minimize our contributions to medical education. The assaults had begun anew after Mort Creditor succeeded Truman Anderson.

One of Truman's last acts as executive dean was to send a final progress report to Jim Schofield and the LCME. He submitted individual progress reports from each regional school as the LCME had requested, but he declined to submit an expected progress report for the college as a whole. He knew the LCME's foremost concern was the college's organizational complexity and explained that at the time that he resigned, both the chancellor and vice chancellor for academic affairs "agreed that the organizational structure of the College of Medicine will be subjected to thorough study…over the next two years [and] changes…difficult to predict" would result.

It did not take long for Mort Creditor to announce who was in charge and to confidently predict organizational reform. In a letter to Schofield, dated February 9, 1979, barely a week after Creditor became acting executive dean, he wrote, "Truman Anderson sent you the unedited reports of the deans of each of the schools: nor would I think of editing those reports. However, I believe it would be useful if I added some commentary which would give you some idea of how the office is supporting the progress which the deans have reported…The VCAA in appointing me to the acting executive deanship gave me the mandate to proceed on these matters with full authority of the deanship…

"The College is large and complex, but its organization is rational. I believe that with vigorous leadership the various concerns can be addressed." To me, it has become clear that by "vigorous leadership," he meant "with Mort Creditor in charge." He went on, "This is not an ingenuous denial of the problems which the LCME has perceptively surfaced…It is our judgment that the current problems can best be addressed by stabilizing the existing governance. This does not rule out orderly examination of administrative organization in the near future as part of continuing long-range planning."

Mort's letter was copied to all of the college deans, President Corbally, Chancellor Begando, and Vice Chancellor Grove.

For all of his pains, Mort Creditor received an unwelcome blast from Jim Schofield writing for the LCME. Responding to Creditor's letter on April 19, 1979, Schofield bluntly chided him. "The members of the LCME…found your progress report to be unacceptable and request, by June 1, 1979, your response to the contents of this communication."

Schofield documented in painful detail the substantial interest shown by the LCME in UICOM since 1970, summarizing six visits by LCME survey teams as well as LCME review of numerous UICOM progress reports. He went on to harangue, "The LCME…has concluded that the time has arrived for the college to respond to the LCME and peer reviewers as well as to internal faculty criticisms by seeking appropriate modifications of the original plans."

Schofield cited a warning from the March 1977 survey report, which said, "(The) administrative/managerial difficulties which many recounted serve as an urgent alarm signal that, at a minimum, the educational system stands in hazard of significant deterioration if remedial actions are not taken by several levels of the university administration." Schofield said this concern had been ameliorated somewhat by comments in a June 2, 1978 letter from Truman Anderson, which said, "I am moving to reunite the School of Basic Medical Sciences in Chicago with the Abraham Lincoln School of Clinical Medicine…The College of Medicine is also moving carefully to consolidate after eight years of rapid expansion. Major administrative realignments are under way to simplify our overly complex system. To me, the future looks promising as a healthy conservative posture is adopted."

Schofield then pointed out the inconsistency between those comments, and Creditor's letter of February 9, 1979, which not only defended the complexity of the system, but which included a flat statement from Mort that "the reunification of SBMS and ALSM will not take place at this time." This was not something the LCME wanted to hear.

Schofield concluded with a threat. "It is the considered view of the LCME…that the college's failure to address the many concerns observed by numerous surveyors now places the quality of your educational system in jeopardy of deterioration. Furthermore, the members of the LCME believe that reasonable doubt exists as to the compliance of UICOM with the criteria for accreditation…Since 1970, the LCME has carefully observed the new and different activities in medical education in several of your schools and the unusual system of administration of your college: however, the LCME now believes that this system has had an adequate trial and that major deficiencies exist in the college as presently administered and organized. The LCME desires to hear from you by June 1, 1979 how you propose to address these and other unsolved problems cited in the reports you and your predecessors have received from the LCME."

Copied to President Corbally, Schofield's letter came down hard. Actually, it came down too hard for there was no objective data that would

lead one to assume that the quality of the educational program was deterio-
rating. Internal squabbling or not, students at UICOM were consistently
doing better than the U.S. mean on standard examinations such as the
National Board of Medical Examiners Parts I and II, and by the objective
criteria we had, the education was probably improving rather than regress-
ing. Nevertheless, the LCME, through Schofield, could not abide the one-
and three-year split between basic sciences and clinical schools and tipped
its hand by showing a definite preference to reunite the School of Basic
Medical Sciences at the Medical Center with the Abraham Lincoln School of
Medicine and to return to a single four-year structure with two years for
basic sciences and two years for clinical instruction.

Creditor, not one to accept misdirected criticism passively, responded to
Schofield in a rational and measured manner. Point by point, he defended
the college's position and sovereignty and although not minimizing the
problems, he gave a detailed defense regarding the ability of the college to
manage them internally.

He closed with a vigorous defense of the existing college structure:
"Finally, I would like to become mildly contentious as I refer to the penulti-
mate paragraph of your letter in which you refer to the guideline documents. As a College of Medicine we are undeniably a medical school by
those guidelines. Only if you choose to look at each of the parts separately,
might one question that fact. But we are unique in that we must be viewed
as a whole; we do not have *branch* campuses in the usual sense, because
there is no *trunk*. Our component parts do not exist in a parent-child relationship. They are siblings—of different size and age, to be sure, but they
exist in an interdependent, not dependent, relationship…This letter has
been broadly circulated among our deans, the opinion leaders of all our
schools, and our Academic Council. Its general content has been endorsed
by all and as evidence of the fact that we are not in a state of disarray."

The reverberations of the UICOM struggle with the LCME shook the
higher levels of the university's administration. Chancellor Begando, at
President Corbally's request, directed Mort Creditor to organize a systematic
review of the organization and administration of the College of Medicine.
In accepting this task, Mort sought a stronger mandate to direct the college
than he believed he had as acting executive dean. He therefore asked for and,
on August 31, 1979, was granted the title of interim executive dean for a
term of two years.

In the fall of 1979, President Corbally stepped down. Stanley Ikenberry, then 44, replaced Corbally. The new president promptly published the word that he wanted to meet with every dean and director in the university in order to receive a frank assessment of each campus unit: its current status, its hopes and aspirations, as well its problems and frustrations. Ikenberry appeared to be interested in learning about campus programs and facilitating their operational quality.

Nurtured as a dean in the waning years of David Dodds Henry's supportive presidency, I had been disappointed to observe that Henry's successor, Corbally, was arguably indifferent to the medical program at Urbana. Now it seemed that a caring president, who would understand and take heart in our development, was on the threshold. Taking the new president at his word without first checking out his biases, I was determined to lay out the case for the overdue transfer of SBMS/SCM-UC to the UIUC campus.

After two weeks of careful preparation, I met with the new president for more than an hour on the morning of September 14, 1979. I handed him an agenda and what was essentially a white paper, complete with charts, graphs, and documentation. The presentation had three parts: (a) the Medical Scholars Program, (b) governance issues, and (c) university issues. He had asked for a frank assessment of current operations and I gave him just that. I described the key issues that had limited our development, the complexity of mission management under current UIMC governance, and the disheartening, bureaucratic frustrations we had repeatedly encountered. The white paper described the Medical Scholars Program (MSP) as our primary mission and as a program like no other in the world, but noted that MSP could not realize its full potential unless and until its governance had been transferred to the campus where it resided. I told him why I believed an SBMS/SCM-UC governance review was entirely appropriate at the end of the 1980 fiscal year. My conclusions were documented in relevant parts of the Treaty, which I read to him, and in the Chancellors' Agreement of January 27, 1976.

I also told him that I was also speaking on behalf of the combined SBMS/SCM-UC faculties who, rejecting their role as a UIMC foreign body on the UIUC campus, unanimously believed that the medical-education program at UIUC would have a better chance to excel if linked to the UIUC's governance and value system. My assertions were documented in tables prepared for the new president that compared elements of quality and

cost that clearly favored UIUC over UIMC. I imparted to him the personal
agonies of dealing with the enormously complicated bureaucracy that
plagued us, including the duplication of committee functions and the travel
stresses that were imposed on our very small faculty.

I exulted over the success we had in delivering our innovative basic-
science curriculum and the excitement we had generated with our new clinical curriculum. I told him about progress in the Medical Scholars Program
and the close integration we had with fifteen to twenty UIUC departments
at that time. Badly needing additional resources, a new medical school such
as ours, with the exciting programs already evident, was a "natural" for university philanthropy. In summary, I told him that through SBMS/SCM-UC
and MSP, the University of Illinois had a great opportunity to excel in medical education and in training future leaders in medicine and the sciences. I
was upbeat and enthusiastic, critical only of the unnecessarily prolonged
and debilitating linkage with Chicago, and sought a sympathetic ear from
his new administration.

Unfortunately, I learned in short order from anonymous, but reliable
sources, that this was not what Ikenberry wanted to hear. He had been
schooled to believe that one medical school per university was one too
many; two were impossible. (He often referred to the university president's
definition of hell as a very attractive campus where the sun always shines,
administrators enjoy unlimited perquisites—and two medical schools are
present.) The new president was unprepared to examine the underpinnings
of the brand-new, less-expensive program that we had developed. As far as I
could determine then and from later meetings with him, he seemed to view
all medical schools as cut from the same cloth.

I don't know what he did with the information I gave him. I assume
that he shared it with the Chicago administration, which only made it more
difficult for me to deal with them. Certainly, they gave me no peace and
remained antagonistic, if not hostile, to SBMS/SCM-UC goals for the rest of
my tenure as dean. The interview with President Ikenberry was memorable
in one additional respect. It was my only face-to-face meeting with him in
which he appeared to listen more than he talked. His style in later encoun-
ters was to monopolize time by talking about his own view of issues and
leaving little time for him to explore alternative opinions. I left his office
feeling just swell, unaware that I had dug SBMS/SCM-UC and myself into a
deep hole. It was a horrendously naive move.

Meanwhile, Mort Creditor was trying hard to overcome some of the nagging problems facing the college. Aside from accreditation, the largest problem he inherited from Truman was the withdrawal of several million dollars of funding support at the state and national levels. Federal funds for medical-school expansion were being phased out. State funding, which was supposed to replace the federal "priming" funds, was inadequate to do the job. The UIMC administration did not place the College of Medicine high on its list of priorities for the limited amount of new state dollars and did not use those funds to reduce UICOM's deficiencies. The ever-problematic university hospital, much higher on UIMC's priority list, was a major drain on funding.

By the fall of 1979, when Mort had been on the job in Chicago for six months, we discussed the economic retrenchment that was going to be necessary throughout the college, and how SCM-UC would have to squeeze into line to get the minimal funding it needed to survive. Mort was sympathetic with Urbana needs at that time and summarized his perceptions in a December 11, 1979, letter that characterized the process of making the budget cuts necessary as "difficult and agonizing." He said that the projected deficit was large and that it was unlikely the problem would be resolved by funding sources outside the college.

"Although I will continue to press for additional funding, we must begin to think in terms of exercising more economy in the uses of college resources and to consider reallocating college resources when that appears to be appropriate," he wrote. "As might be expected, there has been no spontaneous expression on the part of any school or other unit in the College to make a sacrifice on behalf of the common cause."

He added that he could make the task simple for himself by ordering "a uniform reduction in the budget of each school in proportion to its contribution to the total budget. However, such across-the-board approaches, although common, represent failure to exercise responsibility because they do not take into account the fact that different units have different problems."

Then, he turned his comments to Urbana-Champaign. "Deciding how U-C is to contribute to economic retrenchment is a particular problem for me. To be perfectly candid, we must admit that to a large extent the college problem is created by the need to adequately fund SCM-UC. This is complicated by the fact that a whole year (the M-4 year) of medical education has not yet been capitalized at all in Urbana so that the needs are dictated to a lesser extent by new enrollment than assuming the fulfillment of obligation to students already in the pipeline.

"Therefore, we must exercise particular care in protecting those programs that are essential to the fulfillment of your obligations while evaluating your resources."

After a discussion of some costs to be monitored, he added the following: "From my current position, I firmly believe that if this college is to fully exploit its regionalized configuration and to develop to the full potential made possible by its extraordinary resources, then Urbana-Champaign must flourish…I believe that this college is so large and widely dispersed that it needs two central foci sharing what I will call 'nodal responsibility.'…

"Therefore, in my view, as we look beyond 1981 we must think in terms of capitalizing Urbana-Champaign. However, before any new, major long-term investment is made in U-C, there should be some confidence in the long-term strength and viability of U-C, particularly if it is to serve the function I have described."

After this endorsement of our existence, he went on to write that we needed to address problems with the school's governance and minimal residency programs, the same issues that troubled the LCME. In his attempt to resolve these, he laid some impossible short-term tasks upon us. However, this was not the letter of an unsympathetic bureaucrat. It showed considerable understanding of and sympathy for our position, which is, of course, what I expected when I campaigned with Bill Grove to appoint him as acting executive dean.

Little did I know that I was in for quite an unpleasant surprise.

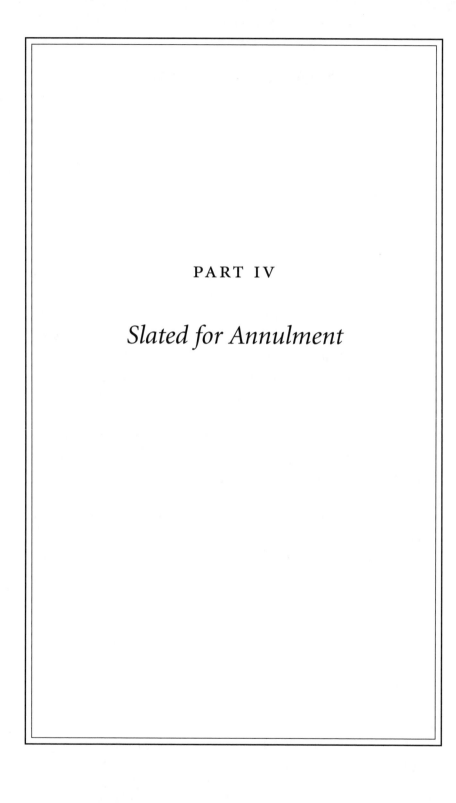

PART IV

Slated for Annulment

CHAPTER 25

Showdown in Chicago

I F THERE WAS ANY ARENA in which Mort Creditor excelled, it was in organization and administration. When he accepted the post as acting executive dean in February 1979, he also received a mandate from higher administration to establish a college governance review process that would satisfy the LCME accrediting agency. To fulfill this mandate, he created the Strategic Planning and Management Committee. This creation was vintage Creditor, and served as a comprehensive, reassuring response to the chancellor's charge. The SPMC process reflected Mort's thorough and systematic approach to the organizational difficulties highlighted in the LCME report. He engaged Dr. Steve Ruma, an independent management consultant who had extensive experience with academic health-science center management issues, and proceeded to outline an orderly process that would begin in July 1980 and be complete by June 1, 1981. In addition to a college-wide SPMC, each school was directed to create an internal SPMC with additional subcommittees to focus on each governance issue. The college SPMC would identify major governance issues and send them for review and comment to the schools' SPMCs, which would return them to the college SPMC for final action.

The SPMC process began with the identification of seven governance issues:

1. The concept of regionalized medical education at multiple sites
2. College responsibility versus school autonomy
3. Missions and priorities of the several schools
4. The one year of basic science and three years of clinical science curriculum split
5. The basic-science school, clinical school separation
6. Responsibility for graduate medical education
7. The relationship of the College of Medicine to the campus, the hospitals, the university, and external agencies

For each issue, an "issue analysis format" was designed. This included the listing of the major positive aspects and the major problems of the existing structure and process. Each problem was to be defined as acute or chronic; previous attempts to rectify the problem were to be identified. Problems were to be described by their major causes in rank order. Each of the six SPMC school committees was directed to analyze the issues from its own viewpoint. The school reports were then to be submitted to the central college SPMC, which included representatives from all units. This body would in turn submit a final recommendation to the Academic Council, which was the executive committee of the College of Medicine, for action. A detailed timetable was established for the process, which included meeting dates, dates for receiving written responses from faculty, retreats for data analysis, reports to the schools, review of the reports, hearings at each of the schools, a retreat by the SPMC to prepare preliminary recommendations, school review of preliminary recommendations, and reformulation of the recommendations. The process was to begin in July 1980 and be complete with a final recommendation to the Academic Council by May 1981. The Academic Council action would then be brought to the general faculty in June 1981. Additional university reviews and approvals would be completed in the summer of 1981.

During this period of instability, of low college morale, of LCME threats to our system, and of growing financial woes, the faculties in Rockford, Peoria, and Urbana were considerably agitated about their future. From 1977 through 1981, rumors flew up and down the state about closing the Urbana clinical school, or cutting Rockford and Peoria to two-year schools, or even dropping either Rockford or Peoria or both. It was natural, then, that both faculty and administrators from the three regional schools would meet from time to time to exchange information, and in doing so, explore other governance options. The desire to communicate with one another became even greater as direct communication with Mort Creditor became more strained from day to day. He seemed to interpret his new role as agent of medical-center policy rather than as champion of the underfunded, downtrodden regional schools. As for those of us who wandered in the wilderness of never knowing which day might be our last, we knew instinctively that we were playing a surreal game of musical chairs. We sensed the music would stop soon and we might be caught by a deficit of one, two, or three chairs. Even though Rockford and Peoria also felt the squeeze, neither of them came close to being "at risk" the way that the foundling at UIUC was. So we looked for options to present to the SPMC.

As the SPMC process got under way, Bill Grove retired on August 31, 1980. His replacement as Vice Chancellor of Academic Affairs was Alexander McKay (Mack) Schmidt. Unlike Creditor, Schmidt was a pragmatist. He had been among the first people I met during my 1970 interviews in Chicago. He was then dean of the Abraham Lincoln School of Medicine. On first blush, he struck me as a down-to-earth individual. He was easy to talk to and had a well-developed sense of humor. A cardiologist by training, Schmidt also had administrative abilities that were brought to Grove's notice early in Schmidt's tenure. Thus, when the Committee to Coordinate Planning was formed to lead the 1969 college reorganization, Mack was chosen to be its guiding force. Subsequently, he was selected to be the first dean of ALSM. It was in his role as dean and in our twice-monthly meetings as fellow members of the Academic Advisory Council (AAC) that I grew to know him better. In that arena, despite his savior-faire, he impressed me as a smart, but inefficient, bureaucrat.

My recollections of those council meetings are crowded with images of Mack Schmidt trying to resolve, in the public atmosphere of the AAC, his insoluble ALSM problems. Sometimes it seemed that our meetings were little more than brainstorming sessions to advise Mack Schmidt on how to run ALSM. It became tedious over the years for those of us from the regions, with paper-thin budgets and countless, complex start-up problems of our own, to spend so much time on the turmoil in the relatively wealthy confines of Chicago. Mack never seemed to find closure to his own problems, and when some of us suggested straightforward approaches, he would resist, citing his view that "finding a simple solution to a complex problem is a form of tyranny."

He once made an unfortunate appointment as his Chief of Medicine. The new chief was a person well connected to the U.S. academic power structure but who was not attuned to function in the fishbowl of a large, publicly funded state medical school. During the three or four years that the individual served, my fellow deans and I gave Mack what seemed to be dozens of management solutions. But Mack could not act on any of them, and the agony of having the wrong person lead the major teaching and research department of the school continued.

Relationships with the university hospital also caused big problems for

Schmidt. Inadequate mechanisms were in place to assure proper billing, collection rates were low, and the hospital and ALSM were losing patients as well as money. The medical staff exhibited little sense of service to the community or to referring physicians. Doctors from around the state would refer patients to the university hospital where they would be diagnosed, treated, and released. But the hospital medical staff was frequently negligent in notifying the referring physician of the patient's hospital course. This was a great annoyance to the referring physician, who would be responsible for follow-up care but ignorant of the recent hospital experience. As a result, referrals in most areas dried up.

Schmidt's tenure at ALSM was interrupted by a two-year stint as head of the Food and Drug Administration in Washington. A lifelong Republican, he was appointed FDA Commissioner by President Richard Nixon and served in an effective, but undistinguished, manner. His most notable brush with national headlines was the "swine-flu epidemic" that failed to materialize in the 1974-75 flu season. Reports of a swine influenza virus spreading to the United States from Asia had prompted some infectious-disease experts to predict that large segments of the U.S. population, particularly the elderly, would be at high risk. Schmidt, trying to sort out conflicting information, prepared for the worst and mobilized the country for a massive immunization effort. The epidemic never reached our shores, and the government was stuck with large quantities of unused swine-flu vaccine. It had been a tough call, and Mack, who had taken a prudent conservative course, took the heat gracefully.

Returning to Chicago, Schmidt was made vice chancellor for health affairs (VCHA) at UIMC, a position that placed him in charge of the university hospital. Schmidt had had his troubles with the hospital earlier as the dean of ALSM. As VCHA, Schmidt was equally ineffective. The hospital still did not thrive. Yet when Bill Grove retired as VCAA, Chancellor Begando elevated Schmidt to that powerful position the next day. Thus a strong, decisive VCAA was replaced by a far more tentative one.

As a result, Mort Creditor was better able to pursue his personal agenda in the review of college governance. If Grove had hung on, it is unlikely that Creditor would have worked vigorously against the split into one-year regional basic-science and three-year clinical schools. That plan was Bill Grove's baby. Creditor was uncomfortable with the one-year, three-year split in medical education for both pedagogical and practical reasons.

Pedagogically, he believed that the basic medical sciences of microbiology, pathology, and pharmacology should be taught in the second year by capable departmental scientists. From a practical viewpoint, he held that the college could not afford to have effective research-teaching departments in those sciences throughout the regions. He concluded that it would be in the best interest of the entire program to have Rockford and Peoria leave the basic-science business and the first two years of medical education to Chicago and Urbana. That would reduce the programs at Rockford and Peoria to two years, save a considerable amount of money, and end any dreams that might be emerging of an independent four-year school at either of those sites. It was a rational position, but one fraught with political danger. The university had traveled too far with the communities of Rockford and Peoria to suddenly trim their sails at this time.

Clearly, Creditor had some very strong ideas about the directions the college reorganization should take, even though he posed as administratively neutral and established an objective process through which the college could deal with its perceived governance flaws. He was aiming at more than just making the LCME happy.

He was not in his new post as acting executive dean very long before he confided to me that, given the opportunity, he would close Rockford. (We were good friends when he left Urbana, and when he first took over from Grove, we were still able to discuss sensitive issues at length.) Creditor felt that Rockford was "pre-Flexnerian," a label that implied the medical-education program was as relevant to modern medicine as the horse and buggy was to the latest luxury sports car. (When Flexner surveyed medical education in the United States in the early 1900s, in the true pre-Flexnerian era, he found many diploma mills and observed that most medical schools in those days were seriously deficient in giving students a solid scientific background.)

In order to maintain his neutral pose, Creditor also had to avoid showing favoritism to his former employer, SCM-UC. Regardless of his strong feelings on these matters, he claimed he was determined to lead the examination of college governance with complete objectivity.

Creditor's SPMC process was a meticulously designed, flawless plan that would have served as a core offering in a management-training course. It was of textbook quality. But it did not work! It did not work because, in reality, in the hearts and minds of the personnel who made up the college, there was no college of medicine. Despite Bill Grove's insistence, despite reams of paper that said otherwise, and despite the countless college committee meetings attended faithfully by loyal faculty, there were in reality four separate medical schools, each with its own agenda. This was not apparent to me or to the other deans in Chicago, Rockford, and Peoria at that time. LCME surveyors came close to the truth and indicated many times a preference to accredit each unit on its own. Still, at an official level, the LCME dealt only with one college—a college that was there only by force of Bill Grove's political will.

It is crystal clear to me now, as I review the events of 1979 and 1980, that the emperor had no clothes. The college, in a spiritual sense, did not exist. We had no collegial unity, no collegial intellectual intercourse, no collegial patriotism, and no collegial loyalty. The phrase "semiautonomous units of the college" applied to us in name only. We dutifully sat for meetings with LCME visitors where we affirmed before them, with one voice, our "one-collegeness." The visitors knew otherwise but did not completely understand the dynamics. And when it came to money, it was readily apparent that a collegial spirit of one for all and all for one did not exist. It was very unlikely that any of the four regional units would agree to make a meaningful accommodation or sacrifice for the good of the college or any of its parts.

Concerned about the problem of local chauvinism, and as one of the few who viewed the college as a single entity, Creditor personally selected the "most statesmanlike" faculty from each school to serve on the SPMC. This resulted in an SPMC membership that was, perhaps, more moderate and less confrontational than he might have had were each school to have freely chosen its own representative. The Urbana-Champaign programs appeared to be well-represented on the SPMC with, potentially, three friendly voices out of eight. But it did not work out that way. Mort Creditor, who chaired the SPMC, seemed to bend over backwards to demonstrate his objectivity toward his former school. The other two Urbana spokesmen selected by Creditor were Arthur Leonard of SCM-UC and C. Roland Leeson, the recently appointed head of the division of Anatomy. Leonard had served as a medical resident at Michael Reese Hospital when Mort Creditor was on the staff and was recruited by Mort to SCM-UC to be CEC director at Mercy Hospital. As a new recruit, Leeson was unaware of the complex political background that existed.

The SPMC process was cumbersome, but to those familiar with the Medical Center's usual heavy-handed governance, it was unexpectedly open and systematic. Nonetheless, the analytic process with its to and fro feedback mechanisms was complex and time-consuming. Given our limited and over-worked faculty at SBMS/SCM-UC, I requested from Creditor the authority to combine SBMS and SCM-UC into a single local SPMC. It was a modest and reasonable request, but he adamantly refused to deviate one iota from his overall strategy. Two separate reports were expected from the two Urbana schools. We gave him his two reports, one from each school, but the reports came from a single set of subcommittees. Despite my streamlining, the SPMC process at Urbana still involved effort by more that sixty people: faculty, students, and staff.

The College SPMC also scheduled interviews with the regional deans, separate from the regional SPMCs, to ascertain their remedies for the observed organizational difficulties. On July 15, 1980 I recommended to the College SPMC that:

- The university's commitment to regionalization of health-professional education should be redefined and reaffirmed.
- The College of Medicine (as it was then organized) should be dissolved.
- The executive deanship and its attendant bureaucracy should be eliminated.
- The autonomy of four health-science education campuses should be acknowledged, with each campus having a well-defined mission, controlling its own certification and degree-awarding process, and seeking independent accreditation for its health-science education programs.
- The Urbana-Champaign medical-education program should be assigned to the Chancellor of the UIUC campus.

These recommendations closely paralleled those prepared by Dean Clifford (Bud) Grulee, Jr., Dean at the Rockford School of Medicine. Dr. Grulee was a member of the LCME site-visit team that surveyed the college in 1970. In his personal comments to the SPMC he stated, "I well remember the feelings of that site-visit team, that the regional units of the college should be separately accredited. It was the university's insistence that all units were to be considered integral parts of a single college of medicine that caused the problems. The question then, as on subsequent site visits, was how a single college of medicine could effectively relate to five very different and geographically dispersed units under a single set of policies, procedures, committees, and administrative rules."

Grulee then went on to recommend a renewed and substantive commitment to the regional concept, a separate budget line for each of the regional schools and the opportunity for the dean of each to defend his budget to the chancellor, and separate accreditation for each of the three regional medical schools.

Our bottom-line message was: Change the structure, remove the asphyxiating micromanagement, and most of the problems will be solved.

At the time the college and the school SPMC committees were formed, those of us in Urbana did not view them with great seriousness. The Strategic Planning and Management process was sarcastically referred to as SPAM, and the SPMC generally seen as a sop for the LCME. The president and the chancellor, who had given Creditor his mandate, knew relatively little about day-to-day college operations, the tensions among its different sites, or its conflicts with the LCME. Had it been otherwise, they would have known that most of the faculty unhappiness could have been resolved by shaping up the Medical Center bureaucracy, providing better service to its constituents, and establishing a teleconferencing system that would have reduced the odious travel demands to attend boring and often inconsequential committee meetings. Such simple, sensitive steps would have significantly increased faculty contentment and morale and removed a major problem identified by the LCME. Instead, we were embarked on this doomed SPMC venture, struggling as best we could to adhere to Creditor's precise timetable.

As time passed, however, our local SPMC committees began to suspect that Creditor was leading the college through the SPMC process into a different arena that went well beyond making peace with the LCME. Outcomes were being debated, and major restructuring was under consideration. As budget and resources were discussed in SPMC meetings, it began to dawn on some of us that the college SPMC was actually engaged in a deadly game of musical chairs. The "music" (read: money) had stopped, and this elegant, regionalized organization, structured for five hundred MD graduates per year, was therefore to be trimmed to 60 percent of its planned size. If the administration were not committed to regional medical education in Illinois, it meant that some of us would be superfluous—there were not enough chairs!

By the end of 1980, as we reviewed minutes of the college SPMC meetings, we saw that not just individuals or resources were vulnerable, but entire regional sites. In such a game, it was not difficult to identify who was most at risk. Being the last kid let into the game, SCM-UC was the most vulnerable. The LCME tension, as seminal as it was in creating the process, had virtually nothing to do with the real game that was now on the Creditor agenda. SPAM was no longer a joke. Indeed, the evolving SPMC process would soon lead us into a bitter contest for survival.

Spurred by the dangers that rapidly became evident, I initiated local discussion with my inner circle to take stock. They agreed that an ill wind was blowing. Politically, SCM-UC was the most vulnerable unit in the college. With only twenty-five students per year, underfunded, not yet perceived as a major player at UIUC, and yet to graduate its first MD, it was a ripe target for the chopping block. Only the Medical Scholars Program shielded it from arbitrary elimination. The MSP was unique in the university and the nation, but it might not carry the day if the SPMC called for SCM-UC to be eliminated. It was important, we decided, to explore other options, and the most attractive was a linkage to Peoria.

Linkage of the Urbana and Peoria programs had always been a reasonable prospect. The two cities were only ninety miles apart and had complementary resources. Peoria had long been a major downstate referral center. It possessed the best tertiary-care facilities outside of the Chicago area and had a full spectrum of residency-training programs. Urbana had all the basic-science potential that any medical school might require. Although PSM had some major town-gown conflicts, we knew that the level of student satisfaction at PSM was high, and that those students from Peoria who took residency training in Champaign-Urbana were well-educated and respected. PSM was a good clinical school and linking it to Urbana would create a program that would, we believed, be readily accredited by the LCME.

I was in frequent contact with several Peoria faculty members to discuss the possibility of a Peoria-Urbana medical school as an outcome of the SPMC process. They also saw the handwriting on the wall and disliked what they read. But achieving a consensus of opinion from the Peoria faculty was a deed worthy of the gods. The Peoria School of Medicine was a house divided. Nick Cotsonas had been the dean at Peoria until 1978, when he was replaced by his associate dean, Jerry Newman. Though very different men, both looked askance at a four-year program at UIUC. Although Cotsonas never came out and directly challenged the concept of a clinical program at Urbana, Newman was not so inhibited and told me up front that he would always oppose a clinical program at Urbana because it would directly compete with the Peoria School of Medicine and its plans to become the major downstate medical center.

Compared with Rockford and Urbana, which both developed with good relationships between school and community, PSM was constantly mired in town-gown conflicts. Cotsonas and Newman were so closely linked to the Medical Center in the minds of the medical community that they might as well have had their offices in Chicago. Their power and authority at Peoria required frequent propping by Bill Grove. Cotsonas had a penchant for stirring up dissent, and Newman, who had a penchant for directness and honesty, was often the center of controversy because his view of the truth did not always coincide with the views of other Peorian power brokers. Grove often had to intervene in these affairs and proved masterful at extracting Cotsonas and Newman from the troubles they engendered in PSM development. In surgical terms (and Grove was reputed to be an excellent surgeon), Grove was very skilled in the repair of self-inflicted gunshot wounds to the feet. It was futile to talk with either Cotsonas or Newman about a separate Peoria-Urbana medical school. They were indissolubly linked to UIMC.

But that was not the case with many other members of the Peoria faculty, who were unhappy with the position of the Peoria administration and thought that Peoria could be greatly strengthened by a link with SBMS/SCM-UC and the UIUC campus. Several major conceptual and operational differences between the two sites needed to be ironed out, however, including the dean's office location, department heads' location, and budget-management issues. Unfortunately, having been subjected to Chicago-based governance for ten years, both Peoria and Urbana were rife with cynicism. The PSM group was very keen on having both the dean and the clinical-department heads permanently seated in Peoria. They argued, quite reasonably, that without such guarantees, they might be completely swallowed up or reduced to insignificance by the powerful UIUC campus. I opposed the presupposition of location because it became a major stumbling block to the Peoria-Urbana consolidation. Of course, not everyone at our campus was in favor of linkage to Peoria at this time. Lowell Hager once made the crack, "Peoria! That's like throwing an anchor to a drowning man."

One of the most powerful and controversial figures in Peoria was Ed McGrath, the administrator of St. Francis Medical Center. St. Francis was the largest teaching hospital in Peoria and, for that matter, in all of downstate Illinois. Before the Peoria School of Medicine arrived on the scene, the hospital, under McGrath's leadership, had already established residencies in a number of basic areas including medicine, surgery, pediatrics, obstetrics and gynecology, and family practice. As such, St. Francis provided a solid base to incorporate into the PSM teaching program. But the relationship between St. Francis and the medical school was very rocky for the first decade of PSM's existence, largely because Ed McGrath and Nick Cotsonas could never agree on the terms of the affiliation. Both Cotsonas and Grove appeared to dislike McGrath intensely. I concluded that if we were going to play ball in Peoria, Ed McGrath would certainly be among the players, and I wanted to get to know him firsthand.

So, sometime in the fall of 1980, I met privately with McGrath in Bloomington, Illinois. McGrath was such an anathema to the Chicago powers that I instructed my secretary not to log the appointment in my office calendar for fear that somehow Grove might learn of the meeting. But Grove never did learn of the meeting, and if he had, it would have been an anticlimax. For all his reputation, McGrath and I got along very well. We barely scratched the surface of potential issues as we talked about a possible Peoria-Urbana combination. The main items that we agreed upon were that a PSM/SBMS/SCM merger was a viable possibility, further discussions with faculty were necessary, and we would keep in touch by telephone.

After my meeting with McGrath, a small group of us went to Peoria for some preliminary discussions. We wanted to know who in Peoria supported our position and would plan with us. The most prominent and outspoken member of the Peoria faculty was the Chairman of Pediatrics, Dr. Sachchida Sinha. He agreed to line up faculty leadership in Peoria for a major meeting to try to work out a definitive plan. The meeting was set for March 3, 1981 and would be attended by senior faculty from both schools. I prepared a formal agenda, which I shared with the Peoria group. We did not consider the meeting confidential, but neither did we advertise our intentions broadly beyond the faculties immediately concerned.

Meanwhile, in commenting about the SPMC deliberations, President Ikenberry gratuitously expressed open opposition to a second medical school within the University of Illinois. This presidential interference in the

SPMC process also tainted it, for his comments could not have been over-looked by Creditor, who chaired the SPMC. Ikenberry's comments also had a dampening effect on our discussions with the Peoria contingent, but we agreed to continue meeting because it was entirely possible to conceive a downstate unit as part of a single college.

I discussed the Urbana-Peoria connection on at least one occasion with Mort Creditor, who was by this time firmly committed to the SPMC process as the sole vehicle for college reorganization. As if he had a proprietary interest in the SPMC process, Creditor strongly opposed any other proce-dure or discussion format that might bear on resolving the college's organi-zational problems. I argued with Mort that his position was ridiculous and anti-intellectual. Because it appeared that the college was in a period of transition, it was completely proper for the downstate schools, or the upstate ones for that matter, to talk among themselves about the future. Mort would not accept that point of view and remained fixated on his own creation, the SPMC process. Although frictions had existed in the past between Mort and me, my relations with him now went from bad to worse—much worse.

Well before the SPMC process had begun, I reminded Mort of what he very well knew, namely, that in all the time SCM-UC had been in the plan-ning stage and into the implementation stage, no one at the Medical Center campus had ever requested line-item dollars to fund it. Even Truman Anderson, supportive as he was, felt too intimidated by Bill Grove to ask for separate and new funds to support SCM-UC. At my administrative peril, I frequently reminded the power structure at the Medical Center campus that the SCM-UC financial problems resulted from neglect by the UIMC campus administration. After putting us through all the approval hurdles, the Administrative Advisory Council consensus, approval by higher administra-tion at UIMC, approval by the Board of Trustees, approval by the Illinois Board of Higher Education, and approval by the LCME, nobody in higher administration requested any specific funding for the program. On one occasion, when Bill Grove was lamenting to a group of Medical Center staff some funding difficulties he was facing, I reminded him, "Bill, you don't get if you don't ask. You've never asked for one extra nickel from the State of Illinois for SCM-UC." Grove bristled as he replied, "I'm tired of hearing that from you, Bloomfield." He did not say that I was wrong, only that he was tired of hearing that from me.

Meeting privately with Mort Creditor, I argued that the failure of the

UIMC administration to request specific funding for SCM-UC was nothing short of malfeasance. Creditor refused to deal with the problem and spoke to me only in terms of a funding predicament that encompassed the entire College of Medicine. He denied it was a UIMC problem and warned me (knowing I had a penchant for proceeding out of channels) that if I bypassed the college and went to the campus with my complaint of malfeasance, the conclusion would be drawn to close SCM-UC. Should I persist in carrying the same argument to the president, the conclusion would be the same. The road to solvency for SCM-UC was blocked all the way to the summit, and stalled as I was in the middle of that road, I found that Mort Creditor was no good Samaritan.

On January 16, 1981, I wrote a memo to file that collected my thoughts on malfeasance. "To deal effectively with UIMC administration, the College, through its faculty, should ask the following: (1) An accounting for $10 million in lapsed dollars which have been used by the UIMC campus over the past five years and whose use has led to vacancy credits and has caused excessive draw down of capitation reserves. (2) Ask for an accounting of the method by which UIMC has replaced federal funds with state dollars for programmatic initiatives that were not authorized by IBHE prior to the regionalization mission. For example, the Office of Continuing Education under the VCAA currently draws $194,000 per year of state dollars rather than AHES (federal) dollars."

In February of 1981, SCM-UC experienced a major disappointment. Our application for an NIH grant to assist in training Medical Scholars was "recommended for approval" but received too low a priority to be funded. Approval and funding would have bolstered our case for survival. The grant had been submitted by Dr. I.C. Gunsalus of the Department of Biochemistry. We'd worked extensively with "Gunny" to develop the proposal, but when one reviewed the names and titles of the special study section of NIH that acted upon this grant, it's little wonder that the low priority was given. We were judged by classicists on the review committee who couldn't see how such a training grant could be funded at a medical school without a university hospital. The chief criticism in the summary statement of the training grant was "there is still little opportunity for students to participate in clinical-research programs." We appreciated the problem but there was little we could do about it.

In warning me of the consequences of charging malfeasance, I am sure that Mort knew what he was talking about, although he rarely let down his guard. Except for venting his concern about Rockford, he never discussed all options frankly with me. Any hope I might have had that my special role in elevating him to the position he now held would give me privileged informational status was thoroughly quashed. Taking shelter behind the SPMC process, he refused to release any additional background information to me and presumably to the other college deans. In retrospect, there is reason to believe that Creditor, in his contacts with Schmidt, Begando, and Ikenberry, had long concluded, even before the SPMC report was made, and before the March 3 Urbana-Peoria meeting had been scheduled, that SCM-UC was doomed and that the announcement of its end was merely a matter of timing. But I was not thinking in those terms when I planned the March 3 meeting or when I scheduled a short mid-February vacation in Arizona.

That was until I received an unwelcome wake-up call in my Arizona hotel room on February 16. It was Mort Creditor, and he was hopping mad. Someone from Peoria had called him about the meeting and had sent him my proposed agenda. Mort explicitly ordered me to cancel the March 3 meeting and demanded that I return to Champaign-Urbana forthwith to meet with him. Arguing that the SPMC provided an established process for examining the UICOM organization, he held that it was improper of me to go through any back channels to influence the outcome. I countered that there was nothing in the SPMC process that excluded faculty from meeting to consider alternative solutions. My executive committees had both endorsed the discussions and directed me to explore the prospects with Peoria, and I was doing just that. We were also aware by that time that the SPMC was considering such a Peoria-Urbana option. I said that I would not cut my vacation short, would return on February 23, and would be willing to meet with him anytime thereafter. He reiterated that I was disloyal to him and that he was scheduling a meeting for the two of us with Vice Chancellor Schmidt on Tuesday, February 24 at 10:30 a.m. in order to clear the air. Mort and I were now on a collision course, and the stage was set for a showdown.

On February 24, 1981, as instructed, I reported to the administrative center in Chicago where I was directed to Mack Schmidt's office. Schmidt and Creditor were waiting for me when I arrived. As I entered the office, I saw that the furniture had been carefully prearranged. A tape recorder was perched on a small table surrounded by three chairs. Schmidt and Creditor already occupied two; the third seat was obviously for me.

Because the meeting had been arranged by Creditor to clear the air, I was not sure what role Mack Schmidt would play. I had brought with me Rick Schimmel, my associate dean for business affairs, because the SCM-UC budget for the 1982 fiscal year was a major concern and I wanted to have a financial assistant present if we were going to talk budget. Furthermore, I disliked going into a tense, potentially confrontational situation outnumbered two to one and wanted Schimmel to remain with me. But Schmidt denied that we would have time to talk about the budget and asked Rick to leave the room but to remain available in case we did enter into budget discussions. This left me alone and under great pressure.

Schmidt began the meeting by saying: "To start with, but not to sound overly ritualistic or formalistic, I want to say that…I view this meeting as very important…important enough to tape."

I responded that taping the proceedings was fine with me, adding that I would like a personal transcript (it was provided to me a few days later and is the source for this account). Given the seriousness of my predicament and being outnumbered two-to-one, I had brought along my own tape recorder in self-defense but did not use it.

"The purpose of the meeting is to transmit some information," Schmidt continued, "a mixed kind of information, but you've got to know it. President Ikenberry asked me to meet with you as soon as I could to convey the information that I am going to convey."

"Oh boy!" I thought. "Even the president is on my case."

Schmidt elaborated. "The information has to do with the College of Medicine and the Medical Center together. As I have said many times, I view the expansion and regionalization of the College of Medicine as an important and noble effort…Around 1977…you could sense a change in the country…a lot of schools that tried innovations were backing away from them; there was feeling that the expansion phase was probably coming to an end, that funding would be leveling off. The state, about 1977, quit providing chunks of funds to the college…I think it would be a safe assumption that in the last two or three years, the state has not funded the College of Medicine or the Medical Center to the extent the programs have needed."

The vice chancellor went on to explain that he had not known much about campus financing before he took the VCAA job, but had since learned that the College of Medicine was overextended financially by a significant amount.

I interrupted him to make my own point. "There is no question that when we started our program in Urbana-Champaign, the Clinical School, I made it very clear to the campus and presidential level that when there was a stop-go decision, we could handle it for the first two years, but that we couldn't handle it after that. And I said unequivocally to the senior administration at the Medical Center, 'Now is the time to stop us. If you are not going to stop us, any other course but planning for our funding would be administratively irresponsible.' I sent that letter to your predecessor, and I copied it to President Corbally and to Truman Anderson. So I made that very clear because nothing you have told me about the financing since 1977 was news to me."

Schmidt listened impassively to my declaration and, unperturbed, proceeded to detail the Medical Center funding problems, which had total deficits in the range of $4 million, not counting the clinical school in Urbana. After detailing deficit after deficit, he summarized, "The point of all this is that if you add all this up, a conservative number of funds that we will need that are in our base now or that are coming in here now or that we need to pay our bills for the next year, the conservative number of the short-fall is $10 million...This translates into base budget cuts of the units ranging from about five percent to twenty percent...It is crystal clear to me that we cannot run all of our [current] programs in all of our locations for all of the colleges next year...and my personal bias is that starting in about 1977 we should have started consolidating.

"I have asked Dean Creditor to speed up the SPMC process so that by the Academic Council meeting [of March 10], which I have asked to attend, I can be provided with the results of the SPMC study...I don't know for certain what options the university will exercise, but I do know that we will have to look at whether, or in what form, we can continue Rockford and Peoria and the clinical activities in Urbana-Champaign...One possibility is to change the nature of Rockford, Peoria, and U-C. And another is to close one or more of them. Those are just logical."

This Chicago-centric mode of thought was typical. Detailing massive deficits associated with Chicago programs, largely related to a mismanaged university hospital and to the Area Health Education System, Schmidt wanted to solve his problems by cutting the regional programs. Under the circumstances, I was not about to challenge his warped logic. To be sure that I understood him, he emphasized his point, "And I want to be explicit that one possibility is to close the Urbana clinical activity, now."

He then initiated a series of vague prohibitions. "There cannot be at this time anything done that compromises in any way the university's ability to exercise its options… You don't want any activity going on that would tend to limit or to foreclose or in any way to inhibit the university in doing what is best for the State of Illinois and the university and the communities involved."

I was versed enough in "admin speak" to know he was getting to the projected meetings with Peoria and probably intended to interdict them. "I am concerned that [the President or the Board of Trustees] not be put in a position where something has gone on in advance of the process, the disruption of orderly process."

"Such as?" I asked with appropriate naivete.

"With specific regard to a meeting that I understand you have planned in Peoria that, according to the agenda of the meeting, is to plan the goals, objectives, and philosophy of a downstate College of Medicine, to talk about avoiding mistakes of the past, talk about departmental structure, committee structure, administrative structure, etc.

"In my view this is highly inappropriate…and I feel strongly enough about this to ask that this meeting be called off…because of the likelihood, whatever it is, there will not be a southern college of medicine…This is important enough that I have written a letter to Mort Creditor saying that in addition to that, I want your pledge that you will work cooperatively and collegially in consensual decision-making with your fellow deans in the College of Medicine…as a member of the team and loyal to this campus and loyal to me and so on. If you can't do that, you shouldn't be in your position."

Schmidt had now laid his cards on the table. If I could not sign a loyalty oath, I should resign. He and Mort were looking for a resignation, but I was not about to give them one. I had learned long ago that resigning in high dudgeon makes you feel good for the moment, but does not get the job done. They could martyr me, but only if they fired me.

"The basic issue," I told them, "is, 'What is the statutory responsibility of a dean?'…It is the faculty in the university which is the strength of the university…It is my faculty upon which, for example, my credibility stands. Do you want me to ignore a faculty request [to work with Peoria] or to tell the faculty that they are wrong? Do you wish to deny them the freedom…to meet with other faculty and to say, 'What is our future? What are some of our options?'"

I steadfastly held to this theme: The proposed discussions between Peoria and us were not designed to interfere with the SPMC process, and the March 3 meeting had been scheduled at the request of the two faculties. I cautioned that if faculty were prevented by administration from talking to one another, some would inevitably wave the flag of academic freedom.

"No matter what I pledge, I am responding to a request from Peoria that has been approved by the Peoria Executive Committee [and by my own Executive Committee]. I need some advice from you on how to handle this because I think the faculty will find such a request as you have made not consistent with statutory freedom. I would like to resolve this amicably. I am not here to get into any conflict with you."

Schmidt said I did not fully understand my role as dean. Prepared for just such an attack, I countered with a copy of the *University of Illinois Statutes*, which specify the role of the dean and said I was following the statutes to the letter. He argued that it was the dean's role to represent the administration of the university to the faculty. We then sparred for some time on university statute semantics, the role of a dean, and the role of faculty in the reorganization process. Both Creditor and Schmidt sought further background on the meetings between Urbana-Champaign and Peoria and appeared surprised when I told them that the March 3 meeting would be the third and most substantive. Then, they asked whether I was disparaging the SPMC study to the faculty.

"It is not complete...I think it is a good study...I have no complaint with the process...What you are telling me is to agree with you [and with the exclusivity of the SPMC process] or resign...I don't think a conversation like this would ever take place on the Urbana campus. I think that UIUC has a different kind of academic administration. At UIUC, there is much more faculty self-confidence...for the ultimate decisions that are taken."

Schmidt, pressed for time at this point, said he was asking me, in writing, for two things. He then became very blunt indeed. "Let me tell you...as a friend...that the reason I put this in writing...is because of your past behavior on many, many, many different occasions when you have given the appearance of not being a part of the Medical Center team, of not being a part of the College of Medicine team, or of having clear desires to be independent of the Medical Center. You have had difficulty in relating to every person you have reported to since coming here…and I've got to tell you that these matters of the past have been discussed by people in the university many, many times, so that this is not just an isolated episode. What I am asking you for is your unswerving loyalty to this Medical Center campus, because if you do not feel you can give that, you do not belong in your position."

Once again, the thrust was obvious. Either sign on the dotted line or resign! The fact was that they always had the authority to remove me from my position and undoubtedly had discussed it on many occasions. But, knowing the uproar that followed the dismissal of Bob Evans, they hesitated to take that last drastic step and I was not about to oblige them by resigning.

"I was hired under a Board of Trustees policy that stated, 'When there is a four-year program or a program that meets all requirements for an MD degree, the program's governance will be shifted to the UIUC campus.' Now that is the functioning Board of Trustees policy under which I was recruited and which I read before I accepted my position. That policy has been opposed by the Medical Center administration. So I ask you, who is not part of the university team? The Medical Center administration has not followed that policy. As a matter of fact, it has opposed that policy all along. So I am confused by what you mean by teamwork, because there is a university team, there is a Board of Trustees which says, 'this is our policy,' and the Medical Center administration has opposed that."

"Well, without going into all those documents, I would say the answer is that you were hired to do a job as part of the Medical Center; and it was agreed that at a certain time, things would be reviewed. In the interim, that should have been set aside and your behavior in the interim should have been as a loyal member of the college administrative team…But many times your behavior has been such as to make one believe that your job during this interim period was to establish an independent school or college [on] the U-C campus, and many times that has created difficulties and has been counterproductive for the Medical Center and has certainly inhibited your functioning as a member of the team up here on many occasions. Many times, you have not been doing what you were hired to do."

I respectfully disagreed with that statement and repeated that I thought I was doing what I was hired to do. Conceding that Schmidt strongly disagreed with this view, I said, "I understand your position. I will be glad to receive the letter from you and write you a response to it."

"I have not written you a letter," he corrected me. "I have written Dr. Creditor a letter that indicates the things I have said and indicates I want your concurrence by signature on that letter, and if I don't get that, then I really can't function."

I did not understand exactly what he meant by his inability to "function," but I did not dwell on it for Creditor now chimed in. "You talk about your responsibility as dean. Of course, I didn't appoint you as dean, so I can't say that when I made the appointment, I made it clear what the responsibilities are. But quite apart from that, I believe you are exceeding your mandate as dean in this particular matter. I told you that before and I say it again now. You are not only exceeding your mandate, but I think you are being very destructive to a process which is fair to everyone involved and which has not excluded the issues and concerns which you profess...I took the same position in relation to other deans in the College of Medicine as far as my view that they were getting inappropriately involved in business that was not theirs. You do not have a mandate on this point—I did not give it to you—to get involved in the issue of the reorganization of the college, except in a certain structured fashion. And as far as I am concerned your involvement in this matter—which you say is faculty-initiated—is inappropriate for you in terms of administrative responsibilities that you have... I think the place where you are causing most damage is in Urbana-Champaign...because I think by your behavior you are almost creating a bias in the college against the Urbana program."

Thus portrayed as a bad boy, the *enfant terrible* of the College of Medicine, I tweaked them on technicalities, pointing out that there were negotiations between SBMS-MC and ALSM in Chicago and that "two separate schools" in Urbana, SBMS-UC and SCM-UC, were also talking to one another. So why could SBMS-UC not talk to Peoria? Schmidt referred to his federal government experience: When he disagreed, he stated his disagreement, but when the secretary or other senior administrators made a decision, that was the decision everyone followed. I retorted that the college-reorganization decision had not yet been made, that we were still in the arguing stage. (In retrospect, it seems clear that we were talking past one another because as far as Schmidt and Creditor were concerned, the "final" decision had already been made between themselves and President Ikenberry. Waiting for the SPMC report from the committee which Creditor chaired would merely provide the necessary academic fig leaf for the preconceived outcome.)

Schmidt remained determined to shame me. "You isolated yourself on many occasions from your fellow deans in the school [sic] and certainly from the college deans and so on, and if you don't believe that, you had better ask some questions. You isolated yourself by your behavior. It's been painful for me to sit and observe sometimes what you have been doing. I have to honestly say that I would not have been able to function as executive dean or VCAA at times in the past with you isolating yourself in the way you have."

This time I responded with measured firmness. I did not want to give them any cause to fire me for inappropriate behavior, but I was weary of the "trash Bloomfield" theme. "I have to look at what has developed in Urbana, what we have done, the resources we have had, and the quality we have been able to develop down there. I am very proud of it. I think we are the best development from all standpoints in the whole expansion project of the College of Medicine, and I have no apologies to make for it. It has sometimes meant that I have had to take strong stands, but the concern that I have here is that disagreement means disloyalty."

Schmidt quickly denied that this was his point, and I affirmed that I was prepared to follow any decision that was made by "the university." Schmidt then brought out his letter to Creditor, dated February 24,1981, and handing it to me, said: "You have one [a university decision] in front of you now."

I took the letter. I figured it told Creditor to direct me to cancel the March 3 Peoria meeting and to show appropriate loyalty, but I purposely did not read it in front of them. Knowing the traps that language can provide, I wanted to have other people read the letter to make sure that I knew exactly what I was acknowledging. I needed time. This was a critical juncture in the development of SCM-UC, and I did not want to do anything rash. Schmidt then demanded that I respond within twenty-four hours. I said I would do my best to respond within that period of time, but Schmidt insisted that it was a simple decision: yes or no, loyal or disloyal. Facing two powerful enemies, I pleaded for seventy-two hours to consider the matter, but they wanted their answers sooner. We settled on forty-eight.

Observing that I had not read the letter, Schmidt was emphatic. "I am telling you right now, the Peoria meeting is to be canceled. Now that is an order." I responded that I would carry out the order and cancel the meeting. But I now brought forward my own agenda for these two key administrators:

the inadequate SCM-UC budget. Schmidt responded that although it might surprise me, he really understood that there were good reasons for the over-draft. But, he added, "I have searched high and low for a financing plan for that school when it began, and what there was was a plan to ask the state for funds, and the state has said, 'No.'"

At this, I could not suppress a degree of anger. "One of my repeated troubles with this office and your predecessor was that he would never openly request funds for the Clinical School in U-C. That is past history, but that sure gave me the reputation for not being a team player...But I am going to have around a $200,000 deficit this year, and Mort Creditor has basically said, 'I can't handle it.' Now if Mort can't handle it and you can't handle it, somebody's going to have to handle it over a number of years. But I need some way to say it is going to be handled."

At this point, Schmidt backed off. "It is really a problem between you and Mort, and then Mort and myself, and then myself and the chancellor, and Vice President Brady and so on."

I was getting nowhere. Neither one of them would give me a thing. Before the meeting terminated, I sought one last clarification. "You started out this dialogue by telling me that President Ikenberry asked you to trans-mit some information to me. What information did the president ask you to transmit to me?"

"He asked me to meet with you very early on," Schmidt replied, "to let you know the serious financial problems that the university is facing in the health professions. It is a very serious situation that will cause the university very quickly to examine the options before it and make some decisions."

I asked him why the president singled me out personally to receive this information, and Schmidt replied, "Because of your activities with the Champaign-Urbana administration, and your activities on the Urbana cam-pus have made him aware of your very strong feelings about not only main-taining the clinical school in Urbana, but also to have an independent college or school or operation down there, he wanted me to let you know early on that, one, you could not say that you did not know what the univer-sity was contemplating (which I went over earlier in this conversation) and, two, that you could guide your behavior accordingly."

By this time I was pretty tired and depressed by all the junk they had dumped on me. I made a final effort. "I hope you won't judge me disloyal or not part of the team if I tell you that it is my personal opinion, my own honest opinion, that if one is looking for quality development in SCM-UC, then SCM-UC, if it is to be continued, should be linked to the Urbana campus, not the Medical Center campus. It may be your belief that under those circumstances, SCM-UC should be discontinued, but before you act hastily, my recommendation would be to get a dispassionate observer from outside the university to assist in these difficult decisions. That doesn't mean I can't be a part of the team or that I am disloyal to the Medical Center. It does mean that if you want the best bang for your buck, SCM-UC is very cost effective, and I think we can continue to be. In that sense, the university will be better served by a linkage of the Urbana medical-education program with UIUC."

The meeting was over. I had survived the shootout. It had been rough, very rough, but at least I was not fired. Sure enough, the letter charged Creditor to direct me to cancel the March 3 Peoria meeting and to secure my agreement to cease such planning activities and to "work closely and in a collegial fashion with [my] fellow deans, you, me, and the chancellor as we proceed through the difficult times ahead. Please have him indicate his agreement with the above by his signature on this letter."

Very neat. Very bureaucratic. And I now had forty-eight hours to respond.

The next day I wrote Schmidt a low-key response that was worked out with the assistance of Allan Levy and Hal Swartz, who both agreed that there was no purpose in further tweaking the tiger's tail. The letter told Schmidt that I had canceled the March 3 meeting, that I looked forward to "working closely with my fellow deans, the executive dean," etc., and that I had signed and acknowledged his February 24 letter to Creditor. That was all. It was clear we could expect no support from the Chicago administration. It would appear that Schmidt and Creditor planned a strategy that would keep us so desperately underfunded that we soon would have no choice but to quit. I also suspected that the SCM-UC clinical program was on the UIMC administration's chopping block, although I could not see at that time how the highly participatory SPMC process would yield the result they wanted. As I analyze the discussion in retrospect, however, it seems clear that a university administrative cabal, which certainly involved Ikenberry and Schmidt, and may have involved Brady, Begando, and Creditor, had already decided to eliminate the SCM-UC program and fashion Urbana as a permanent two-year basic medical-science school. Peoria and Rockford would be limited as two-year clinical schools. They were exploiting the SPMC process as a fig leaf to cover themselves. Creditor and Schmidt were agitated by my conversations with Peoria because the last thing they wanted was another solution when they already had one that pleased President Ikenberry and that concealed the massive deficits being accrued in Chicago, largely because of university-hospital mismanagement. It had worked before, so it should work again: The regions would pay for Chicago's mismanagement and incompetence.

I have often wondered in the years that followed the tumultuous events of 1980–81, how the college-reorganization process went so far awry as to pit Mort Creditor against his friends and colleagues at the Urbana schools that he had been so much a part of. He understood our problems and was in a strong position to help us solve them. Once he had been given his two-year appointment as "interim dean," he was virtually unassailable from above and had no need to worry about being fired for doing the right thing. Mort had sweat blood and tears for almost five years to get the SCM-UC program under way.

Two explanations come to mind. First, Mort had enough experience as a bureaucrat to know when, and when not, to be a "team player." As much as a he would have personally liked to defend against closure of SCM-UC, when central university administration decided that, for monetary reasons, SCM-UC must be eliminated, he had no choice, other than resignation, but to carry out that policy. Mort stood where he sat.

A second and more complex explanation to consider is that Morton Creditor believed he had bigger fish to fry. He was playing the role of an educational Moses leading the largest medical school in the country out of ten years in the wilderness. He was breaking new ground in medical education administration, an achievement that would most likely earn him a deanship, if not at Illinois, then at any one of a number of schools searching for distinguished leadership. Mort had carefully developed a process for resolving a classical confrontation between two titans, a giant state medical school and a powerful national accrediting body. Successful resolution would be an achievement of manifest significance and a high point of his career. But to carry it out, he needed complete control of the process. It was vital, in his authoritarian view, to prohibit any confounding solution. In pursuing his goal, he had the resolute support of the presidential office and the powerful operational support of the Vice Chancellor for Academic Affairs, Mack Schmidt.

The above explanations notwithstanding, my bright idea to send Creditor to Chicago had backfired badly. Not only was he no help whatsoever to SCM-UC, it appeared to me that he had joined the jackals for the kill. He put a stranglehold on our budget that required more and more voluntary effort from our salaried and unsalaried faculty and staff. Recruitment was dead. The outlook was grim. We had much work before us. Our future effort had to be directed at gaining political support from our local and regional constituencies. We needed to get our ducks in line before the hunters from Chicago shot us down.

CHAPTER 26

The Axe Falls

E MERGING FROM THE SHOWDOWN, I was badly shaken, but not mortally wounded. Although there was good reason to suspect that the SCM-UC clinical program was vulnerable to cancellation, there was no certainty. Despite Schmidt's blunt suggestion, I could not see how the highly participatory SPMC process would yield such a narrowly targeted result, unless the process was compromised.

The SPMC was scheduled to make its final report and recommendation to the Academic Council on May 18, 1981. It had been Mort Creditor's intention to bring the SPMC report to the June 1981 faculty meeting where the entire faculty of the college would have the opportunity to review the report and to vote on which model to accept.

But Mack Schmidt had other ideas—ideas that compromised Creditor's process. Creditor had already allowed the process to be tainted by President Eikenberry's condition that the SPMC outcome would only include one medical school and one dean. Now, Schmidt presented his own conditions. For budgetary reasons, Schmidt was in a hurry and did not wish to give the college faculty a chance to vote on all three options that were emerging from the SPMC. He was looking to save some funds through reorganization of the College of Medicine. Schmidt wanted to implement the reorganization in the next fiscal year and worried that a report as late as May would prevent early implementation. With this in mind, he directed Creditor to provide him with the SPMC final report and a choice of acceptable options by mid-March, two months earlier than planned. Schmidt would then select the most desirable option, from his viewpoint, which the college faculty could then vote up or down. To avoid embarrassment, he also directed Creditor to prevent the SPMC from indicating in its final report a preference of its own among the three options.

To no one's surprise, the final report of the UICOM Strategic Planning and Management Committee to the Academic Council recommended three viable governance options. Denied the opportunity to select a preferred option, the SPMC essentially said after a year of hearings and deliberations, "Take your pick." The result was tailor-made for Mack Schmidt, who then could choose the option that, in all likelihood, he and President Ikenberry had already agreed upon.

The Academic Council promptly approved the three-model SPMC report on March 11, 1981, by a vote of twenty yeas, five nays. Four of the five negative votes came from the SBMS/SCM-UC members, who pointed out quite correctly that after all that faculty work, the report did not provide a solution to the administrative difficulties that were the root cause of the UICOM dysfunction. But the AC approval gave legitimacy to Schmidt's next moves. It placed the reorganization decision in the hands of a campus administrator who was given carte blanche to wreak havoc on the college structure.

The first model maintained the existing structure and "improved [its] operation." This would involve identification of problems that required attention and making changes in the operating system to deal with issues as they arose. Model I had the advantage of permitting the continuation of a rational, but dysfunctional, system with the hope that it would be made more functional. Its major disadvantage, aside from its dysfunction, was that it would be perceived as an inadequate response by the LCME, among others.

The second model reorganized the college into a single college with one dean and single, collegewide departments, with associate deans and associate department heads at the regional sites. This had the advantage of reorganizing the college into a single administration with a single faculty that might be encouraged to work together more closely. It would restore the unity of the College of Medicine with a single set of standards and a single committee structure to serve the college. It would certainly have the lowest administrative overhead, and if the two-year, two-year split in medical education could be restored, it would save money by avoiding the need for costly basic-science departments in Peoria and Rockford. Furthermore, the LCME would love it. But that organization was a return to 1969. All power would revert to Chicago and the unique programs that had been developed as labors of love in Rockford, Peoria, and Urbana-Champaign would be diminished or expunged. Therein lay Model II's major disadvantage. It failed to consider eleven years of semiautonomous development at regional sites and would consign legacies that were unique to Rockford, Peoria, and

Urbana-Champaign to the ash heap. You cannot engage an entire community for a decade, ask for its cooperation, money, and hard work, and then,
in the first moment of fiscal stress, say, "Sorry, fellows, we are not getting any
new money, and our university hospital is draining what money we have, so
we can't play the medical-education game with you any longer." Aside from
the ethical aspects of Schmidt's personal decision to select Model II, his
action had political ramifications that would mobilize opposition to
Schmidt and the university administration in the three downstate regions.

The third SPMC alternative was bolder, departing from the one-college,
one-dean concept. Model III proposed that the college split in half to create
two separate medical schools, both of which would report to the VCAA at
the Medical Center. The division would be along the lines of Urbana-Peoria
and Chicago-Rockford. It was a model we had explored externally in both
open and clandestine meetings with our Peoria counterparts and internally
with my advisors and faculty. Model III resolved some of the problems of
geography and simplified both the academic and corporate governance. It
would eliminate the conflict between college authority and school responsibility and would decrease administrative costs by removing the executive
dean layer of administration and consolidating the administrative units
between the sites.

The irony of Model III is that Creditor went ballistic when he learned of
the planned March 3 meeting in Peoria, a meeting designed to deal with
how the two faculties at Urbana and Peoria might implement a Model III
type reorganization. It is entirely possible that had Schmidt not interfered,
the college SPMC might have recommended Model III as the best overall
solution to the reorganization dilemma.

The SBMS/SCM-UC faculty reviewed the SPMC report and accepted
Model III in principle as the best solution under the circumstances,
although they preferred a model that they labeled Model IIIA. Model IIIA
was identical to Model III, except that it transferred the governance of the
Peoria/Urbana-Champaign medical school to UIUC. In a response to the
February 20, 1981 report of the SPMC retreat at which these options were
formulated, Harold Swartz, chairperson of the SBMS/SCM-UC SPMC
Committee, drafted a persuasive response that urged acceptance of Model
IIIA: "While Model IIIA is no doubt disturbing to some elements of the
UIMC administration, it clearly has the greatest potential for academic
excellence and cost-effectiveness for all elements of the present College of

Medicine. We urge that the SPMC, as academicians and scholars, put aside
political questions and pressures and make a faculty recommendation based
on the best interests of the university."

The SBMS/SCM-UC SPMC, by a vote of 20-2, passed the following
resolution:

   a. The administration of the medical-school program on the C-U campus
      should be transferred from Chicago to the Chancellor's Office, UIUC.
   b. The C-U and Peoria medical-school programs should be combined
      to form a single teaching and research unit funded at a level that
      would support the maintenance of further development of academic
      excellence.
   c. If appropriate governance and financial support as outlined above can-
      not be provided, the only reasonable alternative would be to abandon
      the *entire* C-U medical-education program (SBMS-UC and SCM-UC).

There was little doubt that the faculty at Urbana-Champaign had had its fill
of a remote governance that was insensitive to our needs and unresponsive
to problems as they arose. They were prepared to give up medical education
in its entirety at UIUC if the change in governance could not be effected.

I tried to prevent precipitous action by UIMC by reminding the administration of its Treaty obligations. All of them, Grove, Schmidt, Creditor, and
the rest, were visibly annoyed by my institutional memory lessons. Nevertheless, I kept a clear paper trail to prevent Creditor or the Medical Center
administration from acting hastily toward SCM-UC. Just as I had reminded
Bill Grove, I also notified Mort Creditor in March of 1980 that I was keeping
the chancellor of UIUC (John Cribbet) and the vice chancellor for academic
affairs (Ned Goldwasser) informed regarding the organizational relationships between SBMS/SCM-UC and the UIUC campus. In my letter to
Creditor on March 17, 1980, I pointed out that Cribbet and Goldwasser
were well aware that "the initial establishment of SBMS-UC on the UIUC
campus followed thorough discussions and negotiations between the UIMC
and UIUC campuses in the 1968–70 period, a process that ultimately led to
the document which was approved by the Board of Trustees. Informed of
the review process you have initiated regarding the governance of the
College of Medicine, they asked me to inform you that they would consider
any UI College of Medicine change of governance which would affect
SBMS-UC to be subject to a similar participatory negotiation process."

In other words, I reminded Mort and the Medical Center administration that they could not take administrative measures against SCM-UC without full consultation with the UIUC Senate and the UIUC campus administration.

It's interesting to note that Creditor's archives contain the record of a private meeting on December 1, 1980 with Goldwasser, at which the vice chancellor of UIUC said, "If SCM/SBMS is to prosper it *must* transfer to this campus."

Shortly after the SPMC report was approved, Schmidt's office called to arrange for a meeting with the SBMS/SCM-UC faculty, a meeting that was held in a Medical Sciences Building classroom on April 8, 1981. We weren't informed of the agenda. Despite all the adverse signs that existed, we were still, at this time, unaware of Schmidt's plans, but not for long. I introduced Mack to a crowd of SBMS/SCM-UC faculty, staff, and students that numbered one hundred in a room designed for thirty. The close crowd magnified the tension in the air. Newspaper reporters were also present. Creditor did not attend; he remained in Chicago. Schmidt then proceeded to summarize the findings of the SPMC, emphasizing again and again the shortage of funds, and concluded:

> The university has decided that we will follow Model II in the SPMC report. The School of Basic Medical Sciences at Urbana-Champaign will be assigned a cohort of medical students for the first two years of their medical education, after which they will attend Rockford, Peoria, or Chicago for their clinical education. The School of Clinical Medicine at Urbana-Champaign will be discontinued.

Typical of the cavalier style of the UIMC administration, Schmidt did not give me, as dean, advance notice of this bombshell. Prepared though we may have been, we reacted much like a family who loses a loved one from cancer. Though we knew death was nigh, the fatal news still fell on us with dreadful impact. Many in the audience had invested ten years of their lives into building the clinical program. There was widespread anger and disbelief. Schmidt now faced a hostile audience. There were protests that closing SCM-UC was not among the options of the SPMC report. The report instead was silent on the one-year, three-year versus two-year, two-years split. Some faculty complained that Schmidt had dramatically overinterpreted Model II and was using it as club, not as a process. It was true. The

Model II, as reported out by the SPMC, did not recommend the two-year, two-year split or the dismantling of basic-science departments in Rockford and Peoria. Schmidt, however, bent on reducing regional costs to a minimum, and with Ikenberry's backing, tailored Model II to suit this more drastic and less costly design.

Schmidt took the flak straight on and answered one frenzied question after another as best he could. When asked about the Medical Scholars Program, he stated that it could be preserved with the students taking their clinical training off-campus. He remained calm, frequently blaming the lack of state funds as the source of the problem, and repeating the mantra that this was a *University Decision.* I asked whether this had been discussed with UIUC campus administration as had been provided for in the Treaty, and he gave me a carefully hedged "no."

After the first, overwrought round of questions ran its course, and the audience seemed to have absorbed the shock, one of our very bright and capable Medical Scholars, Paul Hattis, a protege of Allan Levy and a candidate for degrees in medicine and law, raised his hand and asked Dr. Schmidt, "Who is the *University?*" Schmidt answered confidently that this was a decision he had made in consultation with Interim Executive Dean Creditor and with the consensus and approval of the Medical Center chancellor and the president of the University of Illinois. But Hattis was unimpressed by the name-dropping. He persisted, and asked again, "Who is the *University?*" Schmidt hesitated, and for a brief period was speechless. He was an administrative Goliath stung by the pellet of a lowly student. Then, he finally realized the implications of the question, and he admitted that termination of any unit would have to be approved by the University Board of Trustees. Only that body made *University Decisions.* Hattis agreed and pointed out that he had reviewed the university statutes before the meeting and that Articles VIII.1.b and VIII.2 specifically provide that the decision to initiate or discontinue any program had to have the approval of the Board of Trustees, not just the authorization of an administrator, even if that administrator was the president. Schmidt conceded the point, and with somewhat shaken confidence, went on to other questions.

But the issue was drawn, the axe fell, and barring a Board of Trustees decision that opposed President Ikenberry, SCM-UC was in the tumbrel on its way to public execution. The meeting broke up shortly after the Schmidt-Hattis exchange. The newspapers leapt upon the story. Headlines blared in the April 9, 1981, *Champaign-Urbana News-Gazette:* "UI to Close Urbana Clinical Medical School." This was followed the next day by the headline: "UI Finances Force Med School Closing." For all practical purposes, SCM-UC was a goner.

Where Mort Creditor stood on closing SCM-UC, at this time, and what his role was in this adverse decision is not clear and never has been clear. According to Martin Kernis, who was Mort's associate executive dean and with whom I discussed this issue twelve years later, Creditor was present during the decision-making process that targeted SCM-UC. Creditor, according to Kernis, fought the decision as best he could, but ultimately, because Schmidt was so convinced that the Medical Center and the University Hospital were virtually bankrupt, gave in to Schmidt's decision. Nevertheless, whether Creditor was being a good, loyal soldier who was just following orders, or whether he had turned on SBMS/SCM-UC for forcefully advocating Model IIIA with a shift of governance to UIUC, Mort Creditor was no longer considered a friend of the Urbana-Champaign medical-education program.

The SPMC deliberations being a completely open process, the gamut of acceptable options was known in advance. What we weren't prepared for was the way Schmidt abbreviated the process, blocked the SPMC from making its own recommendations, and used such an extreme interpretation of SPMC Model II as a vehicle to return the college to its pre-1970 configuration. This was very threatening to the self-image of the regional schools, and it soon became clear that there were many faculty members in Peoria and Rockford who supported the Urbana concept that the separate downstate medical-education program visualized in Model III, might be fashioned out of the present imbroglio.

Unfortunately, SPMC Model III was dead on arrival, not only because Schmidt wanted to implement his version of Model II immediately, but also because the new president remained adamant that regardless of circumstance, he did not want two separately accredited Colleges of Medicine within the University of Illinois. He would hold that position firmly throughout his fourteen-year presidency.

For his pains, Mort Creditor had invested almost two years of personal hard work and demanded an enormous expenditure of energy throughout the college toward an outcome that would not be allowed to stick—a painstakingly open process that masked a covert agenda. Schmidt and

Ikenberry devised a classical case of a university administration co-opting a
blue-ribbon faculty committee to do preordained dirty work. Mort, who
should have known better, presumably allowed Ikenberry and Schmidt to
hijack the process, because he was generally sympathetic with their goals
and lost his own objectivity. Perhaps he believed that in his relatively weak
position as interim executive dean, he could not refuse a mandate received
from senior administrators. Perhaps he was promised a permanent position
when all the reorganization dust had settled. Either way, it is hard not to
assign him some of the blame for the events that followed.

Placed under an economic microscope, the decision did not make sense.
We at SCM-UC were very angry. The Medical Center problems had multimillion-dollar price tags. Closing the College of Medicine's smallest and
most cost-effective unit would not solve them. I was a part of the Medical
Center administration, and had I been a dutiful bureaucrat, I would have
taken my directions from Mack Schmidt and Mort Creditor and planned the
phaseout of SCM-UC. But on reflection, I recalled that I had been hired in
1970 under the provisions of a Treaty that had been ratified by the Board of
Trustees and that had made clear provisions for SCM-UC. That was my
mandate, and that was what I would fulfill. There was too much at stake.
First, I was determined to preserve the Medical Scholars Program, which
was unique in the world, and second, I rejected the idea that UIUC, one of
the leading scientific-research campuses in the world, should be without a
four-year medical school of its own. Regardless of my position either as
dean or fired ex-dean, I would oppose that decision. The day after Schmidt's
announcement, I met with my staff and with Ben Williams, Allan Levy, Hal
Swartz, and Jack Pollard to plan our strategy.

We were not without friends. I had worked assiduously for eleven years
to build up a friendly constituency for SCM-UC. The shock of losing
SCM-UC echoed throughout the Urbana-Champaign community and to
the Danville VA Medical Center. There was immediate mobilization of
resources and of interest. The doctors who had worked on the program were
upset. The hospital administrators who made provisions for medical education and graduate medical education were upset. The administrative team at
DVAMC, although not completely cooperative at that time, expressed its
concern about the closing of the school. Taking note of the white-paper
information that I had provided, and spurred by the awareness that the
presence of a medical school within a community has a very significant

economic effect, measured in millions of dollars, the C-U Chamber of Commerce showed immediate interest in this issue. We also had behind us the power and authority of the UIUC Senate support, which had been carefully cultivated by our faculty members in that senate. Hence, SCM-UC was well-positioned to mobilize a sizable constituency to resist the application of Schmidt's Model II. Aside from the merits of the case, taking on the closure of SCM-UC posed a larger-than-expected political problem for UIMC.

As if closing SCM-UC and the Medical Scholars Program were not enough of a problem for Mack Schmidt and Mort Creditor, they also undertook the task of trimming Rockford and Peoria into two-year clinical schools. That posed an immediate and serious threat to the whole development of RSM and PSM and mobilized significant political opposition in those cities. Working in close cooperation with the forces we could muster in U-C, and with allies of convenience in Rockford and Peoria, we prepared for a fight. We were determined to modify the *University Decision.*

CHAPTER 27

Measures and Countermeasures

ITH SCM-UC SLATED FOR CLOSURE, there could no longer be any pretense about how the Medical Center and the university's higher administration viewed our program. Lined up against us were President Ikenberry, Vice President Brady, Chancellor Begando, VCAA Schmidt, and even Interim Executive Dean Creditor. Their issue was money, plain and simple. Ours was quality. Senior administration was convinced that there was a money shortage before SCM-UC began that was exacerbated by the new four-year program at UIUC. They rejected our appeals that we could do more for less, as if we hadn't already been doing quite a bit for very little.

As the SPMC process wore on, I remained upset at the grossly inadequate funding of SCM-UC. It appeared that the Medical Center strategy, in lieu of my refusal to resign and their desire not to stir a bee's nest by dismissing me, was to starve us to death. In the 1980-81 school year, I was running a four-year medical-education program for 106 M-1 and a total of 84 M-2, M-3, and M-4 students on a budget of barely $2.8 million and 57 percent of that, $1.6 million, was assigned to the M-1 program. Creditor reduced the already inadequate SCM-UC budget by $40,000 in the 1981–82 school year, an impossible cut for a program that he knew was already overspending by $200,000 per year. I was reasonably certain that Schmidt and Creditor hoped I would "throw in the towel."

In this depressing atmosphere, some of my administrative staff members were adding to the gloom. Arthur Leonard, my associate dean for clinical affairs, advised me to give up the affiliations with Danville Family Practice Center and with DVAMC, describing them as an "albatross." He wrote on February 23, 1981, that the family-practice center was "an inferior program because it does not have academic leadership." In the same letter, he said of the VA hospital, "I believe that even if I went out there tomorrow to be chief of staff, that I could never recruit proper faculty to that institution."

I acknowledged Art Leonard's sincere advice. I had little choice but to follow it in the case of the family-practice center. The center received notice of accreditation withdrawal on January 24, 1981. There was little I could do to save that program because the two private hospitals in Danville were not prepared to undergo the transition necessary to become residency-supporting teaching hospitals. We would try again to establish a family-practice residency closer to home.

However, the VA hospital was a different matter. I had talked many hours with the DVAMC director and the chief of staff about the future of medical education and research at the hospital. We agreed in principle that a good, strong medical-school affiliation for DVAMC would first and foremost be good for the veterans whom the hospital served. When that requirement was satisfied, teaching and research would follow. It was not an easy path to follow, however. The road was strewn with all sorts of bureaucratic obstacles, most of which were eventually handled by Dr. Sam Birdzell, the very skilled and experienced hospital director with whom we were fortunate to be working during this trying period.

To save money, I cut savagely into every fringe that we had, instituted an absolute hiring freeze, closed down the office of medical education, restricted copying to verified need, eliminated office-equipment replacement, and severely reduced office supplies. I notified the hospitals that we would not be able to pay our space-rental fees, and physician instructors were invited to contribute their teaching honoraria back to the school, which needed the money. I put all faculty members on notice to avoid all official reimbursable travel if they could possibly do so. Travel costs were virtually eliminated. Of all the steps taken in responding to the heavy and ceaseless budgetary pressure, one and only one bothers me to this day. I was forced to break my word to a very loyal friend and supporter, Dr. Shig Yasunaga.

During the early days of SCM-UC, before the arrival of Morton Creditor, Dr. Yasunaga, a Japanese-American and a very competent pediatrician-neonatologist, contributed much of his valuable free time and energy to the development of the pediatrics curriculum. He also helped other physicians develop their curricula. He offered to work half-time with the school as an academic professional for a very modest salary that fell easily within our budget at that time. He asked whether there was any type of academic tenure he might earn for his contributions, and I told him that academic tenure was impossible. However, noting his valuable contributions,

I assured him "that as long as I am dean, you will have a job." Shig worked diligently for us during those formative years, but when the relentless budget pressure finally became too oppressive, I called him into my office and told him that I would have to let him go. He reminded me of my promise and even protested his dismissal to university legal authorities, who told him that I lacked the authority to make such a promise. To this day, I regret that action more than any other in this tortuous history.

In this way, I labored painfully to reduce SBMS/SCM-UC expenditures. For his part, Schmidt had taken great pains to impress on me months earlier at the showdown how bad the financial situation was at the Medical Center. Of course, one of the better arguments for sustaining SCM-UC was to reduce medical education in Chicago because that was where the trouble was and that was where the major financial problems had been generated. Besides, six other medical schools were in Chicago. The Chicago leadership had unwisely built federal funds into the permanent educational structure in Chicago, and as those funds tapered off, they were scrambling wildly to pressure the Illinois Board of Higher Education for state dollars as a replacement. They also had more that $2 million in vacancy credits, financial obligations that were generated from the use of lapsed or unspent dollars to hire new faculty and staff in excess of those who were identified in the budget. When the IBHE balked on recommending the complete replacement of these deficiencies with state funds, instead of cutting overextended and then-unsupported programs in Chicago, the senior administrators at the Medical Center pointed to SCM-UC as an easy target, even though closing it would relieve their deficits by precious little. As far as I was concerned, Schmidt and Creditor, representing the UIMC administration, had declared war on SCM-UC. I would fight them, even though I was bound to be "collegial and loyal" to them after that dressing-down on February 24, 1981. In order to act properly collegial and loyal and to keep myself out of trouble, I met regularly with my close advisors to plan strategy for the next day, week, or month.

It was not without irony that the same day Schmidt and Creditor were pressing me to fall into line or resign, I returned home from Chicago to respond to a written invitation from Paul Stone, President of the University Board of Trustees, to join him at the board's luncheon on April 16. The invitation, which was "seconded" by President Ikenberry, did not happen by chance. Stone, a lawyer from Sullivan, Illinois, had been unanimously elected president of the University of Illinois Board of Trustees at their January 15, 1981 annual meeting. A graduate of the College of Commerce in 1940 and a 1942 graduate of the College of Law, he had practiced law in Sullivan, in the east central part of the state, since 1942. A lifelong Democrat, he was six times elected as a representative to the Illinois General Assembly, serving on the Higher Education Committee throughout his time in the legislature. While serving in that capacity, he was an important and constant friend to the University of Illinois.

Stone had also been active on a number of state boards and committees dealing with higher education. From 1964 through 1966, he was Chairman of the Illinois Board of Governors of State Colleges and Universities. He was first elected a University of Illinois trustee in January 1979. His wife, Thelma, also graduated from UIUC, and their four children all attended UIUC. A seasoned politician and a devoted alumnus, Stone knew a good thing when he saw it and bought into the concept of the Medical Scholars Program at Urbana-Champaign from the very start. His leadership, guidance, and advice during the months after his election to the presidency of the board proved to be crucial to SCM-UC.

Ben Williams heard through the grapevine early in 1981 that SCM-UC was targeted for elimination by the president's office and particularly by the office of Vice President Ron Brady. Working with Dick Thies, a local attorney active in Democratic politics and a person who knew Paul Stone well, Williams arranged a brief meeting for me with Stone early in February. The meeting was nominally planned for us to just get acquainted, but it did not take long to brief Stone about the major funding difficulties that confronted us and about the rumors that SCM-UC and the Medical Scholars Program might be shut down. Stone took an immediate interest in SBMS/SCM-UC and in the Medical Scholars Program. He stated he would send me an invitation to be his guest at the luncheon after their next meeting in Urbana. After lunch, he would visit our program in the Medical Sciences Building.

To prepare for the months ahead, I was urged by my close advisors to immediately prepare another white paper on SCM-UC for wide distribution to all of our constituencies. The white paper should, above all else, justify our existence. In doing so, it needed to stress our achievements, highlight our programmatic development, and emphasize our cost-effectiveness. The white paper was also necessary to mobilize our sympathetic constituencies and to keep them informed. These included UIUC campus faculty, department

heads, faculty senators, and administrators, 250 clinical associate faculty
(most of whom were practicing physicians); as well as local, state, and
national politicians; other leading MD-Ph.D. programs; newspaper editors
within a seventy-five-mile radius of Champaign-Urbana; and hospital directors of our twenty-one affiliated hospitals. We strove to be all-inclusive.

It was an appropriate time for such a self-serving device. The year 1981
marked the successful completion of ten years and ten classes through
SBMS-UC, and the first SCM-UC class was scheduled to graduate in June,
barely two months hence. We were proud because we had plenty of achievements to crow about. We wrote about our strong medical-education base on
the UIUC campus, the involved and committed medical community both in
Champaign-Urbana and in the region, and the broad support of regional
teaching hospitals. We also noted that SCM-UC combined "the faculty, facilities, and support systems of a world-class, research-oriented university, the
excellent medical personnel and the facilities of major teaching affiliates,
and the resources of community hospitals throughout the region...As a
community-based medical school, supported by an outstanding campus,
SBMS/SCM-UC is able to educate students in a singularly cost-effective
manner. Educational costs per student compare very favorably with state
and national data."

The white paper reinforced the concepts underlying the importance of
the Medical Scholars Program—concepts that made it one that no senior
academic administrator would even think of stopping. It was the Medical
Scholars Program that really placed the Chicago administration on the
horns of a dilemma. They could not attack the Medical Scholars Program,
because it represented an irreplaceable element of interdisciplinary quality
within the university. By the spring of 1981, SCM-UC had twenty-seven
medical scholars enrolled in sixteen disciplines: biochemistry, business
administration, chemistry, computer science, economics, electrical engineering, history, law, microbiology, neural and behavioral biology, nuclear engineering, nutritional sciences, physics, psychology, sociology, and speech and
hearing science. Although the Medical Center in Chicago had occasional
MD-Ph.D. students, they had never come up with an MD-Ph.D. program
that even remotely compared. Now, the Chicago leadership wanted to surgi-
cally eliminate SCM-UC without destroying the Medical Scholars Program
as well. But the program's linkage with the broad spectrum of discipline at
UIUC meant that SCM-UC and the Medical Scholars Program were bound

together, conjoined twins, inseparable. Mort Creditor was soon to argue otherwise, that a clinical program at Urbana-Champaign was not essential to the continuation of the Medical Scholars Program, a fundamental flaw in logic from the originator of logic pathways.

We were so successful in advancing the Medical Scholars Program that President Ikenberry had no choice but to include it as one of the essentials to maintain within any reorganization that took place. In fact, it was the only educational program that he specifically mandated for inclusion in the anticipated reorganization of the college. All other Ikenberry mandates related to administrative functions. Strengthened by the white paper and by presidential endorsement, the SCM-UC Medical Scholars Program achieved sacred-cow status. As if to second the SCM-UC white paper, the *New England Journal of Medicine* in May 1981 came out with an article calling for additional federal funding of MD-Ph.D. programs.

The white paper also stressed cost-effectiveness. Citing our symbiosis with the UIUC campus, the paper presented carefully prepared tables to substantiate our lower cost structure. The data were nevertheless rejected without discussion by the UIMC administrators, who persuaded President Ikenberry to do likewise. These senior administrators went to great pains to denigrate the data because to accept them would have made it less logical to eliminate SCM-UC. Nevertheless, these figures were accurate and showed that the projected costs per student at SBMS/SCM-UC were about 20 percent less than the costs for the college as a whole and 40 percent less, when the burden of a malfunctioning, state-subsidized university hospital was included in the calculations.

The white paper was prepared in the week after my Chicago adventure with Schmidt and Creditor and ten days before the SPMC's final report was delivered to the Academic Council. Keeping all options open was critical at the time, so the paper also contained a financial analysis of Model III, the merger of SBMS/SCM-UC with the Peoria School of Medicine. This was appropriate because Model III was under active consideration by the SPMC and would be reported out as such in less than a fortnight. The paper said, "With judicious use of the available community hospitals and the resources of the UIUC campus, a four-year PSM/SBMS/SCM-UC medical program could be delivered at a cost no greater than the average cost per student in the rest of the College of Medicine and with unquestionably lower overhead costs. There is currently approximately $7 million in the combined budgets of PSM/SBMS/SCM-UC. Assuming a class size of one hundred and a total enrollment of four hundred, the cost per student would average approximately $17,500 per year, a figure almost $4,000 less per student than the present FY82 budget that the College of Medicine calls for (University Hospital excluded)."

Creditor, Schmidt, and Ikenberry hotly contested these figures, but not one of them ever took the time to show us where we were wrong. We were not wrong. The judicious merger of PSM and SBMS/SCM-UC to create a single, downstate medical school, together with the merger of Rockford and Chicago, was a logical and feasible solution to the reorganization problem. This probably would have taken place had it not been for the adamant fixation of the president on the concept of a single college of medicine in a system that would have benefited from more imaginative leadership.

Another major thrust in combating the closure of SCM-UC was to mobilize our UIUC campus allies and particularly to rally that sleeping giant, the UIUC faculty senate. Ordinarily, faculty senate matters are routine, deliberative, and dull. Within the confines of senate meetings, faculty senators are known to engage in complicated, convoluted, and thoroughly boring arguments over educational issues that never approach the consciousness of most non-senatorial faculty. But the faculty senate has real statutory power. The University of Illinois Statutes say, "Each Senate may exercise legislative functions in matters of educational policy affecting the university as a whole or its own campus only. No such Senate action shall take effect until it has been submitted to the University Senates Conference...Each Senate shall determine for its campus matters of educational policy including, but not limited to: ...relations between colleges, schools, and other teaching divisions."

The functions of the University Senates Conference (senators from all campuses of the university) are also well defined: "The University Senates Conference shall review all matters acted upon by each Senate. The Conference shall determine whether Senate actions requiring implementation or further consideration by officials or other groups within the university have been referred to the appropriate officials or groups." Translated, this means that no Senate may take steps that impinge on another campus without review by both Senates. In other words, if the Medical Center campus wants to rid itself of the thorny little program of SCM-UC in Urbana, it cannot do so without a complete review by the UIUC Senate.

We knew that due process would require that the SPMC report be approved by the Academic Council, then by the college faculty, then by the Medical Center Senate (a rubber stamp), then by the University Senates Conference, and finally by the president, who would submit it with his recommendation to the Board of Trustees. It was clear to us that once the SPMC report was submitted, the drastic changes that Schmidt and Creditor wanted, could be advanced through the Medical Center Senate and fulfill the due-process requirements without difficulty. There would be no stopping the adoption of the report unless brakes were applied at the Senates Conference level.

The UIUC Senate had approved the Treaty of 1969. It was our position that the UIUC Senate had to be consulted in any decision that was made regarding the future of medical education at Urbana-Champaign. The Chicago administration, on the other hand, maintained a posture that the issue of SCM-UC was strictly under the jurisdiction of the Medical Center Senate. They claimed that only SBMS-UC, which was the only school to which the 1969 Treaty referred, was a legitimate topic for intercampus negotiation. Knowing that the Medical Center Senate would rubber-stamp the phaseout of SCM-UC, we took great pains to alert the UIUC Senate to stake its claim promptly to ensure that any university decision regarding the status of SCM-UC was not beyond its interest and jurisdiction.

At the heart of our senatorial lobbying activity on the UIUC campus was Allan Levy, professor of medical information science. Because we were obligated to be members of the Medical Center Senate, we could not vote in the UIUC Senate. The UIUC Senate however, noting that we were, de facto, a part of the UIUC campus, granted us the privilege of sending two members of our faculty to their meetings as observers. Allan, who served as both official observer and unofficial lobbyist, had been recruited to SCM-UC in 1975 from Baylor University School of Medicine to lead the SCM-UC medical computing effort. In that capacity, he had developed many important faculty contacts across the UIUC campus. Also, he was a valued consultant for the computer branches and programmatic initiatives at the National Institutes of Health. He was logical, meticulous, and thorough. When it came down to legal interpretation or application of the University of Illinois Statutes, he had no peer. Allan, therefore, was particularly effective as a liaison person between SCM-UC and the UIUC Senate. When, after painstaking and lengthy negotiation, he had achieved a consensus of faculty senators about an issue relating to SCM-UC, he would carefully draft appropriate Senate resolutions for the senators to introduce, which reflected the consensus and over time, put the UIUC Senate squarely behind the concept of clinical education in Urbana-Champaign.

It was no accident, then, that on April 13, 1981, within five days of Mack Schmidt's unwelcome announcement that SCM-UC was slated for closure, the UIUC Senate acted decisively. A Senate resolution noted that "the elimination of the clinical-training component would drastically affect the presently operational joint MD-Ph.D. (Medical Scholars) Program, in which over twenty-five U-C departments are participating formally…and that the proposed reorganization, although following an internal study by the College of Medicine, does not specify any of the models recommended by the Academic Council of the College of Medicine, rather the recommendations have emanated from the Office of the Vice Chancellor for Academic Affairs at the Medical Center. They have not been presented to the faculty other than verbally. The recommendations have not been endorsed by any of the faculty bodies within the College of Medicine nor have the plans been presented to either Senate at the Medical Center or at the U-C campus."

Then as if to add an additional spanking to Mack Schmidt, the Senate resolution goes on to say, "The Statutes of the University of Illinois state that 'when acting on matters having to do with educational policy and organization of the university, the board relies upon the advice of the University Senates, as transmitted to it by the president of the university.' The close linkage between medical education and other campus educational programs warrants this Senate's consideration of the reorganization plan before its implementation.

"Be it resolved that the U-C Senate (1) record its observation that the medical-education programs on this campus are an integral part of the educational programs on this campus and are of concern to this Senate; (2) direct the Senate Council, in consultation with the chancellor, to appoint an appropriate committee to study the impact of the proposed reorganization of the College of Medicine…; (3) communicate to President Ikenberry this Senate's concern with the proposed reorganization, advising that this Senate is now considering the matter and requests the president defer final recommendation to the Board of Trustees concerning the reorganization of the College of Medicine and the closing of the School of Clinical Medicine at U-C until he receives the advice of this Senate as required by the University Statutes."

I could not have asked for a more supportive resolution from the UIUC Senate had I written it myself, and indeed, the resolution had been written by Allan Levy, who also arranged for its introduction on the UIUC Senate agenda. Allan, as usual, had done his homework well. He kept in close contact with me as we worked together to establish this important support linkage. The resolution put the president on notice to defer any decision he might recommend to the Board of Trustees until after he had received the advice of the UIUC Senate. It also provided for a new ad hoc committee to study the impact of the proposed UICOM reorganization and the selective closing of SCM-UC. It was a major tactical victory for us on a playing field that was ordinarily tilted against us. But now the defined interest of the UIUC Senate guaranteed us some breathing room and the opportunity of a hearing before a more sympathetic peer group. The ad hoc UIUC Senate subcommittee would report its findings in the fall.

With the UIUC Senate action fresh in his mind, it became clear to the president, if not to the Medical Center administration, that a significant constituency at UIUC was seriously interested in the future of medical education, the Medical Scholars Program, and SCM-UC. On April 16, the same date that I was to have lunch with the Board of Trustees, Ikenberry acknowledged as much in his remarks to the General Policy Committee of the board.

"I have received from the UIUC Senate a resolution indicating that the matter [the reorganization of the College of Medicine] was discussed by the Senate at its most recent meeting on Monday," Ikenberry told the committee, "and that the issue was referred to the Senate Council for assignment to the appropriate Senate committee. I applaud this move and will take personal responsibility...to ensure that the views of the Senate are considered fully."

The president then backed off from Schmidt's firm position of closing the School of Clinical Medicine by saying, "We must correct the mistaken notion in the minds of some that we are dealing with a *fait accompli*. Discussions in recent weeks have been candid and open, but in nearly every area, further planning by the faculty and members of the academic administration remains to be done."

So what we had here, as we grasped at straws in the wind was a key discrepancy, a slight crack in the armor between the presidential denial of Schmidt's *fait accompli* and Schmidt saying, "It is the University's position that SCM-UC will be closed." Schmidt's declaration definitely and unequivocally implicated the president, but the president, at least, was keeping his options open. The president, however, remained firm and committed in one respect when he confirmed his policy of a single medical college, adding, "We do not propose to escalate further our commitment by fragmenting into two or three or four independent, free-standing Colleges of Medicine with the far-ranging implications attendant thereto."

The tiny crack in the facade notwithstanding, the April 16 trustees meeting was very depressing. As the issues surrounding college reorganization and funding difficulties were laid out by the Medical Center administration, I was tempted on numerous occasions to stand up and cry to the trustees, "Foul! You are not receiving information; you are receiving self-serving misinformation!" However, I remained silent while Begando, Schmidt, and Creditor laid the groundwork for our demise. There were some rays of hope represented by board President Paul Stone and Trustee Ralph Hahn. It was very clear, as information about the SPMC process was presented to the board, that the board knew very little about UICOM and its proposed reorganization. Ikenberry pushed very hard for the board to adopt a policy (actually to change earlier policy that evolved out of the 1969 Treaty) that there would be only one college of medicine within the university. He also discussed the high cost of medical education and directly attacked my figures on the cost of a downstate college of medicine, which were ten thousand to fifteen thousand dollars less than the cost figures he cited of thirty thousand to thirty-five thousand dollars per student per year as typical of medical-education costs. He said that the figures I proposed would lead to an inferior College of Medicine on the cheap.

It was clear that my earlier discussions on medical education with the president had gone for naught. Not only had he not bought into any of my arguments, on the contrary, he became an antagonist to SCM-UC and appeared to take great umbrage at my activities. Of course, he was talking these days to Medical Center administrators, who had plenty of opportunities to poison the well. At the close of the meeting, I was downcast and dispirited and felt like I didn't want to go to the luncheon with Paul Stone. Nevertheless, we met at noon. Stone was his usual ebullient and optimistic self and proceeded with me to the Illini Union Colonial Room. At our table were George Friedman (the president of the UIUC Senate), Hal Swartz, several administrators from Penn State, and others. Avoiding me at another table were Joe Begando and Mack Schmidt.

Conversation at lunch covered the usual generalities, but with the presidents of the Board of Trustees and the UIUC Senate in my audience, I brought the dialogue around to the medical-school program. I pointed out how amazing it was that the UIUC Senate supported the concept that they had a stake in the decision-making process concerning medical education on this campus. Ordinarily a liberal arts and sciences campus would be scared to death by the specter of importing into their midst a resource-devouring monster such as a medical school. George Friedman cautioned that a portion of that support was largely due to the faculty resisting what appeared to be, administrative fiat, and felt that when the time came, there would be many who would speak out against the incorporation of a medical school into the governance of UIUC. Nevertheless, I explained then, as I have explained many times over, that SCM-UC was a different kind of school, which did not require the resources of the typical program. What we needed most was a degree of freedom from the repressive UIMC governance. There was agreement, at least at our lunch table that the basic UIUC campus support for its own medical school was there. Paul Stone mentioned that Joe Begando was also amazed that the UIUC Senate had supported the concept of looking into the possibility of its own medical school so strongly. It took the UIMC administration completely by surprise. Stone urged for caution regarding the governance issue because he felt that in this period of fiscal restraint, Ikenberry and the board were pretty well decided that there would be only one College of Medicine.

After lunch, I was walking out of the Colonial Room with Stone but told him that, as a courtesy, I should bid a civil goodbye to Begando and Schmidt. He agreed and said, "I'm in no rush, take all the time you want to." I gave Begando a courteous goodbye, but Schmidt asked to speak with me for a few minutes. He then spent ten or fifteen minutes informing me that he hoped he had not been misunderstood, that he had really been under marching orders (from the president?) to do what he did, that he understood our problems down here. Then, he proceeded to lavish on me a legacy of defensive statements that exposed some element of guilt that was bothering him. I wished I had a tape recorder to document the unusual occurrence, for I couldn't recall much of it at the time I dictated my diary. The message was clear, however. Closing SCM-UC wasn't his idea, but the idea of his superiors, who had directed him to take the steps that he did. I said to Schmidt that had there been preliminary consultation with the deans before presenting them with a *fait accompli*, some of this difficulty and bitterness could have been avoided. I couldn't believe that Schmidt was as gracious as he was, but it was very clear that someone had chastised him. Later on, Stone told me that Schmidt's recent actions had cost him his credibility with the board and that the board probably would not listen to anything coming from him anymore. That was an amazing statement, since Schmidt appeared to be the odds-on favorite candidate to replace the retiring Joe Begando. Stone's observation placed Schmidt out of the running as long as this board was in power.

After lunch, I took Stone to the Medical Sciences Building, where we viewed a movie about the Medical Scholars Program. Stone was very impressed and asked whether he could show it to others, adding that he thought Ikenberry and the other trustees needed an education. We agreed that we would show the movie whenever he wanted and to whomever he wanted. I then took him to visit some of the faculty laboratories to give him a flavor of some of the excellent work that was being done. We began at Joann Cameron's laboratory, where she explained muscle regeneration in newts, and then went to Paul Wong's laboratory, where he explained problems in viral development. Both of them had enough clinical relevance that I could translate between the scientist and the clinician to give Stone a view of the some of the exciting work that was going on at SBMS/SCM-UC. He seemed genuinely impressed. We then drove to Mercy Hospital to show him the significant capital that Mercy was putting into its building program to develop the laboratories and office space that the Mercy CEC would comprise. After seeing that, we went to Carle CEC where we viewed the laboratory facilities that Carle had created to support Ralph Nelson's nutritional work. Ralph Nelson explained his nutrition research and its relation to various departments on campus. Stone met with some of the clinical students for fifteen minutes and enjoyed the exchange.

We then returned to the Medical Science Building and talked at length about the strategy of survival. By that time, he was convinced that clinical education should remain in Champaign-Urbana. He described it as a political problem that we had to resolve. I raised the issue of the one-college, two-college policy and asked whether he was aware that the president's assertion that there would be only one college of medicine at the university was a change in policy. He said that he did not know that and was unaware that there was any previous policy. I showed him the 1969 Treaty, and he was amazed. He asked for a copy. He knew Lyle Lanier was prominent in creating that document, but he was unaware that there had been agreement on the changes in governance when the Urbana-Champaign program was begun. I informed him that I thought it was unfair and relatively dishonest for this information to be suppressed from the board. Stone agreed completely and stated that there had to be some education not only of the board, but also of the UIMC administration and the president

Stone emphasized that, as yet, nothing in the UICOM reorganization plans was set in concrete, but that some strong pitches had been made and that if we wanted to change the outcome we had our work cut out for us. He asked for me to send him the SPMC report and my comments on the three SPMC options, which the board had never seen. In leaving, he asked me to call Dick Thies and tell him, "I'm working on his problem." He advised me to "keep things stirred up" and to keep information coming to the entire Board of Trustees.

Mr. Stone left with a very positive and favorable impression of our program, believing that with further "education," the president would see the light. He'd come a long way from his response to *News Gazette* reporter, Lex Peterson who quoted him six days earlier as saying, "It is because the University of Illinois Medical Center has to do something to save money that the Urbana campus's School of Clinical Medicine is on the chopping block. I don't like it at all, but whatever else is done, I'm not going to like either."

All in all, April 16, 1981 was a remarkable day during which I visited the depths of despair and returned to a level of cautious optimism.

As a follow-up to that meeting, I sent Mr. Stone a copy of the June 9, 1969 letter from Lyle Lanier to Herb Carter and Bill Grove. The second paragraph on page two of that letter states, "No commitment can or should be made that a full program of clinical training will not be developed in time at the Urbana-Champaign campus. Indeed, both the university's report of December 1967 and the Board of Higher Education's document specifically mention such a possibility. But the 'Campbell Report' gives priority to Peoria and Rockford as the initial locations for expansion of clinical training by the university outside of Chicago. Hence, it seems best to leave the matter of clinical training at Urbana-Champaign indefinite and open—*with the understanding that if and when a four- year medical curriculum emerges there, it would be administered as an independent college under the chancellor at that campus.*" [Emphasis added.]

Lanier's wording was an unequivocal commitment of the university to two colleges of medicine when a four-year curriculum began at Urbana-Champaign, a condition met in 1981.

Stone's initial medical-school visit led shortly to what was undoubtedly the strangest meeting I have ever had. Stone arranged for the two of us to meet with Stanley Ikenberry. Stone informed me that on April 27 he was going to visit the Medical Sciences Building with the president. "All the president needs," said Mr. Stone, "is a little education. We'll educate him."

Stone and Ikenberry showed up as scheduled at 3 p.m., but Ikenberry was clearly unhappy. He had the pained look of an errant schoolboy who was having his ear twisted by the teacher and being told to sit down and listen. He was anything but compliant and friendly. After preliminary greetings, we viewed the Medical Scholars film that had so impressed Paul Stone. It left Ikenberry stony-faced. The three of us then toured the Medical Sciences Building, viewing the biocommunication-arts laboratory, which had been created with AHES funds, which created superb art, and which was now being destroyed for lack of continuing funds. I pointed out that this was a major loss to the school and the region. The teaching programs in this area should never have been started unless continuing monetary support was available. We then went to the laboratories of three investigators: Paul Wong talked about oncogenic viruses, Walter Mangel discussed tumor-cell surface-invasive enzymes, and Willard Visek talked about the relationship of diet and cancer. The president, while maintaining his civility, asked no questions of any of the investigators. Without saying a word, he made it abundantly clear to me through body language that he was attending under protest.

The three of us then retired to my office, where we again discussed the future of SCM-UC. Ikenberry, as he always did with me, took an extremely fixed and rigid stand regarding medical education at Urbana-Champaign. It was a strange meeting of three people trying to harmonize, but all were out of tune. There was Paul Stone, upbeat and enthusiastic. He was a great salesman, but Stanley Ikenberry wasn't buying that day. I was there providing the raw data for Mr. Stone's hard sell, but more importantly, trying to establish rapport with the president of the university, but Ikenberry kept his distance from me.

My diary of the meeting comments:

He (Ikenberry) is convinced that basic medical-science education and goodwill will resolve the problems for the Medical Scholars Program. He called SCM-UC late-coming, underfunded, and something "we" can't afford. He was clearly committed to Mack Schmidt and the Medical Center position. I found it a most disheartening conversation. Paul Stone intervened several times in my behalf, but the conversation went nowhere. I raised every issue I could think of: the Treaty, the 1970 BOT [Board of Trustees] documents, Lyle Lanier's 1969 letter, which plowed the middle ground between UIMC and UIUC, but for every situation, Ikenberry behaved like an antibody. He was armed and thoroughly immunized against any argument I could provide him. He said he was willing to learn, but I am not certain that is true. I finally told him that he had a choice between quality and excellence that could be developed here with the Medical Scholars Program and the mediocrity that he would be left with in UICOM without SCM-UC and the MSP. He said the final UICOM reorganization decision would be academically generated, and advanced through regular UIMC channels, which means the Academic Council, the college faculty, and the UIMC Senate; channels which were rigged against us. While he agreed to "consult" with the UIUC campus, he gave no indication that he would take the UIUC Senate recommendations seriously. What chance do we have?

I was left with the impression that Stanley Ikenberry was not a good listener. He had a very closed, inflexible mind on both the future of SCM-UC, as well as on other options that might have been possible for the UICOM reorganization. He was absolutely rigid in his commitment to preserve a single medical college regardless of prior commitments, merits or consequences. Moreover, it was becoming crystal clear that I was not his favorite dean. All in all, it was a distressing afternoon, Paul Stone's enthusiastic optimism notwithstanding.

All this was taking its personal toll on me. On May 1, I flew down to Springfield from Chicago on an SIU plane provided by Dean Moy. I was planning to attend a meeting of the Illinois Council of Deans. It was one of those warm spring days when the cumulus clouds rise high enough in pockets to blot out the sun and add considerable turbulence to the atmosphere. Seated in the rear of the plane, I began to feel airsick, something I had never suffered during my own flying days. As we disembarked from the plane at

Springfield airport, I collapsed on the tarmac and had to be helped off. According to the reports of others, I was ashen gray, sweating profusely, cold and clammy. I was carried to a waiting limousine and rushed off to the main SIU teaching hospital, Springfield Memorial. On the way, I developed profound vertigo. The diagnosis of acute vestibulitis (an inner-ear problem that interferes with balance) was confirmed by the vigorous nystagmus (involuntary rapid movements of the eye) that accompanied my symptoms. My symptoms were short lived however, and I was able to return to work in 72 hours.

CHAPTER 28

Sustaining the Pressure

P AUL STONE SAW OUR PROBLEM as one of education. We had to
educate the president, the Board of Trustees, our professional constituencies, and the public. He did not think that we could educate
the Medical Center administration, but that was no reason not to try. He
advised us to press our message on all who would receive it. Although he
could not be certain, he believed that the "education program" we had
already begun was helping and encouraged us to keep it up. In response, we
tried to facilitate public and private "educational" pressure on the president,
the Board of Trustees, and the Medical Center administration, while rallying
our primary support base of students and faculty.

Letters and telephone calls from UIUC students and faculty, from scientists external to the university, from prominent public figures, and from
politicians were steadily directed to the president, the board, and the newspapers. Although I was blamed (received credit?) for most of the organized
activity, several others fanned the flames far more effectively than I could.
Both the clinical and the basic-science faculties were offended by the UIMC
leadership and had no reluctance in expressing their discontent; neither did
the students.

As for me, I kept my profile very low, declining on-the-record interviews and sticking as closely as possible to the facts that I believed made our
case. I prepared the white papers, which summarized the SCM-UC position
and which couldn't be criticized as "disloyal" by the UIMC administration.
At the same time, I made certain that news reporters and others who would
be sympathetic to the cause of clinical education in Champaign-Urbana had
all the facts they could handle at their fingertips. Academic issues were
defined in terms of "fairness," "cost effectiveness," "quality of medical education," "waste at the Medical Center," and above all, "the preservation of the
Medical Scholars Program." We publicized economic issues as well, convincing the CU hospitals and business interests that a full four-year medical

school would enhance medicine in the area, a fact that could be translated into millions of dollars annually. The medical school payroll in 1981, which included salary and research funds, totaled $10 million. These numbers were not lost on the Chamber of Commerce either. It was not beyond imagination that a mature medical school with an important clinical-research component could pump $50 million to $100 million annually into the area's economy.

We were now deeply engaged in a political brawl. The faculty, staff, students, and key members of the community all appreciated this fact. All of them, in their own ways, rallied to repel the threat. Even though no threat was posed to the School of Basic Medical Sciences, the basic-science faculty set aside some of its internal difficulties and coalesced with everyone else to resist the assault on our autonomy. At separate faculty meetings, the faculties of SBMS-UC and SCM-UC unanimously approved resolutions that recorded "grave concern" about the reorganization plan, confirmed the faculty's opposition to those fragments of the plan that had been informally announced, endorsed the plan for a Peoria-Urbana merger under the governance of the UIUC chancellor, and directed me as dean of the faculty to immediately communicate to the chancellors at UIMC and UIUC the faculty concerns regarding "the gross abuses of academic processes associated with the proposed reorganization." I dutifully forwarded faculty actions to higher administration, but otherwise kept a low profile, bound as I was to work "collegially" with Mack Schmidt, Mort Creditor, and my fellow deans. Besides, there was little I could do that could not have been done better by my very close advisors, such as Ben Williams, Allan Levy, and Hal Swartz, among others.

SCM-UC students were another constituency that quickly perceived the difficulties facing the school. It did not take much, if any, administrative urging to get the students up in arms. Perhaps more than any other constituency, they loved the school. When they asked the SBMS/SCM-UC administration for facts and figures, they were given them to the best of our ability. At noon on Monday, April 13, five days after Schmidt's closure announcement, the students organized an SOS-Save Our School rally on the UIUC quad. They also promptly put out a widely distributed bulletin that summarized the advantages of SCM-UC. It stated, "We believe that SCM-UC is a unique and valuable part of the UICOM. CLINICAL MEDICAL EDUCATION AT URBANA WILL NOT GO DOWN WITHOUT A

FIGHT! We are asking the UC campus as well as the CU community, to join us in support of quality medical education here!"

As reported in the April 14 *Daily Illini*, about seventy students protested the Medical Center proposal that was "being railroaded through the administrative process." The students addressed their complaints to President Ikenberry and to the Board of Trustees. On April 23, in his answer to the students' complaint, Paul Stone wrote to the president of the University Medical Student Council a letter that must have given the university president and his Medical Center advisors cause for concern, not to mention indigestion.

"I assure you that I have spent considerable time since Dr. Schmidt's proposal became public getting acquainted with the problems of the medical school," Stone wrote. *"I share the concern that you have, and I am hopeful that we can adopt a plan other than the one suggested by Dr. Schmidt."* [Emphasis added.]

In the highly politicized environment we were working in, it was difficult to be certain of how Stone's letter should be interpreted, but we grasped at every straw.

Working at the public level required another strategy. For all our efforts, SBMS/SCM-UC had limited name recognition. Overwhelmed by a thirty-five-thousand-student campus, the two hundred or so students in our program made little impact. We were pleased then, when our local newspaper, the *News-Gazette,* published an Op-Ed guest commentary by Ben Williams headlined, "Why Clinical Medical School Should Stay Here." In it, Williams publicly challenged the university's decision to close SCM-UC: "These decisions are allegedly being forced by an anticipated budget deficit of $10 million to $20 million at the MC campus in Chicago, a problem that promises to become chronic. Yet the relatively young school at CU is to be sacrificed to make up the current deficit, a decision that is neither financially nor academically sound."

The local teaching hospitals, Carle Foundation and Mercy, through their CEOs and their boards, joined in the fray. Both of them had made capital improvements to adapt to our clinical-education program. Mercy Hospital was just completing a $13 million addition, which included office and laboratory space for potential faculty. Carle was in the process of planning similar renovations and space allocations. The CEOs of both hospitals complained to Mack Schmidt that they were disturbed by the university's apparent fickleness. Both hospitals had made good-faith investments in programs, space, and equipment for medical education, and it now seemed as though the rug was being pulled out from under them. Mack Schmidt responded on May 4, 1981 that he appreciated that "both of your hospitals are deeply committed to medical education at all levels. I wish to assure you that the university appreciates this commitment and that the university will continue to identify your role in its clinical activities...In the case of a two-year school in UC, it is unlikely that students would be routinely assigned to full junior and senior years in UC. I assume, however, that many students from Peoria, Rockford, and Chicago would be attracted to clinical electives in your hospitals...We are anxious to support the development of high-quality, successful residency programs in selected disciplines. The major source of funding for graduate education is third-party reimbursement. However, the core clinical funding, which we will continue to allocate, will support a nucleus of full-time clinical faculty, who will serve as the academic focus for undergraduate and graduate education...The university will honor its commitment for space rental at Mercy Hospital, as long as we are mutually engaged in medical and other health-science education. We will continue our commitment to use of the Carle Foundation Hospital Clinical Education Center space. We should review together any new commitments for additional space allocations to medical education."

Thus, Schmidt offered the hospitals a plate filled with indigestible scraps. It was highly unlikely that students from Peoria, Rockford, and Chicago would take elective clerkships at our campus. Furthermore, the development of graduate-education programs without the presence of undergraduate education was unlikely in the absence of a clinical program. Arguably, Schmidt's commitments to the hospitals were hardly worth the paper they were printed on.

Meanwhile we continued to solicit letters and resolutions from key groups and opinion leaders. A very important group was the Bicampus Steering Committee (BSC), which managed the Medical Scholars Program and was our main point of entree into the UIUC academic establishment. We had named it the "Bicampus Steering Committee" with a purpose. We wanted to make sure that anybody tampering with the Medical Scholars Program would realize that their tampering would affect the academic program of two campuses, UIUC and UIMC. The BSC comprised faculty from the many departments that had Ph.D. or other graduate students in the dual-degree program. Many BSC members were upset by what they perceived as an administrative coup. In response to the Schmidt initiative, they deemed it important to establish four core requirements to maintaining a viable MSP at UIUC:

1. Maintaining the distinctive nature of the program, which makes it an important state and national resource.
2. Sustaining a university commitment to provide a substantial amount of clinical training in proximity to the UIUC campus in a way that facilitates integration of the clinical and non-clinical curricula and faculties.
3. Providing substantial local autonomy with respect to admissions, curriculum, and budget.
4. Assuring a viable budgetary commitment to medical education in UC on a recurring basis for progressive development of clinical and academic excellence.

Throughout this entire drama, UIMC and the central university administration attempted to downplay the role of the UIUC campus and Senate in the final decision-making process. Stanley Ikenberry, in particular, "welcomed consultation" from UIUC, but he made it clear that he was perfectly prepared to ignore that advice. His April 21 letter to George Friedman, UIUC Senate president, after that body's resolutions to look into medical education at UIUC and to determine how combined medical and graduate education at UIUC would be affected by the College of Medicine reorganization proposal was cautious and unyielding. "I welcome the initiative taken by the Senate at UC to consult [sic] with the faculty and the administration of the College of Medicine and with the campus and general university administration as the planning within the College of Medicine proceeds," Ikenberry wrote.

We countered by methodically including in our ever-growing white-paper information packet, documents which supported the standing of the UIUC Senate in all College of Medicine deliberations relating to SBMS/SCM-UC.

On May 6, President Ikenberry sent a memo to the Board of Trustees to share with them "the internal process to be followed as the difficult decisions that lie ahead are addressed." The memorandum revealed the prominent personal role that the president was assuming in the reorganization process: "After study and consultation with Dr. Brady and me, the Medical

Center administration decided upon the organizational model considered most likely to lead to an overall strengthening of the college...Meanwhile, because of the need to communicate with the faculty and students about a matter involving them personally and deeply, Dr. Schmidt attempted to keep them informed. Admittedly this was not an easy assignment and, as you are well aware, substantial turbulence has ensued."

This revealing memo confirms the prominent role played by the president in the university's acceptance of Model II and appears to corroborate Mack Schmidt's claim, confided to me at the trustees' luncheon, that he had been given his marching orders to spread the central administration's (the president's) message. He was only doing his job.

Having personally involved himself in the process at this stage, the president, recognizing the "substantial turbulence" caused by the heavy-handedness of his administration, decided then to return the issue of reorganization to a faculty process with what presumably were instructions to Schmidt and Creditor to legitimize his selection of Model II. The renewed faculty process was then described to include a second review by the Academic Council, presentation to the UICOM faculty, the UIMC Senate via its Educational Policy Committee, the University Senates Conference, and the UIUC Senate. What the president did not say in his memo was that despite the opposition, he was not really looking for a consultative academic review of the matter, but an up or down, yes or no vote on the plan that he and Brady had worked out with Schmidt and Creditor. At the end of the memo, Ikenberry reemphasized his high-profile role in the process, writing, "I hope you know also of the high level of personal attention that I am devoting to this issue to ensure that it receives the thoughtful and objective consideration that a matter of this magnitude clearly deserves."

The substantial "turbulence" to which Ikenberry referred was not limited to the efforts that emanated from the UIUC area. Rockford and Peoria were upset as well. They were being reduced from three-year to two-year programs and had no sense of certainty that they would not be dropped from the UICOM program entirely at a later date. The reduced role of both schools was far more threatening to their respective communities, where they were "the only game in town."

The Rockford dean, Clifford Grulee, summarized in a memorandum (titled "A Consensus of Faculty Attitudes at the Rockford School of Medicine") the minimal conditions considered essential to maintain the functioning of RSM. These included a cohort of students for which RSM is responsible for a minimum of two years, continued basic support services, continuation of the department-head system, and an educational program in which the RSM faculty would have significant influence.

In discussing the consequences of following Model II, Grulee estimated that "a minimum of 50 percent of the faculty would disengage…The part-time faculty has a fierce and deep pride in what it perceives to have been accomplished in Rockford…they sense that their efforts are not justly valued or appreciated by the University of Illinois and consequently they focus their loyalty on RSM…They feel free to express their opinions, whether critical or not. Further, they represent a far more potent community influence than do their counterparts in large urban areas."

Grulee concluded, "It may be possible to neutralize the damage that has already been done, it may be possible to alter or modify the intransigent viewpoints…We don't know, but we do feel that it would be a grave error for the university to misread the explosive potential in the Rockford situation."

Peoria was also in substantial turmoil. Headlines and stories that appeared during April, May, and June 1981 in the local Peoria *Journal Star* newspaper tell some of the story:

> April 21, "Letter to Board of Trustees from PSM department chairs"
> April 29, "Peoria Medical School Faculty Hits Plan for Cut to Two Years"
> May 10, Satire on what PSM building will be used for in the future.
> May 12, Story on reorganization. Champaign's views.
> May 13, Story on reorganization. Rockford's views.
> May 14, Interview with Begando on his visit to Peoria.
> May 14, "College Executive Committee OKs one college, one dean"
> June 6, President Ikenberry interview. Visit to Peoria.
> June 25, Report of the General Faculty meeting held in Chicago. All three schools quoted.

Meetings between the Peoria and the SBMS/SCM-UC faculties continued despite my total withdrawal from that sphere after my agreement to do so in February. On April 14, 1981, the president was handed a document titled, "The Champaign/Urbana-Peoria Proposal for the Organization of a Downstate Medical School." It was signed by eighteen faculty members and/or hospital administrators from the two programs.

The only happy UICOM constituency was in Chicago at ALSM. In a position paper dated April 15, the ALSM Executive Committee endorsed Model II, believing it *"unwise and unacceptable to modify the intent of Model II* [emphasis in original] by holding out the possibility of preserving Schools/Deans/Departments in Rockford and Peoria." They also recommended an enrollment reduction of twenty-three per class to parallel "the average per-class enrollment of the only present school [SCM-UC]...to be closed out as a program in the reorganized college."

The president, therefore, appeared to be playing a double game. On the one hand, he was reassuring the Board of Trustees of his commitment to an open academic process, and on the other, he had directed Schmidt and Creditor to bring home one result. Further insight into the Ikenberry, Brady, Schmidt, and Creditor effort to crush SCM-UC is gained from private, if not confidential, letters sent between Schmidt and Creditor. An April 30 letter from Schmidt to Creditor that was shared with the Academic Council two weeks later, informed Creditor that he (Schmidt) was "privileged" to meet with the AC when the council approved the SPMC final report and transmitted it for consideration by the administration at the MC campus (himself). Schmidt then continued with some self-serving justifications for his action and wrote, "A series of recommendations was then developed and discussed with general officers of the university [i.e. President Ikenberry and Ron Brady]." This resulted in Schmidt's recommendation "that the clinical school in UC be phased out as a separate organizational unit but retain certain clinical programs."

The recommendation also diminished the Peoria-Rockford programs by a year, allowing them only the M-3 and M-4 years. He then "suggested" to Creditor that of the three options presented in the final report of the SPMC, Model II, as modified by Schmidt, be adopted by the AC formally. What he proposed was a four-year program in Chicago, two-year programs in Peoria and Rockford, and a two-year basic-science program in UC. This, then, was to go to the college faculty at its annual meeting on June 24 for final ratification within the college and then be handled by the university senates. Schmidt mentioned the Medical Scholars Program only in passing when he said, "The school [SBMS-UC] should maintain the Medical Scholars Program." That is all; it revealed that Schmidt had given little thought to the survival of the MSP in his proposed reorganization.

On July 13, Creditor gave Schmidt a confidential status report on the progress he had made in establishing Model II of the faculty-approved reorganization plan: "Attached is a copy of a proposal relating to the reorganization of the College of Medicine, which was approved by the faculty of the college at its annual meeting on June 24, 1981. As is self-evident, this document represents only a part of the complete model, which will be developed during the coming months. However, this approved proposal does include certain specific decisions about organization and governance, which are significant in themselves. The preference expressed by higher administration for the single-college model has been ratified by the faculty. The structure of the model is further qualified by the specification that it be headed by a dean and that the current committee substructures and the executive deanship be abolished.

"The faculty agreed to the extension of students' initial assignments for basic-science instruction for two years in Urbana and Chicago respectively. A September 1, 1981, merger of SBMS-MC and ALSM was recommended by the faculty. In accord with our recent discussions, I plan to move towards that merger at an appropriate pace."

What Creditor did was to boil down the Schmidt instructions into twelve principles that directly or indirectly did the job that Schmidt wanted done. He then had them approved by the Academic Council on May 13 and by the general faculty of the College of Medicine on June 14. The principles disguised the intent behind them. They were couched in general terms and did not specifically eliminate SCM-UC or truncate the Peoria-Rockford schools. The twelve points were:

1. The University of Illinois College of Medicine would be organized as a single COM, headed by a dean.
2. The basic-science curriculum would be extended to two years and offered at Chicago and Urbana-Champaign.
3. There would be clinical activity at all regional sites.
4. The Medical Scholars Program would be preserved.
5. Policies to assure relative enrollment stability in all regions would be established.
6. The possibility of "linked" student assignments to permit "tracking" of cohorts of students through the educational sites would be considered.
7. ALSM and SBMS-MC would merge by August 31, 1981.
8. The AC's composition would not change during the transition period.

9. The executive dean would appoint an AC subcommittee to serve as an implementation-planning committee during the transition period.
10. Existing college committees would plan and recommend policies and practices in accord with changes during the transition period.
11. Consideration would be given to determining the composition of the executive body (i.e., the AC or whatever else it might be called) on a basis other than the number of students assigned to any particular region.
12. An objective of the reorganization would be to eliminate the then-existing subordinate committee structure and the executive deanship.

Gradually over the preceding year, Mort Creditor had undergone a change in heart. He was no longer the Mort Creditor who talked of the need for Urbana-Champaign to flourish. It seems that he was so hemmed in by the deficits facing him at the Medical Center that he just gave up on trying to preserve the UC clinical program and thereafter sought the quickest way to put it out of its misery. Now a pawn of higher administration, he had tried to fight the good fight through the SPMC, but was preempted in his attempt and never recovered.

Creditor's twelve points contained several ambiguous teasers such as "There will be clinical activity at all regional sites," which was no commitment at all to Rockford and Peoria, and "The Medical Scholars Program will be preserved," a sop to UC. However, it was apparent to anybody who had worked in MD/Ph.D. programs throughout the nation that MD/Ph.D. programs on two separate campuses did not succeed. The recombination of ALSM and SBMS-MC would essentially revert the college to its 1969 configuration, with a four-year program in Chicago and clinical experiences in Chicago, Peoria, and Rockford. What was not appreciated by the UIMC administration was that the UIUC campus made it quite clear to UIMC in 1969, when it first agreed to engage in medical education, that it was not within the mission of the UIUC campus to provide a basic medical-science service course for a Chicago-based College of Medicine. Yet, this is essentially what the Schmidt-Creditor proposal called for.

Creditor wrote to Schmidt again on July 16, this time about budget priorities. In this letter, Creditor openly begrudges "continuing the clinical school in Urbana" because it reduces his ability to "finance new or revitalized programs in the yet-to-be-reorganized college." He closed the letter seeking the authority to move more boldly against Urbana and the other regional programs.

"I am particularly worried that our financial plight may be even worse because we cannot monitor the state of the Urbana-Champaign accounts," he wrote. "We have no way of controlling expenditures due to discontinuities of the way the two campuses have done their bookkeeping...The only solution to the problem...is a meaningful reorganization of the college. I emphasize the word 'meaningful,' because there will be no savings if there is appeasement of every complaint about changes in current structure.

"If in the name of local autonomy or control we are forced to maintain large administrative structures in each region, then the savings anticipated by administrative consolidation will not occur. If we cannot reduce the size of the basic-science enterprises in the regional clinical sites, then the savings anticipated for more effective deployment of resources will not be enjoyed. If we cannot diminish the practice of paying part-time salaries for practitioners whose commitment is no greater than those who volunteer their services in most medical schools, then we will never be able to shift the balance of expenditures from 'costs' to 'investments.' Even as I say this, I worry about what can be done in FY83. We are close to the deadline for issuing terminal contracts for the coming year; therefore, many of the decisions which will permit cost reduction will not be implemented until FY84. I am considering the possibility of putting a 'freeze' on all new appointments to administrative positions and perhaps doing the same for certain categories of part-time faculty. I will need strong support for such a decision."

The next day, July 17, 1981, Creditor again wrote Schmidt confidentially, regarding the closure of SCM-UC. Ignoring the May 9 consensus of the Bicampus Steering Committee and after outlining a theoretical program that no competent student would ever undertake, Creditor concluded: "It is my opinion that the MSP can continue in the absence of a complete clinical program in Urbana-Champaign."

Mort usually knew exactly what he was doing, but in this instance he faltered. He obviously wrote the opinion on demand, probably to satisfy the political needs of the president who wanted to cut SCM-UC, without being criticized for sacrificing the Medical Scholars Program. Creditor's tortured opinion satisfied the president, but cost Mort whatever remaining credibility he had with those of us who once counted on him for better things. The July 17 letter was sent privately to Schmidt. Had the letter been made public, he would have been severely criticized, and he knew it.

The Academic Council of the College of Medicine met at its regularly scheduled time on May 13, 1981, with Creditor's twelve-point proposal for reorganization as a major agenda item. The day before the meeting I had written to Schmidt concerning his recommendations to the Academic Council to let him know the impact his proposals would have. "On the basis of my experience and responsibilities here...the effects of your proposal will include:

1. Reduced effectiveness of the Medical Scholars Program, with a strong possibility of losing it altogether.
2. A sharp reduction in...interdisciplinary efforts between SCM-UC and campus departments.
3. The loss of a biomedical-research support grant...approximately $60,000 per year.
4. An obligation to cancel a $60,000 grant from the National Fund for Medical Education.
5. Forfeit the remainder of HHS funds (approximately $180,000) for a curriculum on environmental health.
6. Withdrawal of pending grant to Exxon Foundation for $80,000...in support of a faculty-development seminar in the humanities and social sciences.
7. Withdrawal of application to the National Endowment for the Humanities.
8. Return of a portion of $25,000 UIUC Graduate College grant for development of interdisciplinary programs with the humanities."

The documentation was more for the record than an attempt to change Schmidt's views; but one never knew what documentary evidence tips the scale of fate in one's favor. With that in mind, we went into the May 13 meeting of the Academic Council with only a faint hope of affecting the outcome.

Nothing could better illustrate the geographical differences within the college than the voting patterns at that meeting. As noted previously, the AC membership was heavily weighted toward Chicago voting. The minutes of this meeting reveal unanimity in only one aspect of its business: a resolution that the College of Medicine, by a vote of twenty-five to zero, opposed any further consolidation of the MC campus and the Chicago Circle Campus of the University of Illinois. (However, Ikenberry was determined to merge UIMC and UI Chicago Circle into a single campus to be called the University of Illinois at Chicago. He would succeed in doing so during the next year, despite nearly unanimous opposition from UIMC. One reason he was successful in the face of UIMC opposition was because the UIMC faculty were so numbed by administrative fiat over the years, that it was assumed that their resolutions were no more than recommendations that could be completely disregarded by the administration at no political cost. Although we at UIUC were concerned about the consolidation in Chicago, we had enough problems of our own without organizing to meet that threat. The Chicago faculty, on the other hand, was passive and acquiescent in nature and style.)

The main agenda item for the May 13 meeting was College of Medicine reorganization. Creditor distributed background information for the discussion, including Schmidt's April 30 letter to Creditor, President Ikenberry's remarks of April 16 before the Board of Trustees, the recent resolution of the UIUC Senate staking their claim to consultation in a UICOM reorganization, and position papers from Rockford, Peoria, ALSM, and SBMS/SCM-UC.

Creditor then presented his proposal that the 1981 enrollment be reduced from 342 to 325, which was approved without difficulty. The dean of ALSM, Phil Forman, then moved to accept Creditor's twelve-point proposal. From this point on, the AC was divided. Allan Levy argued that because there had been a recent UIUC senate appointment of an "Ad Hoc Committee to Study the Impact of Proposed College of Medicine Reorganization on the Urbana-Champaign Campus," consideration of Creditor's twelve points should be postponed until the UIUC Senate had reviewed and acted upon the reorganization of the college. After extensive discussion, the amendment was rejected sixteen to eight, a geographically polarized vote with sixteen nays from Chicago and eight yeas from the downstate regional schools. Leon Librik from Peoria tried to get the AC to approve an amendment that would allow some basic-science training in Peoria and Rockford, but this too was handily defeated by the Chicago supermajority, thirteen nays to six yeas. Librik moved that Creditor's point number seven, which read "The ALSM and the SBMS-MC will merge by August 31, 1981," be amended by adding the following sentence: "The Peoria School of Medicine and the two Schools of Medicine in Urbana-Champaign will administratively merge by August 31, 1981."

This failed even worse than Allan Levy's proposal, because this time the Rockford committee members, who did not want to be the only regional program within the embrace of Chicago, voted with Chicago people to oppose it. It failed seventeen to five. The final motion, to approve the entire twelve-point proposal intact, carried by a vote of seventeen to seven: sixteen of seventeen yeas from Chicago and seven nays from Urbana, Rockford, and Peoria.

The final histrionic portion of the meeting occurred when Schmidt excused Executive Dean Creditor and his staff from the room and announced that it was his statutory obligation to consult with the college's Academic Council before making a recommendation on the annual reappointment of the dean. It being clear that there was no organized opposition to reappointing Morton Creditor for another year from September 1, 1981 through August 31, 1982, and seizing this opportunity to demonstrate to Mack Schmidt how collegial I could be, I personally moved that the AC recommend Creditor as Interim Executive Dean for the period specified. The motion was seconded and unanimously approved, but somehow I felt little satisfaction from being so "collegial."

CHAPTER 29

Summer, Time to Play Hardball

I WROTE TO PAUL STONE to update him on the Advisory Council meeting. At that time, the Board of Trustees was heavily involved in a National College Athletic Association brouhaha over the football program. The eligibility of a star quarterback, Dave Wilson, was at stake. The time-consuming football drama captured headlines in the local papers for weeks on end and left academic issues such as ours languishing on back burners. Fortunately, the football distraction gave us more time to plan and to anticipate moves that might be made against us.

I wrote to Stone that there was virtually no downstate support for the one-college, one-dean option. I reviewed the May 6 discussions that the SBMS/SCM-UC Executive Committees had had with the UIUC chancellor and vice chancellor, and that the committees expressed the "strong opinion that it is foolish for one university campus (UIMC) to insist on domination of a program located on a second campus (UIUC), particularly one as distinguished as UIUC. Chancellors Cribbet and Goldwasser were impressed enough…that they suggested I invite President Ikenberry to a similar meeting."

I also told him that Ikenberry and Schmidt remained very skeptical about the accuracy of my proposed budgets for a combined medical-education program at Urbana and Peoria, but would not discuss the numbers with me. I assured Stone of my confidence in the figures, which were similar to cost figures I recently received from the Association of American Medical Colleges for twenty somewhat similar medical schools. Finally, I thanked him for joining Ikenberry in his first view of the Medical Sciences Building.

"Even though I found the dialogue between Stan and me after our tour unsatisfactory," I wrote, "I am concerned, and individuals have informed me, that I may be subject to some retaliation…for reflecting and balancing the views of my faculty and those of the Medical Center administration. I hope that is not true, but I will let you know in any event."

I tried to get Stanley Ikenberry to meet with our executive committees as Paul Stone and Chancellors Cribbet and Goldwasser had recommended. I wrote to request such an interview, but Ikenberry wrote me on May 19 to reject meeting with my faculty and instead suggested, "I would urge that you and your colleagues work within the structure of the College of Medicine." That structure was so heavily weighted against us that it was impossible to get a fair hearing. He continued, "When these matters move onto my desk, I will be pleased to receive such additional counsel from you and other members of the Executive Committee of the Urbana program."

This strongly suggested, if more evidence was needed, that the president had already made up his mind concerning the outcome of the college reorganization and was determined to stonewall the possibility of receiving added information from the medical school or even from the general UIUC campus faculty. Although he talked about meeting with faculty "for counsel" when the matter had moved to his desk, he had already given Mack Schmidt his marching orders and had told the Board of Trustees that he was taking a singular personal interest in the SPMC process, a confession that the matter had long since been on, through, and off his desk.

Meanwhile, a group of SBMS/SCM-UC and UIUC bioscience faculty leaders, who were also widely respected in the UIUC Graduate College, summarized a faculty position on UICOM reorganization in a memorandum to Ted Brown, Dean of the Graduate College, which they distributed broadly to other UIUC faculty to alert them to the probable loss of clinical education at UIUC and to advertise potential solutions. They drove home their central point, "Over nine years of experience with administration of the Urbana-Champaign program has provided unequivocal evidence that local control is essential to success." The memo listed three reorganization options for the Urbana-Champaign medical program acceptable to the faculty. All of them included administration by the UIUC chancellor. Their first choice was a complete and independent medical school, second was a merger of the Peoria and Urbana-Champaign medical programs, and third was a complete medical school that would be part of UICOM but would be run by the UIUC chancellor and have academic and budgetary autonomy. These options reflected once again the faculty's anger with the cross-campus governance. The faculty had no confidence in and was literally fed up with domination by the Chicago leadership.

It was difficult to appreciate in such tumultuous times, but medical education at SCM-UC was proceeding apace despite the political instability. The thirteen students who started with us down that second-year logic-pathway route had now completed their studies, passed all the required examinations, and were about to receive the MD degree. On June 10, 1981, SCM-UC celebrated its first pregraduation convocation ceremony, during which students received their doctoral hoods and took the Hippocratic oath. That convocation was a significant milestone in the development of medical education in UC, and I had invited Stanley Ikenberry, the chancellors of the two campuses, Paul Stone, Mort Creditor, and Mack Schmidt. Of those invited, only Ikenberry, Creditor, and Schmidt did not attend. It was particularly ironic that Creditor did not attend, because this was the class that he started. He was their teacher for the first six months of their clinical education; he generated the tutorial system under which they learned. But it was clear that Creditor, Schmidt, and Ikenberry formed a triumvirate that was dead set on closing SCM-UC. Their absence from this milestone event in the history of the school was just another piece of evidence that the gloves were off and this was to be a fight to the finish. Interestingly, Medical Center Chancellor Joe Begando was a welcome guest. Although he was in the chain of command between Schmidt and Ikenberry, he seemed to take himself out of the loop when distasteful decisions such as closing SCM-UC came up.

After the showdown with Schmidt and Creditor, my relations and communications with Mort were rigid, formal, and perfunctory. I tried to reach out to Creditor on several occasions, to tell him that his behavior toward us in Champaign-Urbana was unseemly, that he was destroying his own creation, and that he should have known as well as I did that the Medical Scholars Program could not survive without a clinical program at Urbana.

It was apparent that he felt a need to distance himself from me but did so to the disadvantage of SCM-UC. The only unofficial words we had were his personal advice to me (as a friend, he said) on a number of occasions that I was wasting my time trying to save SCM-UC. "The issue was decided," and it would be best for me to get on board. That grim advice together with his general hostility was exasperating. It was time to play hardball.

Both of us were angry. I vented my anger by throwing him a biting personal and confidential curveball in letter form that I faintly hoped might bring him to his senses. In the letter, dated June 1, I told him that "the SPMC process was an abject failure" because he could not protect it from being hijacked by the administration, and I told him that carrying out the reorganization plan announced by Schmidt would not result in "as you dreamed, the salvation of the reorganization of the College of Medicine, but the condemnation of Mort Creditor for being the agent of regional school destruction." I told him that he was being "servile" to the administration.

I went on, "You told me (as a friend) that persons in CU and Peoria were wasting their time attempting to change the reorganization process. I'll tell you (as a friend) to get out now, while you have some dignity and integrity left. I'd have quit my position a long time ago, given the indignities that have been suffered by our program, *but I have something worth preserving—you don't.* You told me I am wasting my time in continuing to work for a clinical school—but look at yourself! Even if you win, you will lose and destroy in the process four to five years of your own creative effort in UC."

It was an all-or-nothing letter that turned out to be nothing. Although labeled "personal and confidential," Mort immediately cried "foul" and took the letter to Schmidt, Begando, and even to Ikenberry for advice concerning a reply. In his view, anything that passed between the two of us was public business. He sent an icy communication to me on June 16: "This will acknowledge receipt of your letter to me of June 1, 1981. Its content has been duly noted."

In the interim, anticipating the phaseout of SCM-UC and the change in our basic-science mission, Creditor directed the office of admissions to reduce the number of M-1 students admitted to SBMS-UC from 106 to 75 and at the same time he began to reduce the SCM-UC budget. On May 29, Creditor notified me of an additional sixty-four thousand dollar reduction in the SCM-UC budget for the 1982 fiscal year. It appeared more and more obvious to me that the Chicago administration really wanted me to quit by making life and administration miserable for me. They wanted me to say that I could not do the job with such a small budget. We were to receive $14,300 per student in the 1982 fiscal year. Peoria and Rockford, at a similar stage in their development, had received respectively $29,600 and $32,000 per student in the 1974 and 1975 fiscal years. We survived the 1982 fiscal year largely because of the dedicated effort of our faculty and staff. They gave the educational program everything they had to give.

I wrote to Creditor on June 9 to say, "Given [the] declarations and assurances by the president that no final decisions have been made regarding the reorganization of the college, it is only fair that enrollments and resources for medical-student education for FY82 be distributed on an equitable basis...I mention enrollments as well because...we were assured that no administrative changes would be made to anticipate a final decision that has not been made. To reduce the enrollment of SBMS-UC from 106 to 75...is prejudicial to the process.

I wrote to Creditor again on June 10, stating that in view of the budgetary cuts I was taking certain steps to reduce expenses. I said I would notify Mercy Hospital that SCM-UC would not be able to pay its $50,000 annual rental fee for space. I put a moratorium, effective July 1, on travel reimbursement for college meetings outside of Champaign-Urbana, and said that absent reimbursements from the College of Medicine or Medical Center, we would use telephone-conference facilities. I also said our schools would send no representative to the Association of American Medical Colleges or Illinois Council of Deans meetings unless his office provided a travel allowance. I also said that although, under Paul Treichler's direction, the Urbana medical schools had interviewed 268 candidates for the College of Medicine in the preceding year, it was doubtful that we would be able to provide such services now.

In addition, I told him that because Art Leonard was leaving as the CEC director of Mercy Hospital, I would personally assume directorship of the SCM-UC provisional Department of Medicine, directorship of the Medicine Clerkships in the Hospitals, and Directorship of the Internal Medicine Residency Program. I therefore asked to be excused from personal attendance at all Medical Center meetings except where such personal attendance was absolutely necessary. And I added, "Any request for my personal attendance at a meeting should be accompanied by an account number for travel expenses."

"A number of SBMS/SCM-UC faculty, who are disturbed both by the budgetary inequities and by the May 13 decision of the Academic Council, have asked to attend the College of Medicine faculty meeting on June 24 to speak directly to the faculty of the college concerning the Academic Council resolution and their perception of the budgetary issues. They have asked that you plan adequate time for full debate of the May 13 Academic Council resolutions while also having available overhead-projector facilities. They also ask that you have ballots available, since there will probably be a request for a secret written ballot on the motions to be proposed."

On June 15, I wrote Creditor a letter related to the potential merger of Peoria with SBMS/SCM-UC. Faculty groups had been meeting regularly, without administrative input, in an attempt to smooth the way for a Peoria-Urbana-Champaign merger. There had been no administrative role in the discussions because I had been interdicted and Dean Jerry Newman of the Peoria School of Medicine opposed Peoria having anything to do with SBMS/SCM-UC. In light of Paul Stone and the university's preference for a full and open, academic discussion of the reorganization process, I asked Creditor to reconsider the orders he and Schmidt gave me to stay out of the merger-exploration process.

On June 24, Creditor sent me a confidential reply to all four of my June letters. I learned later that President Ikenberry had personally edited Creditor's letter. It was reserved and formal, a change-up pitch in our game of hardball, which barely concealed what must have been overwhelming rage.

"You make allegations about my servility and at the same time refer to me as the 'bully boy' and make implications about my motives. You question the level of quality and competency of some undefined cohort of individuals and go on record with your opinion about past and present performance of specific individuals. You interpret actions and activities in such ways as to impugn my integrity." In other words, he read my June 1 letter and didn't like it.

"In another letter you list certain actions you are planning in carrying out your duties as dean. I have concern for the implications of withdrawal from certain responsibilities in your office. Therefore, I feel obligated to make certain stipulations, which I believe to be appropriate in regard to the actions to which you refer…It is implicit in the responsibilities of faculty and staff that they participate in college activities. I encourage the use of conference participation by telephone whenever possible. However, when personal participation is necessary, it will be reimbursed out of your budget." Creditor knew as well as I did that I could not live within the budget that was ultimately assigned to me. At that point, I simply told Rick Schimmel, my financial officer, that we would just spend whatever we had to over budget and worry about the shortfall later.

"Participation in the interview process for applicants for admission to the College of Medicine is a responsibility of each of the schools. Continued SBMS/SCM-UC participation will be required, particularly since the option of interview site is in response to applicant needs.

"I note your intention to direct the Provisional Department of Medicine, the Medical Clerkships, the Medical Residency, and curriculum sequence. I have no objections to your assuming these additional responsibilities as long as they do not interfere with your responsibilities as dean. Participation in activities of the COM, including those at the Medical Center, is a requirement of deanship. Furthermore, the cost of participation is to be borne by your school…

"The issue of merger of Peoria School of Medicine and SBMS/SCM-UC is not on the agenda of the administration of the COM…Therefore I believe it inappropriate that any administrative officer of the college take leadership in any negotiations outside of the duly constituted process." The merger was on the agenda of the SPMC report as Model III, but Creditor and Ikenberry kept that fact suppressed. In my opinion, Creditor's adamancy on this issue reflected a flawed interpretation of a flawed process.

"Because you seem to be having such serious problems as an administrator in this college, campus, and university, I deem it important that I share your letters with Vice Chancellor Schmidt, Chancellor Begando, and President Ikenberry. They agree with me that it is important that your problems on matters of policy and process, as well as personalities and personal confidence involving all of us be resolved. Specifically, we need your assurance that you understand the responsibilities of your office and that you will carry out the responsibilities. They include program management within the limits of available resources, the fulfillment of contractual agreements, and appropriate participation in the affairs of the COM and university. We require affirmation of your confidence in, and ability to work with the administrative leadership of the college, campus, and university. We require your willingness to cooperate in the implementation of institution practices and policies. Furthermore, it is expected that you willingly function within our university system, a system which depends on you to carry out appropriate duties of your major administrative office." Oh gosh! Time for another loyalty oath.

"For purposes of discussing these matters, I would like you to meet in my office either Monday, June 29 at 2 p.m. or Wednesday, July 1 at 9:30 a.m. Dr. Schmidt will be present at the meeting. If either of these times represents an unavoidable conflict, please call my office to arrange an alternate date as soon as possible." Here we go again! Another Bloomfield, Schmidt, and Creditor World Series showdown was in the offing. Creditor copied the letter to President Ikenberry, Chancellor Begando, and Vice Chancellor Schmidt.

Now, "Showdown Meeting Number Two" was on the docket. Creditor was smarting from my June 1 blast at him and sought solace from his senior administrators. He and Schmidt were trying to decide whether they should reappoint me as dean at Urbana for the 1981–82 academic year, or risk the fury of the faculty and the community in the event that they replaced me. For my part, I was on the brink again but not about to pull back. Furthermore, the fact that President Ikenberry was personally involved in this confrontation between Creditor and myself upped the stakes. It was additional disheartening evidence, as if any more were needed, that the president was deeply involved in the micromanagement of this affair. It was my opinion that it was a mistake for him to take sides at this juncture and that he would sooner or later regret his early entry in this summer game of hardball.

PART V

Counterpunching from the Ropes

CHAPTER 30

Bittersweet Affairs

I N THE MIDST OF THESE bitter exchanges, SCM-UC—battered, beaten, starved, and "on the ropes"—graduated its first thirteen students in the convocation of June 10, 1981. The convocation was a bittersweet affair. There was much excitement. Both the basic-science and clinical faculties turned out in substantial numbers to make it a gala affair. We had reserved the outdoor amphitheater of Krannert Center, which provided a beautiful backdrop for the ceremonies, although its concrete seats soon became uncomfortable. We counted on good weather and were so favored, but the price for good weather was a blazing afternoon sun. The amphitheater faced due west, forcing the audience to look directly into the still-bright setting June sun. Photographs of that first ceremony show the audience hugging either edge of the amphitheater, avoiding the sunny view. Nevertheless, the amphitheater was a handsome place for such a rite, and better yet, it was free!

Bill Sorlie set up the graduation ceremonies with his usual care. He arranged for the Parkland College orchestra to provide suitable music for the occasion. Chairs were neatly set up for the students, faculty, and distinguished guests. When the ceremonies began, it was apparent that an enormous amount of concern and effort had gone into ensuring the success of these thirteen graduates. About twenty basic-science faculty members and twice as many clinical faculty, most dressed in academic robes, joined in the festivities. They were determined to witness at least one class graduate.

Sorlie had prepared a souvenir program that listed the students, their intended residencies, their honors during medical school, the faculty, the support staff, and the order of business for the day. One could not survey this scene without a great sense of accomplishment. At the same time, most of the realists among us were downcast as we contemplated the dismantling of our efforts. Joe Begando presented greetings from the Medical Center campus. Sincere and upbeat, he gave no intimation whatsoever of any adverse knowledge about the future of SCM-UC. John Cribbet, Chancellor at UIUC, also spoke. Bill Sorlie, as master of ceremonies, went through the program and soon it was my turn to address the audience.

"As many of you know, this is a bittersweet ceremony to honor a select group of students who have elected to stay with a humble, sometimes uncertain, sometimes brilliant, but always striving educational program to become the first graduating class of the University of Illinois College of Medicine to complete four years of study at the Schools of Basic Medical Sciences and Clinical Medicine at Urbana-Champaign. Whether they will also be the last class to do so remains in the balance at the present time. As a class of medical students they have performed with distinction—on tests, in the clinics, and as individuals who have learned how to learn. These are good students, and I assure all of you here, that when these students receive their medical degrees on Friday, June 12, 1981, they shall be well-qualified physicians who will reflect favorably upon this small program at Urbana-Champaign."

I spoke about the effort of the faculty, staff, and the medical community that had made the event possible, and then I offered the students some valedictory advice.

"I came to Urbana-Champaign eleven years ago with a mandate to create a new medical school on one of the great university campuses of the world…It was the creative opportunity of a lifetime, and while I was already experienced in difficult developmental projects…I knew very clearly that the road would not be easy and that much hard, complex, and exhausting work was ahead. But I had been guided for many years by the philosophy embodied in the comment of the late Golda Meir, who said, 'Nothing in life just happens. It isn't enough to believe in something; you have to have the stamina to meet obstacles and overcome them, to struggle.' There is no more significant thought that I can give to you today: Learn to struggle."

Then, I laid out my thoughts about the fruits of our own struggle. "Last year alone, our faculty, in cooperation with many campus departments, brought into the university, grants and contracts which exceeded $2.7 million, virtually equaling our total operating budget. Far from assuming the traditional role of a campus medical school, in which the medical school has gluttonously absorbed every extra campus dollar in recent past and which, incidentally, frightens every college president into a permanent state of paranoia about medical schools, *this new medical school, SBMS/SCM-UC, is cast*

*in a completely different mold. We have not and we do not absorb resources—
we create them.* That is our past record and that will be our future. The
University and the Urbana-Champaign campus [are] richer today for having
this fragile school in place...

"To put it another way, it is my conviction, a conviction documented by
the record, that the elimination of our Clinical School at Urbana-Champaign
or of meaningful clinical education that is identified with Urbana-
Champaign is an extravagance, not a saving—an extravagance the University
of Illinois, and particularly the Urbana-Champaign campus, can ill afford at
this time."

The talk was well-received. Begando, always proper and always the gentle person, was particularly appreciative. He almost seemed to say to me that
which he dared not say, "Keep up the good work." Paul Stone, who was given
the honor of administering the Hippocratic oath to our first graduates,
heartily endorsed the talk and plainly urged me to "keep up the good fight."
The faculty also got a well-needed boost from my "fighting words." We held
a modest reception for the graduates and their families inside the Krannert
Center and called it a day. Tomorrow there would be new challenges.

Convocation was "feel good time." Now it was back to the real world.
Despite our brave words and posturing, the academic process envisioned by
President Ikenberry ground on. The College of Medicine faculty convened
for its annual meeting in Chicago on June 24, 1981. Ordinarily, this would
have been a perfunctory meeting that reviewed committee reports, ratified
faculty committee assignments, and heard reviews of the year's progress
from the regions and from the executive dean. Rarely were issues of substance, such as the reorganization, placed before the entire faculty. Ratified
by the Academic Council on May 13, the twelve-point proposal was now at
the college faculty level. If the faculty approved it, the proposal would go to
the Medical Center Senate and then to the president, who would "consult"
with the UIUC Senate and the Senates Conference before presenting the
matter to the Board of Trustees. The twelve-point proposal was the skeletal
outline of SPMC Model II as modified by Schmidt and Creditor. Its
approval at all levels of the university would give the Medical Center administration carte blanche to implement Model II and to phase out SCM-UC.

The meeting was held in the Chicago Illini Union, in the heart of
Abraham Lincoln School of Medicine turf. So, right from the start, the
regions were placed at a major disadvantage. As noted previously, the ALSM

faculty, which outnumbered the downstate faculty three to one, was already on record as supporting Model II and, at the same time, the phaseout of SCM-UC. Voting strength at this meeting was clearly weighted toward the ALSM contingent, and as if that were not bad enough, Creditor exploited the Office of the Executive Dean, which was supposed to represent the entire college, to alert all Chicago departments that it would be in their best interest to mobilize their faculty to attend and to vote. Contrary to the usual desultory attendance at college faculty meetings, some four hundred people crowded into the meeting room, which had but two hundred chairs. It was standing room only from wall to wall. Included among the ALSM "faculty" were medical interns and residents, who had nominal appointments in ALSM, but were eligible to vote. We were playing against a stacked deck.

I had traveled to the meeting with my secretary, Melody Simeone, and armed with data: enrollment numbers, annual costs per student, capital expenditures, UICOM budgetary history, SBMS/SCM-UC research success, indicators of student satisfaction, etc. I planned to lay out the entire benighted history of our development. As I entered the meeting room overflowing with ALSM representatives, I recognized very few Urbana-Champaign, Rockford, and Peoria faces in the assembly. I had a Don Quixote feeling in the pit of my stomach.

Mort Creditor presided, and after the disposal of routine business, accepted a motion that the faculty of the University of Illinois College of Medicine endorse the administration's twelve-point proposal, which would guide the reorganization. The motion for approval, coming from the Academic Council, needed no second. When the floor opened for discussion, it was time for me to act. With Ms. Simeone at the overhead projector providing appropriate visuals, I laid out the case for the SPMC Option III, the merger of SBMS/SCM-UC with the Peoria School of Medicine to establish a new entity as a downstate division of the College of Medicine. This was no time to be reticent. I had only one opportunity to change the outcome and threw everything into the struggle.

The thrust of my appeal to the Chicago faculty was that the downstate schools were not draining funds from them, but that Medical Center administrative decisions (such as maintaining the budget-devouring University Hospital) were. I told them that I would agree with many of them that regionalization had weakened the school, but for a different reason from what many of them would cite. I told them that faculty's power had been eroded by regionalization. To back up that argument, I cited a 1978 LCME finding that "the College of Medicine has evolved into an extraordinarily complex organization. As such it presents *an example of unresolved and counterproductive tension* between the need for differentiation of operating units versus central managerial requirements."

"That [LCME] report reflected the unhappiness of faculty and administration of all four regions," I said. "For the Medical Center administration to recommend evolution from the present unsatisfactory managerial system to a conformation that, even in the abstract and before implementation, accentuates the problems delineated by the LCME and…is actively opposed by the entire regional faculty—virtually unanimously—is sheer madness."

I went on to urge them not to approve the twelve-point plan and to consider SPMC Option III plan as an alternative. I told them that the twelve-point plan was opposed by virtually all the faculty in the downstate schools.

"You have a chance today to send a strong message to administration and to rid yourself of the burden of at least two struggling satellites (perhaps three) that drain your energies without adding to your luster. If you opt for the mandates of administration, it will do the College of Medicine in Chicago no good, and it will do those of us in Peoria and Urbana-Champaign much harm."

At one point in my presentation, Creditor stood, interrupted me, and asked for the microphone, announcing that I had used up all the floor time I was allowed. I resisted returning the microphone to him and protested that I had given this university and this College of Medicine the best eleven years of my life and with all that work and achievement at risk, I was not going to be thwarted in providing a thorough and essential historical background to a college faculty that was being asked to vote on an issue with which the faculty members were, for the most part, unfamiliar. I insisted that I had the right and the obligation to take whatever time was necessary to thoroughly explain my views on the matter. Moreover, I noted to Creditor that I had given him ten days advance written notice that I would need sufficient time to carefully explain the SCM-UC position to the college faculty. In view of these facts, I refused to be limited by arbitrary time restrictions.

Creditor backed down and yielded the floor back to me, which I held for another half-hour, explaining exactly the amount of resources the downstate schools used and showing that it was a mathematical impossibility for the Medical Center to correct its budgetary problems by shutting SCM-UC down and curtailing programs at Peoria, Rockford, and SBMS-UC. I laid out the history of the Lanier Treaty and all the other agreements for turning the governance of SBMS/SCM-UC over to UIUC, and how the Medical Center administration was attempting to circumvent them. And I told them about how the administration had interfered with the faculty's prerogatives in the SPMC process through President Ikenberry's one-school, one-dean mandate and Vice Chancellor Schmidt's order that the committee present no recommendation, only alternatives.

"The end result of the SPMC process only emphasizes how politically weak is the college faculty. It is regionalized, it is divided, it is without the cohesiveness that a faculty needs to be strong, to be confident, to be productive, and to resist imprudent moves by an administration which, I fear, knows and seeks to exploit faculty weakness…

"A strong, capable, and independent faculty is the hallmark of a great university. The fundamental difference between UIUC and UIMC is that at UIUC, the administration, to the greatest extent possible, depends upon and follows the lead of its faculty. The Urbana administration has confidence in its faculty. At UIMC, the exact opposite is the case. Paternalism is the name of the game, and paternalism has been devastating to the college. In essence, the campus administration has reduced the college to last among equals among other colleges on the Medical Center campus…"

And I exposed the administration's duplicity. "The college has been and will continue to be euchred by a university administration that has continually emphasized quantity over quality. Witness the process today. I have little doubt that the vice chancellor expects the slavish ratification of an administrative decision that was made many months ago, well before the SPMC was halfway through its course. After all, six months ago, in January, Vice President Brady confidently predicted, 'SCM-UC will be closed.' In February of this year, while the SPMC process was still under way, I was ordered by both doctors Creditor and Schmidt—ordered, mind you—to cancel a meeting requested by the Executive Committees of Peoria and Urbana to explore the basis for a possible merger. Yet, on April 16, 1981, President Ikenberry told the Board of Trustees, 'We must correct *the mistaken notion* in the minds of some that we are dealing with a *fait accompli.*' [Emphasis added.] Well, some notions sure die hard. One month ago, Mort Creditor called me to advise me to 'stop wasting' my time, *it* was all decided. Some notions sure die hard.

So much for the 'academic process' at this medical center."

I concluded with a final push for Option III. "To summarize, there is a firm conviction of our faculty and of the faculty of the Peoria School of Medicine that the best solution for this College of Medicine and this university would be to merge PSM and SBMS/SCM-UC as a separate division for medical education. We believe this is possible within the existing resources of the College of Medicine and the Medical Center campus even in these difficult times. We believe it is not only the best option for Peoria and Urbana, we believe it is certainly the best option for Chicago, and with patience and understanding, the best option for Rockford as well.

"Therefore, I move that this COM faculty endorse a reorganization plan that allows for the merger of PSM, SBMS-UC, and SCM-UC and which establishes the new entity as a downstate division of the College of Medicine."

I was finished, emotionally and physically drained. I had argued not so much because I thought I would change the minds of a faculty that felt threatened itself, but because I wanted to lay out, once and for all, the Urbana position to the major cross section of college faculty before me. Moreover, as I warmed to the task and listened to the logic of my own arguments, I began to think that I might change enough minds to win the vote. Although it was clear from the voting that followed that my appeal had attracted some votes, it did not turn enough heads to overcome the enormous home-field advantage of the Chicago faculty. The twelve-point measure was approved. It was another nail in the SCM-UC coffin.

It was some solace that my spirited defense of the Urbana position was not entirely unappreciated. As the crowd drifted away after the vote, one Chicago member exclaimed, "That Bloomfield! He's the Robert E. Lee of Urbana." That may have been true, but I did not like heading for Appomattox.

We pressed on. One path blocked, try another. On June 25, the day after the faculty meeting, a mixed delegation of faculty from SBMS/SCM-UC and campus departments, led by Willard Visek, met with the president to expound the advantages of clinical education at UIUC. But Ikenberry, no doubt fortified by the UICOM faculty vote of the day before, discouraged the delegation with his rigidity. According to Visek, the president made a number of statements that were selectively self-serving to justify his hard-line position that the reorganization would follow Option II. He cited the fact that people on the UC campus were totally unwilling to talk about reallocation of their own resources to keep SCM-UC (although to the best of my knowledge the president never entertained any serious proposal to transfer SCM-UC governance to UIUC), and that Paul Stone, president of the Board of Trustees, had no alternate suggestion to Option II, a swipe at my relationship with him. He added that no one on the board had suggested altering the one-college, one-dean formula. That, too, was hardly surprising, given the publicly outspoken presidential position. The faculty, in visiting with the president, merely sought reassurance of an open academic process, but found instead, a person with his mind made up. They couldn't talk budget or reallocation with him, because they didn't have the figures. He also told them that my proposal for Option III was unrealistic. He did not believe that with $7 million annually, we could put together a good school between Peoria and Urbana. By the end of the hour with the president, Visek and the remainder of the delegation were convinced that SCM-UC was doomed.

As avenues to a favorable decision were blocked, one by one, we began to lay more emphasis on those that remained open. One of these was the UIUC Wicks committee. Marty Weller, my administrative assistant, and Shari Benstock, who served a similar function with the Medical Scholars Program, prepared exhaustive documentation for the Wicks Committee and for the record. We kept informing the UIUC Graduate College and administrative leadership, the faculty, and our community constituencies about the problems and the proposed Medical Center solution. It was important to convince the UIUC Senate that shutting down clinical education at UIUC would be a disaster for the campus. Information was continuously updated. On July 1, we arranged a meeting between SBMS/SCM-UC Executive Committees and the Wicks Committee.

Hal Swartz presented a detailed memorandum on the loss of quality, the loss of clinical resources, and the loss of research resources if the school closed. Allan Levy discussed qualitative points regarding the program in computer science. He pointed out that there were few similar academic programs in the country. We were one of ten medical schools in the United States with a formal program in computer science related to medicine. Of those, only three or four concentrated on training physicians, and we had approximately one-third of the physicians in the United States training in this field. This computer-science education project had existed for about five years, and at that point, we had our first Ph.D. student. We also had our first Medical Scholar, who had completed the second year of medical training and who the following year would be in the Department of Computer Science, while maintaining clinical activity through SCM-UC. Three Medical Scholars were working on a Masters Degree in Computer Science, a degree that was worked out specifically with physicians in mind, although students in other professional areas also participated.

Concerning the single-college, single-dean issue, Levy spoke about the grand federalism in the college, characterizing it as unworkable because there were too many different environments and too many different goals for centralization of administration.

An extensive discussion followed on the question "Why can't the Medical Scholars Program exist without SCM-UC?"

Lew Winter described our involvement with the Veterans Administration Hospital at Danville, whose relationship to the medical school would be entirely different if there were no clinical school present at UC. Dick Gumport pointed out very simply that without the medical school here, even though the possibility had always existed on paper for earning a Ph.D. here and doing the MD degree elsewhere, there were no takers. It was not done. He also noted that the current MD-Ph.D. program at the Medical Center was very weak. The need for SCM-UC, a clinical school to complement the MSP was affirmed over and over again. Together and separately, people responded in great detail to every aspect of the serious questioning relating to the need for the existence of SCM-UC as a sine qua non for the MSP. Toward the end of the session, Joe Larsen spoke about one graduate student who had been teaching an introductory biology course while simultaneously completing his MD degree and conducting research on the campus, an outcome that could never have been achieved with a geographically split MD-Ph.D. program.

It was gratifying to be listened to by an objective third party. So many cogent reasons were put forth by well-respected faculty peers that the Wicks Committee went away convinced that the MSP needed clinical training in the UC area. Finally, each member of the committee was provided with a meticulously prepared packet containing essential historical material, applicable memoranda from Schmidt and Creditor regarding the SPMC and Option II, the twelve-point proposal, the Bicampus Steering Committee statement on minimal acceptable terms for maintaining the MSP at UIUC, two letters from potential Medical Scholars withdrawing from consideration because of reorganization instability, copies of letters from prominent

American and European scientists and a list of other prominent personages supporting SBMS/SCM-UC and the MSP. We were down, but we were not out!

I was not looking forward to my second grilling from Mort Creditor and Mack Schmidt. Creditor had given me two dates, but both were occupied. I finally agreed to meet with them on July 8. (This time there were no tape recorders at the meeting. The narrative is based on my diary entry of July 10.) Going into the meeting, I did not know whether they wanted to dismiss me on the spot, demand my resignation, require some kind of apology, or ask me again for reassurance.

They began the meeting by asking me how I was going to respond to Creditor's June 24 letter. I responded simply that I would carry out my duties as outlined by the University of Illinois Statutes. Regarding specific elements concerning funds for space rentals and for faculty and staff travel, I said that in view of Creditor's response to my money-saving proposals, I would have to manage somehow.

It quickly became clear that those were not the questions they wanted answered. What they really wanted was an explanation of my personal and confidential letter to Mort Creditor of June 1, which I'd written on my personal stationery and sent to him at his home. I told them that the letter to which they referred was personal and confidential and that I would say nothing else about it in this venue. Creditor argued that labeling such a letter "personal and confidential" meant nothing because anything sent like that was a public document and he had no obligation to keep it personal and confidential. He justified his sharing the letter with Schmidt, Begando, and Ikenberry. Playing the sleuth, Creditor noted that the second page of the letter had no letterhead, but did have a University of Illinois watermark, so that even though it had been typed on my own personal stationery, it was, by this logic, a University of Illinois public document. They persisted in trying to extract from me an explanation of the June 1 letter, but I held my ground steadfastly, telling them over and over again that I did not feel that the letter was a proper subject for discussion in a meeting such as this. The harder they pressed, the more I resisted, and finally told them that I would be happy to discuss the letter with Mort Creditor in a personal, off-the-record setting.

I think both of them were genuinely surprised and, to no small extent, irritated by my position. Mack Schmidt was particularly frustrated and said that I was a "cruel individual" and that he had never been subjected to ad hominem attacks before. I said that I did not know what he was talking about, but if he was referring to the June 1 letter, that was out of the range of discussion—I would not respond to it. Schmidt then made repeated statements to the effect that he was dissatisfied at how the meeting was going. I told him that I could not help that because I did not call the meeting and I had no agenda for the meeting.

Schmidt complained that it was apparent that I did not have confidence in the Medical Center leadership, and asked, in view of this, why I continued to hold my position. Creditor chimed in with a statement to the effect that if he had disagreed this much with senior administration, he would have resigned a long time ago. So here was the hidden agenda surfacing. They were looking for my voluntary resignation. But that was not my style. I responded to both of them that I saw myself as dean of a medical school in UC carrying out a job in accordance with the university statutes.

Finally, Creditor and Schmidt insisted on a written response to the Creditor letter of June 24. Their decision as to whether I would be re-appointed as dean of SBMS/SCM-UC depended on my answer to that letter. They set no deadline this time for the response. I told them that whether or not they recommended me for reappointment was clearly up to them. They also mentioned, as if to add weight, that Creditor's June 24 letter to me had been personally edited by Ikenberry, a fact at which I could only shrug my shoulders. At the end of the meeting, which hardly deviated from the topic of my June 1 letter to Creditor, I asked both of them why Schmidt had to be present at this particular meeting. Both replied that it was because Schmidt was attacked in that letter, to which I made a final comment that I had nothing more to say. All in all, it was a Mexican standoff. I left them waiting for my response to the June 24 letter.

During the conversation, Schmidt made two interesting incidental assertions. He said that he was unaware that, as early as December 1980, Vice President Brady, in the name of fiscal retrenchment, had targeted SCM-UC for closing. Schmidt claimed that he came to the conclusion that SCM-UC should be phased out only after he had received the report of the SPMC. Because the matter had been leaked to me in January 1981, I found it startling and disingenuous that Schmidt would make such an assertion. Schmidt also claimed that he had thorough and detailed discussions with Chancellor Cribbet and VCAA Goldwasser at UIUC regarding the fiscal problems of the Medical Center and the anticipated closing of SCM-UC and that there was complete understanding on both sides. Therefore, he claimed that his actions with regard to SCM-UC were not "unilateral."

In any event, I had a complex letter to compose that would go through repeated drafts in the next two weeks before being sent on July 22. Furthermore, the letter that was actually sent was not the one I really wanted to write. Discretion being the better part of valor, I decided not to send that six-page draft. In it, I maintained my refusal to discuss the personal letter and went down the list of my concerns, as frank as you please.

"The inability of the college and the university to deal with budgetary discrepancies, despite, in the case of SCM-UC, a lead time of four years, is to selectively disadvantage SCM-UC students. This unequal assignment of resources represents a serious failure of administration…which is compounded by what is perceived as a 'Stop the Urbana clinical program at all costs' vendetta.

"Your letter of June 24 assumes that I am having unique problems as an administrator. My problems are no different from other regional deans' and stem from the attitude of central administration to treat us as associate deans rather than as statutory deans. As an example: At no time during the SPMC process did you, as senior administrator of the college seriously consult with your regional deans concerning any of the options proposed by the SPMC…concerning either advantages and disadvantages and/or the budgetary implications of each option. In other words, you avoided an administrative consensus that might have helped you avoid the unfortunate events that followed Vice Chancellor Schmidt's recommendation in mid-April of 1981. Provisions for such consultation, which any reader of the statutes would have to assume, are also called for in the charges to the Administrative Advisory Council of Deans. Even now you would be well advised to seek a real consensus from the deans of the six schools concerning reorganization solutions instead of virtually excluding us from the process and relying upon automatic Chicago-based majorities in Academic Council, Faculty, and Senate.

"We consider it a serious problem when the Vice Chancellor recommends solutions to the reorganization process without any reference to the budgetary or enrollment implications of his recommendations. Furthermore, we note with concern that the Vice Chancellor's proposals were fraught with conflict of interest in the sense that his recommendations

appear to be designed to appeal only to the faculty residing in Chicago, a
faculty which has frequently been critical of regional schools, and a faculty
to which he was under obligation as the first dean of ALSM. Under the circumstances it was particularly important that senior administration carefully brief regional deans on every aspect concerning their proposals.
Instead, we heard a panic response, which in effect said, 'Sorry. No money.
Too bad," and ten years of regional progress were scheduled for dismantling.

"Your March 17 letter of transmittal of the SPMC report to VCAA
Schmidt went far beyond the mandate given you by the faculty to chair that
committee and represented nothing less than an indirect attack on the community-based programs that have been developing for the past eleven years.
We interpret your letter as evidence of your failure to understand what the
clinical programs in Rockford, Peoria, and Urbana-Champaign are trying to
achieve—and, more importantly, what is necessary for the development
process for these community-based schools. To refer to our effort as 'a noble
experiment,' to talk about a 'restoration of the values of the university,' and
to quote the Flexner report of 1910 is to ignore the incredible changes that
have taken place in the dissemination of medical science and knowledge
over the past seventy years. You claim to seek 'yet another experiment'
before you have hardly evaluated or tasted the fruits of the first; but what
you are really doing is trying to turn back the clock. Your Flexnerian
approach seriously prejudices regional school development. You forget that
the Massachusetts General Hospital and the Michael Reese Hospital were
once community hospitals. Your view is shortsighted and destructive to the
entire process of development that you agreed to when I first recruited you
into the College of Medicine. You have thus biased senior administration by
raising flags of multimillion-dollar investments to be made in regional programs if they are to be sustained, rather than properly informing them that
quality development takes time.

"The above leads me to conclude that you and VCAA Schimdt are less
than fully committed to the regionalization process. Regionalization is a
commitment of the university, and your actions appear to us to be an attack
on regionalization. The most flagrant example of this is your condemnatory
judgment of the Rockford School of Medicine and your undisguised hostility toward it as a site for medical education. It is also symbolic of your avoidance of a true consensus and your desire to impose your own administrative
ideas on the faculty of the College of Medicine in its reorganization process.

You have downgraded and widely 'badmouthed' the Rockford School of Medicine without any evidence that the graduates of RSM are any better or any worse physicians than those coming from any other unit of the college or that their education is one whit below that of the program elsewhere. You have freely cited data about Rockford graduates based upon statistics that have not been adequately controlled.

"Your letter speaks of the importance of personal confidence, and I would respond that my confidence in the higher administration is limited only by the perception that there is a tendency in your administration and that of the vice chancellor to interpret disagreement as disloyalty to the university. That perception may be an error, but again, in all my dealings with Bill Grove and Joe Begando, I was always treated with the academic respect of a dean within this university and was never subjected to the indignity of signing the equivalency of a loyalty oath. It was self-evident that both of them respected the differences between line and staff responsibility and between academic and corporate or federal government administration. I believe the record will show SBMS/SCM-UC has been a well-administered, productive, and cost-effective unit of the College of Medicine over the past decade.

"You need have no doubt that I completely understand the responsibilities of my office and will carry out those responsibilities. I will continue to participate in the affairs of the college as I always have with the same gusto and enthusiasm.

"Subject to my comments relating to disagreement versus loyalty, I am completely confident to work with the administrative leadership of the college, campus and university. I have always been willing and will continue to be willing to cooperate in the implementation of institutional practices and policies. Furthermore, I have always willingly functioned and will continue to function within the university system in full accordance with Article III, Sections 3, 4, and 5 of the University Statutes."

Draft letters that you don't expect to send are always fun to compose. They allow you to vent your feelings completely without having to suffer the consequences of any indiscretions that might be contained therein. So having vented my thoughts in the draft, which I shared with Bud Grulee in Rockford and Jerry Newman in Peoria for their comments, I returned to the drawing board to write a letter of record in response to Creditor's request. While this was being composed, other significant activities related to reorganization were taking place.

It was now July of 1981 and Ikenberry wanted a recommendation that he could bring to the Board of Trustees in November. I was following the advice of Paul Stone and others to keep the drums beating to save the school. Stone was particularly insistent about maintaining positive relationships with Rockford and Peoria. He was convinced that SCM-UC could not pull off survival by itself; we needed Rockford and Peoria in the picture. He likened us to a fight of ducks going over a duck hunter's blind and how the hunters generally shoot at the trailing ducks before moving up in the formation. We were the trailing duck, and would get picked off first, unless we stuck closely with the formation.

Our students were wonderful and very effective agitators in their own right. They were loyal, vocal, and active. Several of them were represented on the University Medical Student Council: Paul Hattis, Vice President; Elaine Reed, Secretary; and members Nora Zorich and David Marder. All were excellent students who could argue the case for our program as well as anyone. They led a meeting of the University Medical Student Council on June 28 in Chicago to discuss the reorganization and wrote the following letter on July 1, 1981 to President Ikenberry, Chancellors Begando and Cribbet, Vice Chancellor Schmidt, Executive Dean Creditor, members of the Board of Trustees, other prominent administrators, and to the UICOM-UC faculty and students. The letter stated, "It is our observation that the major motivation for what is occurring in the process of reorganization stems from geopolitical (that is Chicago and non-Chicago) concerns rather than substantive academic ones...It was unanimously decided that UMSC issue the position statement concerning reorganization which follows: 'We believe that the College of Medicine's goals and priorities should be a primary concern in any proposed reorganization: specifically, regionalization of health education (to answer Urban Health and Rural Health needs), and efforts to correct deficits in research and academic medicine...The present process has at best dealt with such goals and priorities in a cursory manner...Of major concern is our observation that the proposal for reorganization, which on paper seeks to encourage unity of the College of Medicine faculty by centralization, has in fact created a strict geopolitical split in the faculty...The resulting animosity has seriously decreased faculty collegiality. A third area of concern is our observation that although a major justification of the proposed changes has been financial, at no point have specific cost-related analyses been discussed."

It was a perceptive statement that was unanimously adopted by student members from all four regions. It earned the students an invitation for a personal discussion with the president, which took place on July 10, 1981. But the SCM-UC students who attended that meeting, Paul Hattis and Nora Zorich, reported back to me their disappointment. They perceived that the president had a strong mind-set for closing SCM-UC. He spoke of clinical training in UC for Medical Scholars only. He talked about "bare bones" clinical education here. He mentioned possibly seven or eight M-3 clerkships, but in the students' opinion, clearly did not understand the meaning or implications of these clerkships. The students saw a president fixated in his views and intent on blaming the victim. He stated, "SCM-UC can't live within its budget and will cost more money in the future." Ikenberry pointed out that Medical Service Plan dollars were earned in Peoria, Rockford, and Chicago, but not in Champaign-Urbana, and he did not want our program run by hospitals that put up the money. Clearly, Creditor and Schmidt had briefed him. In closing, he told the students, "The street fighting has to stop." Indirectly referring to my leadership, he said, "Some people have to join reality." After the meeting, the students were depressed.

I talked to Paul Stone on July 14 because I wanted his input on the letter I was writing to Creditor and Schmidt, which basically would answer their question, "Are you with us or against us?" Stone, who was cautiously optimistic, said that he saw some division between the president's position on reorganization and the Schmidt-Creditor position. Stone thought that the July 1 student letter to the president was very good because it brought up the unsatisfactory geopolitical nature of the present college. Stone added that equal regional representation in the future governance of the college was mandatory. This was the way it had to be. He agreed that the Metro 6 hospitals were taking too much money and that community-based education should be left to the downstate schools. He advised us to continue lobbying with the trustees. He predicted that the downstate trustees would stick together. "Don't leave any of them out," Stone warned. "Any solution we propose must be acceptable to Rockford and Peoria. We hang together, or we hang separately." As usual, it was reassuring talking to him.

On the same day, I received a telephone call from Dr. Sinha in Peoria giving some interesting new insights into the president's mind-set. Mayor Carver of Peoria and three hospital board chairpersons, concerned with the possible downgrading of PSM, had talked with the president and had received assurances from him that Peoria would have a cohort of seventy per class, a proportional budget would be allotted to the school, and departmental structure would be maintained there. Yet the president was noncommittal about the number of classes to be assigned to Peoria, two or three, and he was opposed to the merger of the Peoria and Urbana-Champaign programs.

Although Ikenberry told them he would consider any logical, reasonable plan that was laid on the table, he also said he would reject an organization which in any way looked like two Colleges of Medicine, and he certainly did not want an independent program at Urbana-Champaign. I thanked Dr. Sinha for his information and told him as much as I could about the present status of SCM-UC. We both agreed to "keep the pressure on the President."

The July 15 Board of Trustees meeting at Rockford gave Bud Grulee an opportunity to speak directly to the trustees on the UICOM reorganization. Schmidt and Creditor did not receive his statements enthusiastically, and a brief public dispute ensued. Grulee complained that for all the democracy implied in the SPMC reorganization process, he perceived that the decisions and proposals that emerged from the process had been rammed through by one person, Morton Creditor. Creditor responded, "I think administrators have to be different from faculty members. Administrators, such as Dean Grulee, are obliged to support higher administration's recommendations." Grulee argued to the board that in the academic milieu, one went through an academic process before administrators received reports and made decisions. Once a decision is final, then at that time, but not before that time, the administrators should move out and lead, and Grulee said that he was unaware that a final decision had been made. (Of course Ikenberry, Schmidt, and Creditor had already made the final decision in private, but had not yet shepherded it into the public domain.)

Grulee also emphasized that the regional schools related more closely as partners to their respective communities, a bond that was far more difficult for the medical center to achieve in Chicago. Joe Begando welcomed the comments from Grulee and calmed down the exchange between Creditor and Grulee. In response to questions from members of the board, Bud Grulee described the unique progress and strength of the Rockford School of Medicine. When asked about the high costs per student, Grulee said the costs per student were high because the enrollments had been kept at the low level of forty-eight per year rather than at the planned enrollment level of sixty-four per year.

Meanwhile, I continued to work on the response to Creditor's June 24 letter, and Creditor continued to lead the college toward the Option II. In the 1981 summer issue of *Scope,* an internal public-relations quarterly of UICOM, Mort editorialized: "We grow smaller, creatively. The college of the last decade was great. The college of the next decade has the potential to be even greater."

I composed several drafts, discussing the points to make with my staff and close advisors. I even consulted Grulee in Rockford and Newman in Peoria, because any change in the Champaign-Urbana organization, whether internal or external, affected them as well.

Meanwhile, a lot of political activity went on at Rockford and Peoria, much of which was news to me. On July 20, Dr. William Baskin faxed me copies of what he had written to the Board of Trustees. Baskin, then clinical assistant professor and director of the gastroenterology curriculum at Rockford, criticized the Schmidt-Creditor proposal as an "arbitrary decision by the Chicago administrators that did not have any agreement whatsoever from the regional faculty or administrators...The obvious result of this change will be to eliminate a full medical-school class from each of the regional campuses."

I wrote and thanked Dr. Baskin and encouraged his interest and his continued participation, emphasizing that "if the College of Medicine is to honor its regional commitments, then it should cease to develop 'regional' community hospitals in Chicago (the Metro 6) and leave community-based education to Rockford, Peoria, and UC."

On the other hand, not everyone in Rockford and Peoria was support-ive. Jerry Newman, who succeeded Nick Cotsonas as dean at Peoria, wrote to me after he had reviewed my draft response to Creditor's June 24 letter. I knew that Newman had never been one to support the Urbana clinical pro-gram, which he confirmed bluntly. "As I have stated on numerous occasions, I believe that the university's decision, both initially made and reaffirmed later, to develop a clinical school in Urbana was an error. This is in no way meant to be a reflection on the faculty, the administration, or the communi-ty of Urbana. Two clinical schools within ninety miles of each other in a rel-atively sparsely populated portion of Central Illinois cannot be defended in my mind. The purposes of regionalization are served by a single school in this region." That explains some of the problems I had in forming a close and effective relationship with the leadership in Peoria.

Finally, on July 22, I responded to Creditor's demand that I "state in writing [my] plans for fulfilling the obligations for deanship." Of course, it was clear that the administration would have loved to have me resign, and they indicated this to me in every way possible, both in person and in writing. But I was not about to resign, for reasons I have mentioned earlier. Resignation from political fights bestows a momentary feeling of righteous indignation, but in essence, the resignee loses the war.

Nor would I give them cause for firing me. They would have relished that just as well. I remained determined to act as a dean within the Statutes of the University of Illinois. The statutes provided excellent cover for me.

I refused to discuss my June 1 letter, but did discuss the rest. Regarding my June 9 letter, which complained about the budget, I acknowledged that "this is a very difficult year and you have done all that is possible for you to do with respect to the SCM-UC budget. We shall manage within the budgetary limits provided."

I added that I would comply with all his demands in his June 10 and 15 letters, and closed by stating, "I understand the responsibilities of my office and will carry them out as you have outlined...I assure you that I have confidence in and the ability to work with the administrative leadership of the college, campus, and university [although I was less confident that the leadership had the ability to work with me]. I will cooperate in the implementation of institutional practices and policies and will willingly function within our university system. I regret any misunderstandings that may have arisen between us with respect to these matters."

This letter was copied to Ikenberry, Begando, and Schmidt. It was a very calculated response, designed to provide them nothing to support their desire to supplant me at Urbana-Champaign. In August, I received my reappointment papers, all in order, evidence that they had decided to reappoint me as dean of SBMS/SCM-UC.

On July 21, a group of five SCM-UC medical students, who were a designated subcommittee on college reorganization appointed by the UC Medical Student Government, sent a note to the Academic Council subcommittee on implementation of the reorganization process regarding that topic. The students had outlined a proposal regarding a minimal clinical school to function on the UIUC campus that could sustain the MSP. They deemed it a moderate position. Although some students thought it was too much of a compromise, others looked for a solution that could accommodate those people who desired to take advantage of some of the excellent learning opportunities on the campus without actually working toward a Ph.D. The students went on to recommend a minimum cohort size of thirty students in the M-3/M-4 classes and the capacity to deliver core clerkships, with about eight to ten elective clerkships to be available.

They closed their letter with a final request that they had clearly explained to the president weeks earlier. "We must ask that the College of Medicine stop acting as if it operates in a vacuum. The recent bundle of explosive interaction between the various groups affected by the reorganization has begun to detract from the college's credibility as an academically motivated educational system. If there is to be a clinical school in Urbana, the COM must stand by its commitments and present a good deal more stability than has been demonstrated to this point."

Nothing exemplified the complexity of the situation better than the potpourri of events that occurred on July 22, 1981. The morning began with an interview with Robert Eisner, a strong supporter of the university who sat on the Board of the University of Illinois Foundation. Eisner was peripherally aware of the problems of reorganization of the COM, which we discussed at some length. He indicated his great interest in the problem and understood many of the reasons that it was in the best interest of the university to have a clinical program in UC. Although it would take valuable time, meeting with strong supporters of the university was essential.

When I returned to my office, Allan Levy was impatient to see me. Before I could see him, I had to sign my response to Mort Creditor's June 24 letter. Allan wanted to discuss his draft plan for the reorganization of the COM. He maintained that it seemed to be very well accepted by those individuals to whom he had shown it. These apparently included Ned Goldwasser, among others. I informed him of my political imperative and necessity to get an agreement among Peoria, Rockford, and Urbana, and told him that, when I had shown representatives of those schools the Levy proposal, they had turned it down. Nevertheless, I told him that there was a tentative agreement between the three downstate schools on a plan designed by the Peoria-Urbana Faculty Study Group that postulated one hundred fifty students at Urbana-Champaign for their first forty-eight weeks of instruction.

Allan was anxious and upset. He complained to me that he did not

understand how I could be promoting two separate plans. I informed him
that it was not so much a question of me promoting plans, but of my reacting to plans that had been presented to me. Plans to avoid the adoption of
Option II were coming from all sides. Furthermore, I told him that whether I
liked it or not, agreement between Urbana, Peoria, and Rockford was a basic
principle of the solution. Otherwise, Chicago would win, and we would lose
our clinical school. Allan believed that his plan would be acceptable to the
president and if the president approved it (an unlikely event in my view),
then it did not make any difference what Rockford or Peoria thought.

I called Bud Grulee in Rockford about the problem. Bud felt that
Rockford could support the plan worked out by the Peoria-Urbana Faculty
Study Group or would at least give it a good look. Bud did not particularly
like Allan's plan, which gave Rockford only two years of students, and Bud
was very concerned about the rotating deanship proposed. He did not see
the advantages that Allan thought Grulee should see. Furthermore, Bud
informed me, Rockford and Peoria would not support any position that
would give Urbana both a clinical school and autonomy. They did not necessarily object to a clinical program at Urbana-Champaign, but they would
support it only under conditions that protected their interests. They believed
that if there were a four-year program at Urbana and a four-year program in
Chicago, sooner or later Rockford and Peoria would be cut out.

I tried to explore these very sensitive complexities with Allan. His support and diligence had been very useful, and I did not wish to alienate such
a close friend. If I came out openly for his plan and rejected the tentative
agreements we had among the three downstate schools, it would be regarded
as a double cross by them and there was no way his plan would fly by itself.
Allan rejected that line of reasoning, stating that his plan in itself was so
solid it would gain presidential approval.

Sometime later, Allan returned with Ben Williams to convince me of the
error of my ways. We discussed the issues for about thirty minutes and Ben
was able to see both sides, although he clearly wanted me to support Allan's
plan. I told him that I was simply not in a position to openly support this
plan at this time. Instead, I preferred that the joint efforts of Urbana, Peoria,
and Rockford might emerge within Creditor's implementation committee so
that they could at least put a damper on what appeared to be a Medical
Center juggernaut to effect Option II and reduce all the regional schools to
two-year programs. We agreed it would be desirable to have Allan's plan

shown to the president, perhaps by UIUC Vice Chancellor Goldwasser, and to have the president's view of it before it was shot down by our critics at the Medical Center. Should Allan's plan be reviewed at the Medical Center first, we could expect the president to be prematurely prejudiced against it.

To complicate matters more, a close friend called me at about 8 p.m. the same evening with new and encouraging information. It was really a good-news, bad-news story. The good news was that the friend had learned from confidential, but reliable, sources that Executive Vice President Brady and his entire staff, having reviewed all the facts and figures regarding the UICOM finances, were convinced that the most economical plan was to retain SCM-UC. They had concluded that closing SCM-UC would probably not save any significant amount of money, that there was excess money hidden within the budget of ALSM in Chicago, and that Rockford was seriously overfunded. This welcome news represented an about-face by Brady who, if the rumors were correct, had been a long-time supporter of those who wished to close SCM-UC. However, the bad news was that President Ikenberry had rejected those conclusions because he did not want an independent clinical school at Urbana. Ikenberry said that he was very much afraid that a clinical school at UIUC would become the nucleus of a second college of medicine within the university, and he did not want that to occur. Apparently his entire staff tried to convince him that SCM-UC was the most cost-effective way to develop, but he single-mindedly refused to change his position. The president was unwilling to acknowledge that SBMS/SCM-UC was different—a community-based medical school that did not require a costly university hospital.

I asked my friend if it were possible that the data upon which Brady's figures were based could be exposed, but my confidant was not certain that was possible. This new information also helped to explain why the Medical Center had never disclosed facts and figures concerning the cost of medical education at the various sites that would justify their recommendations. Apparently, Brady showed his report to Schmidt and Creditor, both of whom argued fiercely that its conclusions were false, but Brady's staff did not accept the Schmidt and Creditor denials. I received the impression that Brady was convinced that ALSM played games with its budgetary dollars and had stowed away a great deal of money from its budget. Brady's staff was also convinced that SCM-UC was getting a raw deal. It appeared that we were finally being heard in high places.

I talked with my confidants about ways to make this information public, that is, to somehow get either the ad hoc UIUC subcommittee to inquire about it; to request that our state senator, Stan Weaver, inquire about it; or perhaps to go through Paul Stone. But stealth proved unnecessary. Brady's calculations surfaced in an August 7 letter that he and Begando wrote to the president regarding "Planning and Budgeting for the College of Medicine." However, although the Brady figures confirmed the underfunding of SCM-UC, they generated more sympathy to close the impoverished operation and put it out of its misery than to find funds for its survival.

In late July, Creditor formed a new ad hoc subcommittee from members of the academic council to implement the reorganization implied by the anticipated adoption of the SPMC report's option II. Creditor had already made changes based that premise, reducing the first year enrollment at SBMS-UC from 100 to 75. The subcommittee met in retreat on July 27–28 in order to formulate recommendations for additional steps to effect the changes demanded by the adoption of Option II. A series of preliminary recommendations were presented at the August meeting of the academic council. There were no surprises. The plan was straight Option II, with all the power concentrated in Chicago. The Executive Committee would comprise thirty members, eighteen from Chicago and the other twelve divided among the regions. Creditor asked that the preliminary report be shared with the faculties of the schools for their reactions and responses, and planned that in late August, the subcommittee would reconvene to finish the report for presentation to the Academic Council in September. Technically, the Urbana programs were favored in the ad hoc subcommittee because each school had one representative, and we had two schools, but the constraints under which the committee functioned were so limiting that one could only conclude that its deliberations were an academic farce. The three-year programs at Peoria and Rockford would be cut to two years, and the entire clinical program at Urbana-Champaign would be placed on the chopping block. Mort Creditor was the designated hatchet man.

On July 29, Hal Swartz had the opportunity to debrief Roland Leeson and Don Thursh, our representatives on the ad hoc subcommittee, regarding the July 27–28 retreat that produced the report. As summarized in Swartz's memo to me of August 3, the first morning of the subcommittee's retreat was spent discussing what turned out to be a futile attempt to consider anything but a very rigidly constrained program as defined by Mort Creditor.

Creditor insisted that "the highest University levels" had imposed constraints that included a two-year, two-year split, the one-dean, one-college concept, and the closing of the clinical program at Urbana-Champaign. He emphasized over and over again to a very frustrated committee that these constraints were set in concrete, presumably by the president, and were non-negotiable. Apparently, after the first morning of the retreat went nowhere, the group finally agreed to discuss the implementation of such a program, albeit under protest by some of the committee members. The key element was that the president had imposed those limitations.

Swartz's memo pointed out that this was completely at variance with the public posture of the president, who claimed to be waiting for the academic-committee process to work itself out. The memo declared that if the presidential duplicity could be surfaced in public, Ikenberry might have to choose between repudiating Creditor's claim of being severely constrained by the president or modifying his public position that he did not impose limitations on the deliberations except for the one-college, one-dean concept. Certainly, the limitations that Leeson and Thursh described contradicted the statements the president had recently made to the student delegation headed up by Nora Zorich, his subsequent follow-up letter to the medical students, and his statement to the UIUC Senate.

Leeson and Thursh went on to report that the details of Option II implementation were totally supplied by Mort Creditor with little input from the ad hoc subcommittee. Now, Mort was asking subcommittee members to return to their schools and act as advocates of "their" plan. After review and comment by the schools, the subcommittee was to meet again August 26-27 to prepare the final report, which would include the definitive plan for reorganization. The report would then go to the Academic Council on September 9 to be rubber-stamped, then to an impromptu COM faculty meeting, and then to the UIMC Senate. The student letter from Nora Zorich to the subcommittee, which presumably reflected the president's comments to the student group, was read to the subcommittee by Creditor, was not distributed, and was not discussed by the subcommittee thereafter.

Mort also gave the committee some financial estimates stating that, by the 1985 fiscal year, the reorganization would save the college approximately $1.3 million per year in 1981 dollars. This would involve a reduction of $500,000 at Urbana, $700,000 at Peoria, and $400,000 at Rockford, with an increase of $300,000 in Chicago. Once again, the cuts were in the regions,

and the increases were in Chicago. Future budgeting was planned on a
strict formula assignment with different figures used for basic-science and
clinical-science teaching. The assignment of students would be seventy-five
basic-science students to Urbana-Champaign and two hundred fifty to
Chicago. Clinical assignments would be two hundred to Chicago, seventy to
Peoria, and fifty-five to Rockford.

Creditor apparently confided privately to Thursh that the Chicago
faculty involved would really like to close down the regional programs and
indicated that "only the heroic efforts of Mack Schmidt and Mort Creditor
are saving the regions." They also reported that Creditor argued forcefully to
higher university officials that the presence of a clinical program at UIUC
would inevitably demand a university hospital.

Hal's debriefing analysis opened some strategic possibilities. Because
there were seven members on the committee, if the regions held together
they could defeat the proposal by a four-to-three vote, Chicago having two
votes (ALSM and SBMS-MC), and chairman Creditor one vote. On the other
hand, it was not certain that the regions would stick together, because the
individuals on the committee had been personally selected by Creditor and
did not necessarily reflect the views of the majority of the regional faculty.

The financial figures given to the committee also provided some powerful openings. The overall cost reduction represented little more than 4 percent of current total expenditures and would reduce the Urbana-Champaign
clinical program's chances of attracting research money. Meanwhile, an ad
hoc committee of leaders on the Urbana-Champaign campus came out with
a strong endorsement of Allan Levy's reorganization proposal and sent it to
the Wicks Committee. Although plans and programs were flying in every
direction, it seemed more and more likely that the Medical Center would
have its way.

July 1981 ended with a cautious note from UIUC Chancellor John
Cribbet, who, in responding to the June 3 resolution that had been approved
unanimously by the separate executive committees of the SBMS-UC and
SCM-UC, stated, "Any reorganization plan recommended by the COM will
proceed through normal academic channels for academic/administrative
matters of this type. Both Chancellor Begando and I will have an opportunity to review and comment on such a plan." This was an acknowledgment
that Chancellor Cribbet was aware of the problem and, although not enthusiastically endorsing our position, remained open-minded about it.

CHAPTER 31

Imperfect Attempts to Create
an Irresistible Force

O NE OF THE CONUNDRUMS that was always fun to debate as an
eager college student seeking to understand the universe, was the
impossible proposition, "What happens when an irresistible force
meets an immovable object?" Although none of us working for the survival
of clinical education in Urbana-Champaign imagined ourselves as an irresistible force, we definitely believed that we were working against a university president who was uncomfortably close to being an immovable object.
As Paul Stone admonished me repeatedly, it was essential that those of us in
Urbana, who were struggling to save this school, work closely and join forces
with our counterparts in Rockford and Peoria, who were faced with reductions that were nearly as distasteful. Never mind that the ideal solution for
Urbana was to free the program from the UIMC administration and from
the need to integrate with Rockford and Peoria. Never mind that the
Rockford and Peoria agendas were almost as hostile toward the survival of
our clinical program as the president and the UIMC administration were, if
not more so. Never mind that the Rockford and Peoria leadership would
have agreed to almost any compromise that would have avoided the specter
they feared most—an independent four-year program in Urbana (a fact we
did not fully appreciate at the time). Never mind all these unhappy causes;
the political atmosphere of the day forced the three regional schools to share
the tumbrel. Separately, we were nuisances that could be dealt with in serial
fashion. Together and only together, with Rockford and Peoria working on
the state legislature and Urbana working on the UIUC Senate and on the
moral authority of the Medical Scholars Program, did we constitute something that approached being an irresistible force.

Although most universities that adhere to an academic calendar luxuri-
ate during a summer recess, a break of more than two months that allows

for refreshment, renewal, and improved motivation, that was not an option for us in the summer of 1981. Instead, it would turn out to be a summer of feverish political activity at all three downstate sites. Rockford and Peoria engaged local legislators to plead their cause, while those of us in Urbana concentrated on fellow faculty members, who were also voting members of the UIUC senate, to make certain they were fully informed. We refused to permit our destiny to be decided by others, who were less familiar with our past and blind to the bright prospects for our future.

July's events left us dispirited, and we probably would have been even more depressed had we had timely access to a report from Chancellor Begando and Vice President Brady to President Ikenberry titled "A Preliminary Report on Planning and Budgeting for the College of Medicine," dated August 7, 1981. This extended communication, which came across my desk belatedly in September, after it was distributed to the Board of Trustees, contained a number of features, but in essence it was a point-by-point justification of the Schmidt (or by this time, the Ikenberry-Schmidt) reorganization proposal. Complete with enrollment and budget projections and containing a plethora of self-serving statements and references to other documents with which the regional programs were also unfamiliar, it was carefully designed to be the last nail in the coffin of our downstate hopes. As one of my staffers wrote on the cover page, it was "The Planning Document for the Death Knell." Addressing the board in the document cover letter of August 31, 1981, Ikenberry declared that this document was the most comprehensive review of the current status of planning to date, with a final report to come in November. He added, "While there are many concerns to be satisfied, I believe the current planning responds to the fundamental academic, organizational, and long-term fiscal issues in a responsible way."

The document, supported by the presidential imprimatur was meant to be a compelling argument to the trustees, by which Mack Schmidt and Ron Brady justified Schmidt's maximalist interpretation of Option II and Brady's creative addition of self-serving budget projections. The Brady/Begando letter confirmed the desirability of Option II. The letter then went on to present a budget analysis from data that differed radically from any previously discussed budget. The newly formulated budget favored the Chicago elements of the college and was highly skewed against SCM-UC and the regional programs. For example, for the first time ever in the budget analysis of state funds for medical education, resident physicians in training were suddenly included as part-time medical students. This immediately inflated the number of medical students in Chicago, reducing the calculated annual dollar cost per Chicago medical student significantly, even though the university, through its hospital, was already being paid for its interns and residents by pass-through dollars from third-party payers, and particularly from the U.S. government in the form of Medicare and Medicaid. This seemed to be a prima facie case of "double dipping" by the UIMC administration, but there was no one to blow the whistle. This flawed account made ALSM's annual cost-per-student appear roughly comparable with SCM-UC's, which was false.

The argument that we made repeatedly and that fell on the deaf ears of our immovable senior administrators was that SCM-UC was by far the most cost-effective program in the college. It made no sense to close down the most cost-effective program in favor of the more expensive programs that were present in Chicago and to a certain extent in Rockford. However, a cost model constructed by Brady projected "savings" of $4.3 million by the 1985 fiscal year if his plan were followed.

The Brady/Begando report, however, did not calculate the devastating effect its execution would have on the regions. For those of us in Urbana, the most disturbing revelation in the Begando/Brady report was in a copy of an appended letter Creditor sent to Schmidt dated July 17, 1981, in response to the president's wish to maintain the Medical Scholars Program. After analyzing the current and projected operation of the program, Creditor made the flat summary statement: "It is my opinion that the Medical Scholars Program can continue in the absence of a complete clinical program in Urbana-Champaign."

There are certain defining moments in any career or in any relationship that spell out the credibility and standing of the individual. The July 17 Creditor letter to Schmidt, which those of us who were vitally involved with the Medical Scholars Program did not see until two months after it was delivered, was one of those moments. My relationship with Mort Creditor was probably beyond repair even before the July 17 letter was composed, but until that letter I never believed that Mort Creditor would take a position that rational argument would not support. I could forgive him many things because I knew that Schmidt and Ikenberry placed very heavy pressures on him. The old saw goes, "Where you stand depends upon where you sit," and I knew very well that Mort occupied a very hot and turbulent seat. I was

more disappointed than surprised that from a Chicago desk, he took a
Chicago view. I am sure things look vastly different from behind the executive's dean's desk in Chicago from the way they looked from behind my own
desk, 140 miles or so south. Nevertheless, no position that he took, and no
act that he made against our school lost him as much credibility among our
rank and file as did his misguided assertion concerning the MSP.

The final Board of Trustees decision was scheduled for November of
1981. We had barely two months to reverse what seemed like a *fait accompli*,
and the programs in Rockford, Peoria, and Urbana were hardly united in
our stands, especially given the animus of the other two schools toward our
goal of a four-year program at UIUC. Our position in Urbana was to
emphasize the high road of academic quality that resided in the Medical
Scholars Program. This received powerful support from the UIUC Senate
and the Graduate College. The only solution that Rockford and Peoria saw
was political in nature. This became evident in early August, when a joint
letter by two state legislative representatives from the Peoria area invited all
legislators from areas affected by the regional medical schools to a short
informational meeting that October in Springfield, because "our collective
voice in protesting proposed cuts would be much stronger than individual
action."

The letter was sent to twenty-two legislators from the Peoria, Rockford,
and Urbana-Champaign areas and to deans Newman and Grulee, as well as
myself. The legislature to which the University of Illinois is ultimately
accountable was a sleeping giant, and it began showing signs of arousal.

Also coming to a climax at this time were the on-again off-again meetings of the Peoria, Urbana and Rockford faculties, who were desperately trying to find some common formula to ward off Option II. The three faculties
had plenty of reason to unite, but thus far had been unable to do so. SPMC
Option III was the most logical plan to follow, but there was no consensus
for that.

From the Rockford viewpoint, for instance, Option III's linkage of Peoria
with Urbana and Chicago with Rockford left Rockford isolated and vulnerable as an appendage that Chicago could then cut off with ease. On the other
hand, a linkage that would include RSM in a downstate school with Peoria
and Urbana might stretch the geographic operation of a small medical school
too far. Nevertheless, I steadfastly adhered to Paul Stone's repeated advice
that we abandon neither Peoria nor Rockford in our negotiations.

The faculties could come up with reasonable alternate plans, but there was literally no one to receive them. There was a complete disconnect between regional faculty and higher administration.

Nevertheless, the Peoria-Urbana faculty study group approached a solution based on one college, one dean that was the closest thing to a consensus that had yet been achieved. They called for first-year enrollment at Urbana to be one hundred fifty, while the remaining College of Medicine first-year students would be enrolled in Chicago. For the 150-student cohort, the basic-science year would be forty-eight weeks, equivalent to one-and-a-quarter years of medical education. The succeeding two-and-three-quarters years would be at Urbana, Peoria, or Rockford. They recommended that, of the basic-science cohort from Urbana-Champaign, fifty would move on to Rockford, and one hundred would remain in a program linked between Urbana and Peoria. This program would have clinical departments with heads based in Peoria, with the understanding that clinical training would be divided on a 70 percent-30 percent basis between Peoria and Urbana.

In addition, they recommended collegewide committee structures, which would be senatorial in nature; a full committee structure at Rockford and a single committee structure for Peoria and Urbana to manage day-to-day activities. They also called for the College of Medicine budget to be divided proportionately among the three campuses based on their enrollment, and that enrollment structure would remain proportional. (That is, any increase or decrease in enrollment would be shared by all campuses proportionately.)

And, finally, they called for a single collegewide admission policy and single collegewide senior comprehensive examination before graduation.

This seemed like a workable proposal. The consensus was strong enough that it seemed appropriate to bring Rockford into the discussions. Going to 150 for the M-1 class meant certain problems for SBMS-UC, but they could be managed.

A working group of faculty from the three schools met in Peoria on August 4, 1981. The meeting was chaired by neurosurgeon Pat Elwood of Peoria and with him were doctors Sachchida Sinha, Leon Librik, and Brian Curtis, all from Peoria. Don Wortmann, Dick Novack, and Bernard Salafsky represented Rockford. From Urbana there were Ivens Siegel and Tom Filardo, who supplied me with his personal notes from this meeting.

The issue of Rockford in the downstate school was discussed first. The

An early exploration of Option III followed the forced cancellatio. the March 3 Peoria meeting. Reacting to my proscription from organiz tional meetings, a group of faculty and administrators from Peoria and Urbana met, without my blessing or knowledge, on April 14, 1981, and assembled "The Champaign-Urbana/Peoria Proposal for the Organizatio of a Downstate Medical School." The authors of the document represente not only the major hospitals in Champaign-Urbana and Peoria, but also signing the document was John Pollard, CEO of Carle Clinic Association and several major department heads from the Peoria and Urbana schools. I was an impressive group. The proposal was a succinct, straightforward mes- sage that paralleled SPMC Option III.

The consensus proposal was submitted to President Ikenberry and the Board of Trustees. Although it omitted many details of operation, it was a rational approach that offered a happy solution to the difficult problems the College of Medicine was encountering in its reorganization. Unfortunately, Ikenberry was so fixed on the process already being undertaken, with results that were preordained by this time, and so certain that any budget projec- tions that carried the taint of originating from my office were specious, that the proposal died for want of nourishment. However, the group continued to meet as the Peoria-Urbana Faculty Study Group in an effort to seek an alternative the administration would buy.

At the same time, leading faculty members in Peoria sent a memoran- dum to the members of the Board of Trustees and to President Ikenberry urging adoption of Option III. They called it a "sound plan" and said that under a plan that "utilizes the resources of Urbana and Peoria, medical edu- cation and medical care will continue to improve in downstate." They added, "We urge that no action be taken to implement the vice chancellor's proposal for reorganization and that the issues be reviewed by the president and the Board of Trustees."

So the Urbana-Peoria linkage had much thought and considerable momentum behind it. It almost thrived, even though I was proscribed from participating in the discussions.

By July 1981, the Peoria and Urbana faculty study group seemed close to a consensus. President Ikenberry, despite his public facade of neutrality towards an academic process, had come on so strongly to his subordinates for the single-college, single-dean concept, that the will to continue efforts to create a separate downstate school seemed to dry up as a hopeless alternative.

Rockford faculty stated that they were anxious to support a downstate program both within the present "academic process" and politically. They mentioned that their main political weight was through contacts in the University Board of Trustees. Rockford had defined two main goals it would like to salvage from the reorganization, that the name "Rockford School of Medicine" be retained, and that Rockford should remain semiautonomous, with its own budget.

Rockford also wanted a curriculum written by its own faculty and to preserve the one-year, three-year split to keep current programs viable. The school's representatives felt they needed a minimal class size of fifty-five and an equitable, or senatorial, representation on all college committees. The Peoria faculty indicated that their goals were very similar but that they sought a class size of seventy.

Leon Librik from Peoria, a member of the Creditor ad hoc implementation committee discussed that committee's recent retreat to discuss the process by which SPMC Option II would be carried out. He reported that there was little support among the subcommittee members for whatever consensus Creditor might claim was reached on that retreat. Librik voiced disappointment with SBMS-UC representative Roland Leeson. Librik complained that Leeson, who led the anatomy program at SBMS-UC, "seemed to be in Creditor's corner and rolled over and played dead." When Librik's words came back to Urbana, Leeson was virtually ostracized from faculty society. Leeson had been with SBMS-UC for only three years. He had come from the University of Iowa, which had a magnificent medical school and facility in Iowa City. When he compared our two programs, he saw little future for SCM-UC. Roland briefly mentioned his role on the Creditor committee to me, explaining that given the constraints under which the committee worked and the limited budget available to SCM-UC, he felt he had no choice but to go along with Creditor.

The Peoria and Rockford faculties were also very critical of another aspect of the Urbana role in the search for common ground. They took grave offense at Allan Levy's draft proposal, which they refused to interpret as the recommendations of a single individual. The Levy draft infuriated them. They criticized it first because it came like a bolt out of nowhere and seemed to ignore the considerable negotiations that had already taken place. Just as egregious in their eyes, it provided PSM no formal or informal involvement in the Medical Scholars Program, one of the main reasons that

Peoria wanted to link to Urbana. Peoria faculty saw the MSP as a vehicle to enhance medical research at PSM.

Furthermore, the Levy proposal did not provide for a PSM cohort exclusively from Urbana, something the PSM faculty very much desired. Levy's proposal also denied an interdependent working relationship between SBMS/SCM-UC and PSM. Thus, Peoria faculty described Levy's proposal as "going back to square one" and laid much of the blame for the proposal on me, for I was considered to be the all-powerful one on the UIUC campus. They assumed a proposal as blatantly inimical to the prior bases for consensus must have come from me or have had my blessing.

After agreeing that Levy's plan was a nonstarter, the group worked on the premise that we might possibly win the battle at the level of the Board of Trustees, if RSM, PSM, and SBMS/SCM-UC presented a unified consensus solution. However, the group noted that, alas, even in the gibbet's shadow, we were far from that. Finally, it was noted that time was short. It was already August 4. The Creditor ad hoc implementation subcommittee would draft its report before the end of August, and the adoption of catastrophic Option II might be a *fait accompli* before we reached our own consensus. A second tripartite meeting was urgently required and was scheduled for August 18 in LaSalle-Peru, Illinois, equidistant from the three downstate sites. This would give us time to develop and submit a definitive alternative to the ad hoc implementation subcommittee before its final retreat, which was planned for August 26–27. Leon Librik, who was a member of both the Creditor ad hoc subcommittee and the developing tripartite committee, would carry whatever consensus findings emerged to the implementation committee. So it appeared that the downstate schools were finally on track for a consensus approach to the reorganization structure.

On August 12, the SBMS/SCM-UC faculty representatives to the tripartite effort, Tom Filardo and Ivens Siegel, sent a "Dear Colleague" letter to all the representatives from Peoria, Rockford, and Urbana who planned to meet in LaSalle-Peru on August 18. They told their colleagues, "In coming to a consensus at this time, it is very important that we speak with a single voice and not allow ourselves to be divided in any fashion."

The draft reorganization plan that was distributed by the SBMS/SCM-UC faculty committee accepted the reorganization of the college as a single college with four regional components, respectively identified as the University of Illinois College of Medicine at Peoria, at Rockford, at Urbana-

Champaign, and at Chicago. It modified the projected enrollments to a total of 325 and provided for separate tracks: Chicago as one track and Peoria, Rockford, and Urbana as the second. It also provided for approximately twenty-five Medical Scholars at Urbana, but did not exclude Medical Scholars linked to Peoria and Rockford. The proposal also included the Allan Levy concept of "the weak deanship," which postulated that "the dean shall be appointed for a given term from among the four directors of the schools of the college. The dean would serve as the chairperson of the committee of school directors. The dean will administer the budget of the college, but the Committee of Directors will determine the budget. The college would maintain permanent administrative offices in Chicago, regardless of the regional locus of the Dean and would maintain whatever management staff was necessary in Chicago."

The draft was an amalgam of reorganization ideas that had floated around for the previous two years. I was certain that it would not be adopted without substantial change, but it seemed a useful place to begin. I wanted to attend the August 18 meeting, so I decided to jump channels and go around Mort Creditor to see Chancellor Begando. On August 13, I scheduled a meeting with Begando to clarify a number of problems that related to my participation in the development of a downstate position on medical education. Since February, Creditor had proscribed me from communicating with the faculties of Rockford and Peoria, but I believed strongly that it was important that I be at the Lasalle-Peru meeting and I wanted a go-ahead from the chancellor. Besides, I wanted the chancellor to know about the meeting and about what the regions were thinking. I also wanted to share with him the Urbana draft proposal that would be discussed at the meeting, and I wanted to inform him of the August 7 letter from Peoria area state representatives Judy Kohler and Fred Schraeder, who were mobilizing concerned downstate legislators to oppose the Medical Center reorganization plan.

Joe Begando was very correct and very cool as usual. In dealing with the chancellor that day, I found him understanding and friendly, without taking sides. I think he understood, without actually accepting, many of the points I was trying to make. The difference between Joe Begando and the other representatives of higher administration that I had worked with over the years was that he seriously listened to alternative solutions to complex problems. Entering his office, he informed me that only five minutes previously he had talked to Bud Grulee at Rockford, who brought the same agenda as I had. Grulee had been invited to attend the August 18 meeting by Dr. Sinha of Peoria. Feeling some reservations about attending, Grulee also jumped the Creditor channel and conferred with the chancellor. Begando informed him that in his opinion it would be better if the administrators were present than if they were not. It was welcome advice.

The chancellor requested, almost in return for the favor of permitting me to attend the meeting, that we not exaggerate or exploit the apparent differences between Creditor's emphasis on "higher administration constraints" and the president's public position that we were pursuing an open academic process. Although the president had made "certain requests," Begando believed nothing was "fixed in concrete." I told him that it was my understanding that Creditor presented everything to the ad hoc implementation committee as if it *were* "fixed in concrete." The chancellor understood that difference and again asked that the difference not be exploited. He also showed concern about the letter from the state representatives and asked me to give him a copy to forward to the president. He considered it a very important document, indicating downstate concern.

After we discussed the LaSalle-Peru meeting for some time, the chancellor advised me exactly as he had advised Bud Grulee, to attend the meeting! I welcomed that. The following day, he wrote a letter to Mort Creditor stating, "On Thursday, August 13, 1981, first, Dean Grulee and, later, Dean Bloomfield contacted me, since both you and Vice Chancellor Schmidt were away from the campus. Both were mindful of their obligations as members of the College of Medicine administrative group and asked my advice about their attendance at a meeting to be held at LaSalle-Peru on Tuesday, August 18, 1981. The meeting, as I understand it, is of a small number of faculty from Urbana-Champaign, Peoria, and Rockford medical schools who wish to discuss regional implications of the proposed reorganization of the College of Medicine and to provide additional input into the current collegewide discussion. Apparently the deans at the three locations are being highly encouraged by the faculty to attend.

"My point in writing this note to you was to say that my advice was to attend if they wished to do so. It appeared to me that the deans might serve a more useful role if they were present, rather than absent."

The following day, I received a call from Bud Grulee who had met with his executive committee about the Lasalle-Peru meeting. After considerable discussion, they had mutually decided it would be best if the deans were not present at LaSalle-Peru. I told him I would like him to be there and that I was going to attend under any circumstance. He ultimately followed the advice of his executive committee and did not attend.

Meanwhile, both he and Jerry Newman, who also called later, expressed their anger at the interim de facto merger of SBMS-MC and ALSM into a single four-year college. This was done by Phil Forman, the dean of ALSM, and supported by Mort Creditor. Apparently, both Grulee and Newman had been promised by Creditor and the president that no substantive changes in the college structure would take place until the Board of Trustees had acted upon the reorganization plan, yet this was a very substantive change. Newman expressed his anger to Marty Kernis, Creditor's right-hand man, and shortly thereafter received a call from Mort Creditor, vacationing in Maine. Jerry told me that he and Mort had exchanged some angry words over the telephone since there had been some serious misunderstandings, but whether anything else was accomplished, I could not tell. Jerry, too, decided not to attend the meeting in LaSalle-Peru.

Leaving the chancellor's office, I encountered Tom Gamble who had moved from Urbana to Chicago to be assistant chancellor two years earlier. He had graduated from serving as my right-hand man to serving the chancellor. Tom was always very discreet, and in his new position, I never pressed him for any information that he felt might be improper to transmit. Nevertheless, Tom told me that he believed the president would get his way with the Board of Trustees despite Stone's advocacy of SCM-UC. It was his impression that the trustees were largely supportive of the president they had chosen. It was not the kind of news I wanted to hear.

The anxiously anticipated LaSalle-Peru meeting turned out to be a bust. Our mutual aim on August 18 was to form a solid reorganization consensus among Rockford, Peoria, and Urbana that we could take to our faculties to endorse and thence to the ad hoc implementation committee. However, our consensus broke down on the issue of budget management between Peoria and Urbana. Peoria demanded full control of the clinical departmental structure and full budgetary control of all clinical training in the newly projected Urbana-Peoria medical school. Although we in Urbana were willing to cede clinical department headships to Peoria, we were leery of ceding our entire clinical budget to Peoria as well. We suggested wording to the effect that the clinical-department heads at Peoria would receive their budget allocation for the Peoria clinical-departmental teaching activities from the

Peoria director and those in charge of clinical-department teaching activities in UC from the Urbana director. This was unsatisfactory to the Peoria faculty, who wanted not only to have clinical departmental control, but also to receive the entire budget for the combined Peoria-Urbana clinical-teaching track from the Peoria director.

There was genuine disappointment on both sides that we could not get beyond this impasse. The basic problem was that there was a lack of mutual trust between the schools. We didn't want to run a clinical program with our budget controlled in Peoria any more than we liked running the present clinical program with our budget controlled by Chicago. They in turn suspected us, correctly, of desiring an independent four-year program, and they were determined to prevent that from happening. Before the meeting, the Peoria group had already announced to their newspapers that the downstate units were close to a consensus, but had to return and inform their newspapers that a consensus was not reached and that we stood as divided and as vulnerable as ever.

Had we been able to hammer out an agreement that all three schools could have endorsed and then instructed our representatives on the Creditor Ad Hoc Implementation Committee to advocate that consensus, we could have, at a minimum, caused considerable consternation for all three of our antagonists: Creditor, Schmidt, and Ikenberry. Creditor's implementation subcommittee had seven votes with a majority from four downstate schools. But it appears that Rockford and Peoria were emphatic and more concerned that Urbana-Champaign not gain anything that could possibly lead to an independent four-year program than they were about anything else that might be gained. The only way they could conceive of giving us clinical training at Urbana, was in a venue that prohibited us from any budget authority over the clinical program. From our standpoint that was unacceptable. We didn't want to control the Peoria or the Rockford budget, but we certainly did not want our budget controlled off-campus either.

Lasalle-Peru was the high-water mark for merger discussions among the Urbana, Peoria, and Rockford schools. We were far from being an irresistible force. There was some question whether we could survive separately, but it was also apparent that we could not live together, either. Lasalle-Peru illustrated, once again, if more confirmation were needed, that the so-called College of Medicine, was unified in name only. We were four separate schools with four agendas.

CHAPTER 32

Regrouping

I CALLED PAUL STONE on the day after the LaSalle-Peru collapse and informed him that the potential consensus among Peoria, Rockford, and Urbana broke down over our inability to reach agreement on budget distribution. Peoria insisted on total control of the Urbana-Champaign clinical budget, something that I believed was out of the question. Urbana-Champaign could not compromise on the principle of budget autonomy. We did not believe that a clinical budget managed in Peoria could adequately and effectively integrate with the Urbana-Champaign campus. I told Stone we would regroup and continue to work toward maintaining the clinical school in Urbana-Champaign, but added, "I am afraid we can't help you with a downstate consensus at this time."

Stone responded sympathetically. He noted that some of the legislative letters he had received were raising concern within the university. He confirmed that he and Gaily Day were the two people on the Board of Trustees who were most supportive of regional objectives, but he emphasized that perhaps the strongest issue we had going for us at this time was the university's concern about the stirring legislature. "They don't want to stir the legislature into enacting laws that might interfere with university prerogatives," he declared.

I told Stone about my discussion with Chancellor Begando, how helpful he was and how it was my view that our basic problem lay with Mack Schmidt and Mort Creditor. I also related my conversation with Tom Gamble and Gamble's view that the majority of the board was firmly on the side of the president in the reorganization issue. He thanked me for the information and ended the conversation on a positive note that "just some more education is needed."

The inability to reach a consensus at LaSalle-Peru played into the hands of our adversaries. After the July 27–28 retreat of his Ad Hoc Subcommittee, Creditor prepared a preliminary report to implement Option II. It was very upsetting to those of us in Urbana to see a college organizational chart that did not include SCM-UC. Mort sent the preliminary report to the several executive committees of the college for their "official reaction, responses and comments, which will be considered in drafting the final recommendation." Our combined SBMS/SCM-UC Executive Committees met on August 5 to discuss the preliminary report. Before reacting, they unanimously instructed me to write Creditor. They wanted to know what, if any, administrative constraints limited the agenda and scope of planning in the Ad Hoc Subcommittee's report. So I wrote to Mort on August 18, stating: "The Executive Committees of SBMS and SCM/UC would greatly appreciate an explicit description of any administrative limitations that were laid before the Ad Hoc Subcommittee and the authority for those limitations. The committees also believe that such limitations, if any, should be explicit in the subcommittee report."

We knew what the constraints were and who had laid them out, but the committees felt it would be useful to try to get these constraints documented in writing. We knew the trail led from Creditor to Schmidt to Ikenberry, but the president was still professing the aggravating fiction of an open academic process. Creditor responded on August 21, writing: "I am not sure exactly what you mean by administrative constraints in your letter of August 18, but I will try to respond to what I believe to be the purpose of your letter. I did present the Ad Hoc Subcommittee with what I refer to as the 'boundary conditions,' which already existed as a result of prior actions.

"The first of these was the existence of the single-college, single-dean, model. This condition was imposed by the announcement by higher administration of their choice of options and the unchallenged statement of President Ikenberry to the Board of Trustees of his intention to pursue this choice. This decision was ratified by the Academic Council and the faculty of the college as one of the twelve points in the approved proposal.

"The second 'boundary condition' was the extension of the initial basic science experience through the first two years of medical education and its delivery in Chicago and Urbana-Champaign. This also was implicit in the option chosen by higher administration and explicitly approved by the College of Medicine in June.

"I believe these are the items which might be considered by some as constraints upon the subcommittee."

Not surprisingly, not the slightest hint was given on yielding to the preordained outcome. The Ad Hoc Subcommittee met for the last time at a retreat on August 26 and 27. On September 1, Mort Creditor issued the final report of the UICOM Ad Hoc Subcommittee of the Academic Council. The lengthy report (seven single-spaced typewritten pages) covered no new ground. It did, however, specifically identify a "boundary condition" that Creditor did not mention in his letter: "The vice chancellor for academic affairs in public pronouncement and in his letter of April 30, 1981, to Academic Council had declared the administrative decision that there be no organized clinical program in Urbana-Champaign comparable to what is proposed for Rockford and Peoria. The subcommittee members understood this to be a boundary condition."

Otherwise, the report reviewed the history of the process and laid out in some detail what became known as Option II. The committee however was unable to reach a consensus on the numerical distribution of students in the M-3 and M-4 years. There was no recommendation for a clinical cohort structure that would allow students to identify with a single location for their clinical work. This was particularly upsetting to Peoria and Rockford. Chicago, of course, would be the only site to have the full complement of M-1 to M-4 medical education. Each regional program would be led by an associate dean/director who would report to the dean in Chicago. An annual budget would be assigned to each regional site by the college dean to be administered locally.

The clinical administrative structure of the college called for single collegewide departmental chairs with departmental divisions at the regional sites. Administration of the basic medical-sciences departments at Urbana-Champaign remained vague because of the unknown reaction to the reorganization by the SBMS-UC faculty and their associated departments on the UIUC campus. Two college committees were envisioned: an Executive Committee, in which the Chicago units' voting membership would dominate the regional unit votes by approximately four to three, and an Admissions Committee with an unspecified membership. Lip service was given to preserving the Medical Scholars Program and to sustaining "clinical activity" at Urbana-Champaign.

Finally, the report justified itself "as the best possible outcome of a deliberative process which was influenced by certain conditions and boundaries regarded as implicit or explicit constraints."

The report was signed by seven of the eight members of the committee.

That it was endorsed by the Peoria representative, Leon Librik, and by
the Rockford representative, James H. Topp, was ample evidence that the
Rockford and Peoria faculty were willing to be trimmed to two-year programs
before they would accept an independent four-year program in Urbana. Only
Donald Thursh, our SCM-UC pathologist, refused to endorse the majority
report and issued a one-person minority report. Dr. Thursh's dissent, issued
the same day, elegantly summarized the position that we had held at
Urbana-Champaign throughout all these discussions. He wrote, "I cannot
endorse the majority report of this subcommittee because I am convinced it
(a) will be rejected unanimously by the faculty of SCM-UC and by a substantial majority of the faculty of SBMS-UC and (b) it fails to adequately
address at least two of the twelve principles for the reorganization of the
College of Medicine defined by the Academic Council, namely that there
was to be clinical activity at all regional sites and that the Medical Scholars
Program was to be preserved. Furthermore, I believe the manner of
regionalization as structured in the majority report will prove contrary to
the best interests of the college and will become non-viable within a relatively short time."

Moving to specific objections, he said that the report's implementation
plan was educationally unsound. "I feel very strongly that the constraints
imposed on the Ad Hoc Subcommittee by the often-invoked but never documented 'decisions of higher administration' made it impossible for us to
develop an implementation plan that is educationally and academically
sound. We do our faculty a profound disservice by pretending that we have
done so. I think this is particularly striking with respect to the continued
regionalization of the college."

He said that it had "become abundantly clear to many of us that having
a single college with completely centralized administration in Chicago and
simultaneously preserving regional programs with any potential for long-
range viability are mutually exclusive goals," and added, "I believe the majority report tacitly affirms this, although more in what it does not say than in
what it does say. For example, nowhere in the report is there any statement
that guarantees the regional sites even the limited right to the continued
existence they now enjoy by virtue of their presently defined status as formally organized schools. The regional schools at least have the security
that Board of Trustee action is required to close them. I do not believe it is
particularly far-fetched to interpret the majority report as meaning that

regional programs will be continued only so long as a large enough enrollment and budget are available to sustain them without any major curtail-
ment of programs in Chicago. I do not believe that there is any way that
regional programs will be able to recruit or retain high-quality faculty and
administrators under these conditions; I believe it is inevitable that the
quality of education at the regional sites will deteriorate as a result of this."

He also wrote, "The majority report makes a number of dangerously
naive assumptions regarding the program in Urbana-Champaign, i.e., that
all parties involved in the program, including parties with no intrinsic
responsibility to the College of Medicine, will passively accept the college's
decision on reorganization and continue to participate in its educational
program. The active participation of the local hospitals and medical community and the UIUC campus departments is essential if we are to develop
a two-year basic-science program in UC. Unfortunately, all three of these
groups have reasons to believe that the College of Medicine has reneged on
previous commitments to them. Without their cooperation, it will be
impossible to deliver a full two year program in UC, which will in turn
create very significant problems in the movement of students from one site
to another."

He also warned that the report failed to consider the worst-case
scenario, writing that the Academic Council "should be aware that there is at
least considerable feeling on the UIUC campus that inaugurating an *isolated*
two-year basic medical-science program makes no academic sense whatsoever in 1982, would adversely affect the reputation of the campus, and
therefore should not be undertaken. Should this position prevail, the college
might well be forced to prepare for a further drastic reduction in enrollment. This would immediately jeopardize the continued viability of both of
the other regional sites and would undoubtedly prompt state officials to
review the University's medical education program and budget with extreme
skepticism."

Thursh then discussed the Medical Scholars Program, which he said
would most likely be destroyed under the implementation plan. He noted
that the Academic Council directly mandated the preservation of the program. "What the majority report completely fails to do is to provide adequate commitments to the involved faculty, specifically the faculty of the
involved colleges, schools and departments of the UIUC campus, that the
College of Medicine will provide the resources necessary to preserve the

program, or that the College of Medicine as a whole even appreciates the basic academic elements that make up the program, namely a *real integration* of clinical training and graduate study."

He then noted that most of the SCM/SBMS-UC faculty was skeptical that the program could be preserved "unless the medical scholars' basic clerkships are available locally where they can be directly interfaced with their graduate studies. He noted that the majority report implied that the Medical Scholars would "become part of the administrative cohort of another program for at least two years (the closest of which is ninety miles away)" and called such a setup "impractical and unworkable."

"I recognize how difficult it would have been for the subcommittee to recommend any more rational plan for clerkship training for Medical Scholars in view of the vice-chancellor's views that no organized clinical instruction for junior (M-3) and senior (M-4) medical students be offered in UC, but the existing plan is totally unacceptable to me, to the Medical Scholars I have met with and, I expect, to the overwhelming majority of the faculty I represent."

The Thursh dissent was distributed widely to our faculty and to Mr. Stone.

The final Ad Hoc Subcommittee on Implementation report was submitted to the Academic Council of the College of Medicine on September 9. When the report was on the floor and open for discussion, Mort Creditor stated that he did not want piecemeal action, asking that the report be reviewed and voted upon in its totality. I stated that I had an alternative proposal to present, but Creditor stated that substitute proposals could be presented only after discussion of the Ad Hoc Subcommittee report was finished, a discourse that followed predictable lines. The Chicago members of the Academic Council supported the report as a moderate and appropriate compromise. Regional representatives such as Pat Elwood (Peoria), Bud Grulee (Rockford), Don Rager (Peoria), and Dean Bordeaux (Peoria) all spoke against the document. Don Thursh pointed out that the Ad Hoc Subcommittee had not unanimously accepted the report and that he did not sign it because he felt he would be doing a profound disservice in converting an administrative compromise into a faculty decision.

Allan Levy stated that in his view, it would appear that the Urbana-Champaign clinical program would make the "ultimate sacrifice." He pointed out that President Ikenberry and Vice Chancellor Schmidt did not set up that boundary condition but that the Ad Hoc Subcommittee did and was in error in doing so. Leon Librik then announced, "Some representatives were instructed by their Executive Committees not to approve clinical activity in Urbana-Champaign irrespective of what Dr. Schmidt said." When Allan Levy asked Librik to explain what he meant, Librik stated that although in the preliminary report the Peoria School of Medicine supported clinical activity at Urbana-Champaign, subsequent extensive discussions by the PSM Executive Committee led the panel to instruct Librik to withdraw support of any clinical activity in Urbana-Champaign. What a tawdry revelation!

Tawdry or not, this explained why the merger discussions between Peoria and Urbana were never consummated; heavy sentiment prevailed in Peoria to oppose clinical training in Urbana. Many of the Peoria faculty had already decided that they did not want academic clinical activity in Urbana-Champaign competing with their operation in Peoria.

After discussion of the Ad Hoc Subcommittee report was completed, I submitted a substitute proposal for reorganization. The proposal assigned well-defined missions to each of the four schools, reduced the student load in Chicago to 175, and encouraged Chicago faculty to share their expertise with the regions. It simplified the college committee structure, and it redefined senate jurisdiction so that faculty of SCM-UC, although responsible to the Medical Center for medical education, would otherwise be affiliated to the Urbana campus for faculty promotions, salaries, appointments, and Graduate College membership. Most important of all, the document would preserve the Medical Scholars Program, which I insisted would not survive otherwise. After some perfunctory discussion, the vote on my substitute document was two in favor (Allan Levy and myself) and sixteen opposed, with four abstentions. The original document was then placed on the table, and Allan Levy, never losing hope in rationality, introduced an amendment calling for the formal organization of clinical training for thirty Medical Scholars per year at Urbana-Champaign, together with an appropriate budget. But the opposition to clinical training at Urbana-Champaign quickly surfaced again. This time it was Ed Cohen, Dean of SBMS-MC, who argued that college resources were not adequate to support a clinical program at SCM-UC. Once again, we were smeared: three yeas, eighteen nays. It was clear that our opposition was not limited to the Medical Center administration but was pervasive throughout the other three units of the college that perceived SCM-UC as the sacrificial lamb, whose execution would solve the financial problems of the college.

The representatives from Rockford and Peoria also tried to amend the report to state, "Basic sciences in Rockford and Peoria will be continued." This, too, was voted down. Finally, after two hours of fruitless discussion, the original motion to accept the Ad Hoc Subcommittee report was passed with fourteen in favor, seven opposed, and one abstention. *It was noted for the record that no one from the regions supported the main motion.* Creditor then explained that the report would go before a special faculty meeting of UICOM on September 28 and from there to the chancellor, who would refer it to the UIMC Senate Committee on Educational Policy. Thence, the UIMC Senate and the University Senates Conference would act upon it. Creditor announced that it was the chancellor's hope to present it to the Board of Trustees in November.

That being the case and having failed to reach a consensus with Rockford and Peoria on a reorganization solution, we began to concentrate on our linkages to the UIUC campus. By that time, we had four years of experience with the Medical Scholars Program. Departmental faculty found that Medical Scholars were primarily medical students with research bents. Bright and hard-working, they proved to be very productive in the laboratories, and many faculty members praised their overall excellence. There was never any question, at least at UIUC, that the program could not survive the geographic separation suggested by the final Ad Hoc Subcommittee's final report. One observer wrote on August 28 that, in his experience, a separation of even five to fifteen miles had negative consequences. That comment came from Vincent Price, who as program administrator of the Medical Scientist Training Program at the National Institute of General Medical Sciences, oversaw every NIH-funded MD/Ph.D. program in the country. No one had more experience in this field than he.

Ted Brown, Vice Chancellor for Research, Dean of the Graduate College, and co-chair of the Bicampus Steering Committee, joined me in sending a letter to members of that committee asking them to undertake a review of the consensus document with the UIUC colleges and schools they represented. We also enclosed for their information a copy of the Ad Hoc Subcommittee's final report on reorganization. A BSC meeting was scheduled on September 18 to review their findings and to mobilize for action to alert the UIUC campus that it was likely in the near future to lose the Medical Scholars Program. In response, we received letters from many departments and colleges. Typical was the one from the College of Commerce and Business Administration Executive Committee that stated, "We have reviewed the recent statement developed by the Bicampus Steering Committee and are glad to support it. The elimination of the final stages of clinical training in Urbana clearly would have an adverse effect on the Medical Scholars Program and on the three joint-degree programs that have been developed involving this college."

Meanwhile, the work of the Wicks committee was drawing to a conclusion. On September 14, Don Thursh sent the Wicks committee a copy of his minority report and the following incisive observations: "I think that the single most important long-range effect on the Urbana-Champaign campus will be to deny it a role in clinical education and thereby seriously limit its opportunities for collaborative clinical research…*The fear and loathing that the thought of a complete four-year medical program on the Urbana-Champaign campus evokes among other constituencies within the College of Medicine was something I had long heard of, but never really believed until I became involved in the reorganization process. I am now convinced that it is real, that it is strong, that it is widely held, and that if this campus believes that continued and expanding scholarly access to the health-care establishment is important to its own intellectual growth, it must oppose the current plan to reorganize the College of Medicine as vigorously as possible.*" [Emphasis added.]

Don Thursh hit the nail on the head, but Mort Creditor wasn't listening or responding. He had his report in hand, written the way he desired. He was not disconcerted at all by Thursh's minority report.

On September 14, twenty-seven members of the SBMS/SCM-UC faculty wrote a direct appeal to Chancellor Cribbet and to members of the UIUC Senate ad hoc committee that was reviewing medical education on the UIUC campus. It was also copied to Chancellor Begando, VCAA Goldwasser, VCAA Schmidt, Dean Creditor, and me.

Two plans for reorganizing were enclosed with their appeal: the Creditor plan and our plan. The faculty members noted, "It is significant that the plan adopted at the Medical Center on September 9 was not 'the preferred outcome of any member' of the Ad Hoc Subcommittee, which drafted the report. It was a plan whose creation and development was dominated by the Chicago-based faculty. This is evidenced by the fact that it was not supported by a single member of the Academic Council from Peoria,

Rockford, and Urbana-Champaign but accepted by all the Chicago-based
faculty members.

"We consider the plan we propose to be educationally sound and fair
for the entire College of Medicine…Because we are a small numerical
minority, we have exhausted our ability to influence the content or outcome
of the reorganization process initiated by the administration at the Medical
Center campus. We appeal to you to consider these plans and to recommend
a course of action to higher administration. We believe that in the absence
of strong advocacy of a sound medical education program here, by the
Urbana-Champaign campus, the quality of medical education on this campus will die. We believe that excellent medical education is now attainable at
Urbana-Champaign and we are committed to this goal."

The drama, which we hoped would influence higher administration,
was at least catching the attention of the local press. On September 14, Lex
Peterson, a reporter for the *Champaign-Urbana News-Gazette*, wrote an
article headlined "UI Medical School Drama Leaves Out Urbana Faculty." It
was notable because it quickly summed up the history of the situation from
the point of view of faculty members who believed the decision to close
SCM-UC was preordained by the administration and that it had gone
through the motions of faculty approval to "spiff up the 'process.'"

There was also some fallout because of comments made in the article
by Lowell Hager, head of biochemistry at Urbana-Champaign. Hager was
convinced that the Medical Scholars Program would be destroyed by the
reorganization. Then, he commented on the quality of UICOM's educational programs. Peterson quoted him as saying, "In 1960, the UI's College of
Medicine ranked in the top twenty nationally, but now you can't find them
in the top fifty. Sadly, the UI's medical enterprise could be called the
'Guadalajara of the Midwest.'" Hager's pithy comment did not go unappreciated by the Chicago administration, and I took plenty of heat for it at the
next Advisory Council of Deans meeting. Both Creditor and his aide-de-
camp, Marten Kernis, strongly implied that Hager should be fired for
making such an uncollegial, demeaning public statement about the College
of Medicine. When I reported this reaction to the next SBMS/SCM-UC
Executive Committee meeting, Hager responded acerbically in kind, that he
had also received a letter of complaint from the Dean at Guadalajara.

Time was very short. Because the Medical Center case against us was
based on financial projections, I surveyed state financing of Big10 medical

schools, including Iowa, Wisconsin, Ohio State, Michigan State, Michigan, and Indiana. When the data was returned, it became stunningly apparent that, by any measure, UICOM was very generously funded by the State of Illinois. It was time for another white paper, one that would center on the unequal financing of medical education within UICOM. This new white paper was quickly drafted to directly contest the assumption that there was not enough money to fund SCM-UC. We planned to distribute this hard-hitting, no-nonsense white paper to the faculty and Board of Trustees.

This paper's first premise was "that there is more than adequate funding within the current budget of the College of Medicine to provide for quality medical education for all students enrolled in the College and that there is more than adequate funding to continue the clinical program at Urbana-Champaign."

It went on to accuse the UIMC administration of subterfuge "to obscure the fact that the bulk of new state funds that were supposed to support the expansion and regionalization of the health professions were actually kept within the Chicago region." The paper charged that the administration was "attempting to conceal an inefficient operation connected with the University Hospital and the Medical Service Plan of ALSM" that drained about $30 million per year from the college. Similarly, it accused the administration of seeking "to undermine the academic process and to limit the freedom of discussion and interchange between the several units of the College of Medicine" during the course of establishing a reorganization plan.

The paper also called the reorganization process "a charade totally dominated by Chicago-based interests." We added, "The UIMC administration is not committed to regionalization of medical education," as demonstrated by its efforts to delay and obstruct the development of SCM-UC, and that the College of Medicine and UIMC administration had pursued policies contrary to the Illinois Board of Higher Education's intent regarding regionalization. Our final premise was "that the loss of the clinical program at Urbana-Champaign will result in the loss or serious impairment of the Medical Scholars Program at Urbana-Champaign."

These were very tough statements, but this was no time to pull punches. Our assertions were substantiated by a series of tables that compared the University of Illinois College of Medicine state funding with that of four Midwestern state medical schools, three of which were comparable in size to the University of Illinois. We showed that funding for the University of

Illinois College of Medicine was $6,000 higher per medical student per year
than the average of the other four institutions surveyed. When this was
translated to a medical-student population of 1,389 enrolled, the *excess* state
funding for UICOM amounted to $8,334,000 per year compared with the
peer institutions. This was more than enough to make up deficiencies in
funding downstate programs and particularly the clinical program at
Urbana-Champaign. It was also noted that the average annual expenditure
of state dollars per student in Chicago was $5,400 *more than* the Midwestern
average while Urbana-Champaign spending was $4,800 per student *less than*
the average. Again, multiplying these figures by enrollments yielded an
annual excess of $4.91 million in Chicago and a deficit of $900,000 state
dollars in Champaign.

The white paper also challenged the budget of the Metro-6 Hospitals,
which at this time was $2 million per year. We noted that the University of
Illinois was probably the only institution in the country that owned its own
heavily subsidized university hospital *and* still paid community hospitals for
teaching services.

We attacked the August 7 letter that Vice President Brady and
Chancellor Begando sent to President Ikenberry, labeling it as a self-serving
instrument to justify an attack on the smallest college unit in favor of the
larger established units. We made the case that the university would be the
ultimate loser because SCM-UC, its smallest regional unit, had developed a
cost-effective medical-education process that was not being capitalized upon
and, if closed, would be lost forever.

The white paper challenged the UIMC's first-time incorporation of resident physicians as FTE students in UIMC enrollment figures. We exposed
the fact that in preparation for the transition from personal-influence budgeting to a more legitimate and fair enrollment-based budgeting, UIMC was
changing the rules in order to inflate its enrollments and thus rationalize
Chicago's lion's share of both old and new state dollars. We pointed out that
the funding of resident physicians as students was explicitly excluded from
all other Midwestern medical-school budgets. The charge was made that the
inclusion of the resident physicians as students was particularly devious
because resident education was paid for largely by pass-through funds negotiated with the federal government in Medicare and with insurance companies, figures that did not appear in the UICOM state budget. What the
Chicago operation was doing to justify its bloated dependency on state

dollars is described in polite society as "double-dipping."

The new white paper was done, documented, and tabulated. Consisting of ten single-spaced pages with six detailed tables, it was much too long for politicians or Board of Trustees members. People simply would not have the time to read it, and if they did, it would still take considerable amount of effort to understand the budgetary calculations and manipulations that are possible in figuring out annual costs per medical student or any other standard. Ben Williams and Allan Levy recommended holding the paper for the time being until they had more opportunity to contemplate its use, and so we did.

CHAPTER 33

Orange Crush Time

EFORE WE TOOK ANY STEPS to distribute the new white paper, the
September 24, 1981 *Rockford Register Star* carried a front-page
article headlined, "Bill might save medical school's program." The
piece described the introduction of legislation by two Rockford legislators,
Representative John Hallock and Senator Jack Schaffer, to preserve the
"regional medical schools as they are now." They claimed they had statewide
support for the bill, which they believed was "going to make the UI sit up
and take notice." One of the interesting features of the article was the report
that "word is out that Dr. Stanley O. Ikenberry, University of Illinois President, is trying to make a deal to keep the bill out of the legislature by offering to keep Rockford as a three-year [school] and to cut Peoria and UC to
two years." One of the legislators responded, "There is no way I would agree
to that. If he changes theirs now, he may change ours later. We're going to
stand or fall together."

The forces generated by the regions were beginning to coalesce and to
focus on the president. In the meantime, Mort Creditor was dutifully moving
the academic process through to its preordained conclusion. After the final
reorganization recommendation was presented to the Academic Council on
September 9, 1981, it was submitted to the general faculty of the College of
Medicine in a special session held September 28 and approved overwhelm-
ingly by the dominant Chicago-based faculty. As far as Mort Creditor was
concerned, the issue was signed, sealed, and delivered. He submitted the
package to the UIMC Senate, which approved it on October 7. By that time,
Creditor was no longer in the country. He had been invited to tour medical
schools and medical facilities in the People's Republic of China and had left
October 4 for a twenty-one-day survey of the Chinese medical landscape. He
left with the satisfaction of a job well done and confident that the reorganization's implementation would begin soon after he returned. It was, in his view
at least, the crowning achievement of his UICOM administration.

Apparently, he was unaware of the legislative stirrings in Rockford and Peoria before he left for the Orient. Morton Creditor was also unaware that, on the same Sunday (October 4) that he flew to China, a full-page advertisement appeared in the *Champaign-Urbana News Gazette*, signed by a broad cross section of the medical and political community of Champaign-Urbana. The notice was titled, "An Open Letter to Stanley O. Ikenberry, President of the University of Illinois" with copies addressed to the Board of Trustees. The subject of the letter was "The Proposal to Close the School of Clinical Medicine at Urbana-Champaign." The letter ominously hinted it was to be the "First in a series" and was gratuitously designed "to help the President, the Board of Trustees, and the public to understand better this vital issue affecting our university and our community."

The letter, which borrowed liberally from the new white paper, went on to say that acceptance of the UIMC plan was a mistake; that Chicago was the major drainage on UICOM funds; that the plan would destroy the Medical Scholars Program and leave UIUC, alone among the great American universities, without a full medical school on its main campus. In a century characterized by unprecedented advances in medical research, the absence of a medical school represents incalculable costs in lost research opportunities. The letter also tweaked the president by pointing out that the reorganization plan was contrary to the university commitment to regionalization of medical education. The same open letter appeared in the student-managed *Daily Illini* on Tuesday, October 6, 1981.

The letter was a complete surprise to me. Although nobody believed me, I had nothing to do with it, nor do I know to this day who paid for the letter. Ben Williams and Allan Levy organized the authors and signers, and thirteen years after the fact, Allan confessed to me that Ben had shown him a draft of an "open letter" to Ikenberry. The draft "needed some work," and because Ben was leaving town that day, Allan took the letter, worked on it for the better part of the next twenty-four hours, and personally delivered it to the *News-Gazette* before the Sunday paper's deadline. The open letter was a bombshell! More importantly, those of us who believed in the merit of a full four-year program in medical education at UIUC finally got the undivided attention of President Stanley Ikenberry.

Ikenberry contacted Ben Williams that same Sunday to set up a private meeting at his house the next day. Present at the meeting besides the president and Ben were Vice President Brady, State Representative Virgil Wikoff,

State Senator Stanley Weaver, Chairman of the Board of Trustees Paul Stone, Father Duncan of the Newman Foundation, and Augie Meyer, Sr., owner of Channel 3 Television. Williams subsequently reported to me the events at this first meeting between President Ikenberry and "The Committee to Save the Medical School in Urbana-Champaign."

President Ikenberry expressed his anger at the "Open Letter" and asked the group not to place any more such instruments in the newspaper. "If you keep that up, I'll have to take out my own advertisements," he threatened. There was general agreement by the group to give him some maneuvering time before the "Second in a Series" was placed.

When the discussion focused on the Medical Scholars Program and the future of SCM-UC, the president and Brady talked in terms of a twenty- to thirty-student Medical Scholars Program, funded at $20,000 per student for both the third and fourth years. Ben, who knew the data from the white paper, took the lead and responded that he believed that a minimum of thirty students per year should be funded, but that if we got $900,000 in additional funds we could take thirty M-3 students and probably take thirty in the M-4 year as well. It did not matter whether we had thirty or sixty clinical students just as long as we had the additional $900,000 to support them. Ben reminded Ikenberry that the University of Illinois administration had made a serious mistake ten years earlier that led to two new, and probably unnecessary, medical schools: Rush and SIU. They started up because of the inability of the University of Illinois to effectively lay full claim to public medical education in the state. Rush and SIU had caused expensive losses to the University of Illinois. Ben also pointed out that in light of this history, two Colleges of Medicine would have been a far better solution for the University of Illinois than a single college, but it was the president who had insisted on the single-college concept that was now creating his financial and governance problems. He need not have been surprised at the community reaction because he was, in a sense, causing the mess.

Ikenberry stated that he was preparing a position paper of his own regarding medical education and would have that ready on Wednesday or Thursday, at which time he would make a public statement about where he stood. As the conversation went on, Augie Meyer emerged as one of the most elegant pleaders for the school. Augie and his wife had toured the school a few months earlier, and they were very impressed with what they saw. Augie argued that essentially the medical school was being pulled back to Chicago. Ikenberry and Brady denied this, but Ben Williams said that we needed some hard evidence that there would be funding for thirty students per class in Urbana-Champaign.

There was some discussion about governance. Both the president and Brady stated that UICOM-UC would have budgetary autonomy because it would be funded on a per-student basis. "What else do you need?" they asked. Ben pointed out that autonomy was very important to the faculty of the UC campus. They sought autonomy for appointments, promotions, and tenure decisions at a minimum. The concept of the medical school as an integral part of the UIUC campus was extremely important for recruitment of faculty. One prefers to recruit and to be recruited to a recognizable structure rather than to some abstract college organization under control of a more or less indifferent administration one hundred fifty miles to the north. Ben also pointed out the maddening difficulties we encountered in Medical Scholars Program admissions and our need for more autonomy in this vital area. The UIMC bureaucracy simply could not cope with the flexibility required by this unique program. As a result, the program lost five to ten excellent prospects annually. Finally, there was some discussion about when the issue would come up before the Board of Trustees. Ikenberry pointed out that the Medical Center was pressing for a November decision, but he indicated that some leaned toward delaying the final decision until January. When Ben left the meeting, he had the impression that the president had moved toward agreeing to at least thirty Medical Scholars Program students per year in Urbana-Champaign, funded at twenty thousand dollars per student. Although this was not totally satisfactory, he felt that the group had made good progress. The president also announced that he planned to meet with the entire committee on the afternoon of Friday, October 9. Getting the president to finally listen to Urbana voices was a major achievement, but the fight was a long way from being over. Vice President Ron Brady, virtually unknown at SCM-UC, had to be informed in person about our position.

On Tuesday, October 6, I arranged for a personal meeting with Vice President Ron Brady in Chicago to review calculations of budgets, cost per student, and related material. In requesting the meeting, I emphasized that it was important for all parties to understand the bases of the prolific output of data emerging from so many sources. I informed Brady as gently as possible that I believed there were a number of inaccuracies in the Brady-Begando letter to the president and sought the opportunity to either

understand them or to correct them. The fact that Brady was willing to
listen to me was a genuine relief and perhaps a sign that the university's
central administration was genuinely looking for a better solution than that
offered by the Schmidt-Creditor straitjacket. I drove to Chicago and met
with Brady from 3:30 to 5 p.m. that day. It was our first face-to-face meeting, and in the end, I believe that I convinced him of two basic points: that
the Urbana calculations of medical education costs per student were based
on valid data and, on a more personal level, that I was not the monster I was
made out to be by the Medical Center administration. I had been so demo-
nized by Schmidt and Creditor that Brady was surprised by my apparent
rationality. On one occasion, he confided that he had expected to be meeting with Rasputin incarnate.

The next day, October 7, the president addressed the UIMC Senate at its
regular monthly meeting. He complained, "There remains much misunderstanding of the college's proposed reorganization. The charge has been made
that approval of the proposed reorganization…will effectively mean the end
of medical education at the University of Illinois in downstate Illinois. A.
Such a statement is untrue, uninformed, and unfortunate. B. The commitment of the Board of Trustees and my commitment as president of the
University of Illinois to regional medical education is irrevocable. That commitment means the provision of medical education at Urbana-Champaign,
Rockford, and Peoria as well as Chicago."

He also said, "Of special concern in UC is the preservation of the
Medical Scholars Program. Will the college proposal destroy it as some have
alleged or will it preserve it? Everyone in the College of Medicine has agreed
from the beginning that the Medical Scholars Program would and should be
continued. The only question has been how much of the clinical experience
could be provided in UC, especially in the critical third year. The answer
that comes to me now is all of the required clerkships in the third year could
be provided there, given cooperation from the local hospitals and medical
community."

Ikenberry then went on to distance himself from the reorganization
plan. "As president of the University of Illinois, I frequently am asked what
qualities I will look for in any proposed medical reorganization plan that
eventually reaches my desk. It is inappropriate for me as president to dictate
the curriculum and organization of any college. That is a faculty matter.
When the plan reaches my desk, however, I will want to be satisfied on

certain key points. (a) It must continue the commitment to regional medical education. (b) The funding implications must be equitable among the four locations and realistic overall. (c) There must be a provision for the Medical Scholars Program. (d) It must emphasize quality rather than size. (e) It must cut administrative layers and cost. (f) It must provide for appropriate local control. (g) We must end up with a single College of Medicine capable of self-governance."

It was a good speech from our point of view, but it was not at all clear that anyone at that UIMC Senate meeting heard it. Shortly after he delivered those comments, the UIMC Senate passed the Schmidt-Creditor implementation document by a vote of seventy-one to twenty-nine.

On that same day, the *Champaign-Urbana News Gazette* reported, "University of Illinois President Stanley Ikenberry Wednesday pledged the University of Illinois will continue its system of medical education in Chicago, Rockford, Peoria, and Champaign-Urbana. 'That commitment is irrevocable,' he said at a news spot taping…'I will not bring before the Board of Trustees…any recommendation that does not sustain it.'

"But in keeping with a six-point plan expected to meet easy approval at the Medical Center Senate Wednesday afternoon in Chicago, the four-site College of Medicine will be reorganized as a single entity with one dean. The plan must also go before the UI Board of Trustees for its nod, likely to be sought in January, Ikenberry said. 'This is the only guideline I ever set forth and I took it to the UI Board for articulation of that one-college, one-dean policy. In the final analysis it is a very fundamental issue. If we had the resources, a second College of Medicine would be splendid, but we don't.' To create a second college of Medicine, as some at Urbana and Peoria have suggested, would be 'fiscally imprudent' and 'financially irresponsible,' Ikenberry said Wednesday."

The newspaper article went on to explain the proposed changes at Champaign-Urbana. "Champaign-Urbana will see its clinical school shut down, but has been promised it will keep its Medical Scholars Program…The Medical Center administration is expected to support 'clerkships' in five study areas at Urbana-Champaign to allow twenty or so students to take their third year of clinical education at Urbana despite there being no school as such."

It was interesting that with Creditor in China, the presidential position perceptibly softened. The official line was reflected in the newspaper article

that forecast the closure of SCM-UC. The UIMC Senate voted overwhelm-
ingly, as expected, in favor of the Schmidt-Creditor plan. On the other hand,
the president was backing away from that plan. Having retreated to his fundamental position of "one college, one dean," he appeared to be less inflexible about the exact format of that college organization.

A second item on the UIMC Senate agenda on October 7 was the
announcement by Joe Begando that he was retiring at the end of August
1982. From the president's standpoint, that was very convenient because
now he could merge the two Chicago campuses with a single chancellor and
not be forced to choose between the current leadership. From the standpoint of the reorganization of the College of Medicine, Joe Begando was one
who kept his head when all the others around him were losing theirs. I am
certain that I provoked him on many occasions, but he always answered
with dignity. On balance, I was going to miss him.

By October 9, I wrote another memorandum to file to document some
guarded optimism that was beginning to shine. Most important, I observed
that there really appeared to be definite movement on the part of the president and then the Medical Center administration to acknowledge that an
integrated Medical Scholars Program at UIUC required basic M-3 core clerkships: surgery, pediatrics, obstetrics-gynecology, psychiatry, and medicine.

To exploit this opening wedge and to keep the pressure on the president, we prevailed upon Helen Satterthwaite, our local representative in the
state legislature, to set up a meeting of university administration, faculty,
and community people to discuss the Urbana-Champaign medical-school
issue on Friday morning, October 9. In preparation for the meeting, Hal
Swartz, Allan Levy, and I had met for two hours with Satterthwaite the night
before and stressed to her our goals of a presidential commitment to a
cohort of thirty clerks in the M-3 year and appropriate governance. Allan
Levy extended the concept by implying that, for the fourth year, some of the
twenty to thirty might stay in Urbana and others might take electives here
or elsewhere.

The morning meeting with Representative Satterthwaite produced no
breakthroughs, but it appeared to be helpful in adding pressure on the now-
beleaguered president before his afternoon meeting with the full complement of signers of Sunday's open letter. After the meeting, we alerted those
present who would be at the afternoon meeting with the president to push
for thirty students per class and for suitable governance autonomy.

Jack Pollard, CEO of Carle Clinic Association began the Friday, October 9 afternoon meeting by bluntly telling President Ikenberry that Carle Foundation Hospital was going to teach medical students—if not ours from the University of Illinois, then students from another medical school and specifically SIU. Pollard made it clear that he was not threatening the university administration, but that he and his colleagues at Carle were intent on participating in clinical education. Others spoke their piece, but the essence of the meeting was an attempt to clarify the number of students assigned to the core clerkships in Champaign-Urbana. President Ikenberry's position gradually began to move from a complement of twenty to thirty students over the third and fourth years to twenty to thirty in the M-3 year alone. The group pushed the president very hard toward thirty, and the chance to get that many assigned to Urbana looked bright.

The second major issue discussed at this meeting related to the governance of the Urbana medical-education program. The group urged that the president bring the UIUC campus into the governance discussions because UIUC was so clearly involved through the Medical Scholars Program. The president listened but would make no commitment about governance.

October 9 proved to be an eventful day beyond the meetings with the president. At 1 p.m., Mack Schmidt called me from Chicago to ask if I had some time to talk with him, and I told him that I did. I found his tone of voice unusually friendly and pliable. Having had two séances with him trying to drive me from office, I was naturally wary of this apparently new, friendly demeanor.

So we began to talk. He first discussed the October 7 UIMC Senate meeting, saying that Ikenberry had discussed with the Senate the state of the university, his reasons for supporting consolidation of the two Chicago campuses, UIMC and UI at Chicago Circle, and his views of what was necessary in the College of Medicine reorganization. Furthermore, after conversations the president had with the Executive Committee of the UIUC Senate, Ikenberry had indicated to Schmidt that he now had a better understanding of faculty concerns regarding the Medical Scholars Program (although we had been trying to tell him of these concerns for over six months). Schmidt then professed to have had "a good understanding of these concerns" ever since his April trip here, when he received a hostile reception to his announcement that SCM-UC would be closed. He said that there was concern about the importance of sequential subject integration in

Medical Scholars' training. The problem was how to run the MSP in a satisfactory way.

Schmidt said that he advised the president that he favored core clerkships at UIUC to which Ikenberry had responded, "I'm learning. I don't
know the difference between an elective and a required core clerkship."
Schmidt explained this to Ikenberry, who then said, "I want to be assured
that the Medical Scholars Program can be run in Urbana-Champaign. Has
anybody ever communicated with Dan?"

Schmidt responded to that last question ingenuously. "Having been
rapped by the regional faculty," he said, he had stayed out of these discussions until the issue reached his desk. (He obviously did not count the two
sessions we had together with Mort Creditor as "communicating with
Dan.") Now, by virtue of the ratification of the Option II reorganization
plan by the UIMC Senate, the Medical Scholars Program issue had reached
his desk, and he wanted to talk to me about it. He wanted to make sure that
there was no question either about his belief that the Medical Scholars
Program would continue at UIUC or about his intent to sustain it. Therefore, at that time, definitive planning was needed. I responded that the
requirements were simple. We needed resources for a cohort of thirty M-3
students, mostly Medical Scholars, who would take their core clerkships in
Urbana-Champaign, and we needed to have an agreement on governance.
I said that a unique relationship existed among SBMS/SCM-UC, UIMC, and
UIUC, and that he and Ned Goldwasser (VCAA at UIUC) had to talk. He
agreed with that, and he agreed with respect to a comment I made that the
Urbana-Champaign faculty felt disenfranchised by the Medical Center reor-
ganization process.

I then explained Goldwasser needed to be involved because nothing that
Schmidt and I and Mort Creditor could come up with would have substantial credibility unless a consensus with the UIUC administration developed.
I told him that Lowell Hager was going to introduce an amendment to the
report of the UIUC ad hoc Senate subcommittee that would separate the
governance of UICOM-UC from the Medical Center, an act that I thought
would be unwise at that time. Our budget had been so depleted that we
could not be independent without a significant infusion of dollars to make
up for the funds that Creditor unfairly took away and for the budget dollars
we would have received had there been a fair-share, enrollment-based
budget. But I told Schmidt that I was in no position to dissuade Hager from

submitting the resolution and advised Schmidt to contact Goldwasser and to ask for help in the matter. "In that way," I said, "we might avoid unnecessary polarization at this time."

The conversation with the "new" Mack Schmidt was over. Five minutes later, I called Ned Goldwasser, who was not in his office but the call from Schmidt had already been there. When Goldwasser called me back later, I brought him up to date. My final note in the memo for that day reads, "We may win this thing yet!"

CHAPTER 34

Moving the Immovable

"KEEP UP THE PRESSURE" was the word from Paul Stone, and we did precisely that. From within and without, the university president was virtually besieged by advocates for SCM-UC and the Medical Scholars Program. The legislature was threatening to take legislative action to preserve the three downstate clinical programs. Key UIUC faculty and Senate committees openly opposed his stand, and newspaper advertisements had mobilized community sentiment against him. Students and faculty were openly critical of his inflexible stand. Although some of the pressure on the president was orchestrated by UIUC campus figures who hoped to preserve the Medical Scholars Program, much of the pressure was spontaneous.

One of the most significant statements came from the UIUC College of Engineering's College Policy and Development Committee. Its minutes of October 6, 1981 show that the committee voted unanimously to endorse the four-point May 9, 1981 statement developed by the Bicampus Steering Committee in favor of the continuation of the Medical Scholars Program. The committee went on to approve the following statement: "In addition to our explicit endorsement of the four-point Bicampus Steering Committee statement, we wish to add that the presence of a clinical medicine program at Urbana-Champaign has intellectual merit which extends well beyond the Medical Scholars Program itself. Without a clinical program, this campus will lose the highly productive medical researchers who have already been attracted here and will lose, in addition, unmeasured opportunities for cross-disciplinary actions between medicine and engineering and other disciplines."

The College of Engineering's endorsement was very important, not lightly entertained, because it pointed out the obvious value and necessity for a clinical program at UIUC. The president might ride roughshod over the opinions of lesser colleges and schools, but he could not ignore the strong message from the internationally respected College of Engineering.

Dozens of other departmental statements supporting SCM-UC and the Medical Scholars Program reached the president's desk. Typical of these was the resolution from the October 5, 1981 meeting of the Department of Physiology and Biophysics, which read, "The arbitrary dismantling of the School of Clinical Medicine threatens to render the Medical Scholars Program unworkable...The faculty of the Department of Physiology and Biophysics feels compelled to withdraw from the Medical Scholars Program if adequate clinical experiences at Urbana are eliminated."

Other communications directed to the president were solicited by members of the faculty from medical educators and scientists who were prominent on the national scene. Typical was a letter from James G. Hirsch, President of the Josiah Macy Jr. Foundation, to President Ikenberry: "It has come to my attention that consideration is being given to discontinuing the Clinical Program of the College of Medicine, Urbana, converting the college into a two-year basic-science activity. I realize that these times demand serious consideration of any proposal that would save money, but it is also important to figure into account effects on quality that may result.

"We have all too few centers of excellence on the medical-school scene now...the school at Urbana was designed to meet this need for an academic medical center...if the clinical training is transferred to Chicago or elsewhere, there will surely be a detrimental affect on the Urbana medical operation. No two-year school can hope to receive a reputation for excellence on its own."

However, as late as October 15, the immovable president still maintained that he believed the reorganization plan, which had by that time been "approved by the Medical Center Senate," was the best solution. Until then, Ikenberry may not have been briefed on two compelling reports from independent UIUC blue-ribbon ad hoc committees. The two committee reports, one from the UIUC College of Liberal Arts and Sciences and the other from the UIUC Senate dealt sledgehammer blows to the wisdom of the presidential stand. The first, dated March 9, 1981 was labeled "Report of the Ad Hoc Committee to Examine the Prospects for Medical Education at the Champaign-Urbana Campus." It had been filed by a committee of six senior professors and/or administrators from the chemical, engineering and biological sciences, who were charged by LAS Dean Prokasy to study the problem of medical education at UIUC in depth. They were to determine whether there should be a medical school at Champaign-Urbana and, if so, whether it should retain ties to the College of Medicine. Ultimately, they were to determine under which conditions a separate medical school could be justified.

After briefly reviewing the background of medical education at UIUC, the committee noted that the twenty-two members of the SBMS-UC faculty generated $1.5 million in research support annually, compared with $3.2 million generated annually by the basic-science faculty in Chicago, which was six to eight times larger. "This observation is only one way of documenting a very important difference between the Champaign-Urbana and the Chicago campuses in terms of faculty quality and academic excellence."

However, the report focused primarily on the School of Clinical Medicine and the Medical Scholars Program, which the committee members also saw as inextricably linked. "*It is important to note that the future of the Medical Scholars program is dependent on the successful operation of a C-U clinical school.*" [Emphasis in the original.]

Specific weaknesses cited were no surprise: inadequate funding, faculty isolation associated with their dual roles as members of academic units that have entirely different reporting structures, and lack of full-time, research-oriented clinical faculty.

As a result, the committee advised that there should be a medical school but that local governance was necessary. The committee also advised that a separate medical school would be justified in order to maintain clinical research initiatives, which would seem "less likely without an adequate number of full-time university clinical faculty." However, the committee also advised that such programs needed to be properly funded: "If adequate funds are not available for the operation of the C-U medical program, the program should be terminated."

The final recommendations of the LAS ad hoc committee were that the administration of the medical program at Urbana-Champaign should be transferred to the UIUC Chancellor's office, that our program should be combined with Peoria's, and stressed again that absent adequate funds "the only reasonable alternative would be to abandon the entire U-C medical-education program."

The Wicks Committee, appointed by the UIUC Senate, submitted its final report on October 12, 1981. It was an extremely thorough documentation of the relationship, the opportunities, and the costs related to a college of medicine on the Urbana-Champaign campus. The forty-four-page report was accompanied by forty pages of tables and other documentation, both current and historical. The committee recommended that the UIUC Senate "recognize the excellent progress" made by SBMS/SCM-UC "in the development of a high-quality medical program, which emphasizes and supports both clinical training and research at the clinical-nonclinical boundary" and that the Senate resolve that SCM's contribution to research at Urbana-Champaign was "extremely important to this campus and should not be eroded." In addition, the committee asked the Senate to affirm "the need to preserve those aspects of clinical training necessary to assure" the continuation of the Medical Scholars Program. It also asked the Senate to remind the chancellors of UIMC and UIUC both that the Senate must have the opportunity to act on any specific proposal to alter the basic medical-science program.

The committee's final recommendation read, "That the Senate request that President Ikenberry, Chancellor Begando, and Chancellor Cribbet reaffirm the intent of existing agreements by which UIUC is to have substantial involvement in policies and issues affecting medical-education programs located on this campus."

After receiving the recommendations, a group of faculty representing the School of Life Sciences and Chemical Sciences submitted a friendly amendment to change that final recommendation to read, "That the Senate request that President Ikenberry, Chancellor Begando, and Chancellor Cribbet reaffirm the intent of existing agreements by transferring governance of the UC medical program from the Chancellor's Office, Medical Center, to the Chancellor's Office, Urbana-Champaign."

This was a stunning move that provoked considerable discussion. There were clearly some senators of the 174 present who opposed the transfer of governance, but after debating the issue for almost half an hour, the Senate voted 142 to 32 in favor of the amendment.

At this point, however, UIUC Chancellor John Cribbet told the assembly that he would be cautious about accepting the transfer because of the financial deficiencies that were obvious in the SBMS/SCM-UC budget. He told the senators, "In an era of grave financial crisis for all higher education, I do not see sufficient financial base to support a separate College of Medicine at Urbana-Champaign without imperiling the quality of our other programs. There is a tide in the affairs of educational institutions and, for now, the tide is flowing in the wrong direction. But tides reverse themselves, and our goals should be to so position ourselves that we will be able to take advantage of the reverse flow when it occurs."

One Senator took exception to Cribbet's remarks and described the latter's urging to wait for a proper time as "just whistling in the dark." Also present at the meeting were Joe Begando and Mack Schmidt, who were questioned extensively from the floor on matters of accreditation, budgeting, and the status of the Medical Scholars Program. They stood up well under fire, but in the end, the UIUC Senate unanimously adopted the recommendations of the ad hoc subcommittee together with the amended recommendation on governance. The Senate's vote in support of SCM-UC, the Medical Scholars Program, and a governance transfer to UIUC was a stinging rebuke to the president. Thereafter, Ikenberry dissociated himself more and more from his sponsorship of Option II.

The strong UIUC Senate support for us was not entirely a spontaneous occurrence. Before the October 12 UIUC Senate meeting, I had assembled all the SCM-UC activists, both faculty and students, to discuss the issue before the Senate and to plan for advance lobbying to support our cause. The new white paper, which provided the basic documentation for our arguments, was circulated to every senator. Allan Levy, Hal Swartz, and Willard Visek, faculty members with the closest connections to the UIUC senators, spent hours at meetings or on the telephone to impress upon senatorial friends the importance of the upcoming votes. Paul Hattis and Nora Zorich were two very effective student leaders, who organized the Medical Scholars to lobby their graduate advisors on behalf of the MSP and SCM-UC. A UIUC Senate membership list was obtained and names were assigned so that virtually every member of the Senate was contacted in advance of the October 12 meeting. My own list of senators included friends in the fields of food sciences, plant pathology, economics, civil engineering, fine and applied arts, law, religious studies, mathematics, kinesiology, aviation, labor and industrial relations, and library sciences. Most of those I called appreciated the information and asked for background data that they could study. The new white paper proved very helpful in that regard. Our support was well informed and very strong.

Only the friendly amendment was a surprise, although not entirely unwelcome. No one desired the transfer of governance more than I did, but at that particular moment, SCM-UC, a victim of administrative abuse, was underfunded by at least $1 million. To transfer governance at that time, when the UIUC campus was in severe financial distress and reducing programs and the UIMC campus was professing poverty, would only have relieved UIMC of committing its fair share of funds to SCM-UC and would have left us impoverished and crippled at UIUC.

Barely two days after the UIUC Senate action, the Advisory Council of Deans met in Chicago. With Creditor in China, Marten Kernis, Senior Associate Dean (i.e., Creditor's primary deputy), chaired the meeting. There, for the first time, we talked about reorganization problems, dean to dean. Phil Forman asked for an executive session; all staffers left. Remaining were Kernis, Forman, Dean of ALSM; Ed Cohen, Dean of SBMS-MC; Jerry Newman, Dean of PSM; Bud Grulee, Dean of RMS; and me.

Forman indicated his distress at the way the College of Medicine reorganization plan was going. It was apparent to him that the president had caved in to pressure from Urbana to allow basic clerkships there with twenty students, if not thirty, per year. Forman's view was that he "didn't see where those students were coming from, because ALSM was not going to give them up." Forman also said, not in a belligerent way, that for some time he had asked his faculty at affiliated hospitals to refrain from political activity. He said he was really drawing back from that position. It was not clear just what kind of political action they might take in Chicago. He felt that Chicago faculty had compromised a great deal on what it really wanted. Those compromises were not clear to any of us from downstate.

The discussion became more interesting as it proceeded. Bud Grulee stated, "The appointment of Morton Creditor as Interim Executive Dean was the biggest mistake this college ever made." Although Grulee expressed much respect for Mort's courage and integrity, he thought that an individual who was as resistant as Mort was to external suggestions was probably the wrong individual to lead the college through reorganization. Jerry Newman then conceded that Nick Cotsonas had advised Bill Grove that the appointment of Morton Creditor as Interim Executive Dean would prove to be a big mistake.

The most revealing feature of this confidential chat among deans was our discussion regarding the reorganization and where the problems lay. There was a virtual consensus that Schmidt and the president, together with Brady, had struck a deal on the basic elements of UICOM reorganization almost before the reorganization process had begun. Ed Cohen stated unequivocally that Ron Brady told him that Schmidt and Ikenberry had agreed upon the reorganization plan in 1980. This piece of information was particularly important to me because when Schmidt and Creditor had invited me to our second tripartite meeting, where they discussed my reappointment and/or resignation, I had complained to Schmidt that it was difficult for downstate administrators to participate in a process from which they felt completely excluded. Furthermore, I told Schmidt that the whole SPMC outcome appeared to me to be preordained before any academic process, such as the deliberations of the SPMC or the ad hoc committee for implementation, took place. In response, Schmidt looked me directly in the eye and said any talk of a preconceived solution was absolutely untrue and that he had made up his mind only after the SPMC presented the report to him at the March 1981 Academic Council meeting. I do not suppose that it makes any difference, but if I heard what I thought I heard, somebody was not telling me the truth. Furthermore, over time, Schmidt seemed to contradict himself.

As the discussion progressed, I laid low and kept out of it as much as possible because I didn't want to raise the issue of recent gains made by SBMS/SCM-UC in preserving the clinical program. Neither Newman nor Grulee really understood what had happened at UIUC during the preceding week, and they did not understand the significance of the UIUC Senate resolution. Newman did say that most of the Peoria faculty would be satisfied with a two-year clinical program. Grulee was not so certain about that at Rockford.

Regardless of what Grulee and Newman understood about the UIUC Senate action, it made a significant impact on the president. Although the UIMC Senate had major jurisdiction over SCM-UC, the president was anxious for a process whereby a universitywide consensus could be reached. To add to his woes, on October 15, 1981, the state legislative representatives from Rockford, supported by no less than one hundred co-sponsors submitted House Bill 1976 and Senate Bill 1261 to the General Assembly of the State of Illinois that would add a section to the University of Illinois Act requiring "establishment of regional medical schools with three-year curricula at Champaign-Urbana, Rockford and Peoria effective immediately."

The language was identical in the Senate and House versions. This was another stunning blow to the president and to the UIMC administration, which did not desire to yield academic policy to the state legislature. By

October 10, it was reported that the bill had 101 cosponsors in the Illinois House, with eighty-nine votes required for passage. University lobbyists at the State Capitol in Springfield informed the president that this was a serious threat and that all indications were that if the bill passed, the governor would sign it.

Meanwhile, Mort Creditor, confident that the reorganization plan he had delivered would soon be approved by the Board of Trustees, had already notified fall 1982 admission applicants that they could anticipate that the new structure of the College of Medicine would become effective "on or about September 1, 1982" and that the new entering class would be the "first group to receive the benefits [sic] of the changes."

It is difficult to pinpoint the exact high-water mark in the attempt by UIMC and central administration to close SCM-UC, but it occurred sometime during the first week of October 1981, just before President Ikenberry finally felt enough pressure to listen to downstate views on the reorganization. By mid-October, it was definitely clear that President Ikenberry was looking for new sources of information that were free of UIMC bias. He was receiving relentless pressure from advocates who rejected Option II; the legislature was threatening; key committees at UIUC openly rejected his stand; newspaper advertisements had mobilized community sentiment against him; faculty and students vigorously questioned his position on medical education, and the Board of Trustees, with Paul Stone as president, was not entirely supportive. As a result, he became more and more unwilling to commit himself to the recommendations of the Academic Council's implementation subcommittee—recommendations that were terribly unpopular outside of Chicago.

Cracks in the president's position could be discerned when he addressed the Board of Trustees on October 15. Although he identified seven attributes of an acceptable plan and declared, "I believe the College of Medicine reorganization plan adopted by the UIMC Senate meets these tests," later on in his address, he acknowledged a need for the UIUC Senate to review the proposed reorganization. "In accord with the July 22, 1970 board action, and recognizing the action taken by the [UIMC] Senate on October 7, as well as the recommendations adopted by the Urbana-Champaign Senate on October 12, I have asked Chancellor Begando and Chancellor Cribbet to recommend to me such modifications of the 'Plan for Organization and Administration of a Program of Medical Education at Urbana-Champaign' as they believe to be necessary and appropriate."

Paul Stone stopped by my office to give me some feedback from the Board of Trustees early in the afternoon of Wednesday, October 21. He was very confident at this time that the reorganization had been stopped and the status quo maintained except for proportional adjustments in enrollments. He viewed the legislative action as very significant and believed that the president had to back down before "he is mortally wounded." I asked him if President Ikenberry realized he was getting some bad advice in Chicago. Stone stated that this was a difficult message to get across to the president. Stone had done everything he could personally to neutralize Mack Schmidt and believed at this time that Schmidt felt discredited and was afraid to sign onto any solution that might resolve the problems whether or not the Chicago operation was disadvantaged. He said that Schmidt should have been less authoritarian in his approach.

When we discussed criticism of the president in this matter, Stone asked me to make certain that people on the campus got the message through to the president that the Board of Trustees perceived substantial faculty unrest and that he was in danger. Regarding the possible survival of SCM-UC, I told Paul Stone that, in any favorable resolution of this matter, the board would probably have to insist on approving specific enrollments, budget distributions, and stability because I did not believe that the Medical Center administration would agree to reallocate money to our underfunded programs unless it received direction from above. He told me that might be difficult to achieve. He also advised us to continue to be firm but to ease off on the pressure we were applying at this time because changes were occurring.

That same afternoon, I received a call from the Ikenberry's office stating that he would like to meet with me at about 9 p.m. He told me he was talking to me first before talking to Jerry Newman at Peoria and Bud Grulee at Rockford. We met from 9 to 10:30 p.m. The meeting, like all meetings I have ever had with Stan Ikenberry, was unsettling. I was impressed with the difficulty he had in listening and the crippling lack of flexibility that he exhibited. Two examples from this meeting come to mind. As we discussed the UIUC Senate action, I told him frankly (as earlier that day Paul Stone had suggested I do) that there was considerable dissatisfaction on the UIUC campus about his leadership and his insensitivity to quality issues, and that the MSP and SBMS/SCM-UC governances were considered "quality issues." He immediately interpreted this as saying, "They want quality but they don't want to come up with a nickel." He thought that the dissatisfaction was localized in the SBMS/SCM-UC conflict, and it was difficult to convince him that it went beyond our small school.

The second example of his inflexibility and inability to listen came when he asked my advice on whether to continue with the Medical Center plan for a two-year, two-year split, or accept some kind of compromise, as implied in the legislative bill, and hold on to the one-year, three-year system. I responded that it depended upon how much risk he wanted to take and how badly he needed to survive. I told him that right now the easiest course and the safest course would be to back down to a one-year, three-year system and that I doubted that a two-year, two-year course could be maintained without the support of external consultants or something of that sort. He brushed aside the survival reference by saying, "I'll survive in any case. That's no problem." He simply would not understand the need for governance changes of a significant nature. In his view, the only flaw in the Medical Center plan lay in the balance of votes on the Executive Committee. He thought that simply by giving the deans or the regional directors votes, the votes would be balanced equally between Chicago and downstate. I told him that was not the way it was set up and would leave the count as sixteen votes in Chicago and fifteen downstate, almost (but not quite) equal.

He wanted to know whether Peoria and Rockford would go along with the two-year, two-year plan. I told him that Peoria really had a mixed bag of faculty; some would fight for the one-year, three-year system and others would go along with the two-year, two-year split. I could not be sure where Rockford stood. I told him that I believed there was enough money in the system to fund us properly, but he was not anxious to transfer money out of Chicago. He indicated that he believed that a strong dean in Chicago, "someone like Bill Grove, warts and all," could run the system. I pointed out that rather than look for a strong dean in Chicago, what we needed was four strong regional programs that could run themselves within the context of a single college. It was a strong dean in Chicago who had led us into the mess we were in at the present time. I told him that two colleges remained a feasible idea, but he quickly shut off dialogue along that line by responding, "Not at this time." I recommended to him that we get an external consultation from the LCME, but he wanted a consultation from outside the LCME. I cautioned him that if he did go outside the LCME, he could be tainted with consultants telling him what he wanted to hear.

The president then asked me why the SCM-UC clinical program would be better than the clinical programs in Peoria and Rockford. I told him that, from the standpoint of straight content, it would be equivalent, but, from the standpoint of a scientific learning atmosphere, it had more potential. At this point, Ikenberry confessed that he had not yet read the UIUC Senate ad hoc committee report. He apparently was not yet aware that the UIUC Senate had spoken firmly and unanimously in favor of SCM-UC. I summarized the resolutions that were passed by the UIUC Senate in as level a voice as I could project. The president took the information stoically, without batting an eye. I suspected, given my nefarious reputation, that he would quickly check out what I had told him, but he changed the subject again and asked what the Medical Scholars Program needed to support its presence at UIUC. I told him that we needed enough clerkships at SCM-UC to manage a clinical cohort of Medical Scholars through the M-3 and M-4 years. The very minimum that would be cost-effective would be thirty per year. I added that the Abraham Lincoln School of Medicine did not need all the enrollment numbers they demanded, but instead the faculty there should be reaching out from Chicago, teaching, consulting, and getting referrals for the university hospital, which was losing a great deal of money. This brought absolutely no response from him.

Reflecting on the entire conversation, I was again troubled and dissatisfied. Throughout our conversation, the president made many uncomplimentary remarks about my proposals and, particularly, my cost estimates. He tried to give the impression that he was listening to all options, but seemed to be listening with closed ears. Once again, in taking leave of the president, I had the feeling that Ikenberry was a very slow learner fixated on central control. He gave lip service to the concept of proper delegation of authority, but I did not believe for a minute that he was not micromanaging the UICOM reorganization. As always, I left his office uneasy, unfulfilled, and unsure about his course of action. Of one thing, however, I was absolutely certain—I was not a presidential favorite.

Meanwhile, the UIUC campus, responding to the Senate action, was gearing up to take a stand on issues of governance for the medical-education programs at UIUC. Ned Goldwasser planned for an October 30 meeting with the Wicks Committee to focus on the governance issue, but before that meeting took place some significant events occurred.

On October 22, an embarrassed Mack Schmidt told the Board of

Trustees of the fiscal problems at the university hospital in the 1981 fiscal year, which included a deficit of $1.5 million that he planned to make up with funds from the 1982 fiscal year. He reported that the auditors, a well-known firm, were "unhappy" with the information they received. The auditors described a "need for leadership" at the university hospital. He informed the board that Vice President Brady had moved the Director of Business Affairs at Chicago Circle to the Medical Center campus to monitor the hospital budget, and he stated that a number of personnel changes were taking place. The director of the hospital, whom Schmidt had recruited without consulting anyone, had been dismissed, and other middle-management administrators had been replaced. He reported that the $1.5 million deficit could be accounted for in accounts receivable, and the hospital would increase its rates by 15 percent. He noted also that the hospital had about $60 million in accounts receivable. If this were not enough of an embarrassment, barely two weeks later, on November 8, 1981, the university hospital was shocked by a *Chicago Sun Times* headline that screamed "$418,000 UI Hospital Fraud Probe." The article began, "University of Illinois auditors have uncovered an embezzlement scheme at the University Chicago Hospital in which three tellers are suspected of skimming $418,000."

It was losses and financial mismanagement such as this that reinforced our argument that the money was in the system, it was just being misspent.

The first real crack in the president's position was hardly recognized. A brief article in *Illini Week,* a local publication of the UIUC campus, excerpted comments made by President Ikenberry to the UIUC Senate on October 27, 1981. Although he repeated his regular litany of the seven qualities he would look for in any reorganization plan that came before the board for final approval, he now added, "Although I believe that the college reorganization plan adopted by the Medical Center Senate seeks to meet these general tests, it is also clear *that there is not yet a sufficient level of understanding nor sufficient consensus within the college and the faculties at the four locations;* nor is there a consensus between the two Senates; nor within the University Senates Conference." [Emphasis added.]

He then went on to point out the risks of attracting legislation by the General Assembly and stressed that it was important that the faculties in each geographic region believe the final plan to be fair and equitable. He then asked that the matter be resolved with minimum delay to achieve a working consensus. He ended the statement by saying that he hoped to bring the matter before the Board of Trustees for review in January 1982. Everyone apparently missed this sea change in attitude. It seems unlikely that members of the UIUC Senate who listened to the speech came to the same conclusion as one does by reading the excerpts as reported in the *Illini Week*, or I would have heard of it.

When victory finally came to us, I heard of it in a most unusual way. On Thursday evening, October 29, 1981, I was attending a continuing-medical-education dinner in the Colonial Room of the Illini Union. The speaker was talking about some obscure medical subject when Bill Sorlie nervously appeared at the door of the dining room and asked to see me. I could not imagine what he wanted from me at 7:30 in the evening. Bill, in a very excit-ed fashion, in fact barely articulate, informed me that he had heard directly from the president's office that the president had capitulated completely to the political pressures we and others had placed upon him. He had made his decision on Monday, October 26 (the day before he addressed the UIUC Senate), that UICOM would remain in a one-year, three-year configuration and that, in view of the UIUC Senate action, there would be a no-nonsense fully funded medical program in UC with seventy-five students in the first year and thirty in each of the other three years. This was really great news. No, more than that, it was stunning news! The Urbana clinical program, SCM-UC, had survived against all odds.

Bill informed me further that the president had spent the whole day with key personnel in the Medical Center administration, informing them of his decision. They were reported to be mad as hornets and that was probably an understatement. I could only imagine the reactions of my two nemeses, Mack Schmidt and Morton Creditor, as they learned of the president's change of heart. Instead of draping our Urbana program with black cloth, they were now instructed to revive it and to prepare budgetary-allocation plans to fund it properly. As Bill went on with his tale, I remember pinching myself repeatedly to make certain this was not a glorious dream.

Bill could not tell me the source of his information, but he was confi-dent of its accuracy. We embraced in the Colonial Room entrance in a hug of victory. The elation felt like winning the World Series and the Super Bowl all at once—an incredible high. Our minicelebration ended, we returned to our respective meetings.

The next night it was open house at the Bloomfields'. Word of our suc-cess had spread rapidly across the campus, and for those who had joined us in this veritable crusade for a clinical school, there was a mood of rejoicing. It was one of those heady celebrations that come all too rarely in life. All the SBMS/SCM-UC faculty and staff were there, together with dozens of faculty from the UIUC campus, as well as John Cribbet, Ned Goldwasser, Ted Brown, and Linda Wilson, representing the UIUC leadership. There seemed to be no end of back-patting, testimonials, congratulations, and savoring the sweet smell of success. The party had no beginning and no end. We imported beer and pizzas and reveled until we were too tired to think anymore about it. When the last guest left, I turned to Franny and said quietly, "We made it."

CHAPTER 35

The Grand Compromise

B ILL SORLIE MAY HAVE SCOOPED the grapevine with news of our victory, but not by much. By the next morning, the survival of SCM-UC (and the three-year programs in Rockford and Peoria) was common knowledge on the UIUC campus. By Saturday it was reported widely in newspapers across the state. There was no mistake. The presidential change in position was real. The change itself was public.

I was now perceived by most of the parties affected as the villain behind the presidential flip-flop. The whole reorganization process was deemed "satisfactory" except for the manipulations of Bloomfield, which upset the apple cart. Rockford and Peoria didn't want us to be a four-year school, regardless of their own good fortune. The administrators in Chicago from Schmidt to Creditor, who had been left "swinging in the wind" when the president abandoned them, were absolutely furious with me, as well as the president. Creditor, who I had urged to resign six months earlier, now saw the light and signaled his intention to resign his deanship immediately. He was persuaded to remain as a lame duck until March 1, 1982, when Marten Kernis took his place as acting executive dean. Both Kernis and Creditor, who had worked closely together for two years on the SPMC process, were angry and bitter. Neither was ready to take on the additional hostility that reallocation of funds to Urbana would have generated. Our future remained uncertain even as we luxuriated in our success.

John Cribbet and Ned Goldwasser revealed the SCM-UC stay of execution at their meeting with the UIUC campus-planning group at 10 a.m., October 30. They described the ninety-minute discussion that they had just had with the president. According to Cribbet and Goldwasser, the president told them, "It's now a whole new ballgame." Ikenberry's major concern was the danger that the legislature would pass a bill that threatened the integrity of the University of Illinois. Vice President Brady had described an uncommon legislative hostility directed toward the university. He had little doubt that the bill to legislate three-year clinical programs for Rockford, Peoria, and Urbana-Champaign would pass both houses and that the governor could be pressured to sign it. No one wanted the legislature in a position to run the University of Illinois. The president was also aware that the Chicago faculty might be stirred into political action because the present reversion toward the status quo represented what appeared to be a downstate victory. He stated that he had specifically requested the Chicago people not to approach their legislators and had told them that he hoped a new consensus might generate an internal solution by January or February.

Cribbet said he and the president had been amazed when they discovered that the principals (specifically, the regional deans) had never been in the same room together to discuss reorganization options. The two senior administrators found that fact hard to believe. It was a glaring omission by the SPMC process. As a result, the president assigned Begando and Brady to meet with the UICOM deans individually and then as a group to see whether they could resolve this problem internally at an early date. Goldwasser and Cribbet took the position with the president that Bloomfield was no longer the sole negotiator for the UIUC campus and they requested that a UIUC Senate observer be present at this new round of negotiations. The request was turned down, and no UIUC observer attended the final negotiations. Schmidt and Creditor were also to be excluded from these meetings.

After Cribbet and Goldwasser shared this information with the group, we got down to business. It was agreed that the "Bloomfield draft" of the reorganization plan, which had been submitted and rejected by the Academic Council at the September 9 meeting, would be the working document for this campus in presenting its governance options. Mort Weir advised us to take an absolutely maximal position with respect to governance and to pull back from it if we had to. Goldwasser and Ted Brown were concerned specifically with faculty staffing and space problems relating to different enrollment scenarios and asked me to prepare documents that compared those issues with the various enrollment figures projected, which I was able to provide very promptly. At the close of the meeting, Cribbet suggested to me that I could expect a call from Begando for a meeting with Brady and him at a very early date.

The only hitch in the whole scenario was that it represented another major administrative decision by the president without really involving central characters. I was also concerned that the present reduction of basic-science student enrollment from one hundred to seventy-five, if maintained, could potentially diminish our budget by as much as $300,000 per year. We hoped to be able to make up for such a loss through clinical enrollments. In any event, that was hardly a reason to be concerned at this time. Moreover, in our euphoria over salvation it was hard to settle down once again and complete the necessary follow-up work. The infighting and hassling were not over by a long shot. Even though the president had talked about "full funding" of SCM-UC, the budget still had to be effected by the UIMC administration, a group of officers who had been "mad as hornets" at our survival. They would not be easy to deal with as we sought the necessary reallocations of funds.

On October 30, I wrote to all the signatories of the "First in a Series" open letter to Stanley Ikenberry, thanking them for their support and telling them that the university was reconsidering its original recommendation to discontinue SCM-UC.

That same day, the University Office of Public Affairs issued a press release to announce that the president had asked for consultation with the regional deans to achieve a consensus plan on reorganizing the College of Medicine. The release quoted Ikenberry as saying, "My conversations with faculty members, community members, and members of the General Assembly lead me to conclude that the plan to reorganize the College of Medicine which has been developed to this point has not achieved the consensus necessary to carry it forward. I am aware of the keen interest of members of the General Assembly in this matter and have written them reporting these next steps.

"I believe it is essential that the faculties in each geographic location believe that a plan, which I must eventually present to the UI Board of Trustees is fairly and equitably developed and over the long term will sustain high quality programs in regional medical education within realistic budget limits."

It was clear that the president was making intensive efforts to quiet things down. He also wrote to every legislator who signed on to the bill to acknowledge their "keen concern" regarding the College of Medicine governance and promising them sequential reports on the progress of internal negotiations.

Joe Begando called me on Tuesday, November 3, to invite me to a

November 20 meeting with him and Ron Brady, as well as Deans Forman, Cohen, Newman, and Grulee, to try to achieve a solution to the reorganization problem. In a letter to the regional deans confirming this arrangement, Begando wrote, "I am convinced that the best chance for achieving the necessary consensus is for the deans to reach agreement on a reorganization which each of you can support personally and which addresses the primary concerns of each medical-education site. I assume that a dedication to the achievement of academic quality within fiscal restraints will guide the outcome of our discussions."

Joe Begando met with me privately in Urbana on Friday, November 13. I gave him a draft copy of a reorganization proposal because I anticipated he would have to present a working document. I also presented him with a letter of transmittal that I was sending to him, Ikenberry, Brady, Cribbet, and the four other regional deans to get my position on the record, which said:

> I have taken the liberty of drafting an incomplete proposal for reorganization that might serve as a skeleton working draft [for the consensus negotiations]. I believe that a fresh appraisal is called for because (1) the proposal that was eventually acted upon by the Medical Center Senate was developed upon 'boundary conditions' which are no longer applicable and (2) was rejected by three of the four regions. The new proposal purposely leaves blank enrollment tables, references to 2:2 versus 1:3 splits and numerical representation on the Executive Committee.

I did however suggest that the decision to reduce enrollment from 350 to 325 per class was premature. I said that the intrinsic elements of regionalization preclude a significant cost saving from such a reduction and suggested a return to enrollment projections based on 350 medical students per class. I made the suggestion because as enrollment was lowered people tended to want to cut clinical positions at SCM-UC.

I also wrote, "The proposal refers to an updated agreement between UIMC and UIUC entitled 'Plan for the Organization and Administration of a Program of Medical Education at the Urbana-Champaign Campus.' That updated agreement between you and Chancellor Cribbet has not yet been arrived at, but I assume it will be forthcoming." That was a red flag for my collegial friends in Rockford and Peoria.

Finally, I wrote, "I may not be fully able to express the interests and concerns of the UIUC Senate. These will undoubtedly be addressed in your negotiations with Chancellor Cribbet, but they reflect the fact that there are two consensus processes that are inextricably linked together." This was another red flag for Rockford and Peoria.

My draft-reorganization proposal, which Peoria Dean Jerry Newman petulantly refused even to read, was dead on arrival. Under those circumstances, it could never serve as the basis of a consensus.

But I had completed other tasks before this decisive meeting, including intense preparation for alternative scenarios. Hal Swartz, Rick Schimmel, and I met frequently to hammer out budgeting details for every possible enrollment scenario and to plan my reactions to any political attack that might be launched. Under the enrollment options discussed, first-year enrollment could vary from 75 to 130 students; M-2 enrollment, from 20 to 75; and M-3 and M-4 enrollments, from 20 to 36. Those were the mixes and options. Each permutation and combination had its own effect on faculty requirements and, given the president's new position, which called for enrollment-driven budgeting, its own budgetary implications.

A major issue we decided to avoid was the push for separate LCME accreditation. Unfortunately, because our academic ranks had been so depleted by the punitive budgetary restrictions that Creditor had inflicted upon us, immediate independent accreditation for SBMS/SCM-UC was really out of the question. It would take at least two years of adequate budgeting to recruit and develop the minimum number of full- and part-time faculty to run a program of sufficient quality for accreditation. Our crippling budget also placed us at a disadvantage with our putative suitor, UIUC, which did not want to marry a debt-ridden, underfunded program. On several occasions, President Ikenberry took unfair advantage of our weak budget situation by chiding UIUC faculty voices calling for the transfer of governance. He would ask them whether they were willing to put up the money necessary to fully fund the program. Of course, he knew that sufficient money did not exist on the UIUC campus to make up for the deficits engendered by the hostile UIMC policy toward SCM-UC.

As if such financial problems were not enough to complicate the discussions, our survival was made even more difficult by the generally low levels of state funding. The timing of SCM-UC's entry onto the stage could not have been more inauspicious. The State of Illinois was feeling poor. Budgets to the university were being cut, and university administrators were asked to reduce the number of employees. Employment was reduced by 2.4 percent at UIUC and by 1.6 percent at Chicago Circle. However, at the Medical Center, there was still a 1.6 percent increase and a 2.5 percent increase in state-funded positions. The only UIMC unit that had lost employees was, of course, SBMS/SCM-UC. Anticipating the demise of SCM-UC, Creditor had transferred money out of SCM-UC accounts and we had reduced employment by 10 percent.

The enrollment and budget scenarios, difficult as they appeared to be, were probably easier to resolve than updating the Lanier Treaty. My colleagues on the Advisory Council of Deans boiled over every time I mentioned it. We had already decided not to push for separate accreditation, but we felt it was essential that the Treaty remain recognized and operational. It was eleven years old, and a new agreement had to be reached between UIMC and UIUC. As far as the forthcoming negotiations were concerned, a basic acknowledgment of these facts was all I could expect. In summary, I felt well prepared for the consensus talks, but my guard was held high.

The first of the talks took place as planned on November 20 in Begando's office at the Medical Center. The deans at that time were Phil Forman of the Abraham Lincoln School of Medicine, Ed Cohen of the School of Basic Medical Sciences at the Medical Center, Jerry Newman of the Peoria School of Medicine, Bud Grulee of the Rockford School of Medicine, and myself. Begando opened the meeting with a brief historical review, and then went around the oval table asking each person if something new had come up in the past week that might be of interest. It was a way of breaking the ice. Not much was said by anyone except when it came to me, and I informed the group that there were three issues to be raised at the onset of discussions. One was that this group should know that the UIUC campus administration was drafting a successor document to the 1970 plan for the administration of the medical school at UC. I also distributed the draft reorganization document, and hoped that it might serve as a working draft for the group's deliberations. That hope was quashed by Newman's refusal to even read it.

Finally, I told the group that I had been concerned about a comment attributed to Ron Brady in connection with Forman's mention of Metro-6 hospital political activity. Referring to those circumstances, I directly asked Brady what he meant by the term "we" in his recent public statement, "We will not only welcome that activity, but we'll help them." Did that imply that he was oriented toward a Chicago resolution of this difficulty? Begando showed a little embarrassment at my question, but Brady denied that "we" meant anything other than "the university," and that his entire statement meant that the university wanted to avert a legislative attempt to dictate academic programs. He also believed that political activity by the Metro-6 would help the entire university, not just Chicago. I thought that his answer was an evasion, but accepted it without further ado so that we could proceed. I did not want to appear excessively belligerent, but I had given notice that I was not going to be intimidated by the vice president or by anyone else in this crucial meeting.

Brady described six different plans together with formula-driven budgets he had worked out with various enrollments and 1:3 and 2:2 splits. Only one of those six plans enjoyed enrollments that were even remotely acceptable to the Urbana-Champaign program, and none provided us, by the formulas he used, anywhere near the resources that would have been necessary. Having intensively studied enrollment tables and budget formulas for the preceding six months, I was thoroughly prepared to attack Brady's plans and formulas on substantive grounds. To begin with, I argued that, because we were dealing with state funding, it was unfair to count ALSM residents as part-time medical students. I pointed out that resident training was not to be funded with state dollars. That was clear in all our previous assumptions. Brady defended placing residents in the formula by saying that residents were a part of the ALSM teaching burden at this time. Jerry Newman, Bud Grulee, and I pointed out that residents helped them more than they cost them. Residents' services generated much of the Medical Service Plan dollars earned by ALSM faculty. If they were going to count residents in the totals for the formula for state fund distribution, they would have to take into account the Medical Service Plan dollars that the residents generated. Both Begando and Brady disagreed with this position, but I continued to argue forcefully that there was no tradition or history of counting residents as students and that they would find no documents in all the College of Medicine funding that did so. We had quickly reached an impasse that might have scrubbed the whole meeting, but my goal that day was to leave the discussions with an agreed-upon SCM-UC enrollment for the M-3 and M-4 years. The president had made his new decision that, if Bill Sorlie's informant was correct, included fully funded clinical clerkships for thirty M-3 and thirty M-4 Medical Scholars. Once SCM-UC enrollment was secure and agreed upon within this consensus-seeking group, there would be ample time to argue the niceties of budget allocation. Therefore, rather than take the resident-funding formula to the brink, I suggested that we continue with the agenda, keeping in mind that consensus was not reached on the resident-as-medical-student issue. That strategy relieved enough of the tension so that we were able to move on to enrollment projections.

Things were not too bright in the enrollment sector either. The several draft enrollment schemes that Brady had prepared gave Urbana no more than twenty or sometimes thirty in the M-3 year. None of the Brady options provided for both an M-3 and M-4 cohort of any size. This was a bad start to a difficult day. Enrollment was critical, and as Brady explained his several preconceived options, I became increasingly depressed. This was clearly unsatisfactory, but I did not wish to reach yet another impasse. We argued and discussed enrollment at length. Brady kept control of the blackboard and the chalk (probably to keep me from etching my own numbers onto the slate), and it was very difficult to persuade him to put any number into the empty block that signified M-4 Urbana enrollment. I knew that I absolutely had to get some enrollment number, almost any enrollment number, into that vulgar emptiness before this day was over.

I insisted that students in the Medical Scholars Program required not only the M-3 core clerkships, but also opportunities for M-4 elective clerkships. There was no way we could execute a sound medical-education program for MSP students without a defined cohort of enrollees for all four years.

Like a mantra, I calmly repeated this theme over and over again that day. The message made Newman and Grulee very unhappy and uneasy, but neither denied the verity of the need for clinical clerkships close by the Medical Scholars research site. They acknowledged that a significant geographic separation between the clinical base and the basic-science base of any MD/Ph.D. student was unsatisfactory. Nonetheless, they resisted both an M-3 and an M-4 year for Urbana. From the reaction of Jerry Newman particularly, one would have thought he was in the negotiations with the sole purpose of blocking a four-year program at UC. Grulee was not so adamant, but Newman was absolutely fixated on that negative goal.

As we struggled with the enrollment figures, Phil Forman suggested the possibility of a two-track system for the college: a 1:3 split in the regional track and a 2:2 split in Chicago. He thought such a system might simplify enrollment planning if each of the two tracks were to have a single cohort of students for all four years. There is a time and a place for all good ideas, and this one struck a harmonious chord in all parties. Although the concept of two programs had been the subject of many earlier discussions, especially at LaSalle-Peru, we had never thought of a two-track system within the concept of a single college. The two-track system had something for everyone. It allowed Chicago to basically go its own way as soon as its enrollment was established. For Rockford and Peoria, it guaranteed a 1:3 split and that their programs would be three years and not truncated to two. From my standpoint, it seemed more likely that Chicago, released from the complicated bickering that enmeshed Urbana, Peoria, and Rockford, might be more yielding on its enrollment figures. Furthermore, sometime in the future, a separate track had the potential to be the nucleus of an independent downstate medical school. The two-track system served the needs of all four regional sites and was quickly agreed upon. It was also a morale booster for the group at a time when we seemed to be going nowhere. We returned to the sticky item of enrollment projections with more hope of resolution.

College enrollments in the preceding year had totaled 356 first-year medical students, 250 in Chicago and 106 in Urbana. In the current year, Urbana's first-year enrollment had been cut to 75 while Chicago's remained at 250, so that the total M-1 enrollment was 325. There were external pressures on the university to cut its enrollment even more, to 300 per year, but that would have made our negotiations far too difficult, so we stayed for the time being at 325. Forman did not want to drop below 210 in Chicago, and Peoria and Rockford were currently operating in their second-year classes with 70 and 50, respectively, figures which added up to 330 M-1 students without a clinical cohort at Urbana. The stage was set for some rough negotiations.

It was gratifying to see Ron Brady, somewhat exhausted by four hours of acrimonious debate, finally etch into the glaring empty M-4 box in the Urbana column the number "20." Newman, grimly resigned to clinical training in Urbana, said nothing. Twenty was there for the moment and the box would never be empty again.

We were close, but I knew that the cost per student at 20 per class would be astronomical and would make us highly vulnerable to rescission, so I continued to argue strongly for a minimum cohort of 30. I pointed out that Grulee and Newman had earlier talked in terms of a minimum cohort size of 50 for their schools in Rockford and Peoria. Asking for only 30 per class was a very moderate request. I had done the numbers for 20, 30, 40, and 50 students and knew that cost per student did not really come under control until class size was 36 or greater. But Rockford and Peoria became fixed on holding Urbana to no more than 20 per class before posturing to establish their own "absolute minimum" number of 55 each. This represented a 15-student loss for Peoria that Newman accepted if only to limit Urbana to 20 or less per year. At this stage, Chicago had 200, Rockford and Peoria had 55 each, or 110, and we, at Urbana had 20. We had reached another impasse; it seemed nobody would budge.

At this point, it occurred to me that I would never get the 30 students per class that I believed to be a minimum size cohort. Newman and Grulee, as well as Forman and Cohen, already thought I was getting too much with an enrollment figure of 20. Heels were dug in pretty hard and there was no movement. We were engaged in negotiation by exhaustion. We had talked without a break since 10 a.m., and it was then about 3 p.m. With this in mind, I offered Brady, the man with the all-powerful chalk in his hand, a deal for a consensus solution: I would settle for 25 if we could increase total college enrollment to 331. It was clearly a major compromise on my part, and both Brady and Begando knew it. This would provide 200 for Chicago, 53 each for Rockford and Peoria, and 25 for Urbana-Champaign. This required an enrollment increase of one to 331, but that was no problem. Brady chalked onto the board the numbers I had given him. Jerry Newman scowled, but Bud Grulee indicated his satisfaction and so did Phil Forman and Ed Cohen. At last, the shoe was on the other foot and Jerry Newman was odd man out. Jerry relaxed, and we had achieved an enrollment consensus. Although not explicitly stated, except in the enrollment tables, Urbana would have an M-3 and an M-4 year. We had a deal!

There was palpable relief on the faces of both Joe Begando and Ron Brady. Newman continued to fuss, and said his people were going to be very angry when they learned that a four-year program had been approved for Urbana. Bud Grulee, who wound up with enrollment parity with Peoria, voiced the same concern about his people. Forman and Cohen stated they could accept these particular enrollments on one condition: that the agreement would not affect their budget because: "We've already lost so much money. We can't afford to lose any more." I couldn't let that go by without rebuttal so I made it quite clear that the president was now on record for enrollment-driven "equitable funding." I added that I did not consider the present formula that Brady had developed, particularly as it related to residency funding, equitable. However, as it turned out, even using Brady's formula, were there to be an immediate reallocation on the basis of the consensus enrollment, SBMS/SCM-UC would have received a budget increment of more than $1 million.

Grulee and Newman again attacked the four-year program at UC but this time, consensus in hand, Joe Begando made it clear that Urbana already had a four-year program at the time of this negotiation and had already graduated its first class. A four-year program at Urbana was nothing new.

Joe Begando then listed the items we had agreed upon: the one-college, one-dean concept would be accepted; the regional programs would be headed by directors; each regional program would be called "The University of Illinois College of Medicine (at Urbana-Champaign, Rockford, and Peoria)"; there would be two educational tracks, a Chicago track with 200 students per year and a 2:2 configuration, and a downstate track with 131 students per year and a 1:3 configuration; the Chicago school might not be designated the University of Illinois College of Medicine at Chicago because the entity that resulted from the merger of the two Chicago campuses made them the entire University of Illinois at Chicago; wording would be developed in the Board of Trustees resolution to the effect that although the individual schools would be known as the University of Illinois College of Medicine at Chicago, Urbana-Champaign, etc., each would function statutorily as a school within a college; each school would have its own department heads and chairpersons; the directors of the several schools would report to the dean in Chicago; there would not be an executive dean; and the enrollment agreements noted above would be the official numbers for the indefinite future.

I added to the Begando summary that a protocol was being developed between the UIUC and UIMC campuses to review the conditions under which the newly recognized UICOM-UC would function. Raising such a painful issue at this time did not endear me to my colleagues but I wanted it up front that the treaty was going to be reviewed and revised. That was a fact of life.

I left the meeting feeling pretty good. SBMS/SCM-UC was now on the books in a more permanent fashion than ever before as UICOM-UC. It was assigned enrollment numbers that it could handle, largely with MSP students.

I believed it would have been wrong to press on the budget formula that day because I knew that any formula within reason would require the transfer of major assets from all three of the other schools to Urbana and that would not be a popular issue. So my strategy was to settle for the enrollment agreement and give the other schools time to digest it. There would be ample time to discuss the budget at the next meeting on Friday, December 4, 1981.

On returning to Urbana, I immediately scheduled a meeting with the SBMS/SCM-UC Executive Committees for Wednesday, November 25. I summarized the agreements in hand and described the hard bargaining that went on before this agreement had been reached. I also told them I expected that talks on the budget formula would be even more contentious. I also shared with the committees a proposed draft revision of the 1969 treaty between UIMC and UIUC, which last had formal Board of Trustee review in 1970.

The executive committee members were generally supportive of the consensus agreement. Some stated that a cohort size of thirty in the M-3 and M-4 years would have been better than twenty-five and noted that the governance issue still remained to be resolved. Others pointed to the need for local control of MSP admissions, and others complained that nothing really mattered unless and until the funding issue was resolved.

I explained that I agreed that funding was everything, and because of that I requested and was able to set up a meeting with Vice President Brady to discuss formula funding prior to the next task force meeting. I wanted to make certain that Brady had received our second white paper and that I had the opportunity to go over its details with him.

I met with Ron Brady on December 2, after Hal Swartz and I had spent December 1 reviewing the potentials of formula budgeting in minute detail. As we studied the issue, we could predict with reasonable certainty the distribution of the minimal amounts of money that were needed to support clinical-student cohorts of from twenty to sixty per class per year. We knew the process well enough that when extraneous factors were brought into play, such as counting residents as half-time students, we were well prepared to react constructively as to their budgetary effect on all four college sites. My objective in meeting with the vice president before the next bargaining session was primarily to let him know that I had done my homework on budgeting and that when I spoke up on the matter, I was delivering carefully calculated and thought-through opinions on the budgeting process. With this in mind, I summarized for him my views of problems existent within the current funding formulas and recommended a methodology that would be fair to all parties. I gave him a summary of my recent survey of twenty-eight other state-funded medical schools on the basis of dollars per medical student per year, the amount of state appropriations made in four neighboring state medical schools (Michigan, Ohio State, Missouri, and Indiana). It was a lot of data, but not too much for a senior administrator whose role as Vice President for Fiscal Affairs was well established. Brady gave me every reason to believe that he was impressed by the data per se and by the presentation. He listened attentively as I showed him that state funding per medical student averaged $16,800 in the four states mentioned above, while UICOM received $22,822 per enrolled medical student, $6,000 above the mean of our neighboring states. Although the survey showed that some schools did receive state funds for resident teaching, none of the four schools mentioned above did. I also gave the vice president several journal articles reviewing the current funding status of medical education and graduate medical education in the United States.

Earlier discussions had raised the question of how long residents had been included as part-time medical students in the state funding of ALSM, Therefore, I left the vice president a copy of the November 1981 *UIMC Campus Report*, which under the headline: "Fall Enrollment Up at Urbana and Medical Center, Down at Chicago Circle in Keeping with Reductions" stated, "Although program budgets have been trimmed at UIMC, enrollment increased slightly in the Graduate College's non-degree program and *hospital residencies were included for the first time in the total enrollment figure.*" [Emphasis added.] So much for the UIMC administration's claim that residents had "always" been figured into the state funding formula for ALSM.

I also provided the vice president with data from the 1980 fiscal year that compared the budget expenditures of SIU School of Medicine and UICOM. This information, presented at the September 18, 1981 meeting of the Illinois Board of Higher Education, revealed that SIU, which graduated 75 students per year, had spent $17,431,000 that year. In contrast, UICOM spent $32 million for 330 graduates. Clearly, the University of Illinois administration was either lax for not seeking its fair share of the medical-education dollar, or was lax for not challenging the enormous costs that supported SIU. The figures for Peoria, Rockford, and Urbana totaled just about $7 million, less than half of that allocated to SIU, while the combined productivity of the three UICOM schools, 125 MD graduates per year, almost doubled the SIU output of physicians.

Brady and I also discussed the application of fixed and variable costs as they affect formula budgeting. I showed him curves that I had developed relating medical-student enrollment to total costs and cost per student. These curves showed that the cost per student was relatively high at levels of twenty-five to thirty students per class, but approached a more acceptable cost per student when student numbers exceeded fifty-three per class. It followed at this point that Rockford and Peoria, from a formula budgeting standpoint, should prove to be relatively cost-efficient at the enrollment level of fifty-three students per class, whereas UICOM-UC, which emerged from the grand compromise of November 20 with an acknowledged enrollment of twenty-five per class, would still be perched on the higher cost end of the efficiency curve. Despite this, I ventured to the vice president that we could operate less expensively than either Rockford or Peoria and would manage to control fixed and variable costs more effectively.

Once again, a private meeting with the vice president proved very useful. Unlike his boss, with whom I was never able to establish trust or rapport, Brady was willing to listen and absorb the information presented to him. Given that opening, I argued that in my view, adequate state funds already existed within the UICOM budget to support the regionalized system. What was needed was a fair and equitable distribution of state funds, preferably by an enrollment-driven formula. I added that I was prepared to accept whatever formula was developed so long as it was objectively prepared by third parties without an axe to grind. He accepted the concept of a technical budget committee as a fair approach to the problem. He said that he would review the material I had given him before the December 4 meeting. That was all that I could request.

On December 4, Brady, Begando, Newman, Forman, Cohen, Grulee, and I met once again. In the interim, Cohen had resigned as dean of SBMS-MC to clear the way for its merger with ALSM, reuniting the two units to reestablish UICOM-C. Chicago, at least, would revert to its original traditional form. Nevertheless, Begando invited Cohen to the meeting because he had been present at the original session.

Begando asked each dean to report his executive committee's reactions to the agreements of November 20. Newman reported that the Peoria executive committee accepted the agreement with some reservations. The committee saw a four-year school at Urbana as a threat. The members feared that with four-year programs in Chicago and Urbana-Champaign, the next step would be to eliminate Peoria and Rockford and run two medical schools at the two major campus sites. Grulee reported a similar reaction from Rockford. Cohen reported that the Chicago-based SBMS-MC executive committee refused to either accept or reject the report. That panel saw the report as divisive and felt it would ultimately lead to two colleges of medicine, and the members worried that Chicago enrollment reduction might decrease their budget. The ALSM executive committee supported the agreement in principle, but was concerned about the creation of multiple departments within the college without separately designated schools. That committee too was concerned about a reduction in resources with student enrollment reduced. Furthermore, the members did not like the increased college enrollment to 331, which was made possible to accommodate "just one unit." They, too, did not want Urbana to have a four-year program.

It was clear from the very start of these discussions that Urbana was the big bogeyman, the all-pervasive power that was out to dominate or destroy the innocents at the other three sites. The rampant fear of UIUC campus power perceived by the other three sites was at a level difficult to conceive. Having been in this expansion program since the beginning, I had always sensed the administrative ambivalence and, of course, the sibling rivalry that characterized Peoria's behavior, yet I was still naive with respect to the depth of fear and anxiety that had been present all of the time in Chicago and Rockford. The day promised to be difficult. When we talked budget, I would have no friends. My main hope was that I had presented rational arguments to Brady two days before.

Last of the regions to report, I informed the group that my faculty neither approved nor disapproved of the document. Although they voiced a definite preference for thirty students per class rather than twenty-five, they accepted the latter figure. However, they found the document incomplete because it did not address the governance issues between UIMC and UIUC that, in their view, had to be resolved. The faculty also requested well-defined provisions for the admission of Medical Scholars and an equitable plan to correct the historic underfunding of Urbana.

My report provoked a diatribe from Peoria's Jerry Newman, who remained antagonistic to everything I said for the rest of the afternoon. It was apparent again that Newman was more concerned with any gains made by Urbana than he was concerned with the needs or enrollments of Peoria. Even when the chancellor, in discussing enrollments, commented that perhaps Peoria, which at the time of the compromise had an enrollment of seventy per class, had been reduced excessively to fifty-three, Newman's vitriol toward the Urbana program took precedence over the opportunity opened to him. The chancellor suggested that Peoria increase to fifty-five per year and Rockford remain at fifty (where it currently was), a suggestion that Rockford's Grulee did not oppose. But Newman was so fixated on blocking any Urbana proposal that I honestly believe he never heard the chancellor's suggestion, for he completely passed up the wide-open opportunity to capitalize on the chancellor's unopposed offer. The enrollment increment for Peoria never surfaced again, and the Peoria class size, despite the availability of superior clinical facilities, remained at fifty per class.

I had prepared a draft interim reorganization proposal based upon the November 20 meeting. Although I had circulated it in advance, the deans of Rockford, Peoria, and Chicago jointly refused even to look at, let alone discuss it. They were not interested in its content. They were determined that they would not use anything that I prepared as a basis for discussion for fear of a hidden agenda lurking within the depths of my prose. Joe Begando also had prepared a draft reorganization proposal based on the previous discussions. I had reviewed his document carefully in advance and was prepared to comment on it. But every comment I made and every suggested amendment I submitted was knee-jerk rejected by Peoria's Newman even before I could complete the defining sentence.

Begando's draft was a suitable beginning, but omitted some important details. For example, a budget allocation formula had yet to be adopted. The document was also vague on Medical Scholars admission policy, for which I suggested the following wording: "The Admissions Committee will delegate primary responsibility for up to thirty Medical Scholars Program admissions to the Medical Scholars Steering Committee at UIUC."

I believed that this was a common-sense proposal that should have been accepted without debate, but Newman immediately attacked even this recommendation, and the others passively followed his lead. It was a most disappointing meeting and little progress was made.

The work toward an enrollment-driven budget was particularly difficult. The chancellor's draft had proposed that state funding would be "reallocated to the medical-education sites by the use of a consistent, enrollment-driven formula." However, there was a stipulation that said, "Ultimate allocations will be the result of negotiations between the Dean of the College and the

Directors at Peoria, Rockford and Urbana-Champaign, and will be subject to consideration of special or unique program needs at any medical-education site." To me, this wording seemed to give lip service to an formula, while actually giving the Chicago-based dean a free hand. But every effort I made to change the wording met with stiff resistance from my peers, who were apparently desperately afraid that I would run off with the whole pie.

The atmosphere throughout the meeting was so bad and the tensions generated were so high, that I had difficulty finding the right time to approach the gut issue of equitable distribution of the budget, which, of course, meant proportionately more money for Urbana. There was no suitable time, and when I finally did raise the issue, I was met with a howling chorus from the other three sites to the effect that the Urbana clinical program should never have been started at all. Each time the termination of the Urbana clinical program was urged, I had to remind my fellow deans that Urbana's survival was not an issue for these discussions, and that what we were now about was a modus vivendi for all four sites.

Brady and Begando were no help as they remained on the sidelines as the venom poured forth. There was a consensus all right, but the consensus was three against one. Forman summed it up at one point when he said, "We may have to take a proposal to the Academic Council with only three regions supporting it." There was no evidence that my fellow deans were the least bit interested in budget equity for Urbana, and, as the day wore on, I genuinely feared that they were going to revisit the enrollment numbers that were agreed upon November 20. I wanted to hang tough on the budget issue, but it was apparent that I would get nowhere. None of the three was prepared to transfer a nickel to Urbana, and Brady and Begando were not offering any financial aid either. But I did have that prior agreement with Brady, from our December 2 meeting, that some type of neutral technical committee would be appointed to review the funding formula used for budgeting. So even though Brady's present enrollment-driven funding formula, residents and all, was disadvantageous to Urbana, I decided then and there to support it on an interim basis, with the hope that an independent technical group would later come to its own conclusions.

Because of the hostility exhibited by my fellow deans, I decided upon a new strategy that would:

1. avoid any issue that might change the enrollment tables; the SCM-UC clinical program would settle for twenty-five per year at this time.
2. accept the present budgets that were defined by Brady's formulas. The formulas may have been unfair to SCM-UC, but they still provided for an immediate and sizable funding increment for us.
3. make sure the final resolution of the meaning of an "enrollment driven budget" would be defined by an impartial technical committee.
4. make clear to all parties that the UICOM reorganization, by "treaty," required the concurrence of both campuses, UIMC and UIUC.

I was successful on the first three points. We kept our assigned enrollment at twenty-five per year and the Brady formulas were endorsed pending a technical review. When I raised the fourth point, regarding the governance issue, Newman relapsed into a frenzy of opposition: Bloomfield was a disloyal, ungrateful cad. I had to agree with Joe Begando that the consensus discussions were no place to settle the governance problem.

Begando was very determined to achieve a consensus document that all of us would sign. Because funding was the most controversial issue, he led the discussions on that matter until we finally agreed on the following wording: "State-appropriated funds assigned by the university to the College of Medicine will be allocated to the medical-education sites at Chicago, Peoria, Rockford, and Urbana-Champaign through a consistent and equitable enrollment-driven budget formula, subject to consideration of special, unusual or unique program needs at any medical-education site. *Further, the university will establish a technical task force to continue to refine the budget formula now being used as a point of departure for this planning process.*" [Emphasis added.]

Of course, this was also ambiguous wording, with something for everyone. What medical education program did not have "special, unusual or unique programmatic needs?" Although Brady delivered on his promise to establish an independent technical review of funding, the technical task force mandate was watered down to refining "the budget formula now being used as a point of departure." After all, there had never been an enrollment-driven budgeting formula for the college before the one Begando and Brady dreamed up in their August 7 report to the president, and that formula was more of an attempt to justify the relatively large ALSM budget than to analyze the real fixed and variable costs of medical education. Given the livid hostility toward Urbana from all sides, though, I could live with the wording and joined the consensus on that issue.

It had been a long afternoon. When it was over, we had finally agreed upon or confirmed the following:

1. All four regional programs would be continued.
2. There would be a two-track system, with Chicago alone as one track, and Peoria, Rockford, and Urbana-Champaign as the second track.
3. Each regional program would have a stable cohort of students.
4. Allocation of state funds would be primarily determined by consistent, enrollment-driven formulas.
5. The executive committee of the new college would have no regional unit with greater than 50 percent voting representation.
6. There would be special admissions processes for dual-degree programs, including the Medical Scholars Program.

I am not certain that Forman, Newman, or Grulee truly understood the budgetary implications of item four and how it would give UICOM-UC leverage to receive a significantly larger share of the college budget than was the case at that time. They placed their faith in negotiation by verbal amendment and commentary as Phil Forman did when he agreed to the forthcoming technical task force as long as the ALSM budget would not be reduced. Newman and Grulee were quick to second that view, and neither Begando nor Brady had the stomach to tell them otherwise. My comments on the matter were never heard, drowned as they were, in a sea of Newman's vitriol. They would find out in time and would protest vigorously the reallocations demanded by the formula, but the phraseology of item four was important for our survival. The university, represented by the vice president and the chancellor, was a party to the compromise and would ultimately have to deal with the reallocation issue with real dollars.

Despite the acrimony, we had arrived at a consensus that I will refer to as "The Grand Compromise." By December 9, Joe Begando had prepared a document for our signatures that we could deliver to the college faculty and to the president for their review and approval. We had accomplished in two days of hard bargaining a reorganization plan that would be approved by large majorities of faculty at all four sites, something that Mort Creditor had failed to do over the previous eighteen months.

CHAPTER 36

Clinging to the Consensus

T HE REORGANIZATION IMBROGLIO appeared to be over. We now entered a period of expectant waiting: waiting for our survival to become official through action of the Board of Trustees; waiting for the technical task force on the budget formula to be formally organized and charged; and waiting, rather naively, for the additional dollars that the task force's deliberations should provide. We were waiting also for the stream-lined governance that always seemed just beyond our reach. The fragile consensus we had achieved made all of these goals possible. Our task now was to preserve the consensus.

We agreed on December 4 that the technical task force, or TTF, as it became known, would be made up of school business managers and a representative finance officer from the central administration. I was reasonably confidant that the TTF would give SCM-UC as fair a shake as possible because, for the first time, the UICOM budget was to be analyzed by relatively disinterested parties. Peter Czajkowski, assistant vice president for financial affairs, was to lead the group. He was known to the fiscal people on the Urbana campus as a very level-headed straight shooter. Rick Schimmel, my business manager at SBMS/SCM-UC, was certainly perceptive, level-headed, and effective. Furthermore, Mike Harms, who was business manager for Phil Forman in Chicago and who would represent ALSM on the TTF, was formerly my business affairs dean. I had absolute confidence in Mike's integrity. He could be relied upon to be as objective as possible under the circumstances, and all I really wanted and needed from the TTF was objectivity.

UIUC Vice Chancellor Ned Goldwasser had been keeping abreast of the consensus talks. I told him that I had tried to raise the governance issue but that none of the deans wanted to engage in any form of talk that might loosen the UICOM's ties to our program. At Goldwasser's request we had already prepared bare-bone, yet realistic budgets for eight different enrollment scenarios. For the enrollment scenario in the Grand Compromise, a

budget requirement of $4.222 million had been generated. Characteristic
of his sensible and thorough approach, Ned wrote me on December 10
acknowledging the December 4 consensus agreement. He said that the
"current thinking inclines towards $3.5 million at Urbana." So he asked
for budget projections based on that figure rather than $4.222 million. He
wanted to know specifically what faculty hiring we'd have to forgo "and how
you would do without them in order to live on $3.5 million."

It was not an easy question to answer, but I sent him a revised budget
based upon $3.5 million, showing a reduced number of full-time faculty and
indicating that we would have to rely more heavily on volunteer faculty than
we had planned. It was plain that the UIUC campus, in this era of limited
state resources and significant belt-tightening, did not want to assume the
burden of an underfunded medical school.

I wrote to Paul Stone on December 9, telling him that I was optimistic
that a feasible reorganization consensus was being worked out and that the
Urbana program would have the opportunity to develop the excellence that
the UIUC campus expected. I praised both Joe Begando and Ron Brady,
who had guided the discussions skillfully to a fruitful conclusion. I warned
Stone, however, that we still had a long way to go and that probably continued pressure from the Board of Trustees would be necessary until all the elements were firmly in place. Keeping in mind that the next step called for the
creation of a TTF that would recommend budget allocations to four badly
divided and mutually suspicious academic units, allocations that were to be
based upon a formula that did not yet exist, I appealed to Stone: "It is very
important that I review with you carefully and beforehand any Board of
Trustees items that appear on the reorganization matter."

I knew that what I needed most in order to achieve a satisfactory budget
for the school soon to be known as UICOM-UC was a level playing field. In
fact, the more level it was, the better we would do. But I remained concerned that in the absence of any other source of new funds, when the other
units of the college found out what a level playing field meant, they would
balk at any reallocation whatsoever from their resources to UICOM-UC.

To ensure that the TTF had a complete database from which to work,
I took advantage of my location at UIUC and scheduled a meeting with
Assistant Vice President Peter Czajkowski, who would lead that group. We
met at his Urbana office on December 17. I had sent him a packet of information that was quite similar to one I had sent to Ron Brady before our

December 2 meeting. Included with the materials was a copy of the presidential statement calling for equitable and realistic funding at all four sites, which I explained to Czajkowski was very important because the old, tired, yet oft-repeated disclaimers of "sorry, we have no money for Urbana" were no longer operational. Urbana was finally due its fair share! I told Czajkowski of my earlier meeting with Ron Brady, showing him the same data and the same reprints on costs of medical education that I had shared with Brady. In the packet I laid out the budget case for UICOM-UC as I saw it. Finally, I personally encouraged him to add a UIUC business figure to the TTF.

Pete Czajkowski proved to be a good listener. After explaining every detail of the budgeting process that came to mind, I felt reasonably confident that if there were no constraints or other conditions exacted by President Ikenberry, which appeared unlikely, the UICOM-UC medical-education programs would finally be dealt with fairly and equitably.

With the Grand Compromise signed by all parties to the agreement, our task was to have the package approved by our respective executive committees before a special meeting of the Academic Council was convened on December 23. After that, the proposal would have to be approved by the College of Medicine faculty as a whole. The UICOM-UIUC governance issue remained unresolved, but that was assigned to Chancellors Cribbet and Begando to sort out so that the entire package—reorganization and governance—could be presented to the Board of Trustees in February 1982. At least that was my understanding. But as the old saying goes: "There is many a slip 'twixt the cup and the lip."

By December 21, the Grand Compromise, better known as "the Deans' proposal," appeared to have been approved intact by the executive committees of Rockford, Peoria, and Urbana-Champaign. The proposal did not have easy sledding before the combined SBMS/SCM-UC Executive Committees. After signing the document, I called a special meeting of the committees on December 15 to ratify it. I related in painful detail the hard negotiations that had taken place and summarized the proposal's elements. I tried to explain my strategic views and the problems we faced, concluding that it was about the best deal we could have hoped for at the time. The faculty finally approved the deal, but not without requiring two major commitments on my part. The governance was to be worked out promptly so that Board of Trustees might approve it at the same time as the Grand Compromise, and the reallocation of resources within the college would have to be significant so that the UICOM-UC programs would be adequately funded.

Before the final vote was taken, I advised my executive committees that I would stake my reputation on the successful conclusion of the negotiations. This was not an off-the-cuff statement. I was beginning to weary of the struggle, and unless we came out of these talks with an acceptable operating budget and satisfactory governance, I was prepared to step down as dean.

The proposal was not having an easy time in Chicago either, as I learned from Marten Kernis a week later. Kernis warned me that I should forgo tele-conferencing and be physically present in Chicago at the upcoming special meeting of the Academic Council. I called Phil Forman to learn more about ALSM faculty's problems with the proposal. Phil informed me that some ALSM faculty members were balking at certain specific terms used in the consensus. Many wanted to remove the clause that permitted the regional schools to function as though they were "schools within a college." Others wanted to delete any reference that would define a separate school in Rockford, Peoria, and Urbana-Champaign, they balked at the establishment of regional executive committees, and they wanted to include wording that the directors of Urbana, Rockford, and Peoria would report to the dean in Chicago. Phil assured me that he was not sympathetic to those faculty concerns, and I had no reason to doubt him.

Phil also mentioned that he was aware of the "Cribbet document," which he felt would also cause concern to his faculty, and that was an understatement. I avoided discussing the document with Phil at this time and simply told him that I had read it and had certainly been consulted on its preparation. I was not prepared to discuss with Phil my close relationship to the document, even though that would have been self-evident to anyone reading it. Later, I called Jerry Newman in Peoria regarding the ALSM concerns. Jerry did not believe that anyone in Peoria would support ALSM and declared that Peoria would not agree to any changes in the consensus document. Bud Grulee's position in Rockford was similar.

On December 22, I met with John Cribbet, Ned Goldwasser, and Jane Loeb to review the Cribbet document. Chancellor Cribbet described the December 15 meeting of the university policy council, which included higher administration from all three campuses, in addition to the president and vice presidents. Cribbet reported that Begando said that he believed the reorganization proposal had been carried about as far as it could go in the deans' committee and that any attempt to be more specific regarding

Urbana program governance would have been counterproductive. *He also commented that Peoria was more concerned about Urbana-Champaign than it was about Chicago.* [Emphasis added.] Begando then stated that he and Mack Schmidt had reviewed the Cribbet document and "believed it was premature." He suggested that the term "governance" be dropped from the document because it represented too rapid a movement toward two colleges and that some form of protocol be included for continued study of the problem. He stated that UIUC had accomplished its two major objectives: (a) it had saved its clinical program from dissolution, and (b) it had positioned itself well for the future.

Cribbet reported that it was apparent that the president and general university officers had not reviewed the document, and it seemed to him that they did not wish to do so. He described the president as very anxious to present the UICOM consensus document to the Board of Trustees in February. In light of this, Begando and Cribbet had agreed to accelerate their negotiations on the Cribbet document. Begando had promised to send Cribbet a counterproposal before Christmas.

Cribbet told us that he had two major objectives at this time: (a) to preserve the program and (b) to develop protocols or operating procedures that would facilitate, at an appropriate time, a separate College of Medicine. He reiterated that he did not think the time was now. At this point, I interrupted and advised him that if we somehow received the $4 million necessary to run the program within the next two years that a separate school could be possible. He agreed and mentioned that it might even be less time than that.

Before the meeting ended, I summarized for the group the two major concessions that had already been made by the Urbana program in the consensus document: (a) we had reduced our M-2, M-3, and M-4 annual enrollments from thirty to twenty-five; and (b) we had agreed to remove the term "school" in our title. As for the future, I added, we already had eleven years of delays and hedged promises relating to the 1970 document, and we wished to avoid another eleven years of the same. Because a separate school of medicine was potentially in the works, I said we should develop a transition program to make it easier to effect. I added that, if and when the separation came, I personally hoped it would come without Peoria and Rockford, which would allow them to continue their relationships with the Medical Center.

Creditor convened the special meeting of the Academic Council on

December 23 to act upon the Grand Compromise. Approval of the Deans' proposal was critical to the future of medical education at Urbana. It contained numbers that guaranteed a minimal enrollment and a full four-year program, as well as the framework for budget equality. My goal was to see it through unamended.

At 10 a.m., four hours before the AC meeting, Mort assembled the Advisory Council of Deans to discuss changes in the consensus document requested by ALSM. Phil Forman, speaking for ALSM, repeated that his main desire was to eliminate the phrase that referred to regional units "as though they were schools within a college." Of course, eliminating such a phrase was very objectionable because our whole concept of autonomy derived from it. I had alerted Jerry Newman and Bud Grulee that this was coming right after Phil called me. So they were well primed, and both promptly took exception to Forman's proposal when it was raised in the meeting. For once, I did not have to be the naysayer, but when prodded by Creditor, I agreed that such a change would destroy the consensus. Creditor, Forman, and Newman, in particular, were very anxious that the AC ratify the Deans' proposal on this day without another divisive fight. There remained considerable UIMC concern that the legislature could do the reorganization in its own fashion if there were too much squabbling within the College of Medicine. Phil Forman agreed to try to get those of his faculty who sat on the Academic Council into line, and we adjourned the meeting at about 11 a.m., three hours before the AC meeting. We also agreed to meet again at 1:45 p.m., fifteen minutes before the AC meeting, to discuss what to do if Phil failed in his attempt to persuade his AC representatives to accept the consensus agreement as it stood.

Meanwhile, by telephone, I discussed Forman's statements with Hal Swartz. Hal and I agreed that perhaps it might be possible to work out a deal with ALSM: If they would support the Cribbet governance recommendation and support our efforts to get a $4 million budget, we could support "the schools" issue. I liked Hal's idea and took it to Forman's office, where Forman considered it briefly but concluded that neither of the Urbana goals would be acceptable to ALSM. The money issue was particularly sensitive in Chicago because, although the Medical Center campus had the lion's share of state dollars, the schools there believed that they had too little to prosper and grow in keeping with modern demands. In fact, Phil also wanted to attach an amendment to the consensus agreement that would permit ALSM to retain all of its own indirect cost reimbursements and Medical Service Plan funds, but I told him that I would not agree to such an amendment because that was a matter for the TTF.

The deans' council reconvened as planned at 1:45. Phil said that he had discussed all the sensitive issues with his faculty and thought that the proposal would pass without change. Then at 1:55 p.m., five minutes before the Academic Council was to convene, Phil casually unloaded his own hidden agenda. He cited one issue that remained a problem for ALSM: the so-called "Cribbet document." Forman said that many members of his faculty were disturbed by the document and that he wanted to raise the issue at this time. Needless to say, when there was any mention of Urbana's governance, Newman and Grulee's ears perked up. It looked for a time as though the fat was in the fire because, outside of Urbana itself, there was a uniform consensus throughout the college to never let Urbana even think about loosening its ties with the Medical Center and going its own way.

Creditor worried that discussion of Cribbet's proposal at the AC meeting would "blow the entire consensus," but Phil Forman said that he had drafted a resolution that would not let that happen. Forman added that his proposal was harmless because it simply stated that the 1970 Treaty for the organization and administration of the Urbana-Champaign program would remain in effect and unchanged until after the reorganization was approved by the Board of Trustees; then, it would be renegotiated. But it was a more complicated proposal than met the eye with language that said that revisions "may be proposed following board approval of the reorganization of the College of Medicine and will be considered by the College of Medicine and recommendations forwarded for subsequent consideration by campus and university administration." That was clearly unacceptable language to replace the Treaty of 1969–70. The UIUC campus never ceded the Treaty review process to initial consideration by the College of Medicine.

I puzzled at the maneuver. It was unlike Phil Forman, who had never played a heavy role in the intercampus relationships up until this time. He was seen as a very competent administrator and appeared to be rising as the undoubted leader of the merger that recombined ALSM and SBMS-MC. He had been very constructive at the consensus discussions: suggesting the two-track system and agreeing to reduce the Chicago enrollment. Regarding Urbana governance, Phil seemed to have been an advocate of laissez faire. I was uncertain whether Phil believed that ALSM interests, particularly those of his clinical-department heads, were threatened by SBMS/SCM-UC autonomy or whether Joe Begando (unlikely), Mort Creditor (more likely), or Marty Kernis (doing Mort Creditor's bidding) had a hand in the initiative. (A 1995 discussion with Forman revealed that the opinions of his clinical department heads were dominant.)

In any event, the initiative was designed to thwart the Urbana strategy to strike for a favorable governance change while the iron was hot. The iron was indeed hot at UIUC; the entire campus had been alerted to the problems that SBMS/SCM-UC had with UIMC governance, and the UIUC Senate was on record calling for the transfer of SBMS/SCM-UC governance from UIMC to UIUC at the time of reorganization. That evening, I learned from Ned Goldwasser that Begando had called Cribbet before this meeting to read him excerpts from the Forman resolution. On hearing it, Cribbet told Begando that he was satisfied with the resolution because, in his view, it reaffirmed what the Medical Center had all but denied over the preceding decade, the standing of UIUC in the Treaty and in the governance of UICOM-UC. But John Cribbet had clearly not studied the resolution's fine print, which was expertly designed to maintain the status quo.

Caught off guard and seeing that approval of the Forman amendment would limit whatever leverage we had in Urbana to resolve the nagging governance issues, I avoided discussion of the merits of the Forman proposal, saying only that, as far as I knew, the Cribbet document was prepared in response to a similar one from Chancellor Begando. Both represented only drafts that followed the mandate of the president to have the two chancellors settle the particular problem of UICOM-UC governance. Nevertheless, Forman stated that he was going to submit the resolution as an appendix to the consensus document that was to be placed before the Academic Council.

Mort Creditor then implied that I had acted immorally to negotiate a consensus with my fellow deans with the hidden agenda of separate or different governance behind it. I was nonplussed by the Creditor attack. My agenda regarding Urbana independence was never hidden from the deans. I reminded the group then and there that I had tried to get a reference to UICOM-UC governance into the consensus proposal but that my efforts had been forcefully rejected by Newman's diatribe. I added, "If the UICOM-UC governance was rejected from our discussions then, it certainly should be rejected now." Nevertheless, it looked as though there was a tacit agreement among Rockford, Peoria, and Chicago to attach the Forman appendix to the Grand Compromise.

By that time, it was 2:10 p.m., and we were already late for the AC meeting. We adjourned, but, instead of going to AC meeting directly, I went to a telephone and quickly called Hal Swartz in Urbana-Champaign. I had previously given him instructions that our faculty was to keep silent during the meeting because it looked like the consensus document would be accepted and that was our fundamental ticket to survival. However, at this point I told him to rescind all instructions regarding faculty silence because the whole consensus was in serious trouble if the Forman appendix passed. I asked him to promptly inform our faculty representatives on the Academic Council, who listened by conference telephone, that they should think about a course of action if and when Forman's appendix was introduced.

At the special AC meeting, the only agenda item was the consensus document. After it was introduced, Phil Forman moved to add the appendix as an amendment. This was immediately seconded by another Chicago representative. I raised a point of order that the appendix was not a proper topic for discussion because this was a special meeting with a single agenda item. Mort Creditor ruled against me, declaring that because the appendix was related to the main proposal, it was an appropriate item for the agenda.

At this point, Allan Levy from SCM-UC, via the telephone, made an eloquent argument that the original consensus document had been reviewed by the Urbana faculty and that the faculty had agreed to the proposal as it was distributed, without any amendments. The Urbana-Champaign faculty also believed that it was improper procedure to amend the document at this late date and recommended that the document should go forward intact. Therefore, Levy argued, he would be constrained to vote against any attempted amendment.

An interesting process then took place. Mort Creditor stated that he would, if the movers of the amendment would withdraw the amendment, bring the amendment up after the Deans' proposal was acted upon. But Allan Levy again responded with eloquence that if such a proposal were to be placed on the agenda after the main proposal, he would consider that improper and would vote against both. Mort then, fearful of a divided house once again, said he would then not add it to the agenda. The next item of business was moving and seconding the Deans' proposal. Mort asked for discussion on the proposal. There was no discussion at all. The official minutes of the AC special meeting of December 23, 1981 read: "On motion of

Dr. Bloomfield, the proposal for college reorganization, promulgated by the school deans, the chancellor, and the executive vice president, was approved by the Academic Council. (17-aye; 0-nay; 6-abstentions)"

The ALSM faculty was stunned. It was all over so fast. There was no vote on the amendment, and the consensus document went through without a vote against it. I was quite pleased. Somehow the ALSM contingent was not alert or didn't react quickly enough to Allan's debate to have the amendment approved in some form. Forman was angry and said he would place it on a future agenda, as indeed he did, but this meeting adjourned in peace. However, I felt a cold shoulder from just about everybody else in the meeting room, except for my own Urbana-Champaign faculty.

Chancellor Begando, who was also in attendance at the AC meeting, was prepared to speak for the proposal but relieved that he did not have to. He asked to meet with the deans afterward. When all of the faculty members had left the room, the chancellor asked each of us to sign another copy of the proposal, which we did. At this point, there was further discussion about the proposed appendix. Mort Creditor, with his unfailing moral certitude, again publicly excoriated me because he felt that I, as a dean and a colleague, had double-crossed everybody by negotiating with one hand hidden behind my back holding a separate document. Jerry Newman, not to miss a trick, asked how in the name of ethics and morals I could possibly do such a thing? Chancellor Begando was there. He knew very well that (a) the Cribbet document had been transmitted to him before our first meeting on November 20, (b) I had tried to raise these governance issues during the discussions and that he, Vice President Brady, and I had agreed that we would not raise specific UIUC-UIMC governance issues during the consensus negotiations, and (c) I had tried to introduce merely a reference to the pending UIUC-UIMC governance issue into the consensus proposal and that was completely rejected by the other deans. The chancellor, who might have spoken up at this time to confirm my arguments, simply remained silent and allowed me to take the heat. He did say that he was concerned that the UIUC Senate should ratify the consensus proposal and do so before an agreement was made to amend the 1970 Treaty. He said he was going to ask me specifically for help in getting this consensus proposal through the UIUC Senate. All I could do at that point was remain silent because I was not sure I could help him in that respect.

Before I left Chicago that day, I returned to Mort Creditor's office and privately told him that he was absolutely off base when he accused me of double-crossing anyone. Mort, never one to back down, did not see it that way. There was no further discussion, and our estranged positions grew a little farther apart and a little cooler.

A disheartened Creditor had submitted his resignation to Vice Chancellor Schmidt on November 19, 1981. This was neither acknowledged nor made public until December 15. His given reason for resigning was that the reorganization process was completed, but Creditor was clearly upset by Ikenberry's unexpected shift in position in October. Some years later I talked with Marten Kernis, who succeeded Creditor as acting executive dean. Kernis was well versed in UIMC politics and knew pretty well what was going on at the Medical Center at that time. As Kernis described it, after the SPMC report had been submitted to the Academic Council, Schmidt and Ikenberry had concocted their own reorganization plan without consulting Creditor or anyone else in the college. Schmidt and Ikenberry called their plan "Option II," but it differed significantly from the SPMC Option II.

In retrospect, Kernis believed that Mort should have resigned as soon as it was clear that Schmidt was distorting the process and had selected an option that was one of his own creation and not really a product of the SPMC deliberations. Schmidt had distorted the SPMC Option II so that it would have remade the college into a completely Chicago-dominated organization. Marty added that when Mort informed Steven Ruma, whom he had hired from MIT as his management consultant to guide him through the reorganization process, of the interference by Schmidt and Ikenberry, the consultant wrote Mort a long letter describing how the process would deteriorate as a result and that Mort would wind up being the scapegoat for an aborted reorganization plan.

Furthermore, according to Kernis, when Schmidt and Ikenberry made adverse decisions that were in conflict with what Mort knew to be correct, Mort protested vigorously every step of the way. In a sense, Mort knew what was right for the college, and he knew what wrongs were being done. However, once he had protested and his protest had been rejected, Marty said, Creditor went along "as a good soldier."

I told Marty that I felt that Mort had made a major mistake by not resigning when Schmidt first interfered in the process, but that in my view, Mort had made an unforgivable mistake when he wrote Schmidt to say that the Medical Scholars Program at UIUC could continue in the absence of a clinical program there. Furthermore, Mort never learned to use and trust his faculty. When Schmidt first interfered in the process, Mort could have used the College of Medicine faculty to figuratively blow Schmidt out of the water. Marty knew very well that on many occasions when adverse decisions were directed toward the Urbana program, I shared those decisions with the faculty. When there was resistance to a particular decision, it was never from me personally, but from my faculty. Mort's failure to use the college faculty to rectify a process that was being distorted by higher administration was a fatal omission.

In October 1994, thirteen years after we had broken off contact as a result of the difficult events of 1981, Mort and Una Creditor visited Champaign, called me at home, and invited Franny and me out for dinner. Mort had retired from his leadership position in geriatrics at the University of Kansas Medical School, so that he and Una now had more time for travel and recreation. I was too stunned by the call to refuse, although I must say I was uneasy about meeting Mort again. The battle wounds that drew us apart were not the kind that healed without a scar; and scars that remained sensitive at that. Mort must have felt the same way because it turned out that he had been in Champaign-Urbana a number of times over the years to see his son Peter, an accountant who lives here, but had never before called me. As it happened, the invitation came from Una, not from Mort.

I thought that the positive side of his return was the chance for me to get better insight into the Chicago thinking during his nearly three-year tenure as interim executive dean, but things didn't work out that way. It was apparent from the very beginning of the evening that he was not here to rehash the unpleasant past. We talked about people at SBMS/SCM-UC, where they were, and what they'd been doing since 1981. We exchanged information on illnesses that had crept up on us as we aged. He was 71, and I was fast approaching 68. We talked hobbies and travel, and I gathered information about his background that I had long forgotten but wished to include here.

He was a graduate of Columbia Medical School. His first academic position was with E. Gray Dimond at the University of Kansas. From there, he went to Michael Reese Hospital, IRMP, and SCM/UC. I also confirmed the dates of his 1981 China trip (October 4 to October 25), which were important to the narrative because he left for China at the high-water mark of the Schmidt Option II plan, convinced that he had overcome our opposition to its implementation, and then returned three weeks later to find that the president had responded to those of us who were dissatisfied with the process and had changed his mind. But as important as it was for me to clarify some events in the narrative, neither of us wished to recall, in any detail, those stressful days.

Franny, tired of the small talk that had carried us through cocktails, hors d'oeuvres, and dinner for better than two hours, asked me whether I was going to talk with Mort about the history of the medical school. Both Mort and I ignored the question as we discussed something else. But after another ten minutes, as we were having after-dinner coffee and the opportunity was escaping, I approached the medical-school history from a safe direction by talking about the LCME, its pressures, and its arrogance. I reminded Mort of his initial ingenuous letter to the LCME and Schofield's blistering reply, which was then followed by Mort's elegant defense of the system. So far, so good. Mort was pleased to talk about the LCME because he thought the accreditors were, at best, inconsistent and, at worst, unethical. He pointed out that the University of Kansas had a branch campus at Wichita that was, in Mort's view, far less formally tied to the Kansas City operation than were Urbana, Peoria, and Rockford to Chicago. He believed the LCME pressure on UICOM was heavy-handed and unjust.

He also expressed resentment at not having been invited to either the twentieth school anniversary party or the tenth anniversary of the Medical Scholars Program. "After all," he said, "I gave the program its name." I avoided mentioning that he almost took it away, as well.

I then approached questions of history again by asking Mort whether he had much contact with Ikenberry during the reorganization work. He grimaced and his head flexed backward almost in an avoidance reaction. "Too much," he said, adding that Ikenberry "never acknowledged my letter of resignation for six weeks and then did so only when I threatened to go public with it." I did not understand exactly what he meant by that, nor did I bother to ask, but Mort, the good soldier, must have deeply resented the presidential about-face that pulled the carpet out from under him. That episode and all the activities of that period were not subject to discussion. So we talked more about Kansas and a little about Nebraska, wrapped up the evening, said our farewells and went our separate ways.

CHAPTER 37

The Empire Strikes Back

W E HAD ENTERED INTO a very delicate phase of the whole process. For two months, events had tilted pretty much in our favor until Forman presented his amendment to the Grand Compromise. We had officially survived; we had been instrumental in establishing a process that should have rationalized our budget allocation; and we had mobilized the UIUC campus to work for our long-range goal of increased autonomy and closer ties to that campus. We genuinely believed that recognition of our academic linkage to the UIUC campus was in the best interest of all concerned: the University of Illinois, the College of Medicine, the faculty of SBMS/SCM-UC, and the students. But it was also clear that those who sat in Chicago, Peoria, and Rockford did not see things our way.

In meeting after meeting, I sensed a growing anger within the Medical Center leadership that "Urbana was having everything its own way." Although I had not burned all my bridges to the Medical Center and I maintained a civil dialogue with all of the key personnel, I had very few friends in that neck of the woods. Forman's amendment was the first evidence of a politically calculated UIMC reaction that opposed the Urbana gains and that worked to maintain the status quo, even to the point of permitting our students and school to wither on a "starvation budget." Despite the political progress we had made, there was no recognition of our obvious budget needs.

The last hurdle of the Grand Compromise within UICOM was its approval at the faculty meeting of January 4, 1982. The proceedings were teleconferenced to all four regional sites and to the Danville VA hospital. Attending were 224 members of the faculty: 132 from Chicago, 31 from Peoria, 31 from Rockford, and 30 from Urbana-Champaign and Danville. Chancellor Begando was present ex officio. Almost all discussion of the resolution to accept the Deans' proposal, prior to the vote, came from members of the Chicago faculty, who repeatedly attempted to amend the document by discussion. They wanted to make sure that the agreement that was on the table would not reduce the Chicago budget in any way. They insisted that all indirect cost reimbursements and Medical Service Plan funds that they generated would remain at the Medical Center and that special educational obligations at the Medical Center, such as those related to teaching residents, graduate students, cross-loaded students from other colleges, and disadvantaged students, would be considered in the budgeting formula. In short, they specified that they wanted nothing less than the status quo.

After making these self-serving interpretations, the Chicago faculty leadership then asked each of the deans to confirm that this was also their understanding of the budgeting mentioned in the proposal. It was an effective tactic. Suddenly, we were in a situation of four regional programs in which three already had enough money, and the fourth was a poor Cinderella without a fairy godmother. The questioners promptly put me on the spot. Deans Forman, Newman, and Grulee were satisfied with the budget status quo, and I, of course, was not. I foresaw that acceptance of the current wording of the Deans' proposal would mandate, in the absence of a new funding source outside the college, that a reallocation of funds within the college would have to take place to put UICOM-UC on an equal footing with the other programs. However, I did not want to discuss that eventuality in this hostile forum where in sheer voting strength we were outnumbered almost six to one. The task was to get the Deans' proposal approved, not to win debating points on the budgeting reallocation process.

I remained silent as long as possible until being forced to respond on whether I agreed with the then-current system of resource allocation. Avoiding a direct answer, I took the carefully circumscribed position that I agreed with the reorganization proposal as written, that funds would be allocated to the schools "through a consistent and equitable enrollment-driven budget formula."

Some of my interlocutors continued to press for a "yes" or "no" answer, but all that I could or would say to them was that I agreed to no more and no less than what I signed in the consensus proposal. I also told them that it was my impression that the interpretation of language in the agreement that stated "the university will establish a Technical Task Force" meant that Executive Vice President Brady would form the technical committee to review the budget formula.

At that point, Chancellor Begando took issue with me, stating that it was his understanding that the Medical Center campus would appoint the technical committee and that the TTF would be handled almost entirely at the Medical Center campus. (The old gambit of the fox guarding the hen house.) Surrounded by a faculty that begrudged our existence, I was not about to engage the chancellor in a public debate at that point, even though his surprising interpretation was clearly not mine and was a formula for disaster. Finally, I told an exasperated group of Chicago, Peoria, and Rockford faculty that my signature was on the document as it was written and that I considered it improper to amend the document by discussion. If people had specific amendments, they were welcome to make them, otherwise the document stood as written and presented.

Although I took a verbal beating from the floor, no new amendments were offered. Forman did not raise the issue of his amendment to the proposal either. With the discussion ended, the Deans' proposal (or the Grand Compromise or the Consensus Agreement) was ratified by the College of Medicine faculty: 173 for, 37 opposed, and 14 abstentions. Of the 37 no votes, 33 came from Chicago, and four came from our own faculty in Urbana-Champaign. More importantly, there were faculty majorities in favor of the agreement at all four regional sites. Begando and I were both relieved by the positive vote, but for very different reasons. Begando was fulfilling the president's charge to have the consensus ready for the February Board of Trustees meeting, and I saw it as another punch in our survival ticket.

After the meeting, I telephoned Ron Brady to inform him of the different perceptions that the chancellor and I had regarding the makeup of the TTF. It was his impression that he and Joe Begando would jointly form the task force, that Peter Cjzakowski would chair the committee, and that each dean would appoint one representative. I suggested to Ron that Joe Preissig, the finance officer of the College of Medicine, should be on the committee and recommended that Ned Goldwasser appoint a UIUC fiscal representative as well. To my relief, Brady responded positively to those suggestions.

On January 6, 1982, the UIMC Senate, chaired by Chancellor Begando, assembled at its regular monthly meeting time. The UICOM reorganization was an early agenda item that provoked no discussion and was almost unanimously approved. The Senate then went on to its remaining agenda. The Urbana-Champaign senatorial representatives, believing that there was no further Senate business pertaining to UIUC, left the meeting early for the long ride home. Their departure was probably not observed by any of the Chicago people; in any event, no one sought to inform the Urbana-Champaign senators that a resolution affecting the Deans' proposal would be introduced later.

Toward the end of the meeting, the chancellor introduced Phil Forman, stating that he had a resolution to submit. Forman then submitted a resolution that, in effect, was the same appendix to the Deans' proposal that had been raised but not acted upon at the Academic Council meeting a fortnight earlier. The only person besides Phil Forman, the chancellor, and several ALSM senators who understood what was going on at this point was Paul Hattis, a Medical Scholar from Urbana who happened to be in attendance because of his position as President of the University Medical Student Council. Hattis argued vigorously that this was a major change in the consensus agreement and that such an action would infuriate the UIUC Senate because it was solely a negative, delaying action. He also pointed out that President Ikenberry had requested that the chancellors of UIMC and UIUC resolve the Urbana program's governance issue. Nevertheless, even though the appendix document was defective in its historical references, and even though few members of the assembly were aware of the complex background behind the resolution, it was approved unanimously except for the vote of medical student Hattis.

Paul Hattis called me about the incident at 8 p.m., and that same evening I telephoned Hal Swartz, Allan Levy, and Ned Goldwasser, and discussed the issue briefly with each one. There was little for any of us to do until we actually saw the text of the approved resolution. Paul Hattis brought the resolution text into my office the next morning. It was immediately obvious that although the substance achieved what the Medical Center wanted (i.e., a separation of the Board of Trustees' approval of the Deans' Proposal from any decision regarding Urbana's governance and the filtration of any future governance recommendation through UICOM, where it would inevitably die), the document was in violation of the 1969–70 Treaty that specified that major policy changes, such as the college reorganization, required "mutual agreement…between the two campuses involved."

I arranged to meet at 9 a.m. at Mercy Hospital with Ben Williams, Ron Aldrich, Allan Levy, John Stewart, and Hal Swartz to discuss whether we needed to take any particular action. Ron Aldrich was the first to speak. He saw this issue as reflecting on the integrity of President Ikenberry, who had promised that he would see to it that the two chancellors met to resolve the governance issues by the time the college-reorganization plan was reported to the Board of Trustees. This postponement of the resolution of governance issues was really a reflection on presidential integrity and he should be so informed, Aldrich argued. There was general concurrence with Aldrich's opinion, although no one desired to make presidential integrity a public issue. Ron Aldrich was encouraged to contact the president.

Shortly after we adjourned, Ikenberry spoke in a conference call with Williams and Aldrich. He told them that it was his understanding that the reorganization compromise had been arrived at without any strings attached, including resolution of the governance issue. Furthermore, he believed that the administration was empowered to handle the governance and that it was not really a Senate issue. He also commented that the January 6 action of the UIMC Senate, which approved the Forman appendix, was of no consequence. Ikenberry acknowledged that he was sympathetic with Begando's desire to delay any governance decision until after the Board of Trustees had acted, but both Ben and Ron vigorously opposed this. They argued that a delay would be breaking faith with his agreements to the local group that had published the "Open Letter," as well as to the UIUC faculty. Ikenberry was slow in recognizing this but ultimately suggested that, as he saw it, there were two possible outcomes to the Urbana governance issue. Should Cribbet become a reactor to his faculty, then Begando could also become a reactor to his faculty, and there would be a bicampus faculty impasse. The alternative way, which he still endorsed, was to have Begando and Cribbet resolve the issue by themselves. Ben and Ron informed Ikenberry that they certainly favored the negotiated route and believed that the community and campus would support whatever agreement the two chancellors could achieve. Thus, the telephone conference ended on a hopeful note.

Meanwhile, Joe Begando had proudly reported to the president that the Deans' proposal had been approved by the faculty of the college on January 4, 1982 and by the Medical Center Senate on January 6, 1982. He noted that the January 4 vote represented faculty majorities at all four medical-education sites: Chicago, Peoria, Rockford, and Urbana-Champaign. He added that it was his "hope that the Senate Council and the Senate at UIUC also will indicate their support for the revised reorganization plan...and that action by the Board of Trustees on February 18, 1982 is especially important."

That same Thursday morning, January 7, I tried to contact Ned Goldwasser at about 10:30 a.m., but he was not available. Goldwasser informed me later that he had been busy because he and Ted Brown, Dean of the Graduate College, had been asked to see the president that morning, presumably after the phone call with Aldrich and Williams, and they had discussed the Urbana governance issue for two hours. Ikenberry tried to take the long-range view that settlement of this UIMC-UIUC governance was of no consequence in the immediate future but should be delayed until after the Board of Trustees met. Goldwasser, with Ted Brown concurring, declared to the President, "You have a serious, I mean, a serious Senate problem."

It took very strong talk on the part of Ted and Ned to convince the president that there really was serious faculty concern about the resolution of this issue. Ikenberry suggested that perhaps he would get a working committee of faculty from both campuses to resolve the issue. Goldwasser said that the issue had gone far beyond that. The faculties were far too polarized at that point to come up with any solid solutions. Finally, after two hours of interchange, the president indicated that he was thinking in terms of pulling together Begando and Schmidt, Goldwasser and Cribbet, Ron Brady and himself to resolve the governance issues between the two campuses. Hearing this from Goldwasser, I felt somewhat reassured that perhaps the governance issue would be resolved in the relatively near future, and thus Forman and the Medical Center administration would have achieved exactly the opposite of what they had intended to achieve by the UIMC Senate action.

Since leaving Chicago in the twilight of December 23 after the enervating and discouraging meetings held that day, I had become more certain than ever that the governance for UICOM-UC should be substantially revised. No one at UICOM would forgive us for surviving the reorganization intact, and given the extraordinary suspicion, hostility, and anger directed toward me and Urbana-Champaign during the talks that brought forth the Grand Compromise, I became convinced that our governance should be in line with the "Cribbet document" that was presumed to be in negotiation between UIUC Chancellor John Cribbet and UIMC Chancellor Joe Begando.

The Cribbet document was UIUC's attempt to revisit the Treaty, and it evolved from the draft proposal that was vehemently opposed by Jerry Newman at the initial deans' consensus meeting in November 1981.

However, after I had given my original draft to Vice Chancellor Ned Goldwasser, the proposal had evolved into a UIUC document by the time it was first sent to Joe Begando. Although I continued to advise Cribbet and Goldwasser on wording, I played no role in the final UIUC positions.

The document essentially reaffirmed the original Treaty's long-range goal of a separate College of Medicine at Urbana-Champaign, and asked that one of President Ikenberry's principles for the College of Medicine's reorganization be amended. Ikenberry had declared, "We must end up with a single College of Medicine capable of self-governance." To which the document would add, "until such time as changed circumstances, fiscal and otherwise, make it possible to consider a separate College of Medicine for the Urbana-Champaign campus." The document said, "current realities…include the president's concurrence with John Cribbet's addendum." The document acknowledged that until such time arose, UICOM-UC would be part of UICOM. However, it stated that details of a consistent, enrollment-driven funding formula remained to be worked out *before* the reorganization could go into effect. [Emphasis added.] The document also set programmatic goals and described specific operational and reporting functions that would be delegated by UICOM to the UIUC administration.

The Cribbet proposal was designed to permit UICOM-UC to function optimally while working within the two-campus structure.

So we had high hopes and had generated a wide variety of ideas that would improve function under a more favorable structure. This, together with an equitable formula for budgeting, would relieve many of the major problems and burdens borne by the Urbana program. But the UIMC administration was not prepared to permit that degree of autonomy in a unit that it "owned." For the time being, and in violation of the Treaty, the UIMC strategy was to separate the UICOM-UC governance issue from the reorganization proposal by stalling and delaying action on the governance.

Joe Begando had acknowledged one element of the Treaty obligation: the need for UIUC Senate approval of the college reorganization. At the same time, though, he denied other obligatory elements such as the well-defined linkage between final board approval of the college reorganization and the governance relationships with UIUC.

What should have taken place was an open-ended and frank discussion of the Urbana governance concerns by the consensus group at some time during the reorganization process. However, this did not happen.

The Chicago administration wanted to lock in the reorganization consensus through Board of Trustees action before dealing with Treaty revisions because, once the former was approved, the administration could dally until doomsday with the Treaty revision process. For instance, the counterproposal to the "Cribbet document" that Begando had promised to send by Christmas 1981 to Cribbet never arrived.

Ned Goldwasser prepared a redraft of the Cribbet document and sent it to Begando on January 7, 1982. He wrote, "It remains our hope that you and John Cribbet will be able to reach substantial agreement about some such revised guidelines within the next few weeks." In addition, he told Begando that through discussions with faculty, it had become clear to him that the Grand Compromise "would surely not be acceptable to the Senate unless there were more substance provided regarding the procedures under which the plan would be implemented." He concluded, by saying, "It is to everyone's best interests to have a set of operating procedures under which that program can achieve the highest quality. If it is burdened with bureaucratic and non-essential reporting and approval lines, the program will suffer, the UIUC campus will suffer, and the college of Medicine itself through its overall responsibility for that program, will suffer."

In contrast to Goldwasser's can-do missive, Begando's January 15 response to Goldwasser was an elegant example of bureaucratic double-talk and delay: "I may sound like a broken record, but I believe the revised reorganization plan for the College of Medicine should proceed to the Board of Trustees on February 18, 1982. Representatives from the Medical Center are willing to work with representatives from Urbana-Champaign to update and revise the 1970 document as may be needed. In any event, I thank you and others for working on the 1970 guidelines and forwarding a proposed revision. I will be in touch with Chancellor Cribbet."

With the Urbana governance issue out in the open after the UIMC Senate vote on Forman's proposal, I decided to meet it head on in the Advisory Council of Deans On January 7, I called Bud Grulee, to float a trial balloon by telling him that I would be sending him a copy of the revised Cribbet document for his objective review. Grulee did not seem upset by the prospect of reading the draft. So, on January 12, I sent copies to him and the two other regional deans, Forman and Newman, for their comments. In my letter of transmittal, I specifically asked them: "When you read the proposal, please focus your attention on your own quality concerns and how the

Urbana-Champaign proposal would impinge on them."

All hopes for early resolution of the governance issue were soon dashed. On January 12, Ikenberry wrote to Begando and Cribbet to the effect that he understood that the two chancellors were working on revision of the Cribbet document and that it was a more difficult process than he had anticipated. Therefore, he urged that the chancellors "continue your efforts to recommend revisions to the guidelines and that you report to me your progress on a regular basis and no later than May 30, 1982. Until such time as the revised guidelines are approved by me, the 1970 guidelines for the administration of the program of medical education at Urbana-Champaign shall remain in effect."

It was a very slick way of delaying the Urbana governance decision for five or six months. It was also a worst-case outcome for us. Through a bureaucratic ruse, the president and Begando had co-opted the UIUC administration and succeeded in delaying action for six months on the two issues that were most vital to us: budget and governance. Whether we operated as SBMS/SCM-UC or as UICOM-UC, we were left with gross budgetary inadequacy and within a structure that seemed determined to avoid any reallocation of funds. We were also at the mercy of an angry, hostile administration in Chicago. The empire had struck back, and we were hurting. There was little we could do at this juncture but bide our time.

CHAPTER 38

The Treaty Is Revised

T HE FINANCIAL PROBLEMS facing the Urbana-Champaign campus clouded our prospects for an early resolution to governance and budgetary issues. On January 26, Paula Treichler, Assistant Dean for Student Affairs, told me that Linda Wilson, then the associate dean of the Graduate College, believed that in order to have these issues resolved the UIUC Senate would have to send President Ikenberry "a loud, clear message."

"Even if this message is sent, there still may be problems and she is not sanguine," Treichler reported. "But if this message is *not* sent, she believes the issue may die." Wilson said that UIUC administrators were so over-whelmed by the campus' financial problems that "they cannot help but let issues die which do not cry out for attention, especially the issue of an inad-equately funded medical school."

Treichler told Wilson she was "concerned that they [UIUC administra-tors] do not really know what they are dealing with at the Medical Center and are more ready to take agreements on faith than we are." Wilson agreed and commented, "They don't want to know more than they do because who wants to engage in confrontation politics all the time? So they can't really let themselves see how bad Chicago really is."

Treichler went on to suggest that I talk with several influential people in the UIUC Senate and people who had the ear of Chancellor Cribbet, Vice Chancellor Goldwasser, and Ted Brown, Dean of the Graduate College, in order to move successfully on the governance issue. Our simple message to them and to anybody else who was a potential campus ally was that we really needed rational governance and an adequate budget. Wilson's advice was good, but it came too late. The presidential delay of the governance issue until May 30 had completely deflated our hopes to resolve that prob-lem as a part of the reorganization process, and there was still no money in sight with which to provide SCM-UC with a credible budget.

On February 8, 1982, the UIUC Senate considered a report from its

Committee on Educational Policy regarding the reorganization of UICOM. The committee report served as a useful historical document. First, it summarized the relevant history of past institutional relationships, pointing out that "the program in medical education at the Urbana-Champaign campus rests on a foundation of past history and experience, but it must also be responsive to current realities and to plans for the future."

The committee recommended that the UIUC Senate:

1. Resolve that the program at the School of Medicine, UC is an integral part of the academic programs of this campus and is of major concern to the academic community.
2. Approve the proposed reorganization plan with the understanding that certain issues of vital concern to this campus remain to be resolved.
3. Request that senior administration afford the opportunity for the UIUC Senate to review and act upon a final plan, which incorporates administrative guidelines for reasonable apportionment of governance (currently being negotiated by Chancellor Cribbet and Chancellor Begando).

After submission of the Educational Policy Committee report, Chancellor Cribbet addressed the UIUC Senate to appeal for its support and approval: "There is no ideal solution to the College of Medicine reorganization at this time. Compromises will have to be, and have been, made. We must take the long view of what is best for the total university as well as for this campus. Moreover, there is now an overriding issue that must be resolved in the best interest of the university. As you all know, the reorganization of the College of Medicine became a statewide issue, involving the Peoria and Rockford sites of the college as well as this campus and the Medical Center. There was more than a threat of intervention by the General Assembly with the real possibility that educational policy in this area would be mandated by the state legislature. It is crucial, therefore, that this problem be resolved internally and promptly. This is especially true because we face an unusually difficult legislative year, and we must not allow the real issues to be clouded by possible external involvement in the internal governance of the university…

"The proposal before you is consistent with President Ikenberry's seven basic principles—principles with which I have previously indicated agreement. The seventh principle is that we must end up with a single College of Medicine capable of self-governance. To that principle I suggest an addendum '*until such time as changed circumstances, fiscal and otherwise, make it possible to consider a separate College of Medicine for the UC campus.' Presi-dent Ikenberry has stated his concurrence with that addendum...*[Emphasis added.] I view the fiscal problems as a critical factor in an ultimate decision. The College of Medicine, like the rest of the University, is underfunded and to create a separate College at UC at this time would further compound our present difficulties.

"What remains as the critical issue at the present time is President Ikenberry's sixth principle, 'We must provide for appropriate local control.'" He mentioned that our school was operating under the 1970 Treaty, and that the Treaty called for the assignment of governance of an expanded medical curriculum to UIUC. "One could, therefore, argue that the time has now come for such an assignment. But the fiscal realities of 1982 are not the fiscal realities of 1970, and I have already indicated why this is not the time for a full-scale assignment to this campus, i.e., a separate College of Medicine. Since there is a single College of Medicine, which must be capable of self-governance, there is a difficult problem in providing for appropriate local control. President Ikenberry has asked Chancellor Begando and myself to address these issues promptly and has promised his personal interest and support...I believe my remarks are consistent with the report and recom-mendations of the Senate Committee on Educational Policy, and I hope this Senate will accept this committee's recommendations."

There were more than a few cynics at the meeting, particularly among those who had prior experience in dealing with UIMC. They expressed great skepticism about the negotiating process and believed that unless the SBMS/SCM-UC governance were wrested from the Medical Center there and then, the apocalyptic moment when the medical-education program at UIUC would have sufficient resources to become independent would never come to pass. The Chicago leadership would see to that.

Herb Gutowsky, Director of the School of Chemical Sciences and a per-son intimately familiar with the Treaty, was one of those skeptics. He pro-posed an amendment to insert the qualifying words "on an interim basis" to Senate approval of the reorganization plan, but the amendment was reject-ed. A second effort, which would also have facilitated appropriate transfer of governance to the UIUC campus after a given period of time, was advanced by music professor Alexander Ringer. This too was defeated and the resolu-tion as recommended by the original committee and strongly supported by John Cribbet was approved.

UIUC Senate approval of the college reorganization brought palpable
relief to both Chancellor Begando and President Ikenberry. For my own
part, I was satisfied that we had done all we could do for the time being. The
final details of a new treaty would await the deliberations of John Cribbet
and Joe Begando. To assist them in negotiating and to mediate between the
two campuses, the president assigned Peter Yankwich, Vice President for
Academic Affairs.

I continued to send governance advice, wanted or not, to Joe Begando
and to the entire UIMC administration, if only to let them know that I was
following the negotiations as closely as possible. The most peculiar facet of
the entire process was that I was consulted frequently by Ned Goldwasser
and the UIUC administration concerning treaty specifics, but I was never a
party to any governance deliberations that went on at the Medical Center
even though no one else at UIMC had the insight, experience and understanding of the governance that was required to manage the complex
SBMS/SCM-UC programs. But UIMC remained concerned only with power
and form, not with function. After all, to include the major party that would
be affected by the negotiations would be too logical a step in this administrative asylum.

My advice to UIMC was not always acknowledged, and if acknowledged, was not always accepted gracefully. For example, I sent a letter on
February 19, 1982 to the five negotiating principals: Begando, Cribbet,
Goldwasser, Schmidt, and Yankwich. In it, I made a plea for the logical governance that had been proposed in the Cribbet document and suggested
that the principals meet with UICOM-UC faculty before coming to any final
conclusions.

"You have two options before you; one which recognizes that
UICOM-UC will function best within the reorganized College of Medicine
as a unit which has close and recognized ties with the UIUC campus, and
the other which stands upon narrow statutory legalisms and which would
impose the restrictive and burdensome problems that led to so much dissatisfaction over the past decade. Most of the UICOM-UC faculty have
reviewed the proposal forwarded by Ned Goldwasser [the revised Cribbet
document] and believe that it best serves the essential requirements for a
single college of medicine and allows optimal interaction with the UIUC
campus. It is a thoughtful document, which has within it the ingredients for
a permanent and stable relationship which will permit UICOM-UC to be a

constructive bridge between two great university campuses in Chicago and in Urbana-Champaign."

I said that I believed that to the extent that they deviated from Goldwasser's proposal, "You will harvest a measure of instability within the system, regardless of the leadership in Chicago or Urbana."

That letter was received in silence; but another letter written to Joe Begando on January 25 was not. In the letter, I shared my concerns about Dean Forman's addendum to the reorganization plan: "Regrettably, the statement, which has had wide distribution, contains both factual inaccuracies and errors of interpretation. I know of no agreement between the two campuses which was made in 1974 and which recommended that inter-campus organizational decisions be deferred for seven years. I believe that the document to which reference was intended was the agreement between you and Chancellor Peltason dated January 27, 1976. In that letter, you and Chancellor Peltason recommend 'a review of the organizational structure of the College of Medicine to be initiated after a period of approximately five years (after FY1979–80).' It is the clear implication of the January 6 Medical Center Senate addendum that the agreement with Chancellor Peltason for a structural review of the Urbana program in medical education has been fulfilled by the processes which have led to the present College of Medicine reorganization plan. I believe this is *not* correct. The studies that have taken place in the college over the last eighteen months and the conclusions therefrom have been carried out in virtual absence of input from the Urbana Chancellor's office…I believe that it is fair to conclude that the cooperative review envisioned in your 1976 agreement has not yet been undertaken."

On February 16, 1982, Begando responded, writing: "You are correct that the statement approved by the Medical Center Senate…used an incorrect date in referring to the Begando/Peltason letter of January 27, 1976…Different views may exist as to whether the organizational study of the past year and more fulfills the review requirements agreed to in the Begando/Peltason letter of January 27, 1976. However, it is my belief that one clear outcome of the study was the rejection of an establishment of an independent college of medicine at Urbana-Champaign at this time. I do not see the current discussion of the 1970 operational guidelines as a way to reopen that issue. Revision of the 1970 guidelines should not be a device for achieving a de facto independence of the medical-education program in UC, in violation of the single-college decision. I do plan to work with

Chancellor Cribbet and others as appropriate to see that the 1970 guidelines are subjected to careful review."

That was a severe, bare-knuckled response from the usually mild-mannered chancellor. He did not hesitate to expose the lines in the sand that were drawn between us. UIMC interpreted our governance suggestions to ease bureaucratic overkill as a device to extort de facto independence for our program.

I discussed these two nagging issues, budget and governance, with my Executive Committee at a strategic-planning meeting with Ron Aldrich, Ben Williams, Allan Levy, and Don Thursh on January 25, 1982. I displayed our critical budget situation and distributed copies of my January 25 letter to Joe Begando, whose feisty reply would not be received for three weeks. After due consideration (and again without my advice or direction), Williams and Aldrich reconvened the Committee to Save the Medical School in Urbana-Champaign. The end result was a second Open Letter to Stanley Ikenberry and the Board of Trustees, which appeared in the *Champaign-Urbana News-Gazette* on Wednesday, February 17, 1982.

This time the substance and tone were different. The "Second in a Series," was presented as a "Progress Report on the Reorganization of the Medical School at Urbana-Champaign."

The letter began by praising the president for the progress made in his efforts to preserve regional medical education, his establishment of seven principles for reorganization, and his progress on five of the seven. The open letter then expressed the committee's concern regarding two major, unre-solved issues: governance and budget distribution. (The letter was written in a supportive style, in fact too supportive for my taste. Had I been consulted, I would have pressed him more forcefully on the twin issues of budget and governance.)

The president responded without the defensiveness that characterized his reaction to the "First in a Series." He wrote to the committee on February 19, two days after the open letter appeared, saying, "I...appreciate the supportive tone of your statement...Regarding the two remaining issues...A formula for allocation of resources to the various medical sites was endorsed a few months ago by the college deans, with the provision that the work on refinement [sic] continue...Although I expect refinements, I do not expect major changes or a larger 'pie.'

"On the so-called 'governance' issue...the two Chancellors...are working with Vice President Yankwich and others to formulate their joint recommendations…However, I would caution that until such time as the Board of Trustees elects to establish two or more medical colleges, the chancellors are unlikely to be in a position to recommend the degree of autonomy some would desire."

So the president, who had deflected and delayed the resolution of the governance issue in favor of UIMC, also took the UIMC position that we should not expect too much either from TTF "refinements" of budget or from the Cribbet-Begando negotiations on governance. How difficult it was to fight city hall. The president was bent on supporting UIMC on these issues every step of the way. In his zeal to limit the SBMS/SCM-UC common-sense gains toward parity, he was also limiting the potential of the UIUC campus to fully participate in the biomedical revolution that was taking off in the 1980s. When history evaluates the tenure of President Stanley Ikenberry, I believe it will find that he achieved a good deal in the ways of bricks and mortar, and worked diligently to upgrade the Chicago campus, but that he contributed very little to the academic growth of UIUC, his flagship campus. Fortunately, I did not have to fight city hall alone.

On February 8, 1982, Mort Creditor, then a lame duck, wrote a confidential letter to Joe Begando, expressing concern about the pending LCME accreditation visit scheduled for April 1983. After summarizing the College of Medicine's position with the LCME, he wrote:

> To some extent, the LCME report was an expression of a continuing problem in the college and that is an unwillingness to respect *consensus.* In complex organizations such as ours, unanimity of opinion cannot be expected. If this organization is to function, it must operate on the basis of consensus, which is defined as "a condition in which all parties agree that the proposed alternative is a viable option and agree to carry out that option as if it were the best option."
>
> If those affected by the consensus agreement do not work toward successful implementation of the agreement, if they continue to use every means possible to resurrect their own original position, which was submerged in the consensus view, and if they continue to use every form available to express their disappointment, then they cannot be considered as participants in the consensus.
>
> I belabor this point because I think it important that any such

behavior be anticipated and dealt with. It would be to the college's serious disadvantage if any unit of the college were perceived by the LCME
visitors as being significantly dissatisfied with the reorganized college…
I am suggesting that we guard against the LCME being used as the
instrument for redress of individual grievance. In my opinion, it would
be better to permit or even encourage abdication rather than risk further serious censure by the LCME because of continued complaint from
one or another quarter. It is my personal view that they [the LCME] are
going to be troubled enough by our new structure, so we must assiduously avoid evidence of serious dissent from within, particularly by
those charged with leadership responsibility.

Finally, I think it important that the plan which the LCME is asked
to approve be presented as "completed" and permanent. They will not
be happy if told by anyone that the organization or governance relationships will be reexamined in the foreseeable future. The question of
whether there will be one or more colleges of medicine in the University
of Illinois should be settled now.

This letter was one last dig at Dan Bloomfield before Creditor lost power
entirely. Begando sent the Creditor letter to the president and copied it to
the senior administrators on the two campuses and to Peter Yankwich, with
the following endorsement: "Dr. Creditor's letter contains some very important points to be considered as we move ahead with the College of Medicine
in its reorganization form."

Ned Goldwasser, however, was profoundly disturbed by Creditor's letter,
not because it attacked me, but because it was so illogical under the circumstances. He wrote to Chancellor Cribbet on February 23, 1982:

The gist of the Creditor letter, as I see it, is that he is very concerned
about an LCME accreditation visit in 1983 and that he believes it to be
extremely important that the College of Medicine display a spirit of
collegiality, cooperation, and accord in order for that visit to lead to the
desired, unequivocal accreditation. I agree with Mort on that score.
However, he appears to address that problem as a problem in its own
right, whereas I address it as only one of a number of symptoms of
other problems which are much more basic and which should be of
much greater concern to all of us.

Everyone recognizes that programs suffer from inadequate funding, and everyone recognizes that every subgroup in an organization tends to see itself as disadvantageously funded relative to other subgroups. LCME visiting committees must be very familiar with that kind of a situation and they must be quite capable of discounting that component of discord, which might exist among several units within a single college of medicine.

What is more troublesome to me, and what I suppose might also be more troublesome to them, would be organizational arrangements which impede rather than facilitate the efforts of faculty members to provide the best possible educational experience within the funding constraints that exist. Members of the UIUC faculty who have been engaged, directly or peripherally, in the medical-education program on this campus have felt very strongly, in the past, that their research and teaching lives were made more complicated, rather than less so, by the organizational arrangements under which the UIMC medical program on the Urbana-Champaign campus was governed. The same can be said, and apparently even more strongly so, for the members of the UIMC faculty who teach on this campus. There is a fundamental problem associated with an arrangement in which faculty members of one campus are permanently assigned on another campus to carry out the programs of the first. That, I believe, is why those who drew up the original 1970 guidelines for governance of the new regional program at Urbana-Champaign did so with the assumption that if that program achieved maturity its umbilical cord from UIMC should be severed and it should become a unit of the UIUC campus. I have checked that impression with Lyle Lanier and he confirms it.

We all recognize that the boundary conditions have changed in many ways since the 1970 agreement was enunciated. The economy has changed, the demand for doctors has changed, and many other things have changed. President Ikenberry now sees it to be essential, at least for the near-term future, for the University of Illinois to continue with only one, single College of Medicine. So be it. We all accept that as a premise to the establishment of new guidelines. However, it is foolish to ignore the fact that the problems, which have existed for the past ten years, will continue to exist in the future unless some substantial measures are taken to alleviate them. If those measures are taken, I have no doubt but that the program will work better and, therefore, that the LCME accrediting team will be very well impressed with the progress which has been made both programmatically and organizationally.

If, however, there is not a substantial effort made to alleviate the problems of the complicated relationships between programs and faculty in different regions, particularly those in a regional program which happens to be located within one of the strongest university campuses in the country, then the program itself will not be able to achieve its full potential, the faculty members on this campus will be dissatisfied with the arrangements, the better faculty members who are on this campus will leave, the most promising faculty members who are being recruited to the program on this campus will not come, and the faculty members who are here will express their frustration to an LCME visiting team.

In my view, the last of those circumstances is by far the least. As I have indicated before, it would only be a symptom of the others. Now is our chance to do something, administratively, which will contribute to the effectiveness of the program and which will facilitate the implementation of the program. It is wrong, I believe, for Mort Creditor to impute poor cooperation, or even worse, to members of his faculty who might meet with an LCME visiting team a year from now. I have not the slightest doubt about the loyalty of those faculty members and about their ability and their wish to convey a positive impression to an LCME visiting team. On the other hand, they cannot and they will not create a positive impression if the program in which they are participating is operating under administrative and organizational handicaps, which appear to them to be burdensome and unnecessary. It is our job to see that such should not be the case. Then, we shall not need to be concerned about the LCME visit. I do not believe that, to date, our efforts to develop a revised set of governance guidelines have reflected the kind of flexibility and imagination which are called for.

In dealing with Creditor's vindictiveness, Goldwasser articulated our case better than I could imagine. It would not be the last time he did so. Witness his March 30, 1982 letter to Cribbet.

Every now and then I feel that I am not succeeding well in communicating some of my thoughts, even in our many discussions, and I then try, in some form, to set them down in writing. Such is the case with our somewhat differing views about the development of a code of governance for the medical program on the UIUC campus, and it is particularly the case in our differing views about our readiness to accept responsibility for the medical program on this campus, thereby cutting the umbilical cord which has connected it to the College of Medicine at the Medical Center in Chicago.

In our discussions on that subject, you frequently voice your concern about the voracious appetite of medical programs and about the tension that would develop in the competition for funds between a UIUC medical program, on the one hand, and the rest of the present UIUC programs, on the other. Of course, I share your concern. However, I am frightened by the prospect of a low-quality program on this campus, insidiously spreading its mediocrity among those programs upon which it depends, as well as among those which depend upon it. In the beginning, you may remember, I was sympathetic to the Hager Proposal that we either establish a completely satisfactory mode of governance or that we give up the program completely. At that time, I was quite ready to contemplate termination of medical education on this campus. Since then, I have become more and more aware of the complicated network of interactions between medical education and research on this campus and many of the other programs which we have always provided and shall continue to provide.

Our recent meeting and discussions with a very distinguished and very thoughtful Visiting Committee to our School of Life Sciences has reinforced my changing attitude toward the importance of a strong medical program on this campus. I am still convinced, however, that if we are to have a strong medical program we must have the best possible ambiance within which to develop such a program. The provision of such an ambiance rules out any adherence to an arbitrary and pointless liaison and dependence on a college administration located 150 miles away, dedicated toward an entirely different facet of medical education, and not yet demonstrably capable of sustaining a program of anywhere close to the quality which is the tradition on the Urbana-Champaign campus.

In expressing your concern, you quite rightly focus on the competition for budget and on the incursions which the demands of a medical program might make on other programs on this campus. Yet I believe that there is a much simpler solution to that problem than there is to the problem of governance at a distance by an unsympathetic and differently directed college administration.

We have always insisted that the formula for distribution of funds among the various regional centers of the College of Medicine must be handled by the General University. We seem to have won general agreement on the principle that the distribution of resources among the four regional programs be changed only under the auspices of the General University. That very fact challenges the myth of a single College of Medicine right from the start. One of the principal responsibilities of any single College of Medicine, which supports multiple branches, should be the allocation of budget among those branches. On the other hand, in a single university, which operates multiple colleges of medicine, it is the university, per se, which determines budget allocations among those colleges. It is the latter model, not the former, which we all agree we are forced to adopt. Therefore, the notion of a single College of Medicine is already somewhat elusive.

I can easily imagine a model within which our new, stronger vice president for academic affairs would have *the* responsibility for allocation of university funds between its medical program, on the one hand, and the rest of its academic programs on the other. Admittedly, that is a complication because the new chancellor of the Chicago Campus might see that as infringing on his role. Ignoring that problem for the moment, once that distribution is decided, that vice president would have the further responsibility, as presently projected, of determining any changes in the distribution of medical funds among the four regional campuses. Once those decisions have been made by the *university's* vice president for academic affairs, we would have a well-defined pool of funds to be used for the UIUC medical program. The on-campus competition which you and I both fear need never come before us. What competition for funds would remain would be only a small extension of what is already our responsibility. I do not need any more of that than you do, but that's our job, and it's a lot easier to handle than a responsibility for maintaining program quality under adverse conditions which are gratuitously imposed for the sake of some kind of imagined administrative convenience.

The main substantive stumbling block to the establishment of an independent medical program on this campus has always seemed to me to be accreditation. I have no expertise upon which to draw to predict whether or not the program on this campus is, or should be, accreditable. I cannot, however, think of any other rational basis upon which a decision about independence should be based. Two knowledgeable members of our Visiting Committee to our SOLS have made the guess to me that the medical program on this campus, as it now exists, would probably win accreditation. They based this opinion on the simple fact that graduates of this program have done as well as (in fact slightly better than) those of Chicago on their Medical Boards.

As you can see, I feel extremely uneasy about acquiescing to the president's imposition of an arbitrary decision upon a program on this campus. I feel this all the more strongly since our visitors have reinforced my belief that a medical program on this campus could be and should be one vital ingredient in any attempt we make to exploit the remarkable opportunity we have not only to participate in, but actually to play a leading role in, the revolution which is just gathering force jointly in the life sciences, in agriculture, in veterinary medicine, and in human medicine. If the president believes that that opportunity can administratively be allocated to Chicago, he has absolutely no understanding for or appreciation of the source of the quality of this institution—a quality about which he likes to boast but, in behalf of which, he seldom makes the kind of tough differentiations which are required. We would be doing him a disservice if we permitted him to finesse the importance of cross-disciplinary linkages involving clinical-medical research as well as research in veterinary medicine and agriculture. It is the presence of all of these ingredients on a campus, which is one of the nation's leaders in research and graduate education, which provides this state with an almost unique opportunity to contribute to the revolution in biology and to exploit the fruits of that revolution.

Goldwasser's letters of February 23 and March 30, 1982, condensed into fluid prose the case for the Urbana medical program to become an integral part of the UIUC campus.

Unfortunately, the articulate moral support of Ned Goldwasser could not help SCM-UC with its budget for the 1983 fiscal year. The facts of the matter were that in the spring of 1982, I was dealing with an openly hostile Medical Center administration. Urbana funding was restricted to the maximum extent possible despite my protestations on behalf of the students assigned to Urbana and in the name of equity.

Assuming responsibility as Acting Executive Dean on April 1, 1982, Marten Kernis, Creditor's protege, continued the policy of minimizing the allocation of new resources to SBMS/SCM-UC. What must have galled the UIMC administration further was a delayed realization that unless the reference boundaries for formula budgeting were radically changed, or the TTF recommendations were limited to ultra-refinements, the Urbana program would be the main and substantial benefactor of TTF deliberations. For that reason, there were a number of last-ditch attempts to redefine the TTF charge and the TTF goals. It was as if the consensus agreement could be amended by disputation, as had been attempted in the Academic Council.

I was invited to attend a March 19 dinner to honor Creditor upon his retirement. I approached that dinner with great trepidation, fearful that I might be called on to make a toast to Creditor, a toast that was just not in me because Creditor had done so many unforgivable things over the past year. I was certain, for instance, that his February 8 letter was a swipe at me for disloyalty. Despite my trepidations, I went.

The dinner was held at the Union League Club of Chicago, and liberal amounts of spirits were served before dinner. Heaven knows it was necessary. Mort was a very bright and efficient professional, but he put many people on edge in his presence. The liquor warmed up the guests' moods to make the evening relatively pleasant. As for me, it took a few cocktails to ease the way for me to bridge the difficult interpersonal relationships so that I could engage in civil talk with Mort and with Mack Schmidt, who, as vice chancellor for academic affairs, was also there. It was difficult to make light of what I have always believed was administrative abuse.

Schmidt, however, approached me like an old friend and asked if we might have a private word together. He said he was very anxious to get something off his chest—to clarify an old problem. Naturally, I agreed to listen. Schmidt proceeded to explain the decision to embark upon the recommendation to change Urbana into a two-year basic-science program and Rockford and Peoria into two-year clinical programs. According to Mack, this decision had been made at a meeting at which he, Ikenberry, Begando, and Brady were present. As Schmidt was describing the budget woes of the Medical Center campus and listing alternative approaches and his own recommendations to deal with the problem, the president suddenly interrupted, jumping to his feet as if to say, "Eureka! I've found it." He proceeded to delineate the unhappy Option II solution that had flashed into his mind. According to Schmidt, several of those present (unidentified by Schmidt) counseled the president that his plan was too drastic, but Ikenberry, once he had decided on the way to go, was adamant. He therefore directed Schmidt to inform the units of the College of Medicine of the "university decision" about the reorganization of the college. Schmidt, in coming to Champaign-Urbana in April 1981 was only doing his duty. He was following his marching orders issued by the president.

This was the second time Mack Schmidt had confessed his passive role in the "university" decision to close SCM-UC, the first, being at the Board of Trustees luncheon one year earlier. The Schmidt story seems plausible and certainly explains why the president so vigorously defended "Schmidt's decision," although it never was Schmidt's decision in the first place and one year later, we were still dealing with the political turmoil that flowed out of that decision and the Grand Compromise that repudiated it. In that climate, we still had to plan a second medical-education track for a cohort of medical students who were to begin at Urbana and finish up at Rockford or Peoria, the UPR track. This was no simple task. We had our differences in the political sphere of the reorganization discussions, and some of those antagonisms carried over to the academic domain as we began to work exclusively with Rockford and Peoria to integrate basic-science and clinical instruction.

There was no shortage of doomsayers or gratuitous comments about the Urbana, Peoria, and Rockford "second track." I received the following warning from Paula Treichler: "There is no question but that this new upstate/downstate 'two track' medical school is going to be disastrous for us. All of the best applicants I have interviewed for admission indicate they would have chosen Urbana-Champaign for their first year and then gone to Chicago, but with this combination no longer open to them, they are selecting Chicago for all four years. This will affect not only the composition of our first-year class (which in my estimation will now include higher numbers of the students least suited to Urbana), it will also affect the pool out of whom we recruit students for the Urbana-Champaign clinical program and for the Medical Scholars Program. Many of our current SCM and MSP students were once slated for clinical school in Chicago."

Difficulties were also encountered on the operational level. After the first meeting of the UPR coordination committee, I received a letter from Peoria's Jerry Newman, expressing concern that the Urbana-Champaign faculty was ignoring the interests of Peoria and Rockford. Dated April 6, 1982, it read, "Recently I met, upon their request, with Peoria School of Medicine members of the College Committee on Educational Policy and the chair of our ad hoc curriculum liaison committee, which was charged with developing interface with Urbana and Rockford for the 'second track.' They expressed a high level of anxiety regarding what appears to be limited interest by the college committee in providing direction for the curriculum outside of Chicago. It is their concern that Chicago will appear to have 'its act together' when the next [LCME] accreditation takes place, whereas this may not appear to be the case downstate. Furthermore, they expressed concern that this will provide the Chicago-based faculty the opportunity to say to the accrediting team, 'We could have told you so.'

"A second concern results from the endeavor to develop a liaison with Urbana and Rockford. The reports we have received are that this first meeting was very frustrating and nearly a disaster. A second initiative by Dr. Peterson to continue the dialogue was responded to by Hal Swartz with a 'don't call us, we'll call you' letter…I hope that you will encourage your faculty to accept Dr. Peterson's invitation to take an active role in this important activity."

I was on vacation when that letter arrived so I missed the heat of this discussion, but Hal Swartz wrote me about it, advising that he had discussed this at the Advisory Council of Deans meeting, but found it very difficult to deal with Newman, who was apparently smarting over the four-year program at UICOM-UC. Swartz added that he had been "rather vigorous," but assured me that he would send "a very conciliatory note to both Rockford and Peoria trying to separate out the two intermixed concerns: (1) input into students that come to them; (2) control of curriculum delivery."

Over time, the UPR track has proved to be very successful.

A final complicated reorganization issue that had to be resolved was the makeup of the College Executive Committee. On April 20, Marten Kernis put together an ad hoc committee on the "Executive Committee Structure of the College." It was noted by Kernis that "recent action by the UI Board of Trustees created a single College of Medicine that is required to have an Executive Committee as defined by our statutes." His words were carefully chosen because the referenced statute states: "Not more than one-half of the membership of the Executive Committee shall be from one department or comparable teaching unit of the college." Although the Chicago faculty did not agree that the statute applied to the college as it was reorganized, it was finally agreed that Chicago representation would be limited to twelve members or a 50 percent representation on the Executive Committee, while Rockford, Peoria, and Urbana would each have four members.

Slowly, the reorganized college completed the housekeeping chores that had to be attended to. On April 15, 1982, a nationwide search for an executive dean began. Like a mammoth beast that had been wounded temporarily, the college as a whole began to move forward.

Our money situation in Urbana remained critical. Five months had elapsed since our consensus, and the TTF had yet to be appointed or charged. Dealing with Chicago continued to be painful and difficult. The new acting executive dean, Marten Kernis, was an anatomist turned administrator. He had served as the number-two person for both Truman Anderson and Mort Creditor. Kernis was a savvy person who knew Medical Center and regional politics well. As acting executive dean, he was to hold the position until the reorganization was complete and a permanent dean had been selected. From his comments, his actions, and whatever body language I could interpret, Kernis, a close friend and admirer of Creditor, was very upset by the disaster that had befallen his erstwhile boss. Creditor had been angry at the president's change of heart in October—angry that almost two years of SPMC effort "went down the tubes," angry that SCM-UC had survived intact, and particularly piqued at me for "unprincipled" behavior that had led to all of the above.

Although Marten Kernis would never admit it, his behavior over the next few months confirmed with reasonable certainty that much of Creditor's anger passed on to him. For example, in the trying fiscal times of 1982, Kernis afforded me no relief from the punitive budget cuts that Creditor had initiated. When the university called for an across-the-board 6.2 percent budget reduction, that reduction was passed down to the units of UICOM evenly. I immediately protested that we, as an acknowledged underfunded unit, should not be hit with the whole 6.2 percent, but, as usual in my dealings with the Chicago bureaucracy, my protests were of no avail. My argument was very simple: The clinical program at Urbana had survived, it was a reality Chicago would have to accept. Thus, underfunding the program at this juncture was patently unfair to the students who were assigned there. It was time for acceptance of the full, four-year program at Urbana.

Toward this end I wrote Kernis on March 17, 1982 to say, "In areas of enrollment and budget planning, the University of Illinois College of Medicine should function as closely as possible to the Board of Trustees resolution of February 18, 1982 which included the statement 'the funding implications must be equitable among the four locations.'"

Furthermore, I asked that budget planning for the 1983 fiscal year "be based upon a consistent and equitable enrollment-driven budget formula subject to consideration of special, unusual, or unique program needs at any medical-education site. It is my view that the students of the University of Illinois College of Medicine at Urbana-Champaign should no longer be dis-advantaged by a grossly unequal distribution of state funds...You should immediately freeze all hiring within the University of Illinois College of Medicine until a decision has been made concerning the distribution of state funds in FY83."

I followed up that letter on April 5, 1982, with a memorandum that pointed out other gross inequities in funding such as infrastructure support for continuing medical education at Rockford, Peoria, and Chicago. In those locations, the costs was paid for by state funds from the vice chancellor's office in Chicago, whereas the same continuing-education effort in Urbana-Champaign was being paid out of SCM-UC operating dollars. I told him that, for that reason, I had closed the continuing-education office. As usual, my letters were exercises in futility. The response essentially said that Chicago couldn't care less what happened to continuing medical education at Urbana-Champaign.

On schedule, a new Treaty was agreed upon by Joe Begando and John Cribbet and sent to President Ikenberry on May 27, 1982 with a letter that affirming that "the program in medical education on the UC campus rests on a foundation of past history and experience...It will be our mutual goal to make the University of Illinois College of Medicine at Urbana-Champaign the highest-quality and most-effective operating program possi-ble...It will be the long-range goal of the medical program to develop its capability for academic independence so that the structure for governance of medical education within the university can be simplified and lines of com-munication shortened by the establishment at UC of a separately governed College of Medicine."

The new Treaty itself incorporated phraseology that stated, "These procedures and relationships are intended to implement the revised reorganization plan but have no long-range implications for the previously envisioned development of a separate medical school at UIUC."

In that sense, the new Treaty would facilitate a transfer of governance to UIUC at an appropriate time. That time would be reached when the university leadership realized that the Urbana medical-education program would only reach its full potential as a full participant in the affairs of the UIUC campus. On June 16, 1982, the new treaty was presented to the Board of Trustees and approved.

The new Treaty was a reasonable document and one with which we could live comfortably. UICOM-UC remained solidly under control of the Medical Center, which at this time had become a unit of the University of Illinois at Chicago, or UIC. I was satisfied that, at this juncture, we had achieved as much as we possibly could have. In order to calm the waters around us, on June 21, I sent a memorandum to the UICOM-UC faculty that summarized the main points of the new Treaty and urged the faculty to provide their support in its implementation.

The memo read: "In my view, the 'operational procedures' are a suitable compromise between the requirements of the university that there be, at this time, but one College of Medicine, and the need to provide the medical-education program at Urbana-Champaign and its faculty operational procedures which will allow suitable and cost-effective flexibility and academic control. So long as the College of Medicine retains the efficient and simple organization envisioned under its revised reorganization plan of December 1981, I am confident that our program, UICOM-UC, can participate effectively both as a 'school' within the College of Medicine and as an academic unit closely integrated with the Urbana-Champaign campus…The opportunity is now in place for UICOM-UC to develop as an effective and leading institution for medical education and research."

Stability was returning to the College of Medicine.

CHAPTER 39

Equity for Urbana—A Policy Oxymoron

HE FOOT-DRAGGING TO CREATE and charge the Technical Task Force to create a new enrollment-driven budget formula was disheartening. From the December 1981 consensus on reorganization until mid-February 1982, nothing was accomplished. Finally, after the Board of Trustees approved the reorganization plan, Chancellor Begando got the ball rolling with an indirect approach. He wrote to Vice President Brady on February 17 to say, "As you know, 'a consistent and equitable enrollment-driven budget formula' was used by Dr. Czajkowski and was reviewed by you, me, and the four medical school deans as we discussed a revised reorganization plan for the College of Medicine. As you also know, the revised reorganization plan calls for…a TTF to continue to refine *that* budget formula [Emphasis added.]…Perhaps it would be helpful…to have Dr. Czajkowski report on the areas…of technical exploration which…might benefit from further technical investigation or refinement…such a report might help us determine how best to establish and charge a technical task force."

Joe Begando was really looking for an easy way out. He knew that a major reallocation of funds to Urbana would cause all hell to break loose in Chicago, Peoria, and Rockford. So he put the issue to the vice president and to the college deans in a way that might reassure them all that we were only dealing with the need for "refinement" of the formula that Brady and Czajkowski had conjured up in August 1981. It was letters like that, which pretended that the Brady budget formula was already "consistent and equitable," that I resisted.

I was unwilling to let casual misrepresentations of history slip by unchallenged. It was as though all my protests at the consensus meetings of November and December were for naught. Disheartened, but determined to set the record straight nevertheless, I wrote to Chancellor Begando on February 22 to say that not all of us had agreed that a "consistent and equitable enrollment-driven budget formula" existed. "In point of fact," I wrote, "we agreed upon the concept of such a formula and also agreed upon methodology to apply that concept which was demonstrated by the tables presented by Ron Brady as a 'point of departure.'

"The 'Technical Committee' idea to examine formula assumptions originated because I specifically argued that the assumptions…[in the information] distributed by Vice President Brady, were not equitable and not consistent either with patterns of distribution of state resources at other state medical schools or with the funding history of this College of Medicine, particularly with the proposal to suddenly incorporate residents into enrollment funding formulae. The assumptions [of Vice President Brady] were never agreed upon.

"You will recall that we agreed to limit formula distribution of funds specifically to state-appropriated funds and, in doing so, released the University of Illinois College of Medicine and others from including Medical Service Plan money, even though that money was earned by salaried faculty in state-supported facilities. It is for that reason that I strongly opposed then, and continue to oppose, the inclusion of residents in student-enrollment formulas that will be used for the distribution of state-appropriated funds."

My arguments were confirmed later and independently in the July 13, 1982 report of the Medical Education Committee to the Illinois Board of Higher Education, which stated: "Residency positions in programs in the teaching hospital at the University of Illinois-Medical Center historically have been supported with State funds appropriated to the University *for allocation to the hospital.*" [Emphasis added.] In other words, residency programs were already supported by state funding through a separate allocation to the university hospital. The Brady formula, which would include residents as a part of the undergraduate burden, was plainly "double-dipping."

I concluded my letter with these words: "I would hope, therefore, that the technical committee will examine every single assumption [made by Vice President Brady], even to the point of consulting or visiting individuals with experience at other state-funded medical schools, so that we can achieve what is now Board of Trustees policy, i.e., a consistent and equitable enrollment-driven budget formula."

As far as budget formulae were concerned, I stressed a more literal interpretation of our agreements while others stretched hard to find the barest, most minimal change possible. A distinct minority of one, I had to count on the integrity of the TTF members to do their job with objectivity. I was absolutely certain that an objective report by the TTF would back my position that what was needed was more than a refinement in the budgetary-allocation process.

I personally did an impromptu survey of twenty-eight state-sponsored medical schools from all over the United States, asking each one about the magnitude of their state support, their overall operating budget, and the fraction of that budget supplied by the state. I also asked each respondent to estimate the relative teaching costs of the M-1 to M-4 years. The responses were very revealing and I knew that they would be of great interest to the Technical Task Force.

The data I gathered showed that overall state funding for UICOM, on a per-medical-student basis was significantly higher than the state funding levels at comparable state-supported schools. For example, the raw UICOM appropriation per medical student in the 1982 fiscal year was $22,822. This compared favorably with $16,000 at Ohio State, $16,561 at Michigan, $18,636 at Missouri, and $16,110 at Indiana. It was also the case that in these four peer institutions, the teaching of residents was not budgeted in the medical-school appropriations. *The University of Illinois was not short of funds. It was short of leadership.*

On February 22, 1982, I wrote to Assistant Vice President Czajkowski, who was to chair the TTF, to let him know of the data I had assembled. "The data speaks for itself," I wrote. "You are welcome to review the original material."

On June 1, 1982, six months after the deans had agreed to the concept of a TTF and three months after the Board of Trustees ratified the TTF, Joe Begando issued the charge to Peter J. Czajkowski, representing the General University Administration; James E. Elsass, representing the UIMC administration; and Joseph L. Preissig, representing the UICOM administration, to serve as members of the technical task force, with Dr. Czajkowski as chairman. Begando's charge went on to say, "The TTF is an advisory group, and thus will identify budget formula refinements and improvements and make recommendations to the appropriate college, campus and university administrative officers. The technical task force is not a budget-determining or budget-allocating group."

The TTF was in difficulty from the very start. The TTF was a university responsibility, and not a UIMC operation. Brady or even Ikenberry should have charged the task force, not Begando. The UIMC people never really wanted "a consistent and equitable enrollment-driven budget formula." Such a formula would place Urbana on an equal footing with Chicago, and that was intolerable to the Chicago leadership. UIMC was only seeking approbation of past allocation policy, and was certainly not seeking a radical change in that policy. Begando wanted to limit the impact of the TTF as much as possible by clearly identifying the task force as an advisory group. From the UIMC point of view, the TTF was an academic exercise that was to be so circumscribed in its charge, that the term "hobbled" would be an understatement. Unfortunately, President Ikenberry and Ron Brady, who had the authority to make the TTF function as a university project, abdicated their responsibility and left most of the direction in the hands of the UIMC administration. Once again the fox was left to guard the chicken coop.

Despite these impediments, the technical task force promptly began work with a June 29 memorandum to the four regional deans that placed the deans on notice that the TTF was planning to do a thorough and objective job:

> At our first meeting, we agreed that we had two essential tasks to complete (1) fact finding, with particular reference to (a) developing an understanding of the components of the budget at each region and to assure that comparable activities will be treated in a like fashion and (b) developing an accurate enrollment base; and (2) the development and testing of a set of principles and/or conventions for weighting the enrollments in the formula.
>
> It is our intention to move as rapidly as possible in this first phase…The language of the reorganization plan is necessarily very general. Accordingly, it would be helpful to the task force to hear your specific views or elaboration on how to achieve 'a consistent and equitable enrollment driven budget formula subject to consideration of special, unusual or unique program needs at any medical education site.' Illustrative items that should be addressed are:
>
> 1. Should the task force consider 'non-enrollment driven' requirements?
> 2. Contractual relationships with affiliated hospitals—educational services and facilities provided by hospitals.

3. The number of filled positions in direct and affiliated medical-
    residency programs in the regions.
4. Operation and maintenance costs of university facilities.
5. Provide budget amounts and FTEs [full-time equivalents, a person
    working half-time is considered 0.5 FTE] utilized for student ser-
    vices, business affairs, O & M operations and maintenance super-
    vision, administrative, library costs, and other academic support
    functions.
6. A listing of medical schools/programs to which your region could
    be compared.
7. Should the pending LCME site visit be an element of consideration
    for the task force?"

The memo was so objective, so thorough, and so fair-minded that it brought
an immediate negative reaction from Acting Executive Dean Kernis in
Chicago. To bring equity to the college where none had ever existed previously was not on the Chicago agenda. On July 6, 1982, Kernis sent a lengthy
letter to Chancellor Begando complaining that the TTF document "goes well
beyond your charge, and I strongly urge you to instruct the group to limit
itself to the fulfillment of your objectives. I disagree…with the committee's
stated desire to explore budgetary components in each site and to 'assure'
that all regions treat comparable activities in a like fashion…*Current budgetary components at each site are the products of over a decade of independent
actions and decision unrelated to guidelines or to generally approved processes.
They represent nothing more than the sum total of a series of independent decisions made by numerous executive officers responding to the ups and downs of
total funding available. To the best of my knowledge they are not related to
numbers of students, full-time faculty, part-time faculty, nonsalaried faculty,
length of curriculum, amount of ambulatory care, etc., etc.* [Emphasis added.]
And they don't have to be! Each site is unique and unusual and special in
these distinctions and must be supported in order to permit each site to
maintain its strengths and improve upon its weaknesses."

Kernis thus vigorously confirmed the obvious: The Brady formula was
never used as a basis of allocation, and there never had been a budget formula, enrollment-driven or not. On the contrary, the Brady formula was
designed solely to explain and to fit the current maldistribution of resources
in terms of a formula. What Kernis ignored or could not tolerate was the

prospect of a consistent and equitable, enrollment-driven formula, to be used for the allocation of state funds to the medical-education sites. But that was exactly what the consensus agreement called for.

The basic problem expressed by Kernis, as one in a long line of Chicago administrators, was that they wanted to regionalize medical education without cost to Chicago. Kernis, like his predecessors, simply wanted to keep all the money and power in Chicago and dole it out according to the whims of a Chicago-based leader. He would deny this is exactly what caused so much dissention previously, and he would also deny the progress made in achieving and ratifying the consensus agreements and their translation into university policy by the Board of Trustees. The concept that allocations would be made through "a consistent and equitable enrollment-driven budget formula" was now policy, whether or not Kernis liked it.

Joe Begando reacted to Kernis's letter by writing Czajkowski on July 13, 1982. As was his style he attempted to take a compromise position. In the letter, Begando stated, "It appears that the [Kernis] concerns center about the possibility that the task force may extend its inquiry, activity and recommendations beyond the charge given to it. My personal view is that the charge given to the task force is circumscribed and can best be defined by the organization plan of the College of Medicine...Clearly the emphasis is upon refinement of an existing [sic] enrollment-driven formula. Thus, the concern, as factors not enrollment-driven are introduced. I am confident that the members of the technical task force understand the issues involved and will make recommendations consistent with the charge."

Even with two members of the technical task force coming from Chicago, both Elsass and Preissig being Chicago administrative financial officers, and with Czajkowski representing the General University, Kernis worried that the TTF might actually recommend a process that would give Urbana a fair shake at the expense of Chicago, Peoria, and Rockford and that such an outcome might destabilize the entire college.

So our last best hope for a fair budget, the TTF, was under heavy pressure to do a minimalist job. Concerned by that, I sought advice from Board of Trustees President Paul Stone, writing on July 16, 1982:

> As you know, my remaining concern as Dean of the Urbana medical school is to insure that the presidential principle of the reorganization that "the funding implications must be equitable among the four

locations and realistic overall" is carried out. The principle of equity was forcefully confirmed by the Board of Trustees. For this reason I enclose recent correspondence, which implies that undue pressures from Chicago are already being exerted on the technical task force; pressures that could jeopardize the equity principle and again lead us into unnecessary conflict.

Dr. Czajkowski, chairman of the task force, indicates in his memorandum of June 29 that he has the clear intent to follow the mandate of regional equity. However, the correspondence which follows, and most specifically the letter from Acting Executive Dean Kernis to Chancellor Begando of July 6, 1982, shows that the Chicago leadership is up to its old tricks again in its effort to preserve the lion's share of funds for Chicago...The Technical Task Force was originally conceived because the Chicago formula was so biased against us that there was absolutely no consensus for its adoption.

I am also concerned by Chicago administrative pressure being placed upon the technical task force because two of the three members of the task force (and Kernis as well) are under the direct administrative control of Vice Chancellor Schmidt, who in the view of many, has not been able to demonstrate a balanced approach towards Urbana-Champaign to date. Such pressure from the UIMC administration on the task force is improper and it might be appropriate, in order to protect the integrity of the task force and its membership, for the university to insist on the participation of an outside observer in its deliberations. Several of us from the regions recommended outside consultation to Drs. Schmidt and Creditor during the troubles of 1981, but the UIMC administration repeatedly avoided taking that step.

One final point. It is true, as Dr. Kernis states in his first paragraph, that Chancellor Begando "created and charged" the task force. The consensus agreement, however, specifies that "the university will establish a technical task force." I did not oppose Dr. Begando initiating and charging the task force, but at this point, it might be wise to confirm that the task force is responsible to the university as opposed to the UIMC administration.

Meanwhile, I still had problems with the budget for the 1983 fiscal year. There was an absolute refusal at the Medical Center to shift any funds our way. I again documented the basic needs of our program, but it was like talking to a stone. Confronted by this unseemly conduct, I tried a different, but equally unsuccessful, approach to shaming the UIMC administration into dealing fairly with UC. I sent a draft of SCM-UC needs so the administrators could correct any errors that I might have made in the interpretation of the SCM-UC plight. Moreover, I reminded them that they were punishing the Urbana students in their zeal to get even with me. With those thoughts in mind on June 18, 1982, I wrote to both Kernis and Schmidt: "It is my intention to discuss this budgetary matter, as is my statutory obligation, with my Executive Committee on July 7, 1982 and to seek their advice concerning the management of this budget. I would welcome your presence, or that of any senior UIMC administrator at this meeting, to assist me in explaining to the faculty why apparent funding inequities, which critically affect programs, continue to persist to the degree they do in FY83."

This was followed by a draft letter asking for $150,000 in additional resources for our program in the 1983 fiscal year. I pointed out that Dean Creditor had rejected my request for more funds the previous year. "The irony of this failure to meet the legitimate needs of an underfunded program for which the College of Medicine had full responsibility is that one year later, in FY83, the College of Medicine alone absorbed a budget cut of $1.38 million *without dropping a single student!* That must be considered evidence, if such were needed, that there were adequate funds within the College of Medicine in FY82 to assist the underfunded clinical-medical education program at Urbana-Champaign without reducing student loads at any other site."

In addition, I asked the Chicago's administrators to consider the students. "Furthermore, the first-year enrollment at UC will be increased from 75 to 131 students [in the 1983 fiscal year]. It is a most difficult logistical problem to meet these needs with what is, in effect, a budget reduction. Furthermore, I urge you to consider whether a negative decision on your part is fair to the students assigned to the UC programs. In FY83, the current College of Medicine allocation per medical student in UC remains at the $14,000 [per] student level and continues to exceed $20,000 [per] student elsewhere in the college. Were you to provide the additional $150,000 requested, the allocation per medical student at UICOM-UC would rise to only $14,800 per student."

Kernis's reply lamented the overall weak fiscal position of the college and went on to justify the aggressive and negative actions taken by Kernis and his predecessor toward SCM-UC. He ended the letter with some ad hominem remarks: "Based on the foregoing, I want to make a concluding comment. Considering the woefully inadequate funding of the college, I find it exceedingly difficult to understand your persistence and expenditure of time and energy trying to establish the fact that SCM and SBMS-UC are the poorest in a poor family. I believe the other schools, if they made a similar effort, could demonstrate the opposite more convincingly since only Urbana shows a budget increase and the 1983 Urbana budgets are close to achieving 'an equal footing' as calculated by the Executive Vice President's staff. Obviously, the other schools understand that the college can only lose by such comparisons. The college is trying simultaneously to adjust to enrollment changes, to reorganize, and to respond to an enrollment-driven budget—all of which you played a key role in developing. Needless to say, your proposed letter does not facilitate this process."

It was apparent that I would receive no help from the Chicago administration. Kernis and Schmidt wanted to win this war by attrition. The numbers used by Kernis were so far from reality that I chose not to pick apart the sophistry of his reply, but suggested that we meet with our respective financial officers to see if we could at least sit at the same table and look at the same numbers. On September 30, Marten Kernis, together with Joe Preissig from the Medical Center (and a member of the TTF), met with Rick Schimmel, my dean for fiscal affairs, and me. We reviewed expenditures and budgeting that accurately reflected year-to-year budget comparisons. With both financial officers present, the discussion remained dispassionate. The meeting demonstrated that the figures Rick Schimmel and I had prepared were very accurate. They also showed once again the maltreatment of a disadvantaged SCM-UC, but that had no effect on Kernis's attitude. I summarized our findings in a letter to Kernis on October 7, 1982, and told him that whether he liked it or not, any reasonable formula that the TTF would arrive at, would result in the reallocation of significant funds to SBMS/SCM-UC. I wrote, "I have asked you in the past to freeze positions at the College of Medicine until this transfer is made because it is probable that the total state dollars in each of those three units [Chicago, Rockford, and Peoria] will diminish as this transfer is made. It is imperative to planning that permanent obligations of state dollars not be made so as to preclude a timely transfer of resources."

As the time for technical task force report drew near, I became more and more uneasy over what seemed to be the capture of the process by the Medical Center administration. I told Kernis that I found it incredible that no preparatory steps were being taken in anticipation of what I believed was an imminent mandate for reallocation. Kernis stated that the college had no money to reallocate. He suggested I bring my case to the Chancellor. Therefore, on October 21, 1982, I wrote to Chancellor Begando, stating:

> It is particularly important to UICOM-UC that the task force report its findings to the General University for final arbitration and decision at an early date. Since it may be presumed that significant amounts of state dollars will be transferred from three units to Urbana-Champaign, adequate time prior to FY84 budgeting must be reserved so that each unit can make appropriate plans. UICOM-UC for example, is understaffed in a number of areas, and, before significant recruiting is undertaken, there must be a reasonable idea of the budget that will be available in FY84 and beyond, so that plans may be made to correct the many existing deficiencies. Similarly, those units transferring funds should be alerted early enough in advance so that their state funds are not obligated in such a way as would impede the results of formula budgeting.

> Furthermore, it is my clear understanding that the final decision regarding the formula budget, pursuant to the agreement all of us reached in our discussions, will be a university decision, not a decision arrived at solely within the Medical Center. This was explicit in our agreement, which said "the university will establish a technical task force."

> The decision to go the formula budget route was fundamentally a recognition that equitable distribution of funds between four dissimilar programs, such as now exist in the College of Medicine, was too difficult a task to be undertaken within the existing administration of the College of Medicine and the Medical Center campus. While I did not protest your initial charge to the Technical Task Force (even though it was technically incorrect for you and not Ron Brady to have done so) the imminent departure of Vice President Brady [who was soon to retire from the university] causes me to call this to your attention. It would seem appropriate that the final decision regarding a budget formula be a university decision, free of any taint which might be labeled "made in Chicago."

Chancellor Begando responded on November 2, 1982, writing:

> My latest information is that it will be beyond the middle of November
> before the task-force report will be available. Whether the report can be
> available, discussed, and decisions made prior to the departure of
> Executive Vice President Brady remains to be determined. Obviously, I
> and others would be very pleased to have the effective and experienced
> participation of Dr. Brady in this matter, if at all possible.
>
> You state that it was technically incorrect for me and not Dr. Brady
> to have established and charged the "technical task force." Perhaps you
> did not know that I am a General *University* Officer, as well as a campus
> Chancellor; or that I consulted with and cleared a draft of the letter
> establishing the "technical task force" with Dr. Brady prior to its official
> distribution. The last sentence of your letter states, "It would seem
> appropriate that the final decision regarding a budget formula be a
> university decision, free of any taint which might be labeled 'made in
> Chicago.'" That statement overlooks the legitimate interests of Peoria
> and Rockford in this matter, and at best is an inflammatory declaration,
> which will not be helpful. All major budget decisions regarding distri-
> bution among College of Medicine sites made during the past year or
> more have involved consultation with Executive Vice President Brady
> and often President Ikenberry and so have been, in your words, "univer-
> sity decisions."

I must admit that I was puzzled by Begando's interpretation of my letter as
"inflammatory," but it must have been because Jerry Newman of Peoria
indicated that he had reached the flash point as he complained to Joe
Begando about my October 21 letter in a note of November 4, 1982, which
he copied to all parties involved in the TTF activity:

> Uneasy that my failure to write might be interpreted as a lack of con-
> cern, I am compelled to do so regarding Dean Bloomfield's letter to you
> on October 21, 1982. I am resentful of and angered by what would
> appear to be a unilateral effort to create an unsettling climate regarding
> the development of a budget formula for the College of Medicine. This
> long-existent source of agitation was, in my opinion, a significant factor
> in the failure of the college to fulfill the potential inherent in its 1968
> reorganization. It bodes equally ill for any future success.

> I urge you to use the authority of the Office of Chancellor to assure
> that any and all decisions concerning reorganization be developed
> through thorough and open discussions of all parties concerned.

So the bile spilled out of Peoria! But I remained at a loss to understand
Newman's concern. The simple facts were that if the president's pledge for
equal funding at all four sites and the deans' agreement for a consistent and
equitable, enrollment-driven formula meant anything at all, some reallocation was necessary. If he wanted to call me an agitator for equality, so be it.

The results of the TTF were finally revealed on November 23, 1982. It
was a day to which I had looked forward for almost a year; a day that I
hoped would expose for all to see, the administrative abuse under which we
suffered; a day when some of my colleagues, who chided me for being
"quarrelsome and uncooperative," would be educated by a relatively independent group of observers with green eyeshades and would learn that
SCM-UC students suffered real discrimination by virtue of the unwilling-
ness of UIMC to deal with the problem of budget-allocation equity.

The two-hour meeting to discuss the Technical Task Force report was
scheduled by Joe Begando from 10 a.m. to noon. Present from the General
University were Vice Presidents Brady and Weir (with the imminent departure of Brady, Ikenberry had appointed Weir as Brady's successor); present
from UIMC was Schmidt, and from UICOM were Kernis, Bloomfield,
Forman, Newman, and Bernard Salafsky (who had replaced retiring Clifford
Grulee at Rockford); and TTF members Czajkowski, Elsass and Preissig.

Joe Begando chaired the meeting and promptly asserted that its purpose
was for information purposes only. No decisions were to be made at this
time. The two hours turned into what one might label as a self-serving "talk
fest" by Begando, Schmidt, and Brady. They all had the opportunity to deliver dire messages of financial troubles within the university that had nothing to do with the topic at hand. Brady discussed the financial problems of
the state, concluding that the university was facing the possibility of a five
percent reduction in its budget, and Schmidt chimed in with the litany that
we were an organization that had been originally programmed to turn out
500 MDs per year, but which now seemed destined to be limited to only
330. None of this was new. It appeared that they were taking up valuable
time so that they would not have to deal with the substantive issues raised
by the TTF report. When Peter Czajkowski finally got the floor, he used the

limited time he had to describe the TTF report methodology and to present nine tables to explain how the TTF conclusions were derived. By the time Czajkowski finished, only twenty minutes of the scheduled meeting time remained. To my great frustration, there was no opportunity to discuss the report number by number. Our only option was to make inquiries, so that we knew the basis for the TTF conclusions.

Despite efforts to muzzle the TTF, they made some important observations, especially in regard to the relative M-1 to M-4 cost factors. They were enough to vindicate everything I had said or done about budget allocations. The issues tackled by the task force, in addition to the weightings of M-1 to M-4 students, were the weighting of residents and cross-loading of students, and calculations of fixed costs. The TTF also took a number of independent initiatives, including site visits to four comparable state schools, conference calls to other public medical schools (including California, Ohio State University, University of Michigan, University of Iowa, and the State University of New York), and the Association of American Medical Colleges. The TTF also presented an analysis of faculty activity data to support their cost-weighting data and a review of college overhead budgets in the university. The panel also reviewed a recent Institute of Medicine study on the cost of medical education; acquired cost information from the AAMC; reviewed the "Bloomfield Survey of 28 State Supported Medical Colleges"; and came to its conclusions by "the application of our combined judgments."

Joe Begando summarized the TTF findings by displaying a table he had prepared which was a bottom-line distillation of the TTF reallocations that would be necessary by FY86. It can be seen from Begando's table that the "present" formula, which I have called "Procrustean," for good reason, would transfer funds from Peoria and Rockford to Chicago and Urbana.

Site	Present Formula	TTF Recommendation
Chicago	+419,000	-1,263,200
UC	+639,000	+1,448,000
Peoria	-649,000	-155,000
Rockford	-407,000	+12,000

Begando, as was his want, suggested that both formulae represented "extremes" and that a compromise should be possible. Although I could have lived with either recommendation or an average of the two "extremes," it was unworthy of Begando to cite the TTF recommendation as "extreme."

It was the best representation of real-world funding that had been developed to date, and it was the most objective approach to budgeting the College of Medicine had seen in the twelve years that I had been on duty.

When Phil Forman saw these stark results, he stated that if the recommendations of the TTF were followed, the faculty at UICOM-C would raise the issue of whether we should continue with four sites of medical education. Newman quickly seconded Forman's remark with a dig at Urbana and added that Peoria would soon have seventy-six residents to factor into the formula. Rockford's Salafsky, looking for the moment at a small potential gain of $12,000 rather than a loss from the TTF recommendation, kept silent at this point. I had maintained silence for most of the two hours, but since our meeting time was so limited for such a crucial discussion, and Chicago and Peoria's first thoughts were to solve the formula-budgeting problem by getting rid of a medical-education site (guess which one), I stated that the TTF recommendation looked very solid and objective to me. Yet, I argued, it would be naive to believe that a consensus on how to deal with the TTF recommendations could be achieved within UICOM and suggested that the university employ an external consultant to review the findings of the technical task force and to make recommendations to the president.

I declared that the report put the college on trial on the issue of fairness for all its sites and urged my fellow administrators to separate two well-defined issues: college structure and college financing. The structure had been defined on November 20, I insisted, trying to fend off a new assault on the existence of clinical education in Urbana. Our existence was a Board of Trustees' policy. The trustees also approved the principle of the enrollment-driven budget formula. These two issues should not be resolved through the sacrifice of the UC program, I said.

In this renewed tense atmosphere, Begando stated that he did not see a quick decision on this matter and added that he would set up a second meeting of this group (except for Brady who was retiring from the University of Illinois to take a position at the University of California the next day) to meet sometime after the first of the year.

Weir, trying to avoid presidential involvement, said that he hoped the college could resolve the issue internally and urged us to come to a consensus decision. An internal process was clearly the easiest and most cost-effective way to proceed. I knew that the college could not handle the matter without scapegoating SBMS/SCM-UC, but I held my tongue at this point because nothing was being said that could substantively affect the outcome of the day's discourse.

After the meeting was over, Paula Treichler, my associate dean for student affairs, informed me that she had talked to Pete Czajkowski while we were all waiting for air transportation to return us to Urbana. According to Paula, Czajkowski told her, "Things are trending towards Urbana-Champaign. Dan may not get as much as he wants, but things are looking fairly good for him. It will take longer than he had hoped it would." Coming from the head of the TTF, that was music to my ears, but I knew that the Urbana medical-education program was still at risk. Rockford and Peoria had joined us when Chicago threatened the three of us. Now it was SCM-UC all alone in the cross hairs, a ready target for its sibling schools.

The next day, the Advisory Council of Deans met. After carrying out routine business, we dismissed the staff and met in executive session. I participated by telephone from Urbana. Phil Forman again raised his objections to the report. He felt the TTF had gone beyond its charge by inaccurately taking into account fixed costs. In fact, both Chicago and Rockford were unhappy with the levels of fixed administrative costs reflected in the TTF formula. Czajkowski argued that this was not to cover all administrative costs but was a base administrative cost figure from which one could build.

Forman announced that he was also very concerned that the loss of over a million dollars from ALSM would be very detrimental. I asked him whether the Medical Service Plan (MSP) had not really generated $2 million to $3 million dollars more than usual during the preceding year and whether those funds were not likely to increase in the future. He answered that most of the MSP money was going to the departments that earned it. He cautioned that just because faculty members are earning more MSP money does not necessarily mean that they should give up their state money. Under such conditions, the faculty would conclude that the more they earned in MSP, the more they would lose in state funding.

Rockford and Peoria both made pitches that the funding projected by the TTF recommendations was inadequate to run quality programs. Salafsky reported that he needed additional funds to recruit a full-time Chairman of Medicine. Newman reported that some faculty in Peoria were discussing possible linkage of their departments to the Chicago departmental faculty in order to provide a departmental critical mass that would satisfy the LCME accreditation body. This would have been a spontaneous reversion to SPMC Option II.

I declared that, for the first time ever, the projected UC budget should be considered on a par with the other three regions, adding that Urbana could deliver a full program on the money projected in the TTF recommendation. But the three other sites were not about to stand by passively as money was transferred to Urbana. After considerable discussion, there was agreement that if Urbana were to be equitably funded, the source of those funds had to be external to the college. I did not oppose that position, but it left me uneasy about the possibility that no external funds would be forthcoming. It was clear to me that if there were no additional funds, the college would be forced to carry out an internal reallocation. But the college, in its present mind-set, would never do so on its own. Direction would have to come from the president. The ACD enjoined Kernis to reconvene Mort Weir, Mack Schmidt, Joe Begando, and the directors (as the regional deans would now be known) at an early date to explore solving the problem with additional funds.

It was obvious to me after our Advisory Council of Directors discussions that even though the Urbana program seemed to be approved in perpetuity by the trustees, it was not eternal in the minds and hearts of our colleagues in Chicago, Peoria, and Rockford. One could sense a consensus gelling to the unavoidable conclusion that "painful" as it was (i.e., all my colleagues were prepared to shed funereal tears and offer lamentations at the wake of the Urbana clinical program), SBMS/SCM-UC must be sacrificed to resolve the college's budget problem. Within three months there would be calls from the executive committees of our three sister programs to "regretfully" eliminate the clinical program at Urbana. Instead of a triumphant vindication from the TTF, the UC clinical program was suddenly vulnerable. It existed naked as a plucked chicken. It was right back on the chopping block again.

But I was not for a moment going to allow SCM-UC to be the convenient victim. If we had to think, as a college, about cutting programs to save money, SCM-UC was not the only option. If we were going to reorganize the reorganization, other programs would be explored. For example, there was no good reason to leave Rockford and Peoria as three-year programs. A three-year program is awkward and expensive. Cities like Grand Rapids, Flint, and Kalamazoo, Michigan, had launched perfectly good two-year clinical training programs for Michigan State University at far lower costs in state dollars than had been expended at either Rockford or Peoria. However, my first priority was to get more state funds transferred to the Urbana budget regardless of their source. I did not care whether they came from internal reallocations within the college or from funds available at the campus or presidential levels. Despite all of our triumphs over hardships, the Urbana-Champaign clinical program remained so grossly underfunded that it would continue to exist in a very precarious state until adequate additional funding was actually received.

We had survived thus far because of our unparalleled faculty support, particularly the clinical faculty, who were often unpaid and otherwise underpaid. Double duty was the order of the day. Just taking myself for example, I was dean of SBMS-UC, dean of SCM-UC, chair of the department of internal medicine, and head of the internal-medicine residency program. But our morale was high and our faculty, in both the basic and clinical sciences stood by us with courage and resolve. We were not going to let our antagonists in Chicago starve us into submission.

Our strategy would include several elements:

1. We would vigorously support the recommended TTF formula.
2. We would advocate that those programs that claimed they could not develop quality within the projected TTF budget should be asked to reduce their program to a size and scope for which the TTF budget would be satisfactory.
3. The UICOM-UC position was that its budget was already fixed and that the directors would have had to apply the TTF formula and divide up the resources accordingly.

To confirm my own analysis, I shared a copy of the TTF recommendations with Bud Grulee, who had left the Rockford deanship and who was now Senior Vice President, University of Cincinnati and Director, University of Cincinnati Medical Center. Grulee had left the deanship of RSM in mid-1982. Grulee, who had no axes to grind, in an undated handwritten note, commented: "It seems to me to be a rather even-handed and logical way of cutting the pie, providing that the decision of the Board [of Trustees] last February (1982) is accepted. I suspect that Buzz [Salafsky], Jerry [Newman] and Phil [Forman] have other ideas particularly concerning the development of a clinical program at UC and hope to recapture some of the funds allocated to it. I haven't talked to Buzz lately and therefore [cannot predict] his thinking. What happens from here sure will be an interesting reflection of university politics, to say the least. Especially intriguing is the fact that Elsass and Preissig had significant parts in the process."

Grulee's note was friendly and accurate but hardly reassuring. He knew that my collegial peers vigorously opposed any strengthening of SBMS/SCM-UC. The sum of it all was that the Urbana clinical program was still unaccepted as a permanent institution. Powerful forces were obviously interested in our demise. Within the asylum equity for Urbana remained a policy oxymoron and the college leadership, which had momentarily embraced the fairness concept of enrollment-based budgeting, had since discerned that formula budgeting would favor the clinical program at U-C and would desperately move to renege from its commitment.

CHAPTER 40

Burnout

S O IT WAS THAT MY FELLOW DEANS at Peoria, Rockford, and Chicago, my colleagues and friends for more than twelve years, beset by their own perceived budgetary problems, finally coalesced into a united opposition against the clinical program at Urbana-Champaign. Facing the double-barreled threat of state reductions in funding and the prospect of sharing some of their own inadequate budgets with the new clinical school at Urbana was too much to bear. During Advisory Council of Deans discussions they recoiled from facing Treaty issues. In general, they deeply resented my fixations both on a full four-year program at Urbana as well as on the Treaty, which they perceived as an escape clause from my obligations to the college. They were unsympathetic to my protestations that the Treaty provided for the necessary trust and linkages that SBMS/SCM-UC required to effect its program at UC. The negative attitude of my fellow deems posed a dilemma. If I failed to mention the Treaty while I negotiated I was "immoral and dishonest," but, if I mentioned the Treaty during negotiations, I was "disloyal and not a team player." What they genuinely wanted was for me to deny the Treaty and be fully committed to UICOM, and that I could not do. Nevertheless, the more hostility that I felt from Chicago, Peoria, and Rockford, the more I was certain that a governance change was the most logical way to proceed.

We came out of the SPMC-Reorganization-Technical Task Force crisis with high hopes for adequate funding and the favorable governance. Although we had made some notable gains, they had been achieved at heavy personal cost. It was no fun to be a pariah and I was weary. The Medical Center administration, particularly Schmidt and Creditor, would have dismissed me in a minute had they thought they could get away with it, but they knew that I had a broad constituency of support in Urbana-Champaign, both within the university and in the community. That support notwithstanding, they had also vastly overrated my power to influence events. Somehow, they envisioned me as a diabolical Rasputin, who dominated the decision-making processes of my faculty and of the UIUC campus.

While I dealt with the twin headaches of survival and governance, things were not running overly smooth in Urbana-Champaign. I still had two distinct schools there to deal with, both of which had their problems and their growing pains. The School of Basic Medical Sciences faculty was now a very strong group of tenured individuals who kept close rein on the dean, his expenditures, and his commitments. They wanted to be certain that not too much money was drained from the basic-sciences budget to support the underfunded clinical program. By University of Illinois statute, deans and others in key administrative positions would undergo a complete review of their performance by a faculty committee every five years. I had recently undergone my five-year review, and, although the overall judgment was favorable, there was ample, sharp criticism directed at me.

Certainly, by the late spring of 1982, I had begun to grow weary. I had fought this battle, almost without letup, for twelve years and was getting very tired, or in modern terms, "burned out." However, I was not so exhausted that I was ready to give up the struggle. Not at all. By this time, the program was so effectively established within the university organization that its struggle for survival had given way to the new struggle for acknowledgment and budget equity.

Although it was against my principles to resign in the midst of an ongoing disagreement, I was prepared to consider a strategic resignation if that would help the school. I'd held the deanship for twelve years now and had accomplished most of what I had set out to do. I recognized the symptoms of burnout in myself and that new, vigorous leadership might be healthy for the school. The pettiness in the Chicago leadership might delay future development, but I remained optimistic about the future of UICOM-UC.

With this in mind, I sent up a trial balloon on May 26, 1982, with the following letter to Acting Executive Dean Marten Kernis: "I hereby resign from my position as Dean/Director of SBMS/SCM-UC (UICOM-UC) in order to assume an active academic role in UICOM-UC as Professor of Medicine. This resignation will become effective June 30, 1983 or when a new director is appointed for UICOM-UC, whichever is earlier." However, I made that resignation contingent upon an agreement signed within seven days by Ikenberry, Begando and Kernis to secure specific budget figures for the 1983 through 1984 fiscal years.

Kernis passed the letter along to Schmidt, but neither Schmidt nor Kernis took the bait. Schmidt wrote the following to Kernis on June 19, 1982: "I have reviewed and discussed with the chancellor, Dean Bloomfield's May 26, 1982 letter of resignation contingent upon the signed agreement by President Ikenberry, Chancellor Begando and you that the FY 1983 budget of UICOM-UC be increased by $150,000, the FY 1984 budget be no less than $3,400,000 and the FY 1985 budget be no less than $3,750,000 (in 1983 dollars).

"Since none of us can guarantee much about the future, much less future appropriations to the university, Dr. Bloomfield's request is impossible to fulfill, as I suspect he knows full well. This leaves us with several questions to discuss. You may share this letter with Dan, if you wish."

I was happy that they did not take that bait. Selling out for a quick $150,000 and the bare-boned needs of FY84 and FY85 would have been too little.

In attempting to get the $150,000 we needed for the 1983 fiscal year, I also slipped out of channels and arranged another personal meeting with Executive Vice President Ron Brady on June 3, 1982. I explained to Brady that although we would eventually need one million in additional dollars, the school's immediate needs to support the teaching program totaled only $150,000. That much, together with the sizable amount of goodwill that existed in the community would allow us to proceed satisfactorily. That was the size of my problem, and once the funds were delivered, we could get the teaching job done.

Brady's response was memorable. He tactfully informed me that personalities were in the way. As if I had failed to notice, he told me there was considerable displeasure with me in Chicago. The department heads in Chicago thought that Urbana hadn't played fair in the reorganization and felt that giving Urbana more money would be tantamount to rewarding such behavior. He stated that the department heads formed a significant pressure block on Phil Forman and Mack Schmidt. (I learned how true this was in 1995, when Forman told me that it was pressure from the department heads rather than from Schmidt or Creditor, as I had assumed, that had prompted him to submit his amendment to the Grand Compromise in December 1981.)

Brady further explained that bureaucrats within the Medical Center administration were uneasy because they did not know what changes would occur in the wake of Joe Begando's retirement. Brady also added that finances at the Medical Center were not so bad. The hospital appeared to be moving toward a $3 million positive balance that year rather than the severe negative deficit that had been projected. The Medical Service Plan income had increased to about $10 million annually and, he added, "Things are improving in Chicago. They are not so tight." What he also implied was that there was sufficient money in Chicago to cover my $150,000, but out of spite, it would not be granted.

At this point, I suggested that perhaps I could approach Mack Schmidt in such a way that Mack might consider burying the hatchet. Brady answered that I was naive to think so. "Schmidt" he said, "is the type of bureaucrat who keeps 'book' on his opponents." To emphasize the point, Brady added, "He keeps it right down here in a desk drawer and is ready to pull it from the drawer at the first opportunity. He will *never* forgive anyone who has crossed him. You," he said, pointing at me with an extended right index finger, "have crossed him."

Brady matter-of-factly suggested that as long as Dan Bloomfield remained in charge, the Urbana-Champaign program would be markedly limited. Because I was already considering retirement from the deanship, I asked him whether, if I stepped down, I could be assured that Urbana-Champaign would get a fair shake. He pointed out that that was a "Catch 22" question, and he could not provide an answer for me. Brady mentioned that he had also heard rumors that I was considering resignation provided that Urbana-Champaign was adequately funded. He apparently was not consulted directly on the issue, but he knew about it.

I told Brady that Marty Kernis had visited Urbana-Champaign the previous day for the purpose of reviewing my performance with my executive committee. The committee had given Kernis a strong message not to "rock the boat." Lowell Hager immediately berated him for even considering a change in administration. Allan Levy pointed out that I had just had a five-year review and that unless there was significant new information this should be a pro forma review. Many others of the combined executive committees of SBMS/SCM-UC joined together to support my deanship. After the meeting, Kernis came to meet me. He was clearly upset and tense. I suspected at the time that he was under orders to find fault with my leadership and to remove me from office, but he could not do that in the face of such strong local support. He read notes he had taken in the meeting, including such comments as "good leader, dedicated to quality, much improved in the past five years, etc." The only criticism voiced was that I delegated too much authority to Hal Swartz.

I then told Brady how Kernis hesitated for some time as if he were very doubtful and almost in pain before he finally told me, "Well, I'm going to recommend your reappointment. Mack Schmidt will have to make his own decision." When he heard this information, Ron Brady smiled and whistled softly. I stayed silent. Then, after a pause that permitted Brady to measure what he said, he continued, "Well, that sure puts Schmidt between a rock and a hard place. He thought he had Kernis set up to do the dirty work." This was a clear revelation that Schmidt intended not to reappoint me. Both Brady and I agreed that it would be interesting to see what Schmidt would do next.

I told Brady that Schmidt, as VCAA, a campuswide position, had no business micromanaging the College of Medicine. Brady agreed that it was inappropriate and repeated that he would try to have Schmidt and Kernis act in statesmanlike fashion. I wrote to Brady after our meeting to confirm our discussion and ask that he act in a timely fashion. If we did not get the money, then we had to decide whether Urbana-Champaign would ever get equity within this College of Medicine and this medical administration.

Brady's conversation confirmed what I already knew, namely that the current money shortage under which we were laboring was largely the result of a personal vendetta by Chicago administrators, not the absence of funds. Their egregious behavior was possible only because they were supported by a sympathetic university president, who would not overrule them. It was a shameful performance, unworthy of a great university.

I reported on our progress within the College of Medicine, or lack thereof, regularly to my executive committees. Furthermore, I made no secret of my expectations, knowing that the 1984 fiscal year would be another bad budget year for the university and that no additional state funding would be coming into UICOM. I informed them that I remained confident that the TTF, no matter how skewed it was against us, in a worst-case scenario, would still recommend the reallocation of significant funds to Urbana-Champaign. I told them that I had publicly asked the Chicago administration to immediately place a hiring freeze on all units of the College of Medicine until this matter was settled, a request that, of course, was refused.

Kernis called me on June 25, 1982 and told me that he had sent a letter to Schmidt and Begando recommending my reappointment. That letter was based on the advice of the SBMS/SCM-UC Executive Committees. However, Kernis advised me that he had been directed by Schmidt to offer me two options. Option A was for me to give them a letter of resignation to be effective June 30, 1983. This would be not be made public until a mutually agreed time. Option B was that if I did not resign, I would be reappointed only until June 30, 1983, with a letter specifying that this was my last appointment as dean. So here it was at last. Something I had expected for a long time. Schmidt and/or Begando had finally come to the conclusion that they needed a new, more friendly, and more collegial administration in Champaign-Urbana. I was being fired!

Following the Kernis call, I talked with Ned Goldwasser. He was not at all surprised and told me that the Medical Center administration position all through the discussions was that once there was a completed reorganization, and a new college dean, and a new agreement between the campuses, there should be a change in administration throughout the college. According to Ned, both he and Cribbet advised Schmidt and Begando that this was probably not the time to replace me, and perhaps that is why they both agreed to make the date June 30, 1983. Nevertheless, Ned said that it would be appropriate for a VCAA to "clear the decks for the new dean." It would make it easier to recruit a new dean of the college if that official had the opportunity to appoint his or her own regional directors.

After these discussions, I mobilized my close friends and advisors, including Ben Williams, Allan Levy, Hal Swartz, and Ron Aldrich. We met at 9 a.m. on June 28, 1982, whereupon I told them about the Kernis call, my discussions with Ned Goldwasser, and the options that had been given to me. I also filled them in on Ron Brady's view of current and future UICOM-UC funding. The mood was serious. Ben Williams asked me whether I really wanted to retire from the leadership. He said the choice was mine, because if I intended to stay on they would back me to the hilt. The group asked what my real plans were. Did I want to fight this move? I answered that I was tired—tired of the continuous stress, tired of being the underdog, tired of playing the spoiler, and tired of the continuous fight against city hall. Moreover, I felt somewhat burned out, and I believed that the school at this time could benefit from new and vigorous direction. Furthermore, I explained that Brady had essentially told me that as long as

Schmidt remained in power at UIMC, I would be a funding albatross for the Urbana program. I repeated that I had concluded, on reflection, that I ought to step down at this point and that I did not feel the timing was particularly bad.

On a more personal note, I was not enamored of the provision in the college reorganization plan that called for a single dean in Chicago and "directors" at Peoria, Rockford, and Urbana. I was vain enough to find the demotion from dean to director distasteful.

Friends that they were, they respected my decision, and, from then on, we talked about timing and strategy. I told them that I thought it best for the schools that there be no "acting dean" appointed, because such a person would have far more difficulty in opposing another move to shut us down than I or a new appointee would. They heartily agreed. There was also general agreement that I should send my letter of resignation to the president, who was most likely to accept its single contingency, copying it to all the major administrators on both campuses.

The group wanted to know if I had any particular plans for leaving Urbana-Champaign, and I replied that I did not. I told them that my name had been thrown into the hopper as a candidate for the College of Medicine deanship, but that I knew full well that under no circumstances would either Schmidt or the president appoint me. Some felt that my candidacy should nevertheless be pursued, if only to increase pressure for an outside choice. I advised them that although Phil Forman, in my opinion, was a good inside choice, he remained at the time much too closely identified with Chicago and to its budget interpretations.

I thanked my friends for their unstinting support over the years and told them that since I planned to remain in Urbana, we would remain close. After the meeting, I drafted my letter of resignation and forwarded it to Stanley Ikenberry that same day, June 28, 1982: "Please accept my resignation as Dean of the Schools of Basic Medical Sciences and Clinical Medicine at Urbana-Champaign (University of Illinois College of Medicine at Urbana-Champaign), to be effective whenever a successor is appointed in my place. My reasons for resigning at this time are as follows:

1. The reorganization of the College of Medicine heralds a new era in the development of the college. The new college dean should have the option of appointing key regional administrators.

2. Conclusion of the agreement between the chancellors at UIMC and UIUC has provided an improved governance for UICOM-UC that will allow it the opportunity to develop to the advantage of both campuses and to the university.

3. Planning my resignation at this time will allow adequate time for a search process and avoid the inherent instability associated with the appointment of an acting administrator. I have discussed this aspect with key faculty and community leaders and together we recommend that the search process for my successor begin at an early date, although late enough that the new college dean will be adequately involved in the selection process.

4. The plan for an orderly process of succession at UICOM-UC will provide solid evidence of stability and continuity for the forthcoming LCME accreditation visit in 1983.

5. It is my personal belief that new and vigorous leadership is in the best interest of UICOM-UC at this time. Furthermore, after twelve years as dean, I have achieved those objectives for which I was appointed and am now anxious to step down in order to return as Professor of Medicine to a faculty of teaching and research.

"I consider it a great honor to have served the college and the university as Dean of SBMS/SCM-UC. For the duration of my tenure as dean, I shall make every effort to see that the UICOM reorganization goes smoothly at Urbana-Champaign, that the chancellors' agreement is endorsed by the SBMS/SCM-UC faculty, and that the SBMS/SCM-UC faculty will approach the forthcoming accreditation visit by the LCME as confident members of a single college."

The letter of resignation was sent seven days after my letter of June 21 in which I urged the faculty to accept the college reorganization as the best deal we could get at that time. My resignation was accepted promptly.

News of my resignation was quickly reported on the front page of our local newspaper. Lex Peterson, *News-Gazette* staff writer, noted in her article of July 7, 1982:

A strong-willed and single-minded man, Bloomfield created the Basic Medicine School nearly of whole cloth and a $150,000 budget back in 1970. It took him seven years to pull off the Clinical School, which has tight associations with hospitals in Champaign-Urbana and Danville.

The fate of that school was tested last year when the UI administration attempted, unsuccessfully, to shut it down during a major reorganization of UI medical education. But that was not the only bad time.

"The unhappy times were the repeated delays in developing the clinical program," he said Tuesday. "While Lyle Lanier (former UI Provost) didn't promise a full four-year program in 1970, he asked me to take a good look at the campus and judge how long a complete four-year program could be denied. It was denied longer than my optimistic being could conceive. But it's done."

Characteristically, Bloomfield submitted his resignation directly to Ikenberry June 28 instead of to his College of Medicine superiors in Chicago and stipulated it not be effective until a permanent replacement is named. "Acting" or "Interim" Deans are common at the UI.

The *Daily Illini*, the university student newspaper, also headlined the resignation on July 9, and added:

Joe Begando, Chancellor of the University's Medical Center Campus, which oversees the College of Medicine, said he was not surprised by the resignation. He said Bloomfield "had been Dean for a long time" and felt he had "accomplished his objectives."

Bloomfield agreed. He said one of his major objectives was integrating the medical program here with the entire campus. "One of the highest points of my twelve years here occurred in October 1981, when the Urbana-Champaign Senate endorsed the concept that the medical college was academically important to the campus," he said. Begando said he is glad Bloomfield chose to serve in the interim period before a permanent replacement is named.

"I do personally appreciate that he is willing to serve in the interim period. I'd compliment him on what he's achieved. He built a good program.'"

Thus, Joe Begando was most gracious in my retirement.

I also wrote to Paul Stone, who played such a pivotal role in our survival, to thank him one last time for his critical support. There were any number of other letters sent and received relative to my resignation, but none more appreciated than the letter from UIUC Chancellor John Cribbet, who wrote:

I have received a copy of your June 28, 1982 letter to Dr. Ikenberry resigning your position as Dean of the Schools of Basic Medical Sciences and Clinical Medicine at Urbana-Champaign to be effective whenever a successor is appointed in your place. It was a statesmanlike letter and I read it with a feeling of nostalgia. You have done a great job as dean, and I have enjoyed working with you, both as a fellow dean and as Chancellor of the Urbana-Champaign campus.

In my judgment, you were the right man at the right place, at the right time, and I feel certain that the medical program at Urbana-Champaign would not be at the position it now occupies without your leadership, your drive, and your vision. I am glad that I will still be working with you during the period until your successor is appointed and I am even more pleased that you will be remaining on the campus as a colleague.

I do feel that probably this is a very wise move on your part. I served as Dean of the College of Law for twelve years, and I know that there comes a time when it is best to give someone else the reins of leadership. I had not really thought of moving from the deanship to the chancellorship but, given the circumstances, I think it was probably a wise decision on my part to try the "poisoned chalice" for a while. Like you, I have enjoyed the challenges and one always hopes that he does make some difference in the development of a great institution.

CHAPTER 41

Searching for Solutions

T HE PRINCIPAL FINDING of the Technical Task Force, flawed
though it may have been, was the exposure of serious distributive
inequities. Knowing that I was in a relatively strong position as a
lame-duck administrator, I was determined to expose the skewed distribution of resources within the college, now documented by an impartial
group. By the terms of my 1982 resignation, the Chicago administration
could not replace me, much as they would have liked to, until they found a
permanent replacement. Such a person, going through the laborious search
process, which includes many one-on-one interviews with faculty and staff,
would inevitably learn about our budget problems and would be advised to
demand budget equity as a part of his/her employment contract.

Only at the University of Illinois could a meaningful success such as the
TTF report, which confirmed the administrative abuse of SCM-UC, turn
into a near-disaster for the victim. Our collegial peers interpreted the TTF
report that vindicated the UICOM-UC position as an excuse to close our
program down. It mattered not to them that by comparison with other peer
medical schools, UICOM was generously funded. Nor did it matter that the
TTF, in constructing its recommendations, bent over backward to satisfy the
Chicago need to justify its very generous state budget. Those things didn't
matter because, even with the heavy pro-Chicago bias, the TTF recommendation still would have reallocated more than $1 million from the other
units to SCM-UC. Without the Chicago bias, the reallocation to Urbana
would have been closer to $2 million.

Joe Begando, Mack Schmidt, and Marty Kernis viewed the TTF figures in
a virtual state of shock. Now it was "spin" time, and they were very accomplished at putting the right spin on messages. They immediately emphasized
how they had spoken all along only of "refinements" to the "present" formula, implying that they were prepared to reallocate twenty cents here and
thirty-two cents there, but little else. The TTF recommendation was too

honest and too revealing for them to accept. Even though their signatures were on the operative documents that had defined the TTF role and that had been approved at all university levels, including the Board of Trustees, they balked. Like children who played marbles for keeps and lost more than they could endure, they tearfully complained they wanted their marbles back.

The responses of the three administrators at Chicago, Peoria, and Rockford were initially tempered by the knowledge that the Urbana clinical program had been given legitimacy by the accepted UICOM reorganization plan and by the Board of Trustees so that eliminating SCM-UC was no longer an option they could promote. So they, along with Kernis, Schmidt, and Begando minimized the importance of the TTF recommendation. Their reasoning was along these lines: "It's only a recommendation…If I had ever thought there would be this kind of change, I would never have supported the TTF…Formula budgeting was a bad idea; its time has come and gone…The TTF is biased toward Urbana…Formula budgeting is absurd."

Collectively, they wanted to bury the report so deep that it would never again see the light of day. They called it a nice try that failed and urged reversion to the original Brady formula. My reminders to them that formula budgeting was now Board of Trustees policy fell on deaf ears and closed minds.

On January 10, 1983, Kernis reconvened the administrative group that had received the TTF report six weeks earlier. There being no advanced agenda, I assumed there would be an announcement of how the TTF decision would be handled, or a discussion of methods by which we could have garnered additional external funds in the absence of any will to reallocate. But I was wrong. Kernis had prepared for this meeting a group of tables that demonstrated the serious financial plight of the college, presumably to convince Vice President Mort Weir that reallocation within the college was impossible and that only additional funds from external sources could solve the college's problem with UICOM-UC.

The tables also showed that, during the previous five years, the Chicago campus had received as many new state dollars as had Champaign-Urbana. In fact, however, when the final accounting was done to determine where the medical-expansion money went, it was shown that, instead of the new funds being focused on the regional medical-education sites, more than half of the total wound up in Chicago salaries and buildings.

I distributed copies of the recent chancellor's agreement underlining the role to be played by the TTF in the reallocation of funds. That went over poorly, even with Mort Weir, who held that a literal interpretation of the TTF report was probably not going to solve the college's problem. Weir did point out, however, that although some adjustments might be made in the TTF report relating to fixed costs, "Unless there is a reopening of the college organization, I would recommend the TTF report to the president." When Forman, Newman, and Salafsky cited their many objections to the TTF report, Weir responded that despite its flaws, the report was the best solution in sight. He also said that downsizing the college was politically unwise at this time.

Mack Schmidt posed three questions: 1. How may options be advanced? 2. Who makes the decision? 3. Will any decision stick?

Weir said he could not argue to the Board of Trustees that the college was underfunded. The peer data from other state medical schools was compelling on that issue. He reiterated that, barring another reorganization, the TTF recommendations would stick.

Weir's bluntness was followed by a long and sad lamentation from Acting Executive Dean Kernis about how Urbana-Champaign had never really been funded adequately, and dreadful shame that it was, the reality of the times demanded that there just were not enough funds to go around. As a result, he had come to the "inescapable conclusion" that the Urbana-Champaign clinical program, despite achievements that no one could deny, should be closed. Newman, Salafsky, and Forman immediately chimed in with the equivalent of "Amen."

Instead of posing some novel funding ideas, there was a gathering consensus in the room that the clinical program at Urbana-Champaign had to go. *Deja vu!* Here we go again. Only Mort Weir and I were outside the consensus, and I couldn't fathom at that time where Weir, in his new vice presidential role really stood. Nor was I certain that Kernis and Schmidt had not choreographed this ballet in advance for Weir's benefit, but I reacted to this new assault as quickly as I could gather my wits and told the group that I was not buying it. If we were going to talk reorganization again, then we were going to talk about downsizing Rockford and Peoria to two years and reducing enrollments in Chicago. I challenged my colleagues by again stating that I could deliver my program with the present budget under the TTF formula and asked provocatively, why couldn't they? The talk of another reorganization died down, but otherwise we solved nothing.

I called Paul Stone that evening to bring him up-to-date. I cautioned him that there were still strong thoughts about reorganizing the college again to eliminate the Urbana-Champaign clinical program and that he might be solicited for his opinion on the matter. He was grateful for the information and said he would be in contact with the president about it.

On January 26, 1983, VCAA Schmidt reported to the UIMC Campus Planning Council that the governor's rescission of appropriations for the 1983 fiscal year would amount to at least $515,000 for UIMC, an amount that could be covered entirely by "campus reserves." Further rescissions were to come from pro rata reductions of campus unit's budgets. Although the amount of "campus reserves" was unknown, it became very clear, as if it were not clear already, that money was available to cover UICOM-UC needs.

However, after the January 10 meeting, it became clear that our colleagues in the other regional schools, unleashed by Kernis's "inescapable conclusion" that clinical education in Urbana was a luxury the college could not afford, were now planning collectively and publicly to call for our dissolution. It was as if the other three schools suddenly awakened from a deep sleep to see SCM-UC, not only as a clinical rival, but also as a serious competitor for fiscal resources. It was too much for our regional siblings to bear. For my part, however, having steered UICOM-UC through the long authorization process, an even longer start-up process, and through the 1981–82 threats of closure, I was not about to give up in 1983.

Like pus from a ripe boil came a series of malicious resolutions from our collegial friends in Chicago, Peoria, and Rockford that would eliminate clinical education at Urbana-Champaign. This from a group of administrators bent on selling their educational achievements, but who did not do their fiscal homework. I had believed all along that my colleagues did not know what they were doing when they supported the TTF and enrollment-driven budget. But the item had been on the agenda for fourteen months and one might suspect that they had done some simple arithmetic to shed light on what their negotiated agreements would cost. But alas, neither the regional deans nor the UIMC leadership seemed prepared for the TTF numbers, and the very group that chided me as not being a team player decided to solve their team problem by eliminating clinical education at Urbana.

In what appeared to be an orchestrated fashion, one by one, the executive committee resolutions from Chicago, Rockford, and Peoria, called for our elimination. Resolutions from UICOM-Chicago and Rockford were passed on February 11. The Rockford resolution also asked for elimination of our basic-science program. Peoria's resolution to close the clinical science program at Urbana-Champaign came a month later on March 18. Interestingly, four members of the Peoria faculty dissented and submitted a minority report on March 28, 1983, which said, "We believe that it is important that the four educational sites of the College of Medicine regain a sense of mutual respect and confidence...Our recommendation is that we begin by trying to honor the original agreement to maintain four educational sites within the College of Medicine, including a clinical facility and faculty at Urbana."

Fortunately for us, the timing of these resolutions could not have been worse for their cause. Had they come during the consensus meetings of November and December 1981, or even when the TTF made its report in November 1982, the clinical program in Champaign-Urbana might have been in serious trouble. But this was 1983, and the president and the Board of Trustees were newly recommitted to four regional programs that had been sold to them by the college. A policy flip-flop at this point was very unlikely.

Kernis invited VCAA Schmidt to our February 9 Advisory Council of Deans meeting where we once again, with Mack Schmidt voicing his song of fiscal doom and gloom, engaged in lengthy discussions related to the shortage of funds and possible solutions. Schmidt added one new twist—the state might rescind some of the funds already appropriated for the 1983 fiscal year.

A day later, Kernis wrote to the four deans to say, "Our lengthy conversation yesterday resulted in my reaching the conclusion that Vice Chancellor Schmidt is asking us to provide to him and the General University a series of alternatives relating to budget, the material from the Technical Task Force, and the desirable size of the student body in the college. I concur with Dr. Schmidt that whatever we perceive our problems in the college to be, *we must ultimately be the responsible agents to transmit recommendations forward.* Though it is obvious that we cannot achieve unanimity among the five of us, it is equally clear that each of us is entirely capable of debate and decision-making." He went on to ask us for the pros and cons of the TTF report and any alternatives to the proposal, as well as a detailed explanation of our budget needs in the 1983-85 fiscal years with particular reference to how the TTF recommendations and any alternatives would affect them. He also asked that we supply "a well-supported narrative of your opinion concerning the size of the student body in the college given the conditions that pertain nationally, as well as locally."

Wow! Speaking of sore losers. It was not enough that I resigned. It was apparent that Schmidt and Kernis, one way or another, were going to punish UICOM-UC. The request angered me. He and Schmidt were intent on keeping the decision on either reorganization (read: finally get rid of clinical education in Urbana) or the TTF (read: we cannot follow the TTF recommendation because, in that case, Urbana would win) within the college, where the outcome was certain.

I hated writing long explanatory letters and memoranda. They are grim signs of communication failure and deep organizational divisions. But from where I sat, there was no other way to document my dissent as objectively as possible. Besides, I always entertained the naive hope that the Chicago administration might actually reconsider its miasmatical, ruinous attitude towards us. So on February 23, I replied:

> Before taking up the issues of the memorandum, I first believe it important to point out that in seeking these recommendations from the Advisory Council of Deans, you and Vice Chancellor Schmidt appear to be proceeding contrary to the process upon which the consensus reorganization was developed. The first paragraph of our reorganization proposal states, "The recommendations contained in this proposal...have been constructed by the deans of the schools within the college in a series of meetings with the executive vice president and the chancellor at the Medical Center. The president of the university has requested the group to seek consensus on a reorganization plan for the College of Medicine." The president took that initiative because the college proved unable to present a cohesive reorganization plan. Interim Executive Dean Creditor was purposefully excluded from the discussions, which finally led to a collegewide consensus, and Vice President Brady was specifically identified as a participant to bring the discussions to the university level.

> At the meeting organized [but not attended] by the president, the group achieved consensus on a general plan for reorganization and on the concept of an enrollment-driven formula for budget allocation to

the regions, but did not achieve consensus on the formula per se. For
that reason, the *university* established a Technical Task Force to continue
to refine the budget formula used as a *point of departure* for the planning process. [Emphasis added.]

It seems entirely inappropriate at this time to attempt to reverse an
agreed-upon process already transmitted to and accepted by the Board
of Trustees and to request a lame-duck group of administrators such as
the present Advisory Council of Deans to make recommendations
which may have very important long-range implications for the next
administration of the College of Medicine.

It remains my view, therefore, that the recommendations of the
Technical Task Force should be implemented as soon as possible and the
newly recruited administrative personnel be carefully advised regarding
the budget situation. Even with current budgetary restrictions *there is
enough money in this college to do the job at all four sites in accordance
with the reorganization plan and the TTF recommendation. Towards that
end, the university will find no shortage of acceptable administrative candidates for all four sites, able and willing to manage on the amounts recommended by the TTF. What is sorely needed by the college is stability and
a 'can-do' administration.* What is not needed is a refusal to accept the
results of a long and painful (and imperfect) process which leads to
continued instability, uncollegial resolutions and nonproductive use
of resources.

I went on to say that UICOM-UC's determination to have the TTF budgeting accepted was not the first step in our demanding more and more state
resources. We had already submitted to Kernis (and to Creditor before him)
a detailed staffing plan and budget for each of the four years of the medical-
education program at Urbana. It included the exact number of MDs, Ph.D.s,
teaching assistants, academic professionals, and nonacademic staff required
for the complete program. Also included were salary and fringe-benefit
costs, building-operations and maintenance costs, and all expenses. This
translated into a budget requirement of $4,222,000 by the 1985 fiscal year.
Since the UICOM-UC operating budget for fiscal 1983 was $2,949,000, the
budget shortfall to be made up by 1985 was $1,273,000.

The TTF formula would have given $4,148,000 to UICOM-UC from a
college state budget total of $31,609,000. The figure for Urbana-Champaign

was 13.12 percent of the total. In raw terms, we would serve 15.6 percent of the college medical-student enrollment with that 13.12 percent. Were the college budget to remain the same in fiscal 1985, our shortfall would have been only $74,000. We could work with these numbers.

In light of these numbers, I argued, "Neither UICOM-UC nor the UIUC campus is interested in the development of classical full-time clinical departments that characterize traditional medical schools. The modest amounts of state funds required for UICOM-UC clinical development are planned to provide an academic core around which community and VA hospital physicians will teach." I also pointed out that, even under the TTF recommendation, UICOM-UC would still receive the lowest number of dollars per medical student from the state.

To emphasize the point that we had no greater designs on funding, I outlined a five-year plan that I believed the executive committee would have approved. The key provision was that we would agree to operate UICOM-UC on the 13.12 percent share of the college budget that the TTF recommended, and that, using that budget share, we would in five years be able to qualify for separate LCME accreditation if the university wished to pursue separate governance for our school. The final provision was that there would be no SCM-UC request for a university hospital.

Then, I went on to provide the information Kernis requested: that the Technical Task Force report was the worst possible formula for distribution of funds within the college except for every other formula examined; that it was heavily biased toward the larger units; that the TTF report struck a balance better than anything previously seen; and that we should get on with the job.

Mack Schmidt, in a pathetic defense of Kernis, rebutted on March 16, writing that Chancellor Begando and others had stated over and over again that the Technical Task Force was to recommend refinements of the Brady enrollment-driven formula for state funds.

He said that he was not ready to concede that the Technical Task Force recommendations were the last word, given that several persons had stated that better alternatives could be found. Schmidt essentially saw the Technical Task Force as window dressing for a budget-distribution system that he did not want to change. This was the attitude of the chancellor and all the other deans of the college. I alone in the asylum was innocent enough to believe that the Technical Task Force would restore a semblance of sanity and equity to the management of the College of Medicine. That hope was being ground into the dust.

Kernis received from each region, except Urbana, a justification for ignoring the TTF recommendation. The ambivalence of the others' feelings toward Urbana is illustrated by a quote from RSM Dean Salafsky's reply of March 31, 1983: "If it is a given, for political reasons, that the College of Medicine at UC will be maintained, I will only add, as I indicated to you in our phone conversation, that, at a minimum, Urbana should openly renounce their plans to develop an independent four-year College of Medicine. This, as you know, has been a very sore point here." (What this had to do with budget equity is beyond me.)

From the lengthy replies he received, Kernis produced an even lengthier, comprehensive report, dated April 4, 1983, which he sent to Chancellor Langenberg (who had replaced the retired Joe Begando) and VCAA Schmidt. The report boiled down to a plea for more money for the entire college and for regjection of formula budgeting. He argued, "A new dean will demonstrate the fairness, equity, integrity, and commitment to regionalization" that would make formula budgeting unnecessary. Veering from his main theme, he chided the UICOM-UC and UIUC campus administrations for their rhetoric calling for an independent downstate medical school linked to UIUC, and urged them to rescind it. To make his point, Kernis gratuitously went on to say, "Faculty members and administrators who cannot concur with this basic principle should be invited to seek opportunity elsewhere." There is little doubt as to whom he was directing that last statement.

Kernis ended his report with a discussion of what he saw as five alternatives from which the university could choose. The five were:

1. Do nothing.
2. Implement the TTF formula.
3. Close the clinical program at Urbana-Champaign.
4. Use the "Brady Formula."
5. Delay further development in Urbana-Champaign.

He listed the pros and cons of each position from a decidedly biased view. Although he acknowledged the poverty of the Urbana program, in listing the disadvantages of doing nothing, for instance, he failed to mention that doing nothing would perpetuate UICOM-UC's abysmal funding situation.

Kernis continued to chant the mantra that the college did not have enough funds to reallocate resources. He blamed this situation essentially on having four regional units. Implementing the TTF formula, he said, "offers [neither] recognition nor solution to the generally acknowledged problem that the College of Medicine does not have enough state support to fulfill its programmatic objectives...Four regional programs, in fact, are more expensive to operate. Comparisons with the funding patterns of other medical schools may be of interest, but they fail to provide guidance because our structure is unique and very costly."

Kernis was at his worst when he tried to enumerate the advantages of formula budgeting. All he wrote was that "1. It is a formula-driven budget as was anticipated by reorganization," and "2. Meets the objective of one constituency" (guess which one). Had he been objective, he might have noted the following advantages:

1. It would prevent the dean from favoring one region over another.
2. It was the only form of allocation agreed upon at the consensus talks. As such, formula budgeting was ratified by the faculty, the two Senates and the Board of Trustees.
3. It would have been profoundly simple to administer.

Kernis then went on to lay out factors that "must be accommodated in the development of a strategic funding plan." He listed them as: the university's commitment to a single College of Medicine; the college, as a whole, was inadequately funded; the commitment to the Medical Scholars Program at Urbana and to the MD/Ph.D. program at the other schools was equally shared; an unequivocal commitment to assuring quality at all sites; the Urbana-Champaign clinical program had never been adequately funded; and finally, "the state's fiscal problems that result in continuing decrements in the college's funding preclude the college's ability to reallocate."

He went on:

In addition to these factors, there is the fundamental issue of the validity of even attempting to rationalize a formula through which state funds will be reallocated. If we have developed the need for a formula because of distrust of motivation by one constituency toward another, we have made a very sad and damaging mistake. Formula budgeting within our college is an absurdity that should be stricken from our guidelines promptly. We need commitment within the institution and the resources to fulfill that commitment. I, therefore, propose the following plan, which, in my judgment, accommodates to most needs of the college, reaffirms regionalization, emphasizes the university's commitment to a strong College of Medicine, and permits us the opportunity to go about our business.

In each of the next four years, the college shall receive from the university (General University, Urbana Campus, Chicago Campus, and/or Health Sciences Center) $200,000 of incremental recurring funds that will be assigned to the College of Medicine at Urbana-Champaign. These funds would be in addition to any general salary or price increases that may occur...In order for this proposal to respond completely to the critical shortage of funds facing the college, the university is urged to recognize in addition that Chicago, Peoria, and Rockford continue to be underfunded. There must be a commitment from the university to include in subsequent budget requests from the Board of Trustees, the Illinois Board of Higher Education, the General Assembly and the governor additional program funding at least so that equity with SIU is achieved. Absent such support, there will be continuing confusion as to the degree to which these agencies actually believe in our regionalized program thrusts.

This proposal addresses the concerns that have been voiced regarding future funding of the college as well as its future stability. It is anticipated that the degree of cooperation that recently was achieved among the sites (i.e., election of an Executive Committee, approval of bylaws) will continue and improve. Support by state agencies, the General University, and the two campuses will be imperative as a means of enhancing the effort.

Before he sent this lengthy proposal to Langenberg and Schmidt, Kernis circulated a draft to the deans, which prompted a vigorous response from me on March 31, 1983. First of all, I stated my opposition to another reorganization, which is essentially what the proposal to close the Urbana program represented. I pointed out, "Should the Board of Trustees and the University reverse their policy [on reorganization] then many organizational alternatives, besides the narrow spectrum you suggest, *presumably* will be on the table. Although I appreciate your unambiguous statement regarding 'underfunding' of the program at Urbana, you might consider that when a program has been 'underfunded' for six years, but has carried its share of students during that time, the descriptive terminology becomes suspect; i.e., is it 'underfunded' or is it really 'administratively abused'? You propose, in essence, the same dilatory funding program for UICOM-UC that has existed for the past six years and at the same time condemn formula budgeting. Formula budgeting is university policy that was written explicitly to deny the college administration the opportunity to continue a policy of repeatedly disadvantaging a region, 150 miles away, to avoid painful decisions closer to home. The university administration's first obligation under formula budgeting is to determine the most reasonable formula and to direct the college administration to implement that formula. Then the administration can plan the distribution of new money that comes to the college. The repeated denial of carefully negotiated written agreements by Medical Center administrators is unworthy of this university."

I then described specific areas of concern that we at UICOM-UC "would not only disagree but would dispute as to accuracy." Instead of breaking down the proposal point by point, I stated our general areas of disagreement.

1. *The overall organization of the College of Medicine is not and should not be a variable.* The policy on this has been decided by the university very recently and very firmly and if such a thoroughly reached decision is to be reopened within months after its completion, then the credibility of the College of Medicine, the president, and the university is at stake. Any alternatives that involve a change of organization therefore should not be considered.

2. *Equitable funding at all four sites also is not a valid variable.* Incorporated within the reorganization decisions, as an underlying fundamental principle, is the commitment that all sites would be equitably funded. Therefore, any alternative that either temporarily or permanently proposes anything else should be rejected. The arguments instead should be directed towards the definition of an equitable funding formula. Your statement to discard formula budgeting is contrary to college and university consensus and policy and is therefore inappropriate.

3. *The assumption that the total funding for the College of Medicine is inadequate is not obviously or necessarily true.* If one considers the total

resources available to the College of Medicine they have in fact
increased rather than decreased in the last two years. Arguments which
assume that the total funding within the College of Medicine is inadequate to sustain and nurture the four programs are understandable, but
not necessarily correct.

4. *The new set of arguments which state that regional programs are necessarily more expensive is incorrect.* Not only is the argument incorrect, the
   leadership at Rockford and Peoria notwithstanding, it is completely
   inconsistent with the decision to have equitable funding at all four sites.
   If indeed there are programs within the college that are unable to provide effective medical education with costs comparable to those of the
   other sites, then there may indeed be cause to look into the leadership
   and organization at that site.

5. *Consideration of the Technical Task Force (TTF) report on its merits as a
   report has not occurred and presumably will not occur within the College
   of Medicine.* If the College of Medicine were to have a role in the budget-allocation process, this indeed was its appropriate role. The present
   leadership at the Medical Center has studiously avoided this obligation.
   It was tragic to observe the Executive Committee of a distinguished
   College of Medicine refuse to debate, on its merits, a critical issue, such
   as the development of an enrollment-driven budget formula, which
   virtually every member had supported only a year or so ago. Their blind
   rejection of the carefully drafted TTF document is quintessential
   hypocrisy. Instead of providing guidance in this difficult period of
   financial retrenchment, the leadership, reflected in your astonishing
   assertion that "formula budgeting…is an absurdity," and Vice Chancellor Schmidt's pejorative references to the "veto power of one unit" and
   the "drive for independence of Urbana" provided a goad for dissension
   and sterile debate.

I also commented on the perceptions of funding levels for UICOM programs, saying, "Responses to the Technical Task Force Report indicate the
irrational aspects that have entered discussion under the subject of budget.
Both Rockford and Peoria rejected the TTF formula alternative to the 'Brady
formula,' which probably means that they don't understand the process…
Paradoxically, this means that the Executive Committees and leadership of
Rockford and Peoria have opted for less money…Under the assumptions of

a total budget $31,609,000, the 'present (Brady) formula' would allocate $3,189,000 to Peoria while the Task Force consensus would allocate them $3,683,000. Similarly, Rockford would have been allocated $4,040,000 by the Task Force rather than $3 621 000 by the present formula.

"The major real budgetary issue in the implementation of the TTF formula relates to projections of major reallocations from UICOM-C to UICOM-UC over the next three years. The relationship between funding in Chicago and funding at Urbana-Champaign is germane to this discussion.

"It is fruitless to debate whether present state funding at Chicago is too much or too little. Suffice it to say that the leadership at the Medical Center has, on many occasions, absolutely refused external consultation to evaluate the issue.

"Consider the report of Dean Forman, March 11, 1983. The report complains that 'the programs and departments of the College of Medicine at Chicago have incurred budget cuts of $1,853,000 since July 1, 1981.' But, the report is remarkable for questions it did not address, i.e., Has the College of Medicine at Chicago lost a single academic position among its tenure-track faculty despite the reduction of $1,853,000? While the Forman report states that 'sizable reductions have been made in the funds available for medical education in our affiliated hospitals,' is there any indication that medical education at the College of Medicine in Chicago has been impaired? Is there any objective evidence of impairment?

"The facts are that since July 1, 1981, UICOM-C has recruited more and better people than it ever has before. Units such as the Center for Genetics and the Department of Obstetrics and Gynecology have actually grown in state resources. UICOM-C has even started the equivalent of a Medical Scholars Program. These are not the changes made by a weak, underfunded program.

"Contrast the advances in Chicago with the critical losses caused to our small program at UICOM-UC by what might be considered ambivalent if not hostile management; a management which found $515,000 in 'campus reserves' recently, but couldn't afford $150,000 to meet critical educational needs for students at UICOM-UC six months earlier."

I then listed the setbacks we had faced, including the losses of our Department of Medicine head, our associate dean for clinical affairs, the director of our internal medicine residency, and two key educational-support personnel. We had also replaced two key full-time clinical teachers with a half-time person on an as-available basis, and our recruitment efforts were stymied by the Medical Center administration's refusal to commit funds for the future.

"These and other losses have led to some serious operational problems such as the loss of accreditation for our residency in Internal Medicine and worse yet, a reduction in community confidence in the integrity of the university. Were the 'underfunding' pattern of one or two years standing, it could be understood. After six years, it is difficult to find an excuse."

Then, I presented my thoughts on the Technical Task Force report:

Since the Medical Center leadership and the several college Executive Committees have refused to deal with the merits of the TTF report, this one report will do so. In introduction, it should be recalled that the enrollment-driven formula, by agreement, was to cover only the distribution of state funds. This was a very major compromise to UICOM-C in the consensus discussions. Even with full implementation of the report of the Technical Task Force, the omission of consideration of total funding leaves considerable imbalance in funding at the four sites because it excludes sizable Medical Service Plan (MSP) income funds, the potential MSP subsidy through unrealistically low overhead charges to MSP by the university, ICR funds, and the $12 million hospital subsidy received by the Chicago campus. Virtually all medical schools use MSP funds as a major source of base income. Its omission from consideration by the Technical Task Force coupled with the fact that much of the MSP income is derived from clinical facilities built by or purchased with state money results in a distribution of total funds that still strongly favors the Chicago program.

The TTF report also refers to the "Bloomfield survey." That survey (which is better called *The Twenty-Eight School Survey*) was conducted because it was clear that the ultimate formula to be used was critical to a fair allocation of the college resources. The formula used as "*a point of departure*" for the reallocation process, the so-called "Brady formula," appeared to be out-of-line with the relative costs of other American medical schools. This was confirmed by the "Bloomfield survey" of twenty-eight state schools; it was confirmed by the separate study of the Technical Task Force; and it was confirmed to a great extent by the effort reports of the Health Sciences faculty in Chicago. The raw data of the twenty-eight-school survey is available for inspection.

I then went on to the specifics of the report that dealt with the "weightings" of M-1, M-2, M-3, and M-4 students in determining the effort and resources needed to educate each class, how the funding of residents was to be accounted, the "cross-loading" of students (a formula for determining what effort and resources need to be allocated for graduate students and other students, such as nursing students, who were not pursuing MD degrees), and fixed costs. I took issue with the TTF's determinations on all but one of these issues, fixed costs. I pointed out that whenever a compromise or an assumption had to be made, the compromise or assumption most favorable to Chicago was always chosen. When applicable, I argued that these compromises and assumptions were far from the norm as reflected in my survey of twenty-eight schools and in other reports the TTF used. In regard to the formula for resident funding, I pointed out that of the three schools or systems surveyed by the TTF (Ohio State University, the State University of New York, and Iowa) none received state dollars for resident training. I also noted that the Illinois Board of Higher Education had reported that the residency positions at UIMC had been supported historically "with state funds appropriated to the university for allocation to the hospital," so that they had never been considered part of this area of the budget before the "Brady formula."

Regarding fixed costs, I wrote that we found "the concept of fixed costs reasonably well handled by the Technical Task Force."

I closed by saying, "In summary, the Technical Task Force report remains biased in favor of programs which have larger clinical student loads, higher cross-loads, and larger numbers of residents (i.e., UICOM-Chicago) but is acceptable to UICOM-UC because it represents *the best good-faith effort to solve this difficult problem* to date, It is a rational document which would probably stand up reasonably well to scrutiny by any group of objective outside observers. Failure of the Medical Center leadership to focus debate on rational issues relevant to present university policy has been unfortunate."

As these negotiations went on and on and on, I kept all of our major constituencies informed. When I showed Ned Goldwasser the Kernis solution, he wrote another of his critical masterpieces, which he sent to Vice

President Weir on April 15, 1983:

I cannot refrain from commenting on the message clearly carried in Marten Kernis's April 4 letter to Don Langenberg and Mack Schmidt. To me, the letter and its enclosures represent a vignette of the frustrating world within which members of the College of Medicine on this campus have been living for some time and continue to live today. Dan Bloomfield's memorandum to Marten Kernis appears to me to be both temperate and objective. It is cast within the policies and principles which have been hammered out with so much pain over the past year. Marten Kernis's letter and the accompanying report, on the other hand, are replete with arguments which completely ignore Stan Ikenberry's general principles upon which the Reorganization Plan was based, the Reorganization Plan itself, the following statement of procedures through which the Reorganization Plan might be implemented as it applies to this campus, the forwarding letter signed by Joe Begando and John Cribbet, and the acceptance of that letter by President Ikenberry.

On the first page of Kernis's letter of April 4, it is stated that "the atypical concept of formula budgeting for the College of Medicine could and should be eliminated because it is expected that the new dean will demonstrate the fairness, equity, integrity and commitment to regionalization that will overcome the rationale for including the concept in our organization document." That is a pious hope in which we can all readily join. However, no one of any sensitivity would suggest that we have arrived at that point yet or that we are going to have arrived at it with the mere appointment of a new dean, whoever that may be. It would take Superman himself at least a year to calm the waters and establish the kind of collegiality and confidence which is suggested in the Kernis letter. Interim funding based on a formula established by the Central Administration is an ingredient that is absolutely essential to the implementation of any reorganization plan and of our fond hope for peace in our time. Formula budgeting was one of the fundamental premises of the whole reorganization process. To say that it is inflammatory to suggest that that process should be eliminated at this stage would be a monumental understatement.

On another point, Dr. Kernis suggests that we "could dramatically reduce current tension by issuing a clear, concise, unambiguous statement rescinding the rhetoric regarding an independent medical school in Urbana-Champaign." I assume that the rhetoric to which Dr. Kernis refers is, in part, John Cribbet's addendum to the president's seven "Basic Principles," which were to govern the reorganization of the College of Medicine.

The seventh of those principles stated, "We must end up with a single College of Medicine capable of self-governance." Immediately after the enunciation of that principle, John Cribbet suggested that an addendum should be added, reading: "Until such time as changed circumstances, fiscal and otherwise, make it possible to consider a separate College of Medicine for the Urbana-Champaign campus." That addendum was subsequently endorsed by President Ikenberry himself. Furthermore, I assume that Dr. Kernis refers to the May 27, 1982 letter to President Ikenberry from Chancellors Cribbet and Begando, in which they stated, "Within those same constraints and recognizing the special academic and other support systems available to this medical-education program by reason of its location on the Urbana-Champaign campus, it will be the long-range goal of the medical program to develop its capability for academic independence so that the structure for governance of medical education within the university can be simplified and lines of communication shortened by the establishment at Urbana-Champaign of a separately governed College of Medicine." Many people agonized for a long time about the wisdom of incorporating such a statement. It was included only after careful weighing of pros and cons by John Cribbet, Joe Begando, and others. It was decided that there would be far less chance of achieving our short-range goal if tribute were not paid to the long-range, probable eventuality. If Marten Kernis believes that statement to be merely "rhetoric," destructive of the current single-college program, he really has a total lack of understanding of his program and his faculty on *this* campus.

It is quite reasonable to believe that in the embryonic stage of development of a clinical medical program in a new setting, an umbilical cord connecting it to an established program could be of great value. On the other hand, it is not reasonable to believe that twenty-five years later such a "new" program, situated on one of the leading university campuses in the country, would still require or profit from an umbilical

cord of that kind. When, during those twenty-five years, such an umbilical cord could best be cut is a detailed matter and probably not a very
critical one. But the rhetoric which would be most destructive of a program of that kind on a campus of this kind is rhetoric which presumes
rigidly to impose, forevermore, a subordinate role for that program to a
"parent" program 150 miles away. It is Dr. Kernis's suggestion that
"faculty members and administrators who cannot concur with this
basic principle should be invited to seek opportunity elsewhere."
(Good-bye Stan Ikenberry, John Cribbet, and Joe Begando, to say nothing of Mort Weir and Ned Goldwasser!) It is precisely that kind of attitude which has all but destroyed the opportunity we have had, since last
spring, to mend fences and to begin to establish some kind of cooperation among the faculty of the various sites of the college.

From our standpoint at UICOM-UC, Schmidt could have easily settled the
budgetary issue by funding our school in accordance with the TTF recommendations, perhaps easing the hit on the other units by using campus
reserves to supplement the college pool. Had he taken such a step, we at
UICOM-UC being given the status of equal partner, would have gladly
shared the fates of any subsequent reallocations demanded of the UIMC
campus. But up to this point, SCM-UC/UICOM-UC had never been given
full citizenship in the college, a point of fact that may explain why we
worked so hard for those rights.

CHAPTER 42

The Rocky Road to Peace

THE FURIOUS ACTIVITY to wish away the TTF recommendation was peaking at a time when the LCME was due to visit. Kernis's major effort to bring about a TTF-voiding solution was dated April 4, merely a week before the LCME survey team was scheduled to arrive. I was the only administrator who was not concerned about the visit. I was a lame duck, in the enviable position of knowing that if the UIMC administration wanted to see the last of me, and that was a given, it had to find a way to fund Urbana. (I was not entirely safe from UIMC barbs. As a snide parting gesture, Kernis and Schmidt denied me my portion of a universitywide salary increment in fiscal 1984.) Thus, the possibility of a new reorganization plan that would eliminate SCM-UC faded day by day as a politically palatable alternative solution to the college's financial difficulties. The members of the LCME accreditation team certainly would not need me to tell them that the college was in disarray.

As I noted in my memorandum protesting the draft version of Kernis's TTF-voiding solution, our program had suffered in recent years from the college turmoil and the anemic budget. In fact, the walls were literally crumbling in every direction.

One of the major setbacks occurred as the deans were in the process of forming their consensus on reorganization late in 1981. For it was on December 8, 1981 that our AHES program was stricken from the next year's course offerings. The Area Health Education System, which was funded by the federal Bureau of Health Manpower Employment, had been created in the early 1970s to deal with manpower shortages in the health-care industry. Our participation at Urbana had begun in 1974, and by 1981, we had established forty-three separate courses under AHES. These included the Danville Family Practice Program and programs in the medical arts, dietetics, occupational therapy and physical therapy. Unfortunately, the federal funding commitment to AHES had been tapering off for years, and in 1981, Chicago cut us off completely from the limited pool of funds remaining.

Unfortunately, the Danville Family Practice Program, under the dedicated leadership of Bill Tanner, was a casualty of this decision. It had always
been difficult to recruit residents to Danville. Those residents who were
recruited were not always of satisfactory quality, and that discouraged many
Danville teaching faculty. This was a residency that had been supported not
only with external funding, but also with time and effort on the part of
Mort Creditor and myself for the preceding five years. Both of us had made
the thirty-mile drive once or twice a week in order to make regular teaching
rounds with the Danville residents. (When Creditor departed for Chicago, I
continued to make the Danville rounds alone.) However, with state funds
being withheld and AHES funds being selectively replaced by a Chicago
administration that was hostile to everything we did, the rug was being
pulled out from under us. With the two Danville hospitals unwilling to fill
the funding gap, Tanner had no choice but to close in 1982.

Similarly, our first internal-medicine residency, another residency that
was critical to our clinical program, fell, when it lost accreditation in 1983.
Our early attempts to develop a three-hospital internal-medicine residency
among the Danville VA Medical Center, and Carle Foundation and Mercy
hospitals in Champaign-Urbana had been frustrating. Under the successive
leadership of two well-qualified internists, the program grappled with the
complex problem of developing a high-quality internal-medicine residency
program in spite of the adversities we faced. But progress was slow. And
when AHES funds dried up, I had no money at all to support local residency
programs. In addition, our three hospital partners were not yet prepared to
fund such a residency by exploiting third-party insurance pass-through
funds.

We were not only short of money, we were short of skilled academic
input, with no help in sight from the rest of the College of Medicine. Faculty
morale was fading, particularly among the academicians who had been
recruited to the Danville Veterans Administration Medical Center to serve as
a core full-time faculty for this new medical school. Our chief of medicine
left for a stable opportunity in Denver. Other academicians at the hospital, a
hematologist and two academic surgeons, abandoned what they believed
was a sinking ship. The one academic stalwart who remained, Dr. Lewis
Winter, a specialist in pulmonary diseases, did much to preserve the
DVAMC-UICOM-UC relationship in its time of peril. A veritable Atlas, he

bore the entire burden for the educational transformation of the VA hospital on his shoulders, and, over the next ten years, molded that facility into being an integral part of the UICOM-UC clinical-teaching program and our second, slowly developing, but ultimately successful, internal-medicine residency program.

In July 1982, a prominent local internist who had served the school continuously since 1971 as an MDE died while on a visit to a Western ranch. His death occurred at a time when our primary-care residency programs were on the ropes. Badly needed was a teaching service in one of our affiliated hospitals where all patients would be treated by residents under the guidance, teaching, and direction of the residency program director in coordination with the private physician. But this meant that a significant number of patients had to be identified for teaching purposes. The only possible community source for such patients was the Frances Nelson Health Center, a free clinic designed to serve the underprivileged. I had discussed possible teaching programs with the clinic only to be rebuffed by the argument that the health center did not want their patients exploited by resident physicians who might not deliver the highest quality of care.

It was imperative to residency development that a satisfactory teaching service be available, not only for the purposes of developing a residency, but because the LCME demanded adequate residency programs to support accreditation of a medical school. I bit the bullet and decided to return to the practice of medicine by assuming responsibility for Jack Hull's practice and making it a teaching practice. I negotiated with Hull's widow, arranged to purchase the practice, and began to incorporate it into the three-hospital internal-medicine residency. By September 1982, the practice was mine. As a lame-duck dean, I was now in part-time private practice in addition to my duties as dean of UICOM-UC and my endless battle for resources after the college's attempt to renege on the TTF recommendations.

There had been a three-month gap between Jack Hull's death and my assumption of responsibility for the practice. During that time, many patients were lost to other physicians. I sent a letter to all of Dr. Hull's patients to inform them that I was taking over with the intent of conducting a teaching practice and that they would be cared for by medical residents under my supervision. Those who accepted those terms filled the office, and those who did not saw other physicians. There were, however, enough residual patients to keep me busy with an office practice that took three half-days per week, not to mention the hospital and telephone time necessary to pursue an ordinary solo practice.

The strategy worked well. The concept of having private patients who agreed to participate in a teaching practice was successfully introduced into the local hospital scene and took root. Today, the Internal Medicine Residency Program regularly fills its resident quotas with skilled resident physicians and has proved very successful.

But back in 1982, our backs were to the wall. We were facing a serious residency-accreditation problem, we had no decent budget, and we received nothing but grief from our sister schools and our Chicago leadership. Since we had no head of either the Department of Internal Medicine or the Internal Medicine Residency Program, I had to play the part of a jack-of-all-trades and assume those roles, in addition to handling my new private practice. I had little free time. The days were long and tiring. But the object of the game was to outlast Chicago until some form of fiscal relief came through the vehicle of TTF reallocation, and I was determined to do just that.

In March 1983, we received notice that the American Council for Graduate Medical Education intended to withdraw accreditation from our internal-medicine residency at the end of May. The fundamental criticism cited by the council was that we were dreadfully short of geographic full-time supervisory and teaching faculty: "Evidence is lacking regarding the administrative support of the program, particularly in the division of adequate numbers of teaching faculty."

This was no real surprise to us, but it was a body blow at a time when we were being stabbed in the back by adverse resolutions from the executive committees of our sister schools. However, there was a bright side to the ACGME threat as well, because it was a dramatic act that served to mobilize our resources better than any individual step I might otherwise have taken. I talked with the CEOs of our three major teaching hospitals and laid out our residency problems before them. From that point forward, the three hospitals linked together to establish a viable monetary base for graduate medical education. On March 8, representatives and CEOs from the three hospitals met with our respective staffs and myself to hammer out a funding plan and to establish a joint task force to create a new and credible Internal Medicine Residency Program (IMRP). We decided that the old, disaccredited residency was beyond repair, and that we would not to appeal the ACGME decision to withdraw accreditation. Instead, with our three teaching hospitals fully aware of their support obligations, we agreed to seek outside consultation and to submit a proposal for the brand-new IMRP. Because we wanted the new residency to begin in July 1984, only fifteen months away, we had to move quickly. We had only three months to submit our proposal if we were to meet the ACGME deadline, which was twelve months before start-up. Anyone familiar with the organization and paper work required for such a task will know that three months is barely adequate to achieve what we had to do, but with expert consultation from Armand Littman, MD, from the Hines VA Medical Center in Hines, Illinois, and hard work by all parties on the task force (which included the CEOs of the three community hospitals, and the head of the VA hospital, and me), we met the deadline and received probationary approval to begin the new program in July 1984.

A key to our success was the willingness of E. Richard Ensrud, MD, to assume the mantle of program director, which was now a salaried position supported by the hospitals. A veteran internist and gastroenterologist associated with the Carle Clinic, he proved to be exactly the right person to lead this residency effort.

Vexing as the birth pangs of the IMRP were, more directly problematic was the accreditation of the College of Medicine itself and specifically UICOM-UC. The LCME survey team of April 10–14, 1983, caught the college at rock-bottom morale with Chicago, Peoria, and Rockford having passed resolutions to eliminate Urbana, and everyone complaining of a shortage of funds.

In discussing the organization and administration of the Urbana medical-education program, the LCME survey team reported, "A major administrative issue [at Urbana] is the provisional status of clinical departments…with implementation of a clinical program, a proposal for creation of separate clinical departments was developed. We were told that this proposal has been held up by the UICOM administration and has not been presented to the IBHE, which must approve creation of departments…

"The team was also told that the executive faculties of the Chicago, Peoria, and Rockford campuses had recently proposed that the Urbana clinical program be discontinued. Presumably, the savings thus realized could be used for projects in the other campuses. If the clinical program is not developed, the survival of the excellent first-year program and of the entire Medical Scholars Program at Urbana-Champaign seems extremely doubtful. Since recruitment of departmental needs and full-time faculty is virtually impossible with the departments in provisional status, resolution of this matter should have urgent priority."

The team also commented, "There is a complex and cumbersome organizational approach to a multifaceted institution. The institution has been undergoing the throes of reorganization for the past two years, and there has been no permanent executive dean for the past four years...Other than for some functional relationships on a friendly basis between the pharmacology department in Chicago and the Chairman of the Basic Sciences Department on the Rockford campus, there is no evidence of significant linkages between the departments in either basic or clinical sciences. The departments in each region seem completely autonomous in regard to their discipline. They attempted integration of quality control of educational programs through the educational Policy Committee, made up of faculty from the various campuses. This committee has been effectively non-functional for the past year or so...The college is effectively divided through the reorganization plan into two distinct programs or tracks...The only residual common elements between the two is affected at the upper levels of administration and in the ultimate requirement that all students pass the National Board Examinations and a common Senior Comprehensive Examination. There is no evidence of discipline-based quality control in the system at all...Even with the reorganization, which appears to improve the organization and educational program on the Chicago campus, there remain major administrative problems in this system. One problem relates to the distribution of resources, where there is obvious competition by the various divisions for adequate monies. Recently there was agreed upon a strict formula-driven budget, based on the number of students in the various divisions. This has some major flaws well appreciated by the Vice Chancellor for Health Affairs. [sic] The major problem of the formula-driven budget relates to the need that if one component of the system is to be provided more money for a new or innovative program, the other components are entitled to a proportionate share. Although the Vice Chancellor believes he will have sufficient flexibility to cope with the formula, the widespread distrust evident within the system seems likely to be exacerbated as this new scheme becomes operational." (These gratuitous comments from the survey team may have been solicited by Kernis and/or Schmidt in their campaign to nullify the TTF report. It is not unusual for survey teams to assist a medical school by encouraging a hesitant university administration to make policy changes advantageous to the school.)

In summary, the team found, "The large and complex administration has required resources that perhaps might otherwise be used for educational programs...There is a pervasive sense among the faculty that the organization of medical education within the University of Illinois has been structured more in response to political considerations than as an effort to develop a sound educational program or programs. In a time of limited resources, competition for those resources has led to widespread mistrust among the several components of the college. The reorganization appears to have exacerbated rather than relieved many of these concerns, and the team found considerable doubt that the reorganization will work...The college has not one, but several quite separate and distinct programs leading to the MD degree."

The survey team clearly saw through the facade of reorganization, the chauvinism of the several sites, and the imbalance of resource distribution. At Urbana, they recognized our desperate need for clinical faculty, the problems with the IMRP, and the impossible and multiple roles played by the dean. At the time of the LCME survey, we were almost back to the days of the free-floating apex.

More important, the survey team also noted about Urbana, "The enormous strength in the teaching and research of the departments responsible for the first year of the educational program, which is integrated and appears to function effectively...that Chancellor Cribbet and his staff are knowledgeable about and supportive of the program...that the university faculty, practicing physicians in the community and local hospitals are also highly supportive of the medical program...and that the Medical Scholars Program is unique and has potential to become a national asset."

Despite such strengths, the conclusion of the team added up to a College of Medicine in disarray. At the exit interview with President Ikenberry, the survey team made its distress clear, indicating that they would recommend to the full LCME that UICOM be placed on probationary accreditation status until it got its act in order. It was a wake-up call to the president and the UIMC administration.

Of all the interactions between the college and the LCME in the thirteen years after the college was first reorganized in 1970, none was more productive than the 1983 LCME Survey Team's decision. Here we were, the largest medical school in the country, divided into four squabbling regions, within which students pursued one of two tracks, each of which was contemptuous of the other. There was polarization both in attitude and in curriculum.

And the team essentially said, "The emperor has no clothes."

The president was alarmed, as well he should have been long before this disaster took place. It was quickly decided that given the unstable framework that had led to an administratively dysfunctional College of Medicine, attracting a new dean from a nationwide search was probably inappropriate at that time. Meeting with administrators and faculty, the president was satisfied with a growing consensus that Dr. Phillip Forman, who had been dean of ALSM and now UICOM-C, was the appropriate person to lead the college into the future. Although I had some reservations about Forman's attachment to the Chicago program, I had worked with him on the Advisory Council of Deans since 1978 and found him straightforward and fair. With no significant opposition from within the college, the Board of Trustees ratified Forman's appointment as dean of UICOM on May 19, 1983.

The thorny issue of the underfunded clinical program at Urbana-Champaign still had to be resolved. My advocacy for formula budgeting, which was not endorsed by the timid administrations of Peoria and Rockford, ended up as a voice crying in the wilderness. In conversations with Dean Forman, who had argued the UICOM-C case against formula budgeting, the president flip-flopped again and decided against application of the enrollment-driven formula budget that would have reallocated funds from Chicago, Peoria, and Rockford to Urbana-Champaign to fulfill his principle that funding be equitable among the four sites. Instead, he took the easy way out by deciding to add more money to the college budget in order to fund UICOM-UC and to preserve the Medical Scholars Program. Shortly after the exit interview with the LCME survey team, he met with the Advisory Council of Deans and advised them of his plan to use presidential discretionary funds to increase the college budget by $1 million overall, in four annual installments of $250,000, each earmarked for UICOM-UC. In taking this step, the president also made it very clear to the deans that, barring an unexpected move by the state legislature, there would be no further new funding from the university to the College of Medicine for the foreseeable future. The $1 million was being allocated to bring the Urbana clinical program up to par. There would be absolutely no additional funds thereafter.

Although it was the death knell of formula budgeting, the presidential announcement was met with general relief on all sides. I know I was relieved. It was a great boost for Forman, who quickly made it plain that he would act as dean of the entire college and remained committed to regionalization and excellence at all four sites. It resolved the problem of gross underfunding and the survival of UICOM-UC so that a search could now begin for my replacement.

Having appointed Forman as college dean and taken a major step to resolve the UICOM-UC fiscal crisis, the president wrote to Jim Schofield at the Association of American Medical Colleges on May 31, 1983 in an effort to persuade the LCME that probation was not necessary. He wrote, "First, a new Dean of the College has been appointed, effective with the May meeting of the Board of Trustees. Dr. Phillip Forman, our new dean, served as Dean of the School of Clinical Medicine in Chicago. Team members were unanimous in their praise of his leadership ability, the trust and support he has engendered with the faculty, his administrative skills, and especially his recruiting ability…He is already hard at work.

"It is important to add that Dean Forman has received indications of strong support from all parts of the College of Medicine…

"Second, it is my firm belief that we have put to rest any question about the university's commitment to regionalize medical education and, as part of that commitment, our intent to develop the Medical Scholars Program at Urbana-Champaign. We have made the commitment to add $1 million to the budget of the Urbana-Champaign program, funds required to develop more fully the clinical component of the Medical Scholars Program."

But Jim Schofield and the LCME were not to be diverted from their course by a presidential letter that contained hope and promise, without the substance they demanded. Schofield wrote to President Ikenberry on June 30, "In its meeting of June 28–29, 1983, the LCME reviewed the survey report dated April 10–14, 1983, and has determined that the educational program leading to the MD degree offered by the College of Medicine is not in substantial compliance with the LCME's published accreditation standards. Failure to be in substantial compliance with the LCME's standards constitutes grounds for placing the program on probation.

"Specifically the LCME has determined that a large segment of the educational program is in jeopardy because of the College of Medicine's reaffirmation of its intent to offer a single MD program at multiple sites, a plan which threatens the overall integrity and quality of the educational experience offered to the students. Thus, the LCME finds it necessary to assign the status of probationary accreditation to the MD program."

The letter then followed with four pages of detailed criticism that bore upon the administration, the governance, the faculty, and the educational program. Finally, a procedure to appeal the adverse action was included.

Phil Forman spent his first four months in office preparing the formal appeal, which he presented personally to the LCME on September 15, 1983. The appeal dealt with every single criticism advanced by the LCME survey team.

The appeal said, "The University of Illinois College of Medicine firmly believes it has provided an educational program for its MD candidates at all sites, which has resulted in those candidates meeting acceptable internal and national standards before being awarded the MD degree." This statement was followed with National Board of Medical Examiners results that showed above-average performance by College of Medicine graduates at all levels of the National Boards.

Forman went on in great detail to address all the issues the LCME had raised, including governance, quality assurance among the disciplines taught through the college, and budgeting. (In the course of discussing budget, he said formula budgeting was out, which meant the TTF had been completely buried.) The appeal was acted upon favorably the same day and the threat of probation withdrawn.

Suddenly, there was peace within the college. It came upon us so swiftly and unexpectedly, it seemed as if there was an explosion of tranquillity. With the governance agreed upon by Cribbet and Begando and the $1 million that had been committed to the UICOM-UC budget, I was satisfied that I had accomplished all that was possible for me to do at that time. Although the executive committees of the other three college sites never rescinded their infamous calls for our demise, they didn't press their resolutions either. All of us at the four college sites set aside what remained of our political differences and turned our attention back to our principal job of educating future doctors.

Epilogue

THE ODYSSEY WAS OVER. Peace and tranquillity were established among the four sites of the college. Dean Phillip Forman proved to be very skillful at bringing people together. He demonstrated these skills to me when, knowing that I viewed the position change from "dean" to "director" as a demotion, he graciously allowed me to keep the title "dean" until I retired from the post.

Quiet, forceful, and effective, Forman made a point of visiting the regional sites regularly to meet with faculty and local executive committees. The new College Executive Committee, made up of twelve elected Chicago representatives and four elected representatives each from the other three regions, proved to be effective and satisfactory to all.

On May 15, 1984, almost a full year after Forman took over and shortly before I stepped down from my own deanship, I wrote to Bud Grulee, former Rockford dean who had returned as a senior statesman to the University of Cincinnati, "I thought you'd like a brief update on how things are going in the old college. Actually, things are going pretty well. Phil Forman has done a masterful job of integrating the four units together so that we are thinking about academic problems rather than political problems. The Executive Committee of the College, for all the controversy over its make-up, has functioned pretty well. There are some regional problems, but no particular regional acrimony."

My tenure as dean of UICOM-UC ended May 31, 1984, thirteen years and ten months after I began. Although I disconnected completely from the administration of UICOM-UC, I was elected as one of four UICOM-UC faculty representatives to the College Executive Committee, which allowed me to keep my fingers on the pulse of college political activity. Both within that committee and at the regional campuses, it was evident that faculty and administrations were working harmoniously together for a change, and it felt good. Differences were largely based on knowledge, facts, and opinion, not on geography, and during the four years from 1984 to 1988, not a single committee decision was decided on the basis of geographic chauvinism.

However, there was an incident that echoed all that had gone on before I stepped down as dean. In 1988, the legislature again limited state funds for the University of Illinois. Stanley Ikenberry, who was still president at that time, proved that he was unchastened by prior experience with the Urbana-Champaign medical-education program. He searched for a noteworthy academic scalp that would prove to the legislature that the university, under his leadership, had no further fat from which to absorb funding reductions, and that funding cuts would result in program losses. Suitably armed, he went after the UICOM-UC jugular for a third time when he announced abruptly at the July 13, 1988 Board of Trustees meeting, "I have asked the dean of the College of Medicine to consult with the acting vice president for academic affairs, the two campus chancellors, and appropriate faculty bodies to develop a plan for reducing the size of the entering class in the College of Medicine by 25 percent, effective in the next admissions year, 1989."

Although denying that he had personally selected UICOM-UC as the preferred sacrificial lamb, news releases and letters from his office made the intended outcome unmistakable. In a university news release dated July 13, 1988, he said, "Specifically, the plan should maintain, to the degree possible, a strong commitment to regional medical education while also consolidating the bulk of the basic medical science instruction in Chicago." (Read: Eliminate SBMS-UC and transfer all the teaching of basic medical science to Chicago.) Moreover, in a July 14 letter to Phil Forman, he wrote "In the longer term, the plan should provide for recasting the Medical Scholars Program on a college-wide basis."

On July 22, he sent another letter to Forman, which said, "As to the Medical Scholars Program, I know of no one who wishes to see this program terminated. I am keenly aware of the quality of the program and the importance placed on it, not only by faculty members in medicine, but in other disciplines as well. If the Medical Scholars Program can be sustained in its current or modified form in the plan you set forth, I would welcome that outcome." (Read: The Urbana medical education program has got to go, but try to preserve the MSP if you can.)

But it was not to be. President Ikenberry tripped over the pesky Urbana medical program once again, for the third and last time for his presidency. By the time he made his proposal, with 115 Medical Scholars distributed about the UIUC campus, the Medical Scholars Program was so well embedded and accepted on both the campus and on the national scene, that the thought of closing the school was reversed in a mere thirty days by an outpouring of support (ably orchestrated by my successor, Director C.C.C. O'Morchoe) from students, faculty, community, and indeed from all over the nation. Even the College Executive Committee, in a demonstration of unprecedented unanimity that would not have been remotely possible four years previously resolved that the "elimination of the program at Urbana adversely affects the College of Medicine as a whole." In the end, the college reduced its enrollment by 10 percent, and the medical-education program at Urbana-Champaign, with its *raison d'etre*, the Medical Scholars Program, lived to see another day.

All in all, the college reorganization, as it finally evolved, was a grand success, and much of that success could be credited to the skilled management of Phillip Forman.

I played no role in the selection of my successor. Once Forman had been appointed dean of the college and the president had committed $1 million to UICOM-UC, the search for a director to replace me began in earnest. Dr. Charles C. C. O'Morchoe, a candidate who was then chairman of the Department of Anatomy at Loyola University of Chicago (a position he had held for ten years), was recommended to Phil Forman by the search committee. With Forman's approval, O'Morchoe, a graduate of the Dublin (Ireland) University School of Medicine, was appointed director effective June 1, 1984. Suddenly, there was a finite limit on my term as dean, and I had one more obligation to fulfill. That was to Hal Swartz.

It was clear, however, that the new director would want to make his own administrative appointments. In his capacity as associate dean for clinical affairs, Hal had gradually assumed responsibility for the direction of the MSP. The MSP had begun under the aegis of the Bicampus Steering Committee, co-chaired by the dean of the graduate college and myself as the dean of UICOM-UC. The BSC established policy and acted as an admissions committee to the program. However, the program needed a designated leader, and I believed Hal would be perfect for that post. With the permission of the BSC and the graduate-college dean's approval, Hal was appointed to lead the program for a three-year renewable term.

With that accomplished, I was satisfied that my job was done. I stepped down from the deanship with no regrets and much relief. Although much had been done, a great deal still remained. The clinical program, literally starved for funds for the previous four years, remained precariously on the ropes, although it still was a long way from being knocked out. It would get an infusion of $250,000 per year for four years beginning in fiscal 1985. Recruitment of clinical faculty had to be started immediately. To attract academic leadership, departmentalization, which had been delayed for bureaucratic reasons as well as for a lack of funds, had to proceed apace. The Clinical Education Centers within our affiliated hospitals needed leadership and staffing. The second-year logic pathways, which languished without Mort Creditor's personal commitment to them, were eventually abandoned, and Don Thursh, our main teaching pathologist, needed more academic full-time help, even though he had good support from the practicing community.

In the long run, we had to plan for the day when we would qualify for separate accreditation and become a legitimate party to the UIUC campus. However, I was fully prepared to give up any and all my vestiges of power to younger, more vigorous leaders: the deanship, the headship of internal medicine, and the directorship of the IMRP. The monkey was finally off my back. I looked forward with pleasure to assuming my full-time clinical and teaching responsibilities as a member of the faculty. I was ready for my farewell roast.

The pity of it was that all the years of strife had been so unnecessary and could have been avoided, if only there had been leadership at any level in the college, in the UIMC administration, or in the general university. From the days of Bill Grove through Forman's rise to dean, presidents allowed personalities at the College of Medicine to rule over policy. Vice President Brady made this very clear when he told me that my problems could be solved, except that personalities were in the way. The turmoil had been a story, then, of how petty administrators can force bad decisions on a great institution.

For instance, as I look back today on the revised treaty of 1982, I'm inclined to think that the UIUC Senate cynics of 1981, who disagreed with John Cribbet's appeal to delay the transfer of SBMS/SCM-UC governance until fiscal conditions were more favorable, were right in their prediction that the Chicago administration would never release its control over us and in demanding a transfer of governance forthwith. In 1982, there was a massive and forceful coalescence of interests at UIUC for the transfer of UICOM-UC governance. But, ultimately, a second College of Medicine at UIUC was frustrated largely by the unyielding stand of an adamant President Ikenberry. The moral of this element of the story is that bureaucracies should be viewed as they are, not as one would wish them to be. Hunkered behind their defenses and condemned by their own negativity, they exercise their power as the power to say "no." They hate to say "yes" because that brings on their greatest fear: change. We had painstakingly mobilized major forces on the UIUC campus that would have supported our transfer of governance and would have accepted us warts and all, but we were unable to overcome the president's intransigence. Today, under a different administration both in Chicago and in Urbana and with a new president, the Gordian knot that ties UICOM-UC to Chicago remains intact and appears to be more puzzling than ever.

Before the most recent LCME accreditation visit in November 1994, I wrote a letter as a faculty member, with presumed academic freedom, to the members of the site-visit team suggesting that they might view the Urbana-Peoria-Rockford track as a separate medical school that should be independently accredited. This was met with a lively response from the keepers of the asylum, a response somewhere between hysteria and pandemonium, from some UICOM administrators. In the end, for better or for worse, the four regional programs of UICOM were accredited as a single medical school.

As far as state dollars are concerned, there is little change in the overall pattern that the Chicago programs swallow up the lion's share of new funds received by the university for health-education initiatives. The loss of formula budgeting remains a problem to this day, and UICOM-UC continues to do more than its share of teaching in proportion to its budget than any other UICOM unit. The TTF formula, which was heavily biased in favor of UICOM-C, was not good enough for Chicago. Indeed, since 1989, UICOM-C has not only received a more favorable fraction (by the unchallenged TTF criteria) of the annual state operating funds allocated to UICOM, it has also benefited enormously from a $40 million-plus annual subsidy and a favorable Medicaid reimbursement rate that the state provides for the University Hospital. None of this has been shared downstate.

UICOM-UC remains a minimally funded, if not underfunded, medical-education program that is still tied to an indifferent, but not necessarily hostile, Chicago administration. For instance, the new Chicago administration, now functioning as the University of Illinois at Chicago (the combined Medical Center and Chicago Circle campuses), searching for a theme that would attract attention both as a relevant university goal and as a political ploy to increase support for UIC, has developed the "Great Cities" initiative. To develop funds for the new program, all UIC units in 1993 were taxed 1.5 percent of their operating budget. I protested in vain against the tax, which served to reduce our minimally funded program one more turn of the screw, and which supported a program that it would be somewhat difficult for us outside the "Great City" of Chicago to exploit. On the other hand, the UIC administration approved a tuition increase that offset the tax loss and left us coming out slightly ahead, for the moment.

The medical program at Urbana-Champaign has enjoyed its share of successes. For instance, the Internal Medicine Residency program grew out of its humble origins into a thriving program. Today, it enrolls about forty-five residents in the three hospitals and is fully supported by them. As I make teaching rounds with the residents, during the writing of this book in 1998, it is difficult to recall the angst involved in getting to here from there.

However, despite the great success of the Medical Scholars Program, which now enrolls about 135 dual-degree students and interacts with as many as thirty-five UIUC departments or programs that award advanced degrees, UICOM-UC, as a result of its Chicago governance, remains an orphan outsider at UIUC, particularly in the areas of campus priorities and philanthropic support.

On March 2, 1995, I received a personal communication from Director Charles C.C. O'Morchoe, my successor at UICOM-UC, that the Medical Scholars Program "did make the 'B' list" in that year's University of Illinois capital campaign for $1 billion. Although that in itself was noteworthy, it was observed that the MSP position on the B-list program priorities was twenty-one of twenty-one with $27,428,000 in competing B-list programs and an unknown quantity of A-list programs ahead of it.

As of May 9, 1995, UICOM-UC, with or without the Medical Scholars program, was not listed on any of the UIC priority lists, according to R.J. Schimmel, UICOM-UC's associate dean for business affairs.

The school, which in the past decade has just begun to build an alumni base, has, by reason of its governance, virtually no access to other university philanthropic support. In dealing with the University of Illinois Foundation, the university's main repository for gifts to the academy, it is the painful experience of UICOM-UC that it is not truly a part of the UIUC campus and therefore shows up rarely, if at all, on Urbana campus priorities. Our actual fund-raising success has been minimal compared with what it might have been given were the school freed of its burdensome governance.

However, that is not to say that the school has been totally devoid of external support. I have personally, without assistance from the University of Illinois Foundation, raised about $250,000 in endowment gifts to the

Medical Scholars Program from friends, relatives, grateful patients, and myself. As of May 9, 1995, Schimmel reported, the school had received a total of $1,262,768 in gifts since its inception. That total is probably inflated because it includes some research grants that were categorized as gifts.

There is no evidence that UICOM-UC is anywhere on the Chicago list of priorities, either. In other words, at a time when medical schools, both private and state-supported, are depending more and more on external philanthropic support, UICOM-UC remains seriously disadvantaged by its adverse governance. Looking beyond the fourteen years of my deanship at the whole UICOM-UC experience, the failure of the University of Illinois to garner significant philanthropic support for this unique medical school and particularly its Medical Scholars Program, and contrariwise its success in preventing the natural bonding of UICOM-UC to the UIUC campus is a singular commentary on the ascendancy of politics over quality within this element of the University of Illinois.

Returning to that roasting ceremony of May 1984 (and I can assure you that it is far more enjoyable to be roasted by friends than by enemies), the final talk of the evening was given by Chancellor John Cribbet, who was also stepping down from his more lofty position at the end of the academic year. A consummate after-dinner speaker, John was in great form when he summed up my deanship. As you may imagine upon reading them, laughter interrupted many of his comments.

"You know, toasting and roasting is a hazardous business even for a Chancellor in the waning months of his reign. True, I shall continue to defy chance only until the end of August, so I can speak with little fear for reprisal. But I do wish to leave with dignity and not be ridden out of office on a rail. Therefore, I shall be less than frank.

"I shall praise all doctors and I shall note that working with Dan Bloomfield has been a bed of roses. You may well recognize that that is an ambiguous phrase since most roses are secreted in the interstices of some rather thorny branches. But I will let that stand.

"As you know, Dan did not report directly to me—thank God! But insofar as he reported at all, he was responsible to the thorny thicket of the College of Medicine in Chicago. Of course, he was located on the Urbana-Champaign campus, and we heard occasional rumors to the effect that he ran a consistent last in the College of Medicine's frequent popularity contests. He always seemed to think that we, too, were responsible for the howling orphan in our midst, and he kept involving us in internecine wars with the best and brightest of our Chicago colleagues. Whatever Dan's virtues (and I assume he must have some), at the top of the list is his sheer staying power. His administrative life extended beyond that of two chancellors in Chicago and a whole bevy of assorted executive deans, deputy executive deans, associate deans, assistant deans, and so forth. Indeed when Dan finally announced his return to the professorate, I lost all interest in sitting on the administrative counsels and announced my own return to the classroom...

"And so I announced my own return to the College of Law to help educate lawyers who will do their best to keep the medical profession in line. The great professions of law and medicine have much in common. They are both learned callings, unappreciated by the public, which seems to think we charge too much for our services. We seem to be under steady attack even by such astute gentlemen as Derek Bok, President of Harvard, who last year noted that the legal system was not working well and that the law schools were to blame. And he has recently issued a report, which minces no words about the medical schools. So, welcome to the club.

"Oddly enough, many of Derek's criticisms and some of his panaceas parallel what Dan Bloomfield has been saying for well over a decade. Maybe Dan could get an appointment at Harvard if he tires of life in the soybeans and corn. I doubt, however, if Bok could receive tenure in the Health Sciences Center of Chicago.

"Dan, as we both lay aside the administrative baton, let's concentrate on the unfinished business of medicine and law, and let the deans, chancellors, and presidents quake in their corridors of power. They have nothing to lose but their chains. We have a world to win. (My apologies to the Communist Manifesto.)

"Seriously, although I really dislike being serious at a roast, Dan has had a vision of a different type of medical school, and he has fought for that vision with the energy and tenacity of a Menachem Begin. Most of you will realize how true is that remark. *I doubt that the College of Medicine at Urbana-Champaign would be where it is today without the leadership of Dan Bloomfield. Indeed, that is an understatement. I know it would not be where it is today without his leadership.* And I hope the College of Medicine at Urbana-Champaign has a great future and that it will live up to the goals, which Dan has helped establish. Good hunting, Dan."

And I conclude: Good hunting, UICOM-UC.

Other Fine Titles From Five Star Publications, Inc.

Shakespeare: To Teach or Not to Teach
By Cass Foster and Lynn G. Johnson

The answer is a resounding "To Teach!" There's nothing dull about this guide for anyone teaching Shakespeare in the classroom, with activities such as crossword puzzles, a scavenger hunt, warm-up games, and costume and scenery suggestions.

ISBN 1-877749-03-6

The Sixty-Minute Shakespeare Series
By Cass Foster

Not enough time to tackle the unabridged versions of the world's most widely read playwright? Pick up a copy of *Romeo and Juliet, A Midsummer Night's Dream, Hamlet, Macbeth, Much Ado About Nothing* and *Twelfth Night*, and discover how much more accessible Shakespeare can be to you and your students.

Letters of Love: Stories from the Heart
Edited by Salvatore Caputo

In this warm collection of love letters and stories, a group of everyday people shares hopes, dreams and experiences of love: love won, love lost, and love found again. Most of all, they share their belief that love is a blessing that makes life's challenges worthwhile.

ISBN 1-877749-35-4

Linda F. Radke's Promote Like a Pro: Small Budget, Big Show
By Linda F. Radke and contributors

In Linda F. Radke's *Promote Like a Pro: Small Budget, Big Show*, a successful publisher and a group of insiders offer self-publishers a step-by-step guide on how to use the print and broadcast media, public relations, the Internet, public speaking and other tools to market books—without breaking the bank!

ISBN 1-877749-36-2

Other Fine Titles From Five Star Publications, Inc.

The Economical Guide to Self-Publishing
By Linda F. Radke

This book is a must-have for anyone who is or wants to be a self-publisher. It is a valuable step-by-step guide for producing and promoting your book effectively, even on a limited budget. The book is filled with tips on avoiding common, costly mistakes and provides resources that can save you lots of money—not to mention headaches. A *Writer's Digest Book Club* selection.

ISBN 1-877749-16-8

That Hungarian's in My Kitchen
By Linda F. Radke

You won't want that Hungarian to leave after you've tried some of the 125 Hungarian-American Kosher recipes that fill this delightful cookbook. Written for both the novice cook and the sophisticated chef. It comes complete with "Aunt Ethel's Helpful Hints."

ISBN 1-877749-28-1

Kosher Kettle: International Adventures in Jewish Cooking
By Sybil Ruth Kaplan, Foreword by Joan Nathan

With more than 350 recipes from 27 countries, this is one Kosher cookbook you don't want to be without. It includes everything from wheat halva from India to borrekas from Greece. Five Star Publications is donating a portion of all sales of *Kosher Kettle* to MAZON: A Jewish Response to Hunger. A *Jewish Book Club* selection.

ISBN 1-877749-19-2

Household Careers: Nannies, Butlers, Maids & More: The Complete Guide for Finding Household Employment
By Linda F. Radke

There is a wealth of professional positions available in the child-care and home-help fields. This award-winning book provides all the information you need to find and secure a household job.

ISBN 1-877749-05-2

Other Fine Titles From Five Star Publications, Inc.

Nannies, Maids & More: The Complete Guide for Hiring Household Help
By Linda F. Radke

Anyone who has had to hire household help knows what a nightmare it can be. This book provides a step-by-step guide to hiring—and keeping—household help, complete with sample ads, interview questions, and employment forms.

ISBN 0-9619853-2-1

Profits of Death: An Insider Exposes the Death Care Industries
By Darryl J. Roberts

This book still has the funeral and cemetery industries reeling from aftershocks. Industry insider Darryl J. Roberts uncovers how the death care industry manipulates consumers into overspending at the most vulnerable time in their lives. He also tells readers everything they need to know about making final arrangements—including how to save up to 50% in costs. THIS IS ONE BOOK THEY CAN'T BURY!

ISBN 1-877749-21-4

Shoah: Journey From the Ashes
By Cantor Leo Fettman and Paul M. Howey

Cantor Leo Fettman survived the horrors of Auschwitz while millions of others, including almost his entire family, did not. He worked in the crematorium, was experimented on by Dr. Josef Mengele, and lived through an attempted hanging by the SS. His remarkable tale of survival and subsequent joy is an inspiration for all. Shoah includes a historical prologue that chronicles the 2,000 years of anti-Semitism that led to the Holocaust. Cantor Fettman's message is one of love and hope, yet it contains an important warning to new generations to remember—in order to avoid repeating—the evils of the past.

ISBN 0-9679721-0-8

Other Fine Titles From Five Star Publications, Inc.

Most titles are available through www.BarnesandNoble.com and www.amazon.com

For the Record: A Personal Facts and Document Organizer
By Ricki Sue Pagano

Many people have trouble keeping track of the important documents and details of their lives. Ricki Sue Pagano designed *For the Record* so they could regain control—and peace of mind. This organizing tool helps people keep track and makes it easy to find important documents in a pinch.

ISBN 0-9670226-0-6

Tying the Knot: The Sharp Dresser's Guide to Ties and Handkerchiefs
By Andrew G. Cochran

This handy little guide contains everything you want (or need) to know about neckties, bow ties, pocket squares, and handkerchiefs—from coordinating ties and shirts to tying a variety of knots.

ISBN 0-9630152-6-5

Phil Rea's How to Become a Millionaire Selling Remodeling
By Phil Rea

All successful remodelers know how to use tools. Too few, however, know how to use the tools of selling. Phil Rea mastered the art of selling remodeling and made more than $1,000,000 at his craft. He has shared his secrets through coast-to-coast seminars. Now, for the first time, you can read how to make the most of the financial opportunities remodeling has to offer.

ISBN 1-877749-29-x

Joe Boyd's Build It Twice...If You Want a Successful Building Project
By Joe Boyd

In *Joe Boyd's Build It Twice...If You Want a Successful Building Project*, construction expert Joe Boyd shares his 40 years of experience with construction disputes and explains why they arise. He also outlines a strategy that will allow project owners to avoid most construction woes: Build the project on paper first!

ISBN 0-9663620-0-4

Other Fine Titles From Five Star Publications, Inc.

Light in the Darkness
By St. George T. Lee

Physician St. George T. Lee's sex addiction cost him his career and nearly his family. In Light in the Darkness, Dr. Lee talks openly of his treatment and how he fought to regain the respect of his family. His book will serve as a beacon of inspiration for others affected by addictive behaviors of any kind.

ISBN 0-967891-0-1

Getting Your Shift Together: Making Sense of Organizational Culture and Change
By P.J. Bouchard and Lizz Pellett

Few things are inevitable: death, taxes—and change. In today's fast-paced business environment, changes come in staggering succession, yet few corporate change initiatives succeed. *Getting Your Shift Together: Making Sense of Organizational Culture and Change* offers solutions to make change an ally that boosts morale, productivity, and the bottom line.

ISBN 0-9673248-0-7

The Proper Pig's Guide to Mealtime Manners
By L.A. Kowal and Sally Starbuck Stamp

Of course, no one in your family would ever be a pig at mealtime, but perhaps you know another family with that problem. This whimsical guide, complete with its own ceramic pig, gives valuable advice for children and adults alike on how to make mealtimes more fun and mannerly.

ISBN 1-877749-20-6